WORKS ISSUED BY
THE HAKLUYT SOCIETY

A TRAVELLER IN THIRTEENTH-CENTURY ARABIA

Ibn al-Mujāwir's *Tārīkh al-Mustabṣir*

THIRD SERIES
NO. 19
(Issued for 2007)

(to whom queries and application for membership may be made)
Telephone: 0044 (0)1428 641 850   E-mail: office@hakluyt.com   Fax: 0044 (0)1428 641 933

Postal address only:
The Hakluyt Society, c/o Map Library, The British Library, 96 Euston Road,
London NW1 2DB, UK

http://www.hakluyt.com

Registered Charity No. 313168   VAT No. GB 233 4481 77

INTERNATIONAL REPRESENTATIVES OF THE HAKLUYT SOCIETY

Australia	Dr Martin Wood, Curator of Maps, National Library of Australia, Canberra, ACT 2601
Canada	Dr Joyce Lorimer, Department of History, Wilfred Laurier University, Waterloo, Ontario, N2L 3C5
France	Contre-amiral François Bellec, 1 place Henri Barbusse, F92300 Levallois, France
Germany	Thomas Tack, Ziegelbergstr. 21, D-63739 Aschaffenburg
Japan	Dr Derek Massarella, Faculty of Economics, Chuo University, Higashinakano 742–1, Hachioji-shi, Tokyo 192–03
New Zealand	John C. Robson, Map Librarian, University of Waikato Library, Private Bag 3105, Hamilton
Netherlands	Dr Leo M. Akveld, Hammerfeststraat 48, 3067 DC Rotterdam
Portugal	Dr Manuel Ramos, Av. Elias Garcia 187, 3Dt, 1050 Lisbon
Russia	Professor Alexei V. Postnikov, Institute of the History of Science and Technology, Russian Academy of Sciences, 1/5 Staropanskii per., Moscow 103012
Spain	Carlos Novi, C/ de Vera 26, E-17255 Begur (Girona), Spain *and* 39 Hazelmere Road, Petts Wood, Kent BR5 1PA, England, UK
USA	Edward L. Widmer, The John Carter Brown Library, Box 1894, Providence, Rhode Island 02912

DONATIONS

The Hakluyt Society gratefully acknowledges donors in 2006–2007 including donors to the American Friends of the Hakluyt Society

The inclusion here of a record of recent financial contributions to the work of the Society is an innovation which we trust members will approve. The need for such contributions has grown inexorably in recent years and Council has thought it right that the generosity of individuals and institutions in this respect should be acknowledged, not just in the relatively ephemeral Annual Report or Newsletter but in the more permanent form of the pages of our published volumes. Certainly, the Society is extremely grateful for the contributions and bequests it has received. These help to make possible the endeavour which Richard Hakluyt himself inspired, and which the Society has continued for 161 years – the endeavour to record, to understand and to interpret the means by which, for better or worse, different regions and different peoples of the world have become connected with one another.

Mr Edward Alsip
Mr Robert C. Baron
Mr Herbert K. Beals
Dr Sanford H. Bederman
Mr Matthew S. Blum
Dr John Bockstoce
Mr Bruce P. Bogert
Mr James Breckenridge
†Mr Brian Bridges
Mr Charles Elk
Dr Norman Fiering
Mr Joseph H. Fitzgerald
Mr Richard H. Float
Mr & Mrs Albert & Mary Fullerton
Mr Martin L. Green
Mr Manuel Guerra
Mr Todd Hanson
Dr William L. Harris
Mr Warren Heckrotte
Mr Paul Herrup
John Carter Brown Library
Mr Stephen A. Kanter
Mr John Levin
Mr John H. Libcke
Mr Caedmon A. Liburd
Mr Stephen F. Lintner
Dr & Mrs Ross D. E. MacPhee
Mr Kenneth MacPherson
Mr William McKinstry
Mr Glen McLaughlin
Mr & Mrs Robert M. Norris
Dr James C. Orcutt
Mr R. David Parsons
Dr Norman C. Peeler
Mr Brian R. Pinto
Dr Hugh Raffles
Mr William S. Reese
Mr & Mrs Curtis & Joan Roy
Professor David Harris Sacks
Mr Robert F. Scholl
Mr Werner Schuele
Mr & Mrs Harold & Michelle Schwab

Mr Neil M. Silverman
Mr Kenneth J. Siple
Mr Stephen A. Skold
Mr David H. Stam
Mr Elmer Templeton
Mr Stuart Thro
Professor Andrew Walls (per the Scottish Institute of Missionary Studies)
Mr Edgar L. Weber
Mr F. David Westcott
Mr Peter H. Wood

The President and Council would like in particular to express their gratitude for a substantial bequest from the estate of the late Mr Raymond Jagger, a member of the Society for over thirty years. As with all donations and bequests to the Society, this will go directly to defraying the costs of publication.

Grants made to assist the publication of specific volumes are acknowledged in those volumes and in the Annual Report.

The medieval port of Aden. Huqqāt bay and Ṣīrah island. Courtesy of Salma Samar Damluji

A TRAVELLER IN THIRTEENTH-CENTURY ARABIA

IBN AL-MUJĀWIR'S *TĀRĪKH AL-MUSTABṢIR*

Translated from Oscar Löfgren's Arabic text
and edited with revisions and annotations
by

G. Rex Smith

Published by
Ashgate
for
THE HAKLUYT SOCIETY
LONDON
2008

Published for The Hakluyt Society by

Ashgate Publishing Limited
Gower House
Croft Road
Aldershot
Hants GU11 3HR
England

Ashgate Publishing Company
Suite 420
101 Cherry Street
Burlington
VT 05401-4405
USA

Ashgate website: http://www.ashgate.com

British Library Cataloguing in Publication Data
Ibn al-Mujawir, Yusuf ibn Ya'qub, 1204 or 5–1291 or 2
A traveller in thirteenth-century Arabia : Ibn al-Mujawir's
Tarikh al-mustabsir. – (Hakluyt Society. Third series ; no.19)
1. Ibn al-Mujawir, Yusuf ibn Ya'qub, 1204 or 5–1291 or 2 –
Travel – Arabian Peninsula 2. Arabian Peninsula –
Description and travel – Early works to 1800 3. Arabian
Peninsula – History – To 1500
I. Title II. Smith, G. Rex (Gerald Rex)
915.3'042

Library of Congress Cataloging-in-Publication Data
Ibn al-Mujawir, Yusuf ibn Ya'qub, 1204 or 5–1291 or 2.
[Tarikh al-mustabsir. English]
A traveller in thirteenth-century Arabia : Ibn al-Mujawir's Tarikh al-mustabsir / translated by G. Rex Smith.
p. cm.
Includes bibliographical references and index.
ISBN 978-0-904180-91-6 (alk. paper)
1. Yemen – Description and travel – Early works to 1800. 2. Mecca (Saudi Arabia) – Description and travel – Early works to 1800. 3. Saudi Arabia – Description and travel – Early works to 1800.
I. Smith, G. Rex (Gerald Rex) II. Title.

DS206.I2613 2007
915.304'2–dc22
2007017576

ISBN 978-0-904180-91-6
ISSN 0072 9396

Typeset by Waveney Typesetters, Wymondham, Norfolk
Printed and bound in Great Britain by
the University Press, Cambridge

To the memory of
Oscar Löfgren and Robert Bertram Serjeant,
two great Mustabsirologists,
and
Charles Beckingham,
a wise counsellor

We are like dwarfs on the shoulders of giants, so that we can see more than they, and things at a greater distance, not by virtue of any sharpness of sight on our part, or any physical distinction, but because we are carried high and raised up by their giant size.
(Bernard de Chartres)

Also to the memory of
CWS,
who wanted this translation published as much as I did,
and to AMM-S, this volume is dedicated.

CONTENTS

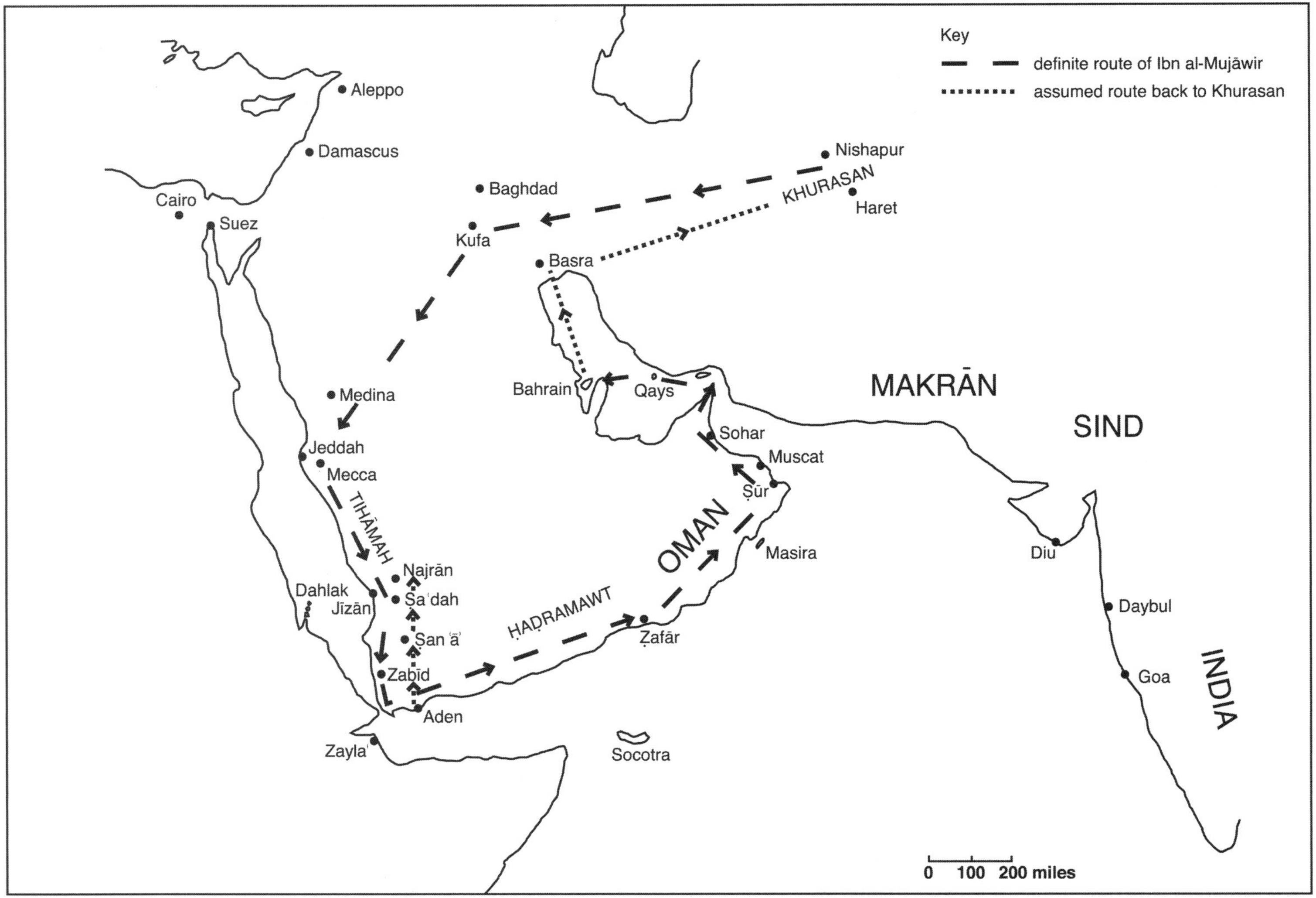

Map 1: Ibn al-Mujāwir's World

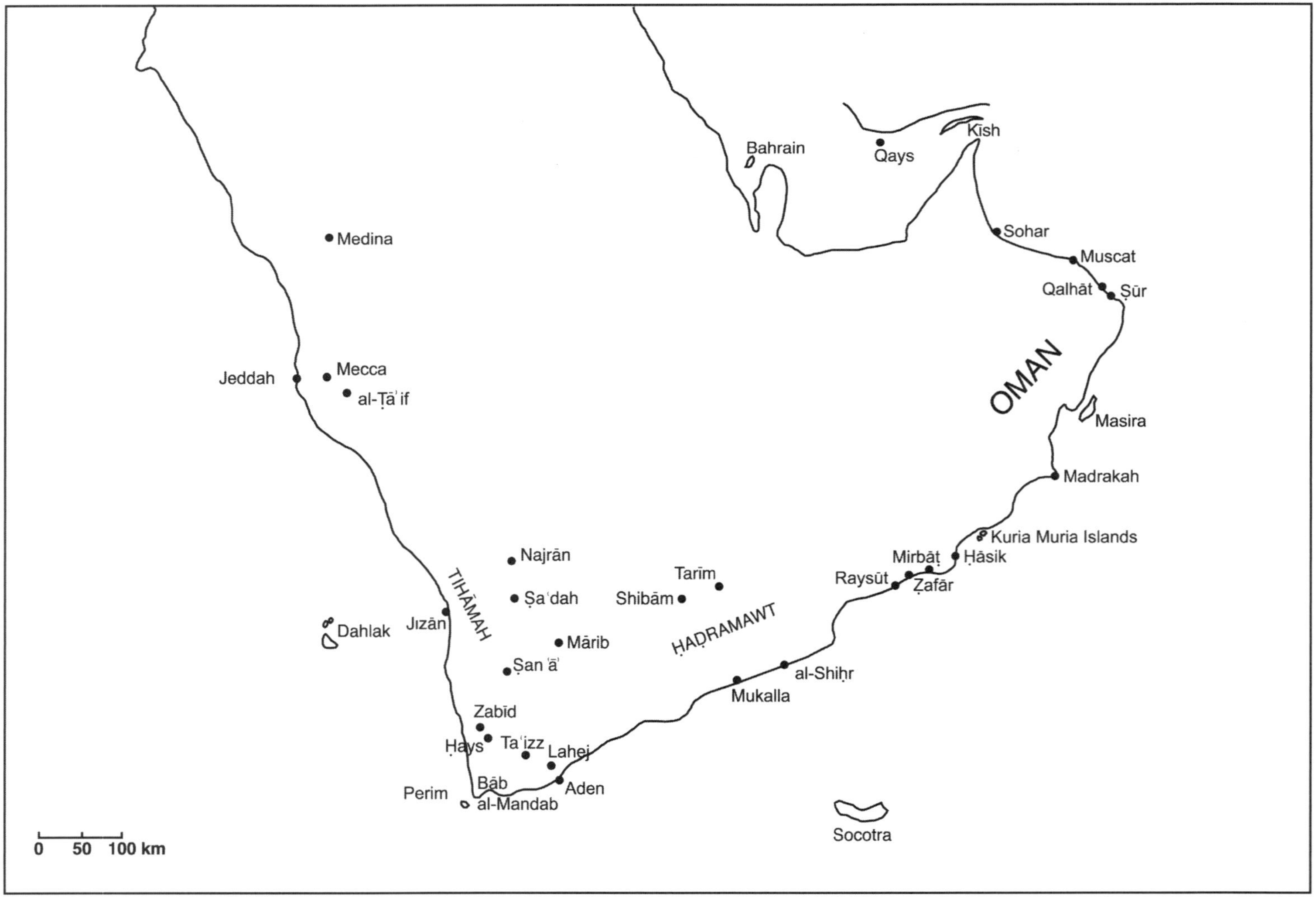

Map 2: Seventh/Thirteenth Century Arabia

LIST OF PLANS AND DIAGRAMS ACCOMPANYING THE TEXT

The reader should consult the explanation below the caption of each illustration where it occurs in the body of the text together with the text itself; it will be noted that there are sometimes differences between the two.

All these illustrations are reproduced from the sixteenth-century Istanbul MS of *Tārīkh al-Mustabṣir* in the Sülaymaniye Kütüphanesi.

PREFACE

> There is ample fodder for the [Hakluyt] Society in these three languages, [Arabic, Persian and Turkish], but I hope I have convinced you that it is rather indigestible fodder. If they are to deal with it adequately our editors will need all a cow's stomachs and ample time to chew the cud.
>
> Beckingham, 'Arabic Texts', p. 13.

I have been chewing the cud and operating on all stomachs for well over twenty years now and, blemishes and all, it is high time that Ibn al-Mujāwir's *Tārīkh al-Mustabṣir* saw the light of day in the English language.

I first discovered the edited text in the University Library in Cambridge in about 1965 after it had been recommended to me by the late Robert Bertram Serjeant, my then PhD supervisor, primarily as a good source of Yemeni place names. Oscar Löfgren's published Leiden edition of the Arabic text[1] contains only a brief list of contents and no indices of any kind and one had to work hard to find exactly what one was looking for. However, compensation came in the reading of this amazing account of an early seventh/thirteenth-century traveller in Arabia, a stranger from the East, no great scholar he, though a man with a curiosity for all things wonderful and unusual, commercial and economic, agricultural, historical and social. I suppose I was captivated from the start.

I can no longer be sure when I began to think of serious work on *Tārīkh al-Mustaṣbir*, but it must have been over twenty years ago. Although he had carried his copy faithfully for years during his stays in the Arabian Peninsula and had annotated it copiously, Serjeant told me that he could have no plans for further work on it and he willingly handed over his copy to me so that I could make use of all the notes taken over a period of many years. He suggested that I should consult Oscar Löfgren, the original editor, and I learned from the latter that he too had no plans to work more on the text. With great generosity he sent me draft indices and many valuable notes he had made, material which had not been published in the Leiden edition.

It was not difficult to see which way my work would proceed. Had other manuscripts appeared over the years, a new edition of the Arabic text might have been possible. It was clear to me at an early point, however, after exhaustive and futile attempts to track down manuscripts other than those which Oscar Löfgren had used, that an annotated translation based on Oscar Löfgren's edition, where some gaps could be plugged, some suggestions and corrections made, a translation proposed and at times possible alternative readings noted, was the only possible course to follow.

[1] Oscar Löfgren, *Ibn al-Muǧāwir: Descriptio Arabiae meridionalis, praemissis capitibus de Mecca et parte regionis Ḥiǧāz. qui liber inscribitur Ta'riḫ al-Mustabṣir.* Secundum codicem Constantinopolitanum Hagiae Sophiae 3080 collate Codice leidensi or. 5572. Cum adnotatione critica, Leiden, Brill, 1951–4.

Work has continued on and off ever since. Years of heavy teaching loads, endless committees and other research demands delayed the project seriously until my retirement in 1997. Even then Fate continued to intervene and my wife's illness and death in 1998 inevitably caused further postponements. Acceptance in 1999 by the Hakluyt Society of my proposal of an annotated translation in their rolling publication programme gave the project a great fillip and serious full-time work has been possible for some time now.

The difficulties presented by the text are many and will become clearer as the reader passes through the introduction, the translation and the notes below. Suffice it to say here that Ibn al-Mujāwir's strange language (even by Middle Arabic standards, and doubtless much mutilated over the centuries by well-meaning scribes who thought they were doing the world a favour by 'correcting' the original), his frequent habit of getting hold of the wrong end of the stick, his myriad oblique references to any number of persons, places, events and so forth, all these contributed to adding to my work and prolonging completion. Heavy annotation has been absolutely necessary and I make no apology for a total of more than 2,800 notes, some of them of some length. Perhaps unusually for a Hakluyt publication, many of these concern lexicographical and other linguistic and textual matters. Yet they are too important to allow to slip through unobserved.

So broad are the contents of *Tārīkh al-Mustabṣir* they ideally require the treatment of a whole committee of scholars. In the absence of such a committee, I asked the following to cast their eagle eyes over my manuscript before it was submitted for publication and they all agreed to read it in full: Dionisius Agius, Clive Smith, Francine Stone and Daniel Varisco. Numerous suggestions for improvement and corrections were proposed by them, the majority of which I have been able to incorporate into my work. I shall never be able to thank them adequately for all their time and for their wonderful scholarly efforts.

The full list of all those others worthy of my thanks follows. They are Hussein al-Amri, Edmund Bosworth, Bill Donaldson, Bernard Haykel, John Healey, Leila Ingrams, Paul Luft, Charles Melville, Fatima al-Muhairi, Venetia Porter, Marie-Claude Simeone-Senelle, Noha Sadek, Jack Smart, Yasir Suleiman and Mohammed Thenayian. I also extend my gratitude to all those PhD students in Durham and Manchester who, over the years, humoured me and my obsession with the text and who appeared to enjoy reading it with me almost as much as I did (Ali al-Dosari, Moshalleh al-Moraekhi and Mohammed Thenayian spring particularly to mind in this context) and also to those MA students who took my Middle Arabic Texts course in Manchester and from whom I learned much.

Much as all these kind friends and colleagues have helped me, responsibility for the final translation and the notes, as well as for the introductory essays, lies solely with me. Many problems and lacunae remain and I can make no claim to comprehensiveness in this work. Perhaps someone in the future will be inspired by these pages to make an attempt to solve at least some of the problems, complete some of the lacunae and confirm or otherwise some of the educated guesses. I fear, however, we shall never arrive at comprehensiveness after all this time with the sources now available to us.

I acknowledge with particular pleasure the cheerful assistance rendered to me by the staff of two libraries where I have worked for the most part on this book: both the staff of the John Rylands University Library, Manchester, UK, and that of the Branford Price Millar Library at Portland State University, Oregon, US – I should mention by name in the context of the latter the Director, Tom Pfingsten, and also Kristen Kern, Rex Marshall and Kay Sellman. I wish also to place on record here the warm welcome extended to me by Jon Mandaville and Jean Campbell in the Middle East Studies Center at Portland State University.

I must add a word of particular gratitude to my original Hakluyt series editor, Robin Law, and to my main series editor, Michael Brennan, who answered my sometimes silly questions with great patience and humour and did so much to improve this work, and to Will Ryan who wrestled with the diacritics and prepared the final version for publication. My gratitude is also extended to the Society for accepting this annotated translation for publication.

Bronwen and Stuart Campbell have helped in a number of practical matters and I am very grateful to them. Muammer Ülker, then director of the Sülaymaniye Kütüphanesi, kindly permitted me to see the Istanbul manuscript in 1996 and I am much in his debt. On that occasion my son Jonathan proved an invaluable and highly competent interpreter and I record my thanks to him here. Dr E. van Donzel, then secretary of the Stichting De Goeje, with great courtesy informed me in 2000 of the Foundation's authority to use the Löfgren printed text for this translation. I acknowledge with pleasure his help in this matter and thank the Foundation warmly. Dr J. J. Witkam of the University Library, Leiden, personally arranged for me to have a microfilm of the Leiden manuscript and to him I offer my sincere thanks.

Finally I dedicate this volume to the memory of Oscar Löfgren and Robert Bertram Serjeant, both of whom had already done so much to tease out the problems of this difficult text; to the memory of Charles Frasier Beckingham, who generously dispensed wisdom; and to the memory of my dear, late wife, Cerries, who over the years protected me from interruptions and distractions and who rendered more help than she ever realized. I also dedicate it with much love to my wife and new inspiration, Maggie.

Dyserth, Denbighshire, 2005

LIST OF ABBREVIATIONS

CHIr	*Cambridge History of Iran*
CHIs	*Cambridge History of Islam*
DMV	Daniel Martin Varisco
EI	*Encyclopaedia of Islam*, 2nd edition
EIran	*Encyclopaedia of Iran*
EJ	*Encyclopaedia Judaica*
FLS	Francine Stone
I MS	Istanbul MS of *Tārīkh al-Mustabṣir*
L MS	Leiden MS of *Tārīkh al-Mustabṣir*
OL	Oscar Löfgren
RBS	R. B. Serjeant
SEI	*Shorter Encyclopaedia of Islam*

INTRODUCTION

The text of *Tārīkh al-Mustabṣir* is the early thirteenth-century account of a journey made by a businessman (or someone profoundly interested in business) in the Arabian Peninsula. The author undoubtedly came from the east of the Islamic world. The annotated translation published here is based in the edited text of Oscar Löfgren and the two important manuscripts, that of Istanbul (late sixteenth century), here designated I MS, and that of Leiden (nineteenth century), here designated L MS.

THE AUTHOR

It was in 1864 that the text of *Tārīkh al-Mustabṣir* first appears to have come to the attention of scholars when Aloys Sprenger took over a copy of it from 'M. Schefer' and used it extensively for the Arabian section of his work.[1] Thereafter, three other scholars entered into a discussion of the important question of the true authorship of the work. De Geoje in 1899,[2] questioning the correct identification of Yūsuf b. Yaʿqūb as author, Derenbourg in 1901,[3] supporting the identification of Yūsuf b. Yaʿqūb as it is found on the title page of the manuscripts and the 1950s printed edition, and Jawad in 1938,[4] agreeing with De Geoje's view, all expressed their opinions on the matter. Having read their arguments and, perhaps more importantly, having studied very carefully the internal evidence of the text, I am of the opinion that we may now state as follows regarding the author of *Tārīkh al-Mustabṣir*. Despite the title page as it appears in all the manuscripts I am able to check, and in Oscar Löfgren's printed edition of 1951–4, the author was Abū Bakr b. Muḥammad b. Masʿūd b. ʿAlī b. Aḥmad Ibn al-Mujāwir al-Baghdādī al-Nīsābūrī.[5] The name provided on the title pages, Yūsuf b. Yaʿqūb b. Muḥammad Ibn al-Mujāwir al-Shaybānī al-Dimashqī, was, I suggest, an error which crept in at some point in the copying process which went on through the centuries and was slavishly repeated from scribe to scribe. It found permanence because there was a known scholar of that name who died

[1] De Goeje, 'Communication', pp. 23, 30. Schefer's copy used by Sprenger is of the Istanbul manuscript. See also Sprenger, *Reiserouten*, pp. 125 ff. and my 'Dhofar and Socotra', pp. 79–80; 'Eastern Connection', pp. 78–9.

[2] 'Communication', pp. 30 ff., where he has spotted the references in the text to Ibn al-Mujāwir's father, brother and uncle.

[3] *Manuscrits arabes*, p. 18, very brief and with no evidence for his disagreement with De Goeje.

[4] 'Petites découvertes', p. 286, his argument focusing on the *early* 7th/13th-century dates in the text and reminding the reader that Yūsuf b. Yaʿqūb died in 690/1291. It might be added here that Landberg with the publication of his *Etudes* (1901–13) and *Glossaire daṯînois* (1920–42) was the first after Sprenger to exploit the text for scholarly purposes.

[5] This can be deduced by reference to the text at p. 220 below, where on this one occasion the author writes, 'qāla Abū Bakr …' (he usually writes, 'qāla Ibn al-Mujāwir …) and by reference to his mention of his brother, p. 121 and of his father, p. 254.

in 690/1291.[1] In fact, the Yūsuf b. Yaʿqūb, of whom we read in the biographies, was rather a scholar of the Islamic discipline of the sayings and doings of the Prophet (our author was certainly no *muḥaddith*!) and there is no evidence in them of any particular interest on his part in the Arabian Peninsula.[2]

Not only does the text itself tell us who wrote *Tārīkh al-Mustabṣir*, but we should perhaps remember that the figure whose name occurs on the title pages died more than sixty years after the final date mentioned in the text: 627 (1229–30). He would have been a remarkably young man making his Arabian journeys in the early seventh/thirteenth century – and then he wrote nothing else for the rest of his life.[3]

If more evidence is required in order to establish the true author, it surely comes from almost every page of the text. The writer was connected and acquainted with the east of the Islamic world.[4] He was in all probability a native Persian-speaker (see 'The language' below) and he quotes Persian poetry on occasions, some of it, he says, of his own composition. All his comparisons are with the Islamic east. Scrutiny of the names of Ibn al-Mujāwir's informants shows a noticeable minority from the east, as compared with a negligible number of Syrians.[5] On p. 14 of Oscar Löfgren's edition of *Tārīkh al-Mustabṣir*, Ibn al-Mujāwir tells us Khurasan was his home. Baghdad too is of some importance to him and all this evidence adds up to the appropriateness of the two *nisbah*s al-Baghdādī and al-Nīsābūrī rather than al-Shaybānī and al-Dimashqī.

What else do we know about the author? Our sole source in trying to answer this question is *Tārīkh al-Mustabṣir* itself. Perhaps the first thing which strikes the reader of the text is the author's great interest in trade and commerce. If he was not a businessman himself, who travelled firstly to perform the pilgrimage and then on from the Hejaz into the Yemen via Tihāmah and who from time to time visited India and East Africa to ply his trade, then he must surely have been someone with a remarkably keen interest in business wherever he found himself. From such an interest, it might be suggested that he held the distinct philosophy that one should know the people with whom business might be done. He was thus a keen student of humankind and the clothes, the food, the agriculture and the social customs of the peoples of the Arabian Peninsula are all observed with a particularly keen eye. In view of this passion for trade, it is not at all surprising that he tells his reader of such things as the prices and customs taxes of the different commodities which passed in and out of the area, of the markets and currencies, and the weights and measures.

Another golden thread running through the whole of the text is Ibn al-Mujāwir's love for – one might even say obsession with – magic and the bizarre, sorcery and the jinn, and weird and wonderful tales from the distant past. Equally, he displays an extraordinary sense of humour and fun, for no opportunity is lost to tell the amusing anecdote, the funny story, perhaps after long hours rehearsing it and perhaps even stealing it from friends and acquaintances. There is the distinct feeling that many such tales are the product of all-male gatherings where they are told and told again, with additions and exaggerations each time they are recounted.

[1] See Ibn Tirghī Birdī, *Nujūm*, VIII, p. 33; Ibn al-ʿImād, *Shadhar*, V, p. 417; Ziriklī, *Aʿlām*, IX, p. 341.
[2] Smith, 'Eastern Connection', pp. 85–6.
[3] Smith, 'Dhofar and Socotra', pp. 79–80.
[4] Smith, 'Eastern Connection', pp. 80 ff.
[5] Ibid., pp. 80–82.

It should perhaps finally be said that our author was no great scholar or deep religious thinker. He does, it is true, quote from several literary texts (some identifiable, some not, see 'The Text, Ibn al-Mujāwir's sources – literary works' and Appendix C below), but these do not constitute a large proportion of *Tārīkh al-Mustabṣir*. He is not averse to a little poetry now and again, and some of it he says he has composed himself. Even his Quranic quotations can be off the mark and the opportunities to elaborate on the tenets and ideas of the religious groups he encounters are not seized. Rather, more often than not there appears some rather absurd, tongue-in-cheek caricature of the group or one of its members.

To sum up, it is suggested that our author was Abū Bakr b. Muḥammad b. Masʿūd b. ʿAlī b. Aḥmad Ibn al-Mujāwir al-Baghdādī al-Nīsābūrī. He may have come from Khurasan or at least he lived there at some point in his life and he knew the eastern provinces of the Islamic world well. He knew Persian and was in all probability a native Persian-speaker. Since the dates in the text are the 620s/1220s, the latest being 627/1229–30, we can assume that he was born in the second half of the sixth/twelfth century and that he died in the first half of the seventh/thirteenth. The contents of the text (see 'The Contents' below) indicate that he was either a businessman himself, or at least someone with an enormous interest in business. A man of some humour and with a deep interest in the world of magic and those who practised it, he travelled to the Arabian Peninsula on at least one occasion and visited the Hejaz, Tihāmah, the southern coastal area of Arabia, the Gulf region and some inland locations. The text is essentially his account of those travels.

HISTORICAL BACKGROUND

We can safely assume from several clues in the text that Ibn al-Mujāwir was on his travels in the first quarter of the seventh/thirteenth century and was writing his account at some time perhaps during the years 624–27/1226–30, just as Ayyubid rule over much of the Yemen was coming to an end and just before their successors, the Rasulids, assumed power. To be sure, he travelled in areas of Arabia outside the Yemen and not controlled from the Yemen. Nevertheless, it is clear that it is the Yemen which must hold our major attention here in order to understand well the historical background of his journey and the historical comments he makes in the text before us. Perhaps the other part of the Peninsula which requires such an introduction is the region of the Holy Cities. The reader's attention is drawn to Appendixes B.2–B.11 below. Any other historical remarks in the text can be dealt with adequately in the footnotes.[1]

The Yemen

Ibn al-Mujāwir mentions the following Yemenite ruling families in *Tārīkh al-Mustabṣir* in sufficient detail to warrant our attention here: the Ziyadids, the Najahids, the

[1] This includes the immensely important Zaydīs who are mentioned but rarely by Ibn al-Mujāwir, no doubt because he did not travel in their territory in the northern highlands of the Yemen. I have assigned Appendix B.2 to them, however, and have attempted a dynastic list of the imams of the relevant period.

Sulayhids, the Zuray'ids, the Mahdids and finally the Ayyubids.[1] Relying on previous publications,[2] I now proceed with some brief notes on these dynasties which I hope will be useful for the reader's greater understanding and appreciation of the translated text. In the case of the last in the list, the Ayyubids, they would have been in control of Tihāmah and the southern highlands, including Aden, even as Ibn al-Mujāwir went on his travels.

The Ziyadids, 203–409(?)/818–1018

The dynasty takes its name from Muḥammad b. Ziyād who in Iraq became the protégé of al-Faḍl b. Sahl, the vizier of the Abbasid caliph, al-Maʾmūn. In 202/817, news reached the Abbasid court in Baghdad that two Arab tribes of Tihāmah, the Red Sea coastal plain of the Yemen, had rebelled against the Abbasid governor in Ṣanʿāʾ and against the caliphal house. Al-Faḍl b. Sahl suggested to the caliph that Ibn Ziyād be despatched to the Yemen to quell the revolt. The latter thus left Iraq and was given the additional command to found and build a new capital in Tihāmah. After attending to his pilgrimage duties in 203/819, Ibn Ziyād travelled south into the Yemen and fought many hard battles before he could assert his control over the coastal plain. In 204/819, he built the new capital, to be called Zabīd.

Ibn Ziyād died in 245/859, by which time, we are told, he had extended his territories as far as Ḥaḍramawt, along the southern Indian Ocean coast to Mirbāṭ in modern-day Oman, and also north along the Red Sea coast as far as Ḥaly Ibn Yaʿqūb.

We know little more of Ziyadid history than a list of rulers who followed the dynasty's founder: his son, Ibrāhīm (d. 283/896), the latter's son, Ziyād (d. 289/902), another Ibn Ziyād (d. 299/911) who was finally succeeded by the last name history records in connection with the dynasty, Abū al-Jaysh. The latter died in 371/981 and this is the last firm date we have. There is an indication in our sources that the house finally fell in 409/1018.

The Najahids, 412–551/1021–1156

This was a black Abyssinian slave dynasty with sovereignty over Zabīd and northern Tihāmah. From 412/1021, the area fell into the hands of two brothers, Najāḥ and Nafīs, the latter soon ousted by the former. Najāḥ received an official diploma from the Abbasid caliph in Baghdad and struck his own coins. He was murdered by the Sulayhids in 452/1060 and Tihāmah passed into their hands for a while.

Najāḥ's son, Saʿīd al-Aḥwal, attacked and killed the Sulayhid ruler, ʿAlī b. Muḥammad, and kidnapped his wife, though later she was rescued and Saʿīd compelled to flee to the Red Sea island of Dahlak. Tihāmah swung to and fro under the control of the Najahids and the Sulayhids until Saʿīd's death in 481/1088. His brother,

[1] A check on the text of *Tārīkh al-Mustabṣir* with my dynastic lists in 'Political History', pp. 138–9, reveals that he all but ignores the Yuʿfirids (232–387/847–997) and makes very brief mention of the Sulaymanids (latter half of 6th/12th century) and the Hamdanid sultans (492–c. 569/1098–c. 1173).

[2] In particular, my *Ayyubids and Early Rasulids*, II, 'Political History' and the following *EI* entries: 'Ziyādids', 'Nadjādids', 'Ṣulayḥids', 'Zurayʿids', 'Mahdids', 'Tūrānshāh b. Ayyūb'.

Jayyāsh, succeeded him and built up the town of Ḥays, purposely bringing over Abyssinians to populate it, Ibn al-Mujāwir tells us. Jayyāsh died in 498/1104 and Najahid power was then exercised by his son and two grandsons, all named Fātik, and then a series of slave ministers. The last of these was murdered by the Mahdids in c. 551/1156 and the Najahids passed from history.

The Sulayhids, 439–532/1047–1138

This Fatimid Ismāʿīlī dynasty can be divided between the Ṣanʿāʾ (439–c. 480/1047–c. 1087) and the Dhū Jiblah periods (ca. 480–532/ca. 1087–1138). The founder who figures on more than one occasion in the text of *Tārīkh al-Mustabṣir* was ʿAlī b. Muḥammad who had been brought up an orthodox Sunnī in the mountains of Ḥarāz, south-west of Ṣanʿāʾ, and later converted by a Fatimid *dāʿī*. From 439/1047, he rose to arms and took the Ḥarāz region. By 455/1063, he controlled the whole of the south of the Yemen below Ṣanʿāʾ and the capital itself. When he was murdered by Saʿīd al-Aḥwal, the Najahid, in about 473/1080, his son, Aḥmad, succeeded him.

A long struggle with the Najahids ensued and at times they made serious inroads into Sulayhid territory. In about 479/1086, Aḥmad handed over the affairs of state to his wife, Arwā bint Aḥmad, who, perhaps in 480/1087, moved the capital to Dhū Jiblah. Thus began Sulayhid rule from there over Tihāmah and southern Yemen, a period of some brilliance, presided over by this legendary queen known as 'Bilqīs the Younger'.

The rest of the history of the dynasty centres on the queen and her trusty henchmen and the continuing struggles against the arch-enemy, the Najahids. Arwā died in 532/1138 at the ripe old age of eighty-eight. There was no one to continue the dynasty.

The Zurayʿids, 473–569/1080–1173

A Fatimid Ismāʿīlī dynasty centered on the southern port of Aden, the Zurayʿids were installed as representatives of the Sulayhids in 473/1080 in recognition of their past services to the family, and their joint leaders were brothers, al-ʿAbbās, and al-Masʿūd, sons of al-Mukarram b. al-Dhiʾb. Al-ʿAbbās died in 477/1084 and his son, Zurayʿ, who gave his name to the dynasty, took over as joint ruler with his uncle, al-Masʿūd. In 504/1110, the Zurayʿids decided to cast off their agreement with the Sulayhids and declared independence.

The period of rule was dogged by family quarrels resulting from the rivalry between its two branches, the descendants of al-ʿAbbās on the one side and those of al-Masʿūd on the other. It was only in 533/1138 that ʿAlī b. Sabaʾ b. Abī Suʿūd b. Zurayʿ united the family, and his brother and successor, Muḥammad b. Sabaʾ, took sole control over Aden, much of southern Arabia and Ḥaḍramawt.

Muḥammad's son and successor, ʿImrān, died in 561/1166 and the affairs of state fell into the hands of their slave ministers, including one Yāsir b. Bilāl, who was put to death after the entry of the Ayyubids and their vast army from Egypt into Aden in 569/1173.

The Mahdids, 554–569/1159–73

This short-lived Tihāmah-based dynasty was, like the Zurayʿids, brought to an end by the arrival of the powerful Ayyubids in the country.

The first date in fact marks the entry into Zabīd of ʿAlī b. Mahdī after some years of struggle in Najahid Tihāmah where he had endeavoured to spread his religious message. He died soon after taking the town and his son, ʿAbd al-Nabī, continued the policy of cruel plundering and looting undertaken by his father before him. Combining a policy of peace making here and armed struggle there, ʿAbd al-Nabī gained much territory for the Mahdids, even outside Tihāmah in the southern highlands. His exploits were brought to a sudden halt when he and his brother, Aḥmad, were arrested by the conquering Ayyubids and were finally strangled by them in 571/1176.

The Mahdids were commonly branded Khawārij, particularly because of their doctrine that all sin is infidelity.

The Ayyubids, 569–628/1173–1230

IM must have been undertaking his journey (or journeys) in southern Arabia during the time the Ayyubids firmly controlled Tihāmah and the southern highlands of the Yemen. This family was by origin Kurdish and its high-ranking officers were mostly Kurds and Turks. For the first time in the Islamic history of the Yemen, we see the entry into the country of a major foreign force. The Ayyubid army under Tūrānshāh b. Ayyūb, the brother of Ṣalāḥ al-Dīn (Saladin), was vast, well equipped, well disciplined and with exceptionally large numbers of horse. They were to sweep away the local dynasties and to establish a strictly Sunnī unity within their territory. The date 569/1173 is of great significance in Yemenite history, for here surely are the beginnings of a single political unit called the Yemen, controlled by the Sunnī Ayyubids in the south and in Tihāmah and by the Zaydīs in the northern highlands.

These brief historical notes cannot include a comprehensive discussion of why this Ayyubid army marched out of Egypt against southern Arabia in 569/1173.[1] Strategic and commercial reasons may have been well to the fore in the thinking of the Ayyubids. It had also been reported to them that the Yemen had more than its fair share of Ismāʿīlīs, religiously and politically closely linked with the Fatimids in Egypt, whose caliphate Saladin, the brother of the conqueror of the Yemen, Tūrānshāh, had brought to an end two years earlier in 567/1171.

The Ayyubid sultans of the Yemen, with their steady supply of men, materials and horse from Egypt, conquered southern Yemen and Tihāmah as it had never been conquered before. With military successes came administrative development: a system of governors and government officials, the institution of fiefs and the regularization of customs dues and taxes, sometimes building on earlier Zurayʿid models, though more often than not they brought in innovations imported from Ayyubid lands to the north.

There were six Ayyubid sultans in the Yemen and their list can be consulted below in Appendix B.1. When the final one, al-Masʿūd Yūsuf, left the Yemen for the last time in 626/1228, he cast around among his senior Ayyubid amirs, but found no one of the

[1] See in particular on this question Smith, *Ayyubids*, II, pp. 31–49.

family to hold the fort. The Rasulid, Nūr al-Dīn ʿUmar, of Turkish origin incidentally, was finally appointed his deputy to hold the country in the name of the Ayyubid house until relieved by another member. But no Ayyubid was ever to set foot in the Yemen again. By the year 628/1230 after Ibn al-Mujāwir had composed *Tārīkh al-Mustabṣir*, one can assume, the new Rasulid regime was officially confirmed in authority by the Abbasid caliph in Baghdad.

The Hejaz

The historical background of the Hejaz need not detain us long. Ibn al-Mujāwir, like all good Muslim travellers and businessmen, no doubt performed the pilgrimage on his way through the Hejaz down into the Yemen. He has much to say about Mecca, some of his data of immense social and economic interest, though there is also much unoriginal material concerning the etymology of the name. He mentions the sharifs in his writings and for this reason I append some remarks on them here and direct the reader's attention also to Appendixes B.9–B.11 below.[1]

We may perhaps suggest that the sharifs under review in the context of the *Tārīkh al-Mustabṣir* can be divided into three houses: the Musawids (mid-fourth/tenth century to the second half of fifth/eleventh century), B. Hāshim (from the second half of fifth/eleventh century to 597/1201) and B. Qatādah (from 597/1201 to the mid-seventh/thirteenth century). All were descended from Mūsā al-Jawn, a direct ancestor of ʿAlī b. Abī Ṭālib, through his son al-Ḥasan (see p. 36, n. 6 below). It might be stressed here that frequently during the early seventh/thirteenth century the Ayyubids from Egypt and from the Yemen (and the Rasulids after them from the latter) played an active role in Meccan affairs and directly and indirectly controlled the city.

The Musawids, 350s–450s/960s–1060s

The first to make himself master of Mecca and to become known as sharif had been Jaʿfar b. Muḥammad in the early years of the second half of the fourth/tenth century. The sharifate during this period made every attempt to assert its independence and the third ruler of the house, Abū al-Futūḥ (reg. 384–432/994–1039), proclaimed himself caliph in 402/1011. The last ruler of the dynasty, Shukr, died without heirs in 453/1061 and power passed to the B. Hāshim.

B. Hāshim, 455–597/1063–1201

The name was taken from Abū Hāshim Muḥammad, the first ruler of the line, in 455/1063. He had originally been appointed deputy by ʿAlī b. Muḥammad al-Ṣulayḥī (see Sulayhids above), who had gone on pilgrimage to Mecca in 455/1063 and remained

[1] See in particular the Arabic histories in Wüstenfeld's *Chroniken*, Ibn Fahd's *Ghāyah*, Snouck Hurgronje's *Mekka*, De Gaury's, *Rulers* and *EI*, 'Hāshimids', 'Ḳatāda b. Idrīs', 'Makka'.

there as ruler. It is sufficient here to refer the reader to the list of their amirs which can be found below in Appendix B.10.

B. Qatādah, 597/1201 – mid-seventh/thirteenth century

In 597/1201, Qatādah b. Idrīs, then lord of Yanbuʿ, himself an ardent Arabian 'nationalist' and invited by those of Mecca tired of outside interference, seized the city from the last Hashimite, Mukthir, and the latter and his immediate family left the town for good. Qatādah was already over the age of seventy when he became ruler and died in 617/1220, when he was succeeded by his son, Ḥasan. The latter, expelled from Mecca by Ayyubid forces, left for Baghdad to seek the aid of the Abbasid caliph. He died there and never returned to Arabia. As the Ayyubids lost their control of the Yemen to the Rasulid amirs and as quarrels between the two houses over the Holy Cities continued to rage, Rājiḥ, another son of Qatādah, ruled as a Rasulid governor until he was finally ousted by direct Ayyubid intervention in 638/1240.

THE CONTENTS

We cannot be sure how many visits Ibn al-Mujāwir made to the Arabian Peninsula. Indeed, there may have been only one. I am assuming that, coming from the north-east, he would have followed either the Kufa–Mecca road, the Darb Zubaydah, or the Basra–Mecca road and Map 1, 'Ibn al-Mujāwir's World', is marked accordingly.[1] He then presumably did first what all Muslim travellers to the area would wish to do, namely perform the pilgrimage. Assuming that he was there on business, this would appear to be a classic case of *ḥajj wa-ḥājah* ('pilgrimage and business'), an age-old Arabian practice.

From Mecca and al-Ṭā'if (he says nothing of Medina), he travelled south, down into Tihāmat al-Yaman, the Yemen section of the Red Sea coastal plain, where he has much to say of Zabīd, traditionally a centre of learning. He continued south to the Bāb al-Mandab, the extreme south-western point of the Peninsula, whence a route along the southern coast of Arabia brought him to Aden which, given his keen observations of all aspects of trade and markets, one might suggest is the highlight of his expedition.[2] We cannot be sure to what extent, or even if, Ibn al-Mujāwir travelled into the mountains of the Yemen, for how much of *Tārīkh al-Mustabṣir* is personal observation and how much second hand we can only surmise, relying on the hints, and nothing stronger, which we find in the text (see below, 'The Text, Ibn al-Mujāwir's sources'). He certainly mentions important places in the southern highlands like Taʿizz and Dhū Jiblah; further north, Dhamār and the chief town, Ṣanʿā', and further north still, Ṣaʿdah, about which he says a great deal, and Najrān in present-day Saudi Arabia.

[1] For an excellent study of the Kufa pilgrim route, see al-Rashid, *Darb Zubaydah*, *passim*. Rashid's inside rear cover map of al-Rabadhah indicate the two routes extremely well. In order not to confuse the issue, my own Map 1 shows the route of the Darb Zubaydah from Kufa only.

[2] Apart from the relevant sections of *Tārīkh al-Mustabṣir*, see also my articles, 'Trade and Commerce' and 'Port Practices'.

He then proceeded along the southern coast. He perhaps cut inland and continued his way via Wādī Ḥaḍramawt, for he writes of Shibām and Tarīm there. Then he travelled down into the area of present-day southern Oman. The medieval town of Ẓafār which gave its name to what is now the whole area of Dhofar features in the text. Ibn al-Mujāwir then made his way as far as Ra'➚s al-Ḥadd, the furthest easterly point on the map of the Arabian Peninsula. Turning left into the Gulf of Oman, he called in, we assume, at Ṣūr and Qalhāt, then Muscat and Sohar before travelling the length of the Musandam Peninsula on the eastern side right to the tip at Kumzār. From somewhere on the western side, now in the Gulf proper, he takes us over the sea to the island of Qays, only a few miles off the coast of present-day Iran. We leave him as he tells us something of the island of Bahrain and perhaps we should assume that he returned home (to Khurasan?) through the head of the Gulf and eastwards. This is a quick summary of the ground covered by Ibn al-Mujāwir in *Tārīkh al-Mustabṣir*.

Ibn al-Mujāwir's introduction

Ibn al-Mujāwir's own introduction to his text is couched in an elevated classical Arabic rhymed prose (*saj'*) style which promises a much more orthodox and staid geographical text to follow.[1] He is engaged in the superior discipline of *fann al-tārīkh*, he tells us, which I translate historical geography or topography:

> The discipline of historical topography (*fann al-tārīkh*), especially what concerns the inhabited parts of the earth, the lengths and breadths of its territories, the sites of its buildings, the distances between its settlements, the presentation of its countries and the explanation of the conditions of its towns ... is one of the most marvellous, the most extraordinary, the most intellectual ... and the most pleasing.[2]

There is then, he is clearly saying here, a real historical approach in what he is writing. That and the elevated style deceive the reader for the time being into believing that this is a geographical reference book in the long tradition of such works in Arabic and perhaps one to be assigned to the 'post-classical' genre of Arabic geographical writings (see section below on 'The Place of *Tārīkh al-Mustabṣir* in Arabic Geographical and Travel Literature'). I am even inclined to suggest (and I hope I am not unduly maligning him) that he has lifted his introduction, or at least the inspiration for his introduction, from another source (as he sometimes did lift the words of others). Or, I suppose we may admit, this was in truth his own articulation of his idealistic intention, namely to produce a geographical reference work in the traditional mould with a bias towards the historical, an intention which, as he composed his work, he was unable to fulfil.

He further stresses the historical in his work:

> The old pages [of historical topography] renew for you razed towns with their archaeological remains and castles while the lifeless sections and chapters bring to life within their letters and lines centuries long gone by.[3]

[1] See also below, section: 'The Place of *Tārīkh al-Mustabṣir* in Arabic Geographical and Travel Literature'.
[2] P. 1 of Oscar Löfgren's published Arabic text.
[3] Ibid., p. 1.

The following, while still a little too lofty for the main text which follows, lacks the historical emphasis and begins to tell us a little more genuinely and more accurately what is in store:

> So in this book I have concentrated on the following two areas [Mecca and the Yemen] by recording what is related to them in this field of study, a statement concerning [different] sites, areas, towns, mountains and seas and also an explanation of [different] dwelling places and settlements, as well as the measurements of distances across both deserts and centres of habitation. ... [There is also] a picture of every place, so that it is as if you can actually see it with your own eyes and you become acquainted with it in its entirety, so meanwhile you are relieved of your fatigue. Every place has its own rare piece of poetry which has been strung together of old. But now it is the time to begin [to tackle] the objectives of the book, to ease back the curtain and open the door.[1]

By highlighting the most important of the contents of the text below, we shall see that it did not emerge quite as he describes.

Ibn al-Mujāwir's route descriptions

Below in Appendix A, I have provided a comprehensive list of the forty-two routes described by Ibn al-Mujāwir in *Tārīkh al-Mustabṣir*. These route descriptions form the foundations of the structure of the work and are usually in the following pattern: to place A – x parasangs; to place B – y parasangs; and to place C – z parasangs. To be sure, he does on occasions abandon the route before completion, seemingly forgetting that he has started. Some of his routes too, it should be said, are highly doubtful, possibly composites of more than one route, and I have drawn attention to such in my notes.[2] I get the feeling that some of his Hejazi and ʿAsīrī itineraries in particular are second-hand (and frankly second rate) and that confusion, whoever is at fault, he or his informant(s), has entered into the equation. Often he completes a fairly lengthy list without distraction; more often than not he starts his list, digresses at a certain point, sometimes at great length, for one thing often reminds him of another;[3] then he picks the itinerary up again several pages on when his digression is over. Usually, the route is summarized in a simple heading: from place A to place B. An elaboration of the digressions, the true contents of the work, will follow below after mention of Ibn al-Mujāwir's measurement of distance, the parasang.

Ibn al-Mujāwir's parasang

It is of interest to note that the original meaning of the word *farsakh* (plural *farāsikh*) which Ibn al-Mujāwir employs in all his route lists is the distance covered on foot in

[1] Ibid., p. 2.

[2] Such problems are not confined to Ibn al-Mujāwir. Ibn Baṭṭūṭah, the North African 8th/14th-century traveller, similarly baffles scholars: where exactly did he travel and where did he take his information second-hand? See Dunn, *Adventures*, pp. 314–16.

[3] In a sort of stream of consciousness and I am much reminded of al-Mubarrad's remark in his *al-Kāmil fī al-lughah*: 'al-shay' yudhkaru bi-al-shay'', 'one thing is brought to mind by [another similar] thing'.

one hour.[1] It had disturbed me from the start that the *farsakh* was generally taken as a fixed measurement of distance[2] and this set me off on a series of calculations in order to try at least to discover what precisely Ibn al-Mujāwir means by the word.[3] Selecting twenty routes given by Ibn al-Mujāwir in *Tārīkh al-Mustabṣir*, I calculated the distances in miles as best I could, though often as the crow flies. My calculations, necessarily rough, revealed an average of 4.42 miles per parasang, which is high, and a figure below three miles per parasang had been expected. The outcome of these calculations was, however, the strong belief that we are dealing here with a word, *farsakh*, whose precise meaning we should trace back to its origin; I am now fairly confident that Ibn al-Mujāwir's parasang is the distance he found he could travel in one hour.[4] It goes without saying that this is a sensible way of expressing his distances; in this way his figures reflect the ease or difficulty of the terrain over which the traveller passes.

Place names in the text

Not surprisingly in a work of this nature, something in excess of 1,200 place names are mentioned in *Tārīkh al-Mustabṣir*, most of them situated in the west and south of the Arabian Peninsula. Unfortunately, many of these remain of dubious reading. Many too cannot be traced in other geographical and allied sources and I deliberately draw the reader's attention to this fact by a one-word note, unidentified.[5] Tedious as this may appear, it seems to me important that this fact is highlighted in this way and it should indicate that there is the strong possibility that Ibn al-Mujāwir's recording of the name in question is unique.

As evidence of Ibn al-Mujāwir keen sense of humour, I have already discussed his amusing attempts to provide the derivations of certain place names.[6] His ingenious etymologies of places such as Zabīd,[7] Ḥays[8] and Qalhāt[9] may be mentioned, again[10] comparing them to those of the famous Iraqi third/ninth-century belleletrist, al-Jāḥiẓ.[11]

[1] Except on p. 42 of the published text, where the mile (*mīl*) is used (on three occasions), a sure indication that Ibn al-Mujāwir is taking the route from an informant, and on p. 83, the stage (*marḥalah*), though not in a route list. The word *farsakh* is Parthian in origin: *frasakh*; Greek παρασάγγης (Liddell and Scott, *Lexicon*, s.v.) and Syriac *parseḥā* (Payne Smith, *Dictionary*, s.v. See also *EI*, 'farsakh').

[2] Hinz (*Masse*, p. 62) gives 'about 3 miles, 1000 *bāʿ* or approximately 6 km'.

[3] See my 'Dhofar', pp. 82–3.

[4] Discussing this problem with Dr Francine Stone, she suggests that walking with a good, fit donkey, even laden, rather than walking without, could well push up the average distance covered in an hour.

[5] I do not include Sprenger's *Reiserouten* in these sources, as he takes the whole of his Arabian section direct from Ibn al-Mujāwir's *Tārīkh al-Mustabṣir*.

[6] 'Wondrous', pp. 115–17.

[7] See p. 96 below.

[8] See p. 238 below.

[9] See p. 269 below.

[10] See 'Wondrous', p. 115.

[11] See *al-Bukhalā'*, p. 106, with such tongue-in-cheek derivations as *yaStaLlu wa-yulQī* for *salūqī*, the Arabian hound, and *ʿaṣā wa-FaRra*, for *ʿṣfūr*, the sparrow or any small bird.

Agriculture, crops, fruits, vegetables and food

As part of his interest in trade and also in the people he meets on his travels, Ibn al-Mujāwir often catalogues their agricultural produce and their food. Lists of wells may be provided, including the assessment of the salinity of each – or at least whether they are brackish or sweet. Flood irrigation is mentioned but very rarely, in detail at any rate, and one might deduce from the text that almost all agriculture was well- or *ghayl*-watered. Surprisingly, nothing is said of terraced agriculture. Lists of cereal crops (wheat, barley, sorghum, millet and so on) occur, as do those of fruits (particularly the citrus varieties) and vegetables (for example, cucumber, radish, leeks, Chinese chives). Such catalogues of produce often lead neatly into a description of the food a particular people eat. We may be told of the different types of bread available from the cereals and lists of fish occur on more than one occasion. *Harīsah*, not surprisingly in the coastal areas usually made with fish rather than the more common meat, is the dish which he recalls most frequently.

Dress and social customs

The two fit neatly together in Ibn al-Mujāwir's text and can overlap. It is true, our author does tend to emphasize the sartorially bizarre, or at least the unusual. There are, however, statements that leather is worn because it is warm in a cold mountain winter. But for the most part he delights in teasing his readers with somewhat ridiculous descriptions of strange, and often titillating, costumes. The female leather garment which is simply a rectangle with a hole in the centre for the head and which without a belt is embarrassingly revealing to the visitor not used to such displays of flesh is described with some gusto.[1] So too is the *futūḥī*, also a lady's dress, worn as the sole garment and so abundant and with such ample sleeves that a man is described as slipping inside the garment of one woman and round a complete circle of women, remaining inside their garments and emerging only after doing the complete round.[2]

Perhaps Ibn al-Mujāwir's descriptions of the social customs of those with whom he came into contact are some of the most interesting, as well as entertaining, aspects of the book. To be realistic, however, those which highlight sexual behaviour can be nothing more than an illustration of Ibn al-Mujāwir's puckish and humorous nature. His coterie of friends, all assembled to enjoy the company and the stories they produce, is brought to mind and one can imagine how such tales become stranger and stranger and more and more salacious as they are repeated time and time again.

To be charitable, we can perhaps say that this is just a part of Ibn al-Mujāwir's endeavours to understand people of different backgrounds, religious affiliations (including non-Muslims) and cultures from his own and the anecdotal aspect of his social comment should not be overemphasized. My 1993 contribution to the Dostal Festschrift, '"Anthropological" Passages' was only to some extent written with tongue in cheek, for such subjects as dress, preferred names, marriage ceremony traditions,

[1] Arabic text, p. 52.
[2] Ibid., p. 189.

burial customs, Jewish purification rituals and how to marry off both virgin and non-virgin, to mention but a few, are of genuine social interest in the context of seventh/thirteenth-century Arabia.

Magic, the wondrous and the bizarre

I have previously written on this subject[1] and can once again deal with it in general terms under four sub-headings: magic,[2] the jinn,[3] the supernatural[4] and amazing geographical changes.[5]

Examples of magic abound: a woman enormous enough to sit in the wadi bed and divert with her body the flood waters on to the land prepared for crops;[6] humans turning into lions to terrorize their fellow human beings;[7] how to become a sorceress;[8] women who can travel all the way to Java and return in one night;[9] the Socotrans in particular are all sorcerers, as well as Christians, and so powerful is their magic that they can make the island disappear as Ayyubid warships patrol up and down seeking it out in order to make a landing and capture it.[10]

The jinn appear in different shapes and sizes. Three mountains in Tihāmah are in fact three jinn metamorphosed. The jinn build; they dig canals and underground tunnels. One participates with a poet in a poetic competition and, in a fit of rage, tears the poet's favourite young she-camel to pieces.[11] In a wadi where flows of water are allocated on a tribal basis (when the wrong tribe tries to take the water, it dries up), we are told it is a jinni who has been appointed agent over the wadi in order to control and allocate the flow appropriately.[12]

Supernatural happenings often occur in nature: flowers which bloom with the flashing of lightning; flowers which open only on moonlit nights; plants which turn with the sun. There are no snakes or scorpions in Dhamār, Ibn al-Mujāwir tells us, for they die as they enter through the gates; what is more, soil taken from Dhamār and sprinkled over snakes will kill them instantly. Birds are described which dance as they sing and even birds with two bills.

There are, according to Ibn al-Mujāwir, three major amazing geographical changes which in effect bring into being the Red Sea, separating Arabia from Africa, the Gulf of Aden and the island of Socotra. One such change is wrought by the hand of God, whereas the other two through the deeds of the legendary figure Dhū al-Qarnayn.

[1] See 'Magic', *passim*.
[2] Ibid., pp. 9–11.
[3] Ibid., pp. 11–13.
[4] Ibid., pp. 13–14.
[5] Ibid., pp. 14–16.
[6] Arabic text, p. 100.
[7] Ibid., p. 194.
[8] Ibid., p. 248.
[9] Ibid., p. 266.
[10] Ibid., p. 266. Another story which fits neatly also into the humorous category. Perhaps one of the themes of the evening's conversation with his friends was the poor standard of Ayyubid navigation – and so the story developed.
[11] Arabic text p. 207.
[12] Ibid., p. 255.

History and buildings

The two are perhaps best linked in this introductory essay, as the buildings which exercise Ibn al-Mujāwir mind are often historic.

Surprisingly, in view of his introduction which focuses so precisely on his intended historical bias, it has to be admitted that Ibn al-Mujāwir is not a reliable historian. Fairly frequent remarks to that effect will be found below in my notes and I regularly correct his careless historical comments. Anything which it is possible to get wrong, he may get wrong, be it a date, the name of a person or place, or the details of some particular event. One example will suffice here.[1] He tells us of the slaying of al-Malik al-Masʿūd Ismāʿīl b. Ṭughtakīn b. Ayyūb in Wādī al-ʿIrq. Firstly, he provides no date of death. Now Ismāʿīl b. Ṭughtakīn was the nephew of the famous Saladin and the third Ayyubid ruler of the Yemen. His cognomen was in fact al-Malik al-Muʿizz, not al-Masʿūd. We know well too from reliable sources that al-Muʿizz was killed at a place called al-Qawz close to Wādī al-ʿIrq in Rajab 598/April 1202. This was only, of course, less than thirty years prior to the writing of *Tārīkh al-Mustabṣir* and was almost certainly during the lifetime of Ibn al-Mujāwir. The irony concerning his lack of accuracy with dates is that he tells us from time to time of his dreams which he invariably dates precisely.[2] The moral of this observation is that Ibn al-Mujāwir's text, at least when he purports to pass on his own piece of historical information, must be very carefully checked against other sources. Fortunately, such sources do exist and the reader accepts Ibn al-Mujāwir's historical comments without further investigation at his peril.

One more observation is necessary under the heading of history. This is to highlight Ibn al-Mujāwir's propensity for lifting historical texts verbatim and sometimes he quotes from them at great length. There are two or three lengthy quotations from ʿUmārah's *Tārīkh al-Yaman*, for example, which we can keep an eye on, as well as quotations from one work which is no longer extant.[3] He does tell us his source (see below 'The Text, Ibn al-Mujāwir's sources'), it should be pointed out, and it is true that the finger of suspicion in the cases of the occasional *lapsus calami* which occurs might well be pointed in the direction of the scribes of the manuscripts over the centuries, rather than at Ibn al-Mujāwir himself.

Buildings are a favourite topic of Ibn al-Mujāwir: castles, walls, sometimes houses and the structures of wells. In the main, they are ancient curiosities, although some contemporary structures are mentioned, albeit with little detail, except perhaps of the materials, and sometimes with the dimensions of the stone or brick, if it is used.

[1] The passage is on p. 63 of the Arabic published text. See also my 'Eastern Connection', p. 77. Ibn Baṭṭūṭah, is equally accused of such lapses (Dunn, *Adventures*, p. 313).

[2] E.g. p. 186 below, 'On 22 Ramaḍān 620 [19 October 1223], I saw in a dream ...' and there follows a description of the contents of some fairly trivial dream.

[3] The work of ʿUmārah is called *Kitāb al-Mufīd fī akhbār Zabīd* in the text, but it appears to read exactly as that of his *Tārīkh al-Yaman*. The best edition of ʿUmārah's history is that of Kay, *Yaman*, and my notes keep the reader *au fait* with any differences that have been discovered between the two texts. An example of a work no longer extant is *Kitāb al-Mufīd fī akhbār Zabīd* of Jayyāsh, the third Najahid ruler in Tihāmah (reg. 482–500/1089–1107) (see Appendix M below). There is nothing really surprising or new to be found in this text, though it is always good to rescue snippets of lost works in this way. Medieval Yemenite historians had no compunction in copying their predecessors verbatim, with or without acknowledgement, and plagiarism did not exist in their culture. I am not therefore making a value judgement here.

More in keeping with the subject of this section of the introduction is his passion for the building and renovation of ancient buildings and in particular of town walls (see next section). Materials used (stone, gypsum, mud, mud brick, baked brick etc.), dimensions and the builder or renovator are all usually presented, the latter perhaps one of the rulers of old: Decius, a Sasanian emperor, or a tubbaʿ for example. It is of little import who, for all these names merely signify the ancient, usually pre-Islamic, foundation of the building and whichever name he happens to choose can be taken with a pinch of salt. We are usually told of the number of gates in the town wall and their names. It is the subject of building and renovation which brings us closest to Ibn al-Mujāwir's stated historical aims in his introduction.

Maps and plans and diagrams

Integrated into the text are thirteen town plans or maps and these are reproduced with this translation.[1] Full captions have been written for each, rather than comprehensive translations of the notes. Briefly they are as follows: the town plans of Mecca, Jeddah, Zabīd, Jabal Ḥarīz, Aden, Taʿizz, al-Janad, Mārib, Ṣaʿdah, Biʾr al-ʿĀṣimiyyah, Ẓafār and Qalhāt and the map of Socotra. In addition, there are two diagrams to illustrate features of the text: a pointed hat and what is in all probability a levelling board to be pulled by oxen preparing land for cultivation (p. 69 of the Arabic text) and also benches used for relaxation and reclining (ibid., p. 259).

Trade and commerce

There are three aspects of trade and commerce in seventh/thirteenth-century Arabia with which Ibn al-Mujāwir deals. The first and most obvious is his lengthy description of the port of Aden and its administration, the second his mention of commercial land routes and the third his catalogues of currencies and exchange rates and weights and measures.

Pages 138–46 of the published Arabic text are given over to Ibn al-Mujāwir's detailed description of trade in Aden, the most important port in the Peninsula at the time of his writing.[2] The lowly look-out who is supposed to spot arriving merchant ships, the chain of events after his correct recognition of an Aden-bound ship, the official arrangements once the ship has anchored in the harbour, the off-loading of commodities, the instituion of the galley-tax, the goods for which taxes are payable, the goods for which they are not, other taxes and dues to which merchants are liable, the market of slave-girls and the law of sale and defect in action; all these topics are dealt with by our author. My instant comment on all this information is that he must have spent a great deal of time in Aden investigating all aspects of the port administration and how imports were handled. My further observation is how valuable the information is (see below '*Tārīkh al-Mustabṣir* as a source of social and economic history').

[1] See pp. 11, 44, 77 (Zabīd, reproduced here), 103, 129, 157, 162, 198, 205, 220, 261, 269 and 273. Noha Sadek ('Zabīd', p. 215) refers to them as 'schematic maps with varying degrees of detail, they offer the reader additional information not found in the text proper'.

[2] See my 'Maritime Trade', especially pp. 129–34.

Before moving on to land routes – the second aspect of Ibn al-Mujāwir's treatment of commercial matters – it should be stressed that Ibn al-Mujāwir writes from the merchant's point of view and he articulates the resentment and unhappiness felt by merchants when they were confronted by the Ayyubid customs administration in Aden.[1] Unlike their successors, the Rasulids, who established a relatively benign customs regime in later years, the Ayyubids in the Yemen, who, it must always be remembered, were still trying to bring about military and political stability there, had not yet had the opportunity to develop and refine their administration and to win the confidence of the merchant classes.

Ibn al-Mujāwir describes to us a number of commercial land routes. For example, there is the old route from Ẓafār, in the extreme south of what is now Oman, to Baghdad[2] and he tells us how the bedouin traders brought in horses from Iraq and took away perfume and cloths (or perhaps, though less likely, wheat). He also recalls a paved(?) route from Raysūt, across the bay from Ẓafār, to Baghdad,[3] along which commodities were brought from Iraq and brass, cinnabar, rose-water and silver originating in India taken back there.

Thirdly, Ibn al-Mujāwir's keen interest in exchange rates, commodities and weights and measures is particularly evident when he writes of Mecca, where he clearly spent some time examining the market places, and Zabīd.[4] In a passage of some complexity, he looks first at units of currency in Mecca and compares them with values in Egypt, the headquarters of the Ayyubid house. He then turns to the Yemen, telling us what unit of measurement is used for what commodity. Reverting to Mecca, he makes the interesting comment that measurements change in and out of the pilgrimage season. Further comparisons with the commercial situation in Iraq follow, before he turns his attention for some time to the trade in leather. He writes of the quality of different leathers, how they are sold in Mecca and how in the Yemen. He informs us of the different types of leather and which are preferred where. Equally valuable is his description of the markets of Zabīd, the commodities found there and the units of measurement used.

Tārīkh al-Mustabṣir as a source of the economic and social history of Ayyubid Yemen

Tūrānshāh, the brother of Saladin, and his Ayyubid successors gradually imposed firm political control over Tihāmah and the southern highlands of the Yemen over a period of time beginning with the arrival of their large army in the north of the Red Sea coastal plain in 569/1173. They remained in the country for a period of only about fifty-seven/fifty-five years (569–626/1173–1228), when, by default almost, the Rasulids, their protégés, took over this same territory. Perhaps because they were only in the country for such a relatively short time, all the efforts of the Ayyubids appear to have been directed at a thorough military conquest of Tihāmah and southern Yemen. Local states,

[1] 'Maritime Trade', p. 130 and note 15.

[2] Arabic text, p. 263, and see my 'Eastern Connection', pp. 82–3.

[3] Arabic text, p. 268, and see my 'Dhofar and Socotra', p. 87.

[4] Arabic text, pp. 12–14, for Mecca and pp. 88–9 for Zabīd .

like those dealt with above in 'The Historical Background', were swept aside by the conqerors from Egypt with their superior numbers of men and horse and with their good discipline and military organization. It was their successors, the Rasulids (628–858/1230–1454), who could reap the benefits of these military successes and it was they who were able to build up a government administration of unequalled brilliance. It is not therefore surprising that we have no commercial documentary material on Ayyubid Yemen, in contrast incidentally to Ayyubid Egypt and Rasulid Yemen, no material, that is, except what Ibn al-Mujāwir is able to convey to us in *Tārīkh al-Mustabṣir*.[1]

Writing as a businessman, or as someone in sympathy with the merchants of the day, Ibn al-Mujāwir conveys to us a wealth of commercial information on Ayyubid Yemen, that is described in 'Trade and commerce' above. It is unique in two ways: firstly, it is unique in itself; there is nothing else which has so far come to light and it can be said with confidence that nothing else is likely to come to light. Secondly, it is unique when compared with other similar material from contemporary Ayyubid Egypt and later Rasulid Yemen: all the data we have from such sources were collected by state officials and the authors write from that standpoint, not, as Ibn al-Mujāwir does, from that of the merchant.[2]

If *Tārīkh al-Mustabṣir* is a unique commercial source, then there remains the question of the quality of the information provided. It seems to me that the passages of commercial interest speak for themselves in this regard. Ibn al-Mujāwir deals in some detail with the various aspects of Aden trade. He was undoubtedly there in the field and writes, if not always with great clarity and organization, with authority and with a manifest experience of what he saw during his travels.

Much the same can be said of *Tārīkh al-Mustabṣir* as a source of the social history of the Yemen. It seems unlikely that more sources will be found and there is nothing in existence which can even remotely match the passages of social interest written by Ibn al-Mujāwir anyway. One must confess that in the sphere of social customs, Ibn al-Mujāwir can certainly make a meal of the unusual dress and behaviour which he encountered. These reports, moreover, are more likely to have formed the subject of debate during meetings with what I imagine to be his male cronies than, say, the minutiae of trade and commercial taxation in the area, and therefore to have become exaggerated and distorted. Even with this in mind, however, I would suggest that Ibn al-Mujāwir's observations on the social customs of seventh/thirteenth-century Arabia are there for all to see and presented with some conviction and authority. It is easy to decide, I would suggest, when Ibn al-Mujāwir has his tongue in his cheek and when he does not.

Essentially then, Ibn al-Mujāwir's information on the commerce, trade and social behaviour of the inhabitants of Arabia is unique and is likely to remain so. The reader must make up his own mind, but it is my contention that we have in this text an excellent source, as far as it goes, of these aspects of life in the seventh/thirteenth-century Arabian Peninsula.

[1] From Ayyubid Egypt, I am thinking in particular of such works as Ibn Mammātī's *Qawānīn al-dawāwīn* and from Rasulid Yemen, *Nūr al-ma'ārif* and Ḥusaynī's *Mulakhkhaṣ al-fiṭan*, the former a treatise on the Ayyubid administration in Egypt (both now published, Smith, *Medieval Administrative and Fiscal Treatise and Nūr*), and the latter two texts concerning the Rasulid administration in the Yemen. See my 'Port Practices', p. 210.

[2] I exclude here the enormous mass of Geniza material; they were original documents written by both merchants and civil servants and others, but rather the raw materials, while here we speak of administrative treatises.

Assessment of the contents

Let us begin on the debit side. The reader may find the text a little disorganized and Appendix A below is meant to serve at least to clarify the route lists Ibn al-Mujāwir has in his text. The reader will certainly discover so many amendments and corrections, both in the translation itself and in the notes, that he may even be excused for wondering whether *Tārīkh al-Mustabṣir* is anything other than a simple linguistic curiosity and a catalogue of funny, sometimes obscene, stories. It must certainly be admitted that Ibn al-Mujāwir does get his information confused and sometimes just plain wrong. This is perhaps clearest when he is dabbling in history and dates, names and even events can be presented erroneously. He is full of good intentions to provide information on such topics, far removed in time and space, as pre-Islamic happenings for example, and Indian names and myths too, but he lacks the detailed data from which to work. With the former, it seems, anyone may be involved, perhaps Dhū al-Qarnayn, a Sasanian emperor or a South Arabian tubbaʿ; when he deals with India, tedious and confusing lists with distorted and corrupted names can be dished up.

Let us concede also that our author is no great intellectual. He misquotes on occasions (if only slightly) the text of the Quran. He fails time and time again to tell us more of the ideas of the religious groups with whom he comes into contact. The poetry he quotes is often carelessly presented, and even the long passages copied verbatim from the prose works of others can contain errors.

On the debit side too, it must be admitted that what may begin as genuine social observation and comment often degenerates into a smutty anecdote, picked up perhaps, laughed and sniggered at, by Ibn al-Mujāwir and his companions.

Certain firm and positive statements can be made, however, on the credit side of the balance. Firstly, this is a major, sometimes unique, source for the historical geography of the west and south of the Arabian Peninsula. This latter is badly served on the whole by the medieval geographers and travel writers (with the exception of Hamdānī and his *Ṣifah*). Where one can have confidence in a route, it may often be that *Tārīkh al-Mustabṣir* uniquely documents its topography.

The text is also without any shadow of doubt a unique and extremely informative source for the economic history of the Zurayʿid and Ayyubid periods of Yemenite history, before the country settled down under the Rasulids to a life of administrative and cultural brilliance. Again Ibn al-Mujāwir's detailed comments on the major port of Aden must be mentioned.

Likewise it can be said that *Tārīkh al-Mustabṣir* is so far a unique, and on many occasions an enlightening, source for the social history of seventh/thirteenth-century Arabia. Since descriptions of social customs and mores may develop in his work into what appears to be a titillating tale, the reader must beware and decide for himself whether he is reading informative medieval sociology, or simply the repartee of a comedian with a penchant for blue jokes. My own opinion is that he is reading both and it is not difficult to decide the nature of each passage.

That the text is linguistically challenging and of immense interest is a gross understatement (see below, 'The language'). Suffice it to say here, this is a major milestone in the history of the Arabic language. It is one of the very few works available to us which is written in what can be termed Middle Arabic and composed by a Muslim. It must surely be compared with Usāmah Ibn Munqidh's *Kitāb al-Iʿtibār* and be brought into consideration when future discussion is comtemplated concerning the nature of Middle Arabic, particularly Muslim Middle Arabic, as opposed to Judaeo-Arabic and Christian Arabic, especially the question why – why would any Muslim brought up with the Quran and the discipline of classical Arabic and all the emotional attachments which that involved even think of writing in Middle Arabic?

Finally, it might be said that this is a monument to a seventh/thirteenth-century traveller who had an extraordinary sense of humour and who allowed that sense of humour to shine through. This is to his eternal credit. Far from your finding its sections and chapters 'lifeless', as Ibn al-Mujāwir himself puts it, 'you are relieved of your fatigue', above all by the author's humour and fun.

THE TEXT

Ibn al-Mujāwir's text generally speaking follows the geographical route which he took and which has been described above ('The Contents'). While perhaps somewhat disorganized, the work is essentially based on a series of route lists (see Appendix A below), with digressions, short and long, inserted where he feels he needs to elaborate on some geographical or indeed any other feature. The information he imparts is derived from three sources: his personal observations, his informants and named literary works.

Ibn al-Mujāwir's sources – personal observations, informants, literary works

The most obvious indication which the text provides that Ibn al-Mujāwir is writing from personal observation is his common third person intervention, 'Ibn al-Mujāwir said'. Frequently this is followed by an opinion on a particular subject, but also it is the prelude to any observation which has come to mind. The reader should also be aware that any stray first person pronoun also heralds Ibn al-Mujāwir's actual involvement in an event or situation and therefore that personal, rather than second-hand, information is being provided. My experience too is that where no indication is given at all in the text to the contrary it is as well to assume that Ibn al-Mujāwir's own thoughts are being conveyed to the reader.

Fortunately, Ibn al-Mujāwir is meticulous in naming his informants before he passes on their information and a total of seventy are quoted by name in the text. These make up the second source of his information. Only rarely is he vague: 'A Jewish silversmith in Aden informed me ...';[1] 'A certain Christian said ...'.[2] Unfortunately, however, almost all his informants are impossible to identify. Some, I believe, belong to his group of chums to whom I have already alluded, those who gather together with our author to enjoy good conversation and a fine yarn and add much colour to the subject in question. Did some of these chums travel with him, we should perhaps ask? Incidentally, seventeen out of the seventy of his informants can be identified as 'eastern' by origin. Others assuredly were informants whom Ibn al-Mujāwir met on the road.

[1] Arabic text, p. 32. On the question of Ibn al-Mujāwir's informants in general, see my 'Eastern Connection', pp. 80–81.

[2] Arabic text, p. 33.

The identifiable exceptions are his family and their clients: Aḥmad b. Masʿūd, his uncle;[1] Aḥmad b. Muḥammad b. Masʿūd, his brother;[2] Mubārak al-Sharʿabī, client of Muḥammad b. Masʿūd, his father;[3] Muḥammad b. Masʿūd, his father;[4] and Rayḥān, client of ʿAlī b. Masʿūd, his uncle.[5]

Ibn al-Mujāwir's third source of information is certain literary texts which he names and from which he quotes.[6] A comprehensive list of these texts can be found below in Appendix C. It is not surprising, given his declared interest in the history of the regions he describes, that we should find quotations from historical writers. His only Hejazi historian is the third/ninth-century figure, al-Fākihī from whom he quotes fairly briefly on three occasions. This reflects the lesser emphasis on events of the Hejaz and what he quotes is in the main 'old hat' being the somewhat fanciful etymologies of the Arabic Makkah, Mecca. Not surprisingly, his debt to the Yemenite historian ʿUmārah (d. 569/1173) is much greater, for Ibn al-Mujāwir spent more time in the south of the Peninsula and was clearly more involved in contemporary happenings there, which in turn led him to investigate some of the more recent history in the area. From ʿUmārah in some lengthy passages (see Kay, *Yaman*, p. xii for his remarks on the *Mufīd*), he took much on the Sulayhids (see above, 'Historical Background, The Yemen', and below, Appendix B.5), and on the Zurayʿids (see above, 'Historical Background, The Yemen', and below, Appendix B.6), the dynasty holding Aden prior to the Ayyubid conquest in 569/1173. His only other source of Yemenite history is a work by the Najahid ruler, Jayyāh (d. 498/1104), which is no longer extant.

He twice quotes from the well-known encyclopaedist, historian and geographer, al-Masʿūdī (d. c. 345/956). Neither quotation is of any great import.

His one quotation, at the head of which he names the renowned medieval scientist, al-Bīrūnī (d. after 441/1049), is from the *Tafhīm* and concerns the signs of the zodiac, in particular the nature of women born under different star signs. Its sexual nature may have caught Ibn al-Mujāwir's eye. He also quotes from al-Bīrūnī without acknowledgement, and at some length, concerning the Jews and their festivals. This I associate strongly with Ibn al-Mujāwir's interest in the people he meets and on more than one occasion he comments on the lives and behaviour of non-Muslims.

Other acknowledged quotations need not detain us much further: a work on religions (*adyān*), which I cannot trace, by the exegete, philosoper and traditionist, Fakhr al-Dīn al-Rāzī (d. 606/1209), detailing a legal problem among the Jews concerning circumcision; a work of Quranic exegesis (although the quotations concern legends of old rather than profound religious matters); an unknown work entitled the *Tarjamah*; and, predictably, a pilot guide, *Kitāb al-Rahmānj*.

[1] Ibid., p. 86.

[2] Ibid., p. 97.

[3] Ibid., p. 111.

[4] Ibid., p. 252. His father is not so much an informant here, but rather Ibn al-Mujāwir is quoting what he once wrote.

[5] Ibid., pp. 97, 115, 120, 243 and 245, one of his common informants.

[6] I leave out of the reckoning here his numerous quotations from the Quran, one or two of which are slightly inaccurate. It would be very strange in any case if he did not quote from this source.

The language

In 1996, I published a detailed study of the language of Ibn al-Mujāwir's *Tārīkh al-Mustabṣir*[1] and this serves as the major source of this section of the introduction. The prime conclusions then were that the language of the text of *Tārīkh al-Mustabṣir* is Middle Arabic and that the text was composed containing more non-classical Arabic features than we find in the version now before us. I return to the various arguments here and add a new dimension to those of my 1996 study.

I should firstly offer a definition of exactly what I mean by Middle Arabic. I use the term here in the strict sense of a literary Arabic which is a mixture of non-classical Arabic elements and pure classical Arabic elements – and by classical Arabic, I mean the language described by the classical grammarians.[2] Middle Arabic is not a chronological term; its earliest examples are the Arabic papyrus texts which date from the first/seventh century. The papyri are particularly valuable examples of Middle Arabic, since they are all original documents, uncorrupted by later scribes and, what is more, written before the classical grammarians put pen to paper. Then again, the language of Middle Arabic can be found right down to the present day.

Most examples of Middle Arabic were written by Jews, Judaeo-Arabic, and Christians, Christian Arabic. Complete, full-length Middle Arabic texts written by Muslims are rare and only one to my knowledge has so far been published, Usāmah Ibn Munqidh's *Kitāb al-Iʿtibār*. Such has been its impact on scholars that it has also been translated and studied.[3]

The first question of great importance, it seems to me, is what is the process of composition and how exactly do Middle Arabic texts come out as this mixture of non-classical Arabic and classical Arabic. The second, much more difficult, question is why a Muslim, presumably steeped in classical Arabic as the language of the Quran to which he would be deeply emotionally attached, should wish to compose in Middle Arabic.

As good fortune would have it, we have in the example of *Tārīkh al-Mustabṣir* a reasonable guide on the first question posed above. How did the text as we have it now in Oscar Löfgren's edition come about in the form we have it? The oldest manuscript dates from 1003 (AD 1595) i.e. almost four hundred years after its composition. The only other manuscript which Oscar Löfgren chose to take seriously enough to include in his edition is that of the University Library, Leiden (Or 5572), which was copied in the nineteenth century. What first of all happened to the text between the early eleventh/late sixteenth century and the nineteenth? While the two manuscripts have a common recension, the latter has undergone a major 'correcting' operation, with the great majority of non-classical Arabic features of the earlier manuscript rendered into classical Arabic. It therefore seems reasonable to me to assume that the copying process between the early seventh/thirteenth century, when the text was composed, and

[1] 'Language'.

[2] Joshua Blau is the name which first comes to mind in the context of Middle Arabic. He has changed his mind over the years and from 1965 (*Emergence*, pp. 24–5), when he interprets Middle Arabic as being the non-classical Arabic elements in an Arabic text, to 1981 ('State of Research', *passim*), when he suggests that Middle Arabic means the mixed language, i.e. more or less the definition I have just given.

[3] Published by Derenbourg, *Ousama* and Hitti, *Usāmah's Memoirs*; translated by Hitti, *Memoirs*, and studied by Schen, 'Usāma Ibn Munqidh's Memoirs'.

the eleventh/sixteenth century, the date of the oldest extant manuscript, had been much the same, that therefore the original text was 'corrected' by disapproving scribes over the years and was much more heavily laced with non-classical Arabic features at the time of its composition. Both the papyri and the *I'tibār* support this theory. The former have an extremely high level of non-classical Arabic elements.[1] We have only one manuscript of the *I'tibār*, and that dating from a time close to composition in the sixth/twelvth century. Without scribal interference, the non-classical Arabic features of the *I'tibār* have remained large in number, certainly larger than those of *Tārīkh al-Mustabṣir*.

The second question posed was why should a Muslim compose in Middle Arabic? In the case of the *I'tibār*, two theories have been advanced. Firstly, Landberg suggests[2] that the text is that which was dictated by Usāmah as he lay old, sick and dying. This suggestion is supported by Schen[3] and seems to me to be a plausible explanation of why Usāmah, who had previously composed in classical Arabic (including a whole *dīwān* of poetry) should for the first time write in Middle Arabic.

A second suggestion was that made by Blau.[4] He rejects the idea of a dictated text. His argument is that the *I'tibār* did not fall 'within one of the recognized categories of "literature" and so did not require an elevated style'. In the narrow context of the *I'tibār*, I find this less plausible, though not out of the question. Perhaps both this and the dictation explanation should be borne in mind.

Returning to *Tārīkh al-Mustabṣir*, the idea of the text having been dictated is not an outlandish one and there are even one or two clues in the text which have been highlighted in the notes and which could point to a process of dictation. The suggestion, however, to quote Blau on the *I'tibār*, that Ibn al-Mujāwir's text was not written 'within one of the recognized categories of "literature" and so did not require an elevated style' is clearly not sustainable.

One further point should be raised here. In my 1996 study of the language of *Tārīkh al-Mustabṣir*, I wrote, 'That he may have been a native Persian speaker ... certainly does not mean that he was incapable of writing Classical Arabic'.[5] With the passage of time and further concentrated study of the text in the process of making this translation, however, I have come to recognize that there is at least the possiblity that Ibn al-Mujāwir's knowledge of Arabic was less than perfect. The more I have read the text, the more I am inclined to think that this is not just Middle Arabic before my eyes, but perhaps also the writing of a Persian speaker who had a less than complete grasp of the Arabic language. I shall not labour the point further; but I do feel now that it should be added to the conclusions of my 1996 study.

To sum up very briefly: *Tārīkh al-Mustabṣir* was written in Middle Arabic by a non-Arabic speaker; the process of copying between the oldest (1003/1595) and the nineteenth century Leiden manuscript was one of 'correcting' the non-classical Arabic

[1] Blau (*Emergence*, p. 123), in my view, underestimates the amount of non-classical Arabic features in the papyrus texts. Cf. Hopkins, *Studies*, p. xlvii.

[2] *Critica Arabica*, p. 30.

[3] Schen, 'Usāma Ibn Munqidh's Memoirs', p. 228.

[4] Blau, 'State of Research', p. 191, n. 23. See also Nöldeke, 'H. Derenbourg', pp. 237 ff. and Schen, 'Usāma Ibn Munqidh's Memoirs', pp. 228–9.

[5] 'Language', p. 348. The remark is a perfectly reasonable one, and have not some of the greatest names in Arabic literature been Persians?

features, and we can assume that the same process was taking place between composition of the text (early seventh/thirteenth century) and the oldest manuscript (early eleventh/late sixteenth century). This is the reason that *Tārīkh al-Mustabṣir* is less heavily laced with non-classical Arabic features than, say, the Arabic papyri and the *Iʿtibār*. We shall perhaps never know why a Muslim should choose to write in Middle Arabic, even our author, Ibn al-Mujāwir, a man of business and humour, rather than of learning and deep religious conviction.

The manuscripts and the published edition

Löfgren used extensively two manuscripts in order to arrive at his edition: one of the Ayasofya, Istanbul, Nr. 3080, now preserved in the Süleymaniye Kütüphanesi, and the second of the University Library of Leiden, Or. 5572 (Ar. 2450). Although he lists a third, of the University Library of Uppsala, Landberg 69, its siglum does not figure in Oscar Löfgren's apparatus.

Löfgren's Arabic text was published in two parts with continuous pagination, part I in 1951 and part II in 1954. Apart from the text itself and the apparatus which is presented as footnotes, the publication contains only the following: in part I – an Arabic title page, a list of contents of part I using the headings found in the text, a brief table of errata; in part II – a Latin title page, a dedicatory page in Latin, dedicating the book to the memory of De Goeje and Snouck Hurgronje, a two-page foreword in German, a list of references with sigla and the abbreviations used in the apparatus, a list of contents by location and plans for part I in the Roman type, a second one-page foreword in German, a list of contents by location and plans for part II in the Roman type and finally, following the Arabic headings of the text, a list of contents of part II. For some reason, an introduction and indices were never included in the publication and Löfgren was kind enough to send me some draft introductory remarks and complete draft indices when I first corresponded with him about the work in the 1980s.

Using the Istanbul manuscript (I MS) as the basis of his edition, Oscar Löfgren's Latin footnotes contain in the main variant readings from the Leiden MS (L MS). It came as no surprise to discover quickly that the huge majority of these variants arise from the apparent need of the scribe of L MS to 'correct' the non-classical Arabic features in the I MS version.[1] Where the editor has discovered that the author is taking material from elsewhere, he identifies it precisely and where necessary provides variant readings. Similarly, where he has discovered that other modern scholars have quoted a passage from *Tārīkh al-Mustabṣir* (usually Landberg), he will give the precise reference. All Quranic references are given, as are all the metres of the poetry where possible. Oscar Löfgren provides aid with many lexicographical problems and frequently gives a precise reference to one of the classical Arabic lexica or European dictionaries with a definition. Similarly, he endeavours to provide assistance with unclear place and personal names. Where the text is of dubious reading or corrupt, Oscar Löfgren, with truly remarkable skill and understanding, frequently suggests a reading or alternative reading, very, very few of which I have found necessary to reject out of hand.

[1] See previous section 'The language' above.

The end product is a seemingly uncluttered treasure trove of erudition and enlightenment. It is true that no one today would think of composing a Latin apparatus for an Arabic text, and in the West at any rate throwing in all useful references together with variant readings (the 'dustbin' method!) would now be frowned upon – though perhaps not in the Arab world. Oscar Löfgren too, it might be said, was no traveller and many lacunae might have been filled and many dubious readings confirmed in his text if he had been. I am thinking particularly of all the light which R. B. Serjeant was able to shed on the text by simply taking the text with him on all his travels in the Arabian Peninsula. But it must be said at the end of the day that Oscar Löfgren's edition is a superb effort of precision and meticulousness; I do not recall a single misreading of all the many manuscript readings I have checked during work on this translation. I know he was proud of his efforts and laboured many years on *Tārīkh al-Mustabṣir*. Perhaps he published far too much for any one of his works alone to be counted a memorial to his name, although I would like to think that this edition is precisely that.

Other manuscripts

A brief word concerning the other manuscripts of *Tārīkh al-Mustabṣir* which have come to light might be in order here. The following is, as far as possible, a list in order of date of copying:

1) Istanbul, Sülaymaniye Kütüphanesi, Ayasofya 3080, 1003/1595
2) Leiden, University Library, Or 5572, 19th century
3) Paris, Bibliothèque Nationale, Schefer collection 6021, 1279/1862 (Derenbourg, *Manuscrits*, p. 18)
4) London, British Library Add. 25,603, 1862 (Playfair copy of the Paris MS)
5) Uppsala, University Library, Landberg 69 (Zettersteen, *Handschriften*, pp. 102–3).[1]

THE PLACE OF *TĀRĪKH AL-MUSTABṢIR* IN ARABIC GEOGRAPHICAL AND TRAVEL LITERATURE

A comprehensive survey of Arabic geographical literature cannot be attempted here.[2] Suffice it to mention the major trends and schools and their exponents, to examine the essential features of *Tārīkh al-Mustabṣir* and to attempt to see where the work might fit into the grand scheme. The astronomical, mathematical and geodetic approach to geography may be disregarded for our purposes, as too navigational literature, although these were extremely important in early Islamic scholarship and culture.

Human geography was born in an eastern, particularly Iranian, milieu and is closely associated with *adab*, general knowledge and culture. Government officials and administrators needed information concerning the Islamic world and this new

[1] See also Brockelmann, *Geschichte*, I, p. 482, S I, p. 883.

[2] For a detailed discussion of Arabic geographical literature, see Miquel, *Geographie humaine*. Hopkins's survey ('Geographical Literature') is chapter-length and more up-to-date. I use the term 'geographical' in the widest possible sense.

kind of geographical writing, which not only sought to inform and edify such people, but also to bring recreation and enjoyment more generally to the literate classes, was born.

The first of such writers, often thought of as the 'classical' school of Arabic geographical literature, was Ibn Khurdādhbeh, a Persian who died c. 300/911.[1] Others were al-Iṣṭakhrī (fourth/ninth century),[2] Ibn Ḥawqal (d. c. 380/990)[3] and al-Muqaddasī (d. after 380/990).[4] Such works may perhaps be called 'ways and kingdoms' a literal translation of the title of Ibn Khurdādhbeh's and al-Iṣṭakhrī's works, and they are basically personal descriptions of routes and of regional features.[5] Continuing the tradition, yet introducing more biographical and historical material, is the 'post-classical' school[6] as epitomized by al-Idrīsī (560/1165).[7]

Finally,[8] mention must be made of travel literature (*riḥlah*). Two names quickly come to mind in this context: Ibn Jubayr (d. 614/1217)[9] and Ibn Baṭṭūṭah (d. c. 770–79/1368–77).[10] As the name of the genre implies, these are personal accounts of travels and voyages, in which the authors record their impressions of their travelling experiences and of the sights they see.

What then can be said of *Tārīkh al-Mustabṣir* after this very cursory account of the genres of geographical and travel literature in Arabic? Although there can certainly be no suggestion that Ibn al-Mujāwir aimed to instruct government officials, we can see that there is an element of the 'ways and kingdoms', the 'classical' genre, in *Tārīkh al-Mustabṣir*. His, albeit disorganized, route lists and descriptions of geographical features are there for all to see and he certainly had the aim to instruct and entertain. Perhaps, nevertheless we should emphasize 'the ways' rather than 'the kingdoms', for Ibn al-Mujāwir does not show any great propensity for discussions on 'political regions'.[11] The work teems with *adab*, whether in the form of anecdotal material of various sorts or of general – and sometimes specific, and even technical – knowledge. His declared interest in all things historical (even if he does not always get his facts correct) is clearly laid out in his introduction.[12] There can be no question too that *Tārīkh al-Mustabṣir* is a *riḥlah*

[1] *al-Masālik wa-al-mamālik*. See also Miquel, *Géographie*, pp. 87–92.

[2] Also *al-Masālik wa-al-mamālik*.

[3] *Ṣūrat al-arḍ*.

[4] *Aḥsan al-taqāsīm fī ma'rifat al-aqālīm*. See Miquel, *Géographie*, pp. 313–15.

[5] The *mamālik*, literally 'kingdoms', would appear to mean 'political regions' (Hopkins 'Geographical Literature', p. 314).

[6] This is Hopkins's term ('Geographical Literature', p. 317).

[7] *Nuzhat al-mushtāq fī ikhtirāq al-āfāq*. See Bibliography, s.v. *Opus Geographicum*.

[8] Geographical dictionaries and encyclopaedias also form an important and exceptionally useful genre and may thus be mentioned here in passing, though it is not suggested that they are relevant to this precise discussion. Surely the grand master was Yāqūt b. 'Abdallāh (d. 626/1229, i.e. about the time Ibn al-Mujāwir was writing *Tārīkh al-Mustabir*) and references to his *Mu'jam* will be found profusely scattered throughout the notes below.

[9] *Riḥlat Ibn Jubayr*.

[10] Also called *Riḥlah*, though the real title is *Tuḥfat al-nuẓẓār fī gharā'ib al-amṣār wa-'ajā'ib al-asfār*. See Bibliography, s.v. *Travels*.

[11] It might be recalled that Ibn al-Mujāwir takes from Ibn Ḥawqal, a 'classical' geographer, passages verbatim the subject of which might be termed 'political regions' (pp. 39–40 and 231 of the Arabic text). It may not be an exaggeration, therefore, to suggest that he has very little or nothing of his own to contribute to the subject.

[12] See above: 'The Contents; Ibn al-Mujāwir's introduction'.

work; disorganized it may be and by no means strictly chronological, but one can read of the personal journey(s) in Arabia of this Khurasani traveller on every page. Without too much imagination, then, one can detect features in the text of the 'classical', 'post-classical' and *riḥlah* genres, as they have been set out above.

TRANSLATOR'S NOTES

On the translation

Using essentially the printed text, though having had frequent recourse to the two manuscripts, I MS and L MS, throughout, I have endeavoured to translate the whole of Ibn al-Mujāwir's work. The numbers in square brackets refer to the page numbers of Oscar Löfgren's printed Arabic edition. Only serious and/or substantial insertions on the part of the translator have been enclosed in square brackets and supplying a noun for a pronoun, or, more likely in *Tārīkh al-Mustabṣir*, a pronoun for a noun, for example, is not so indicated. I have retained the original headings of the author's Arabic text and translated them in italics. I have used the word 'section' at the head of the many passages headed by the one Arabic word, *faṣl*. Where I feel absolutely sure that there is an error, I correct and indicate this clearly in the note. Where I only suspect that a correction is required, I leave the original and include my suspicions in the note. I have taken every opportunity to anglicize; I see no merit, for example, in al-Baḥrayn, al-Ḥudaydah and Juddah/Jiddah, when Bahrain, Hodeida and Jeddah are used commonly – sometimes officially – and completely understood by all. Persian and Turkish names I have preferred to write as such as far as possible and not simply to transliterate the Arabic. Words like amir, qadi and wadi, even tubbaʿ (the word used in Islamic texts for the pre-Islamic ruler in the Yemen) I have regarded as English. Otherwise all non-English words other than proper names are italicized in the normal way. Ibn al-Mujāwir's frequent third person intervention, 'qāla Ibn al-Mujāwir', I have left as the bland, 'Ibn al-Mujāwir said' and remind the reader that this is the one clear indication that our author is directly involved in the happenings of the text, or is about to voice his own opinion, or give his own version. I have tried to give verses of poetry the appearance of such, though I make no claim to poetic translations of the same. How to deal delicately with sexual matters I have found something of a problem. I have finally decided the only course of action is to consider carefully the context in which they occur: in a court of law I have been clinical; translating the obscenities of quarrelling fishwives I have used what would seem to be appropriate colloquialisms. Ibn al-Mujāwir's frequent and exaggerated tautology I have tended to avoid in English. I have usually tried to run the component parts together with what I judge to be the right amount of emphasis.

I have often struggled long and hard with dubious and corrupt passages. On occasions, one has simply to go along with the context; on others, no amount of teasing out will provide anything like satisfactory translations. In such circumstances, I have transliterated the passage concerned in the note. Whatever the circumstances, I have always indicated what I am doing in the note. Where two or more interpretations of a passage seem to me possible, the most likely is included in the translation and the other possible renderings are given in the note.

On the notes

I have tried to make the reader's task easier and more enjoyable by the inclusion of no fewer than 2,800 notes on the text. The latter is replete with all manner of references to persons, tribes, religious groups, historical events, places and so on, sometimes relatively obvious, sometimes downright obscure, of which identification has been my first duty. While the identification of the first four in this list has not been particularly taxing (excluding here the identification of Ibn al-Mujāwir's named informants who are doubtless in the main members of his coterie about whom I have already talked), the fifth, toponyms, has at times proved extremely difficult. It should be noted in particular that I have adopted the practice of mentioning my inability to trace the place name elsewhere in my *literary* sources by a simple one-word note, 'unidentified'. The reader should remember that such a note (or indeed a whole series of such notes) in all probability indicates that Ibn al-Mujāwir's description of a place or of a whole route is unique. Such places may have been found on modern maps and the note concerned indicates this.

There is also the question of Ibn al-Mujāwir's errors which occur throughout the work and it has been a major task in composing the notes to include corrections for the reader's information. I hope the note concerned illustrates clearly what I am trying to achieve.

In a work like this, with its cast of thousands and pot-pourri of any number of different subjects, I have not hesitated to repeat brief notes on important individuals and topics, rather than have the reader, through the relevant index, return to an earlier note in order to follow the text.

It will be noticed that on occasions Arabic words in the notes are provided with the root letters purposely in capitals. This is to help explain some particular reference in the text to some etymology or such which Ibn al-Mujāwir is trying to highlight. A good, straightforward example might be on p. 161 below, where the author suggests the place named al-Muzayḥifah is to be derived from the Arabic verb *ZaḤaFa*.

On the glossary, appendixes and bibliography

These generally speak for themselves and in any case the first has a clear note at the beginning. I refer the reader once again to the great linguistic interest which the Arabic text holds, some of that interest a lexicographical one. The text contains a plethora of Persian and more generally 'eastern' words, many of Indian origin, and the author too is much influenced by the language which he finds in the Arabian Peninsula, particularly, it seems to me, in the south. The glossary reflects this dual influence on Ibn al-Mujāwir in what he wrote.

While carrying out this work, it has struck me from time to time that the reader would be well served to have certain specific information or a particular list provided for him. These subjects and lists make up the Appendixes below: A – his routes; B – a genealogical table and dynastic lists; and C – a list of Ibn al-Mujāwir's literary sources.

The bibliography includes all the literary works and maps which I have used personally during the translation of *Tārīkh al-Mustabṣir* and in the writing of these introductory essays. I have not included those sources used by others who have commented on my draft text and whose observations appear in the notes.

On the maps

I have included two maps at pp. xiii and xiv.

Map 1, 'Ibn al-Mujāwir's World', includes part of India, Sind, Makrān, Persia, the Arabian Peninisula, Khurasan, Iraq, the Levant and part of Egypt. My wish here is particularly to show Ibn al-Mujāwir's travels as recorded in *Tārīkh al-Mustabṣir* and those about which I am confident I have drawn in long broken lines. This includes the strong theory that he travelled from Khurasan and took either the Basra–Mecca or the Kufa–Mecca pilgrim route.

More doubtful journeys, north of Aden into the highlands of the Yemen for example and his return to Khurasan from Bahrain are drawn in short broken lines. This method allows that he either made the journey or that he took the information he provides from informants.

Map 2, 'Seventh/Thirteenth-Century Arabia', highlights some of the more important geographical features of the Arabian Peninsula of his day.

TĀRĪKH AL-MUSTABṢIR: TRANSLATION

[1] In the name of God, the Compassionate, the Merciful. Praise be to God who raised up heaven as an example to those who look, and spread out the earth, placing on it signs for those who are sure. He left [thereon] a variety of languages and different things, with differing climatic zones and countries, proofs for those who are able to see and testimonies of the universality of His mercy and the abundance of His favour [bestowed] upon the whole of mankind. God bless our lord, Muḥammad, him chosen from His creation in the heavens and on earth. [God bless also] his worthy family and all his Companions.

To proceed. The discipline of historical [topography],[1] especially what concerns the inhabited parts of the earth, the lengths and breadths of its territories, the sites of its buildings, the distances between its settlements, the representation of its countries and the explanation of its urban features,[2] is one of the most marvellous, the most extraordinary, the most intellectual[3] and the most pleasing. The old pages [of historical topography] renew for you razed towns with their archaeological remains[4] and castles while the lifeless sections and chapters bring to life[5] within their letters and lines centuries long gone by.

There can be no doubt that for the intelligent and the religious Mecca – God increase her honour – is the Mother of Settlements [Umm al-Qurā] and the centre[6] of the inhabited earth. [She is] the best loved to God and His Apostle of all God's places within the well-known practices [of Islam].[7] The most auspicious of countries around [Mecca] and indeed the most fortunate realm is the Yemen, especially endowed[8] from way back in time with the three prophetic blessings within the genuine practices [of Islam]: the fount of wisdom, the mine of knowledge [2] and that of the Faith.

So in this book I have concentrated on the following two areas by recording what is related to them in this field of study: a statement concerning [different] sites, areas, towns, mountains and seas and also an explanation of [different] dwelling places and settlements, as well as the measurements of distances across both deserts and centres of habitation. [There is also] a picture of every place, so that it is as if you can actually see it with your own eyes and you become acquainted with it in its entirety, so meanwhile you are relieved of your fatigue. Every place has its own rare moment of history and its

[1] Arabic *fann al-tārīkh* (Smith, 'Eastern Connection', p. 71).

[2] Arabic *amṣār*.

[3] Arabic *wa-[min] ab'adi-hā ghawran*, i.e. *ba'īd al-ghawr*.

[4] Arabic *raṣāṣ*. OL's *apparatus criticus* refers to Lane, *Lexicon*, IV, p. 1092, 'stones cleaving to the circuit of a running spring', and to Dozy, *Supplément*, I, p. 532, 'môle'. I prefer to take it in the wider sense given.

[5] Reading *yuḥyī*.

[6] Arabic *surrah*, 'navel'.

[7] Arabic *sunan*, plur. of *sunnah*.

[8] Reading *al-makhṣūṣ* with the I MS.

own piece of poetry which has been strung together of old. But now is the time to begin [to tackle] the objectives of the book, to ease back the curtain and to open the door. God facilitates the means [of attaining one's goal]; He is generous, giving.

The names and qualities of Mecca. God – He is exalted – has given Mecca four names: Mecca, the Town [al-Balad], the Settlement [al-Qaryah] and the Mother of Settlements [Umm al-Qurā]. God – He is Almighty – has said, 'It is He who kept their hands from you and your hands from them within Mecca.'[1] Thus there is some discussion about this name. Al-Zajjāj said,[2] '[The Arabic word] Makkah [Mecca] cannot be fully inflected, because it is both feminine and definite. It is legitimate to derive it from *bakkah* [squeezing, pressing] with a *mīm* in place of a *bā'*, as one would say *lāzib* and *lāzim* [necessary]. It is also legitimate to derive the word from people's saying, "*Makaktu* the bone", meaning "I sucked it hard until there was nothing left on it." Thus [the name Mecca] is likened to the violent pushing and shoving of people there.'

Ibn Fāris said,[3] '"*Makakta* the bone", meaning, "You extracted the bone marrow." The word *makk* has the meaning of going right through to the end of something.' Also in the tradition there is [the following], 'Do not press your debtors.'

There are four theories concerning the naming of Mecca thus. One is that the distance which people come 'from every deep ravine',[4] so it is as if it is Mecca [3] which attracts them to her.[5] The Arabs say, 'The young camel suckled[6] what was in its mother's udder.' The second thing they say is '"You pressed[7] the man", meaning, "You wanted to frighten him." So it is as if Mecca presses hard upon anyone who oppresses there, i.e. she destroys him.' [The poet] has said,

> Oh, pressing hard[8] upon the immoral! Press hard!
> But do not press hard upon Madhḥij and 'Akk![9]

The third [thing they say] is that [Mecca] was so named because of the effort of its people and fourthly because there is so little water there.[10]

[1] Quran 48:24. I use the Egyptian text provided in *The Glorious Koran*. The Quranic translations are my own. For Mecca, see the roughly contemporary Yāqūt, *Mu'jam*, V, pp. 181–8, where much of Ibn al-Mujāwir's comments are to be found verbatim. Not surprisingly, the chronicles of Mecca have similar accounts of the origin of the name: e.g. al-Nahrawālī, *Kitāb al-I'lām bi-a'lām bayt Allāh al-ḥarām* in Wüstenfeld, *Chroniken*, IV, p. 17. See also the lexicographical sources: Ibn Manẓūr, *Lisān*, X, pp. 490–91, al-Zabīdī, *Tāj*, XXVII, pp. 342–6, al-Fīrūzābādī, *Qāmūs*, III, p. 330.

[2] Al-Zajjāj is Ibrāhīm b. al-Sarī, an Iraqi who died in 311/923 (*EI*, 'al-Za<u>dj</u><u>dj</u>ā<u>dj</u>').

[3] Ibn Fāris is Abū al-Ḥasan Aḥmad who lived in Hamadhān, wrote in particular on lexicography, also on grammar and poetry, and died in 395/723 (*EI*, 'Ibn Fāris').

[4] Quran 22:27. Or 'every remote ravine' (Lane, *Lexicon*, V, p. 2157 and Penrice, *Dictionary*, p. 101).

[5] Ibn al-Mujāwir does not explain this point well. He uses the verb *jadhaba*, 'attract'; *makka* can have the same meaning (Zabīdī, *Tāj*, XXVII, p. 343).

[6] Arabic *iMtaKKa*.

[7] Reading *MaKaKta*.

[8] Arabic *MaKKah*.

[9] Two well-known Arab tribes. Madhḥij is a branch of Kahlān with numerous sub-tribes. Their original territory was in the east of the Yemen in the present-day areas of Dhamār, Radā', Murād, 'Ans and al-Ḥadā (Smith, *Ayyubids*, II, p. 232 and *EI*, 'Ma<u>dh</u>ḥi<u>dj</u>' and also Ibn Rasul, *Ṭurfah*, pp. 9, 35–6, 139–40; Ḥajarī, *Majmū'*, IV, pp. 699–702 and Maqḥafī, *Mu'jam*, pp. 576–7). As for 'Akk, it is a tribe of al-Azd, inhabiting Tihāmah from about Wādī Mawr to Wādī Rima', as FSL informs me (Ibn Rasūl, pp. 63–6; Kaḥḥālah, *Mu'jam*, II, p. 802; Ḥajarī, *Majmū'*, III, pp. 608–9; Maqḥafī, *Mu'jam*, pp. 455–6 and *EI*, "Akk').

[10] Both meanings are given in the lexica under the root *m k k*.

Scholars agree that Mecca is a name which refers to the whole area. But they disagree about Bakkah, [offering] the following four theories.[1] One, it is the name referring to the area in which the Kaʿbah is situated; this is what Ibn ʿAbbās[2] – God be pleased with him and his father – said. Two, it is the area around the House, while Mecca is what is beyond; ʿIkrimah held this view.[3] Three, it is the name referring to the mosque and the House, while Mecca is a name referring to the Ḥaram, as al-Harawī suggested.[4] Four, Bakkah is in fact Mecca; al-Ḍaḥḥāk made this suggestion,[5] using Ibn Qutaybah[6] as an authority to confirm this. He said, 'The *bā'* was changed from a *mīm* and one says both *ḍarbat lāzim* and *ḍarbat lāzib*.'

The etymology of the word Bakkah is *bakk* ['squeeze', 'press', 'break', 'tear']. One says, 'The people pressed one another', meaning 'pushed'. There are three theories regarding naming Mecca Bakkah. One, because of the jostling of the people there; this is what Ibn ʿAbbās said. Two, Bakkah breaks[7] the necks of tyrants, i.e. she strikes them, so no tyrant makes his way there without God destroying him; this is what Ibn al-Zubayr said.[8]

On the question of Mecca being called al-Balad [the Town], God – He is mighty and glorious – said,[9] 'No, I swear by this town', meaning Mecca. *Balad* in popular speech means 'the best of settlements'.

On the question of Mecca being called al-Qaryah [the Settlement], God – He is mighty and glorious – said,[10] 'God coined an example: a settlement which was secure and content' – i.e. inhabited by its people who were in no need of moving away from it out of fear or anxiety – 'its provision coming to it in plenty[11] from every side'; 'provision' means 'plenty which is in great abundance'; one says, 'So-and-so had in plenty',[12] meaning 'he attained abundance and opulence' – 'but it did not believe in God's favours', i.e. it rejected Muḥammad – God bless him and grant him peace – 'so God forced upon it the garb of hunger and fear.'[13] The origin of 'provision' is divine favour. Most often it is derived from [this idea]. [Evidence of] this is that God – He is almighty – punished the unbelievers of Mecca with [a period of] hunger [lasting] seven years until

[1] See Yāqūt, *Muʿjam*, I, p. 475 and Balādī, *Muʿjam*, I, pp. 246–7; Azraqī in Wüstenfeld, *Chroniken*, I, p. 50 and Nahrawālī in Wüstenfeld, III, p. 17; Ibn Manẓūr, *Lisān*, X, p. 402; Zabīdī, *Tāj*, XXVII, p. 80 and Fīrūzābādī, *Qāmūs*, III, p. 305.

[2] Ibn ʿAbbās is ʿAbdallāh, the cousin of the Prophet and ʿAlī b. Abī Ṭālib, and a prominent scholar who died in 68/686. See *EI*, "Abd Allāh b. ʿAbbās'.

[3] The slave of ʿAbdallāh b. ʿAbbās (see above n. 2), noted for his scholarship in the field of prophetic tradition, who died in 105/723 (*EI*, "Ikrima').

[4] Abū al-Ḥasan ʿAlī b. Abī Bakr, a 6th/12th-century ascetic and pilgrim who wrote a work called *al-Ishārāt ilā maʿrifat al-ziyārāt*. He spent his last days in the Ayyubid court in Aleppo and died in 611/1215 (*EI*, 'al-Harawī').

[5] Unidentified.

[6] Abū Muḥammad ʿAbdallāh b. Muslim, a theologian and belletrist, a prolific writer who died in 276/889 (*EI*, 'Ibn Ḳutayba').

[7] Arabic *taBuKKu*.

[8] ʿAbdallāh, the son of al-Zubayr b. al-ʿAwwām of Quraysh, an anti-Umayyad figure who died in 73/692 (*EI*, 'Ibn al-Zubayr'). It will be noted that Ibn al-Mujāwir lists only two theories.

[9] Quran 90:1.

[10] Quran 16:112.

[11] Arabic *raghadan*.

[12] Arabic *arghada*.

[13] Literally, 'so God made it taste the garb of hunger and fear'.

they ate [4] corpses and burnt bones. They were afraid of the Messenger of God – God bless him and grant him peace – and of his raids. The word *qaryah* [settlement] is the name given to a place in which a large group of people gather. It is a noun derived from the [idea] of collecting. One says, 'I collected[1] water in the cistern', meaning the same as *jamaʿa*. This type of cistern is called a *maqrāh*.

On the question of Mecca's being called Umm al-Qurā, God – He is mighty and glorious – has said,[2] '... that you may warn the Mother of Settlements and those around her', meaning Mecca. There are four theories concerning the naming of Mecca Umm al-Qurā. One, the earth has been spread out beneath her, as Ibn ʿAbbās suggested. Ibn Qutaybah said it was because she is the oldest [settlement]. Two, because she is a place to which people turn in prayer and visit. Three, because she is the most important settlement. Four, because she contains God's House – He is mighty and glorious. The view of military leaders ... is that which is given precedence over [other] places is called a mother,[3] because [places called] mother given precedence [over others] are [those] in which people are secure.[4]

Ibn al-Mujāwir said: One of the things I read in al-Fākihī's book[5] was as follows. A Meccan told him that one of his shaykhs gave him a book in which were written the following names of Mecca: Bakkah, Makkah, Barrah [obedience to God],[6] Bassāsah,[7] Umm al-Qurā, al-Ḥaram, al-Masjid al-Ḥarām [the Sacred Mosque] and al-Balad al-Amīn [the Secure Town]. [People] also have said that one of her names is Ṣalāḥ[8] [what is right and good]. Someone said in this regard, '... Ṣalāḥ'.[9]

In the pre-Islamic period she was called al-Nashshāshah, since she drives out[10] those who are there, i.e. removes them.[11]

Ibn al-Mujāwir also said: An Indian in India told me that the Indians call her Makkī Masīr. Some erudite people have stated that her name is Kūsā,[12] using the following poem as evidence:

[5] I questioned ʿAmr about a young man called Yaḥyā and a second called ʿĪsā.
He replied, 'I saw Yaḥyā sitting in the ravine, trimming his hair with a razor.[13]
ʿĪsā I saw entering a settlement called Kūsā.'

Merchants call her 'the sources of gold',[14] while she is called by Baghdadis 'the woman who brings up orphans'.

[1] Arabic *QaRaYtu*.

[2] Quran 6:92.

[3] Arabic *umm*.

[4] This final sentence of the paragraph is clearly corrupt and assigned by OL to his *apparatus criticus*.

[5] Abū ʿAbdallāh Muḥammad b. Isḥāq al-Fākihī, author of the 3rd/9th-century *Tārīkh/Akhbār Makkah*, written in 272/885 (Wüstenfeld, *Chroniken*, II, Arabic title page; Brockelmann, *Geschischte*, I, p. 143, cf. Fawwāz ʿAlī al-Dihās [ed.], *Akhbār Makkah*; see also Ibn Faraj, *Silāḥ*, p. 24, n. 16). See also Wüstenfeld, *Chroniken*, II, pp. 1–51, *Tārīkh Makkah*.

[6] See Nahrawālī in Wüstenfeld, *Chroniken*, III, p. 18.

[7] Ibid.

[8] See Balādī, *Muʿjam*, V, p. 159.

[9] A corrupt and unintelligible sentence, confined by OL to his *apparatus criticus*.

[10] Arabic *taNuSHSHu*.

[11] Arabic *tukhriju-hu*.

[12] Possibly an error for Kūthā (Yāqūt, *Muʿjam*, IV, p. 488; Nahrawālī in Wüstenfeld, *Chroniken*, III, p. 18).

[13] Arabic *mūsā* to rhyme with 'Kūsā'.

[14] Arabic *ʿurūq al-dhahab*.

Al-Masʿūdī in *Kitāb Murūj al-dhahab*[1] has reported that Mecca is of the second climate zone, is associated with Mars and was built by Abraham the bosom friend[2] – peace be upon him. Her air is healthy and her climate good. Her nights are pleasanter than days, since rain[3] falls at night on all those who are there. Her water comes from wells, the sweetest being that of al-Shubaykah,[4] al-Wardiyyah[5] and al-Wāsiʿah,[6] the latter the well beyond Jabal Abī Qubays.[7] There a poor man can make a living. All this was built by Umm al-ʿAzīz Zubaydah bint Jaʿfar b. Abī Jaʿfar al-Manṣūr.[8]

Her inhabitants are Arabs and sharifs descended from al-Ḥasan b. ʿAlī b. Abī Ṭālib.[9] Her remaining inhabitants are Qurashīs, [following] the school of Imam Zayd b. ʿAlī b. Abī Ṭālib.[10] They are dusky people since most of their partners are black slave girls from Abyssinia and Nubia. They are physically tall, speak correctly, are poor, but belong to numerous families and tribes and are content. The Prophet – God bless him and grant him peace – said, 'Contentment is riches.' He also said, 'Contentment is a treasure which can never be exhausted.' One of the inhabitants of Mecca used to survive on bread cakes and a little ghee for [the period of] three days and nights. On this subject Imam Abū ʿAbdallāh Muḥammad b. Idrīs al-Shāfiʿī composed the following poem:[11]

[6] I put my desires from my mind and gave it rest; for as long as it covets, it belittles itself.
I brought contentment back to life after it had died and by doing so my honour was preserved.
If covetousness occurs in the heart of a servant [of God], weakness and baseness get the better of him.

[1] See *Murūj*, II, p. 161,

[2] 'Al-Khalīl', Abraham's usual epithet in Islamic tradition.

[3] Arabic *raḥmah*, literally 'mercy'.

[4] Yāqūt (*Muʿjam*, III, p. 324) mentions three places with this name, though no specific well: a wadi near al-ʿArjā'; a place between Mecca and al-Ẓāhir, one of the stages of the Basra pilgrimage; and a third, a place belonging to B. Salūl. Balādī, himself a Hejazi, (*Muʿjam*, V, p. 18) states it is a large quarter of Mecca near the Kaʿbah and then goes on to quote Yāqūt, though insisting that the last two places are in al-Qaṣīm on the Iraqi pilgrim route, one now known as al-Shubaykiyyah. Snouck Hurgronje (I, end plan) locates a cemetery and a district of this name, the former in the SW, N of Jabal ʿUmar (Djèbèl Omar) and the latter (ès-Schebēkah) close by.

[5] A well mentioned by Fāsī in Wüstenfeld, *Chroniken*, II, p. 121.

[6] See Fāsī in Wüstenfeld, *Chroniken*, II, p. 122.

[7] One of the two mountains of Mecca, lying to the E of the town (Wüstenfeld, IV, plan; Snouck Hurgronje, I, plan; Ḥarbī, *Manāsik*, p. 474).

[8] Zubaydah was the wife of Hārūn al-Rashīd and the mother of Muḥammad al-Amīn. She was a patron of the arts and of public works and died in 216/831 (*EI*, 'Zubaida bint D̲j̲aʿfar').

[9] See Smith, '"Anthropological" Passages', p. 162. I.e. descendants of the Prophet through his grandson, al-Ḥasan b. ʿAlī.

[10] The statement here that the 7th/13th-century Meccan Qurashīs were Zaydīs is of great importance. Quraysh, the tribe of the Prophet, formed the majority of the inhabitants of the town (*EI*, 'Ḳuraysh'). Zayd b. ʿAlī (d. c. 125/743) was the eponymous founder of the Zaydiyyah, generally a liberal branch of the Shīʿah, the prominent school in the north of the Yemen and often known as the 'fifth school'; i.e. fifth after the four orthodox schools, the Ḥanafīs, the Ḥanbalīs, the Mālikīs and the Shāfiʿīs (*EI*, 'al-Zaydiyya'). On the question of Zaydism in Mecca at this time, see Mortel, 'Zaydī Shiʿism', pp. 455–72.

[11] Abū ʿAbdallāh Muḥammad b. Idrīs, the eponym of the Shāfiʿiyyah who died in 204/820 (*EI*, 'al-Shāfiʿī' and also *Dīwān*, p. 108, reading *fa-araḥtu* for *wa-araḥtu*, *ʿirḍun* for *ʿirḍī*, *yaḥillu* for *aḥalla* and *mahānatun* for *madhallatun*).

The inhabitants of Mecca wear fine Nishapuri cloth of silk and linen,[1] using the other half of it as a girdle and throwing away the excess. Their womenfolk wear bonnets[2] – bonnets have already been mentioned in the [section on] the areas of Ṣanʿāʾ – and veils.[3] They eat meat, ghee and bread. Their names are Sālim, Muslim, Ghānim, Ghannām, Farrāḥ, Fāriḥ, Qāsim, Hayyāb,[4] Nahhāb, Waththāb, Muṭāʿim, Fārij, Qāʾim, Ḍāḥik, Ḍaḥkān, Sallāl, Fallāl, Sayyār,[5] Habbār, Rāshid, Rashshād, Rashīd,[6] Shākir, Mushkir[?], Fāḍil, Faḍāʾil, Ṭālib, Ẓālib, Wāṣil, Ḥāṣil, Rajī, Murtajī, Rājiḥ, Nājiḥ, Fātik, Mālik, Mahyūb, Hayyāb, Wahhāb, Raʿʿāsh, Ḥawwās, Kannās, Qādim, Muqdim[?], Mushammar[?], Hānī, Muhannā,[7] Zākī, Ṭāʾib, Ẓāfir, Nājī,[8] Munajjā,[9] Jābir, Lāḥiq, Sayyār, Ṣābir and ʿĀris.

Marriage among the inhabitants of Mecca.[10] On 10 Dhū al-Ḥijjah,[11] Zayd becomes engaged to the daughter of ʿAmr[12] and on 10 al-Muḥarram[13] all [those getting married] go in to their wives, publicly and making a show.[14] We asked, 'Why is this?' They replied, [7] 'Because we are all involved with pilgrims in every kind of activity, both legal and illegal. So when the pilgrims leave, people continue their engagements, marriages, family festivals and marriage celebrations.' When a Meccan gets married, agrees on how much the dowry should be and wants to consummate the marriage with the woman, he dyes his hands and feet in a decorative manner, just like all the people of the Yemen and Ḥaḍramawt. All his friends, both family and relatives, are present, each one carrying in his hand a piece of paper which is tied up,[15] on which is written the name of

[1] See Smith, '"Anthropological" Passages', p. 162 and also Dozy, *Supplément*, II, p. 680. The significance of 'the other half' in the next sentence would seem to be the connection between the words *naṣāfī* (sing. *naṣfiyyah*) and *niṣf*, 'half'. Dionisius Agius has kindly drawn my attention to his *Arabic Literary Works*, pp. 247–9, where he records the word *naṣīf*, 'a kind of turban'. Nishapur (Arabic Naysābūr) is a town, one-time capital, of the eastern province of Khurasan, from which Ibn al-Mujāwir claims one of his *nisbahs*, al-Naysābūrī (Yāqūt, *Muʿjam*, V, pp. 331–3 and Le Strange, *Lands*, pp. 382 ff. and map VIII). The 8th/14th-century traveller, Ibn Baṭṭūṭah, writes of the silk and other fabrics of Nishapur (Ibn Baṭṭūṭah, *Travels*, III, p. 584).

[2] Arabic *qunūʿ*, sing. *qināʿ*. Dozy, *Supplément*, II, p. 413, has *qunūʿ* and defines it as 'sorte d'étoffe'. The comment in the margin of the L MS that the word is synonymous with *qarāqīsh* was confirmed to me by a Ṣanʿānī lady who also gave me the singular, *qināʿ* (Lane, *Lexicon*, VIII, 2993; Dozy, *Vêtements*, pp. 375–8; Landberg, *Glossaire datînois*, III, p. 2534; Rossi, *L'Arabo*, p. 156). Despite Lane's definition, my own experience confirms the rendering I have given. I am very grateful to Dionisius Agius for his comments on this word.

[3] Information on Ṣanʿāʾ is in fact yet to come; see pp. 187–221 below.

[4] See Dhahabī, *al-Mustabih*, p. 656.

[5] Ibid., pp. 78, 379.

[6] The text has R.sh.d and I read Rashīd with OL.

[7] Dhahabī, *al-Mustabih*, p. 618.

[8] Ibid., p. 109.

[9] Ibid., p. 617.

[10] See Landberg, *Etudes*, II, pp. 858–61 and Smith, '"Anthropological" Passages', p. 163.

[11] The Muslim month of pilgrimage, the last month of the year.

[12] Ibn al-Mujāwir frequently uses two imaginary characters named Zayd and ʿAmr in his narrative in this way, just as the classical Arabic grammarians did in their linguistic examples.

[13] The first month of the Muslim calendar, so Ibn al-Mujāwir means here exactly one month later, presumably when the town settles down after the upheavals of the pilgrimage.

[14] This is a tentative translation of *bi-al-naẓrah wa-al-taẓhīr* which is Landberg's and OL's suggested reading.

[15] Reading Arabic *maṣrūr* with Landberg.

the guest, together with the weight and number of everything which he presents to the bridegroom,[1] each according to his situation and financial means. The women do exactly the same. The bridegroom goes out to the Ḥaram and circumambulates it seven times. He prays two *raqʿahs* at the Station of Abraham and kisses the Black Stone. He goes out with candles to the house of the bride and she is revealed to him. He consummates the marriage and remains with her for seven days. On the seventh day he leaves, collecting up the marriage money[2] which he has been given and using it as working capital. Immediately he opens up a shop from which he can earn his living. These marriage monies become a debt which he has to repay. As for all those who have attended the wedding and who [then themselves] get married, he pays back to each one of them [at the time of their wedding] the same amount which they gave to him or even more. They do the same in most of the provinces of the Yemen.

Previously[3] the inhabitants of Mecca used to buy slaves and imposed a financial contribution[4] on them which was to be paid to their master daily. Similarly the women imposed a contribution on their slave girls in order to get money.[5] So the slave girl [simply] hopes for alleviation [from her financial burden][6] or she gives freely of her vagina[7] to the man and promiscuity[8] runs amok.[9] This is still found in Aden among outsiders and locals and they do not regard this practice as a shameful act. On the contrary, women [even] boast of doing this.

It was the same in pre-Islamic times. Every slave girl who did not give freely of her vagina was disapproved of until the following verse was revealed:[10] 'Do not force [8] your slave girls into prostitution if they wish to remain chaste.' So it dates from this time, but they still follow this practice.[11] When the master, the slave and the slave girl leave for their work, the woman is left in the house alone. Then she kneels on all fours, since she has nothing to do. Also sitting on her haunches becomes something familiar and they [all] get used to it. It is said that, when a man and his wife are quarrelling and she loses her temper completely, she says to her husband, 'You really want me to break "it"!' The meaning of this is, 'You really want me to sit on my bottom!' Her husband replies to her, 'Please, no, don't do that!'[12]

Section. Sayf al-Dawlah [ʿAlī] b. ʿAbdallāh b. Ḥamdān[13] came in upon his cousin on his father's side – some say on his mother's side – as she was down on all fours

[1] Reading Arabic *al-ʿarīs* with Landberg.

[2] Arabic *ṭarḥ* (Landberg, *Glossaire daṯînois*, III, p. 2200).

[3] See Landberg, *Etudes*, II, p. 927 and Smith, '"Anthropological" Passages', p. 163.

[4] Arabic *qiṭʿah* (Serjeant, *Portuguese*, p. 192).

[5] Arabic *fī taḥṣīl al-dhahab*.

[6] Arabic *faraj*.

[7] Arabic *farj*.

[8] Arabic *ḥaraj/ḥirj*.

[9] Arabic *fī harj wa-marj*.

[10] See Quran 24:33.

[11] This is not clear; either the Meccans, or the Adenese, or both.

[12] Ibn al-Mujāwir is suggesting that, although still angry with her husband, the wife permits sexual intercourse from behind so that she, on all fours, can threaten to injure him during penetration simply by adopting a sitting position.

[13] Ruler of Syria and renowned for his patronage of the famous Arabic poet, al-Mutanabbī, Sayf al-Dawlah died in 333/944 (Bosworth, *New Islamic Dynasties*, pp. 87–8 and *EI*, 'Ḥamdānids').

arranging the pearls of her necklace. Sayf al-Dawlah said to her, 'What price to do it like that?' She replied, '[I would want] Mosul!' He said to her, 'It's a deal!', to which she replied, 'It's a deal!' He had his way with her ...[1] and in the morning her servant came to exact payment for what he had bought [from her]. So Sayf al-Dawlah told his vizier to write an official note[2] for her to take over Mosul. But the vizier was far from happy with this order and held back from writing [it]. So Sayf al-Dawlah said to him, 'Write [it] for her! Indeed, I have taken from her something which is equal in value to a red thoroughbred camel.'[3] A variant is 'an Iraqi camel'. As the poet has said:

> Yes, I proclaim – if what I have to say is acceptable -
> passion remains and talk goes on for a long time.
> A greeting [in itself] does not cure the heart of serious illness,
> without any kissing and cuddling going on!
> No lover can be satisfied with his loves
> until he triumphs over the contents of their trousers!

Because of this [constantly being on all-fours], the buttocks of Hejazi women are large, since they increase them in size on purpose.

[9] All kinds of vegetables grow in [the area of Mecca], like melons,[4] cucumbers,[5] snake cucumbers,[6] egg-plants and leeks.[7] These they eat with dates, radishes[8] etc. There are also there good quality *barnī/birnī* and *maktūm* ripe dates.[9] It is also said that in olden times all kinds of flowers, fruits, produce and sweet basil were to be found there. [It is reported] also that saffron was cultivated among Zahrān.[10]

Every year after expenditure and tax contributions,[11] 80,000 dinars were submitted to Baghdad. Another report says 18,000 dinars and this is more accurate. All this was from cultivation, livestock, income from trees, the fruit harvest, irrigation channels and camel pastures, as well as from the date palm income. But when times changed, all that which we have mentioned decreased in quantity because people had different intentions and became dishonest.

[1] The I MS has an illegible phrase not found in the L MS. It might possibly read *fa-laysa bi-shay' maḥjar*, 'and this is nothing unlawful' (Lane, *Lexicon*, II, pp. 517–8), perhaps an aside from Ibn al-Mujāwir himself.

[2] Arabic *manshūr*.

[3] Arabic *jamal aḥmar*. See Lane, *Lexicon*, II, p. 641; this expression is proverbially applied to anything highly prized.

[4] Arabic *baṭṭīkh/biṭṭīkh* (Varisco, *Agriculture*, pp. 183–4).

[5] Arabic *khiyār*, *Cucumis sativus* L. (Dimyāṭī, *Mu'jam*, p. 55; Varisco, p. 182).

[6] Arabic *qiththā'* (ibid., pp. 182, 210).

[7] Arabic *kurrāth* (Dimyāṭī, p. 133, *Allium Porrum* L. or *Euphorbia aculeata* Forsk., 'leeks'; cf. Varisco, *Agriculture*, pp. 182, 20–10, 'Chinese chives').

[8] Arabic *fijl*, *Raphanus sativus* L. (Dimyāṭī, *Mu'jam*, p. 116; Varisco, pp. 211, 213, 'long, white radish').

[9] For *ruṭab*, 'fresh, ripe dates' (Varisco, *Agriculture*, p. 193). For *barnī/birnī*, see Dozy, *Supplément*, I, p. 78, 'espèce de dattes', 'espèce de raisins'. For *maktūm*, ibid., II, p. 444, 'espèce de datte'.

[10] A large tribal group of northern 'Asīr in modern Saudi Arabia, inland from al-Līth, about 200–250km SE of Mecca (Kaḥḥālah, *Mu'jam*, II, pp. 481–2; Bindagji, *Atlas*, p. 11, Tribes, and also Zahrānī, *al-Mu'jam al-jughrāfī*, II, fold-out map between pp. 304–5, showing Bilād Zahrān due N of the provincial capital of Bilād Ghāmid and Zahrān, al-Bāḥah).

[11] Arabic *mu'an* (Dozy, *Supplément*, II, pp. 573–4, 'impôt', 'contribution').

Everyone in [Mecca] uses perfume, both men and women. Everyone carries a sword and they put down their weapons only in God's month, Rajab the Deaf[1] – God increase reverence for it.

The construction of the ground floor[2] [of their houses] is in stone and gypsum and the building of the first floor[3] is in the same way. This [dates] from the time of Muʿāwiyah b. Abī Sufyān.[4] Later in the time of Abū ʿAbdallāh Muḥammad al-Mahdī bi-Allāh, Commander of the Faithful,[5] when he built the Noble Ḥaram, every house was like a fortress because it was so solidly built. Amir Hāshim[6] built a town outside Mecca between Darb al-Thaniyyah[7] and al-Masfal[8] called Murabbaʿat al-Amīr.[9] His troops, servants and dependents lived there and the town remained inhabited. But it fell into ruin during the rule of Amir ʿĪsā b. Fulaytah[10] and remained in ruins until the rule of Amir Qatādah b. Idrīs b. Muṭāʿin b. ʿAbd al-Karīm.[11] He renovated certain remains there and various [other] places. He wanted foreigners and Quraysh to live there, while he and all the sharifs lived in Mecca. But he died all of a sudden and all the work he hoped to carry out came to nought. Amir Qatādah b. Idrīs built a wall around Mecca made of stone and mud which followed the [10] mountain tops and the wadi beds. He put four gates into it: Darb al-Maʿlā gate leading to ʿArafāt;[12] Darb al-Thaniyyah gate leading to Madīnat al-Rasūl[13] – God bless him and grant him peace – and also called

[1] The usual epithet of the 7th month of the Muslim calendar, probably because it was one of the sacred months during which no warfare, with all its clamour, was permitted (Lane, *Lexicon*, IV, p. 1724).

[2] Arabic *balad* (RBS, 'ground floor').

[3] Arabic *al-ṭabaqah al-thāniyah*.

[4] The first Umayyad caliph, reg. 41–60/661–80 (Bosworth, *New Islamic Dynasties*, p. 3; *EI*, 'Muʿāwiya b. Abī Sufyān').

[5] Abbasid caliph, reg. 158–69/775–85 (Bosworth, *New Islamic Dynasties*, p. 6).

[6] Hāshim b. Fulaytah b. Qāsim al-Ḥasanī, known as Ibn Abī Hāshim, who was amir of Mecca 527–49/1133–54 (Ibn Fahd, *Ghāyat al-marām*, I, pp. 521–2 and also Fāsī in Wüstenfeld, *Chroniken*, II, pp. 212–13; Appendix B.10 below).

[7] There are a number of towns with the name al-Thaniyyah in the Hejaz, though I can trace no Darb al-Thaniyyah. However, it must have been to the N or NW of Mecca (see n. 13 below) (Balādī, *Muʿjam*, II, pp. 89–94). The plan of the town, OL's published *Tārīkh al-Mustabṣir* text, p. 11, Tabula I, confirms this, although it should be noted that in general the captions of the plan appear so corrupt as to be of little value.

[8] I can trace no place of this precise name in the sources available to me. However, perhaps al-Masfalah (the reading of the L MS) is meant (see below p. 38, n. 1), referring to the S of the town. The main wadi of Mecca is called Wādī al-Masfalah and an area of the town of this name is found in Balādī's map of Mecca (*Muʿjam*, VIII, opposite p. 249; Snouck Hurgronje, I, plan). The plan in OL's published *Tārīkh al-Mustabṣir* text, p. 11, indicates a SW position and that the road through this gate leads to the Yemen.

[9] I can trace no place of this name in the sources available to me. The plan in OL's published *Tārīkh al-Mustabṣir* text, p. 11, positions the town of Murabbaʿat al-Amīr SW of Mecca.

[10] ʿĪsā b. Fulaytah b. Qāsim, amir of Mecca 556–70/1160–74 (Ibn Fahd, *Ghāyat al-marām*, I, p. 527 and Fāsī in Wüstenfeld, *Chroniken*, II, 213; Appendix B.10 below).

[11] Qatādah b. Idrīs b. Muṭāʿin (cf. text Muṭāʿim) b. ʿAbd al-Karīm b. ʿĪsā, amir of Mecca 597–617/1200–1220 (Ibn Fahd, *Ghāyat al-marām*, I, pp. 550–77; Fāsī in Wüstenfeld, *Chroniken*, II, 214; Appendix B.11 below).

[12] ʿArafāt is a hill about six hours to the east of Mecca where the address is given on 9 Dhū al-Ḥijjah each year as part of the pilgrimage (*SEI*, "Arafa/ʿArafāt'). In Wüstenfeld's plan the road out of Mecca to ʿArafāt leaves the town in the NE and, if this is accurate, the gate must therefore have been in the NE (see also Snouck Hurgronje, I, plan, indicating a cemetery, el-Maʿlā in the north of the town). The plan in OL's published *Tārīkh al-Mustabṣir* text, p. 11, here written al-Maʿlāh, indicates a gate due N of Mecca, through which the road to ʿArafāt runs.

[13] The Medina road leaves Mecca in the NW of the town; the Jeddah road leaves in the due W and one can perhaps assume the gate was situated at the fork in the Medina and Jeddah roads in the W (Wüstenfeld's plan).

Juddah gate and al-ʿUmrah gate; al-Masfalah gate[1] leading to the Yemen; al-Ṣaghīr gate leading to al-Ṣafā[2] and al-Ṣaḥīfah,[3] a wadi having no road [out of Mecca]. God Almighty knows best what is correct.

The rulers of Mecca from the family of al-Ḥasan b. ʿAlī b. Abī Ṭālib – God honour him.[4] Amir Manṣūr b. Mukthir b. ʿĪsā b. Fulaytah[5] b. Qāsim b. Muḥammad b. Jaʿfar b. Muḥammad b. ʿAbdallāh b. Abī Hāshim b. Muḥammad b. al-Ḥusayn b. Muḥammad b. Mūsā b. ʿAbdallāh b. Mūsā al-Jawn b. ʿAbdallāh,[6] the adornment[7] of B. Hāshim b. al-Ḥasan [b. al-Ḥasan] b. ʿAlī b. Abī Ṭālib.[8]

Amir Ḥasan b. Qatādah b. Idrīs b. Muṭāʿin b. ʿAbd al-Karīm b. ʿĪsā b. al-Ḥusayn b. Sulaymān b. ʿAlī b. ʿAbdallāh b. Mūsā al-Jawn[9] – and here the two genealogies come together in one.

There are also those who settled in Mecca from the time of the caliph, Imam ʿAbdallāh Abū Jaʿfar [al-Maʾmūn], [son of] Hārūn al-Rashīd,[10] down to 619.[11]

In that year [Mecca] was taken over by Sultan al-Malik al-Masʿūd Ṣalāḥ al-Dīn Abū al-Muẓaffar Yūsuf b. Muḥammad b. Abī Bakr b. Ayyūb b. Shādhī b. Marwān b. Muḥammad.[12]

[11. Plan of Mecca, see Fig. 1]

[12] *Equivalent values.*[13] The local currency is Egyptian gold and [coins] are struck in [Mecca] according to the standard of Egyptian [coinage], a dinar being equal to

[1] See p. 37, n. 8 above.

[2] Al-Ṣafā is a mound, part of Jabal Abī Qubays, to the SW of the Kaʿbah within Mecca between which and al-Marwah the pilgrims run as part of the pilgrimage, a run called the *saʿy* (Ḥarbī, *Manāsik*, p. 433, which confirms also a gate, al-Ṣafā gate, leading up to the mound, and also Wüstenfeld, *Chroniken*, IV, plan of Mecca; Snouck Hurgronje, I, plan; *SEI*, ʻal-Ṣafāʼ; Balādī, *Muʿjam*, V, p. 143, and plan of Mecca, VIII, opposite p. 249.) The word following al-Ṣafā in the text, al-Ṣāfī/al-Ṣāfā/al-M ṣāfī/al-M ṣāfa, is a mystery and perhaps best ignored as a scribal error.

[3] Al-Ṣaḥīfah appears in none of the geographical sources at my disposal.

[4] I.e. the descendants of the Prophet through ʿAlī b. Abī Ṭālib and his son, Ḥasan, the Ḥasanī sharifs.

[5] I have corrected from ʻMukthirʼ.

[6] The correct genealogy of Manṣūr is as follows: Manṣūr b. Dāʾūd b. ʿĪsā b. Fulaytah (see p. 37, n. 10 above) b. Qāsim b. Muḥammad b. Jaʿfar b. Muḥammad b. ʿAbdallāh b. Muḥammad b. Muḥammad b. Ḥusayn b. Muḥammad b. Mūsā b. ʿAbdallāh b. Mūsā al-Jawn (Snouck Hurgronje, *Mekka*, I, Stammtefel, I; also below n. 9).

[7] Arabic *dībājah*.

[8] Again the Ḥasanī sharifs are intended (*EI*, ʻHāimidsʼ).

[9] Ruler of Mecca from 617/1220 (or 618/1221) to 619/1222 (or 620/1223) (Fāsī in Wüstenfeld, *Chroniken*, II, p. 215; Ibn Fahd, *Ghāyat al-marām*, I, pp. 580–89; Snouck Hurgronje, *Mekka*, I, Stammtafel I; Appendix B.11 below).

[10] Abbasid caliph 189–201/804–17 (Bosworth, *New Islamic Dynasties*, p. 6).

[11] Begins 15 February 1222.

[12] Ibn al-Mujāwir has the titles and pedigree of the sixth and final Ayyubid ruler of the Yemen, al-Malik al-Masʿūd, correct. He died in Mecca in 626/1229 on his way to Egypt to take up the the governorship of Damascus (Zabīdī, *Tarwīḥ al-qulūb*, p. 79; Smith, *Ayyūbids*, II, p. 50, Appendix B to chapter 2; Smith, ʻTransferʼ, pp. 9–10; Introduction, Historical background, the Yemen, the Ayyubids above; Appendix B.8 below). The date 619/1222 is perhaps a little late for the beginning of Ayyubid rule in Mecca. They were much involved in the town from about 617/1220 onwards (Ibn Ḥātim, *Simṭ*, pp. 175 ff.).

[13] Arabic *muʿāmalāt*. The word might be taken in a more limited sense, ʻcurrenciesʼ (Dozy, *Supplément*, II, p. 177; Khoury, *Chrestomathie*, p. 222).

[11]

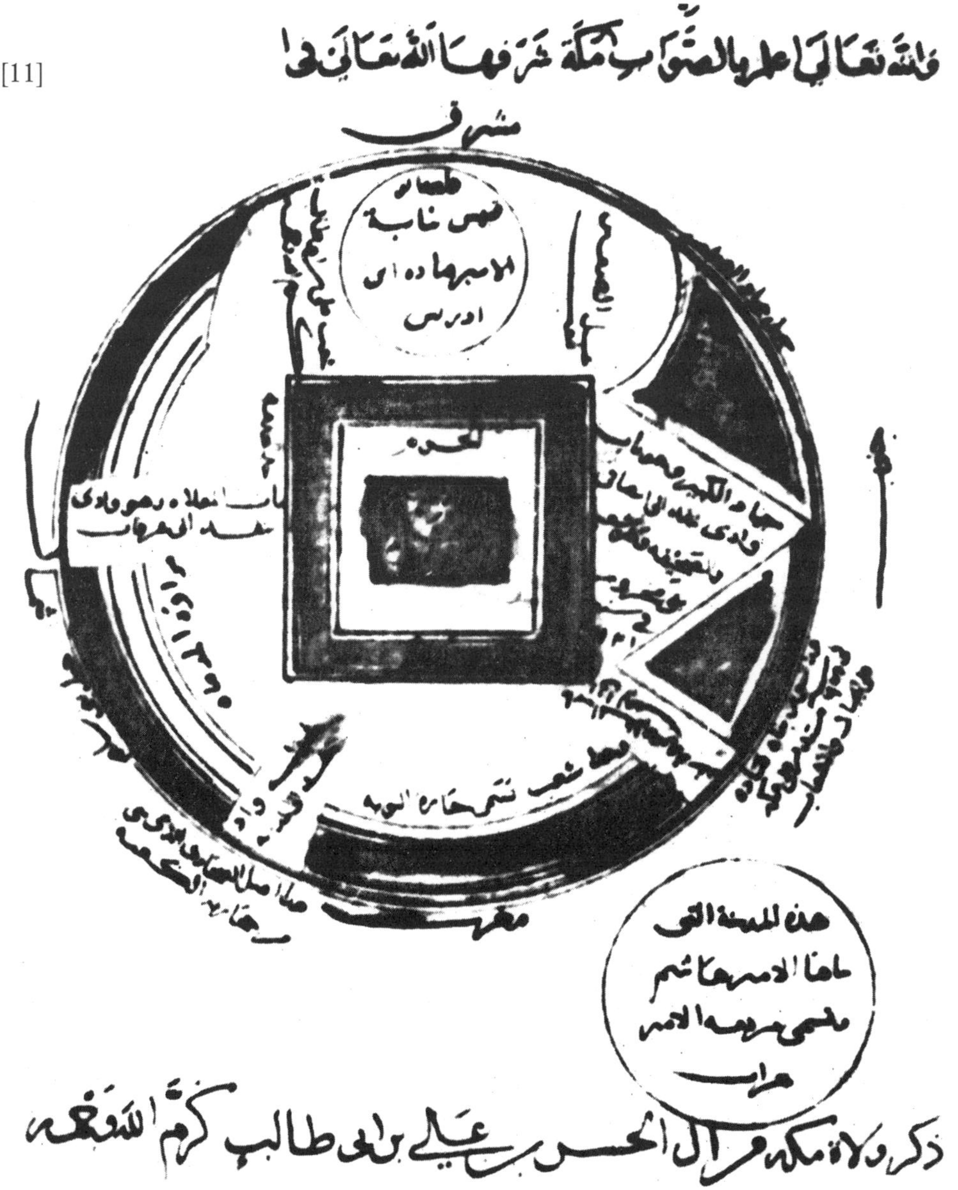

Figure 1. Plan of Mecca (I MS, f. 5b, text, p. 11, tabula I)

Mecca is depicted in circular form with the Kaʿbah a rectangle in the centre, surrounded by the sacred area (*ḥaram*) in the form of an exact square. The circular plan of the town is marked with E at the top of the page, S on the right, W at the bottom and N on the left. The small circle at the top of the large circle and within the latter is labelled 'castle of Abū Qubays, built by Amir Qatādah b. Idrīs' (d. 617/1220) (see above 'Historical Background, The Hejaz, B. Qatādah'). The gates are marked as follows: in the S, on the right of the plan at three o'clock, al-Kabīr (? and cf. al-Ṣaghīr gate in the text), 'a wadi leading to ? (read al-Ṣafā from the text?) and al-Ṣaḥīfah'; in the SW position at four o'clock, al-Masfal gate, 'a wadi leading to the Yemen'; in the NW position at seven o'clock, Thaniyyah gate, 'a wadi leading to Medina'; in the N position at nine o'clock, al-Maʿlāh gate, 'a wadi leading to ʿArafāt'. Outside the town at the NW gate, Thaniyyah, Jabal al-Ṣaḥārī is marked with the remark that the Kaʿbah was built from its stone. The outside wall of the town, we are told, was built by Qatādah in 608 [1211–12]. The small circle outside the town near the Masfal gate marks the town called Murabbaʿat al-Amīr, a ruin.

twenty-four *'alawī*,[1] each *'alawī* reckoned four dirhams and each dirham six *fals*. When authority passed to the Ayyubids,[2] they struck 'large' dirhams.[3] It is reported that the first to strike this 'large' dirham there was al-Mu'izz Ismā'īl b. Ṭughtakīn [who was sultan] in the Yemen.[4] The first to strike 'large' dirhams in Mecca according to the legal standards of the Yemen was al-Malik al-Mas'ūd Yūsuf b. Muḥammad. The Egyptian dinar is equal to four and a half *malakī* ones,[5] equivalent to eighteen dirhams. Every four dirhams[6] is reckoned a Meccan dinar, each dirham being three *jawzah*,[7] each being eight *fals*, each being four *dāris*.[8] Ibn al-Mujāwir said that everything which was in the beginning worth an *'alawī* has now become a 'large' dirham. The *raṭl*[9] is [equivalent to] 130 dirhams, which is six *ūqiyyah*,[10] each one reckoned to be twenty-one and one third dirhams, by which all spices[11] and perfumes are sold.

The *mann*[12] of the Yemen is 320 dirhams, in which clothes, sugar, honey and all sweet commodities are sold. The *mann* used for meat is 400 dirhams, in which meat, suet,[13] *harīsah*,[14] cheese cake[15] and sheep's rump[16] are sold. The *mann* used for ghee is 800 dirhams, in which ghee, oil, vinegar and sesame oil[17] are sold.

The cubit is the 'hand cubit'[18] during the pilgrimage season[19] and at the time when alms are given.[20] When a whole month has passed after the pilgrimage, there is an

[1] I can trace no reference to such a coin elsewhere.

[2] This must mean Ayyubid authority in the Yemen, i.e. after the Ayyubid conquest of the Yemen in 569/1173.

[3] Arabic *kibār* (Serjeant, *Portuguese*, pp. 146–9).

[4] Third Ayyubid sultan of the Yemen, 593–8/119–1201 (Appendix B.8 below).

[5] A type of dinar struck in great numbers in Aden by the Sulayhids (439–532/1047–1138) and their successors, the Zuray'ids. The first was struck in 497 (begins 5 October 1103) ('Umārah, *Tārīkh* [Kay, *Yaman*], p. 37; Bikhazi, *Coins*, 87). They were still being used under the Ayyubids (Lowick, 'Mint', p. 305; Smith, 'Maritime Trade', pp. 129, 135).

[6] The text is here corrupt and it is not clear whether dirhams or dinars are meant. The context seems to indicate the former.

[7] The singular is *jawzah* or *jā'iz* (see following line). The plural may be read either *jūz* or *juwwaz* (Löfgren, *Texte*, II, p. 27; Hinz, *Masse*, p. 12).

[8] Tritton, *Rise*, p. 132, has a plur. *dawāris*, bronze dinars (and also Piamenta, *Dictionary*, I, p. 148, *dūrisī* and *dāris*, bronze coin).

[9] Hinz (*Masse*, pp. 29–33) has a long excursus on the *raṭl* throughout the Islamic world. See also Serjeant, *Portuguese*, p. 144, Donaldson, 'Pre-Metric Weights', pp. 88–9 and Allouche, *Economics*, p. 90.

[10] See Hinz, *Masse*, pp. 34–5; for the *ūqiyyah* in Mecca in some detail, see Mortel, 'Weights and Measures', pp. 181–2. See also Serjeant, *Portuguese*, pp. 144–5 and for medieval Egypt, Allouche, *Economics*, pp. 56, 90.

[11] Arabic *ḥawā'ij*. The more usual South Arabian meaning is 'spices'. It can mean 'necessaries', 'requirements', 'things', 'household comestibles' (Serjeant, *Portuguese*, p. 66, especially n. 6).

[12] See Hinz, *Masse*, pp. 16–23 and Mortel, 'Weights and Measures', pp. 180–82.

[13] Arabic *shaḥm*.

[14] This is a boiled meat dish with wheat or rice (Arberry, 'Baghdad Cookery Book', pp. 198–9, 'beat well and set in a smooth paste'; Pellat, *Avares*, p. 316, 'mets fait de froment cuit et de viande pétris en pâte'; Serjeant, *Misers*, p. 236, appendix 34, with the complete recipe).

[15] Arabic *mujabbanah* (Dozy, *Supplément*, I, p. 172).

[16] Reading *alyah* (Lane, *Lexicon*, I, p. 87).

[17] *Shīraj*, a Persian word (Steingass, *Dictionary*, p. 773; Dozy, *Supplément*, I, p. 810).

[18] Arabic *dhirā' al-yad*, 24 fingers (Hinz, *Masse*, p. 61; Mortel, 'Weights and Measures', p. 177).

[19] Arabic *mawsim*. Presumably prices are high during the pilgrimage.

[20] I.e. at the end of Ramaḍān.

increase in the cubit. In 622[1] there was an increase in the cubit and it became the Egyptian cubit.[2]

One hundred Meccan 'stones'[3] in Baghdad are the equivalent of ninety-five dinars. [13] When Ṭughtakīn al-Kāmilī[4] assumed power over the Hejaz, he decreased [the value of] one hundred dinars, so now a hundred Meccan [dinars] are equivalent to ninety-four in Baghdad. But every transaction in Mecca by direct sale[5] is carried out in an unofficial way.[6] Wheat and all [other] grains are sold by the *ṣāʿ*,[7] [that] reckoned to be four *mudd*,[8] each *mudd* being four *rubʿ*.[9]

Leathers are sold by the *bayʿah*,[10] each one being a hundred *mann*. The *ḥiml*[11] is equivalent to two and one half *bayʿah*. Defects [in leathers] are reckoned to be of three kinds: [firstly] that in the middle of the bale,[12] scratch marks of a knife at the outer edge of the bale; two, [a defect called] *shaʿrānī* which is in the hair; and [thirdly] shrivelled [leather]; the grain[13] is shrivelled up from the skin [itself]. The [leather] which is free of grease, light and black is [in] the same way [a defect]. Quality leather is heavy, clean and pure, with a striped surface,[14] mingled together and free of the defects which we have [just] mentioned.

Ibn al-Mujāwir said: The following is the situation in the Yemen and its surrounding areas. A hundred *mann* in Khwārazm[15] equals seventy dinars according to the description we have given. Leather is tanned in every province of the Yemen and the Hejaz and the surrounding areas and is sold by the number [of skins] in bales,[16]

[1] Begins 13 January 1225.

[2] Presumably this is the *dhirāʿ al-ḥadīd al-Miṣrī* of Serjeant, *Portuguese*, p. 160. See also Mortel, 'Weights and Measures', p. 177.

[3] Ibn al-Mujāwir's *ṣanjah* is the Persian *sang*, 'stone', 'rock' (Steingass, *Dictionary*, p. 701; Dozy, *Supplément*, I, p. 690). It can thus be compared with the English 'stone' weight.

[4] This must be the mamluk of the Ayyubid al-Malik al-Kāmil Muḥammad b. Abī Bakr b. Ayyūb, the nephew of Saladin, Ṭughtakīn b. ʿAbdallāh al-Kāmilī. He was briefly amir of Mecca about 629–30/1231–3 (Ibn Fahd, *Ghāyat al-marām*, I, pp. 612–4).

[5] Arabic *muqābaḍatan*. I interpret this after reference to Dozy, *Supplément*, II, p. 300, who quotes the use of *taqābuḍ*, 'délivrance et payement de marchandises'.

[6] Ibn al-Mujāwir here uses the Persian expression *kaj ba-kaj* which Steingass (*Dictionary*, 1016) defines 'very much crooked' (not in the criminal sense!) and equates it with *kaj-maj*, 'crooked', 'distorted', as an adverb 'crookedly', e.g. 'walking crookedly'. I.e. rates are agreed between the parties without regard necessarily to official ones. I am very grateful to Dr Bill Donaldson with whom I have discussed this problematic sentence and who made some extremely useful suggestions.

[7] See Hinz, *Masse*, p. 51; Mortel, 'Weights and Measures', p. 180; Allouche, *Economics*, p. 88; Donaldson, 'Pre-Metric Weights', pp. 89–90.

[8] See Hinz, *Masse*, pp. 45–7; Allouche, *Economics*, p. 87.

[9] See Hinz, *Masse*, pp. 50–51; Donaldson, 'Weights and Measures', pp. 88–9.

[10] See Hinz, *Masse*, p. 10; Mortel, 'Weights and Measures', p. 182.

[11] See Hinz, *Masse*, pp. 13–14; Mortel, 'Weights and Measures', p. 182.

[12] Arabic *ṭāq* (Lane, *Lexicon*, V, p. 1894; Kazimirski, *Dictionnaire*, II, p. 122; Dozy, *Supplément*, II, p. 70, both the 'bale' and a 'layer' making up the bale). RBS found *ṭāqah* on Socotra meaning a component of a bale (*Socotra*, p. 179).

[13] Ibn al-Mujāwir uses the Persian *kīmukht*. Dozy, *Supplément*, II, p. 506, gives simply 'espèce de cuir'. Steingass, *Dictionary*, 1070, gives 'shagreen', 'the grains of such', 'wrinkled skin'.

[14] Arabic *ʿattābī al-wajh*.

[15] See Le Strange, *Lands*, pp. 446 ff., Yāqūt, *Muʿjam*, II, 395–8 and Bosworth, *Islamic Dynasties*, p. 179. This is the province N of Khurasan, bounded on the eastern side by the Oxus. See also Le Strange map X. It may be that the town is meant here, i.e. Jurjāniyyah, in the very N of the province; see Le Strange, *Lands*, p. 448.

[16] Ibn al-Mujāwir here uses a plural *ṭāqāt*.

and also in Abyssinia and its surrounding areas. The Persians call it *khūsh* leather.[1] It is [also sold] in Kashk in India.[2] Hides are tanned using only acacia leaves.[3] The hides of camels, cattle and gazelles are tanned in Mecca and travellers from Khurasan buy the pelts of stallion mules from the district[4] of Mosul[5] and from the area of Irbil[6] and they are tanned in Mecca. But all this came to an end in 610[7] because of the appearance of the [Mongol] infidel[8] in Khurasan and al-Rayy.[9] Light leather is considered good by the Iraqis and Syrians because they can spread out the bales to work on the actual skin. In Khwārazm and Khurasan, they only want heavy [leather] because they use it to line their footwear. On the subject of prices, it is said that the Khwārazmī and heavy leathers[10] are worth four Zangī *dānaq*[11] and the boot [made from] them ten dinars. It is the same [among] the Byzantines. It is said that a friend has the status [14] of the head, while an enemy has that of the foot. So the people of these districts put the best of what they wear on their feet.

Muḥammad b. Rizq Allāh said to me, 'Can you see Canopus in Khurasan?'[12] 'No, indeed', I replied. 'For this reason they cannot tan leather', he said. I asked why. He replied, 'In every area where Canopus rises, tanning can be carried out, because it gives [the leather] a dark green appearance[13] and produces the softness and smoothness which you can see.'

[1] *Khwush* or *khwash* (Steingass, *Dictionary*, p. 485) means 'good', 'excellent', 'beautiful' and the meaning here may be simply 'good-quality' leather.

[2] Idrīsī (*Opus*, I, p. 500) calls Kashk a district (*rustāq*) from which the river Asrūdh flows. It must be close to the town of Kush, two stages from Samarkand. Ibn Khurdādhbah, *al-Masālik*, p. 196, places Kashk eight parasangs from Kūram and ten from Rā'īn.

[3] Arabic *qaraḥ*, the leaves of the *salam* (*Acacia ehrenbergiana* Hayne) (Dimyāṭī, *Muʿjam*, pp. 123–4; Varisco, *Agriculture*, p. 149; Hepper and Friis, *Flora*, p. 174). However, DMV informs me that *qarāḥ* [*sic*] in the Yemen generally refers to *Acacia etbaica* Schweinf. He quotes Wood, *Handbook*, 169.

[4] Ibn al-Mujāwir uses *rustāq*, from the Persian *rōstāk* (Morony, *Iraq*, p. 534).

[5] The well-known town on the Euphrates about 220 miles from Baghdad (Le Strange, *Lands*, pp. 87–90).

[6] Irbil is a town in the Jazīrah province of Iraq to the E of Mosul between the Upper and Lower Zāb rivers (Le Strange, *Lands*, map II).

[7] Begins 23 May 1213.

[8] Arabic ... *li-ẓuhūr al-kāfir bi-Khurāsān*. Although the date is somewhat early (we can never trust Ibn al-Mujāwir with dates!), this must be a reference to the Mongol conquest of the Islamic world. The dates 616–20/1219–23 are assigned by the author to the Mongol conquest of the empire of the last Khwārazm shah in *EI*, 'Mongols'. More specifically, the Mongols crossed the Oxus to take Khurasan in 618/1221 (*EI*, 'Çingiz-Khān'; Barthold, *Turkestan*, pp. 424 ff).

[9] A town close to modern Tehran in the NE corner of the Jibāl province, one of the four capitals of the province (Le Strange, *Lands*, pp. 214–17, and map V; Yāqūt, *Muʿjam*, III, pp. 116–22).

[10] Reading *al-thiqāl*. This problematic passage has been put together with much assistance from RBS, including a personal note to me dated 20 March 1989.

[11] For *dānaq*, see Hinz, *Masse*, p. 11, s.v. *dāng*. RBS reads *Zankiyyah*, suggesting that this *dānaq* might well have been struck by the Zangids of Mosul and Aleppo or in the Jazīrah. Bosworth, *Islamic Dynasties*, p. 190–99, notes that the famous ʿImād al-Dīn Zangī (reg. 521–41/1127–46) struck coins, as did most of his successors of the line and all those of the Jazīrah line (Lowick, 'Coinage of the Jazīra', pp. 163 ff).

[12] This is one of the very few hints in the whole of the text that Ibn al-Mujāwir is a Khurasani.

[13] Or 'black', reading *yukhaḍḍiru-h*, although OL prefers *yuḥammiru-h*, 'gives it a red appearance'.

From Mecca to Medina via the B. ʿUṣayyah route. They are al-Sarw.[1] From Mecca to the bed of [Wādī] Marr four parasangs.[2] This is a fertile wadi where a certain amir of Mecca from the east built a palace which is now in ruins. To al-Hadah four parasangs.[3] To Burzah four parasangs.[4] To Shābah four parasangs.[5] To Medina the amount of four parasangs.[6] To Hajar[7] the amount of seven parasangs, fine land, [belonging to] B. Sulaym,[8] which was conquered by the Commander of the Faithful, ʿAlī b. Abī Ṭālib[9] – God honour him.

The conquest of these mountains by the Commander of the Faithful, ʿAlī b. Abī Ṭālib. ʿĪsā b. Abī al-Barakāt b. Muẓaffar al-Baghdādī informed me in Mecca as follows: I read in a certain book that in pre-Islamic times B. Sulaym had many bees. When any enemy attacked them, they smoked out the bees from their nests[10] and they would fly high up into the air, appearing to anyone looking at them like a cloud, so numerous were they. Having reached a great height, they came down, descending upon the horse of the enemy and harassing them. Thereupon the horse of the enemy would flee before them. B. Sulaym had defeated all their enemies [15] in this way. They remained as they were until God – He is ever Mighty and Glorious – made Islam triumph and until the Prophet – God bless him and grant him peace – accompanied by some of his Companions, moved out into these areas. B. Sulaym did what has just been mentioned. But when the bees went up into the air and descended upon the troops of Islam, the Prophet called out, saying, 'Where is the religious leader?'[11] But no one answered. So he said, 'Where is the commander of the bees?' But no one answered. So he said, 'Where is ʿAlī b. Abī Ṭālib?' When ʿAlī b. Abī Ṭālib – God's approval be upon him –

[1] B. ʿUṣayyah are a group of Bajīlah, the large Hejazi tribe (Kaḥḥālah, *Muʿjam*, II, p. 509, and p. 53, n. 10 below). Kaḥḥālah (*Muʿjam*, II, p. 786) gives ʿUṣayyah b. Khufāf of B. Sulaym. See also Caskel, *Ǧamharat an-nasab*, I, table 122. Al-Sarw are a group of B. Sulaym (see n. 8 below), inhabiting Wādī Kulayyah, a well-known wadi of western Hejaz (Balādī, *Muʿjam*, VII, p. 228).

[2] Balādī (*Muʿjam*, VIII, pp. 98–9) lists three wadis of the name Marr. It may be his first, a large Hejazi wadi which takes water off the lava field (*ḥarrah*) of B. Sulaym. He also mentions a Marr al-Ẓahrān, another important wadi of the Hejaz (ibid. pp. 100 ff.). See n. 3 below.

[3] Reading thus with OL's apparatus after consultation with Balādī, *Muʿjam* (IX, p. 166) who says it is a wadi running from E to W, parallel with Wādī Marr al-Ẓahrān.

[4] A place name famous from pre-Islamic times as the venue of a battle involving B. Sulaym (Balādī, *Muʿjam*, I, p. 204; Wāqidī, *Maghāzī*, III, p. 878). Bindagji, *Atlas*, p. 53, has Barzah, about 60 km N, slightly W of Mecca.

[5] Shābah appears to be a mountain, though its exact position on the Mecca–Medina route which Ibn al-Mujāwir is describing is not clear (Balādī, *Muʿjam*, V, pp. 5–6 [quoting Yāqūt, *Muʿjam*, III, p. 304]; Ḥarbī, *Manāsik*, p. 337, n. 2, the editor quoting information on Sulaym sites).

[6] OL is right in his apparatus to query 'Medina' here. See below as the route continues.

[7] Hajar is mentioned by Ḥarbī (*Manāsik*, pp. 518, 532, 620, 621), but it is not sufficiently clear to give a precise location.

[8] Sulaym b. Manṣūr b. ʿIkrimah b. Khaṣafah b. Qays etc. down to ʿAdnān, a huge Hejazi tribe (Caskel, *Ǧamharat an-nasab*, I, Taflen 92, 122; Kaḥḥālah, *Muʿjam*, II, pp. 543–6).

[9] The well-known fourth Orthodox caliph, nephew and son-in-law of the Prophet.

[10] Ibn al-Mujāwir uses the word *akwārāt*, the plur. of the plur. of *kūr*, which usually means the nest of a wasp or hornet (Kazimirski, *Dictionnaire*, II, p. 942).

[11] For *yaʿsūb*, see Lane, *Lexicon*, V, p. 2041 (also for *yaʿsūb al-dīn* in particular) and Kazimirski, *Dictionnaire*, II, p. 249. The word is used for the 'leader' (i.e. queen) of bees, thought by the Arabs to be a male, and by extension any 'leader' or 'chief'.

heard what the Prophet had uttered, he drew [his sword], Dhū al-Faqār,[1] and attacked the bees. The latter retreated against B. Sulaym and stung them. B. Sulaym fled before the bees to the tops of the mountains and into the beds of the wadis. God conquered the mountains of B. Sulaym at the hand of the Commander of the Faithful, ʿAlī b. Abī Ṭālib. When the conquest was complete and victory accomplished, one of his Companions said to the Prophet, 'Apostle of God, you likened ʿAlī b. Abī Ṭālib to a leader [*yaʿsūb*], [a term used for] the bee?' The Prophet replied, 'The Believer is like a bee which eats only what is good and out of which only good comes.' From the time of this event the Commander of the Faithful, ʿAlī b. Abī Ṭālib, was given the honorific title Yaʿsūb al-Dīn [Leader of the Faith] and Amīr al-Naḥl [Commander of the Bees]. Until now honey[2] is taken from these mountains, some of which is bought by pilgrims, the [whole of] Hejaz and some Yemenis.

Wādī Anẓar.[3] Ibn al-Mujāwir said: On the eve of Saturday, 6 Shaʿbān 624,[4] I had a dream and someone was saying to me, 'In the area of Medina, Yathrib,[5] there is a hidden[6] wadi with mountains and side wadis which no one knows how to enter.' I asked what it was called and he replied, 'Wādī Anẓar.' I asked him what the meaning of this was and he replied that someone asked a shaykh of the inhabitants of this wadi where he was from. The shaykh said he was from Wādī Anẓar. I asked [again] [16] what the meaning of this name was. He answered it was a wadi associated with Islam and renowned.[7] I asked from where its inhabitants came. He replied, 'They are a people descended from Ham, son of Noah – peace be upon him. Moreover they are not Arabs, Persians, Indians, Abyssinians, Turks, nor Nabataeans, but they have a language all of their own which is used among themselves.' I asked what the circumference of [the wadi and its surroundings] was. He replied two parasangs or the distance of two days.[8] Amir Qāsim b. al-Muhannā b. Jammāz al-Ḥusaynī[9] is still pasturing his camels and livestock there. Its land is cultivated and there are springs, also security and calm. But [the land] has become empty [of people and I asked him what][10] the reason for this was. He replied, 'God has turned it upside down.' Ibn al-Mujāwir said: During this period, Amir Qāsim b. al-Muhannā b. Jammāz killed his cousin, Shīḥah.[11] After his death Amir

[1] The well-known sword of ʿAlī b. Abī Ṭālib, originally obtained as booty by Muḥammad (*EI*, 'D͟hu 'l-Faḳār').

[2] Ibn al-Mujāwir uses the word *naḥl* here to mean 'honey' and then goes on to define the word.

[3] Unidentified.

[4] 19 September 1227.

[5] Yathrib is the pre-Islamic name of Medina.

[6] Ibn al-Mujāwir uses the term *masrūq*.

[7] Arabic ... *bi-h ʿizz*.

[8] I think the only way to interpret this sentence is to take it as a clear alternative offered to the character of the dream or to the shaykh by two different informants, i.e. the circumference of the area was either two parasangs, perhaps two hours' walk, or it was much greater, the distance of two days.

[9] See Fāsī in Wüstenfeld, *Chroniken*, II, p. 214, and Ibn Fahd, *Ghāyat al-marām*, I, p. 545, where he is described as amir of Medina, appointed governor of Mecca in 571/1175, but he remained there only three days.

[10] There is a lacuna in the text and both of OL's suggested readings are acceptable. The translation of the other would read, '... for some time and I asked him what ...'.

[11] Not true, according to the Hejazi sources. Shīḥah b. Hāshim b. Qāsim b. al-Muhannā al-Ḥusaynī is described as lord of Medina. In 637/1231, he entered Mecca at the head of 1,000 cavalry. He did not die in fact until 647/1249, killed by B. Lām (Fāsī in Wüstenfeld, *Chroniken*, II, p. 217; Ibn Fahd, *Ghāyat al-marām*, I, pp. 267–8).

Hāshim b. Qāsim assumed control of Mecca. Moreover it is possible that this wadi among [all] these wadis, mountains and side-wadis is hidden and none of the bedouin knows of it other than its inhabitants. God [alone] knows.

To al-Khaḍrā'[1] from Yathrib is four parasangs. There there are springs and palm groves and its inhabitants still to this day live in hair tents.[2] To ʿAyn al-Nabī four parasangs.[3] It is a flowing spring, irrigating date palms, situated where the mountains and wadis end and where the desert sands begin. To [al-]ʿUmaq[4] four parasangs where there are springs and palm groves. In 615[5] Amir ʿIzz al-Dīn Abū ʿAzīz Qatādah b. Idrīs burnt its date palms. To Najd four parasangs.[6] It is [also] called Mabrak,[7] a desert land where there is a huge reservoir built by the Merciful One. It is said that the Prophet washed in it and used its water, so the water is still throughout all this time one of the blessings of the Prophet. [17] You pass by three mountains called al-Barānīn.[8] If you want to get to Medina, keep two of them on your left. But if you want to get to Mecca, keep them on your right. Walk close to the mountains so as not to get lost, since it is a wadi containing sand as white as flour.[9] There is certainly no road through other than at this place. To Bi'r ʿAlī b. Abī Ṭālib four parasangs.[10] This is a well with a large construction from which pilgrims drink, as well as those bedouins who live around it and all of their livestock.

To Qubā four parasangs.[11]It used to be a town before Medina and it has been said that it was built in the time of the Prophet. In its mosque there are two *qiblah*s, one in the direction of the east and the other towards the Kaʿbah because of the order given by God – praise to Him – to the Prophet to direct his face towards the Kaʿbah as follows:[12] 'Direct your face towards the Inviolable Mosque and, wherever you are, direct your faces towards it.' Then on to Medina a parasang among 'lofty, high-standing'[13] date palms.

[1] Ḥarbī mentions al-Khaḍrā' on two occasions; firstly (*Manāsik*, p. 298) wells and sweet water two miles from a place called al-Thaʿlabiyyah, whose inhabitants use the water; *Manāsik*, p. 332, tells us that al-Khaḍrā' is a well of al-ʿUmaq (see n. 4 below), the latter belonging to B. Sulaym. Balādī (*Muʿjam*, III, pp. 131–3) lists eight features of this name. See also Fākihī in Wüstenfeld, *Chroniken*, II, p. 83.

[2] Arabic *akhdār*, plural of *khidr*.

[3] In Ruhāṭ, watering various crops taken to Mecca and al-Ṭā'if (Ḥarbī, *Manāsik*, p. 349; Balādī, *Muʿjam*, IV, p. 106).

[4] I correct after reference to the Hejazi sources. Ḥarbī (*Manāsik*, p. 332) says the place belongs to B. Sulaym and has a castle, mosque and well, the latter named al-Khaḍrā' (see n. 1 above). The editor of *Manāsik*, Ḥamad al-Jāsir, comments (n. 2) that the place is still known, a watering place N of Sharawrā.

[5] Begins 30 March 1218.

[6] Unidentified.

[7] Unidentified.

[8] I am inclined to think the text is here corrupt, as the name as given does not appear in the sources available to me.

[9] Arabic *daqīq al-samīd* (Steingass, *Dictionary*, p. 698, 'white bread'; Fīrūzābādī, *Qāmūs*, I, p. 314; Zabīdī, *Tāj*, VIII, p. 212; Lane, *Lexicon*, IV, p. 1424).

[10] Unidentified.

[11] Perhaps correctly with final *hamzah*, plural of *qabwah*, 'vault'. (Yāqūt, *Muʿjam*, IV, pp. 301–2). Burton (*Pilgrimage*, I, pp. 279, 406–7, 410–11) has much to say on the place.

[12] Quran 2:144, 150.

[13] After Quran 50:10 and 77:27.

From Mecca to al-Ṭā'if. From Mecca to Minā a parasang.[1] To al-Mashʿar al-Ḥarām a parasang.[2] To Jabal ʿArafāt a parasang, the source of Wādī Naʿmān[3] where there are arak trees[4] and date palms.

> Oh, will the days of al-Muḥaṣṣab[5] ever return?
> Shall I [ever again] alight at these domes?
> Will the nights of al-Khayf return in al-Khayf?[6]
> Will there be any way of passing the night at al-Jimār?[7]
> Shall I be able to stop at the landmarks of al-Muʿarraf?[8]
> And take a siesta by the eel woods[9] in Wādī al-Arāk?[10]

To al-Burqah three parasangs,[11] where there is the grave of Amir Shukr b. Abī al-Futūḥ[12] who conquered Jeddah. To al-Marzah four, or more accurately six, parasangs.[13] To al-Ḥajar [18] two parasangs.[14] You should pass by a high mountain called ʿUfr.[15]

[1] A place to the E of Mecca on the road to ʿArafāt, about 5 miles from the holy city. It is where the pilgrims cast stones and, after a journey on to ʿArafāt and the return to Minā, the pilgrimage ends. See *SEI*, 'Minā'. Burton, *Pilgrimage*, II, pp. 180 ff., has a detailed description of Minā. See also Sprenger (*Reiserouten*, p. 125) using the whole of Ibn al-Mujāwir's passage here.

[2] By al-Mashʿar al-Ḥarām ('the sacred place for religious ceremonies'), Muzdalifah is meant. Situated between Minā and ʿArafāt, the sources confirm that it is the same distance from Minā as Minā is from Mecca, as the text suggests (Ibn Jubayr, *Riḥlah*, p. 172; Burton, *Pilgrimage*, II, p. 181; and *SEI*, 'al-Muzdalifa'; Ibn Faraj, *Silāḥ*, p. 41). For an overview of the area Mecca-Minā-Muzdalifah-ʿArafāt, see Farsi, *National Guide*, p. 42, also *SEI*, 'Ḥadjdj', map opposite p. 121.

[3] Balādī, *Muʿjam* (IX, pp. 70–73) confirms the vocalization and tells us that the wadi belongs to Hudhayl, two nights from ʿArafāt. He calls the place Naʿmān al-Arāk (see n. 8 below).

[4] *Arāk* (often reduced to *rāk*) is *Salvadora persica* L, the well-known toothbrush tree (Dimyāṭī, *Muʿjam*, p. 10; Miller and Morris, *Plants*, p. 254–5 with coloured illustration; Hepper and Friis, *Plants*, p. 226).

[5] Place between Mecca and Minā, much nearer to the latter. It is also the name of the place where stones are thrown in Minā itself, so named after *ḥaṣab*, 'stones', 'place of stoning' (Fāsī in Wüstenfeld, *Chroniken*, II, p. 94; Lane, *Lexicon*, II, p. 581; Balādī, *Muʿjam*, VIII, pp. 43–5).

[6] There are several places of this name given in the Hejazi sources, including that of the mosque of Minā, Masjid al-Khayf (Burton, *Pilgrimage*, II, p. 180; Balādī, *Muʿjam*, III, pp. 180–87).

[7] The plural of *jamrah*, 'pebble'. The name originates from the three heaps of pebbles, supposedly pelted by Adam at Iblīs, the origin of the pilgrimage practice of casting stones to ward off the devil (see n. 5 above). The places of this name are all in Minā (Lane, *Lexicon*, II, p. 453; Balādī, *Muʿjam*, II, pp. 169–70; *SEI*, 'al-Djamra').

[8] Balādī (*Muʿjam*, VIII, p. 196) says that this is the name of the place of the ritual 'standing' (*wuqūf*) of the pilgrims at ʿArafāt. He then goes on to quote the poem found here in Ibn al-Mujāwir's text.

[9] Arabic *sarḥ*, *Cadaba farinosa* Forssk., a shrub not uncommon in Arabia (Dimyāṭī, *Muʿjam*, 71; Miller and Morris, *Plants*, 90–91; Hepper and Friis, *Plants*, 91 [Niebuhr calls the tree *Sārah*]; also Dīnawarī, *Plants*, p. 38, quoting the *Mufaḍḍaliyyāt*, and mentioned by Aṣmaʿī, *Nabāt*, 19). It might also be taken as a place name.

[10] There are any number of wadis in the Hejaz of this name (Balādī, *Muʿjam*, I, pp. 80–82). In view of the mention of Wādī Naʿmān and its arak trees above, this may be the wadi meant here.

[11] I follow Balādī's vocalization. There are any number of places in the Hejaz of this name (Balādī, I, pp. 206–9).

[12] Shukr b. Abī al-Futūḥ al-Ḥasan b. Jaʿfar b. Muḥammad … al-Ḥasanī, amir of Mecca, died in Ramaḍān, 453/October, 1061, although there is no mention of his grave in the sources at my disposal (Ibn Fahd, *Ghāyat al-marām*, I. pp. 497–9; Fāsī in Wüstenfeld, *Chroniken*, II, p. 209; Ibn Faraj, *Silāḥ*, 81–2; Appendix B.9 below).

[13] A tentative vocalization, since I cannot trace any reference to this place in the sources available to me.

[14] Of all the possibilities offered by Balādī, *Muʿjam*, II, pp. 228–33, I tentatively suggest this vocalization, 'a village belonging to B. Sulaym'. See Sprenger, *Reiserouten*, p. 125.

[15] I vocalize tentatively after Yāqūt (*Muʿjam*, IV, p. 131) who says it is the plural of *aʿfar*, 'dust-coloured inclining to white', but who has nothing more useful than 'sands in the desert in Qays territory' and 'Najd ʿUfr, a place near Mecca', though neither fits in with Ghazwān which follows. Sprenger (*Reiserouten*, p. 125) has Ghafar.

Ibn al-Mujāwir said: It is [also] without doubt called Ghazwān.[1] A poet recited as follows about it:

> If sometime you fear the punishment of some amir,
> I have a lodging place at al-Liwā[2] at the top of Ghazwān.

The building of al-Ṭāʾif. I read in al-Fākihī's book as follows:[3] al-Ḥusayn informed me, saying ʿAlī b. al-Ṣabbāḥ[4] informed me, saying Ibn al-Kalbī[5] informed me on the authority of Iyād b. Nizār[6] – another version is on the authority of his father,[7] on the authority of Abū Ṣāliḥ, on the authority of Ibn ʿAbbās – who said: There were among the Nakhaʿ[8] and Thaqīf[9] two men of Iyād b. Nizār, one called Thaqīf, Qasī b. Munabbih, son of Bint Afṣā b. Duʿmī b. Iyād b. Nizār, the other al-Nakhaʿ b. ʿAmr b. Ṭahmān b. ʿAbd Manāh b. Yaqdum b. Afṣā b. Duʿmī b. Iyād b. Nizār.[10] They went off, taking with them a few flocks, including a she-goat in milk and they drank from her milk. There appeared to them an alms collector of a certain king of the Yemen, who wanted to take alms on their flock. They told him to take whichever of them he wanted and he chose the milch goat. They said, 'Our lives and that of this kid depend on her milk.' But he refused to take any other, so one of them killed him. One said to the other, 'We cannot remain together in the same place, nor even in the same land. Either you take the high road and I'll take the low road or you take the low road and I take the high road.' Al-Nakhaʿ said he would take the high road. He [eventually] came to Bīshah and remained there.[11] Thaqīf went off to Wādī al-Qurā,[12] where he took refuge with an old Jewess, hiding with her at night and working during the day. She took him as a son and he took her as a mother. As she was on the point of death, she said, 'My son, when I die, take these dinars and these

[1] Yāqūt, *Muʿjam*, IV, p. 202, says this is the mountain upon which al-Ṭāʾif is situated and Balādī, *Muʿjam*, V, p. 223, confirms this.

[2] A not uncommon place name in Arabia, though none of Balādī's entries (*Muʿjam*, VII, pp. 264–6) appears appropriate in the context. The word means 'fine, twisting sand' and may not even be a place name here (Ibn Manẓūr, *Lisān*, XV, p. 262; Fīrūzābādī, *Qāmūs*, IV, p. 389; Tibrīzī, *Sharḥ*, p. 1; Smith, 'Masqaṭ', p. 148, n. 3).

[3] See p. 32, n. 5 above.

[4] Unidentified.

[5] Hishām b. Muḥammad Ibn al-Kalbī, author of 141 books, including *Jamharat al-nasab* and *Kitāb al-Aṣnām*, died in 204/819 (Caskel, *Ǧamharat an-nasab*, I, pp. 75 ff.; Ibn al-Kalbī, *Aṣnām*, pp. 19–21).

[6] See Caskel, *Ǧamharat an-nasab*, I, Tafel 1, 174.

[7] Ibn al-Kalbī's father was Muḥammad b. al-Sāʾib who died in 146/763 (Caskel, *Ǧamharat an-nasab*, I, p. 72). He may mean the father of Iyād.

[8] See below n. 10.

[9] Thaqīf, alias Qasī b. Munabbih, was not directly 'of Iyād b. Nizār' on his father's side, but rather the famous tribe of al-Ṭāʾif was originally of Qays (see n. 10 below) (Caskel, *Ǧamharat an-nasab*, I, Tafel 92, 118; also Kaḥḥālah, *Muʿjam*, I, pp. 147–51, mentioning a claim of descent from Iyād, p. 148).

[10] We have here a strange pedigree of Qasī. On his mother's side he was of Iyād b. Nizār, the son of the daughter of Afā b. Duʿmī b. Iyād b. Nizār. I think Ibn al-Mujāwir is confused here: al-Nakhaʿ b. ʿAmr is a tribal group of Madhḥij (Kaḥḥālah, *Muʿjam*, III, p. 1176); Ṭahmān b. ʿAmr is a tribal group of Kilāb (Kaḥḥālah, *Muʿjam*, II, p. 685); one of Yaqdum's sons was called ʿAwdh Manāh and Ibn al-Mujāwir's ʿAbd Manāh would appear to be an error (Caskel, *Ǧamharat an-nasab*, I, Tafel 174).

[11] A wadi, town and area, belonging to Khathʿam, now in northern ʿAsīr about 230 km N of Abhā, though historically part of the Yemen (Hamdānī, *Ṣifah*, pp. 121–2, 127, 151; Yāqūt, *Muʿjam*, I, p. 529; Iṣfahānī, *Bilād al-ʿArab*, p. 5; Bindagji, *Atlas*, p. 36; Farsi, *Guide*, p. 35).

[12] Between Medina and Syria, a wadi containing many settlements, hence its name, *qurā*, plural of *qaryah*. The wadi is on the Syrian pilgrim route (Yāqūt, *Muʿjam*, IV, pp. 338–9). So Nakhaʿ went S and Thaqīf N.

vine shoots. When you settle anywhere, plant the vines and you will never lack sustenence from them.' Thaqīf did this. [19] He came and settled in a place near al-Ṭā'if. [There] he came across an Abyssinian slave girl on a piece of high ground, pasturing one hundred ewes for her master. He kept his designs on the ewes secret, saying [to himself] that he would kill her and take her sheep. But she realized what he intended to do to her and said to him, 'You there, do you intend to kill me and take my sheep?' He confessed that he did. She replied, 'You have done wrong! If you were to kill me and take the sheep, you would not get away with it, for I am the slave girl of 'Āmir b. al-Ẓarib b. 'Amr b. 'Abbād b. Yashkūr b. 'Adwān b. 'Amr b. Qays b. 'Aylān b. Muḍar,[1] lord of the inhabitants of the wadi. I think you are [just] a frightened stranger!' He confessed that he was. She continued, 'Can I not point you in the direction of something better than what you were intending?' 'Oh, yes, please do!' was his reply. She said, 'When the sun rises, my master comes to this [certain] rock, puts down his clothes and his bow and his quiver there and goes down into the wadi to relieve himself and to perform his ablutions in the wadi spring. Then he returns, takes what he has left and goes to his camp, ordering someone to shout, "Anyone who wants food and company should come to the house of 'Āmir b. al-Ẓarib!" He will receive anyone who wishes [to join him]. Lie in wait for him under the rock; take his clothes, his bow and his quiver and if he sees you and asks who you are, say, "I am a stranger; give me shelter; I am afraid; give me protection; and I am an equal,[2] find me a wife, if you are noble and good."' He told her he would do everything she had suggested.

The narrative continues. 'Āmir came out as usual and Thaqīf lay in wait for him. When he went into the wadi, Thaqīf did everything the slave girl had told him. 'Āmir b. al-Ẓarib told him to go with him. He did so and he went down to his people. Someone gave a shout and the people came hurrying to him. They ate and enjoyed one another's company. 'Āmir said to them, 'Am I not your chief?' 'Indeed!', they cried. He continued, 'You have given protection to anyone to whom I have given protection; you have granted safety to anyone to whom I have granted safety; and you have given a wife to anyone to whom I have given a wife?' 'Indeed!', they cried. 'Āmir said, 'This is Qasī b. Munabbih!' And he married him off to his daughter straight away. She bore Thaqīf sons, 'Awf, Dāris and Salāmah. Then he married her sister after her death and she bore him Qāsim. He remained in al-Ṭā'if and planted the vine shoots. They grew and bore fruit. The place became built up and was called [20] al-Ṭā'if, because he had gone round[3] the area and settled there.

It was said that he was called Thaqīf, because his father had not given him discipline[4] and he had come across[5] 'Āmir, when he granted him safety and married

[1] His great-grandfather was 'Iyādh rather than Ibn al-Mujāwir's 'Abbād and he figures in some of the early Arabic literature. In the *Sīrah* (Ibn Isḥāq, I, pp. 121–2, Guillaume, *Life*, p. 51), he is 'an arbitrator who makes decisions' (*ḥakamun yaqḍī*), on acccount of his wisdom and decisiveness and much sought after in difficult litigation. He had a slave girl called Sukhaylah who pastured his flock, perhaps the very slave girl here mentioned. He is called 'arbitrator of the Arabs' (*ḥākim al-'Arab*) by Ibn 'Abd Rabbi-h (*'Iqd*, I, p. 62) in pre-Islamic times (*'Iqd*, III, p. 94). See also Ibn Qutaybah (*Ma'ārif*, p. 80) who with the *Sīrah* takes up his decision concerning the treatment of a hermaphrodite (*khunthā*), a point particularly important in the context of inheritance.

[2] Arabic *kafī'*.

[3] Arabic *ṭāfa*, *ṭā'if* being the active participle, 'he who goes around'/'going around'.

[4] I read *THaQQaFa* here; cf. OL who vocalizes *thaqufa/thaqifa*.

[5] Arabic *THaQiFa*.

him off. Also he tended[1] the vines when he had planted them, so he was called Thaqīf.

Muḥammad b. Abī ʿAmr informed us, saying that Shaʿbān b. Jurayj informed him on the authority of Mujāhid concerning God's word:[2] 'If only this Quran had been revealed to a great man of the two settlements.' It was said that the two settlements were Mecca and al-Ṭāʾif. It was also said that the man in question[3] was ʿUtbah b. Rabīʿah, the bounty[4] of Quraysh from that time on. [Others] said he was Masʿūd b. Muʿattib.[5]

Ḥiṣn al-Hujūm.[6] Abū ʿAlī Aḥmad b. ʿAlī b. Ādam al-Yazanī informed me, saying: Ḥiṣn al-Hujūm is a circular mountain in the middle of the desert plain. The Nabataeans, descendants of the Christian Greeks – it is also said of the Byzantines – arrived.[7] Some reminders of them remain: the casing of the canals and the spring-water channels, and also the mill stones on which acacia leaves are ground for the tanning of leather. The informant continued: The circumference of these stones is seven to eight cubits in height. This is not the work of Arabs – no such work occurs to them, nor are they competent to carry it out; it does not even figure in their thinking. Rather, this and similar work is carried out by the tyrants of old[8] and based on the wise ways of the ancients. I only mention this good workmanship because of our description [which follows] of the building of the fortress. The Nabataeans came and built around the mountain square, dressed[9] stones, each one seven cubits by three in breadth. They continued to build it up until the structure reached as high as the top of the mountain. When building was complete as they intended, they built the walls [21] and towers according to previous descriptions. One gate was put into it and a large deep well dug out in the interior of the castle. At the completion of the huge fortress there appeared in the well water as sweet as honey, as sweet-smelling as rose-water and as pure as the spring of life. As the months and years passed by, the feeling of nearness and togetherness within the community began to wear thin and their destruction came gradually nearer and they became more remote from one another. Finally God caused Islam to triumph and the Prophet conquered them by force. The fortress remained as it was

[1] Arabic *THaQQaFa*.

[2] Quran 43:31.

[3] Presumably an alternative to Thaqīf in the anecdote above.

[4] A fiercy anti-Muḥammad Qurashī Meccan chief. He was killed at Badr in 3/624 (Guillaume, *Life*, 118–19, 132–3, 298–9). The text uses *rayḥānah* to describe ʿUtbah, which might also mean 'offspring' (Lane, *Lexicon*, III, pp. 1181–2).

[5] A Thaqafī whose only mention in Ṭabarī is in the context of the arrival in al-Ṭāʾif of the Abyssinian conqueror, Abrahah, in the mid-6th century AD (Ṭabarī, *Tārīkh*, II, p. 132 and *History*, V, p. 223).

[6] There is no mention of this name in the sources at my disposal. The word means 'attack' or 'charge'.

[7] There is broad agreement today among scholars that the Nabataeans were Arabs, at least the ruling classes were. Their official language was a dialect of Aramaic. I am not sure what the distinction is between Ibn al-Mujāwir's 'Christian Greeks' and 'Byzantines'. The Nabataeans thrived in the area of Greater Syria and Northern Arabia from about the 4th century BC to 1st century AD. Petra in present-day Jordan was their administrative and commercial capital and Madāʾin Ṣāliḥ, near al-ʿUlā in northern Saudi Arabia, is usually regarded as their southern boundary (Healey, *Tomb Inscriptions*, pp. 14, 18).

[8] Arabic *jabābirah*. Ibn al-Mujāwir uses the word frequently and it seems to mean nothing more than pre-Islamic rulers.

[9] Arabic *manqūsh*.

until Amir ʿIzz al-Dīn Abū ʿAzīz Qatādah b. Idrīs came to power in the Hejaz and ordered the fortress to be destroyed. It was destroyed for fear that some bedouin might rebel against him there. The fortress has remained in ruins until now and is called among the people there Ḥiṣn al-Ghurāb [Fortress of the Crow].

Al-Waht.[1] Maʿbad b. ʿAbd al-Raḥmān al-Makhzūmī informed us saying that Shuʿayb[2] on the authority of ʿAmr b. Dīnār[3] informed them saying: ʿAmr b. al-ʿĀṣ[4] made provisions in his will for al-Waht and made it [a place on whose produce] the legal poor-rate [was to be taken].[5] It could not be sold, nor given away, nor bequeathed. [He wrote]: It is to belong to my eldest son and the one there who obeys my prescription and my command. If he does not carry out my prescription and my command, he will no longer have any say in [how it is run], meaning by this al-Waht, until God inherits it, who is able to watch over His own principles. Muḥammad b. Manṣūr[6] informed us saying that Sufyān[7] on the authority of ʿAmr b. Dīnār informed them saying: In al-Waht ʿAmr b. al-ʿĀṣ planted[8] 100,000 [22] [vine] shoots, each worth a dirham. Al-Waht is a settlement in the district of al-Ṭāʾif, three miles away from it. All fruit in al-Ṭāʾif and Mecca [come] from this same Waht.

Muḥammad b. Mūsā al-Qaṭṭān informed us as follows, Muḥammad b. al-Ḥajjāj al-Thaqafī[9] informed us as follows, ʿAbd al-ʿAzīz b. Abī Rawwād informed us on the authority of ʿAṭāʾ,[10] on the authority of Ibn ʿAbbās who said that al-Ṭāʾif had been part of Palestine. But when Abraham said,[11] 'Our Lord, I have settled some of my posterity in a wadi without cultivation at Your Inviolable House', God moved it to where al-Ṭāʾif is now. Muḥammad b. Fāris al-Qurashī informed me saying, 'Only one black mulberry tree[12] has remained in al-Waht and they must still regard it as a pious endowment.'

[1] The word means 'plantation', 'shrubbery' and the anecdote concerning the association of the place with ʿAmr b. al-ʿĀṣ is told in other sources (Yāqūt, *Muʿjam*, V, p. 386; Balādī, *Muʿjam*, IX, pp. 150–51).

[2] This early transmitter (*rāwī*) might be Shuʿayb b. Ibrāhīm al-Tamīmī, found frequently in histories such as al-Ṭabarī (Ṭabarī, *History*, XIV, p. 2 and passim).

[3] A transmitter who died in 126/743 (Rosenthal, *History*, p. 381).

[4] Hero of the early Muslim conquests and conqueror of Egypt, who died in c. 42/663 (*EI*, "Amr b. al-ʿĀṣ').

[5] The Arabic *ṣadaqah* must here be used in this meaning, synonymous with *zakāh*, a payment which is obligatory, rather than in the meaning of 'voluntary alms'; *SEI*, 'Ṣadaḳa'.

[6] This transmitter might be Muḥammad b. Manṣūr al-Ṭūsī who lived in Baghdad and died in 254/868 or 256/870 (Ṭabarī, *History*, VIII, p. 79).

[7] There are two well-known transmitters of this name: the so-called Sufyān al-Rāwī, Sufyān b. ʿUyaynah, who died in 196/812 or 198/814 (Ṭabarī, *History*, I, p. 176; Rosenthal, *History*, p. 293); and Sufyān b. Saʿīd al-Thawrī who died in 161/777 (Rosenthal, *History*, p. 276).

[8] OL chooses to take *ʿarasha*, 'erect a trellis' from Yāqūt (see n. 1 above), although the MSS have *gharasa*, 'plant' and I retain the latter in translation. It is therefore necessary to point out that the 'shoots' are vine shoots.

[9] See Ṭabarī, *History*, XII, p. 166.

[10] There are one or two likely transmitters with this name, notably 'Aṭāʾ' b. al-Sāʾib who died in the 130s/747–57 (Ṭabarī, *History*, XIV, p. 118).

[11] Quran 14:37. The 'wadi without cultivation' is Mecca.

[12] Arabic *tūt*, *Morus nigra* L. (Dimyāṭī, *Muʿjam*, p. 29, 'black mulberry'; Varisco, *Agriculture*, p. 197).

Sulaymān b. ʿAbd al-Malik b. Marwān[1] and his arrival in al-Ṭāʾif. Muḥammad b. Ṣāliḥ al-Balkhī[2] informed me saying, Muḥammad b. Ibrāhīm[3] informed us saying: We were with ʿAbd al-ʿAzīz b. Abī Rawwād in the Inviolable Mosque when we were caught by a tremendous rain storm and strong wind. ʿAbd al-ʿAzīz said: Sulaymān b. ʿAbd al-Malik was going to al-Ṭāʾif and something similar came upon them on the way. They were terrified by this, so they sent for ʿUmar b. ʿAbd al-ʿAzīz.[4] Now when they were afraid of something, they sent for ʿUmar. Sulaymān b. ʿAbd al-Malik said to him, 'Can you not see what [a state] we are in?' He replied, 'Commander of the Faithful, this is the noise of His mercy. It cannot be the noise of His punishment!'[5] Sulaymān set off [again] for al-Ṭāʾif. When he reached there, he was met by Abū Zuhayr, one of B. Thaqīf, who said, 'Commander of the Faithful, make your home with me.' [Sulaymān] said, 'I am afraid of headaches.' 'No, not at all; [this will not happen]', replied [Abū Zuhayr], 'God has made me very well-off.' But [Sulaymān] dismounted in the wadi bed. It was suggested to him that [he put down] something to make it softer,[6] but he said that he preferred [just] the wadi bed. He was in need of something to eat[7] and was brought five pomegranates which he ate up. They brought him five [23] more and he ate them. Then he said, 'Do you have any more?' They said that they had and began to bring him five at a time until he had eaten seventy pomegranates [in all]. Then he was given a lamb and six chickens which he ate. They brought him some raisins, the measure of a *makkūk*[8] on a leather spread. He ate the lot and then fell asleep. When he awoke, he called for food and ate with his companions. When he had finished, he called for napkins, but there were so many people and so few napkins, there were not enough to go round them all. He said, 'How shall we solve this, Abū Zuhayr?' 'I'll solve it', replied Abū Zuhayr, and he gave instructions for eel wood[9] and lavender[10] and other similar trees to be brought on which Sulaymān could wipe his hands. Then [the latter] smelt it and said, 'Abū Zuhayr, leave these trees with us and take these napkins and give them to the people!' Then he added, 'Abū Zuhayr, are these trees which grow with you camphor trees?'[11] He replied that they were not and told him [all] there was to know and Sulaymān was amazed.

Imruʾ al-Qays al-Kindī recited as follows:[12]

[1] The fourth Marwanid caliph of the Umayyads, reg. 96–9/715–17 (Bosworth, *New Islamic Dynasties*, p. 3; *EI*, 'Sulaymān b. ʿAbd al-Malik').

[2] There are several well-known transmitters of this name.

[3] Perhaps al-Sabbārī; see Ṭabarī, *History*, XXXII, p. 253.

[4] The fifth Marwanid caliph of the Umayyads, reg. 99–101/717–20, he succeeded Sulaymān (see n. 1 above) (Bosworth, *New Islamic Dynasties*, p. 3).

[5] I.e. the storm brings rain; *raḥmah* 'mercy' is not infrequently used for 'rain'. See p. 33, n. 3 above.

[6] Arabic *waṭāʾ* (Kazimirski, *Dictionnaire*, II, p. 1560).

[7] Arabic *lazima-h baṭnu-h* (Dozy, *Supplément*, II, p. 526).

[8] A not inconsiderable weight, variously in different parts of the Islamic world 7½ *mann*, 15 *raṭl* etc. (Hinz, *Masse*, pp. 44–5).

[9] Arabic *ṣarḥ*; see p. 46, n. 9 above, *sarḥ*.

[10] Arabic *khuzāmā*, *Lavandula spica* Cav. (Golius, *Lexicon*, p. 707; Lane, *Lexicon*, II, p. 734; Dīnawarī, *Plants*, p. 32; Aṣmaʿī, *Nabāt*, p. 15).

[11] Arabic *kāfūr*, *Laurus camphora* L. (Dimyāṭī, *Muʿjam*, p. 131).

[12] Author of the famous pre-Islamic *muʿallaqah*, he was descended from the kings of Kindah (Nicholson, *Literary History*, pp. 103–7). For the poem in question see Ayyūbī, *Dīwān*, pp. 102–3.

'Tis as if the wine, the rain-bearing clouds,
the aroma of lavender and the diffusion of [the sweet odour] of aloes[1]
Once again bring about cool canine teeth,
when the dawn bird sings.

When [Sulaymān] had finished, Abū Zuhayr ordered the gates to be opened and Sulaymān, along with [all] the people, went in. [There] they found a garden with [flowers all] in bud, full of all sorts of good things and fruits. They made for the fruit and Sulaymān remained there the whole of that day and the next. Then he said to ʿUmar, 'Do you realize that we have caused the man inconvenience by [all] this?' So he left, casting a look over the wadi, its verdure and its sweet scents, and saying, 'How wonderful is any wadi in which [Abū Zuhayr] Qays has settled!' He saw the bunches of grapes and thought they were black stones, but ʿUmar told him, 'Commander of the Faithful, these are bunches of grapes!' So he remained there for seven [more] nights, then returned to Mecca.

[24] A certain [poet] recited as follows, describing the orange:[2]

Many's the meadow whose flowers have left me
speechless by their beauty and splendour!
I shall sing the praises of the orange of [all the flowers]
for it has not been described before.
I cried out to the people, 'Oh, who can imagine
a chrysolite bearing a sapphire?'

[A poet] recited as follows on the lily:[3]

[Let there be] abundant rain for a land in which, as I am falling asleep, I am awoken
by the sound of bells before I [actually] slumber!
'Tis as if its lilies in every water channel
in the fields are the tails of peacocks.

[A poet] recited as follows on the stock:[4]

Many's the stock I've stopped at,
when the sun is already up,
Like dirham pieces of every kind,
large mixed with small.

[A poet] recited as follows on the jasmine:[5]

Many are the jasmine [flowers] which have come to you on a tray,
intoxicating people ... with their clinging perfume;[6]
Lovers have shaken off the after-effects of
separation by [imposing] their own colours on the leaves [of the jasmine].

[1] Arabic *quṭr* or *quṭur*, the latter pattern necessary here for the metre. The European lexica (e.g. Lane, *Lexicon*, VII, p. 2543, and Kazimirski, *Dictionnaire*, II, p. 766) use the term 'aloes-wood' and the Arabic lexica gloss with the word *ʿūd* (e.g. Fīrūzābādī, *Qāmūs*, II, p. 123; Zabīdī, *Tāj*, XIII, p. 445). The word does not figure in the technical botanical sources and I take it to mean here any wood which, when burned, gives off an aromatic vapour.

[2] A Persian word *nāranj*, *Citrus Bigaradia* Duh. (Dimyāṭī, *Muʿjam*, p. 149; Varisco, *Agriculture*, p. 182). DMV adds that the sour variety is *Citrus aurantium* L.

[3] A Hebrew word, Arabized as *sawsan*. DMV informs me that it is *Lilium elegens* Thumb.

[4] Arabic *manthūr*, usually for *Matthiola incana* (L) R. Br. DMV would translate 'gilliflower'.

[5] *Yāsamīn/yāsimīn*, *Jasminum officinale* L., white jasmine (Varisco, *Agriculture*, p. 201; Hepper and Friis, *Plants*, p. 207).

[6] There is a lacuna in the line which renders the translation tentative.

[A poet] recited as follows on the lotus:[1]

Many's the azure blue [lotus] which is lost with its blueness
among the meadows with their blue sapphires;
'Tis as if they, dyed layer upon layer, are
wicks[2] on fire with a [blue] sulphur [flame].

[A poet] recited as follows on the narcissus:[3]

Many are the pupils [of the eye], kept awake and held captive,
which have stolen the enchantment of those of women in no need of adornment![4]
[The latter], rising up with rods of chrysolite,
comprise [all] the qualities of a fire of wild chamomile,[5]
With pupils fashioned of camphor,
and eyelids made up with saffron.

[25] *Description of al-Ṭā'if.*[6] Al-Ṭā'if is high, with cool water and a healthy climate. It abounds in fruits and their [basic] agricultural produce is Luqaymī wheat which is like pearls.[7] Its inhabitants are of Thaqīf and Quraysh and they eat and dress like the Meccans. The people of al-Ṭā'if inherit from a daughter when she dies, but no one leaves his daughter any money. It is the same with B. Hudhayl,[8] Muḍar,[9] Bajīlah,[10] all the Sarāh,[11] [indeed] all the Arabs living in the Hejaz and around Mecca. The people [in al-Ṭā'if] show a tremendous community spirit. When some one dies there, the young men carry the bier. They say, 'God bring you peace! This is what He has promised. What an excellent judge He is!', as they take turns to carry the bier to the cemetery. They it is too who dig the grave.

Al-Zubayr b. Abī Bakr informed us saying, 'Umar b. Abī Bakr al-Ramlī[12] informed us saying: A certain scholar of Quraysh informed me, saying, 'It was not the practice for

[1] *Laynūfar/līnūfar* or *naynūfar* or *nawfar*, *Nymphaea lotus* L. (Dimyāṭī, *Mu'jam*, p. 154; Hepper and Friis, *Plants*, p. 207).

[2] Arabic *dhabā'il* (Landberg, *Glossaire daṯînois*, p. 922).

[3] *Narjis* or *nirjis*, used for *Narcissus poeticus* L. (Aṣma'ī, *Nabāt*, p. 32; Varisco, *Agriculture*, pp. 198, 200) and other species.

[4] The poet likens the narcissus to eyes so beautiful that they require no make-up.

[5] DMV kindly informs me that *uqḥuwān* and *bābūnaj* are often interchangeable and refer to several types of chamomile. The two main varieties in the region are *Matricaria chamomilla* and *Anthemis nobilis* (Kahl, *Sābūr*, p. 245). Dīnawarī (*Plants*, pp. 29–30) quotes several lines of poetry comparing the 'fire' of the camomile to white front teeth. The most important point here is the whiteness of the women, a fine quality, according to Arab tradition.

[6] See also Smith, '"Anthropological" Passages', p. 164.

[7] I.e. wheat originating from Wādī Luqaym in the vicinity of al-Ṭā'if (Balādī, *Mu'jam*, VII, p. 263; Kazimirski, *Dictionnaire*, II, p. 101; Fīrūzābādī, *Qāmūs*, IV, p. 178).

[8] Hudhayl b. Mudrikah, a large Hejazi tribe in the region of al-Ṭā'if and between Mecca and Medina (Kaḥḥālah, *Mu'jam*, III, pp. 1213–5; Caskel, *Ǧamharat an-nasab*, I, Tafel 3; *EI*, 'Huḏhayl').

[9] Muḍar b. Nizār, an enormous tribal confederation of 'Adnān which includes the Arabian branches of Khindif and Qays (Kaḥḥālah, *Mu'jam*, III, p. 1107; Caskel, *Ǧamharat an-nasab*, I, Tafel 1; *EI*, 'Rabī'a and Muḍar').

[10] A Qaḥṭānī tribal group of some size, occupying the mountain regions of the Yemen and the Hejaz (Kaḥḥālah, I, pp. 63–5; Caskel, *Ǧamharat an-nasab*, I, Tafel 221; *EI*, 'Baḏjila').

[11] The chain of mountains which runs from the Yemen in the south up to Syria in the north. See Hamdānī (*Ṣifah*, p. 48) who comments that the Arabs call it the Hejaz.

[12] If this name is correct, the man cannot be identified. It may be, however, a MS error for al-Mu'ammalī, a transmitter mentioned by Ṭabarī (*History*, VI, p. 39).

wailing women [to cry out], "Alas, what grief for Ḥarb!", until after the death of Ḥarb b. Umayyah.[1] His wailing women cried out, "Alas, what grief for Ḥarb!", so wailing women began to cry "Alas, what grief for Ḥarb!" for everyone from that time on.'

There is in al-Ṭā'if the grave of ʿAbdallāh b. al-ʿAbbās – God be pleased with both of them.

The whole of their work effort [goes into] tanning leather. Leather is tanned in al-Ṭā'if which is of excellent quality, heavy and well known there. It is [that leather] which is used in Khwārazm.

Every nabk[2] which is planted in this area shoots up in full leaf.[3] The [fruit of the] nabk tree is ground in al-Ṭā'if [to produce] a drink made of its juice; [it is] from the nabk of Iraq which has no thorns.[4] It is the same as a tree in Zabīd in the part close to al-Qurtub.[5]

From al-Ṭā'if to Jabal Badr.[6] From al-Ṭā'if to al-Maʿdā six parasangs.[7] There stone cooking pots are hewn, the stone of which surpasses all others. An old man involved in this informed me saying, 'Only the purest iron[8] works on the smooth stone.' To Khabt ʿAntar five parasangs.[9] This is ʿAntar b. [26] Zabībah al-ʿAbsī. It is a land of mountain tracks and winding wadis in flood,[10] where there is a well of exceedingly sweet water. To Ḥaddān six parasangs.[11] To Karā five parasangs,[12] where wheat is cultivated with two harvests a year, every six months, which is different from everywhere else as far as crops are concerned. To al-Darb two parasangs.[13] To the land of Laylā al-ʿĀmiriyyah and Qays b. al-Mulawwaḥ.[14] It is said that Laylā al-ʿĀmiriyyah and Qays b. al-Mulawwaḥ lived on this land and died there. Concerning her family the poet recites as follows:

[1] Ḥarb b. Umayyah b. ʿAbd Shams b. ʿAbd Manāf of Mecca (Lane, *Lexicon*, II, pp. 540–41).

[2] Arabic *nabq /nabiq*, the fruit of the nabk tree (*Ziziphus spina-christi* L.) (Dimyāṭī, *Muʿjam*, p. 71). The tree is called *sidr* in Arabic, or *ʿilb* and sometimes *dawm*, though the latter also appears to refer to the fruit (Dimyāṭī, *Muʿjam*, pp. 59, 70–71; Dīnawarī, *Plants*, pp. 35, 38, 51; Miller and Morris, *Plants*, pp. 242–3, the latter with illustration and much on the fruit and its medicinal properties).

[3] Reading *muktasī* for *muktasiyyan* (Wehr, *Dictionary*, p. 828).

[4] See n. 2 above.

[5] Al-Qurtub is only half a parasang from Zabīd town to the SSE (Ibn al-Mujāwir, *Tārīkh al-Mustabṣir*, pp. 74, 236; information from FLS).

[6] See Spenger (*Reiserouten*, p. 31) who lists the places on this route. The mountain is unidentified.

[7] Unidentified.

[8] *Fūlādh* is from the Persian *pūlād* (Steingass, *Dictionary*, p. 942; Zakī, *Silāḥ*, p. 34).

[9] I find reference to the place nowhere in the sources available to me. ʿAntar/ʿAntarah is the famous warrior-poet of pre-Islamic times, ʿAntarah b. Shaddād of the tribe of ʿAbs. His mother was a black slave girl, Zabībah (Norris, 'Fables', p. 141; *EI*, "Antar'; "Antarah').

[10] Arabic *mukassarāt* (Kazimirski, *Dictionnaire*, II, p. 897).

[11] The vocalization is tentative, but see Yāqūt (*Muʿjam*, II, p. 227; Sprenger, *Reiserouten*, p. 131).

[12] Sprenger's 'Baḥry' (*Reiserouten*, p. 131) looks just as unlikely as the Baḥrā of the text. My tentative suggestion is Karā, written with final *alif* according to Balādī (*Muʿjam*, VII, pp. 207–8), but which might also be written with *alif maqṣūrah*. Balādī says it is a large mountain between Mecca and al-Ṭā'if, difficult of ascent, nevertheless fertile and yielding many crops.

[13] This is an extremely common place name in the Arabian Peninsula, meaning in the south 'wall', 'tower-house', even 'citadel' (Landberg, *Glossaire daṯînois*, pp. 726–46; Smith, *Ayyūbids*, I, p. 122), rather than classical Arabic 'narrow path' or 'street'. See Balādī, *Muʿjam*, III, pp. 215–17.

[14] Laylā bint Saʿd Umm Mālik al-ʿĀmiriyyah and Qays b. al-Mulawwaḥ, better known as Majnūn, were lovers in Arabic literary tradition (Iṣfahānī, *Aghānī*, I, p. 167-II, p. 17). They were both of the tribal group ʿĀmir b. Ṣaʿṣaʿah, many of whom were in the Ṭā'if area (Kaḥḥālah, *Muʿjam*, II, pp. 708–10; Caskel, *Ǧamharat an-nasab*, I, Tafel 92).

Oh, would that my mother, an ʿĀmiriyyah, were at al-Minā;[1]
when oppression afflicts her, she calls out, 'O Āl ʿĀmir!'

To Nawā a parasang,[2] the first part of Bajīlah territory, and these people are called al-Sarw.[3]

Al-Sarw.[4] Al-Sarw are [made up] of Arab tribal groups under the authority of no ruler, but rather under that of tribal shaykhs from among their number. They are scattered tribal groups.[5] When one of them goes on a journey, his wife approaches her replacement husband,[6] i.e. the wife's lover, who sleeps with her until her husband returns. When the traveller approaches his house, he shouts at the top of his voice, 'You unwelcome replacement, time to go!',[7] and he goes straight into the house unannounced. If he finds the replacement there, he kills him. But if he has already left, then God pardons him for what he has just done. I asked one of them in Mecca, saying, 'My good man living in [the Holy City], what does a replacement do?' He gave me the most direct reply,[8] 'He grinds [the grain for] bread and burns up the wife!'[9]

The most these people do by way of the pilgrimage is the Lesser[10] on 1 Rajab. They were given the guarantee by the Commander of the Faithful, [27] ʿUmar b. al-Khaṭṭāb[11] – God be pleased with him – that this lesser pilgrimage would be accepted as a complete pilgrimage. When they go into Mecca, they fill it with wheat and barley, nabk juice, ghee, honey, sorghum,[12] millet,[13] almonds and raisins etc. So the Meccans say, 'The Iraqi pilgrims are our father through whom we acquire our gold and the Sarw are our mother through whom we acquire our food!'

It is said that the district of Nawā is [made up of] 200 villages or more and included in these 200 settlements are al-Maslam,[14] ʿUqdah,[15] al-?fūʿ,[16]

[1] The line is nowhere quoted in the *Aghānī*.

[2] I vocalize after reference to Yāqūt (*Muʿjam*, V, p. 306) who takes it as the plural of *nawāh*, 'date stone'. Neither of his two places of this name fits the context of the text.

[3] A branch of Bajīlah (Kaḥḥālah, *Muʿjam*, II, p. 509). Cf. Ibn Jubayr (*Travels*, p. 132), who suggests that the Sarw are various different tribes, '... like Bajīlah and others ...', who inhabit the Sarāh and take their name from it.

[4] See also with variant readings and translations the following: Landberg, *Etudes*, II, pp. 911–13, Serjeant, 'Zinā', pp. 150–51 and Smith, 'Wondrous', pp. 118–19.

[5] See n. 4 above.

[6] Arabic *mukhlif.*

[7] Arabic, the following doggerel: 'ayyuhā al-mukhlif al-lajūj / fa-qad ḥān waqt al-khurūj.' 'Lajūj' might mean rather 'quarrelsome' (Dozy, *Supplément*, II, p. 516; Kazimirski, *Dictionnaire*, II, p. 967).

[8] Arabic *aswā al-jawāb* for *aswā jawāb* might mean 'proper reply'.

[9] Arabic *yasḥaqu al-khubz wa-yamḥaqu al-marʾah*! Both have a strong sexual connotation.

[10] Arabic *ʿumrah*.

[11] The third of the Orthodox caliphs, reg. 13–23/634–44.

[12] Arabic *dhurah* (Varisco, *Agriculture*, p. 165; cf. Serjeant, 'Cereals', p. 45, 'millet').

[13] Arabic *dukhn* (Dimyāṭī, *Muʿjam*, pp. 56–7; Varisco, *Agriculture*, pp. 167, 250, n. 18).

[14] Many of the following village names appear doubtful and corrupt. A Maslam is mentioned by Balādī (*Muʿjam*, VIII, pp. 157–8), though the entry is imprecise.

[15] FLS informs me that these ʿAsīr mountains were mapped by Thesiger in 1946, though having also been mapped by the British in 1837 and the French in 1840. They also figure on Philby's map which bears no title, nor scale, 1933 add 1934. She suggests that al-Maslam is the French map's Aqdah Salam at c. 2040 3850. The mountain of Abraham is Jabal Ibrāhīm, which FLS locates at 2030 4105. It appears on Thesiger's map, on the French map (*Carte d'Acir et du Hodjaz*, dressée à Djeddah d'après les renseignements pris dans le pays par M.M. le Colonel Mari et le Docteur Chadufan par M.M. Ferret et Galinier, ..., 3/4,000,000, Paris, 1840). FLS takes the coordinates from the *Saudi Arabia Official Standard Names* gazetteer.

[16] Unidentified.

Ḥaddā,[1] al-Rāhin,[2] Saʿmūm[3] and ?r?f.[4] In the latter there was the incident of the Commander of the Faithful, ʿAlī b. Abī Ṭālib and the viper which he killed. There too is the mountain of Abraham the Friend – peace be upon him. [Of the 200 settlements] are also Manhūr,[5] al-?rawāt,[6] al-Shiʿbayn,[7] al-L qāʿ,[8] Ḥ r f[9] and al-R j ʿayn.[10] These settlements form a group. In these districts there took place the incident of B. Tamīm and Bakr b. Wā'il.[11] In one war there, Laqīṭ b. Zurārah, brother of Ḥājib b. Zurārah and Ḥasan, perished.[12] To al-Fardā' six parasangs.[13] To al-Malḥā' six parasangs, a huge mountain.[14] God knows best!

Jabal al-Malḥā'. Abū ʿAlī Aḥmad b. Muḥammad b. Ādam al-Yazanī informed me saying: When a tubbaʿ[15] became king of the land of the Yemen, Ḥaḍramawt, the area of al-Aḥqāf[16] and the Hejaz and wished to journey out in the direction of Iraq, he came to this mountain, intending to dig out a huge underground tunnel. He excavated[17] beneath the earth the distance of three parasangs or more, [all the time] descending lower. When he had dug for this distance, he commanded that there be excavated a huge town (or more accurately, a huge market area) at the end of the tunnel with shops opposite one another in one row, in each 1,000 shops. He hewed out behind the shops houses and [other] properties. When the work was complete, he filled every single shop with one kind of [28] goods, food, commodities or herbal medicines,[18] everything which was needed, heavy and light, as a storehouse for himself. In the middle of the market he dug out a well which was both broad and deep. Collecting together all the wealth he had, he stored it in the well. [The presence] of gold began to become obvious, so he set up a beam, extended over[19] the curb

[1] *Sic* for Ḥaddā'. See Baladī (*Muʿjam*, II, pp. 241–2) where four places of this name are given, including one of Bajīlah, about 160 km south of al-Ṭā'if.

[2] Unidentified.

[3] This looks doubtful and cannot be identified.

[4] Unidentified.

[5] Unidentified.

[6] Unidentified.

[7] Unidentified.

[8] FLS suggests the is a corruption of al-Qaʿ [*sic*] on Thesiger's map and locates it at 2027 4103.

[9] FLS suggests that this is Jabal Harfah [*sic*] on Thesiger's map at c. 1930 4200.

[10] Unidentified.

[11] B. Tamīm b. Murr was a large tribal group of Najd (Caskel, *Ǧamharat an-nasab*, I, Tafel 59; Kaḥḥālah, *Muʿjam*, I, pp. 125–33). They and Bakr b. Wā'il fought many battles, both in the pre-Islamic period and after Islam. Bakr b. Wā'il of Rabīʿah was also a large tribe of Najd (Caskel, *Ǧamharat an-nasab*, I, Tafel 141; Ibn Ḥazm, *Jamharah*, p. 307; Kaḥḥālah, *Muʿjam*, I, pp. 93–9; *EI*, 'Tamīm b. Murr', with genealogical chart).

[12] Laqīṭ b. Zurārah, a poet, sayyid and chief of Dārim of the 6th century AD (*EI*, 'Laqīṭ b. Zurāra').

[13] Unidentified.

[14] See Baladī, *Muʿjam*, VIII, pp. 254–5. FLS adds that the Milḥa range is on Philby's map and that the *Saudi Arabian Official Standard Names* gazetteer places it at 1950–2003 4240–4250.

[15] The word used of the pre-Islamic rulers of the Yemen by later Muslim writers.

[16] Sing. *ḥiqf*, meaning literally 'winding tract of sand', the name is used as the title of chapter 46 of the Quran. It is sometimes used to indicate the sands in the region of al-Shiḥr, the Ḥaḍramī port, home of ʿĀd, or, as Ibn al-Mujāwir indicates below on p. 253 of the Arabic text, Wādī Ḥaḍramawt itself. Hamdānī (*Ṣifah*, p. 87) states it is a wadi running between Ḥaḍramawt and Mahrah territory, a distance of three days. See also Ḥajarī, *Majmūʿ*, I, p. 60.

[17] Reading with the L MS *fa-ḥafara*.

[18] Arabic *ʿaqāqīr*, plur. of *ʿaqqār* (Dozy, *Supplément*, II, p. 152; Kazimirski, *Dictionnaire*, II, p. 316).

[19] Probably what is meant by *muʿarraḍan*.

of the well and containing a talisman. When anyone put his foot down on the obliquely positioned beam, it would swing round and, since it had a sharp, well-made sword [attached] to it, it would cut him in two and cast him down the well. Ibn al-Mujāwir said: I think the origin of this particular sword can only be the 'thunderbolt' which Japheth, son of Noah – peace be upon him – fashioned.

'Thunderbolt' swords. 'Īsā b. Abī al-Barakāt b. Muẓaffar al-Baghdādī informed me saying: Thunderbolt swords are three, though some say seven. Others say that rather there were fourteen swords fashioned in the time of Japheth, son of Noah – peace be upon him. When Noah died, disagreement broke out among his sons as they sought the leadership and they scattered. Japheth made for the west and built there the town of Jābalqāh, whereas his brother, Ham, went east where he built the town of Jābarsā.[1] What happened to Japheth was that he collected together the wealth of the inhabited earth[2] and piled it up as treasure. He made a talisman over it, setting up swords on [different] talismans. The treasures remained as they were until the time of Dhū al-Qarnayn.[3] Then al-Khiḍr[4] nullified the effect of the talismans and Dhū al-Qarnayn took away these treasures.

Ibn al-Mujāwir said: One of these swords is on Jabal al-Malḥā' in the well in which the treasure was placed by a tubba'. It is also said that it was moulded out of a thunderbolt, the weight of a mustard grain[5] in purest iron, and a sword was fashioned from it for which no scabbard had to be carried,[6] [29] but rather it was placed in an earthenware sword-case. It was also said that, when the thunderbolt struck, it did not come to rest until vinegar was allowed to come into contact with it. When it reached water [also], it stopped. When no vinegar was allowed to come into contact with it, it would reach the extremities of the earth. It was originally a pillar made of the iron of hell – we take refuge with God from it.

Section. God – He is ever mighty and glorious – said,[7] 'Abiding therein [in hell] for ages.'[8] Somebody has commented that a *ḥuqb* is 4,000 years, the year being 14,000 months, the month 4,000 days, the day 4,000 hours and the hour is the period of 70,000 earth years. Ibn Sallām said,[9] 'The inhabitants of [hell] are a miserable lot; we ask God to give us refuge from its evil. The comparison of [the intensity of] its fire and steel is to be drawn from that of [the length of] its days and hours.'

It is said that the swords mentioned above are of four types: Ṣan'ānī – struck in Ṣan'ā', an infantry [sword],[10] short, since it is the sword used by a foot-soldier, cutting alike

[1] Yāqūt (*Mu'jam*, II, p. 91) agrees with Ibn al-Mujāwir that Jābalqāh is the western town, whereas Ṭabarī (*Tārīkh*, I, p. 69 and *History*, I, p. 237), calls it the eastern town. Yāqūt (pp. 90–91) calls Jābarsā the eastern town (cf. Ṭabarī, loc. cit.).

[2] Arabic *al-rab' al-maskūn*, a favourite expression of Ibn al-Mujāwir.

[3] Alexander the Great. He is mentioned in the Quran 18:83 etc. (*EI*, 'al-Iskandar').

[4] A rather vague legendary figure (*EI*, 'al-Khaḍir').

[5] Perhaps to be taken literally, but it should be noted *khardal* was also used as a unit of weight (Hinz, *Masse*, p. 14).

[6] Reading ... *lam yuḥmal la-hu al-ghimd* with the L MS.

[7] See Quran 17:37.

[8] Arabic *aḥqāb*, sing. *ḥuqb* (Quran 73:23).

[9] Ibn Sallām al-Jumaḥī perhaps, a traditionist and philologist who died in 231 or 232/845 or 846 (*EI*, 'Ibn Sallām al-Djumaḥī').

[10] Arabic *mutaqaddim* which might mean rather 'of good quality'.

both what is dry and what is moist. Its hallmark is that it has grooves[1] in the centre, or rather one [such groove]. These swords are frequently found among the Arabs in the mountainous regions of the Yemen.

Kirmānī – an ancient [sword] which was fashioned at the time of the dynasty of Persian kings in Kirmān.[2] It is sharp,[3] neither short nor long. The origin of these pure steel swords is Herat[4] and it is reported that they had [there] a mine from which the iron was extracted. These swords are invariably found among the Shārūnī Kurds,[5] the Baluch,[6] also Kūshān,[7] the Afghans[8] and Sarhadiyyah[9] of the area of Ghaznah.[10]

Ifranjī – an exceedingly long and slim sword,[11] elongated only for [the use of] horsemen. [It is] originally from pieces broken from horseshoes and moistened from the dew of their agricultural produce. [It is] very flexible, cutting into what is soft, but not [30] what is dry. It would often cut through the meat in the body, but the bone remained intact! Invariably these well-known swords are conveyed by them in wooden boxes. Its hallmark is that it has [the handle shaped for] a human palm which is excellent.[12] It is also reported that the man who incised this on his swords fashioned 400, the like of which have never been fashioned throughout the habitable earth. When the Byzantine emperor saw this high-quality craftsmanship, he commanded his right hand be cut off. When this had been done, he moved away from the town in which he lived and settled in another. With his left hand he fashioned 400 more swords, incising in them [handles especially for] human hands.[13] None of these swords would become rusty,[14] without your noticing it, they being white iron, with grooves in the middle.

[1] Arabic *marāzib*, plur. of *mirzabah*.

[2] Perhaps Ibn al-Mujāwir has the Buyids in mind here who ruled in Kirmān between 324/936 and 440/1048 (Bosworth, *New Islamic Dynasties*, p. 155). The reading 'Arab kings' of the L MS would not seem possible. Kirmān is the province immediately E of Fārs, its capital city having the same name (Yāqūt, *Mu'jam*, IV, pp. 454–6; Le Strange, *Lands*, pp. 299 ff. and map VI).

[3] Arabic *qaḍīb* (Kazimirski, *Dictionnaire*, II, p. 760).

[4] Herat is on the river of that name in the province of Khurasan (Yāqūt, *Mu'jam*, V, pp. 396–7; Le Strange, *Lands*, pp. 407 ff. and map VIII).

[5] A Kurdish tribe of Fārs (*EI*, 'Kurds').

[6] Sometimes written Balūṣ in Arabic. Baluchistan is the SE part of the Iranian plateau, from the Kirmān desert to the western borders of Sind and the Punjab (*EI*, 'Baluçistān').

[7] 'Mountain dwellers' of SE Persia. Professor Edmund Bosworth kindly points me in the direction of his article, 'Qufṣ' and informs me that Kūç v Balūç (i.e. Quf/Kūfiçī) were regularly paired as a kind of rhyming phrase to denote the wild tribes beyond the civilized lands.

[8] All the MSS read al-Awghān.

[9] For Sarḥaddiyyah, the people of the mountainous districts of the Sarḥadd-i Chahār Dānga, SE Persia, in the modern Persian province of Baluchistan (Busse, *History*, p. 225 and nn. 48–5). I am grateful to Edmund Bosworth for this reference. See also *EI*, 'Sarḥadd'.

[10] About 145 km SW of Kabul and 150 W of the Indus in province of Sijistān; Yāqūt (*Mu'jam*, IV, p. 201) says it is on the borders of Khurasan and India. See also Ibn Baṭṭūṭah, *Travels*, III, pp. 589 ff. and map p. 588 and *EI*, 'Ghazna'.

[11] Arabic *sayf ṭawīl mādd bi-al-marrah*, the latter being a very common South Arabian colloquialism (Landberg, *Glossaire datînois*, III, p. 2684).

[12] This is how I interpret ... *yakūnu bi-h kaff* ..., i.e. the handle is especially shaped for the hand of the swordsman.

[13] See previous note.

[14] Arabic *jariba*; this might be read *ḥurriba*, 'could not be sharpened'.

Hindī – there are various types, including the Bākhirī[1] which is fashioned in Sind, but originally of Herat iron and pure steel. Its hallmark is that it is black in colour, like beet.[2] Some of them are red similar to the colour of fire ...[3] There is also another type made of finest Indian steel,[4] fashioned in some areas. [The grain][5] twists – but it is sharp and long with a dust-coloured grain – but [again] the parts in between are straight. The third type has double edges[6] fashioned in Khawr Fawfal,[7] or rather ... [They are] very long, broad swords with a grain, not [too] thick, nor [too] thin, but in between; it only cuts into something soft. One type is the 'shāhī', a high-quality steel sword,[8] fashioned in al-Kūz[9] or in ... [They are] very long, broad swords, light and very thin. Its hallmark is that its grain width is four fingers and it is thick and rough like green leeks when they first come up, some intermingled with others like twisting snakes, and four fingers of the sword are like ants collecting on something sweet. The grain can be seen on the surface of the sword like silver, inlayed with iron. Its grain can be seen pure and white, while its surface is [31] sky-blue. It is said that seventy cross-belts[10] for these swords, plus seventy chains were presented to King Quṭb al-Dīn Aybak al-Abthal.[11] [The swords] have a watery and moist appearance, like the white of an egg. When you raise it, it droops; when you move it down, it rises – [it is so flexible]. [It is] dry, [but] will cut into anything moist. With [this sword] the throats of cattle are cut in front of their houses on their feast days. A special property it has is that, if someone's heart is in pain and he washes one of these swords and drinks the water, the pain of which he was complaining leaves him.

There are many types of swords in the world, fashioned in every town and region, apart from the four types which are superior to all others and known one from another as their own [distinctive] kind. Some we have placed above others in order of superiority.

Let us return to the original account.[12] People nowadays have begun to bring in balls of animal wool, taking with them a lantern, a needle, a hook and some wool. The latter is fastened to the top of the entrance of the cave. When anyone goes in, he plays out the

[1] I do not understand the reference here.

[2] Arabic *silq*, *Beta vulgaris* L. (Dimyāṭī, *Muʿjam*, p. 74).

[3] The text reads 'yarfaʿu /yurfaʿu al-dirham wa-...ā marsagh al-jamal!'

[4] Ibn al-Mujāwir uses the word *rūhīniyā*, Persian *rohan*, *rohinā*, *rohīniyā* (Steingass, *Dictionary*, p. 579).

[5] Arabic *jawhar* '... usually refer[s] to the style in which intermingled lines of different colours and forms cover sword blades, but can also denote smooth chains of patterns which divide the sword blade into symmetrical circular or rectangular cartouches, or possibly curved or parallel incisions along the surface of the blade.' (*Weapons*, p. 16, with plates). See also Lane, *Lexicon*, II, p. 475 and Dozy, *Supplément*, I, p. 237. This is my tentative interpretation of 'yatalawwā wa-hwa qaḍīb mādd fī-h jawhar shibh al-ghubār wa-hwa mā bayn dhālik qawāman'.

[6] Arabic *ahillah*, plur. of *hilāl*; I translate tentatively after reference to Kazimirski, *Dictionnaire*, II, p. 1435, who gives '... à deux tranchants' in the context of both lance and halberd.

[7] Unidentified.

[8] *Falālak al-shāhī*; Persian *palālak* (Steingass, *Dictionary*, p. 254). I am not sure of the significance of *shāhī*, but it may mean nothing more than 'regal'.

[9] Unidentified.

[10] Arabic *band al-sayf* (Dozy, *Supplément*, I, p. 117).

[11] This might well be Quṭb al-Dīn Aybak (reg. 602–7/1206–10), 'Malik of Hindūstān in Lahore for the Ghūrids' (Bosworth, *New Islamic Dynasties*, p. 300).

[12] I.e. to p. 56 above, Jabal al-Malḥā'.

wool [attached to] the hook.[1] When they reach the shops, they realize there that all the goods and cloths have become spoilt after such a long period of time, that the iron has become entirely rusty and that the brass is covered with verdigris. So he takes everything which he finds which has some remaining use for himself. Some people find gold, silver and money. When these people return, they wind the wool into a ball, as they get back to the mouth of the tunnel. This is what people do.

It is said that there are there three routes: one leads to the market of ʿUkāẓ,[2] the second to Jabal al-Malḥāʾ and the third to the desert of Fayd,[3] which is the shortest.

Abū ʿAlī [Aḥmad b. ʿAlī] b. Ādam al-Yazanī informed me saying, 'Many [32] shepherds whose flocks have been attacked by wolves hunt down the wolf, intending to kill it, and find themselves unexpectedly where the treasure is. This is a road leading straight to the well which has been mentioned above. There is a middle road which leads to Jabal al-Malḥāʾ. There is also a distant route which is close to the market of ʿUkāẓ. The place remains to this day and can be visited by anyone wishing to do so, as mentioned above.'

To Abīdah one parasang, a fortified settlement in a pleasant wadi.[4] To al-ʿAqīq six parasangs,[5] an area where leathers are tanned and from which acacia leaves are brought to Mecca.

Amir Abū al-Ḥasan b. al-Muʿallim says of [this place]:[6]

> Tell [me], o love-sick companion,
> when the love-sick will recover;
> These are the abodes and al-ʿAqīq;
> Where are Laylā and the tents?

He also said:

> Stop at al-Khiyām overlooking the protected pasturage
> and mingle your tears with blood at its [past] abodes which provided them with all they wanted.
> When you pass by al-ʿUdhayb, say to it,
> 'Is there any water which will quench the thirst of an echo?'[7]

[1] Arabic *nashara al-ghazl wa-al-khuṭṭāf*; I interpret this to mean that the person entering the underground passage attaches a hook to the entrance and ties the wool to the hook.

[2] The sight of a well-known commercial and literary fair near Mecca existing from pre-Islamic times (Yāqūt, *Muʿjam*, IV, p. 142; Nicholson, *Literary History*, pp. 101–2, 135).

[3] Yāqūt (*Muʿjam*, IV, pp. 282–3) does not provide a very precise location of Fayd: 'on the road to Mecca', 'on the road between Kufa and Mecca', 'halfway between Kufa and Mecca on the pilgrimage road'. This latter location is confirmed by al-Rashid (*Darb Zubaydah*, pp. 75, 225 and map II), though, if this is the Fayd in question, it is difficult to reconcile this location with Ibn al-Mujāwir's statement that this third route is the shortest.

[4] Unidentified.

[5] Yāqūt (*Muʿjam*, IV, pp. 138–40) mentions several places of this name, with and without the article, which he says means 'a place where flood water flows', 'a wadi'. This one must be near Mecca.

[6] An unidentified poet. Both poems are part of the amatory prelude usual as an introduction to the classical ode in Arabic. The lover, often with a companion, pines and weeps over the remains of the encampment of his estranged beloved who had been compelled to move on with her tribe.

[7] Al-ʿUdhayb is a watering place on the Kufa pilgrim route near al-Qādisiyyah (Yāqūt, *Muʿjam*, IV, p. 92). Using the expression 'the thirst of an echo', the poet is making reference to the lover's emaciation after his grieving over the departure of the beloved.

I feel remorse for those who departed
on the day of al-Ghuwayr.[1] It is right that I feel remorse.
I wanted them to allow me to return just once,
where the wounded eye is free from blindness.
O eye! Let not blindness take away your sight;
perhaps, perhaps the dwellings are near.
If my body spends the night in Sahām,[2] yet I have
a heart, alone and enslaved, in al-ʿAqīq.

To Tabālah eight parasangs.[3] To al-Jabal eight parasangs, the mountain of B. Badr.[4] All those there are Jews and the fortress is solid at the furthest edge of a high mountain. God knows best.

Nahr al-Sabt.[5] The people of the covenant[6] claim that it is in the wilderness.[7] But a Jewish goldsmith in Aden told me that Nahr al-Sabt is in a land called Ṣayūn.[8] More correctly, [however,] it appeared in the Hejaz, as a river [33] of flowing sand which runs from Thursday evening until [Sunday] morning.[9] No one can cross it, because it flows with such violence on that particular day, but is still for the remainder of the week. Beyond this river are 100,000,000 Jews, both men and women, more than can be counted, innumerable.[10] They are Arabic-speaking and pronounce the *qāf* as a glottal stop in their dialect.[11] Among them are the descendants of Moses, son of Amram – peace be upon him.

It is said that these Jews only arrived in these regions after the attack of Nebuchadnezzar the Babylonian on the Jews in Syria and Egypt.[12] More accurately it

[1] The name of several watering places according to Yāqūt (*Muʿjam*, IV, p. 220). Probably the one between Iraq and Mecca is the one meant here. The 'day' here means 'battle'.

[2] This place is in al-Yamāmah, the scene of an important battle in the days of Abū Bakr, the first caliph (reg. 11–13/632–4) (Yāqūt, *Muʿjam*, III, pp. 288–9).

[3] This ancient town in the present-day emirate of ʿAsīr in Saudi Arabia on the Yemeni pilgrim route, just over 60 miles due west of the major town of Bīshah (Ḥarbī, *Manāsik*, p. 644; Farsi, *National Guide*, map 34; *EI*, 'Tabāla').

[4] It is impossible to pinpoint this mountain precisely and I can find no reference to a Jewish tribe, B. Badr.

[5] The Saturday River is a clear reference to the Sambatyon in Jewish tradition. The latter is a river flowing so strongly that it hurls bolders along before it. Also it flows every day *except* the sabbath, not as Ibn al-Mujāwir's river does! Beyond it the ten lost tribes of Israel are supposed to be exiled (*EJ*, 'Sambatyon'). Rather than indicating Ibn al-Mujāwir's 'abysmal ignorance' of central and northern Arabia, as Rentz suggests (*EI*, 'Ibn al-Mud̲j̲āwir', p. 881), this anecdote in *Tārīkh al-Mustabṣir* is to be read in the context of his predilection for wondrous, and often much embellished, stories based on the legends and myths of old.

[6] Arabic *ahl al-dhimmah*, referring mainly to the Christians and Jews (*SEI*, 'D̲h̲imma').

[7] Arabic *arḍ al-tīh*.

[8] I find no reference to such a place name. Could Ibn al-Mujāwir have misheard Ṣayūn for Ṣahyūn, Zion, in Arabic. The L MS reads Miyyūn (Maqḥafī, *Muʿjam*, p. 650)/Miyūn (Tibbetts, *Navigation*, p. 421), not a name of any great antiquity, the island situated in the Bāb al-Mandab strait at the southern end of the Red Sea and anglicized as Perim. This is hardly likely to have been the location of the Saturday River.

[9] I have corrected the error 'until Saturday morning'.

[10] Arabic *khārijūn ʿan al-ḥadd*.

[11] Arabic 'wa-al-qawm ʿarab yaʿqidūnu al-qāf al-alif fī lughati-him' (Dozy, *Supplément*, II, p. 148). They are Arabic-speaking Jews.

[12] This is a reference to the destruction of the Judean kingdom and the Babylonian captivity in 586 BC (Ṭabarī, *Tārīkh*, I, p. 539 and *History*, IV, p. 45).

was because of God's causing Muḥammad to triumph and they fled from Khaybar[1] and Wādī al-Qurā and settled on these lands. To this day, if a pilgrim goes astray on his way to Mecca and comes across these people, some of them will kill him, while others receive him and put him back on his way in the best possible condition.

Section.[2] One of the things mentioned by Imam Abū ʿAbdallāh Muḥammad b. ʿUmar b. al-Ḥasan al-Rāzī in *Kitāb Maʿrifat al-adyān*[3] is the following. A legal question – the Jews have one day on which, if one does something, he may be killed, and even if he does not, he may still be killed. We asked what it is. The reply was if a child is born to a Jew and on the seventh day[4] the child is circumcised and if the child's seventh day falls on a Saturday and the child is circumcised, the Jew may be killed, since he has broken his religious observance.[5] Also if the child is not circumcised, the father's blood may be shed, because he has not then adhered to the law.[6] This is their law. [This situation comes about] because [the father] has [technically] advocated setting aside [certain religious] prescriptions.

Section. Some Christians have said, 'Islam is amazing!' I asked what he found amazing and he replied, 'If someone does not become a Muslim,[7] killing him is lawful,' i.e. because of his refusal to embrace the Islamic faith.[8] 'If he becomes a Muslim, [34] he is cut,' i.e. he is circumcised. 'So in either case there is bloodshed.' In the same way, going back to the previous passage, the Jew may be killed in either case. God knows best.

The Jewish Months are lunar and run as follows: Tishri, Heshvan, Kislev, Tevet, Shevat, Adar, Nisan, Iyyar, Sivan, Tammuz, Av and Elul.[9] All the Jews of the inhabited earth use these months.

What is the [festival of] the Passover?[10] Among the festivals of the Jews, [it is] the one when the Israelites fled from Egypt after they had been delivered from bondage and made their offerings, as had been shown to them. They are seven days called the Faṭīr [when] they are not permitted to eat bread, nor even keep it among their supplies.[11] On

[1] A well-known town inhabited by Jews in pre-Islamic and early Islamic times situated about 170 km N of Medina (Balādī, *Muʿjam*, III, pp. 170–71 and map p. 179, which includes Wādī al-Qurā; Farsi, *National Guide*, p. 79).

[2] See Smith, 'Wondrous', pp. 117–18.

[3] This must be the famous Fakhr al-Dīn al-Rāzī who died in 606/1209, although I can trace no mention of the work in question (*EI*, 'Fakhr al-Dīn al-Rāzī').

[4] By 'seventh' Ibn al-Mujāwir must mean the seventh day after the day of birth, i.e. the eighth day of the child's life. While it seems clear that this legal problem has been settled in Judaism, it is interesting to note that a dispute must have raged among medieval Jews. It is now accepted that, if the eighth day falls on the sabbath or on a festival day, the circumcision must nevertheless take place (*EJ*, 'Circumcision').

[5] Arabic *sunnah*, an interesting term in this Jewish context.

[6] Arabic *sharʿ*, another interesting term in this context.

[7] Reading the I MS marginal note *lam yuslim*, rather than the text *tanaṣṣara*.

[8] Arabic *al-dīn al-ḥanīfī* (Lane, *Lexicon*, II, p. 658; *SEI*, 'Ḥanīf').

[9] I have used the forms of the months as they appear in the *EJ*.

[10] Hebrew Pesaḥ (*EJ*, 'Passover'; Bīrūnī, *Instruction*, p. 175; *Chronologie*, p. 271).

[11] *Faṭīr* means literally 'unleavened bread' and the Passover is called ʿĪd al-Faṭīr in Arabic (Lane, *Lexicon*, VI, p. 2417). *Laḥm* must here mean unleavened bread as its Hebrew cognate does. Leaven is not even permitted in the house at the time of Passover.

the last day Pharaoh was drowned in the Sea of Sūf, the Red Sea, and this day is called the Keseh.[1]

What is the [festival of] the Pentecost?[2] It is on 6 Sivan, called ʿAshar and derived from [the sense of] assembling.[3] It is also one of their pilgrimages [made] in order to acquire [good] crops.

What is the [festival of] the Kippūr?[4] It is on 10 Tishri. This is perhaps also called the ʿĀshūrāʾ.[5] Kippūr is [derived] from the expiation of ones sins.[6] Only on this day is fasting binding on the Jews and death on those who do not. The period of the fast is twenty-five hours beginning before sunset on 9 [Tishri] and ending one hour after sunset on 10. The Kippūr is not permitted on Sunday, [35] Tuesday or Friday.

What is the [festival of] the Tabernacles? In their language it is Muṣallā.[7] It is [a period of] seven days, the first of which is 15 Tishri. All of them are festivals during which they sit in the shade of branches, Egyptian willows,[8] vines and olives. They are commanded to rest at this time in remembrance of God's giving them the shade of clouds in the wilderness.

What is the [festival of] the ʿArabā? The meaning of the word is 'willow'.[9] It is the last festival day of the Muṣallā. By this I mean 21 Tishri and it is also one of their pilgrimages.

What is the [festival of] the Benediction[10] It is a festival, [the name] derived from divine blessing.[11] It [falls] two days after ʿArābā.

What is the [festival of] Dedication?[12] It is a festival whose name is derived from cleansing.[13] It is eight days, the first of which is 25 Kislev when they light one lamp at the doors of their houses on the first night, two on the second, until eight days are up [and there are] eight lamps. This is to remind them of the youngest of eight brothers[14] who were killed at a time when they were conquered [by a Greek king] who deflowered some of their virgins and went round Jerusalem on his mule.

[1] Yam Sūf, the latter meaning 'reeds', and originally applied only to the arms of the Red Sea (Brown, *Lexicon*, p. 693; *EJ*, 'Suf'; Bīrūnī, *Instruction*, p. 175, n. 4).

[2] Hebrew *ʿaṣārāh*. See Bīrūnī, *Instruction*, p. 175; *Chronologie*, p. 281.

[3] Arabic *ijtimāʿ*. See also *EJ*, 'Shavnot' and 'Sivan'.

[4] Hebrew Kippūr. See *EJ*, 'Day of Atonement'; Bīrūnī, *Instruction*, p. 175; *Chronologie*, p. 276.

[5] The Muslim voluntary fast day on 10 Muḥarram. For the Jewish background of this day, see *SEI*, "Āshūrāʾ'.

[6] Arabic *tafkīr al-dhunūb*.

[7] The festival of Sukkot, the Feast of the Tabernacles. Booths or tabernacles are built from the leaves and branches of these trees (*EJ*, 'Sukkot'). The Arabic *miḥallah* means 'a goat's hair tent' (Lane, *Lexicon*, V, p. 1917). See the *ṣālal* root in Hebrew (Brown, *Lexicon*, p. 853, entry III, 'be/grow dark etc.'). See also Bīrūnī, *Instruction*, p. 176; *Chronologie*, p. 277.

[8] Arabic *khilāf*, *Salix aegyptia* L.; see Dimyāṭī, *Muʿjam*, p. 53.

[9] Hebrew *ʿarābāh*, which, however, is probably the Arabic *gharab*, *Populus euphratica* Oliv. (Brown, *Lexicon*, p. 788). The Hebrew word is translated 'willow' in Psalms 137:2 (Dimyāṭī, *Muʿjam*, pp. 112–13). The pilgrimage is to Jerusalem. See also Bīrūnī, *Instruction*, p. 176.

[10] Text Tabarrīk (Bīrūnī, *Instruction*, p. 176; *Chronologie*, p. 277).

[11] Arabic *barakah*.

[12] Text Ḥanukkah (*EJ*, 'Hannukah'; Bīrūnī, *Instruction*, p. 176; *Chronologie*, p. 278).

[13] Arabic *tanḥīf*, i.e. of the temple (Bīrūnī, *Instruction*, p. 176, n. 3).

[14] The text is perhaps corrupt here and reads: '... qatalū-hum bi-mutaghallab ʿalay-him kāna yafraʿu min ʿadhārī-him wa-yaṭūfu Bayt al-Muqaddas ʿalā baghli-h!' See OL's apparatus.

What is the [festival of] the Purim?[1] It is a name derived from casting lots and divining. It is on 14 Adar followed by Nisan. It is also known as the Festival of the Majallah, i.e. Maghallā.[2] The reason for it is that Haman, the minister of Ahaseuerus, namely Abruwīz, son of Anūshirvān, used to plot against them when they were [36] in Babylon.[3] He schemed to bring about their downfall and asked for permission to crucify them. But the tables were turned on him on this particular day and he [himself] was crucified. For this reason they make crucified effigies and take delight in burning them. During this festival the Jews [observe] fasting and superogatory prayers. The reasons for these are what has been related, so they made it sacred and made abstention from food obligatory.

When one of their women menstruates, they isolate her and vessels are put aside for her to eat and drink. No one approaches her until she leaves off her bleeding, i.e. her menstruation. When she has finished, she goes to the bath and washes and combs her hair. Next she comes to a well structure called Ṭūmī. Ibn al-Mujāwir said: In Baghdad they have a well called the Ṭūmī well in a ruined place among the stones of an enclosure,[4] a well built in layers.[5] Across the middle of the well a beam has been placed over the curb and a long chain fixed to the beam, the end of which reaches down to the bottom of the water.[6] The woman strips off her clothes and holds on to the chain, ducking herself under and emerging [continually] until some woman above the well tells her that she is clean, i.e. purified. When the woman hears this, she knows that she is cleansed of the impurity of menstruation. Only then does she put on all her clothes. All the Jewesses meet her when the woman is cleansed.

The proverb says:[7] Seek advice from Muslims; sleep in the houses of Christians; sup with Jews. It is also said: The Muslim has his sex,[8] the Christian his wealth, the Magian his home comforts[9] and the Jew his belly!

[37] *From al-Ṭā'if to Ṣa'dah.*[10] Muḥammad b. Zankal b. al-Ḥusayn al-Kirmānī informed me saying: From al-Ṭā'if to al-Ma'din is four parasangs.[11] To al-Rān eight parasangs.[12] To Maḥrā eight parasangs.[13] To al-Dawrab four parasangs.[14] To Yāfi'

[1] Meaning 'lots' (*EJ*, 'Purim'; Bīrūnī, *Instruction*, p. 176; *Chronologie*, p. 280).

[2] Purim falls on 14 Adar and I have corrected Ibn al-Mujāwir's erroneous 24 Adar. Hebrew *m^egillah*, the scroll of Esther (Brown, *Lexicon*, p. 166 and Esther 10:20 ff.).

[3] For Ahaseuerus, king of Persia, ruling from India to Ethiopia, see *EJ*, 'Ahaseuerus'. See also Esther 10:24.

[4] Reading *jadarah* with OL.

[5] Arabic *mudarraj*.

[6] The text is corrupt: '... ilā an yaṣila ilā ākhir al-silsilah thumma ilā qarār al-mā''.

[7] See Smith, 'Wondrous', p. 118.

[8] Arabic *inna li-l-Muslim farja-h*.

[9] Reading *riyāsh* with OL.

[10] This must amount to part of the Yemeni pilgrim route N from the northern Yemeni town, situated about 180 km N of Ṣan'ā'. For Ṣa'dah, see Smith, *Ayyūbids*, p. 196, with full references and *EI*, 'Ṣa'da'. For the route, see Sprenger, *Reiserouten*, p. 130 and Theniyian, *Study*, *passim*.

[11] This might well be the Ma'din al-Birām of Hamdānī (*Ṣifah*, p. 121; Ḥarbī, *Manāsik*, p. 654; Balādī, *Mu'jam*, VIII, p. 193). See also Sprenger, *Reiserouten*, p. 131.

[12] Unidentified.

[13] Unidentified.

[14] Unidentified; al-Durūb.

eight parasangs.[1] To ʿAdā eight parasangs.[2] To Rān Kīsah(?) four parasangs,[3] a tall, extensive mountain, over which there is a pedestrian track. To Ṣafī four parasangs,[4] a market which is held on Friday. To Khafan four parasangs.[5] To Madar four parasangs,[6] a market frequented[7] on Thursday evening. To ʿAḍḍat ʿArīn four parasangs.[8] To Bilād B. Qaran four parasangs.[9] To Bilād B. ʿAbd al-Dār twenty parasangs.[10] To al-Dhahbān seven parasangs.[11]

A description of these areas. The [previous] informant, [al-Kirmānī], informed me as follows: All these areas [are made up of] settlements similar in size to one another to a greater or lesser degree. Each settlement has its own people. Every Arab tribal group[12] and every bedouin section[13] is [represented] in a settlement. As a result of their behaving badly[14] [towards others], no one can settle with them, either on a temporary or a permanent basis.

A stronghold of stone and plaster has been built in every settlement and everyone living in the settlement has a store in the stronghold in which he keeps all his possessions, taking only from it what he needs on a daily basis. The inhabitants of the settlement surround the stronghold on all four sides. Each settlement is ruled over by an old shaykh of some power, clever and intelligent. When he gives a ruling, no one else shares in, nor opposes, what he advises them to do and what judgement he gives. There is no other authority ruling over all those in these areas and they pay no tax,[15] nor [38] do they hand over any levy[16] at all, except whatever each one wishes. Thus they are constantly fighting, one getting the better of another's wealth and the relatives of Zayd taking the wealth of ʿAmr.[17] They do this all the time.

Their crops are wheat and barley; their trees are vines, pomegranates and almonds. All [kinds] of fruits and choice things are to be found among them. Their food is ghee and honey and they [bask] in their God[-given] ease and security. They are tribes who go back to Qaḥṭān[18] and others in their family trees.

[1] Unidentified in this context, although the root is common in place names, meaning 'climb up', 'ascend'.

[2] Unidentified.

[3] Unidentified.

[4] Unidentified.

[5] Unidentified.

[6] Unidentified.

[7] Arabic *yaltām*, for *yaltaʾimu*, *iltām* for *iltaʾama* (Kazimirski, *Dictionnaire*, II, p. 953; Dozy, *Supplément*, II, p. 508). It is much preferred by Ibn al-Mujāwir to, say, *ijtamaʿa*.

[8] Unidentified.

[9] B. Qaran b. Radmān may be meant here (Caskel, *Ǧamharah*, I, Tafel 271; Kaḥḥālah, *Muʿjam*, III, p. 946).

[10] The territory of ʿAbd al-Dār b. Quṣayy, a ʿAdnānī Hejazi tribe (Kaḥḥālah, *Muʿjam*, II, p. 723; Caskel, *Ǧamharat an-nasab*, I, Tafel 4).

[11] A mountain in ʿAsīr on the Yemeni pilgrim route (Hamdānī, *Ṣifah*, p. 227; Balādī, *Muʿjam*, III, p. 260; Ḥajarī, *Majmāʿ*, II, 351; Maqḥafī, *Muʿjam*, p. 253; Akwaʿ, *Buldān*, p. 115 [a mountain]).

[12] Arabic *fakhdh*.

[13] Arabic *baṭn*.

[14] Arabic *jawr*.

[15] Arabic *kharāj*. This term originally in Islam meant 'tribute'. It was only later that it took on the meaning 'crop tax' (Ṭabarī, *History*, XIV, p. 29, n. 158; *EI*, 'Kharādj'; Ben Shemesh, *Taxation*, pp. 19–20).

[16] Arabic *qiṭʿah* (Serjeant, *Portuguese*, p. 192).

[17] Arabic *ḍaraba ʿalā* (Dozy, *Supplément*, II, p. 5). Ibn al-Mujāwir again introduces these imaginary characters.

[18] The ancestor of all the southern, Qaḥṭānī, tribes (Caskel, *Ǧamharat an-nasab*, I, Tafel 176; *EI*, 'Ḳaḥṭān').

Dhahbān. It is the centre of the settlements, a wealthy area. It is said that the circumference of the area is forty parasangs. It is the highland[1] of the Yemen, or more accurately the extremities of the regions of the highland of the Yemen to the east of Tihāmah. It has few mountains and flat plains. Najd al-Yaman is not the same as Najd al-Ḥijāz, but rather the south of Najd al-Ḥijāz joins up with the north of Najd al-Yaman.

To Bilād Qaḥṭān four parasangs.[2] To Rāḥat B. Shurayf two parasangs, a wadi also called Darb al-ʿAqīq in which the town of al-Barah was situated.[3] To Ṣaʿdah twenty parasangs, a town of habitation and cultivation, pleasant land and a secure citadel.[4]

Ibn al-Mujāwir said: On this route there are countless communities, areas, towns and settlements, too many to be included in official records, i.e. in making [tax] calculations.[5] The local people drink from flowing streams, and some drink from wells the water of which is light on the constitution, aids digestion and is delicious to the taste.

From al-Ṭāʾif to Mecca, taking the route back from al-Ṭāʾif. To Ḥadab al-Ranj two parasangs.[6] This is a mountain cave. To al-Ṭawd al-Aʿẓam three parasangs,[7] a tall mountain and it is this which is called al-Ḥijāz.

[39] *The Hejaz*. Al-Aṣmaʿī said:[8] The Hejaz was so called because it is surrounded by[9] the five lava fields,[10] including Ḥarrat B. Sulaym[11] and Ḥarrat Wāqim.[12] One also says, 'The man put on a waist-wrapper',[13] that is he tied it around his waist. From this too one says 'the waistband[14] of the trousers'. The word used by everybody, *ḥuzzah*, is wrong.

Al-Khalīl[15] said that [the Hejaz was so called] because it separates the low ground[16] and Syria[17] [on the one hand] and the desert area [on the other].

[1] Arabic *najd*.

[2] Unidentified.

[3] A Rāḥah is mentioned by Hamdānī (*Ṣifah*, pp. 116, 169, 199) in the region of Najrān and this could well be the place in question here. It might be Yāqūt's (*Muʿjam*, III, p. 12) first al-Rāḥah, 'a place at the beginning of the Yemen; I think it is a settlement.' The other two names are unidentified. B. Shurayf could be Kaḥḥālah's (*Muʿjam*, II, p. 592) 'al-Shurayf, *fakhdh* of Qaḥṭān 'Asīr'. FLS also kindly mentions 'Shuraif, sub-section of Qaḥṭān' on Thesiger's map of 'Arabia, a journey through the Tihama, the 'Asir and the Hijaz Mountains in 1946 by W. Thesiger'.

[4] See p. 54, n. 13 above.

[5] Arabic *wa-lā taḥwī-h aqlām al-dawāwīn*. Does this mean that Ibn al-Mujāwir had access to such records?

[6] See Balādī, *Muʿjam*, II, p. 244.

[7] Yāqūt (*Muʿjam*, IV, pp. 46–7) says this is another name for al-Sarāh, the long mountain chain stretching right down to the Yemen. It is evidently on occasions, as here, another name for the Hejaz. The word means 'mountain'.

[8] Abū Saʿīd ʿAbd al-Malik al-Aṣmaʿī, a well-known philologist who died in 213/828 (*EI*, 'al-Aṣmaʿī').

[9] Arabic *uḤtuJiZat*.

[10] Arabic *ḥirār*, plur. of *ḥarrah*.

[11] See Balādī, *Muʿjam*, II, p. 271.

[12] There are two lava fields of Medina so called (Balādī, *Muʿjam*, II, pp. 283–8).

[13] Arabic *iḤtaJaZa*.

[14] Arabic *ḤuJZah*.

[15] Al-Khalīl b. Aḥmad al-Farāhidī/al-Furhūdī, a well-known philologist who died in 160/776, or 170/786, or 175/791 (*EI*, 'al-Khalīl b. Aḥmad').

[16] Arabic *ghawr*.

[17] Arabic *shām*.

Al-Jawharī[1] said that it formed a barrier[2] between Najd and the low ground. The Yemenis claimed that Mecca belongs to the Yemen and what illustrates the proof of this is what the Prophet, standing on a couch, said, 'This is north and this is south.'[3]

The inhabitants of al-Ṭā'if claim that Mecca belongs to Tihāmah, because everything between Najd and Tihāmah is mountain called al-Ṭawd al-Aʿẓam, since everything to the west of it is Tihāmah and everything east Najd. The Iraqis claimed that Mecca is the land of the Hejaz.

Ibn al-Mujāwir said, 'On this basis al-Ṭawd al-Aʿẓam is the Hejaz itself, because it forms a barrier[4] between Najd and Tihāmah.' It is also said that it is a mountain which joins up with the Yemen.

The home of the Arabs[5] is the Hejaz which includes Mecca, Medina, al-Yamāmah and its mountain districts[6] and Najd al-Ḥijāz which joins up with Bahrain, the desert of Iraq and that of the Jazīrah.[7] (In all regions there is nothing better and more healthy than the weather and climate of the Hejaz – as [the poet] has said:

> Alexandria would be my home,
> if I were [able to] settle there;
> But [I spend] my nights in Najd
> and my days in the Hejaz.)

[The home of the Arabs also includes] the Syrian desert and also the Yemen, including Tihāmah, Najd al-Yaman, Oman, Mahrah, Ḥaḍramawt, the area of Ṣanʿā', Aden and the rest of the mountain regions of the Yemen.

The border of al-Sirrayn as far as the district of Yalamlam,[8] ending up at the elevated land of al-Ṭā'if [in the north], stretching as far as Najd [40] al-Yaman [and] as far as the Persian Sea in the east, [all this] is part of the Yemen. So this [amounts to] about two thirds of the Arabian Peninsula.

The land from al-Sirrayn as far as the Persian Sea over to the vicinity of Midian and going back on the eastern boundary via Hajar to Jabal B. Ṭayy', extending over to the elevated land of al-Yamāmah, as far as the Persian Sea [again] is part of the Hejaz and Midian.[9]

[1] Abū Naṣr Ismāʿīl al-Jawharī was a lexicographer who died c. 397/1006 (*EI*, 'al-Djawharī').

[2] Arabic *ḤaJaZat*.

[3] Using the words *shām* (also meaning Greater Syria) and *yaman* (also meaning the Yemen), presumably indicating that the latter included Mecca.

[4] Arabic *ḤaJaZa*.

[5] Arabic *diyār al-ʿArab*. Here Ibn al-Mujāwir begins to copy Ibn Ḥawqal, pp. 18–19, and not very accurately. As some of this text is clearly corrupt, I have followed that of Ibn Ḥawqal. The differences are well indicated in OL's apparatus.

[6] Arabic *mikhlāf*, plur. *makhālīf*. For al-Yamāmah, a region of Najd in earlier times, see *EI*, 'al-Yamāma'.

[7] Ibn al-Mujāwir loses the thread here in his eagerness to comment on the climate and quote his little ditty. I follow Ibn Ḥawqal and keep Ibn al-Mujāwir's insertion in parentheses.

[8] Al-Sirrayn is an island off the Red Sea coast a little south of al-Līth (Balādī, *Muʿjam*, IV, p. 199). Yalamlam, also known as Alamlam, is a town and wadi about 80 km S of Mecca, a meeting-place for pilgrims (Hamdānī, *Ṣifah*, pp. 120, 125, 175; Balādī, X, p. 28; Farsi, *National Guide*, map 32).

[9] Madyan is between Tabūk (see p. 68, n. 3 below) in the NW of the Peninsula and the Red Sea coast, only about 80 km from the latter (Balādī, *Muʿjam*, VIII, pp. 68–70). Ṭayy' b. Udad is a hugh tribal confederation of Qaḥṭān. Originally from the Yemen, they migrated to Najd, Hejaz, Iraq and al-Yamāmah. The 'two mountains' are the two ranges of Ajā' and Salmā and called Jabalā Ṭayy' (Ibn Ḥazm, *Jamharah*, pp. 398–9, 476; Ibn Rasūl, *Ṭurfah*, pp. 36–7; Kaḥḥālah, *Muʿjam*, II, pp. 689–92; *EI*, 'Ṭayy'').

The land from the border of al-Yamāmah as far as the vicinity of Medina, going back over the Basran desert and stretching over to Bahrain as far as the sea, is part of Najd. The land of ʿAbbādan as far as al-Anbār and its surrounding area as far as Najd and the Hejaz including Ṭayyʾ, Asad and Tamīm and the rest of the tribes of Muḍar is part of the Iraqi desert.[1]

The border of al-Anbār as far as Bālis and its surrounding area to the Syrian desert including the land of Taymāʾ and Barriyyat Khussāf to the vicinity of Wādī al-Qurā and al-Ḥijr is part of the Jazīrah desert.[2]

The land of Bālis as far as Eilat, facing the Hejaz, over to the Persian Sea, as far as the area of Midian, opposite the land of Tabūk[3] until it joins up with the territory of Ṭayyʾ, is part of the Syrian desert.

However, there are scholars who divide up these areas [differently] and who have asserted that Medina is of Najd because it is close to it and that Mecca is of Tihāmat al-Yaman because it is close to it.

From Mecca to Jeddah. From Mecca to ʿAyn Abī Sulaymān one parasang,[4] a flowing spring where date palms have been planted and also nabk trees.[5]

To Maqtalat al-Kilāb one parasang.[6] The reason for [this name] is that there was a dog belonging to a certain bedouin and the dog attacked a man of the village, bit him and made him blind in one eye. So the man killed the dog. Whereupon the owner of the dog assembled his paternal relatives, while the man bitten assembled his people and war broke out between the two parties. They continued [41] fighting until they were all killed. So the place became known as Maqtalat al-Kilāb. To al-Rikābiyyah one parasang, a well surrounded by two mountains, called Rashshān, on the left of the road.[7] A certain bedouin recites as follows about this:

> O two mountains of Rashshān, tell indeed
> when did Badr of the Hejaz cross over you?[8]

[1] ʿAbbādān is on the Gulf at the Tigris and Euphrates estuary (Yāqūt, *Muʿjam*, IV, pp. 74–5). Al-Anbār is on the Euphrates, W of Baghdad (Le Strange, *Lands*, pp. 65–6 and map II).

[2] Bālis is on the Euphrates, due W of al-Raqqah (Yāqūt, *Muʿjam*, I, pp. 328–9; Le Strange, *Lands*, p. 107 and map III). Taymāʾ is about 400 km N of Medina (Balādī, *Muʿjam*, II, pp. 52–7; Wohaibi, *Northern Hijaz*, 277–83; Farsi, *National Guide*, map 95). Barriyyat Khussāf is a desert area between Bālis and Aleppo (Yāqūt, *Muʿjam*, II, p. 370), between al-Raqqah and Bālis (Idrīsī, *Opus*, I, p. 352). Jazīrah here is of course the Jazīrah of Iraq.

[3] Eilat (Arabic Aylah) is at the head of the Gulf of ʿAqabah. Tabūk is about 200 km SE of Eilat in the NW of present-day Saudi Arabia (Balādī, *Muʿjam*, II, pp. 10–14; Wohaibi, *Northern Hijaz*, pp. 272–6; Farsi, *National Guide*, map 109).

[4] The place does not figure in the sources at my disposal. The route is about due E and it must be just outside Mecca in that direction.

[5] Arabic *sidr*.

[6] Unidentified, meaning 'place where dogs are killed'.

[7] Yāqūt has an entry al-Rikābiyyah (*Muʿjam*, III, p. 63) which he says is ten day's journey from Medina where Rikābī oil comes from or to which oil is brought from Syria on pack camels (*rikāb*). Rashshān does not figure in other sources. OL in his apparatus wonders if this should read Rayshān. ' ... on the left of the road'; *al-darb* may be a place name.

[8] Badr may be a personal name here, or the tribal one.

To Ḥaddah one parasang.[1] It used to be cultivated land belonging to B. al-Badriyyah,[2] but they sold it and it was bought from them by Sulaymān b. ʿAlī b. ʿAbdallāh b. Mūsā and he dug out the spring. It was reported that the spring remained as it was in the hands of these people for a long time as they made use of it to produce their crops. Sharif al-Ḥusayn b. Thābit al-Sadīdī[3] bought it from them. He planted over the whole area date palms, 20,000 of them, his people [remaining] as their owners until 622.[4] Then Amir Ṭunbughā made it so that al-Malik al-Kāmil was in control of the province of the Hejaz.[5] He took possession of the palms of the sharifs, making himself the owner of them. He took possession of these date palms among everything else he seized and they now belong to the sultan. It is said that Ḥaddah was known by this name because it is the last part of Wādī Nakhlah.[6] But, more accurately, it is part of Wādī al-Ṣafrāʾ.[7]

To al-Qurayn one parasang,[8] built by Amir Hāshim and he kept there a garrison of cavalry to protect the caravans on the roads. They took an *ʿalawī* dinar on every camel. It is a small, square fortress, built on a hill [and made] of stone and gypsum. On its outside wall[9] were built thirteen small towers under which was a well with good, sweet water. When water is scarce in Ḥaddah, its inhabitants draw water from them. It is said that al-Qurayn is only called by that name because it is exactly half way between Mecca and Jeddah.[10] It is said that by building it there were united together [42] justice and security.[11]

To Kitānah one parasang.[12] It is said that God – He is ever mighty and glorious – destroyed on this very spot the Abyssinians who were bringing elephants from Ṣanʿāʾ.

To al-Thadyayn one mile,[13] among high mountains, the last part of the flat, low land and the first part of the wadi [area]. It was a stronghold built in stone and gypsum, but now in ruins.

[1] Yāqūt (*Muʿjam*, II, p. 229) tells us that this place is halfway between Mecca and Jeddah and was called Ḥaddāʾ by the ancients. Balādī (*Muʿjam*, II, p. 241) lists the place under the latter name and confirms its location 29 km from al-Ḥudaybiyah (see Farsi, *National Guide*, map 41). See p. 70, n. 8 below.

[2] Perhaps the same tribe as Badr.

[3] This sharif cannot be identified. The *nisbah* might read 'al-Sudaydī' or 'al-Sudayrī'.

[4] Begins 13 January 1225.

[5] There is some error here. There must be two persons and we must therefore read *mallaka* and translate thus. Anyone called al-Malik al-Kāmil in this context would be an Ayyubid leader, though none of the Ayyubids with this name could be in question here. The name Ṭunbughā is not found in the Hejazi histories of the period.

[6] Arabic *ākhar ḥudūd*. Balādī (*Muʿjam*, IX, pp. 39–47) mentions several wadis of this name, called after its date palms, and quotes extensively from Yāqūt (*Muʿjam*, V, pp. 277–8), but from the information given it seems none is the one in question here.

[7] It is impossible to relate this wadi to those of this name mentioned in Yāqūt (*Muʿjam*, III, p. 412) and Balādī (*Muʿjam*, V, pp. 148–53). I have a distinct feeling that Ibn al-Mujāwir has taken this route from an informant and that it is, in this middle section at least, not entirely accurate. See n. 13 below.

[8] A small, though prominent, hill, according to Balādī (*Muʿjam*, VII, p. 126), on the edge of the region of Baḥrah (see Farsi, *National Guide*, map 41). The editor of Ibn Jubayr, William Wright, has accepted the reading al-Qarīn (*Riḥlah*, 80), although his MS indicates an initial *ḍammah*. Presumably Hāshim b. Fulaytah (d. 549/1154) is in question here. See Appendix B.10, B. Hāshim, below.

[9] Arabic *dawr*.

[10] Arabic *aQRaNa niṣf al-ṭarīq*.

[11] Arabic *uQRiNa al-ʿadl wa-al-amn*.

[12] I follow Balādī's vocalization (*Muʿjam*, VII, p. 189). This may be the place in question. FLS finds 'El Kattana' at about 2126 3925 on map *Medina-Mecca*, 1916 and 'Kathana' on Philby, 1933 add 1934.

[13] Meaning 'the two breasts', this place is not found in other sources. The mile is not Ibn al-Mujāwir's usual unit of distance and its mention here and below (p. 70, n. 6) seems to me to suggest that this route is taken from an informant. See also n. 7 above.

To Wādī al-Sidrah one parasang.[1] There is a small *sidr* tree on the right of the road and [once] the Prophet returned this way. Everyone who travels along the wadi takes some of its leaves for the purpose of acquiring good luck. But the *sidr* tree remains in the same state and to this day it has not diminished in any way.

To al-Ghār half a parasang.[2] To al-Fajj al-Akhḍar half a parasang.[3] To al-Farʿ half a parasang.[4] To Mathwab half a parasang.[5] To Abū al-Raḥim one mile, a small mountain on the left of the road.[6] To al-Nuhūd one mile, twelve separate mountains like a young girl's breasts.[7] To al-Mīnah half a parasang, called also al-Ḥudaybiyyah.[8] It is said that the Prophet got as far as this and the further he walked, the longer the route became. So he went back, saying, 'How far away you are, God curse you!' The place is a long salt-pan in low ground as flat as the scale [of a balance].[9] To Jeddah half a parasang.

The building of Jeddah. Mūsā b. Masʿūd al-Nassāj al-Shīrāzī informed me saying: When Salmān al-Fārisī[10] – God be pleased with him – became a Muslim, news filtered through to his people and they made their way to him and accepted Islam through the Apostle of God – God bless him and grant him peace. They lived in Jeddah because they were merchants. One of them said that rather Khusrau Fīrūz b. Yazdgird b. Shahriyār b. Bahrām built it.[11] One of the things reported by Abū ʿAbdallāh Muḥammad b. Isḥāq b. ʿAbbās al-Fākihī in his book was as follows: The first one to adopt Jeddah as a port was ʿUthmān b. ʿAffān.[12] Previously it had been in a place called al-Shuʿaybah.[13] Ibn al-Mujāwir said: Al-Shuʿaybah is a large inlet [43] and ancient anchorage opposite Wādī al-Muḥram.[14] There can be no doubt that this [came] before Jeddah since in these regions there was no anchorage nearer, nor safer, than it. The Persians said that, when Sīrāf fell into ruins, its

[1] See Smith 'Wondrous', p. 113. The wadi is not mentioned in other Hejazi sources and I am no longer confident that the Shiʿb al-Sidrah reference is relevant (cf. Smith, 'Wondrous', n. 10).

[2] Meaning 'the cave'. If this is the site of the famous cave in Jabal Ḥirāʾ in which Muḥammad, accompanied by Abū Bakr, took refuge during the *hijrah* to Medina in AD 622, it is surprising that Ibn al-Mujāwir does not elaborate. Balādī (*Muʿjam*, pp. 248–9) makes it clear that Ḥirāʾ is E of Mecca.

[3] The name as Ibn al-Mujāwir has it appears nowhere in other sources. Balādī (*Muʿjam*, VII, pp. 14–15) mentions a ravine called Fajj Liḥyān which he says in between Mecca and Jeddah.

[4] This place name is common with a number of different vocalizations: al-Farʿ, al-Furʿ, al-Furaʿ, al-Furuʿ etc. The one in question does not appear to find a place in the other sources.

[5] I vocalize this name after Yāqūt (*Muʿjam*, V, p. 55), although the location he suggests does not fit in here.

[6] The place is unidentified. Ibn al-Mujāwir uses the word *darb*, apparently with the meaning 'road' here.

[7] Arabic *nuhūd*, plur. of *nahd*.

[8] No other source gives this alternative name of al-Ḥudaybiyyah and I am highly suspicious of its presence here. The plan of the town, Tabula II, in the printed text has M.n.yat al-Ḥudaybiyah, the name of a mountain. For al-Ḥudaybiyah, which, it is clear, may or may not double the final *yāʾ*, and the famous Willing Homage, see Ibn Hishām, *Sīrah*, I, pp. 308 ff. and Guillaume, *Life*, pp. 499 ff. Yāqūt (*Muʿjam*, II, pp. 229–30) and Balādī (*Muʿjam*, II, p. 246) say it is a stage from Mecca.

[9] Arabic *kaff* (see Dozy, *Supplément*, II, p. 475). Perhaps this image is more appropriate than 'the palm [of a hand]', which is another possible meaning.

[10] The conversion of the Magian Salmān during the Prophet's lifetime is featured at some length in Ibn Hishām (*Sīrah*, I, pp. 214 ff. and Guillaume, *Life*, pp. 95 ff.). This passage regarding the wall of Jeddah is also found almost verbatim in Ibn Faraj, *Silāḥ*, p. 5 (English), pp. 13–4 (Arabic).

[11] That is, ignoring Ibn al-Mujāwir's 'son of' before Fīrūz. He is thus a son of Yazdgird III, who reigned AD 459–84 (Ṭabarī, *History*, I, p. 369; *CHI*, III, pp. 147–8; *EIran*, 'Fīrūz (Pīrōz)').

[12] The third Orthodox caliph, reg. 23–35/644–56.

[13] See Yāqūt, *Muʿjam*, III, pp. 350–51, and Balādī, *Muʿjam*, V, pp. 72–4.

[14] Unidentified.

inhabitants moved out to other coastal areas.[1] Some of them came [here], including two men, one called Sayyār, the other Mayyās. They lived in Jeddah and threw around the town a wall made of hard, solid rock[2] with gypsum. It was when they had begun to settle there that they built this wall, making it ten spans wide. The wall remained as it was until they were able to stay [longer and] they built along the face of the wall a second wall made of *kāshūr* stone[3] which was carved out, that is hewn and squared, together with gypsum. They made the width of [this] wall five spans, so the [total] width of both walls together was fifteen spans. Four gates were made in it: al-Dawmah gate; al-Madbaghah gate, on which was a stone with a talisman inserted into it – if anyone stole in the town, the name of the thief was found next morning written on the stone; Makkah gate; and al-Furḍah gate on the sea side.[4] A huge ditch, both wide and deep, was excavated around [the wall], so sea water would run right round the town and the excess flow back into the sea. The town itself became like an island in the midst of the sea. When the Persians had completely fortified the town, the inhabitants were afraid of a lack of water,[5] so they built sixty-eight reservoirs inside and the same number outside. More accurately, 500 reservoirs were built inside and the same number outside the town. God knows best.

Some of the reservoirs.[6] Abū al-Ṭīn ʿĀmir, al-Marzubānī[?], al-Ḥafīrah,[7] al-Nakhīlāt,[8] the reservoir of Abū Bakr, al-Ḥajarī, al-Ṣarḥī, the reservoir of al-Sidrah, al-Ḥawār, al-Faraḥī, the reservoir of Yaḥyā [44 – Plan of Jeddah, see Fig. 2] [45] al-Sharīf, al-Waddiyyah, al-Mabādir, the reservoir of al-Bayḍah, al-Birkah, the reservoir of Umm Ḍirār, the reservoir of Barakāt, the reservoir of Sulaymān al-ʿAṭṭār, al-Ṭūlānī, al-ʿArḍānī. When rain fell and the reservoirs outside the town filled up, slaves used to transport the reservoir water on animals and transfer it into the reservoirs which they have in their houses. There was also the reservoir of al-Akhmīmī, the reservoir of Masjid al-Abnūs,[9] the reservoir of the Friday Mosque,[10] the reservoir of Radriyyah, the reservoir of Muḥammad b. al-Qāsim. The water remained with them from year to year. They could eat, drink and wash; [sometimes] they joked, [sometimes] they were serious and in turmoil.[11]

The destruction of Jeddah. The lord of Mecca sent to the shaykh of the merchants in Jeddah, asking him for a load[12] of iron. The shaykh told his servant standing beside him to give him a load of iron. So the servant came and gave the messenger a load of iron. But when he

[1] Sīrāf, on the Persian Zuhayr coast, fell into ruins as a result of an earthquake in 366 or 367/977 (Le Strange, *Lands*, p. 258 and map VI; Whitehouse, 'Sīrāf', p. 3).

[2] Arabic *ḥajar aṣamm*.

[3] I have not been able to identify this stone. I wonder if coral is meant.

[4] The gates are all mentioned by Ibn Faraj (*Silāḥ*, p. 5/14). I correct Ibn al-Mujāwir's al-Rūmah gate to al-Dawmah, the northern gate. Al-Madbaghah (the tannery) is the southern gate and Ibn Faraj says the stone is green. Makkah is obviously the eastern gate and al-Furḍah (the customs house), the western gate on the sea side.

[5] Reading with Ibn Faraj (*Silāḥ*, p. 15) *ḍayqah*.

[6] Many of the following names of reservoirs in Jeddah are tentative.

[7] Or al-Ḥufayrah.

[8] Or al-Nukhaylāt.

[9] See Ibn Faraj (*Silāḥ*, p. 18/58), who says this is one of the Friday mosques of the town and the first one built there.

[10] Ibn Faraj (*Silāḥ*, p. 15/51) says there are three.

[11] Arabic *harj wa-marj* (Wehr, *Dictionary*, p. 1025).

[12] Arabic *ḥaml/ḥiml*. See above p. 41, n. 11.

[44]

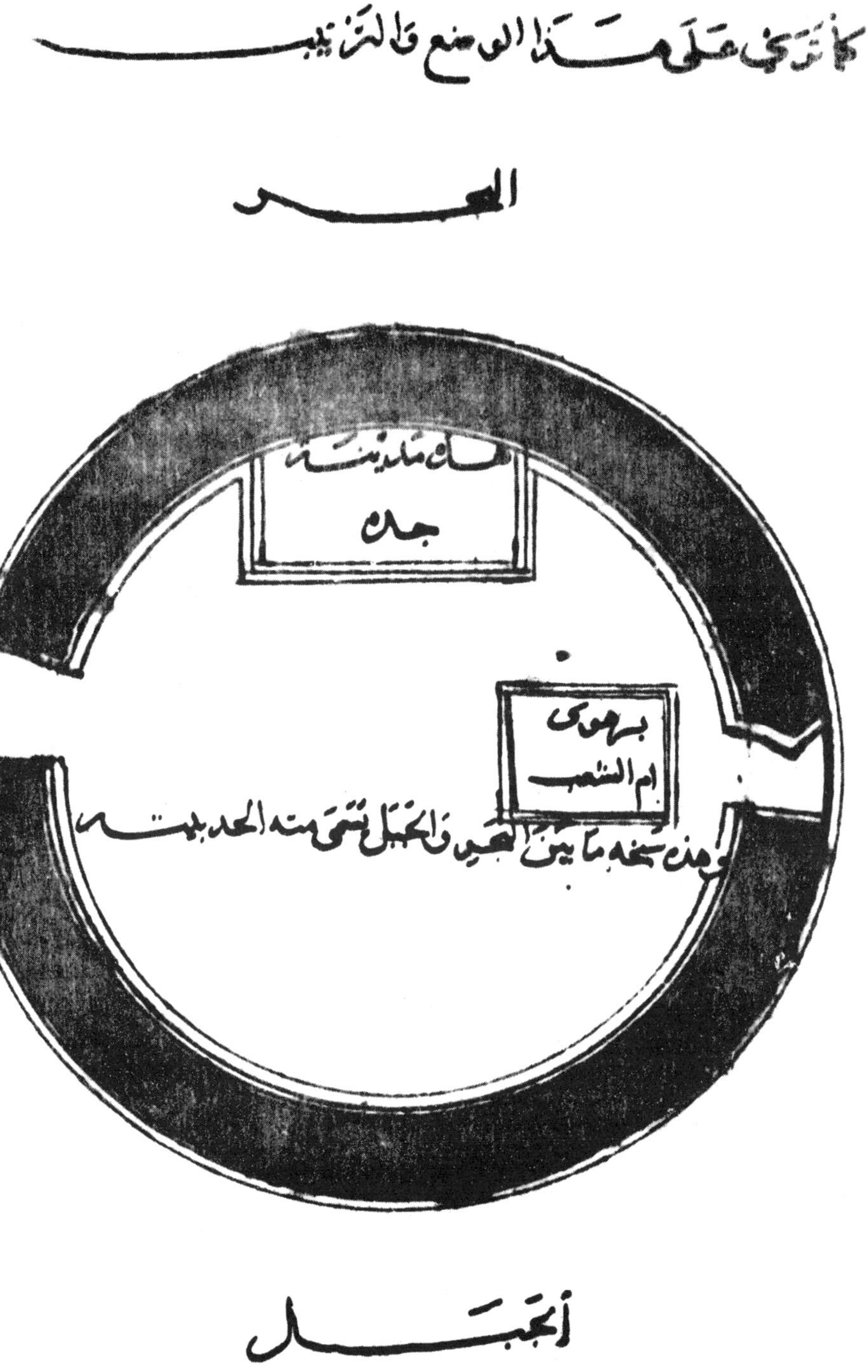

Figure 2. Plan of Jeddah (I MS, f. 18a, text, p. 44, tabula II)
This is a simple circular plan of the town of Jeddah with few markings. The top of the page above the circle of the town is marked 'sea' (i.e. W) and at the bottom outside the circle 'mountain' (E). The caption in the rectangle attached to the top of the circle within it announces that 'this is the town of Jeddah'. The rectangle within the circle at three o'clock depicts the tomb of Eve, 'mother of the people'. The large, bare area below the rectangle is marked, 'This is a salt pan called Maniyyat al-Ḥudaybiyyah between the sea and the mountain.'

opened up the load of iron before the amir in Mecca, he discovered that it was bars of gold. The amir sent the messenger back and told him that he should inform the shaykh to be kind enough to send him another load of iron of this same type. When the merchant realised what was happening, he called the servant and asked him what he gave the man [on the previous occasion]. He replied that [he had given him] a load of iron which had been buried for such a long time that it had turned yellow and gone rusty. The shaykh then realised that the load was gold bars. He knew too that [the amir] was out to get the same [again]. The shaykh went to another old shaykh among them and asked his advice and what he should do. The [other] shaykh replied, 'In my opinion, you are well off, so take everything you need. Everyone should embark on his ship and sail off over the open sea. Whichever place he likes best, he should stop and live there after you leave the town [of Jeddah] as empty of the belly of an ass or as a head [46] which has no covering.' At this, they filled their ships with their belongings and each one set sail, putting out to sea. This was in 473.[1]

Another report suggests that Arabs came and besieged the inhabitants. When the water was getting low, they took to their ships and sped across the sea. Some of them settled in al-Sirrayn, al-Rāḥah,[2] ʿAththar,[3] al-Jarʿah,[4] al-Darʿah,[5] Dahlak,[6] Beilul,[7] Juddah on the island of Farasān,[8] Mocha,[9] Ghulāfiqah,[10] al-Ahwāb,[11] al-Thamīd,[12] the island of Dhahbān,[13] Kamarān,[14] Bandar Mūsā[15] and Bāb Mūsā.[16]

[1] Begins 22 June 1080.

[2] See p. 66, n. 3 above. A list of maritime settlements follows whither the Persian inhabitants were scattered.

[3] On the coast of ʿAsīr, just N of Jīzān (Hamdānī, *Ṣifah*, pp. 52, 54 etc.; Kay, *Yaman*, end map; Stone, 'Gazetteer', pp. 164–5).

[4] The printed text and the MSS clearly have al-J.r.ʿah. I have corrected on the advice of FLS who also refers me to Kay, *Yaman*, p. 11 and to her as yet unpublished paper 'Kay Page Eleven' delivered at the Seminar for Arabian Studies, 2000.

[5] The printed text and the MSS clearly have al-D.r.ʿah. I have corrected on the advice of FLS.

[6] An archipelago in the Red Sea, close to Maṣawwaʿ on the African coast and due W of al-Luḥayyah (Kammerer, *Routier*, pp. 66–7 and Pl. XI; *Western Arabia*, pp. 121–2; *Red Sea*, pp. 226–40; Serjeant, *Portuguese*, end map; Tibbetts, *Navigation*, end map, Red Sea; Smith, *Ayyubids*, p. 144; Stone, 'Gazetteer', pp. 178–9).

[7] A port and bay on the African coast due W of Mocha (*Western Arabia*, p. 124; van Donzel, *Embassy*, p. 30).

[8] I cannot trace a Juddah on the Farasān islands, but it is scarcely surprising that the people of Jeddah should use the name of their native town after their dispersal. The islands lie in the Red Sea, directly opposite Jīzān (*Red Sea*, pp. 343 ff.; Tibbets, *Navigation*, end map, Red Sea; Stone, 'Gazetteer', pp. 246–8).

[9] Arabic al-Mukhā (with or without final *hamzah*), a port of some importance in medieval times about 90 km up the Red Sea coast from Bāb al-Mandab (*Western Arabia*, pp. 548–9; for a detailed account of the port in the 17th century, see Brouwer, *al-Mukhā*).

[10] A port between Hodeida and al-Ahwāb (see n. 532 below) (Kay, *Yaman*, end map; Stone, 'Gazetteer', pp. 218–19).

[11] On the Red Sea coast or close to it, S of Wādī Zabīd (Kay, *Yaman*, end map). See also Stone, 'Gazetteer', pp. 128–29.

[12] Unidentified.

[13] Other sources suggest this place is on the Red Sea coast, rather than an island. Kay (*Yaman*, end map, inset) places it just above the 18 degree latitude line, whereas Serjeant (*Portuguese*, end map) places it about halfway between Ḥaly in the N and Jīzān in the S. FLS kindly directs me to Niebuhr's map, 'Mare Rubrum …' in his *Description*, Amsterdam, 1776.

[14] Off the Yemeni coast opposite al-Ṣalīf, between al-Luḥayyah and Hodeida (*Western Arabia*, pp. 135–7; Serjeant, *Portuguese*, end map; Stone, 'Gazetteer', pp. 423–4).

[15] A port on the N coast of the island of Socotra (RBS E of Qalansiyyah [called by Ibn al-Mujāwir Fatk]; War Office map; Serjeant, 'Coastal population', p. 141; Smith, 'Ibn al-Mujāwir on Dhofar', pp. 86, 90–91).

[16] I cannot identify Bāb Mūsā and it is perhaps dittography.

When the town of [Jeddah] was [finally] empty of [these] outsiders,[1] the bedouins took control of it during the rule of Amir Dā'ūd b. Hāshim.[2] Ibn al-Mujāwir said: I saw in a dream someone telling me that only Muḍar b. Hāshim sought to take Jeddah from the Persians, or more accurately Shukr b. Abī al-Futūḥ.[3] From their time it fell into ruin and was wiped out. It remained empty. As the poet has recited:

May God not deliver my heart to the object of its desire in you!
If the abode is far away after you have gone, my situation will become worse.
I have appointed my tears guardians of the remembrance of you;
tears are an indication of hidden grief.
My eyeball has sworn an unimaginable oath;
I keep remembering and it causes my tears to flow down.
Many are those who have said to me, 'They are here!' I replied,
'God has made the distinction between the eyelid and deep sleep.'

The following is by Abū Bakr al-'Abdī:[4]

O you spending the night resting in Alexandria ...!
He who spends the night awake in rapture, then I [too] spend it awake.
I observe the star to remember seeing him,
even if the tears of my eyelids flow bringing him to mind.
I look at the full moon rejoicing at seeing him;
perhaps the eye of the one whom I desire looks upon it [also].

[47] Ibn al-Dumaynah recited as follows:[5]

O east wind of Najd, when did you spring up from Najd?
Your night journey has increased my rapture even more.
When a dove[6] coos in the bright morning light
on the twigs of a ben-tree branch[7] and a sweet bay,[8]
I weep as a young lad with no steadfastness weeps,
but I show [the feelings] which he does not.[9]
They have asserted that the lover, when he is close,
grows weary, and that absence cures physical separation.
We have administered every drug, but our illness remains uncured,
for having [our lover's] abode near is better than it being far away.

[1] Arabic *ajnāb*.

[2] I think the amir of Mecca, Dā'ūd b.'Īsā b. Fulaytah, is meant here. He was amir 570–89/1174–93 (Ibn Fahd, *Ghāyat al-marām*, I, pp. 534–7; Appendix B.10 below).

[3] Ibn al-Mujāwir is right to correct: Shukr b. Abī al-Futūḥ al-Ḥasan b. Ja'far al-Ḥasanī, who died in 453/1061, ruled over the Hejaz for 23 years before his death (Ibn Fahd, *Ghāyat al-marām*, I, pp. 497–9; Appendix B.9 below).

[4] This poet cannot be the Yemeni literary figure, Ibn al-Adīb, as suggested by OL in his apparatus, who was born long after this text was written (661/1262) and did not die until 725/1324. This man is Abū Bakr Aḥmad al-'Abdī and not Abū al-'Atīq Abū Bakr b. Aḥmad Ibn al-Adīb al-'Īdī (cf. OL, *Texte*, II, pp. 242–4, quoting al-Janadī).

[5] 'Abdallāh b. 'Ubaydallāh (Iṣfahānī, *Aghānī*, XV, 151–7, where the lines are quoted, p. 156; Brockelmann, *Geschichte*, S I, 80).

[6] Arabic *warqā'*, literally 'ash-grey'.

[7] Arabic *bān*. DMV tells me that this is *Moringa peregrina* Forssk. (previously *M. aptera*), but that it appears to be rare in Tihāmah (Wood, *Handbook*, p. 128)

[8] Arabic *rand*, *Laurus nobilis* L. (Dimyāṭī, *Mu'jam*, p. 64). DMV: *rand* is also used for wormwood (*Artemisia arborescens* L.) (Wood, *Handbook*, p. 300).

[9] I.e. I show my emotions even more than a young lad does.

Someone else has said:

> Oh, nights [we spent] in Dhū al-Athalāt, return!
> Return to come into leaf among the tamarisk hills.[1]
> The conversation we had with you is sweeter in my heart
> and more melodious than the sound of a lute.

The excellence of Jeddah. One of the things Abū ʿAbdallāh Muḥammad b. Isḥāq b. ʿAbbās al-Fākihī mentioned in his book was: Muḥammad b. ʿAlī al-Ṣāʾigh informed us, Khalīl b, Rajāʾ informed us, Muslim b. Yūnis informed us, Muḥammd b. ʿAmr informed us on the authority of Ḍawʾ b. Fakhr who said:[2] I was sitting with ʿAbbād b. Kathīr[3] in the Sacred Mosque and said to him, 'Praise be to God who has placed us in the best and noblest majlis!' 'What about Jeddah?' he replied, 'One prayer there is worth 19,000 prayers [elsewhere]; one dirham there is worth 100,000 dirhams [elsewhere] and good deeds here are the same.[4] God forgives him who has Jeddah in the range of his vision.'

Ibn al-Mujāwir said: I think this divine good fortune comes only from the mother of the human race, Eve – God's blessings upon her – since she is buried outside Jeddah.[5] It was the Persians who built over her [48] a tomb solidly made of baked bricks and gypsum. It remained until the year 621.[6] At that time it fell into ruin bit by bit, but it was never rebuilt. I actually saw it when it was standing and in use and I have also seen it in ruins, when it had become old and worn bit by bit. It is a blessed site where prayers are answered.

Taking taxes from Maghrebis.[7] Ismāʿīl b. ʿAbd al-Sayyid b. al-Bayʿ al-Baghdādī informed me as follows: Amir ʿAlī b. Fulaytah b. Qāsim b. Muḥammad b. Jaʿfar b. Abī Hāshim[8] used to take a tax in Jeddah from the Maghrebis when they came for the pilgrimage. He took seven Yūsufī [dirhams][9] from everyone, the weight of each Yūsufī being thirteen

[1] Arabic *athalāt*, plural of *athlah*, must be read in both hemistitchs (Lane, *Lexicon*, I, p. 21), Dhū al-Athalāt, '[place] having [many] tamarisks', in the first clearly a place name. DMV: in the Yemen three species are represented: *Tamarix aphylla* (L.) *Karst*, *T. arabica Bunge*, *T. mascatensis Bunge* (Wood, *Handbook*, p. 113).

[2] This chain of authorities cannot be identified (Ibn Faraj, *Silāḥ*, p. 4/10).

[3] A Thaqafī traditionist (Ibn Faraj, *Silāḥ*, p. 84).

[4] Ibn al-Mujāwir's 19,000 prayers becomes 17,000,000 in Ibn Faraj (*Silāḥ*, p. 4/10). The last part of this sentence might mean 'and its environs the same'.

[5] See Tabula II (Fig. 2 above), a plan of Jeddah, where the tomb is clearly marked. See also Ibn Faraj (*Silāḥ*, Plate 4, a copy of Niebuhr's 18th-century plan where the tomb is marked no. 13 outside the town to the N).

[6] Begins 24 January 1224.

[7] For *jizyah* with a more general meaning of 'tax', see p. 65, n. 15 above. The *maghāribah* may simply mean those coming from the west.

[8] There was no amir of Mecca called ʿAlī b. Fulaytah. OL in his apparatus suggests it isʿĪsā b. Fulaytah in question (d. 570/1174) and that is certainly possible. Other sons of Fulaytah to hold the office and to be in a position to levy such a tax were Hāshim b. Fulaytah (d. 549/1154) and Mālik b. Fulaytah (d. 577/1181). Anyone of these could be meant here and we are thus talking of the 540s, '50s, '60s and '70s/1140s, '50s, '60s and '70s (Ibn Fahd, *Ghāyat al-marām*, I, pp. 520–22, 523–6 and 527–32; Appendix B.10 below).

[9] The Yūsufī silver dirham was first minted by Yūsuf b. ʿUmar al-Thaqafī, Umayyad governor of Iraq until 126/743. It was struck initially in Wāsiṭ. It seems a long time and distance between the original striking of the Yūsufī in Iraq and 6th/12th-century Jeddah of which Ibn al-Mujāwir is here talking, but the coin was certainly known in Mamluk Egypt and is mentioned by Maqrīzī (d. 845/1442) (Allouche, *Economics*, pp. 63, 135; Walker, *Coins*, pp. lxiii, 198–9; DeShazo and Bates, 'Umayyad Governors', pp. 107–15).

carats and a *ḥabbah* according to the weight of Mecca.[1] The guides used to make the Maghrebis pay also one Yūsufī per head of people as dog bloodwit. The reason for this was that a dog came to Jeddah and took a loaf of bread. The Maghrebis gathered round and killed it, so the guides made to kill the Maghrebis. When the latter were on the point of being killed, they agreed that each one would pay a Yūsufī as the dog's bloodwit. This was imposed upon them, so they would pay seven Yūsufīs to the amir and one to the guides. The total came to eight Yūsufīs on each one of them. Anyone who did not pay up would be taken and dangled in one of the Jeddah reservoirs, or more precisely in the reservoir of the Masjid al-Abnūs. It is said [also] that they would take them away to the island of Ṣandalah[2] – it is also said to the island of Abū Sa'īd[3] – and suspend one of them by his waistwrapper where beams of wood had been erected for this purpose. When all the [other] pilgrims had performed the pilgrimage, had carried out their rituals and each one had returned to where he was going, then they would remove the Maghrebis from the reservoirs and from the islands and disperse them on their ships, [some] returning to Egypt and [others] to 'Aydhāb[4] and Suez. [49]

Section. One of the guides[5] was asked why they took [only] this [one] Yūsufī from them, when they were the stingiest and most irascible of all creation. He replied quoting from a poet as follows:

> Take a little from a miser and blame him;
> A little from a miser is [in fact] a lot!

Al-Ḥasan b. Muḥammad b. al-Ḥūt said: The situation is not in fact thus. Each one ofthem used to pay seven and a half Yūsufīs, each Yūsufī being twenty-six carats and two *ḥabbah* according to the weight of Mecca. For the dog bloodwit there was half a Yūsufī, the total being eight Yūsufīs.[6] This was established during the rule of Amir 'Īsā b. Fulaytah and remained as it was until late on in the rule of Amir Mukthir.[7] When rumours abounded and news of this reached the ears of the whole world, Ṣalāḥ al-Dīn Abū al-Muẓaffar Yūsuf b. Ayyūb[8] sent 4,000 *irdabbs*[9] of wheat to Amir 'Īsā – or more

[1] For the carat (*qīrāṭ*) and the *ḥabbah*, see Hinz, *Masse*, pp. 27 and 12–3. The former was originally the bean of the carob tree, Greek κεράτιον (Yule and Burnell, *Hobson-Jobson*, pp. 160–61). Allouche corrects Maqrīzī's 'seven' to six *dānaq*, the equivalent of one Yūsufī (Allouche, *Economics*, p. 63).

[2] Perhaps the island of Ṣandal in the group E of Java (Tibbetts, *Navigation*, p. 499 and map of the Indian Ocean).

[3] FLS kindly suggests that this is the 'Jazīrat Abu Sa'd' of *Red Sea ... Pilot*, p. 304, in the channel of Jeddah.

[4] A port on the western Red Sea coast, serving medieval Upper Egypt and about 350 km N of Suakin (Garcin, *Centre musulman*, Pl. XXIV).

[5] I.e. the guides employed, as still to this day, to look after the pilgrims.

[6] This does in fact make a total of 8 Yūsufī dirhams so I correct from the text's 'Ya'qūbī'. There is evidence of a Ya'qūbī dirham, however, struck at the beginning of the Marinid dynasty in the early 7th/13th century in North Africa about the time Ibn al-Mujāwir was writing (Ḥakīm, *Dawḥah*, p. 88; Bosworth, *Islamic Dynasties*, pp. 41–2).

[7] I.e. from c. 557/1161 to c. 589/1193. Mukthir was another son of 'Īsā (Ibn Fahd, *Ghāyat al-marām*, I, pp. 520–22, 538–44; Appendix B.10 below). But see n. 9 and p. 77, n. 1 below.

[8] I.e. the famous Saladin, Ayyubid ruler in Egypt who died in 589/1193 (Gibb, *Life*, p. 76; Lyons and Jackson, *Saladin*, p. 362–3).

[9] A Egyption grain measure, a Coptic word (*ertab*) by origin (Sobhy Bey, *Common Words*, p. 6). See also Hinz, *Masse*, 39–40; Khoury, *Chrestomathie*, p. 187. The text says erroneously 'Mukthir', whose rule did not begin until 589/1193, the year Saladin died.

correctly 6,000 to Jeddah and Mecca – and he said to him, 'Take this amount and stop charging the Maghrebis a tax together with the dog bloodwit.' So Amir ʿĪsā brought this whole business to an end in 586.[1] There the matter remained, [but] in the days of Amir Qatādah b. Idrīs b. Maṭāʿin b. ʿAbd al-Karīm,[2] he intended to return to the previous arrangement, i.e. taking the tax from the Maghrebis. However, death overtook him and [the threat] was lifted from them.

Abū al-Rabīʿ Sulaymān b. al-Rabīʿ al-Ṭarābulsī informed me as follows: The Fatimid rulers[3] used to impose on all Maghrebis a tax of two dinars and two carats.

Section. Ibn al-Mujāwir said: I had a dream on the eve of 13 Dhū al-Qaʿdah 624,[4] I was given some information by Amir Nāṣir al-Dīn Fārūt, the governor of Aden,[5] [50] who on that date assumed authority over the pilgrims in addition to his own original position as governor (and the pilgrims had already returned from Mecca to the Yemen), as follows. He was saying [in my vision], 'Every pilgrim who returns to India is made to pay ninety-two *fals*[6] tax per head by ʿAbd al-Ghafūr b. Aḥmad b. Muḥammad b. Muḥammad al-Ṣanādīqī al-Barī.[7] If the pilgrims were to get wise, they would simply travel on to India in my ship and I would "give a crack of the whip" on their behalf,[8] so that they would all be secure from the evil of ʿAbd al-Ghafūr when he takes taxes from them.'

As for B. Mahdī, governors of Zabīd,[9] they regarded taking taxes[10] from anyone except pilgrims as unlawful. Instead of one dirham, they would take three.

Al-Jār.[11] It is an anchorage near Jeddah, where ships coming from Egypt drop anchor. It is a dark sea of death[12] with terrible waves where the skill of the swimmer is useless.

Section. I heard something from a group in Mecca and others as follows: An axe dropped from the hand of one of the Barāmikah[13] in this particular place. So he tied a leather bag

[1] Again I correct: ʿĪsā for Mukthir. The year begins 8 February 1190.

[2] Amir of the Hejaz until his death in 617/1220 or 618/1221 (Ibn Fahd, *Ghāyat al-marām*, I, pp. 550–77; Appendix B.11 below). I have corrected the name of his grandfather from Ibn al-Mujāwir's Muṭāʿim.

[3] Ismāʿīlī rulers of Egypt, southern Syria and North Africa 297–567/909–1171 (Bosworth, *Islamic Dynasties*, 63–4).

[4] 25 October 1227.

[5] He is Nāṣir al-Dīn Nāṣir b. Fārūt, governor of the Ayyubid ruler of the Yemen al-Malik al-Masʿūd Yūsuf b. Muḥammad (612–26/1215–28) (Löfgren, *Texte*, I, pp. 20, 64, II, p. 237; Smith, 'Political History', p. 139).

[6] Ḥakīm specifically mentions *fulūs al-Hind* (*Dawḥah*, p. 64).

[7] An unidentified Indian official.

[8] Ibn al-Mujāwir uses the word *miqraʿah*, any instrument used for striking, including a whip. I.e. 'I would make a strong complaint', 'kick up a fuss'.

[9] A dynasty centered on Tihāmah, 554–69/1159–73 (Smith, *Ayyubids*, II, pp. 56–62; Smith, 'Political History', pp. 134–5; *EI*, 'Mahdids'; Appendix B.7 below).

[10] Arabic *mukūsāt*, plur. of *mukūs*, itself a plur. of *maks*. *Maks* carries a definite stigma and is usually, as here, regarded as an illegal tax outside the *sharīʿah* (Lane, *Lexicon*, VII, 2729; Løkkegaard, *Taxation*, pp. 159–60, 186; *EI*, 'Maks', 'He who takes *maks* is in hell!').

[11] The ancient port of Medina about 250 km N of Jeddah, 80 km S of Yanbuʿ and called today al-Buraykah (Yāqūt, *Muʿjam*, II, pp. 92–4; Balādī, *Muʿjam*, II, pp. 104–8 with a local map on p. 107).

[12] The text is here corrupt and the translation of *baḥr aswad jīfah* tentative.

[13] The MSS have *al-sarāmilah*. If OL's assumption is correct and we should indeed read al-Barāmikah, this must be the account of an informant and not Ibn al-Mujāwir himself speaking. The Barmecides were a 2nd/8th-century dynasty of Persian viziers at the Abbasid court (Shaban, *History*, pp. 35–9; *EI*, 'al-Barāmika').

round his middle and went down to retrieve the axe. When he had descended, he heard someone shouting to him, 'Where are you going down to, servant of God?' He replied, 'I've come down to retrieve something which slipped from my hand. An anchor[1] fell from a ship in this place.' He replied, 'It's still going down [and will continue to do so] until the Day of Resurrection!' God is most knowing, wise.

[51] *The islands of Maṭārid al-Khayl.*[2] It is said that in ancient times this [area] was not sea, but a stretch of land,[3] so there was no division between the Arabian Peninsula and Africa. For this reason the blacks were in possession of the province of the Yemen in its entirety on a permanent basis, both in pre-Islamic and Islamic times. When the sea water became too much[4] and the difficulty involved [in walking across it] became obvious, [people] began to cross it in ships. When the sea drowned out these lands[5] and every piece of high ground became an island, [these particular islands] were called the islands of al-Maṭārid, i.e. Maṭārid al-Khayl.[6] It is said that the Arabs in ancient times when it was dry land used to catch horses where it is [now] the depth of this sea. There is another version [of the name] in these parts: Marābiṭ al-Khayl;[7] fodder and trees can be found [there].

A description of Jeddah. It is a small town on the sea shore, the port of Mecca. It is impossible to live there because of the crowds of people during the pilgrim season. People gather in it from the ends of the earth, the inhabited world and populated islands,[8] from Egypt, North Africa, India and the Yemen. When its people run short of water, they carry it from al-Qurayn, half way between Mecca and Jeddah.

Its inhabitants are of Persian stock and they build in *kāshūr* and palm leaves, all their buildings being khans. The one well-known khan there is Khān al-Baṣar[?] and there are two khans standing face to face with large stores. It is said that a huge khan was built outside Jeddah by Amir Shams al-Dīn Ṭunbughā in 623.[9] Every one who builds a palm leaf house there pays the sultan three *malakī* dirhams a year. Houses [built] in stone and gypsum [52], have no tax on them because they are the actual property of those who live in them and their owners can do what they like with them.

It is said that Jeddah was called Jaddah [grandmother], simply because the mother of human beings, Eve – peace be upon her! – is buried there and she is the ancestor of the

[1] Text *anjar*. Dionisius Agius informs me that it is the Persian *langar*, the *lām* then becoming part of the Arabic article *al-*. See Kazimirski, *Dictionnaire*, I, p. 60.

[2] I find no mention of this name, 'places where horses are hunted' or '... herded together' in the geographical sources. See below n. 7.

[3] Reading *'arṣah* (Lane, *Lexicon*, V, p. 2001).

[4] I.e. in the Indian Ocean in general and in the Gulf of Aden in particular. There was so much water that it forced its way up between Africa and Arabia to form the Red Sea.

[5] I.e. the lands which ended up under the Red Sea.

[6] The name gives the impression that, before the Red Sea was formed, there were vast areas where wild horses were hunted and herded together.

[7] This alternative version of the name of the islands means 'places where horses are tethered'. Tibbets (*Navigation*, p. 406) writes of 'a shoal called Murābiṭ al-Khail' on the Farasān bank S of latitude 8 2/3 degrees in the Red Sea. This must be Marābiṭ al-Khayl, the plural of the noun of place. See also Tibbetts' end chart, Red Sea and Gulf of Aden.

[8] Arabic *al-baḥr al-ma'mūr*.

[9] Begins 2 January 1226.

whole world. When this town was built, it was known by the name Jaddah, i.e. Eve, the wife of the father of mankind – peace be upon him. It is also said that Arabia was called a peninsula because it is surrounded by seas and rivers[1] in its [various] countries and regions. So Arabia became one of the peninsulas of the Arabs.

From Mecca to al-Maḥālib.[2] From Mecca to al-Qurayn a parasang, built by Amir Hāshim.[3] To al-Bayḍā' two parasangs.[4] To Idām[5] three parasangs, a well dug by the Commander of the Faithful ʿAlī b. Abī Ṭālib and renovated by Commander al-Ḥusayn b. Salāmah.[6] To Wādī al-Muḥram three parasangs, from where the Yemeni pilgrims don their pilgrim garb.

To Farʿ five parasangs,[7] territory of B. Shaʿbah.[8] Their women wear only leather. The woman takes two pieces of leather and stitches them together, cuts a round hole in it and puts it on. When she walks, the whole of her body can be seen, above and below. If a stranger sees the woman dressed in this style, he says to her, 'Cover yourself up!' Her husband answers him, 'You clothe her!' But if a woman appears naked, even though she is wearing [this garment], and if [the stranger] provides her with a garment, the husband kills him [nevertheless], because they say, 'He who covers up brings jealousy!'[9]

There is no one in the whole world more foul-smelling, more negligent, more sinful and viler than these people in taking the wealth of the pilgrims, since they call pilgrims 'God's begging bowl'! If this is mentioned to them, they say, 'When God's begging bowl is there for his people, all going out and coming in eat from it.' If you say to one of them, 'God cut off [53] any sustenance which you have which is unlawful', he will reply, 'No, rather God cut off any sustenance which you have which is lawful! You can see the only goodness we have is these black mountains; we have no agriculture, no livestock, no income and nothing to give away. All the shameful acts you perform and booty you take are [when you are dealing] with another pilgrim who comes face to face with the Kaʿbah. So God has given us the advantage over you [in our own region], so that we get back what is just for the pilgrims among you and a third of what is unjust.' Thus the Persians recite in their poetry:[10]

[1] Is this a reference to the Tigris and Euphrates?

[2] An inland place S of Wādī Mawr and N of Surdud, close to both, in northern Tihāmat al-Yaman (Kay, *Yaman*, end map, about level with Kamarān; Schuman, *Political History*, p. 57, 'place of some importance in the region of Wādī Surdud'; Smith, *Ayyubids*, II, p. 176 and map I; Ḥajarī, *Majmūʿ*, IV, p. 689; Maḥqafī, *Muʿjam*, p. 564). Its ruined site has been located by FLS near Wādī ʿAyyān at about 1533 4306.

[3] I.e. Hāshim b. Fulaytah b. Qāsim, amir of Mecca 527–49/1132–54 (Appendix B.10 below).

[4] This would seem to be Thenayian's pass of al-Bayḍā' (*Study*, pp. 93–5 [with full references], maps 13 and 13.5), just off the pilgrim route and about 100 km, as the crow flies, W, slightly S, of Mecca.

[5] I correct after reference to Yāqūt (*Muʿjam*, I, p. 125), describing a place Udām, a wadi of Tihāmah, the lower part of which belongs to B. Shuʿbah (see below, n. 8) and which has a well called Idām.

[6] A black Nubian freedman and vizier of the Ziyadids, the Tihāmah dynasty, c. 203–409/818–1018. The sources (e.g. ʿUmārah in Kay, *Yaman*, pp. 9–13; Janadī in Löfgren, *Texte*, II, pp. 59–62) tell us that he died in 402/1011 and mention his splendid works and well excavations.

[7] See Landberg, *Etudes*, II, p. 918 ff. See also p. 70, n. 4 above.

[8] A tribal group (*baṭn*) of Kinānah (see p. 80, n. 5 below) owning a well called Idām (see n. 5 above). See also Kaḥḥālah, *Muʿjam*, II, p. 596.

[9] This difficult and corrupt Arabic reads 'wa-in kānat imra'ah ʿuryānah wa-hya lābisah fa-yaqūlu la-hu zawju-hā aksi-hā fa-in kasā-hā wa-illā qatala-hu li-'anna-hum yaqūlūna man satara ghayyara'.

[10] I am extremely grateful to Edmund Bosworth for his ready assistance with this verse. The translation as it stands depends on the reading *gawāfil* with Minori/OL's apparatus.

Neither a bridge nor a religious building comes from the money of caravans,
Since they steal all the pilgrims' travelling provisions.

To al-Sirrayn three parasangs, built by the Persians on the sea shore. To Wādī al-Athalāt three parasangs.[1] To Ḥaṣārah five parasangs.[2] To Ḥaly seven parasangs,[3] a town in which there is a Friday mosque and a minaret. The first person to destroy it was Ghāzī b. Matkalān[?] b. Ḥārith al-Kurdī during the rule of Sayf al-Islām Ṭughtakīn b. Ayyūb.[4] The place remained as it was until Mūsā b. ʿAlī b. ʿAṭiyyah, its present owner, restored it. All these regions belong to B. Kinānah.[5] The name Ḥaly is derived from the ornaments [*ḥaly*] which the Israelite al-Sāmirī[6] collected in the days of Aaron, son of Amram – peace be upon them – and made from them the shape of a calf. As God – He is almighty – has said, 'He brought out for them a calf with bodily form, lowing.'[7]

In the east of these regions there is a people called the Bahīmiyyah who are descended from Āl ʿĀmir, who [in turn] are descended from Sanḥān.[8] If a guest is staying with them, [the host] says to him, 'What would you like for dinner?' [The guest] will reply that he would like such and such a dish. 'What would you like for lunch?' [The host] brings him only what he has requested and expressed an appetite for. When [the guest] has eaten dinner, the host will say to his wife, 'Go and honour the guest.' So the wife comes and sleeps in the guest's arms until morning without fear or caution. In the morning each one rises and goes about his business.

If Zayd asks for ʿAmr's daughter in marriage and the latter gives [54] a positive response, Zayd goes into ʿAmr's daughter and deflowers her, remaining with her all night. In the morning, he departs, leaving his shoes in the daughter's room, so that ʿAmr knows that Zayd finds her pleasing. The marriage contract is then drawn up. But if he puts on his shoes and leaves, ʿAmr knows that Zayd is not pleased with his daughter. This happens even among the most distinguished of them. Their ornaments are made of brass, iron and lead; their clothes are tanned skins and their stones cowries. Their occupations are cutting the road and highway robbery.

[1] See above p. 55, n. 1.

[2] FLS writes: South of al-Līth at c. 2004 4033; see Philby's untitled map 1:750.000, 'Philby 1951–54'.

[3] Ḥaly Ibn Yaʿqūb is on the Red Sea coast about 18 degrees 50' (Kay, end map; *Western Arabia*, p. 133; Smith, *Ayyubids*, II, p. 156; Stone, 'Gazetteer', pp. 280–81).

[4] I.e. 579–93/1183–97, the second Ayyubid ruler of the Yemen. I can find no reference to this Ghāzī, nor indeed to any Ayyubid activity so early so far north. I read '... Matkalān b. Ḥārith ...', rather than '... min Banī Ḥārith'.

[5] Hamdānī (*Ṣifah*, p. 154) confirms that Ḥaly belongs to the tribe of Kinānah. See also Kaḥḥālah, *Muʿjam*, III, p. 996.

[6] He first appears in Quran 20:85. Much ink has been spilt on this man and his name: Bayḍāwī (*Anwār*, pp. 420–21) says his name comes from the Israelite tribe of the Samaritans. His name was Mūsā, son of Ẓafar. See also Sale, *Koran*, p. 237, and Rodwell, *Koran*, p. 99.

[7] Quran 20:88. See also Penrice, *Dictionary*, pp. 28, 45.

[8] This passage occurs in Landberg, *Etudes*, II, p. 909 ff. and Smith 'Wondrous', p. 119. Both Kaḥḥālah (*Muʿjam*, II, p. 558) and Ḥajarī (*Majmūʿ*, III, p. 432) confirm an ʿAsīrī Sanḥān, as well as a tribe of Janb SE of Ṣanʿāʾ. In view of the remarks of the ʿAsīrī scholar Zulfa ('Village Communities', pp. 77–8), I wonder if Ibn al-Mujāwir is mistaken about the descent of Āl ʿĀmir from Sanḥān; Zulfa has Āl ʿĀmir descending from Rufaydah, another of the six sub-tribes of Qaḥṭān (see also below p. 81, n. 5).

To al-Dabsā' five parasangs,[1] the mouth of a deep wadi, on the coast[2] and [also] know as Sharm al-Jāriyah,[3] an inlet from the sea which can be waded across. It is known by this name because, when the pilgrims forded it and they were in the middle, a camel with a young girl [*jāriyah*] slipped and she fell into the sea and was carried off by the rising tide. So it was known as al-Sharm, i.e. the inlet, because of the young girl.

To Dhahbān four parasangs.[4] Its inhabitants are Arabs made up of B. Asad, B. R ..., B. Ma'āṣim and B. Rufaydah.[5] When a guest is staying with them, they say to him, 'Kiss, fondle, nibble and embrace [her]', that is the lady of the house, 'but don't put anything into her!' (That is have intercourse with her). 'If you do, we shall put this dagger into you!'

[Dhahbān] is [also] called Wādī al-Dawm, simply because of the abundance of doum palms there, that is the *muql* tree.[6] Of Wādī al-Dawm the poet recites:

> The last time I saw you was the day you met me
> in lower Wādī al-Dawm, you with your garments washed.[7]

Jabal Kudummul[8] can be seen from the sea shore.

Jabal Kudummul. It is half way between the Hejaz and the Yemen. The first flat land is 'Aththar,[9] also called Khabt 'Aththar. [55] It is said that Kudummul, his wife and donkey are three mountains. Jabal Kudummul is [actually] in the sea. At the foot of it is a small mountain called al-Ḥimār [The Donkey] and opposite it on land is a mountain called al-Kulyatān [The Kidneys],[10] which is [also] called al-Mar'ah [The Wife]. It is [also] said that Kudummul, his wife and donkey were certainly jinn, or humans who have been

[1] See Theniyian, 'Riḥlat al-Sulṭān', p. 170, nos 3–4.

[2] Reading *sāḥil*.

[3] 'The cut/canal of the young girl'.

[4] See Landberg, *Etudes*, II, pp. 909–10.

[5] The text is here corrupt and the second and third tribal names in the list are unidentified by Landberg, Löfgren and myself. It is not possible to identify with accuracy B. Asad in this context. With Landberg, I read B. Rufaydah who are dealt with extensively in Zulfa's excellent article ('Village Communities', pp. 77–96). For the anecdote, see Serjeant, 'Zinā', p. 158, n. 33. FLS kindly provides me with the following information: Thesiger's RGS map identifies the 'Asam and Rabi'a wa Rufaida, 'Asīrī tribes in W Dhahban good for this passage. Thesiger, 'A Journey through the Tihama, the 'Asir and the Hijaz Mountains', *Geographical Journal*, 110, 4/6, 1947, pp. 188–200.

[6] Dimyāṭī (*Mu'jam*, p. 146) states that *muql makkī* is the fruit of the doum palm (Arabic *dawm*, *Hyphaene thebaica* Mart.) and this is perhaps what Ibn al-Mujāwir is trying to say here. See also Smith 'Dhofar', p. 89 and Varisco, *Agriculture*, p. 136.

[7] The poet is in fact the famous Kuthayyir (d. 105/723) (Iṣfahānī, *Aghānī*, VII, p. 85 [Wādī al-Rūm in the second hemistitch!] and VIII, p. 27; Brockelmann, *Geschichte*, S I, p. 79).

[8] That this is a mountain is clear, both from the text and other sources. Hamdānī (*Ṣifah*, p. 51; *Ṣifah*, ed. al-Akwa', p. 90) says it is near a place called Ḥam(i)ḍah and al-Akwa' vocalizes the name for us. Kay (*Yaman*, p. 241 and end map) has found a 'Kotumble' on an Admiralty chart, a small island near the coast. 'Aqīlī (*Jāzān*, p. 363) lists a mountain Kutumbul which he says is S of the port of al-Qaḥmah (at about 18 degrees latitude) and attributes the *dāl – tā'* change to the local dialect. See also Stone, 'Gazetteer', pp. 466–7.

[9] Given a tentative location on Kay's end map (*Yaman*), a little N of Jīzān. This is probably about right and Hamdānī (*Ṣifah*, pp. 52, 54) confirms that it is the port of Baysh. 'Aqīlī (*Jāzān*, pp. 285–91) deals with the port at some length and lists the Arab geographers and others who mention it. See also the excellent entry in Stone, 'Gazetteer', 164–5.

[10] OL suggests in his apparatus either the reading al-Kalbatān (the two bitches) or al-Kulaybān (the two puppies). The sources (even those he cites) do not appear to confirm either reading.

turned into mountains and stones. Jabal Kudummul was originally an iron mine. Ibn al-Mujāwir said: How often have I enquired in order to get at the truth about them, but I have not succeeded!

To Bayḍ four parasangs, a wadi.[1] To al-Rāḥah four parasangs. It is also called Maḥall Abī Turāb and also Rāḥat al-Mu'ayyad, i.e. al-Mu'ayyad Aḥmad [b. Ghānim] b. Qāsim b. Ghānim.[2] It is ancient and was built by the sharifs.[3]

Section. Ibn al-Mujāwir said: I saw in a vision on the eve of Thursday, 1 Ramaḍān 620[4] and I was reading an inscription engraved in stone, the stone having been built into other stones of the prayer niche of the Friday mosque. There was written on it, 'al-Rāḥah and al-Ḥawī[5] were built by Persians'. ʿAbdallāh b. Muḥammad al-Rāḥī informed me in Zabīd in 619[6] that there could be found written on the gate of al-Rāḥah, '"O my Lord, leave me not childless, though you are the best of inheritors!"[7] On the evening of Friday a thousand cameleers[8] left this town, followed by a thousand stallion camels on which were a thousand virgins. The next morning, Saturday, there was no further reference to them, or the earth had swallowed them up, nor was there any news of them at all. "Learn by example, o you who have eyes to see!"[9] We also found a line of something written as follows: We have exchanged a load of pearls for a load of wheat and no harm has come upon us. God is the one whose help is to be sought.'

An inscription was also found in the town of Abū Sayyār in the regions of Ḥarrān:[10] We asked for wheat in exchange for pearls, but we did not find it. There are 360 wells in the town. [56] At each well is a rock on which is written: There is no god but God; Moses is the interlocutor of God. This is followed by: Trust them to dig [it] up. Dig with your hand and you will drink water. To Hajar four parasangs. From here as far as Ḥarrān is known as al-Darb.[11]

[1] Clearly between ʿAththar and Jāzān (Hamdānī, *Ṣifah*, pp. 73, 120, 188 and ʿAqīlī, *Jāzān*, p. 84; Stone, 'Gazetteer', p. 191).

[2] ʿAqīlī (*Jāzān*, p. 195) has an entry for this place and confirms that it is also known as Rāḥat al-Mu'ayyad, N of Wādī Baysh. I am puzzled by Ibn al-Mujāwir's remark that it is also known as Maḥall Abī Turāb, as the latter is reckoned to be an alternative name for Ḥaraḍ (Kay, *Yaman*, end map). Al-Mu'ayyad Aḥmad was the grandson of the Ḥasanī Sulaymānī sharif, Qāsim b. Ghānim, who corresponded with the Ayyubids in Egypt concerning their conquest of the Yemen in 569/1173, and who then allied himself with them when they arrived in Ḥaraḍ in the north of Tihāmat al-Yaman. Al-Mu'ayyad was active in that area in the early 7th/13th century during the Ayyubid rule over the Yemen (Smith, *Ayyubids*, II, pp. 52–5 and I [the text of Ibn Ḥātim's *Simṭ*], pp. 68, 78, 123, 140, 160, 164, 170; Yaḥyā b. al-Ḥusayn, *Ghāyah*, 403, where al-Rāḥah is called Rāḥat Banī Sharīf).

[3] Presumably the earlier Sulaymānī sharifs.

[4] 28 September 1223.

[5] Unidentified, but presumably close to al-Rāḥah. This conflicts with what Ibn al-Mujāwir says above, namely that al-Rāḥah was built by the early Sulaymānī sharifs (see n. 2 above).

[6] Begins 15 February 1222. Ibn al-Mujāwir's informant, it will be noted, is a local from al-Rāḥah whom he met in Zabīd. This adds to the impression one gets that these Hejazi and ʿAsīrī itineraries are presented second hand and were never covered personally by Ibn al-Mujāwir.

[7] Quran 21:89. It is not absolutely clear from the text where al-Rāḥī's information ends.

[8] If the word is *jarīr*, as OL suggests from the L MS, the meaning is unclear. The word means 'camel rope' and I have translated it tentatively after reference to an otherwise unexplained note in my field notebook.

[9] Quran 59:2.

[10] Both the town and the region are unidentified.

[11] Hajar is known and is located in Wādī Ḍamad, one of the major wadis of the Jīzān area (Hamdānī, *Ṣifah*, p. 86; ʿAqīlī, *Jāzān*, pp. 425–6, pp. 266 ff., map p. 97). Al-Darb is perhaps Darb Banī Shuʿbah (ʿAqīlī, *Jāzān*, p. 181).

From these boundaries as far as Zabīd their inhabitants are called al-Shamah,[1] since these regions are called al-Shām and also al-Sāʿid[2] in Zabīd. Night in these regions is good, whereas day is melancholy. It is also said that night in Ḥaraḍ is a sweet thing, whereas day is hard [to endure].[3] God knows best.

Marriage among the inhabitants of these regions.[4] From the time she reaches puberty until she gets married, they do not allow the girl to remove [her pubic hair]. Rather the hair grows longer and longer as time goes on. She allows it to grow until she [is able to] plait it into a tress.[5] It is said that it, that is the hair, is greased, combed and washed with *sidr* and earth.[6] On her wedding night she plaits her hair in two, each tress being let down[7] on to each of her thighs. She is then displayed to her husband. When he is in private with her and has assumed a man's [normal] position [for intercourse] with his wife,[8] he then grasps these two plaits and pulls them out by the roots. When he has removed them, he deflowers her. The next morning her female relatives visit her, each bringing a plate of butter. They say to her, 'How's it going with your beard?!' To which she replies, 'Fine, like the seller of the pumpkin!'[9] [Each relative] anoints the place with butter to remove the pain, since [her husband] has pulled out skin along with the hair. This is their custom.

To al-Hiliyyah eight parasangs,[10] from where fresh ginger comes. To al-Maḥālib two parasangs. This is the land of ʿAntarah al-ʿAbsī and his people.[11] It has a wadi called Mawr.[12]

[57] *The presenting of these regions as a gift by Imam Abū Mūsā* al-Amīn bi-Allāh.[13] I was informed by ʿAbdallāh b. Muḥammad b. Yaḥyā al-Mahjamī[14] as follows: When the sharifs were many in the Hejaz, a number of them left for Iraq during the caliphate of Imam Abū Mūsā Muḥammad al-Amīn bi-Allāh Commander of the Faithful, son of Hārūn al-

[1] OL vocalizes 'al-Shumah' from the I MS, whereas Landberg, *Etudes*, pp. 866 ff., prefers 'e-Śammah' with no further comment. In view of what follows it seems clear that the Zabīdīs are simply calling them 'the northerners' and I am inclined to take this as a corruption of something like 'al-Shāmiyyah'.

[2] Al-Shām means here 'the north'. *Sāʿid* means primarily either 'forearm' or 'upper arm'.

[3] Arabic *muṣlābah*. The translation is tentative.

[4] See also Landberg, *Etudes*, II, pp. 866–9 and Smith, 'Wondrous', pp. 119–20.

[5] Arabic *dabbūqah*.

[6] See Dozy, *Supplément*, I, p. 641, who mentions the use of *sidr* leaves for cleansing as one would use soap.

[7] Reading *yusdalu*.

[8] I.e. kneeling between her opened legs (Landberg, *Etudes*, II, p. 837).

[9] The Arabic produces a piece of doggerel:

'Kayf ḥālu-k maʿ al-zubbah. Bi-khayr, ka-bayyāʿ al-dubbah!'

For *zubb/zubbah*, see Lane, *Lexicon*, III, p. 1208, 'beard' and Kazimirski, *Dictionnaire*, I, p. 968, 'grande quantité de cheveux', the feminine form being necessary for the rhyme. There is no deep and hidden meaning which Landberg thinks he has missed (Landberg, *Etudes*, II, p. 869)!

[10] I vocalize after ʿAqīlī, *Jāzān*, p. 427; a place on the Wādī al-Khums, S of Jāzān. See also Smith, *Ayyubids*, II, p. 160, with various vocalizations and references. See also Stone, 'Gazetteer', pp. 330–31.

[11] See above p. 54, n. 9.

[12] The most northerly of the five great Yemeni Tihāmah wadis running E to W into the Red Sea: from N to S, Mawr, Surdud, Sahām, Rimaʿ and Zabīd (Smith, *Ayyubids*, II, p. 181 with full references; Kay, *Yaman*, end map).

[13] The 6th Abbasid caliph, reg. 193–8/809–13 (Bosworth, *Islamic Dynasties*, p. 6).

[14] I.e. an informant from al-Mahjam on Wādī Surdud.

Rashīd. They asked him to grant them a gift of some land where they [could] stay and cultivate it. So he granted them as a fief [the area] from Mecca as far as al-Hiliyyah in length and from Ṣaʿdah[1] as far as the coast in width. These regions remained in the hands of the group [of sharifs] and they lived a healthy life, '... their sustenance comes to them in abundance from every direction.'[2] They continued to occupy it until 615.[3] They grew weak and the hand of the Ghuzz[4] fell upon them and the land was no longer under their control and came into the possession of the Ghuzz. One of those in power was Sharīf al-Muʾayyad Aḥmad b. Qāsim b. Ghānim. But they vanished and there is no longer news of them in the land. As has been recited:

> The valley is effaced and his former abode empty;
> the situation as it was has changed from what I used to know.
> Why stay in a place whose good qualities are no longer
> evident and for whose today and tomorrow there is no hope?

From al-Maḥālib to Ṣaʿdah. From al-Maḥālib to Ḥirdah three parasangs.[5] To al-Madārah three parasangs.[6] This is Wādī al-Ṣ mā[7] and there are lots of wild animals there. To Shamr two parasangs.[8] To Qalḥāḥ one parasang.[9] To al-Afrūr three parasangs.[10]

To al-Ẓuhayrah two parasangs and [the area] is known as Wādī al-Yamānī.[11] This place is called al-Ẓuhayrah simply because it is the spine of land[12] at the confluence of two wadis in Wādī Mawr, Wādī Ḥūth and Wādī Ḥarf, the first one [one comes to], [the spine being a part] of the mountains to the east.[13] When the wadi comes into flood, the

[1] See p. 64, n. 10 above.

[2] Quran 16:112. Ibn al-Mujāwir misquotes: *min kulli jihatin*, for the correct *min kulli makānin*, 'from every place'.

[3] Begins 30 March 1218.

[4] In general, the term Ghuzz, an Arabic corruption of the Turkish Oghuz, was used by medieval Arab writers to denote non-Arabs, especially Turks and Kurds. In particular here, the term is used of the Ayyubids who were Kurdish in origin and who conquered the Yemen from Egypt in 569/1173 and remained in control of much of the southern highlands and Tihāmah until about 626/1228 (Smith, *Ayyubids*, II, p. 91).

[5] See Sprenger, *Reiserouten*, p. 133 ff. for this itinerary. Al-Maḥālib must be further N than Kay's end map indicates, perhaps about 1550 N. Al-Ḥirdah, with the definite article in Hamdānī (*Ṣifah*, pp. 52, 120), cannot be the place in question here and it would appear to have been the port of al-Mahjam (Stone, *Tihāmah*, p. 36; 'Gazetteer', p. 335). I have been able to discuss this difficult, and at times corrupt, itinerary with FLS and am very grateful for her comments on it. We are convinced Ibn al-Mujāwir did not pass this way himself and FLS adds that several of the stations on the route are localities rather than specific settlements.

[6] DMV kindly draws my attention to his *Agriculture*, p. 306, 'an area in Wādī Surdud from which honey was exported'.

[7] Unidentified.

[8] I vocalize after consultation with FLS who knows of a present-day Jabal Shamr on this route at coordinates 1552 4322.

[9] Vocalization probably thus, after Jabal Qalḥāḥ (FLS).

[10] Unidentified.

[11] Ẓuhayrah (literally 'small, raised stretch of land') is known at coordinates 1550 4330. Wādī al-Yamānī is also known (1552 4331) and is given by Ibn al-Mujāwir in order to indicate the general area on Wādī Mawr where al-Ẓuhayrah is situated (FLS).

[12] Arabic *ẓahr*. FLS proposes this translation here.

[13] Wādī Ḥūth does not exist and never has. I tentatively take Ibn al-Mujāwir's Wādī Ḥarf to be Wādī Akhraf (the two could be easily confused in Arabic) and thus in fact Wādī Ḥūth must be Wādī Thaʿlān and called Ḥūth in the text because of its flowing from the general direction of the town of Ḥūth (see Wilson, *Gazetteer*, map 2, p. 31). The text is particularly corrupt here and I translate with some diffidence.

two streams reach as far [58] as the spine of land at the same time [on either side], and each one retains the other. But whichever is stronger dams up the other and pushes back its flow. The other remains in the wadi[1] until [the stronger's] force abates, then the weak one takes over from the strong because of the waning of the latter's force and it peters out. Thus they remain until the wadis have finished running with flood water. This always happens when [the flood] reaches the confluence of the two wadis at the same time.[2]

To Shaẓab five parasangs,[3] built by the family of Barmak, or the last of the Barāmikah who lived in this town. It is said their posterity are still there, but they are in weak circumstances and their wealth is small.

To Ḥūth ten parasangs, the seat of the sharifs of the family of al-Ḥasan b. ʿAlī b. Abī Ṭālib.[4] To Ṣaʿdah fourteen parasangs, seat of ʿAbdallāh b. Ḥamzah al-Ḥasanī.[5]

From al-Maḥālib to Zabīd.[6] From al-Maḥālib to al-Mahjam[7] three parasangs. It is said that al-Mahjam is called by this name because the sharifs regularly attacked[8] its inhabitants and when the army returned to their own lands, they would be asked, 'Where have you been?' So they would reply, 'To al-Mahjam [the place of attack].' Its name is [also] Surdud and it has a wall round it which has fallen into ruin and been erased. There is a mountain overlooking it which [is so high that] it blends in with the sky and is called Milḥān.[9] Its summit is covered in cloud. A mosque built on top of it was called al-Shāhir because it became famous[10] for its high altitude in all the regions around. It is said that it was the abode of al-Khiḍr – peace be upon him. It is a high mountain which could not be taken by the kings in the Yemen. There are there amazing fortress houses [looking like] chess pieces the tops of which can be seen by anyone looking [even] from the furthest place, i.e. from Tihāmah. Its inhabitants are of Ḥimyar[11] and one of them recited as follows:

[1] Reading perhaps *masīl* where the text has *sayl*, though DMV informs me that the latter is used colloquially for 'watercourse'.

[2] FLS has been able to try out this out on expert hydrologists. Firstly it is clear that such a phenomenon occurs frequently in nature and that it has been reasonably accurately observed here. The correct terminology is 'dynamic backwater in tributary', 'hydraulic backwater', or 'dynamic/hydraulic ponding' and can occur even without flooding. I am extremely grateful to Mark New of the University of Oxford School of Geography and the Environment for his comments on which the above is based.

[3] FLS directs me to Wilson (*Gazetteer*, p. 203 and maps 3, p. 33 and 4, p. 38 with full Arabic references). It is often written Shaṭab, as in the text. See also Smith, *Ayyubids*, II, 202–3.

[4] A well-known town about 75 miles N of Ṣanʿāʾ (Smith, *Ayyubids*, II, pp. 163–4; Wilson, *Gazetteer*, p. 149). What is meant by the Ḥasanī sharifs here is the Zaydī imams. Perhaps 'a seat' would have been more accurate, for they certainly had others.

[5] I have corrected from 'al-Ḥusaynī'. Either Ibn al-Mujāwir is wrong here and thinks the Zaydī imams, of which ʿAbdallāh b. Ḥamzah was one, were Ḥusaynī sharifs, or this is a scribal error which has been repeated and found a place in OL's edited text. ʿAbdallāh b. Ḥamzah rose to power as Zaydī imam in about 583/1187 and died c. 613–4/1216–7 (Kay, *Yaman*, 302–3; Smith, *Ayyubids*, II, pp. 77, 80, 81; Wāsiʿī, *Tārīkh*, pp. 29–30; Appendix B.2 below).

[6] See Sprenger, *Reiserouten*, pp. 148 ff.

[7] A town of Wādī Surdud (Kay, *Yaman*, end map; Smith, *Ayyubids*, II, p. 176 with references).

[8] Arabic *taHJuMu*.

[9] Kay (*Yaman*, end map) places Milḥān to the E of the town. See also Hamdānī, *Ṣifah*, p. 68; Wilson, *Gazetteer*, p. 318.

[10] Arabic *iSHtaHaRa*.

[11] A large tribal confederation inhabiting from pre-Islamic times, according to Hamdānī, much territory to the W and NW of Ṣanʿāʾ (Smith, *Ayyubids*, II, p. 229; Wilson, *Gazetteer*, p. 147).

[59] My people will recall my courage and my noble deeds
and what they have done to Qays.
I built majesty for them out of a star and the heights
and they became the best and most eloquent of men.
For Ḥimyar are the lords of kings, the best of them;
from ancient times they were the best.

And on this mountain the small melon grows.[1]

To al-Kadrā' five parasangs,[2] built by King Decius[3] on the side of the wadi among arak and other trees. I was informed by ʿUmar b. ʿAlī b. Muṣabbaḥ who was informed as follows by Yūsuf Ibn al-Hamdānī: I set my horse to jump over the wadi and it jumped right over the bed. Now its width at that time was three cubits and its depth the same. [This was] at the end of the rule of the Abyssinians and at the first part of the Mahdids.[4] It has now become a huge wadi whose width is more than 3,000 cubits since the flood has eaten it away. In ancient times it was not a [normal] wadi, but the wadi in the middle of the town, which had a wall round it, a trench and gates. He continued. Its inhabitants drink water from the wadi side and for other than drinking they use water from their wells, since their well water is salty. They build their houses in baked brick because they [can] take it from the remains of [earlier] buildings. The length of each baked brick is one half a cubit and the same in width from the building of their ancestors.

I was informed by ʿUmar b. ʿAlī b. Muṣabbaḥ as follows: A huge flood came down one day, bringing with it a dead man sucked dry by the earth and who had become like a dried animal skin, seven cubits in length. Another version is that he was five cubits and wearing a sword. So they excavated the ruin and found that he had been buried standing up in the days of King Decius. I infer from this that these people used to bury their dead standing upright. It is said that Abraham the Friend – peace be upon him – was buried in this way. ʿAbd al-Mu'min b. ʿAlī al-Kūmī and Muḥammad b. [60] al-Ḥusayn b. Tūmart al-Barbarī were buried [standing up] in Ḥuṣn al-Ghār, which is [also] called Ḥuṣn al-Mahdiyyah.[5] They do this simply in order that the king is standing among them until the Day of Religion. However, this is simply madness.

[1] This is corrupt. After some reflection, I would suggest ' …*tanbutu al-shammāmah*', *Cucumis* Forsk., a small melon the size of a colocynth (Dimyāṭī, *Muʿjam*, p. 84; Hepper and Friis, *Plants*, p. 147, where the location of the plant is specifically mentioned as 'Surdud', although the vernacular name given is not the same).

[2] A town of Wādī Sahām, inland of Hodeida (Kay, *Yaman*, end map; Smith, *Ayyubids*, II, p. 168; Stone, 'Gazetteer', pp. 420–22).

[3] The Roman emperor, AD 249–51. His persecutions led to the flight of the seven sleepers of Ephesus who hid from him in a cave. See below p. 174, n. 9 (Serjeant, 'St Sergius', p. 574; Cross, *Oxford Dictionary*, p. 1246).

[4] Ibn al-Mujāwir means the Abyssinian Najahids and the Mahdids, both dynasties having their power base in Tihāmah. The former petered out under various slave ministers in the early 5th/12th century and the Mahdids could be said to have assumed power in 531/1136 and were destroyed by the conquering Ayyubids some time after 569/1173 (Smith, 'Political History', p. 138; *EI*, 'Nadjāḥids' and 'Mahdids'; Appendixes B.4 and B.7 below).

[5] Ibn Tūmart, as he is usually known, was the founder of the dynasty of the Muwaḥḥidūn, the Almohads, in North Africa and Andalucia and died in 524/1130 (*EI*, 'Ibn Tūmart'). ʿAbd al-Mu'min b. ʿAlī al-Kūmī (I have corrected his tribal *nisbah*, which derives from the Berber tribe of Kūmya) assumed leadership of the movement after Ibn Tūmart's death. He died in 558/1163 (*EI*, "Abd al-Mu'min b. ʿAlī al-Kūmī'). Al-Mahdiyyah is a port on the Mediterranean coast, on the east coast of present-day Tunisia, created by the Fatimids in the early 4th/10th century (*EI*, 'Mahdiyya'). See also Yāqūt, *Muʿjam*, V, pp. 229–32; Watt, *Spain*, pp. 103–6; Abun-Nasr, *Maghrib*, pp. 103–12 and map p. 94; Bosworth, *Islamic Dynasties*, p. 39.

One of the things mentioned by 'Umārah b. Muḥammad b. 'Umārah in *Kitāb al-Mufīd fī akhbār Zabīd*[1] is that Commander al-Ḥusayn b. Salāmah founded the town of al-Kadrā' on Wādī Sahām and the town of al-Ma'qir on Wādī Dhu'āl.[2] It is said that the area of al-Kadrā' is from al-Dawmayn as far as somewhere near al-Mazḥaf in length,[3] as far as the mosque built by Ibn Wahb near al-Qaḥmah, and from the mountain as far as the sea in width.[4] Its daily income is 1,000 dinars. Sahām is called [thus], as the poet has recited:

I see that Syria is getting nearer every day and night,
whereas Surdud and Sahām are getting further away from me.
My heart and soul are in Damascus, whereas my heart's blood
and my body, already possessed by leanness, are crushing [me].[5]

Another poet has recited as follows:

How can I cope with the valley dwellers?
If they make an agreement, they break it, or if they are reminded, they disown it.
How dear is the wadi side when play therein
branches [of trees] and its song-bird sings!

Section. Commander Bilāl became governor of the regions of al-Kadrā' during the rule of Amir Fātik b. Muḥammad.[6] Now Commander Faraj b. Isḥāq[7] grew up during Fātik's time [in office] and he used to eat and drink until his eating passed beyond [all reasonable] bounds. His maternal uncle, Bilāl, was disgusted with him. When he noticed this, Faraj b. Isḥāq left, accompanied by a black slave, and they became highwaymen between Ḥaraḍ and al-Maḥālib for two and a half years. While they were thus engaged, [61] the black slave said to Faraj, 'Master, I am afraid that, if you are reconciled with Bilāl, you will forget me.' But Faraj recited the following poem:

[1] A native Yemeni who went to Egypt in 552/1157 and was executed there in 569/1173, the same year as the Ayyubid conquest of the Yemen, having become implicated in a pro-Fatimid conspiracy against Saladin. His *Kitāb al-Mufīd* is not to my knowledge extant and his fame as an historian rests on his *Tārīkh al-Yaman*, the best edition of which remains that of Kay (Kay, *Yaman*, pp. iv–xii). Comparing this passage with his *Tārīkh*, however, reveals, in this particular section and those below (pp. 120 and 172 of *Tārīkh al-Mustabṣir*) at least, that the two were identical. See Kay, pp. 9 (English), 7 (Arabic).

[2] Kay (end map) locates al-Ma'qir on Wādī Dhu'āl (Stone, 'Gazetteer', pp. 231–2, itself a tributary of Wādī Rima'). Hamdānī (*Ṣifah*, pp. 54, 71) confirms this. FLS believes 'Old Manṣūriyyah' (*Tihāmah*, pp. 54–5) is the actual site of al-Ma'qir, not al-Qaḥmah, as had been supposed.

[3] Both unidentified.

[4] Jamāl al-Dīn 'Alī b. al-Ḥasan Ibn Wahb is unidentified. Al-Qaḥmah appears close to Wādī Dhu'āl upstream of al-Ma'qir (Kay, *Yaman*, end map). The end of the sentence is corrupt and I have corrected from: *wa-fī* (read *wa-min*) *al-jabal ilā al-baḥr ṭūl* (read *'arḍ* for *'arḍan*).

[5] The two lines of poetry have the rhyming scheme *-āmu*, ... *wa-sahāmu* (i.e. the name of the wadi) and ... *suhāmu*, 'leanness', thus employing two words in close proximity with the same root letters, but with different meanings, a neat poetic device called *jinās* in Arabic.

[6] Fātik b. Muḥammad b. Fātik b. Jayyāsh, who died in 553/1158, was the last of the slave ministers who had kept the Najahid flag flying in Tihāmah after the death of his great-grandfather, Jayyāsh, in 498/1104, and who appears as Fātik III in the *EI* family tree (Kay, *Yaman*, p. 95 ['Umārah's account]; *EI*, 'Nadjāḥids'; Appendix B.4 below). Bilāl does not figure in 'Umārah's *Tārīkh*, the main source of our knowledge of the Najahids.

[7] Mentioned only incidentally by 'Umārah (Kay, *Yaman*, p. 115).

When the noble are well-off, they remember
those who were friendly towards them in hard times.

The slave kept on repeating the verse until he had learned it off by heart. Commander Bilāl died and Faraj b. Isḥāq was summoned. When he arrived, they appointed him governor of the region of al-Kadrā' and he was put in full charge, giving out orders and prohibitions, of income and expenditure. When the slave had been a long time away, he went in search of his master and entered al-Kadrā'. He wrote the verse quoted above in a note and submitted it to Faraj b. Isḥāq. When the latter read the note, he searched for the slave and brought him in. He treated him with the utmost kindness and he assigned a place to him where he [could] live for the rest of his life. The following poem is about him:

Gazelles appeared in the waterless desert;
they gave, but were given nothing.
They hunted, but were not themselves hunted;
They caught [the prey] and did not turn away.
They killed a young man in love,
saying they were joking.
Oh, may their archers be paralysed!
Do they not know whom they wounded,
the one killed by their arrows?
They agreed to [shed] his blood.
He was made to drink red wine, mixed,
drinking morning and evening.
O you riders and
the caravan who have departed,
How depressed the world has become!
This matter too is depressing, so rejoice!
Be off to al-Kadrā'
and praise the commander of its army.
You must concern yourself with Ibn Isḥāq;
for in freedom from grief, there will be joy for you![1]

He opened up the door of giving to anyone who sought him out, anyone coming as a delegation, near or far. So he was criticized [62] for what he was doing in wasting wealth and income. He gave instructions that the following should be written on the door of his house:

He who is strong takes and no one is secure from his evil deeds;
while he who is humbled is devoured and blamed.
May God never bless the wealth which I leave behind
for my heirs, while my honour is reviled!

To al-Qaḥmah a parasang and a half, also called Dhu'āl. Now Dhu'āl is the whole area between the sea and the mountain opposite. Good quality bananas and delicious pomegranates are found there. It is said they are brought in from the Liwā mountains,[2] since

[1] A clever pun on his name, Faraj, which means 'joy'. The last word of the second hemistitch must be *faraḥu* to fit in with the rhyming pattern *-ḥu* or *-ḥū*. The gazelles here are girls and 'their prey' elligible young men. The image of blood and red wine is common in Arabic poetry.

[2] Unidentified.

in al-Qaḥmah there is no landowner. It is said that al-Mafālīs[1] and al-Qaḥmah acted in a high-handed manner.[2] This is because, when iniquity appeared in the west of the country and dissension became clear, the Ash'ūb[3] plundered al-Mafālīs and the Ma'āzibah[4] plundered al-Qaḥmah in the twinkling of an eye, because these tribes were against these towns, [the former] being rebellious and [the latter] tyrannical. Jamāl al-Dīn 'Alī b. al-Ḥasan b. Wahb had built Ḥuṣn al-Aḍwaḥ[5] opposite al-Qaḥmah on a mountain on 1 Shawwāl 622.[6] It was ancient, reduced to ruins by an Arab ruler[7] and renovated by Ibn Wahb who made it an extremely well-fortified building.

From al-Qaḥmah to Maḥall Ibrāhīm three parasangs.[8] To Sufākā three parasangs,[9] which is a fortress built on the highest point of a mountain which could not be taken by the rulers of the Yemen. From it is brought tamarind,[10] i.e. *al-tamr al-Hindī*, to the whole area. In this territory are areas of land not penetrated, the trees being too numerous and the terrain too difficult. From these wooded areas wood is cut down. It is called roka,[11] from which arrows[12] are made. Payment is made in advance from the state to carpenters for arrows at the rate of two *malakī* dinars per thousand. In these wooded areas oranges, citrons, lemons and bananas are left neglected, having no owner. These trees are among streams and springs, but in their water are huge snakes.

To Zahrān one quarter of a parasang,[13] a fortress built by Arabs on a flat, depressed piece of land like the pan [of weighing scales]. Al-Malik al-Mas'ūd Yūsuf b. Muḥammad conquered it in 620.[14]

[1] A village and mountain pass in al-Ma'āfir, now al-Ḥujariyyah, in the southern highlands of the Yemen (Smith, *Ayyubids*, II, p. 176; Ḥajarī, *Majmū'*, IV, p. 715; Maqḥafī, *Mu'jam*, p. 616). My assumption is that Ibn al-Mujāwir remembers a similar situation in the southern highlands and he thus brings in al-Mafālīs into his text along with the case in point, namely al-Qaḥmah.

[2] Arabic *'alā ṭāli'*. The expression cannot be taken literally as 'in a high position', as FLS tells me al-Qaḥmah certainly is not so elevated. This is an exceedingly difficult sentence which, I think, is trying to explain that the need on the part of the inhabitants of al-Qaḥmah to bring in fruits from the surrounding area is because of the lack of landowners, and that in itself due to general unrest in this part of Tihāmah (which Ibn al-Mujāwir here calls 'the west of the country').

[3] *Mashāyikh* of Ḥimyar would seem to be in the southern highlands from the text and perhaps Redhouse's note (Khazrajī, *'Uqūd*, III, p. 148, n. 958) that they are near al-Dumluwah and al-Juwwah is not far off the mark, N of Ta'izz (Ibn Rasūl, *Ṭurfah*, pp. 12, 136; Smith, *Ayyubids*, II, p. 226; Maqḥafī, *Mu'jam*, p. 33). The Ash'ūb behaved towards al-Mafālīs exactly in the same way as the Ma'āzibah did towards al-Qaḥmah.

[4] A tribal group of 'Akk inhabiting northern Tihāmah (Ibn al-Dayba', *Qurrah*, II, p. 72, al-Akwa''s n. 3; Smith, *Ayyubids*, II, p. 232).

[5] Unidentified.

[6] 6 October 1225.

[7] It is difficult to see what Ibn al-Mujāwir means precisely by 'Arab' here. He uses the term frequently to mean either Arabs, as opposed to conquering Kurds and Turks, or Arab tribesmen, as opposed to those of African origin who lived in great numbers in Tihāmah. Perhaps he means here that the fortress had originally been built in pre-Islamic times, 'ancient', and was destroyed 'by an Arab ruler' in Islamic times.

[8] Unidentified.

[9] Kindly identified by FLS from YAR50 as Jabal Sufākah at 1438 4331 – 1436 4331.

[10] Arabic *ḥumar*, *Tamarindus indica* L. The acid pulp of the pod makes a refreshing drink for one suffering from a fever. It is also a laxative (Dimyāṭī, *Mu'jam*, p. 46; Yule and Burnell, *Hobson-Jobson*, pp. 894–5; Löfgren, *Texte*, p. 30; Varisco, *Agriculture*, p. 182).

[11] Arabic *ruqa'*, *Trichelia emetica* Vahl (Dimyāṭī, *Mu'jam*, pp. 63–4; Hepper and Friis, *Plants*, p. 200; Wood, *Handbook*, p. 201).

[12] Arabic *nushshāb* (Smith, *Ayyubids*, II, p. 126, *sub f r d*).

[13] This particular Zahrān is unidentified.

[14] Begins 4 February 1223.

The wadis from where wood is cut for buildings. Of the region of Dhu'āl are Wādīs Nab', Raymān, 'Arm[?], Jābiyah and al-Madārah.[1] In Wādī Zabīd are Sakhmal[?] and al-Fā'ishī.[2] Vegetation there is in general spinage[3] and sesban.[4] In the plains[5] of the Yemen is Wādī Nakhlah, apart from that of Mecca and of Wāsiṭ.[6] Among the wadis of the north[ern Tihāmah] are Wādīs Rimā', al-Kadrā',[7] Surdud and Mawr. From all these wadis wood is cut for the purpose of building.

To Fashāl four parasangs,[8] which is made up of seven sand dunes and seven wadis. In it are about 800 villages whose inhabitants cultivate only millet and sorghum using rain water. Shaykh Muḥammad b. Mu'aybid[?] planted wheat and barley there and it grew to maturity in 623.[9] His nephews al-'Ijl and Mu'aybid planted rice, which, when planted and matured, was pulled out by its roots in 624.[10]

To Wādī Rima' half a parasang. It is a huge wadi and it has been mentioned in writing as follows.The flood continued to eat into the wadi as far as al-Khayf, a mountain in Bura'.[11] When it reached there, a treasure of gold became visible, sufficient for all the people of the Yemen.

To Qūniṣ half a parasang, [also] called Wādī al-'Irq[12] where al-Malik al-Mu'izz Ismā'īl b. Ṭughtakīn b. Ayyūb was killed.[13] To Zabīd four parasangs and God knows best what is correct.

[1] *Nab'* in Arabic is the name of a tree from which bows are made. DMV informs me that the reference may be to *Grewia tenax* Forssk (Wood, *Handbook*, p. 100). FLS writes: Wadi Nab' [*sic*] is today 1437 4315 – 1437 4308 and 1439 4318 – 1437 4315 (YAR50). Raymān is probably a corruption of Rummān, today so named at 1437 4314 – 1437 4259 [YAR50]; and for Jābiyah, see Stone, 'Gazetteer', p. 385.

[2] Tributaries of Wādī Zabīd. Yāqūt (*Mu'jam*, IV, p. 234) mentions a Fā'ish, a wadi in the Yemen and see Stone, 'Gazetteer', p. 244.

[3] Arabic *isḥil*. DMV says this is probably in reference to the abundant *Salvadora persica* L., also known as *(a)rāk*, the toothbrush tree.

[4] Arabic *sīsbān*, *Sesbania grandiflora*. DMV: the most widely planted trees in Tihāmah (Wood, *Handbook*, 153).

[5] I take *ṭaḥawāt* as the plural of *ṭaḥan*, strictly speaking the *maṣdar* of *ṭaḥā*, *yaṭḥū*, to arrive at this translation and assume he speaks of Tihāmah (Lane, *Lexicon*,, V, p. 1832; Kazimirski, *Dictionnaire*, II, p. 62; Nashwān, *Shams*, VII, p. 4074, *imtadda* and quoting Quran 91:6).

[6] A large, well-known wadi of Tihāmah. Hamdānī (*Ṣifah*, p. 71; *Ṣifah*, p. 86 [Akwa''s n. 3]; Kay, *Yaman*, end map) says it joins Wādī al-Milḥ at Ḥays. Wāsiṭ ('middle') in Iraq was so called because it was equidistant from Kufa, Basra and Ahwāz. It is on the Tigris, about 150 miles downstream from Baghdad (Yāqūt, *Mu'jam*, V, pp. 347–53; Le Strange, *Lands*, pp. 39 ff. and map II).

[7] I.e. Wādī Sahām.

[8] Between al-Qaḥmah and Zabīd in Tihāmah, about 20–25 miles N of the latter (Smith, *Ayyubids*, II, p. 151 and map I).

[9] Begins 2 January 1226.

[10] Begins 22 December 1226.

[11] I take al-Khayf as a place name here (it means 'mountain slope' among other things; Lane, *Lexicon*, II, p. 833; Kazimirski, *Dictionnaire*, I, p. 656), one of the mountains making up the Bura' range. The latter is a huge mountain range due E of Hodeida and al-Kadrā' (Hamdānī, *Ṣifah*, p. 103; Kay, *Yaman*, end map).

[12] Qūniṣ is vocalized Quwayḍ by Sprenger (*Reiserouten*, p. 149) and Kay (*Yaman*, p. 288). For Wādī al-'Irq, see Smith, *Ayyubids*, II, p. 164 and Stone's excellent entry in 'Gazetteer', p. 371.

[13] I have corrected Ismā'īl's honorific title from the 'al-Mas'ūd' of the text. He was in fact killed at al-Qawz in 598/1202 (IbnḤātim, *Simṭ*, p. 81–2; Smith, 'Eastern Connection', p. 77; Introduction, Contents, History and buildings above).

[63] *Zabīd and what it was like in ancient times*. It was said that all the territory of Zabīd used to be the pasture area[1] of Muhalhil and Kulayb,[2] this being from the border of al-Ḥajf[3] as far as the prominent part of Qūniṣ mountain. It [also] has his palace, water reservoir and stable where his horses were tethered. This [64] is on the summit of a lofty mountain overlooking Tihāmah. He used to sit in the palace, surveying the land below like an emerald with water channels and rivers flowing. It was said that there were 600,000 springs there. Another version is that there were 60,000 springs, and yet another 6,000 springs. The most accurate account is that there are 600 springs. It is also said that there are 60 springs flowing on the surface of the earth, every one of them pure and sweet. Because of the dampness of the earth, the land has become permanently green, with gardens, trees and wild animals. The pasture land remained as it was until war broke out among the people, [lasting] for a period of forty years. The account is well known and there is no need to mention it [here].[4]

A king came after the people had blocked up the springs there and there is no doubt that he was Maʿn b. Zā'idah al-Shaybānī.[5] The proof of the accuracy of what we are saying is that the two millstones discarded at Ghulāfiqah gate in Zabīd used to be turned by these waters and springs. It was [also] unhealthy on account of the very wet earth and water and any area in this condition is bound to be unhealthy.

I was informed by Jaʿfar b. ʿAbd al-Malik b. ʿAbdallāh b. Yūnis al-Khazrajī al-Jurjānī as follows: I came to the Yemen during the rule of Sayf al-Islām Ṭughtakīn b. Ayyūb[6] and we used to draw water from the wells manually and drink. The water level dropped during our time, 625,[7] until the depth of the well reached fifteen *qāmah*s.[8] So the unhealthiness ceased and the water and the climate became moderate. The wells on the road to the town, [Zabīd], are sixteen *qāmah*s deep and around it about twelve *qāmah*s. As for the boundaries of the pasture land of Kulayb and Muhalhil, they [stretch] from al-Ḥajf as far as the prominent part of Qūniṣ as far as the head of Rimaʿ. All the plots of land[9] and wadis of Zabīd [reach] as far as the border of al-Nawbatayn and Qawārīr,[10] as broad as they are long. When the springs were blocked and the water became scarce, arak and tamarisk trees[11] sprang up in the scrub[12] and therefore it became an area with much vegetation.

[1] Arabic *ḥimā*.

[2] The two sons of Rabīʿah b. al-Ḥārith b. Zuhayr ... b. Taghlib. The whole story of Kulayb's murder which became the *causus belli*, as B. Taghlib went to war with B. Bakr, the war of Basūs, in the late 5th century AD is told in Nicholson (*History*, pp. 55–60). See also Hamdānī, *Iklīl*, X, p. 42; Ibn Rasūl, *Ṭurfah*, pp. 16, 23; Kaḥḥālah, *Muʿjam*, pp. 120–23; *EI*, 'Taghlib b. Wā'il'.

[3] An area to the W of Zabīd (Stone, 'Gazetteer', p. 273).

[4] The war of Basūs is meant here which is reputed to have lasted for 40 years; see n. 2 above.

[5] Governor of Aden on behalf of the Abbasids from 145–51/762–67 (Kay, *Yaman*, p. 245).

[6] I.e. 579–93/1183–97.

[7] Begins 12 December 1227.

[8] The word means literally the length of the adult human body, a fathom, about 6 feet. It is used to this day to measure in particular the depth of a well (Hinz, *Masse*, p. 54, s.v. *bāʿ*).

[9] Reading *ḥawāzz* (RBS), plural of *ḥāzzah* for OL's *jawāz*.

[10] The former perhaps also capable of the vocalization al-Nūbatayn. I take it as the colloquial word *nōba*, meaning 'circular tower', 'watch tower', 'tower house' (Serjeant, *Ṣanʿāʾ*, p. 589; Landberg, *Glossaire daṯînois*, III, p. 2831 ['tour d'angle carrée', 'chateau fort']; Landberg, *Etudes*, I, p. 728). FLS locates Qawārīr precisely for me: 1416 4331.

[11] Arabic *ṭarfāʾ* which may include all the Tamaricaceae (Dīnawarī, *Plants*, p. 43). DMV: in the Yemen, this may refer to *Tamarix arabica* Bunge which is widespread (Wood, *Handbook*, p. 113).

[12] Arabic *khabt*, '... scrubland at best, sand and gravel with sparse shrubbery' (FLS).

[65] *The building of Zabīd.* I was informed as follows by ʿAbd al-Raḥmān b. Aḥmad b. al-Rājī:[1] In the area of Zabīd there was land with many tamarisk and arak trees, around which were palaces and a number of settlements. One of them was al-Matāmah and also al-Nafīr[2] to the west of the town. They were two great towns. One of the [illustrations] of their greatness is the fact that 500 dancers[3] used to leave them every Thursday and Friday evening to visit the pious.

Junayjir,[4] east of the town [of Zabīd], was built by Decius. Wāsiṭ is south-west [of Zabīd][5] and every day 600 cavalry left this place, which is still inhabited until now, to fight in the area of Zabīd. So they remained for a long time until they became weary of each another. The local shaykhs left for Iraq during the rule of Imam Commander of the Faithful al-Amīn [Muḥammad] b. Hārūn al-Rashīd[6] and told him all about themselves and what had happened to them. They said, 'We are folk of al-Ashāʿir,[7] all of us relatives. But we fight amongst ourselves.' Al-Amīn replied, 'Who is the senior of you?' They indicated one man. 'Who is after him?', he asked. They indicated another. He kept on asking them and they informing him until they had enumerated five people. He appointed the senior shaykh over them, saying to those present, 'When this man dies, appoint the second one after him. When the second one is appointed and then dies, appoint the third. When the third dies, appoint the fourth and when the fourth dies, appoint the fifth.' He imposed the shaykh [as leader] over his people and his relatives. They all left the city of peace, Baghdad, to return [home]. Now the shaykh for whom al-Amīn imposed the oath of allegiance died and the second was appointed after him. He died and the third was appointed. He died and the fourth was appointed. When he came near to their home town, the fourth died, so the fifth refused to take up the position [as leader] and withdrew for fear of dying. He put in charge there one of his relatives. As soon as he entered the town, he collected taxes there and sent the revenue to Baghdad. When al-Amīn was killed and al-Maʾmūn took over the caliphate, the man appointed in the Yemen rebelled [66], and took over the area and its different regions, storing the revenue in his own treasury.

In 199[8] some people were brought to al-Maʾmūn, including a descendant of ʿUbayd Allāh b. Ziyād. One of them gave out his pedigree, saying his name was Muḥammad b. So-and-so b. ʿUbayd Allāh b. Ziyād.[9] Another of them claimed descent from Sulaymān

[1] This might also read al-Rāḥī from al-Rāḥah.

[2] The former is mentioned by Hamdānī (*Ṣifah*, p. 168), the second, which may read al-Nufayr, unidentified.

[3] Arabic *raqīṣ*. The rest of the sentence suggests they might have been Sufis.

[4] Unidentified.

[5] Maqḥafī (*Muʿjam*, p. 688) says it is one of the dependencies of Zabīd. FLS informs me that she has evidence of a Wāsiṭ Zabīd.

[6] The sixth Abbasid caliph, 193–8/809–13 (Bosworth, *Islamic Dynasties*, p. 6).

[7] A well-known Tihāmah tribe, whose name is derived from al-Ashʿar b. Udad b. Zayd of Kahlān b. Sabaʾ, inhabiting Wādī Zabīd. Full references can be found in Smith, *Ayyubids*, II, 225. See also Ḥajarī, *Majmūʿ*, I, pp. 78–80; Maqḥafī, *Muʿjam*, pp. 32–3.

[8] Begins 22 August 814.

[9] The history of the Ziyadids, who were eventually to rule as a dynasty in Tihāmah from about 203–371/818–981, is shrouded in mystery. Ziyād, whose name gave the dynasty its name, appears to have had two sons, Muḥammad and ʿUbayd Allāh, and Ibn al-Mujāwir is suggesting here that the Ziyadid sent to the Yemen and the dynasty's first ruler there was descended from Ziyād through ʿUbayd Allāh. ʿUmārah in fact (Kay, *Yaman*, p. 2) says Muḥammad was the grandson of one ʿAbdallāh. The claim that Ziyād was the son of Abū Sufyān and thus the brother of the first Umayyad caliph, Muʿāwiyah, should, however, be taken with extreme caution (Kay, *Yaman*, pp. 218–9). If this were so, ʿUbayd Allāh was the consecrator of the murdered

b. Hishām b. ʿAbd al-Malik.[1] A descendant of this man was Khalaf b. Abī al-Ṭāhir, the minister of Jayyāsh b. Najāḥ.[2] Al-Maʾmūn said to this Umayyad, 'Imam Abū Jaʿfar al-Manṣūr ʿAbdallāh b. Muḥammad b. ʿAlī b. ʿAbdallāh b. ʿAbbās[3] cut off the head of Sulaymān b. Hishām and his parents in one single day.' The Umayyad replied, 'I am descended from his youngest son. From us are descended people in Basra.' [Another] man claimed descent from Taghlib,[4] his name being Muḥammad b. Hārūn. So al-Maʾmūn wept, saying, 'How can I forget Muḥammad b. Hārūn?', meaning his name was the same as that of his brother, Muḥammad al-Amīn b. Hārūn al-Rashīd. Al-Maʾmūn said, 'The two Umayyads will be killed, but the Taghlibī will be pardoned, to remain mindful of his name and his father's name.' Ibn Ziyād said, 'What liars people are, Commander of the Faithful, who claim that you are lenient, much given to forgiveness and abstaining from shedding blood unjustly. If you kill us for some transgression, we shall not withdraw our obedience, nor dissociate ourselves from the opinion of the community on the question of the oath of allegiance given to you. If you kill us, Commander of the Faithful, for the crimes of the Umayyads against you, then God – He is almighty – says, "No [soul] bearing a burden will bear the burden of another".'[5] Al-Maʾmūn approved of what he said and pardoned them all. They were more than one hundred men. Then he added them [to the followers] of Abū al-ʿAbbās al-Faḍl b. Sahl, 'him of the two commands'. Another version is [to the followers] of his brother, al-Ḥasan b. Sahl.[6]

The oath of allegiance was given to Ibrāhīm b. al-Mahdī[7] in Baghdad in al-Muḥarram 202[8] [67] and this coincided with the arrival of news from the Yemen of the rebellion of al-Ashāʿir. Al-Ḥasan b. Sahl praised Muḥammad b. Ziyād, [Sulaymān b. Hishām] al-Marwānī and the Taghlibī in the presence of al-Maʾmūn, they being men of prominence and totally dependable. He advised that they be sent to the Yemen, i.e. that Ibn Ziyād should be commander, Ibn Hishām minister and the Taghlibī a judge and mufti. From the offspring of the Taghlibī Muḥammad b. Hārūn were the qadis of Zabīd, B. Abī ʿUqāmah.[9] The office of judge was passed on from father to son until they were

body of Ḥusayn b. ʿAlī b. Abī Ṭālib at Karbalāʾ in 61/680, a story told by Gibbon (*Decline and Fall*, VI, pp. 275–7, using Ockley's account (*History*, pp. 410–12)). See also Smith 'Political History', pp. 130, 138; *EI*, 'Ziyādids'; Appendix B.3 below.

[1] I.e. the son of the tenth Umayyad caliph (reg.105–25/724–43) (Bosworth, *Islamic Dynasties*, p. 3).

[2] The third Najahid ruler in Tihāmah, 482–98/1089–1104 (Smith, 'Political History', p. 138; Appendix B.4 below).

[3] The second Abbasid caliph, 136–58/754–75 (Bosworth, *Islamic Dynasties*, p. 6).

[4] A huge ʿAdnānī tribe found in Iraq and areas of the northern Arabian Peninsula and particularly famed for their pre-Islamic warlike activities (Kaḥḥālah, *Muʿjam*, I, pp. 120–23; *EI*, 'Taghib b. Wāʾil').

[5] A common funerary quotation, it occurs in several places in the Quran, e.g. 6:164.

[6] Al-Faḍl b. Sahl ('he of the two commands', an honorific title, d. 202/818) is the famous Persian minister of al-Maʾmūm (*EI*, 'al-Faḍl b. Sahl'), his brother, al-Ḥasan (d. 236/850) (*EI*, 'al-Ḥasan b. Sahl'), being less well known. It is generally accepted that Muḥammad became al-Faḍl's protégé (Smith, 'Political History', p. 130; *EI*, 'Ziyādids').

[7] The brother of Hārūn al-Rashīd and uncle of al-Maʾmūn who was proclaimed caliph by the Iraqis, fearing Persian domination led by al-Faḍl b. Sahl (*CHIs*, IA, pp. 121–2 and IB, Table III, p. 732).

[8] July 817.

[9] Kay (*Yaman*, p. 4) vocalizes ʿAqāmah and I correct after reference to Maqḥafī (*Muʿjam*, p. 453), himself a Yemeni, who calls them Zabīd ulema. FLS points out to me that Sayyid (*Ṭabaqāt*, p. 241) and Zetterstéen in Ibn Rasūl (*Ṭurfah*, p. 16) also vocalize ʿAqāmah.

destroyed by 'Alī b. al-Mahdī, when he had [already] put an end to the Abyssinian dynasty.[1] The army which al-Ma'mūn had levied to send to Baghdad departed to make war on Ibrāhīm b. al-Mahdī.

In 203[2] Ibn Ziyād and his followers performed the pilgrimage. He marched on the Yemen, conquered Tihāmah after wars which took place between him and the Arab tribes and laid the foundations of Zabīd in Sha'bān 204.[3] On this date Imam Abū 'Abdallāh Muḥammad b. Idrīs al-Shāfi'ī died in Cairo.[4]

Ja'far, the client of Ibn Ziyād, made the pilgrimage from the Yemen in [20]5,[5] [taking] wealth and gifts, and journeyed to Iraq, where he had a audience with al-Ma'mūn. This Ja'far returned to Zabīd in [20]6,[6] accompanied by a thousand cavalry of those carrying the black banners of Khurasan, [plus another] seven hundred.[7] Ibn Ziyād became very important and ruled the whole of the province of the Yemen, mountains and plains. This same Ja'far assumed authority for the highlands and laid the foundations there of the town of al-Mudhaykhirah, [a place] of rivers.[8] The territory which was Ja'far's is called Mikhlāf Ja'far to this day.[9] Ja'far was one of the shrewdest and wisest [of men] and through him the rule of Ibn Ziyād reached its zenith. This was the man who stipulated that the Arabs in Tihāmah should not ride horses.

Ibn Ziyād ruled over Ḥaḍramawt, Kindah territory, al-Shiḥr, Mirbāṭ, Abyan, Lahej, Aden and the coastal regions as far as Ḥaly.[10] In the mountains, he ruled over al-Janad and its regions, Mikhlāf Ja'far, Mikhlāf al-Ma'āfir, Ṣan'ā', Ṣa'dah, Najrān and Bayḥān.[11] Ibn Ziyād kept the Friday address in the name of the Abbasids, but carried off wealth and valuable gifts, he himself and his sons after his death, [firstly] Ibrāhīm b. Muḥammad, who was ruler.[12] After his death, Ziyād b. Ibrāhīm remained ruler, [but his period of rule did not last long,[13] [68], then his brother Abū al-Jaysh Isḥāq b. Ibrāhīm ruled

[1] The first Mahdid ruler in Tihāmah, 531–54/1136–59. By the Abyssinian dynasty he means the Najahids, the last minister of whom was murdered by the Mahdids in 551/1156 (Smith, 'Political History', pp. 132, 138; Appendices E and H below).

[2] Begins 9 July 818.

[3] February/March 819.

[4] Al-Shāfi'ī is in fact thought to have been killed by a Mālikī on the last day of Rajab 204 (rather than in the following month, Sha'bān)/20 January 820 (*EI*, 'al-Shāfi'ī').

[5] Begins 17 June 820.

[6] Begins 6 June 821.

[7] I.e. Abbasid cavalry.

[8] Kay (*Yaman*, end map) places it about 45 miles N of Ta'izz. It is in the region of Dhū al-Kilā' and in the district of Saḥūl (Hamdānī, *Ṣifah*, pp. 68, 100; Maqḥafī, *Mu'jam*, p. 578).

[9] The area in medieval times is usually reckoned to be centered on Dhū Jiblah, itself about 20 miles S of al-Mudhaykhirah (Kay, *Yaman*, end map; Smith, *Ayyubids*, II, p. 182).

[10] This is an impressive list of territories and would seem to be somewhat exaggerated! Kindah is the well-known tribe Kindah b. 'Ufayr who inhabited vast areas of Ḥaḍramawt in its widest geographical sense (Kaḥḥālah, *Mu'jam*, III, pp. 998–1000; Caskel, *Ǧamharat an-nasab*, I, Tafeln 176, 233). Al-Shiḥr is on the southern Arabian coast about 40 miles E of al-Mukallā (Serjeant, *Portuguese*, end map); Mirbāṭ is about 40 miles E of Ẓafār, present-day Ṣalālah, the chief town of southern Oman. Abyan is an area E and NE of Aden and Lahej due N (Serjeant, *Portuguese*, end map; *EI*, 'Laḥdj').

[11] Al-Janad was an important medieval town, now almost a suburb of Ta'izz in the southern highlands. Al-Ma'āfir is the area S of Ta'izz now called al-Ḥujariyyah. Bayḥān is an area about 150 miles NE of Aden and about 75 miles SE of Mārib as the crow flies.

[12] Reg. 245–83/859–96.

[13] About 6 years, 283–9/896–902 (Smith, 'Political History', p. 138).

after his death] and ruled for a long time.[1] When he became old and had spent eighty years ruling, some of his family parted company with him. One of those who showed his opposition was the ruler of Ṣanʿāʾ, a descendant of the tubbaʿs of Ḥimyar, whose name was Yūsuf b. Asʿad b. Yuʿfir,[2] but he had the Friday address delivered in the name of Abū al-Jaysh [Isḥāq] and his ancestors. The wealth of this man Asʿad b. Yuʿfir was collected, not exceeding 400,000 dinars a year, and he would spend some of it on good causes and on those who came to him [for a good reason].[3] As for the lord of Bayḥān, Najrān and Jarash, he decided to rebel against Ibn Ziyād.[4] The lord of Ṣaʿdah did likewise; the Ḥasanī sharif, known as al-Rassī, rose there in revolt.[5]

There is another version of what happened as follows. The Commander of the Faithful Muḥammad al-Amīn made Muḥammad b. Ziyād b. Maḥmūd b. Manṣūr governor of the Yemen. Muḥammad b. Ziyād came to the region of al-Ḥuṣayb[6] and found people fighting with each other every day until late morning, then dispersing. He intervened between them and made peace. He built a palace at Ghulāfiqah gate and its remains are there until now. He lived there and bought one thousand slaves.

Another version is that he came bringing a large number of troops from Iraq. He said to them, 'If anyone comes to be entertained, put them to the sword!' He invited some of the shaykhs of the area and the important tribal groups of al-Ashāʿir. He brought them food which had been prepared. When they were busy eating and being entertained, the slaves took up their arms and put those present to the sword. Not one of them escaped. He also put to the sword those Arabs from the villages and settlements around them. This situation continued until the people asked for his protection. Everyone who showed obedience to him had a mark left on his head in the shape of a conical hat which looks as follows: [69] [diagram of conical hat] He would [also] give him a pair of oxen and a levelling board,[7] shaped as follows: [diagram of a thin piece of wood], that is to till the land. The people tilled the land and settled in this place and the mark and piece of wood have remained traditional gifts until now.

I was informed by Aḥmad b. Saʿīd b. ʿAmr b. ʿAwīl who was informed by an old shaykh who had reached one hundred years old and he had been informed by his father on the authority of his grandfather as follows: I used to pasture my cattle at Masjid al-Ashāʿir,[8] where there were then trees and a pool of water. When Ibn Ziyād left Mecca,

[1] Reg. 299–371/911–81.

[2] I.e. Asʿad b. Ibrāhīm b. Muḥammad b. Yuʿfir (290–344/903–55) (Smith, 'Political History', pp. 130–32, 138).

[3] Reading *fī al-mabarrah wa-li-qāṣidī-h*.

[4] OL has 'Jurash', though a Najrānī informant has given me 'Jarash', a settlement in ʿAsīr. FLS reminds me that these places are very far apart. Ibn al-Mujāwir has this wrong, I suggest, and in any case I know of no historical corroboration of this uprising.

[5] This is the Zaydī imam. Since Abū al-Jaysh Isḥāq's rule was about 70 years in length, it cannot be said with certainty which imam this would have been: it could have been the third, al-Nāṣir Aḥmad, the fourth, Yaḥyā b. Aḥmad, or the fifth, al-Dāʿī Yūsuf b. Yaḥyā (Smith, *Ayyubids*, II, pp. 76, 81).

[6] I.e. the region where Zabīd was eventually built.

[7] This is a tentative translation of *mihār*. The classical lexica (Ibn Manẓūr, *Lisān*, V, p. 185; Zabīdī, *Tāj*, XIV, p. 159) give us the probable vocalization and define the word as a 'thick piece of wood', adding it is used in the nose of a Bactrian camel, presumably in order to control the animal. It might be some sort of plough, but the diagram does not give this impression. The image of oxen dragging a levelling board in order to prepare arable land for sowing crops is a common one in the Yemen and this fits in well with the meaning here. DMV adds that this is usually called *maḥarr*.

[8] An unidentified settlement presumably in the territory of the Ashāʿir.

he would take the soil of every place he passed through, sniff it and build a village on that spot. This continued until he reached the land of al-Ḥuṣayb, where he took a handful of soil, sniffed it and said to his Abbasid followers, ' Stay here with us !' They asked why and he replied it was because this was good land,[1] the best[2] of this area. They asked him what proof he had of this and he replied, 'Because it is good and between two wadis,' meaning Wādīs Zabīd and Rimaʿ. When he settled in the place, he built a town called Zabīd. Zabīd is derived from the word *zubdah*, on the basis of what happened on the first day [after their arrival].

Section. ʿAbd al-Nabī b. ʿAlī b. al-Mahdī said to those present:[3] I am amazed at the people of these two wadis.[4] They asked, 'What have you observed of their amazing characteristics?' 'I notice,' he replied, 'that every man [70] has the characteristics of virility and masculinity except those living between the two wadis. Their characteristics incline to effeminacy and to those of women.' 'How can you be certain of this?' they asked. He replied, 'Every human being inclines to anything which promotes his religion and his life in the present world except the inhabitants of Zabīd. They incline to food and drink, fine clothes and footwear,[5] and to smelling perfume. Their characteristics incline more to those of women than of men.' One of those present at the meeting said, '[Zabīd] has been placed between two wadis exactly like a man with two wives. He inclines to the one his personal taste chooses and the one upon whom his needs[6] rest.' Ibn al-Mujāwir said: The majority of their men speak, make amorous gestures to each other, ...[7] and frolic around like women.

I was informed by Aḥmad b. ʿAlī b. ʿAbdallāh al-Jumāʿī al-Wāsiṭī as follows. The Yemen was ruled over by a tubbaʿ named al-Zabā. Someone else asked, 'Whatever became of Zabā?' He replied, '*Bīd*',[8] i.e. he perished, so the area was called 'Zab bīd'.

Others say that Zabīd was called by that name because it had a wadi called Zabīd, so the town was called after the wadi.

Yet another suggested, 'Camels were pasturing in land abounding in herbage.[9] Among them was a she-camel called Zabīd and she champed away at the vegetation to

[1] Read *arḍ barrah*.

[2] Arabic *zubdah* (Lane, *Lexicon*, III, p. 1209).

[3] The second ruler (reg. 554–69/1159–73) of the Mahdid dynasty of Tihāmah (531–69/1136–73), strangled by the Ayyubids in 571/1176 after their conquest of Tihāmah and southern highlands in 569/1173 (Smith, 'Political History', p. 134–5; *EI*, 'Mahdids'; Appendix B.7 below). For this passage, see also Landberg, *Etudes*, II, pp. 930 ff.; Smith, ' "Anthropological" Passages', p. 165.

[4] I.e. Wādīs Zabīd and Rimaʿ.

[5] Arabic *al-markūb al-waṭī'* (Dozy, *Vêtements*, p. 191; Landberg, *Glossaire datînois*, II, 1387, *markūb* 'chaussure' and III, p. 2927, *waṭī'* 'sandale'; Brockett, *Khābūra*, p. 220, has *waṭiyya* 'a pair of sandals', the latter a dictionnary of the Arabic of the Bāṭinah coast of Oman).

[6] Reading *ḥawā'ij* with Landberg.

[7] I have been compelled to leave a gap here. The text appears to read *y.t.m.q.ṭ.ʿūna*. *Yamṭaʿūna*, 'they nibble', is possible, but this does not fit in well with the context.

[8] For the whole of this passage, see Smith, 'Wondrous', p. 115. It is tempting to take the word *bīd* as a dialect form of *bād*, 'he has perished' and this may be what Ibn al-Mujāwir is trying to indicate by his gloss. If, however, we take the word as non-Arabic, Sabaic, one possible explanation of *bīd* is that it is from the root *bʿd*, but with the medial *ʿayn* devoiced and thus not pronounced in this form. There is attested in Sabaic (Beeston, *Sabaic Dictionary*, p. 25) a verb, *b ʿ d*, presumably causative, *b ʿ ʿ d*, 'take away', 'carry away', i.e here reading a passive 'Zabā has been taken away' (*buʿʿida* > *buʿʿid* > *bīd* ?).

[9] Arabic *ʿuqdah*.

such an extent that the area was named after her. There certainly was rich vegetation and many arak trees which remain to this day close to al-Darb,[1] and especially a place called Ḥāfat Masjid al-Hind[2] and other places.'

Yet others say that there was a woman living at the head of Wādī Zabīd called Zubaydah. Ibn al-Mujāwir said: I think this is none other than Zubaydah bint Jaʿfar b. Abī Jaʿfar al-Manṣūr,[3] for Muḥammad b. Ziyād[4] built a residence for her between Wādī Zabīd and Rimaʿ. She it was who strove to build up the place during the caliphate of the Commander of the Faithful al-Amīn.[5]

[71] *End of the story of the Ziyadids.*[6] When al-Ḥusayn b. Salāmah died, control passed to a child of the Ziyadid family called ʿAbdallāh.[7] His paternal aunt and his slave and major-domo, called Marjān, one of al-Ḥusayn b. Salāmah's slaves, were his guardians. The vizierate rested with Marjān who had two intact Abyssinian slaves of his own. He reared them when they were young and gave them authority when they grew up. One was called Nafīs who was in charge of the administration and the other Najāḥ, [later] one of the rulers of Zabīd destroyed by ʿAlī b. al-Mahdī in 554.[8] This Najāḥ was the father of the ruler Saʿīd al-Aḥwal, the killer of ʿAlī b. Muḥammad al-Ṣulayḥī who was charged with the mission in the Yemen of al-Mustanṣir.[9] [Najāḥ] was also the father of al-Mukarram al-Fāḍil Abū al-Ṭāmī Jayyāsh.[10] The rule continued in the line of Jayyāsh until the above mentioned date. Najāḥ was in charge of the regions of al-Kadrā', al-Mahjam, Mawr and the two wadis [Zabīd and Rimaʿ]. These are the areas north of Zabīd. Then a quarrel broke out between Nafīs and Najāḥ, the slaves of Marjān, on the question of the vizierate. Now Nafīs was tyrannical and violent, while Najāḥ was just and compassionate. However, their master Marjān inclined towards Nafīs against Najāḥ. It was malevalently reported to Nafīs that Ibrāhīm b. Ziyād, his master,[11] and his paternal aunt were in correspondence with Najāḥ and that she was on his side. So [Nafīs] complained about what she had done to their master, Marjān, who seized her and her nephew, Ibrāhīm b. Ziyād, the last of the Ziyadids. He handed them over to Nafīs who built a wall around them, as they stood imploring him to spare them, until they were sealed up. Ziyadid rule came to an end and passed to the slaves of their slaves.

[1] It must be close to Zabīd and is a common place name in the Yemen. Unidentified.

[2] Unidentified as the name is given. It is possibly the same place as Ḥārat al-Hunūd (Stone, *Tihāmah*, p. 4).

[3] The well-known granddaughter of the second Abbasid caliph (see p. 33, n. 8 above).

[4] Ibn al-Mujāwir also calls him 'al-Manṣūr'. He was never given this name, as far as I am aware, and I delete it here, taking it as dittography of the previous name.

[5] Reg. 193–8/809–13.

[6] See ʿUmārah (Kay, *Yaman*, pp. 13–15).

[7] This name is doubtful and rightly queried by Kay (*Yaman*, 13).

[8] Begins 23 January 1159.

[9] The first of the Sulayhid rulers of the Yemen (reg. 439–59 or -73/1047–1066 or -88) (Smith, 'Political History', pp. 132, 138; *EI*, 'Sulayḥids'; Appendix B.5 below). They were Ismāʿīlī Shīʿīs and held the title *dāʿī*. *Faute de mieux*, I translate *daʿwah* 'mission'. Al-Mustaṣnir is the eighth Fatimid caliph, Maʿadd b. al-Ẓāhir (reg. 427–87/1035–94) (Hamdānī, *al-Ṣulayḥiyyūn*, genealogical table 7; Bosworth, *Islamic Dynasties*, p. 63).

[10] The third Najahid ruler of Tihāmah, reg. 482–98/1089–1104 (Smith, 'Political History', p. 138; Appendix B.4 below).

[11] ʿUmārah is responsible for confusing the name of this Ziyadid. Ibn al-Mujāwir, like ʿUmārah from whom he is copying (Kay, *Yaman*, pp. 13, 234–5, n. 13), would appear here to be referring to the same person who is called ʿAbdallāh above (see n. 7). The complete conundrum is discussed in Kay's n. 13 cited above.

Ziyadid rule lasted in the Yemen for 203 years: they had founded Zabīd in 204[1] and it passed from them in 407.[2]

[72] *Section*. When the Ziyadids heard of the disorder of the Abbasid dynasty,[3] the killing of al-Mutawakkil[4] and the deposition of al-Mustaʿīn,[5] they took over control of the revenue[6] of the Yemen and rode out with the ceremonial parasol. However, they kept control over their subjects by keeping the Friday address in the name of the Abbasids. When Ibrāhīm b. Ziyād was killed and his aunt seized, Nafīs took over, rode out with the ceremonial parasol, struck coins in his own name and in the name of al-Ḥusayn b. Salāmah.[7] When Najāḥ finally heard what Nafīs had done to his subjects, he rode out against Nafīs in Zabīd and a number of battles took place between the two, including Rimaʿ and Fashāl, which went against Najāḥ, and al-ʿUqdah and al-ʿIrq, in which Nafīs was killed at Sahām gate. Five thousand men were killed from both sides. Najāḥ conquered Zabīd in 412[8] and said to Marjān, 'What has your master done with our masters?' He replied, 'They are in this wall'. So Najāḥ got them out, prayed over them and built a shrine over them. He put Marjān where they had been and built a wall over him and the corpse of Nafīs.

Najāḥ rode out with a ceremonial parasol, struck coins in his own name and corresponded with the Iraqis, giving them his obedience.[9] [A communication] was sent to him granting him the honorific title al-Muʾayyad bi-Naṣr al-Dīn and the appointment of qadis and the administration of the Yemen were entrusted to him. Najāḥ continued to rule over the coastal regions and to hold sway over the highlands. He was addressed as 'our lord' and granted the title king in the Friday addresses. Of his sons were Saʿīd, Jayyāsh, Muʿārik, al-Dhakhīrah and Manṣūr. The governors of al-Ḥusayn b. Salāmah were in control of the [highland] fortresses. Aden, Lahej, Abyan, al-Shiḥr and Ḥaḍramawt were controlled by B. Maʿn b. Zāʾidah (though it is also said that they were not of the offspring of Maʿn b. Zāʾidah al-Shaybānī).[10] Some Ḥimyar called B. al-Kirandī[11] controlled

[1] Begins 28 June 819.

[2] Begins 10 June 1016.

[3] See ʿUmārah (Kay, *Yaman*, p. 15).

[4] The eleventh Abbasid caliph, Abū al-Faḍl al-Mutawakkil, was killed in 247/861; (Kay, *Yaman*, p. 15; Bosworth, *Islamic Dynasties*, p. 6).

[5] The thirteenth Abbasid caliph, Abū al-ʿAbbās al-Mustaʿīn, was deposed in 252/866 (loc. cit.).

[6] Arabic *irtifāʿ* (Kazimirski, *Dictionnaire*, I, p. 898).

[7] No coins struck by Nafīs or al-Ḥusayn b. Salāmah have been found to my knowledge. See n. 9 below.

[8] Begins 17 April 1021.

[9] See Lowick, 'Coins of the Najāḥids', pp. 545–50. Lowick published four such coins, all struck in Zabīd: not later than 422/1031; 437/1045 or 439/1047; ditto; 440/1048. By Iraqis, Ibn al-Mujāwir means the Abbasids.

[10] Ibn al-Mujāwir is correct to cast doubt on the claim that B. Maʿn, the dynasty centered on Aden prior to the Zurayʿids (473–569/1080–1173) and representatives of the Sulayhids, were descended from Maʿn b. Zāʾidah. The claim appears to have come from Ibn Khaldūn who is not to be relied upon as a historian of the Yemen (Kay, *Yaman*, p. 245, n. 20).

[11] I vocalize after reference to Maqḥafī (*Muʿjam*, pp. 536–7), but cf. Kay, *Yaman*, p. 16. See also Hamdānī, *Ṣifah*, pp. 54, 99. They were rulers of al-Maʿāfir until the 6th/12th century when they were wiped out by the 'Ghuzz' (the Ottomans, according to Maqḥafī!), the Ayyubids. Remnants of the tribe continued down to the 10th/16th century.

al-Samadān,[1] Ḥuṣn al-Sawā',[2] al-Dumluwah,[3] Ṣabir,[4] Dhakhir,[5] al-Ta'kar,[6] Mikhlāf al-Janad[7] and Mikhlāf al-Ma'āfir. The following were controlled by [73] Sultan Abū 'Abdallāh al-Ḥusayn al-Tubba'ī:[8] Ḥuṣn Ḥabb,[9] Ḥuṣn 'Azzān,[10] Bayt 'Izz,[11] Ḥuṣn al-Sha'irayn,[12] Ḥuṣn Anwar,[13] al-Naqīl,[14] al-Saḥūl,[15] Ḥuṣn Khadid[16] and al-Shawāfī.[17] The following were controlled by some of Bakīl of Hamdān:[18] Ḥuṣn Ashyaḥ, the seat of Dā'ī Saba' b. Aḥmad al-Ṣulayḥī,[19] Ḥuṣn Muqrā,[20] the fortresses of Wuṣāb and its regions.[21] Ṣan'ā' and its regions was controlled by some Hamdān. Ḥuṣn Masār[22] and Jabal

[1] Ibn al-Mujāwir is here describing the larger area of Ta'izz, particularly to the S. Clearly a site of great inaccessibility and importance in medieval times. Ḥajarī (*Majmū'*, p. 431) confirms the vocalization and calls it a fortress in the Ḥujariyyah. Maqḥafī (*Mu'jam*, 325) quotes from al-Akwa''s note (Ibn al-Dayba', *Qurrah*, I, pp. 334–5). The latter says it had only one gate and great buildings, water, grain and treasure storage. Its remains can still be seen. See also Kay, *Yaman*, p. 245.

[2] Al-Akwa' says (Ibn al-Dayba', *Qurrah*, I, p. 335, n. 1) it is adjacent to Jaba' (featured on Kay's end map) and called today Qal'at B. Khawlān.

[3] About 20 miles E, slightly N, of Ta'izz (Kay, *Yaman*, end map; Smith, *Ayyubids*, II, map I). See also Hamdānī, *Ṣifah*, p. 76.

[4] The mountain overlooking Ta'izz to the S (Smith, *Ayyubids*, II, p. 196; Botta, 'Extraits', pp. 369–81).

[5] The mountainous area SW of Ta'izz (Kay, *Yaman*, end map; Ibn al-Dayba', *Qurrah*, I, p. 335, n. 2).

[6] The huge mountain to the S of Dhū Jiblah about 30 miles N of Ta'izz (Smith, *Ayyubids*, II, p. 209; Smith, *Lightning*, pp. 49, a plan of the summit, pp. 52–5).

[7] I.e. the area around al-Janad.

[8] A ruler of B. al-Kirandī (Kay, *Yaman*, p. 242). His *nisbah* implies descent from the pre-Islamic kings of Ḥimyar.

[9] Near Ibb, just over 30 miles N of Ta'izz, less than 10 miles NE of Dhū Jiblah (Kay, *Yaman*, end map; Lamare, 'Arabie', map on p. 3, pp. 13–15; Smith, *Ayyubids*, II, p. 153–4; Smith, *Lightning*, p. 7, map 2).

[10] In the Ba'dān mountain range overlooking Ibb (Ibn al-Dayba', *Qurrah*, I, p. 336; Smith, *Lightning*, p. 7, map 2).

[11] In the vicinity of Ḥabb (Smith, *Ayyubids*, II, p. 140).

[12] Ḥajarī (*Majmū'*, III, p. 454) lists al-Sha'ir in the district of Ibb.

[13] S of the town of Ibb (Ḥajarī, *Majmū'*, I, pp. 91–2; Maqḥafī, *Mu'jam*, pp. 49–50).

[14] I wonder if Naqīl Ṣayd is meant, the mountain road N of Ibb, present-day Sumārah (Kay, *Yaman*, end map).

[15] A settlement and a wadi, the latter flowing eventually into Wādī Zabīd (Kay, *Yaman*, end map; Smith, *Ayyubids*, II, p. 197).

[16] S of Ibb in Mikhlāf Ja'far (Hamdānī, *Ṣifah*, p. 78; Smith, *Ayyubids*, II, p. 169; cf. Smith, *Lightning*, p. 7, map 2).

[17] An area to the W of Ibb (Ibn Samurah, *Ṭabaqāt*, p. 319; Smith, *Ayyubids*, II, p. 203; Ibn al-Dayba', *Qurrah*, I, p. 337, n. 2).

[18] The division of the great tribal confederation of Hamdān mainly in the highlands N of Ṣan'ā' is that of Ḥāshid and Bakīl (Hamdānī, *Ṣifah*, pp. 110–11; Caskel, *Ǧamharat an-nasab*, Tafeln 227, 230; Smith, *Ayyubids*, II, p. 226; *EI*, 'Hamdān').

[19] Kay (*Yaman*, pp. 173–4) includes Ibn Khaldūn's description of Ashyaḥ which confirms Dā'ī Saba''s association with the fortress, although it is not clear exactly where it was from this account. Maqḥafī (*Mu'jam*, p. 34) says it is 25 km NW of Ḍūrān, near Dhamār. The Sulayhid dā'ī, best known for his undying hostility towards the Najahids in Tihāmah and for his vain attempt to consummate his marriage with the famous Sulayhid queen, Arwā bint Aḥmad, died in 492/1099 (Kay, *Yaman*, p. 257; Hamdānī, *al-Ṣulayḥiyyūn*, pp. 159–60; Smith, 'Political History', p. 132).

[20] Thus in all my sources, with the exception of Maqḥafī (*Mu'jam*, p. 624), who clearly vocalizes Muqrī. It is in Ānis, SW of Ṣan'ā' (Hamdānī, *Ṣifah*, p. 104; van Arendonk, *Débuts*, p. 246, n. 7; Smith, *Ayyubids*, II, p. 185).

[21] Also Uṣāb. An extensive mountainous district between Zabīd and Ṣan'ā', about 30 miles NE of the former and lying between the upper reaches of Wādīs Rima' and Zabīd (Smith, *Ayyubids*, II, p. 214; Maqḥafī, *Mu'jam*, pp. 699–700, confirming the correct vocalization; Wuṣābī, *Tārīkh*, *passim*, but especially pp. 81–3).

[22] The highest point of the Ḥarāz mountain range about 45 miles SW of Ṣan'ā' (Kay, *Yaman*, end map; Smith, *Ayyubids*, II, p. 179).

Tays[1] were controlled by a group from Ḥarāz, where al-Ṣulayḥī arose with the mission of al-Mustanṣir.[2] In [Sulayhid] times al-Ḥusayn b. Salāmah was governor and he died in 402.[3] After his death, Amir ʿAlī b. Muḥammad al-Ṣulayḥī ruled, but he was killed on 12 Dhū al-Qaʿdah 473.[4] After his death, al-Sayyid al-Aʿẓam ʿAẓīm al-ʿArab al-Mukarram Aḥmad b. ʿAlī al-Ṣulayḥī ruled, who himself died in 484.[5] The mission was entrusted to Saba' b. Aḥmad b. al-Muẓaffar b. ʿAlī al-Ṣulayḥī.[6] After his death, Saʿīd al-Aḥwal ruled, but he was killed beneath Ḥuṣn al-Shaʿirayn in 481.[7] In this year, his brother, Jayyāsh b. Najāḥ and Khalaf b. Abī al-Ṭāhir al-Umawī, the vizier, left to travel to India. The first person to wall Zabīd was al-Ḥusayn b. Salāmah and after him the Abyssinians.

After their disappearance Shaykh ʿAlī b. al-Mahdī al-Qurtubī[8] assumed control. He ascended the throne on Friday 14 Rajab 554.[9] ʿAlī b. al-Mahdī remained there for the remainder of Rajab, Shaʿbān and Ramaḍān, then he died in Shawwāl of this year.[10] The period of his rule was two months and twenty-one days and he also laid claim to the caliphate. About him, the following was recited:

[74] Mankind, old and new, were led on by
joy of the heart and the garden of pleasure,
More desirable than cool, sweet water to the thirsty
and more delicious than the age of weak-sighted youth.
Today the caliph uses as an example after him
the two up-standing guides and his bloom,
His two young lions, his grandsons to whom
Belongs the honour of the office of amir, whilst the caliphate comes to an end.

He means by the two of them al-Mahdī and ʿAbd al-Nabī, for they both ruled over Zabīd and some of the highlands for a period of ten years and put a second wall around Zabīd.[11]

[1] A mountain range W, slightly N, of Ṣanʿā', about 40 miles distant (Kay, *Yaman*, end map).

[2] Ḥarāz is a massive mountain range about 50 miles SW of Ṣanʿā'. ʿAlī b. Muḥammad al-Ṣulayḥī who lived in the area was befriended in the early 5th/11th century by a Fatimid dāʿī in the Yemen and began actively to support the cause. Al-Mustanṣir was the eighth Fatimid caliph, reg. 427–87/1036–94 (Kay, *Yaman*, end map; Smith, 'Political History', pp. 132, 138; *EI*, 'Ṣulayḥids'; Bosworth, *Islamic Dynasties*, p. 63).

[3] Begins 4 August 1011.

[4] 24 April 1081, or, according to some sources, 459/1066 (Smith, 'Political History', pp. 132, 138).

[5] Begins 23 February 1091. Ibn al-Mujāwir means Aḥmad b. ʿAlī who had the honorific title of al-Mukarram and I have deleted his '… b. Muḥammad …'. In 467/1074 or 479/1086, he had handed over the affairs of the Sulayhid state to his wife, Arwā bint Aḥmad. It should be understood that Sulayhid dates are in great confusion and Hamdānī (*al-Ṣulayḥiyyūn*, genealogical table 2) gives Aḥmad's date of death as 477/1084. See also ʿUmārah (Kay, *Yaman*, pp. 42, 254).

[6] See above, p. 99, n. 19.

[7] Begins 27 March 1088.

[8] The first of two Mahdid rulers of Tihāmah, reg. 531–54/1136–59 (Smith, 'Political History', p. 134–5, 138; *EI*, 'Mahdids'; Appendix B.7 below). Al-Qurtub is only half a parasang from Zabīd (*Tārīkh al-Mustabṣir* text, p. 236).

[9] 22 July 1159. This is not entirely accurate. ʿAlī b. Mahdī was active in Tihāmah from about 531/1136. Certainly he did not take Zabīd until 554/1159 (Smith, 'Political History', pp. 134–5).

[10] November 1159.

[11] I have corrected Ibn al-Mujāwir's 'Muʿādh', as he surely means al-Mahdī, who with ʿAbd al-Nabī, was the son of ʿAlī b. al-Mahdī (the *sibṭ* of the text of the poem, 'grandson', should be regarded as poetic licence). It was ʿAbd al-Nabī who was the real successor of ʿAlī (ʿUmārah, Kay, *Yaman*, pp. 124–9 [beware his extremely pro-Mahdid bias!]; Smith, 'Political History', pp. 134–5).

After them the Ghuzz[1] ruled over the land, the first one to rule over it for two years being Shams al-Dīn wa-al-Dawlah Tūrān Shāh b. Ayyūb.[2] After his death, Sayf al-Dawlah Mubārak b. Kāmil b. Muqallad b. Munqidh and after his death, his brother, Khaṭṭāb, [ruled] for two years.[3] After him, Sayf al-Islām Ṭughtakīn b. Ayyūb walled the town – and put four gates in the wall: Ghulāfiqah gate, leading to Ghulāfiqah, Sahām gate, leading to Sahām, al-Shubāriq gate leading to Ḥuṣn Qawārīr, and al-Qurtub gate, leading to the mountain[4] – with earth and unburnt brick, ten cubits wide. Ibn al-Mujāwir said: I counted the number of towers of Zabīd and found them to be 109 in number. From one tower to the next was eighty cubits, while each tower was twenty cubits long, making one hundred cubits. The true circumference of the town was 10,900 cubits and it remained fortified for ten years.

One of those in Masjid al-Sidrah informed me as follows on Thursday 15 Dhū al-Qaʿdah 624:[5] Sayf al-Islām[6] intended to put a second wall around the town, long and wide. He gave orders for the troops to live between the two walls with their animals and belongings. But when he had built the wall and finished it, he died and he was not able to carry out [fully] his intention. After his death, al-Malik al-Muʿizz Ismāʿīl b. Ṭughtakīn ruled for six years.[7] After him, the Kurds for a year and after them Atabeg Sunqur for ten years.[8] After him, al-Malik al-Nāṣir Ayyūb b. Ṭughtakīn for two years and after him the Noble Ladies for three months. After them, Ghāzī b. Jibrīl for three [75] days (it is also said for seven days).[9] After him, Sulaymān Shāh b. ʿUmar b. Shāhanshāh b. Shādhī,[10] it is said for seven months, and after him al-Malik al-Masʿūd Yūsuf b. Muḥammad b. Abī Bakr b. Ayyūb.[11]

[1] I.e. the Ayyubids who controlled much of Tihāmah and the southern highlands between the years 569–628/1173–1228 (Smith, 'Political History', pp. 135–6; Appendix B.8 below).

[2] The brother of Saladin. The latter in 567/1171 had rid Egypt of the Fatimid caliphate (*EI*, 'Tūrān<u>sh</u>āh b. Ayyūb').

[3] Between 571–9/1175–83, the Yemen was controlled by deputies stationed in various parts of the country on behalf of the Ayyubid house. Mubārak was one of these deputies and put in charge of 'Zabīd and its environs and the whole of Tihāmah' (Ibn Ḥātim, *Simṭ*, pp. 20–21; Smith, *Ayyubids*, II, p. 93). There is a problem with his brother's name: Abū Makhramah (Löfgren, *Texte*, II, p. 69) also calls him Khaṭṭāb, though all the MSS of Ibn Ḥātim's *Simṭ* (p. 22), the most authoritative early source on the period, clearly have Ḥaṭṭān (Smith, 'Political History', pp. 135–6).

[4] Ghulāfiqah would have been the western gate, Sahām the northern, al-Shubāriq the eastern and al-Qurtub the southern.

[5] FLS refers me to Khazrajī (*ʿUqūd*, V, p. 142) from whose text it is clear that the mosque is opposite the gate of al-Shubāriq in Zabīd. The date is equivalent to 27 October 1227.

[6] I think here al-Malik al-ʿAzīz Ṭughtakīn b. Ayyūb, the second Ayyubid ruler in the Yemen and brother of Saladin and Tūrānshāh, 579–93/1183–97, is meant.

[7] 593–8/1196–1201.

[8] 598–609/1201–12.

[9] Al-Nāṣir was the fourth Ayyubid ruler in the Yemen, reg. 609–11/1212–4. Ibn al-Mujāwir becomes a little confused. Ghāzī b. Jibrīl had been al-Nāṣir's personal servant and had been given the fief of Lahej, N of Aden, in the time of the atabeg. He may have been responsible for the murder of al-Nāṣir in 611/1214 by giving him poison to drink. He then seized power for a brief time until he was in turn killed by the Ayyubid troops and mamluks. These same troops and mamluks decided then to grant power to al-Nāṣir's sisters. Ibn Ḥātim does not say how many they were, but I am assuming that they are Ibn al-Mujāwir's 'Noble Ladies' (Ibn Ḥātim, *Simṭ*, pp. 148, 152–4). Ibn al-Mujāwir uses the plur. (*khawātīn*) of the Persian word, *khātūn* (Lane, *Lexicon*, II, p. 704; Steingass, *Dictionary*, 437).

[10] Al-Malik al-Muʿaẓẓam Sulaymān b. ʿUmar b. Tūrānshāh b. Ayyūb b. Shādhī is his true genealogy and he was the fifth Ayyubid ruler in the Yemen, 611–2/1214–5 (Smith, *Ayyubids*, II, p. 50; Appendix B.8 below).

[11] 612–26/1215–28. The reason that Ibn al-Mujāwir gives no period of reign for al-Masʿūd, the sixth and final Ayyubid ruler in the Yemen, is that in all probability he was writing during his period of rule.

Al-Janābidh[1] *and the killing of al-Ṣulayḥī.* These are three domes built of smooth bricks[2] and gypsum, each one being four cubits from another. They were built by Amir ʿAlī b. Muḥammad al-Ṣulayḥī. He intended to build a mosque every stage of the way from Zabīd to Mecca, and also a hospice.[3] He would be remembered by [this deed] after his death. He went on building until he reached al-Mahjam and he stopped outside the town in a garden called Biʾr Umm al-Duhaym and Biʾr Khaymat Umm Maʿbad.[4] Saʿīd al-Aḥwal b. Najāḥ said, 'When we entered the encampment, no one noticed us except ʿAbdallāh b. Muḥammad [al-Ṣulayḥī],[5] who rode off, saying [to his brother], "Ride on, my lord. This is indeed al-Aḥwal b. Najāḥ and the gang about whom [the warning letter] of Asʿad b. Shihāb[6] arrived yesterday evening from Zabīd."' Al-Ṣulayḥī said to his brother ʿAbdallāh, 'I shall die only in Umm al-Duhaym and Khaymat Umm Maʿbad', thinking that she was the Umm Maʿbad with whom the Prophet stayed – God bless him and grant him peace – when he emigrated, accompanied by Abū Bakr.[7] Someone said to ʿAlī, 'Fight for your life for this is Biʾr Umm al-Duhaym b. ʿAbs and this mosque is Khaymat Umm Maʿbad bint al-Ḥārith al-ʿAbsī!'[8] Jayyāsh said, 'Al-Ṣulayḥī despaired for his life and wet his trousers. But he did not budge and we cut off his head with his own sword. I was the first person to pierce him, but ʿAbdallāh b. Najāḥ took part with me in dealing a thrust. I cut off his head with my own hands and set it up on the pole of the parasol.' Al-ʿUthmānī recited as follows about him:

> What an ugly face he had in the shade [of the parasol]
> and what a fine head on the pole![9]

Saʿīd entered Zabīd on 16 Dhū al-Qaʿdah 473.[10] [76] Saʿīd al-Aḥwal was killed in the battle of Ḥuṣn al-Shaʿirayn in 481.[11] When the dynasties of the Sulayhids and the Abyssinians came to an end, ʿAlī b. al-Mahdī ruled over [Tihāmah]. After his death the Mahdids, ʿAbdallāh, al-Mahdī and ʿAbd al-Nabī[12] assumed control and they built a

[1] Persian *junbadh*, *gunbad*, which means 'dome' (Löfgren, *Texte*, II, p. 26, 70; Serjeant, 'Tihāmah Notes', pp. 47–8).

[2] It is suggested that Ibn al-Mujāwir's *maḥkūk* might be a misheard *maḥrūq*, 'burnt' (Serjeant, 'Tihāmah Notes', pp. 48, 58 n. 10).

[3] Arabic *ribāṭ*.

[4] Cf. ʿUmārah (Kay, *Yaman*, pp. 82–5) for the true context of the anecdote which follows. ʿUmārah calls the garden simply Umm al-Duhaym and perhaps Ibn al-Mujāwir's 'Biʾr' should be deleted. It is necesssary to understand that, after the Sulayhids had reached the garden of Umm al-Duhaym, Saʿīd al-Aḥwal arrived there. See also Stone, 'Gazetteer', p. 241.

[5] ʿAlī's brother (Hamdānī, *al-Ṣulayḥiyyūn*, genealogical table 2).

[6] He was the brother-in-law of ʿAlī b. Muḥammad al-Ṣulayḥī and his governor of Zabīd. He had clearly been trying to warn ʿAlī of the arrival of the Najahids, his great enemies (ʿUmārah in Kay, *Yaman*, pp. 25–6).

[7] She was a Kaʿbiyyah of the tribe of Khuzāʿah. According to a poem quoted by Ṭabarī, *Tārīkh*, II, p. 380/*History*, VI, p. 149, she gave hospitality to the Prophet and Abū Bakr as they journeyed from Mecca to Medina during the *hijrah* and they rested in her 'two tents', *khaymatay Umm Maʿbad*.

[8] I.e. two local Yemeni women. The *nisbah* is in all probability derived from the town of ʿAbs, NW of Ḥajjah, although there is also a district of al-Maḥwīt and a village near Radāʿ (Maqḥafī, *Muʿjam*, p. 425).

[9] These verses are quoted by Abū Makhramah (Löfgren, *Texte*, II, p. 163) and the otherwise unidentified poet is called al-Qāḍī al-ʿUthmānī.

[10] 28 April 1081.

[11] Begins 27 March 1088.

[12] The text actually reads 'After his death the Mahdids assumed control, ʿAbdallāh, Muʿādh and ʿAbd al-Nabī, ...'. There is some confusion about the succession after the death of ʿAlī in 554/1159. There was a quarrel among his three sons, al-Mahdī, ʿAbdallāh and ʿAbd al-Nabī, the latter eventually coming out on top (ʿUmārah, Kay, *Yaman*, p. 129).

tomb for ʿAlī. They used to call their troops the Muhājirūn and the Anṣār and say, 'Circumambulate the tomb of Shaykh ʿAlī b. al-Mahdī as they circumambulate the garden of the Prophet – God bless him and grant him peace.'[1] It was commonly said that Jabal Qawārīr is ʿArafāt, al-Janābidh the Kaʿbah, the Zamzam well and this tomb the garden of the Prophet – God bless him and grant him peace.

It is said that Sayf al-Dawlah[2] took great wealth from the domes, but now a group of the poor from the descendants of Shaykh Muḥammad b. Abī Bakr b. Abī al-Bāṭil al-Ṣarīfī live there.[3] Badr al-Dīn Maḥmūd b. Jammāz al-Fallāḥ al-Mawṣilī built a square wall around the domes.[4] Jamāl al-Dīn Abū al-Ḥusayn ʿAlī b. Muḥammad b. Wuhayb[5] had already built some steps by means of which one could climb up above the domes by donkey. The inhabitants of Zabīd used to say when they saw someone doing this, 'Muḥammad has mounted al-Burāq[6] and climbed to the highest point of heaven.' Others used to say, 'Jesus has mounted his donkey.'

It is said that mosques were constructed; another version is that it was the tomb of some of its inhabitants. There was some writing inside the domes in gold and lapis lazuli and an inscription has been made in the gypsum which will last forever and the following is an illustration of it.[7]

Ibn al-Mujāwir said: I arrived at the mosque during the latter part of Dhū al-Ḥijjah 626.[8] I saw the place where al-Ṣulayḥī was killed. A mosque had been built on a hill near it called Masjid ʿArafāt, but nothing remains of it except ruins. All these lands round the mosque are the property of Qadi Ibrāhīm b. Ṣāliḥ, the judge in al-Mahjam. The following is a plan of the town of Zabīd; God – praise to Him – knows best and is most wise. [77. Plan of Zabīd, see Fig. 3]

[78] *Description of Dār Shukār b. Jaʿfar.*[9] When Ibn Ziyād was in Zabīd,[10] Shukhār b. Jaʿfar built the ruler's residence there, long and wide, [made of] baked bricks and gypsum, a building safe against robbers. Every ruler in Zabīd lived there. It had a very high door through which they could see anyone on the road at a distance of two parasangs. A huge, wide trench was dug around it. The door remained as it was until al-Masʿūd Yūsuf b. Abī Bakr destroyed it in 618.[11] Amir Aybak al-ʿAzīzī[12] had also tried

[1] Imitating the names allotted to the followers of Muḥammad in Medina, 'those who emigrated', those who had been in Mecca with him, and the 'Helpers', his supporters in Medina. 'the garden of the Prophet' is the Kaʿbah in Mecca.

[2] Ibn al-Mujāwir may mean Sayf al-Islam, al-Malik al-ʿAzīz Ṭughtakīn b. Ayyūb (see above p. 101, n. 6).

[3] Al-Sharjī (*Ṭabaqāt*, pp. 282–3) lists one Abū ʿAbdallāh Muḥammad b. ʿAbdallāh b. Abī al-Bāṭil al-Ṣarīfī who died in Aden, although no date is given. If Ibn al-Mujāwir's pedigree is correct, he would be the cousin of the above. B. Ṣarīf are of the tribe of ʿAkk in Tihāmah (Maqḥafī, *Muʿjam*, p. 380).

[4] Unidentified. Since he is from Mosul, he may well have been in the train of the Ayyubids in the Yemen. There is no wall shown in the plan of Zabīd.

[5] Unidentified.

[6] The fabulous animal on which the Prophet travelled from Mecca to Jerusalem and thence ascended into heaven (*SEI*, 'Burāḳ').

[7] There is in fact no illustration.

[8] November 1229.

[9] Somewhat surprisingly not mentioned by ʿUmārah and not identified.

[10] I.e. some time after 204/819 when the town was founded.

[11] Begins 25 February 1221.

[12] Presumably a mamluk of al-Malik al-ʿAzīz Ṭughtakīn, the 2nd Ayyubid ruler in the Yemen (reg. 579–93/1183–97) (Smith, 'Political History', p. 138).

[77]

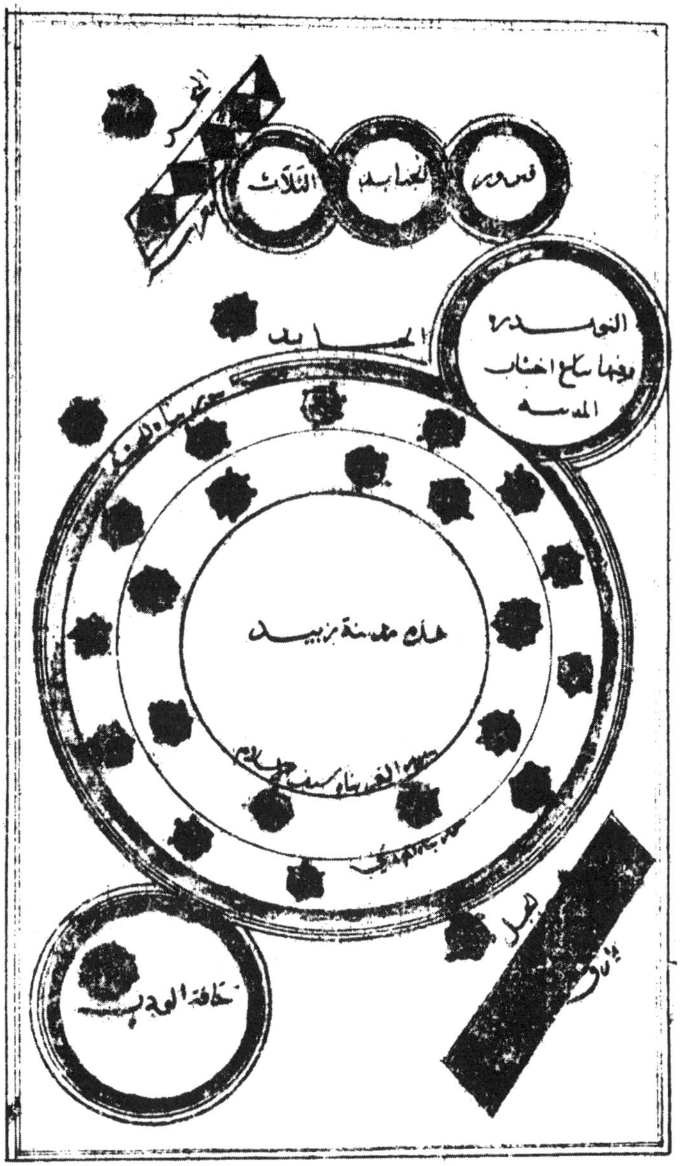

Figure 3. Plan of Zabīd (I MS, f. 31b, text, p. 77, tabula III)

The main concentric circles represent the various walls of the town: the outer built by the Abyssinians (i.e. the Najahids, – see 'Historical Background, The Yemen, Najahids'), next the wall built by al-Mahdī – he means the Mahdids (531–69/1136–73, see Historical background, the Yemen, Mahdids); finally the inner circle, the Ghuzz wall, built by the second Ayyubid ruler of the Yemen, Ṭughtakīn b. Ayyūb, reg. 579–93/1183–97 (see 'Historical Background, The Yemen, Ayyubids'). Three small circles at the top depict the three domes mentioned in the text. The larger circle attached to the main outer wall at two o'clock reads, 'al-Nuwaydirah[?], where the town's woods [i.e. for construction] are sold'. The small circle directly opposite at eight o'clock is marked Ḥāfat al-Widn. There are also two rectangles with diamond-shaped patterns: that at the top to the left of the three domes reads, 'sea, west'; that at the bottom to the right of Ḥāfat al-Widn reads 'mountain, east'.

[The reader is urged to refer to the excellent article by Sadek ('Zabīd'). She surveys the town throughout the medieval period, specifically relating this plan to her findings in the Yemenite histories. One interesting point which she makes is that the circular (or more correctly in reality, pear-shaped) lay-out of the town was a deliberate copy of Baghdad. Zabīd has been referred to as the 'Baghdad of the Yemen'.]

to destroy it. When [al-Masʿūd] did demolish it, he took the bricks and anything which remained of them and built houses with them. The building was destroyed from the very foundations. Traces of this door and the steps [going up] like a lofty mountain have remained until now. God knows best.

The removal of the Arabs from Tihāmah. When the Arabs had settled in numbers there, Commander Rayḥān al-Kahlānī, the client of Saʿīd b. Najāḥ, made a surprise attack by night[1] on the Arabs stationed at the gate of Zabīd. They numbered 3,000 cavalry and 10,000 infantry. He attacked them and only a small number of them escaped; the rest perished and the Arabs gave up Tihāmah after this. God – praise be to Him – knows best, is wisest.

Date palms. The first person to plant date palms was Amir ʿAlī b. Muḥammad al-Ṣulayḥī. It is also said it was the Abyssinians at the beginning of the rule of ʿAlī b. al-Mahdī.[2] When the Abyssinians were there, a caravan arrived from the Hejaz, carrying dates. They would eat the dates and throw the stones down. Because of the dampness of the soil, date palms grew.[3] [79] When the inhabitants of the area saw this,[4] they learned how to plant [palms]; they planted them and they became numerous. They are [planted in] ten strips of land: al-Abyaḍ, al-Kudayḥā, al-Majrashiyyah, al-Maḥallah, al-Athil, al-Majāziʿ, Karwah, al-Maḥjar, al-Qahīrā, al-Maghāris and Ḥujnah. Each one of these strips was one quarter of a parasang wide and [the same measurement] long.

As for the fully ripe dates[5] there, they were of three varieties: *ḥumārī*, *ṣufārī* and *khuḍārī*,[6] each one of them having different kinds. When the palm was full of fruit, everyone would have a leasing contract[7] drawn up according to what he could afford. People would come there from Ḥaraḍ, as far as the furthest regions of Abyan and the mountain dwellers would come down to Tihāmah. How many women were divorced on account of the date palm! How many women were given sexual pleasure on account of the date palm! A poet recited as follows:

> This is the reddening, the pollinating, while the spadix has already opened up.[8]
> O spinning women, spin [your charms], for the dates are already beginning to ripen![9]

[1] Reading *bayyata al-ʿArab* with ʿUmārah (Kay, *Yaman*, p. 33).

[2] 'The Abyssinians' would appear to mean simply the black population of Tihāmah who, after the policy of the Najahids to import people in large numbers from Africa to populate Tihāmah, would probably have been in the majority (Smith, 'Wondrous', p. 115, quoting Löfgren's *Tārīkh al-Mustabṣir*, p. 235).

[3] Arabic *ṭalaʿa al-nakhl* which I take here in the general sense given. Cf. Lane, *Lexicon*, V, pp. 1867–9, 'the palm trees put forth the spadix (*ṭalʿ*)' (see below n. 5).

[4] I.e. the area around Zabīd. Among the names of the strips below, FLS has given me the al-Kudayḥā reading and suggested the Ḥujnah vocalization.

[5] Arabic *ruṭab*. See p. 36, n. 9 above.

[6] So called because of their colours: red, yellow and green respectively.

[7] Arabic *yataqabbalu*, i.e. he has a *qabālah*, a contract which permits him to exploit the land in return for a tax in cash or in kind (Dozy, *Supplément*, II, pp. 305–6).

[8] See Varisco, *Agriculture*, p. 158. *Shaqaḥ* perhaps for *tashqīḥ*, *laqaḥ* for *talqīḥ*.

[9] *Balaḥ* is the date in its first stage of development after pollination and difficult to translate, the stage before the *busr*, the nearly ripe, and then the *ruṭab*, the fully ripe date (Varisco, *Agriculture*, pp. 193–4, an excellent description of date cultivation). DMV is right in noting the reference here to the carousals about to take place between the sexes (*Agriculture*, p. 158).

Another recited:

> He who has experience of date palms and leasing contracts
> becomes weak in his heart.
> Because of them he lives an unhappy life
> and debt takes hold of him, no doubt about it!

The people remain among the palms for two or three months, most of them eating bitter and salty plants and playing, laughing and drinking. Wine called *faḍīkh* is made from dates, wheat and ripe dates and its manufacture takes exactly one day and one night. The women drink with the men. They say that it is beneficial, but its harm outweighs its benefit.

The first person to make it in this region was a Syrian.[1] He would earn 90,000 dinars a year, apart from what went into the treasury, to the sultan's workers and civil servants,[2] apart from the [income of] royal palm groves and pious endowments and apart from [the income of dates] belonging to high-ranking people and members of the ruling house. The total income of what we have mentioned above is exactly [80] 130,000 dinars. Tax[3] [on dates] during the Abyssinian dynasty and in the days of the Mahdids was 70,000 dinars per annum. This was not taken in cash, but rather in dates. Credit slips[4] were issued and the rate of conversion was three *jā'iz* to a dirham, four dirhams to a dinar and four and a half dinars to a gold dinar.[5] The tax[6] on date palms was only thus because Sayf al-Islām enjoined Ṭughtakīn b. Ayyūb[7] to act justly towards the farmers and oppressively towards the date palm growers. This is something which they started during his time. Someone said to him on this subject, 'The peasant ploughs, waters, sows, harvests, digs and winnows, experiencing great hardship; you must treat him kindly. Date palm growers, however, pick the fruit from year to year without working hard or becoming exhausted. God – He is ever almighty – has said, "... and the date palms, lofty, they have flowers in rows".'[8] If any owner of a date palm deserts it, the sultan takes it for himself as tax from him. All those palms taken by the sultan are called *ṣawāfī*, i.e. taken exclusively[9] for the treasury.

Ibn al-Mujāwir said: The wealth of the date palms in 624[10] was 110,000 dinars cash, apart from what was put into the treasury. The inhabitants of Zabīd recited as follows in this year:

> It's what the palm trees want, not what Zabīd wants;
> it is forced to depend upon the stroke of fortune and is knocked about by a palm branch.[11]

[1] Arabic *rajul min ahl al-shām*, which might also mean someone from the north of Tihāmah.

[2] Arabic *nuwwāb al-dīwān*.

[3] Arabic *ḍamān*.

[4] Arabic *ḥawālāt* (Dozy, *Supplément*, I, p. 341, 'une lettre de crédit').

[5] Arabic *dīnār aḥmar* (Dozy, *Supplément*, I, p. 322).

[6] Arabic *kharāj*.

[7] Ibn al-Mujāwir gets these honorific titles confused. I think this must refer to Tūrānshāh, giving advice to his brother, Ṭughtakīn, the first and second Ayyubid rulers of the Yemen respectively.

[8] Quran 50:10. *Ṭal'* here meaning rather the flowers or first fruit (Lane, *Lexicon*, V, p. 1869; Penrice, *Dictionary*, pp. 91, 148).

[9] Arabic *yuṢFā*. See also Dozy, *Supplément*, I, p. 838, *al-ṣawāfī*, 'ce qui a été confisqué'.

[10] Begins 22 December 1226.

[11] This line is corrupt and difficult to interpret, the second hemistitch in particular where I read *mulimmah* with OL; the message is that Zabīd's prosperity, or lack of it, depended entirely on the date crop.

It was only the governor, Amir al-Ṣārim ... al-Kāmilī,[1] who appropriated this wealth. If anyone weighed out [some dates] in front of him, he would weigh out twice as much [for himself]. When the dates had finished, the young and the old and the good and the bad would go forth with drum and pipe, after dressing up a camel in full attire, with bells and pellet drums[2] and veils and ornaments tied round its neck. Four people would ride to a camel and others in litters, and they would process to a mosque overlooking the sea shore. The place is a blessed place containing the footprint and the mark of the chest of the she-camel of Muʿādh b. Jabal.[3] When he returned [81] from the Yemen [on his way] to the Hejaz after the Prophet's death – God bless him and grant him peace – he passed through this area and along these shores. This place is called al-Fāzah;[4] it is where they go down to the sea. The women go into the sea with the men, all mixed together,[5] drinking, playing, dancing and revelling. They only go out to these places on two days of the week, Monday and Thursday. When they return from there, they enter the town in a body.

The fragrant screw-pine.[6] It is a tree that grows in the area of the mosque of Muʿādh b. Jabal. It is like a date-palm. [It has] a flower like the aloes[7] which is cultivated in Iraq and India in the main centres on the roofs of tower-houses.[8] But the leaves of the fragrant screw-pine are thin, like the leaves of the date-palm, thorny and rough. Its flower is formed only by the flashing of lightning. If there is lightning flashing, it will

[1] The given name eludes me and I assume he was a mamluk of al-Malik al-Kāmil Muḥammad, nephew of Saladin, Tūrānshāh and Ṭughtakīn, and father of the sixth and final Ayyubid ruler of the Yemen, al-Masʿūd Yūsuf (*EI*, 'Ayyūbids'; Smith, *Ayyubids*, II, Appendix B.1, p. 50).

[2] I am very grateful to FLS for her suggested meaning which I am happy to follow here (Stone. *Tihāmah*, p. 106, with a drawing of a *qulqulah* at fig. 7.3). We have here only the plur. form, *qalāqil* and I had originally taken the word to indicate the *qilqil* plant (D. II, p. 399). Of this plant, DMV writes: In the herbals this generally refers to a kind of wild senna. The species in the Yemen is probably *Cassia obtusifolia* L. (Miller and Morris, *Plants*, p. 162 [the whole genus]; Wood, *Handbook*, p. 165).

[3] He was an early representative of the Prophet in the Yemen (Serjeant, *Ṣanʿāʾ*, p. 53; Guillaume, *Life*, p. 644). Perhaps his most famous religious foundation was the mosque of al-Janad, now a suburb of Taʿizz, studied by Costa ('Mosque', 43–68). This is *not* the mosque mentioned in my Addenda and Corrigenda concerning p. 121, n. 13 of my 'Wondrous' article (*Studies*, Add. and Corr., p. 2) and this should now be corrected accordingly. The mosque in the text is evidently 'overlooking the sea shore' and FLS now makes it clear to me that the other Masjid Muʿādh is where Wādī Zabīd '*debouches onto the plain* of Tihāmah'.

[4] This place name may be al-Fāzzah (Cf. Smith, *Ayyubids*, II, p. 151 and map 1). At any rate it is a natural deep water harbour which served Zabīd as early as the Ziyadids (Maqḥafī, *Muʿjam*, p. 489; Stone, 'Gazetteer', p. 252–53).

[5] Arabic *khulayṭ mulayṭ*. D (II, p. 612) has *khalṭ malṭ*, 'pêle-mêle', also Landberg, *Glossaire daṯînois*, I, 634, although *m l ṭ* also carries the connotation of mixing (Kazimirski, *Dictionnaire*, II, p. 1148).

[6] Arabic *kādhī*, *Pandanus odoratissimus* L (Dimyāṭī, *Muʿjam*, p. 131; Varisco, *Agriculture*, p. 199). For this passage, see Smith, 'Wondrous', pp. 113–14.

[7] Arabic *ṣabirah*. Often identified as *Aloe soccotrina* Dec. (Dimyāṭī, *Muʿjam*, p. 87; Forbes, *Natural History*, pp. xxxiv and 509 ff.). However Miss Rosemary King of the Royal Botanic Garden, Edinburgh, informs me (letter 25 July 1985) that *Aloe soccotrina* is not recorded in the Arabian Peninsula proper. Wood, 'Flora' in Stone (*Studies*, pp. 15, 17) states that *ṣabir* is *Aloe vera* and this may be what is meant here. I am extremely grateful to Miss King for her botanical assistance here and throughout this passage. DMV adds: There are 17 species of aloe in the Yemen, one of the more common being *Aloe vera* L. (Wood, *Handbook*, p. 401).

[8] I.e. perhaps in the early stages of growth. For *darb*, see Smith, *Ayyubids*, II, p. 122. Cf. Landberg, *Glossaire daṯînois*, I, p. 731, 'sur les plates-formes des murailles'.

develop in great profusion. But if there is no lightning, nothing of it appears. This is a wondrous thing. '[God] creates what you do not know.'[1]

In the same way mariners seek direction to the region of Sumatra simply by means of the frequent flashes of lightning, since in the season of travel to Sumatra the rains are abundant, the sky completely overcast and the sea very rough.[2]

Others have remarked that many *sandarūs* trees grow in these parts[3] and when the resin runs from the tree, the sea appears to travellers like the flashing of lightning. This is because of the great number of waves which throw the ship up and dash it down.

They say the fragrant screw-pine develops with lightning. In the same way the flower of the henna[4] is open only on moonlit nights. The cucumber turns around with the sun, as does the lily[5]. The tide is higher on a dark night. Any piece of wood cut on moonlit nights is attacked by woodworm and any wood cut when the moon is on the wane is destroyed by woodworm.[6] Millstones are cut out only on moonlit nights. All the waters of the earth are cut off when Canopus is in the ascendant.

The tanning of leather can only be done without blemish [82] during this time. Rabbān b. Jubayr said, 'When Canopus is in the ascendant, the water of the sea drops forty cubits.' There is nothing more sweet smelling among all odoriferous plants than the fragrant screw-pine flower. Its juice is cool, drying and beneficial for anyone with fever and bathed in sweat. The Indians call it *keora*.[7]

Description of Zabīd. The Prophet – God bless him and grant him peace – called it the land of al-Ḥuṣayb. [We know this] because the Prophet said to Muʿādh b. Jabal, 'Muʿādh, when you arrive in the land of al-Ḥuṣayb, hurry on, for there are women there like the houris [of paradise].'

[1] Quran 16:8.

[2] Arabic al-Jāwah, i.e. Sumatra (Ibn Baṭṭūṭah, *Travels*, IV, p. 873, Beckingham's n. 18). Arabic 'wa-yastaddu al-ufuq bi-al-ghamām wa-yashtaddu hayajān al-baḥr'.

[3] *Tetraclinis articulata*, whose resin is called sandarac(h), is named 'alerce' in Britain and 'arartree' in America (Dallimore and Jackson, *Handbook*, pp. 602–3). Miss King informs me that it belongs to the same family, the Cupressacceae, as the junipers (hence, one assumes, the corruption of the Arabic *ʿarʿar* in the American name), but the two genera are not closely related. See Dozy, *Supplément*, I, p. 693; Steingass, *Dictionary*, p. 701. The alerce has not been recorded in the Arabian Peninsula, nor in Sumatra, and we must therefore confess that Ibn al-Mujāwir's words 'in these parts' remain unclear. With reference to Ibn al-Mujāwir's remarks on the effect of lightning, Miss King writes, 'there can be sufficient light intensity in moonlight and lightning to affect the photoperiod of plants ... I would guess the author's suggestions are coincidence, that the flowers occur at the same time as a period of electric storms or are perhaps more noticeable at this time.' We should perhaps add that it is a typical Ibn al-Mujāwir story!

[4] Arabic *ḥannūn*, *L. inernis* Linn. in the Yemen (DMV) (Lane, *Lexicon*, II, p. 654).

[5] The cucumber in Arabic is *khiyār*, *Cucumis sativus* Linn. The text reads *laynūfar/ naylūfar*. DMV: This term usually refers to the water lily. The only recorded variety from modern Yemen is *Nymphaea coerulea* Sav. (Wood, *Handbook*, p. 65).

[6] A not untypical Ibn al-Mujāwir aporia! There is perhaps a negative missing here: 'Any piece of wood cut on moonlit nights is *not* attacked by woodworm.' There may rather be a distinction between 'attacked by woodworm', unsuccessfully, and 'destroyed by woodworm'. Dionisius Agius informs me that he discusses the best time for the cutting of wood in Gulf and Oman tradition in a forthcoming book, *Seafaring in the Arabian Gulf: the People of the Dhow*. DMV adds: See my *Agriculture*, p. 103... I can see the logic of not cutting when the moon is waning (there are parallels with other agricultural acts), but I cannot find evidence for or against the first part. I suspect Ibn al-Mujāwir is not using the classical sources, as the almanacs tend to do.'

[7] The Persian word *kiyūrā* (Steingass, *Dictionary*, p. 1071). Miss King writes, 'oil distilled from the bracts of the male flowers ... is called "Keora" in India.'

Al-Hubaytī recited the following:

Tell her gardens I will change them
[by producing] a violent flood like that of Mārib.
Will wine be drunk in the hills of Aden,
while brown and white go thirsty in al-Ḥuṣayb?

By him is also the following:

Oft-times I went down to al-Ḥuṣayb
with a chieftain who showed most hatred towards the Persians![1]
Violent winds in Ḥuṣaybah blew against
its Abyssinians and there was grumbling against the false claimant.[2]

The following is by Ibn al-Mujāwir:

Fate has sentenced the lover and the beloved
to be far apart; can there be a platonic reunion?
One of them is frantically murmuring in the land of the Hejaz,
while the other is love sick in the land of al-Ḥuṣayb!

[83] The land is called Tihāmah which is a part of the Yemen.[3] The latter is a series of mountain chains, all of them overlooking the Red Sea to the west. East of it is the region of Ṣaʿdah, Ḥaraḍ and Najrān, north of it the borders of Mecca and south of it from Ṣanʿāʾ for a distance of about ten stages. [Tihāmah] is called al-Shām in Aden and al-Yaman in al-Mahjam. It is called Kūsh among Āl ʿImrān[4] and in general parlance Zabīd. [It is called] the province of the Yemen, because it is [the land to] the right of the *qiblah*. The Prophet – God bless him and grant him peace – said, 'I can indeed find the essence of the Merciful One through the Yemen.' The meaning of this lies in what he said to Uways al-Qaranī[5] who used to sigh, yearning for the Prophet. Because of this, the Prophet gave him the following information, saying, 'The Kaʿbah is Yemeni, the right corner is Yemeni and the faith is Yemeni.' The Prophet mentioned many different connections with the Yemen: Canopus of the Yemen, onyx of the Yemen, carnelian of the Yemen. A poet recited as follows:

By the lord of the throne, may you be far removed from one you love!
Your desire is in Iraq, while you are a Yemeni!

Another said:

She said to one of her sisters who reminds her [of her lover],
wanting through her only to trouble me,
'Say to her indeed without any blame,
"What do you want by delaying so long in the Yemen?"'

[1] I take this as a reference to the conquest of the Yemen by the Persians under Wahriz in AD 575, driving out the Abyssinians, but replacing one colonial rule for another (Serjeant, *Ṣanʿāʾ*, p. 51).

[2] Presumably a reference to the Najahids, and I wonder if the 'false claimant' is ʿAlī b. Mahdī who was the object of any number of attacks on his political and religious aims (Smith, 'Political History', pp. 134–5; *EI*, 'Mahdids').

[3] See Landberg, *Etudes*, p. 868, n. 1.

[4] Kūsh, the eldest son of Ham in the Bible, is linked vaguely with Arabia and the Red Sea area (*EI*, 'Kūsh'). Āl ʿImrān remains something of a mystery in this context. DMV makes the very plausible suggestion that this is a reference to the ancient civilizations, i.e. *ʿumrān* in a generic sense.

[5] Unidentified.

Yet another said:

> There is no foreign traveller, even if he shows his endurance,
> who will not remember his native land after a long journey,
> Except an Iraqi and an Egyptian, for they
> do not return if they get as far as the Yemen.

Qays b. al-Mulawwaḥ al-ʿĀmirī recited as follows:[1]

> Oh, the only eagle I love is one soaring up;[2]
> the only lightning that which is Yemeni.

[84] Ibn al-Mujāwir said [in Persian]:

> What did I not fix on to this? What have I seen like the sea of Aden?
> The sigh of the son of man burns up everything there is; oh woe, alas…

The following is by al-Ḥusām al-Kirmānī [in Persian]:[3]

> I said, 'What is your face [made of], red rose or jasmine?'
> He replied, 'It is a rose, scattered over a leaf of jasmine.'
> I said, 'Are your lips made of sugar or of carnelian?'
> He replied, 'They are both sugar and carnelian, but not from the Yemen.'

The interpretation of this Persian poem by al-Ḥusām al-Kirmānī is as follows in Arabic: I said to him, 'Is your face a rose or jasmine?' He replied, 'It is a rose scattered on a jasmine leaf.' I said, 'Are your lips sugar or carnelian?' He replied, 'Of both sugar and carnelian, but not carnelian which is from the Yemen.', i.e. the place called ʿAqīq al-Yaman [the carnelian of the Yemen].

The following is by Ibn al-Rujā[?]:[in Persian][4]

> Because of that rosy cheek and that down like wild rose,
> They call him 'spring' in every gathering.
> This time it is more marvellous, for his face is like spring,
> And then again his face looks like Canopus of the Yemen.

The interpretation of these two verses in Arabic is as follows: Because of that fiery cheek and streak like a wild rose [85], he is called 'meadows' in every gathering place. More wondrous than this is that his cheek is like meadows and the prominent part of it like Canopus of the Yemen.

Outside this town, [Zabīd,] it is hot, while inside it is cool and dry. Its climate is not conducive to [producing] saffron because it is eaten by woodworm within a few days. But a more accurate statement is that saffron dries up of its own accord; when the top of the sack is opened, the dryness flies out into the air. This is saffron [itself], while the body of the plant changes into dust. The water of the town is from wells.

The people [of Zabīd] are dusky, dark-eyed with scanty beards,[5] a weak physique and their heads shaved. It is the same in the whole of North Africa, Alexandria, the

[1] See p. 54, n. 14 above.

[2] Reading *nasr* with OL.

[3] Ibn al-Mujāwir's lines in Persian are corrupt and obscure. Edmund Bosworth has kindly looked into this poetry for me and draws my attention to de Blois, *Persian Literature*, pp. 337–8, no. 205, where the author cites Ibn al-Mujāwir's quotation. Nothing else is known of the Persian poet.

[4] Unidentified Persian poet.

[5] Persian *kawāsij*, *kawsaj/kūsaj* (Steingass, *Dictionary*, p. 1062).

Meccans, the Abyssinians and the Beja,[1] but no one [of the latter] shaves his head until he kills someone. The women of Zanzibar, black slave girls, the inhabitants of Khwārazm, Shaʿshaʿīn,[2] the Bulghars, ...,[3] Allān,[4] the Daylamites,[5] all these people, including qadis, mystics, imams and the general public are like pilgrims, as God – He is ever powerful and glorious – has said, '... shaving your heads, cutting [your hair] short.'[6] There are also children, the Jews, Indian pilgrims and all the regions of the Yemen, mountain folk and those of the coastal plains [who all shave their heads].

Their womenfolk are of sweet disposition,[7] with loose trouser waists,[8] extremely flirtatious in what they say, this being an indication that desire in their womenfolk is stronger than that in their menfolk; thus they use perfume because it arouses sexual passion. Makḥūl al-Shāmī said, 'You must use perfume; anyone with a good smell has more intelligence and anyone with a clean robe has little anxiety.' ʿUmar b. al-Khaṭṭāb[9] – God be pleased with him – said, 'If I were a merchant, I would choose to deal in perfume; if I cannot make a profit out of it, I still have its sweet smell!'

The wives of the inhabitants of [Zabīd][10] do not take a dowry from their husbands; taking a dowry is with them a great disgrace. Every woman who takes a dowry from her husband is called 'hated'.[11] That is her husband has given her her dowry and has grown to hate her,[12] i.e. has divorced her. If this happens, men's desire for her diminishes, because a [prospective] husband would say the following, 'I am afraid she will take [86] a dowry from me, as she took it from someone else.' Perhaps the man will not have the ability to pay back the dowry and the women will say among themselves, 'Her husband can only drive her away with her dowry [returned to her] because he has little desire for her and she is in disgrace.'

When a man intends to marry a woman, the women of the quarter come to the woman without fear and say to her, 'Hate your husband before he hates you!' That is, give him the dowry and leave before he pays it and drives you out. At festivities and weddings, they give monetary gifts – as has already been mentioned in the description of Mecca.[13]

If a woman gives for a wedding, the same sum is returned for a wedding [in her family]. If it is for a circumcision, it is returned to her for a circumcision; if it is for a birth, it is returned for a birth and everything is done on the basis of strict reciprocity.

[1] The Sudanese tribe inhabiting the African Red Sea coastal plain from about ʿAydhāb in the north down to the Abyssinian border in the south (Ḥasan, *Arabs*, map and *passim*).

[2] Unidentifed.

[3] The text is corrupt and unintelligible here.

[4] A conjectural reading. One of the districts of the Khazars in the province of Arrān (Le Strange, *Lands*, p. 179).

[5] Living in the highlands of Gīlān, SW of the Caspian Sea (Le Strange, *Lands*, pp. 172–4 and map V; *EI*, 'Daylam').

[6] Quran 48:27, a direct reference to pilgrims.

[7] Arabic *khaliqāt* (Kazimirski, *Dictionnaire*, I, p. 625).

[8] Arabic *rikhawāt al-tikak*.

[9] The second Orthodox caliph, reg. 13–23/634–44.

[10] See Landberg, *Etudes*, II, pp. 826–30.

[11] Arabic *mafrūkah*.

[12] Arabic *farika-hā*.

[13] Pp. 34–5 of the *Tārīkh al-Mustabṣir* text above.

Aḥmad b. Masʿūd[1] informed me saying, 'A woman in the Yemen becomes corrupt only in the practice of the monetary gift.' I asked why this was. He replied, 'Because [other] women give her a loan in advance and she has nothing to pay it back with, so she strays from the straight path and is lost. She will be in need and writes [an IOU] for them until she [herself] is paid back and so can return people's money to them. No oath is accepted from her, nor any male witness, but it is only what one woman says against another that is taken as the truth.' The men dye their hands and feet [with henna].

Their cooked dish is *mulūkhiyyah*;[2] their food is millet and sorghum, from which *khafūsh*,[3] *kubān*,[4] *laḥūḥ*[5] and *faṭīr*[6] are made. They eat [the last] with sour milk and fish and call it *multaḥḥ*.[7] [They also eat] cheese, bananas, sugar cane and milk. They have no [topic of] conversation except food. Zayd says to ʿAmr, 'What did you have for your morning meal today?' He replies, 'Millet bread and *qaṭīb*',[8] or, '*multaḥḥ* and oil.' Muḍar says to Jaʿfar, 'What quarry did you hunt?' He replies, 'A loaf of wheat bread for a *fals* and a piece of sweetmeat for four *fals*, so that makes a total of six *fals*!' Khālid says [87] to Zayd, 'Today I ate enough food for three days, unleavened bread, milk and "eastern" sugar cane. I enjoyed myself and ate my fill!' On this subject, ʿAlī b. Abī ʿAlī al-Sanawī recited as follows:[9]

> One day, I spoke to Riʾm, a marvellous girl,
> with ample bosom and round, swollen breasts,[10]
> A slim figure and slender like a pole when
> it sways over a sand dune, not granting trust.[11]
> She had waved with her hand, as she turned away
> and [then] approached like a gazelle in the herds,
> Wanting to make contact with me. I said, 'My dear,[12]
> Be gentle with me for hunger has made me miserable.

[1] In all probability Ibn al-Mujāwir's uncle (Smith, 'Eastern Connection', p. 81).

[2] These dishes are left in their original Arabic form in the translation. It is clear from information kindly supplied by DMV and FLS that their meanings differ in different areas of the Yemen. The following notes therefore contain information from both sources, the former's from his 'Production of Sorghum' article, with data from al-Ahjur, the latter's from her fieldnotes made in Bājil in 1992. DMV and FLS prefer the vocalization *mulūkhiyyah* to that of the lexicographical works, *malūkhiyyah*, and tell me it is *Corchurus olitorius* L. in the Yemen (Wood, *Handbook*, p. 102).

[3] DMV directs my attention to Zabīdī (*Tāj*, XVII, p. 192) who gives *kafūsh*, a kind of sorghum bread.

[4] Varisco ('Production of Sorghum', p. 86) says this is a variety of sorghum bread made with egg, ghee and yeast; cf. FLS: 'a soup like mixture of wheat and cowpeas (*dijrah*)'. Wheat today was probably sorghum in Ibn al-Mujāwir's day.

[5] 'A variety of sorghum bread which is spongy' (Varisco, 'Production of Sorghum', p. 87); cf. '... a sour batter pancake/crepe, very common' (FLS).

[6] This ought to mean unleavened bread; but cf. 'a mixture of wheat, eggs, spring onion and tomatoes, fried and when put into a crepe is called *multaḥḥ* [see n. 7 below]' (FLS). It should be noted that Ibn al-Mujāwir specifically says that all these dishes are made from sorghum and millet.

[7] One assumes that, in view of the findings of FLS, although the name is connected with the word *laḥūḥ*, *multaḥḥ* is perhaps applied to the dish which includes the *faṭīr*.

[8] FLS tells me this is buttermilk, but cf. Nashwān (Shams, VIII, p. 5549), '*qaṭībah*', and K (II, p. 765), 'camel and goat milk mixed together'.

[9] Unidentified poet.

[10] Arabic *akʿābi* plur. of *kuʿb* (Piamenta, *Dictionary*, II, p. 432).

[11] Arabic *rayyābi*.

[12] Arabic *yā sakanī*.

Bring *tharīd* when you come back
to me, don't bring musk and perfumes.
Prepare some unleavened millet bread with some milk
and give me it one morning at the door.
For my heart inclines towards a love of bread;
it does not incline towards a love of women!'

Their fruits are melons (and they call melons *barṭīkh*),[1] bananas, grapes, snake cucumbers[2] and cucumbers. They eat gourd melons cooked in a tandoori oven. They are offered for sale by shouting out, 'Water melon gourds, juicy, not many pips!'

Their odoriferous plants are *buʿaythirān*, which is white wormwood,[3] and the fruit of the henna,[4] that is the henna flower.[5] Ibn al-Mujāwir said: The first time I smelt it was in Mūltān.[6] This was when Lord ʿIzz al-Dīn Shams al-Mulk, leader of the merchants, Yaḥyā b. Asʿad al-Baladī gave me three or four bunches. I had never seen it, nor sniffed it before that. He said to me, 'What is this?' I replied it was the fruit of the henna. He asked me how I knew this and I replied, 'By three things: its colour, its smell and its freshness.' It has been mentioned above. The first time I saw it in Daybul[7] was in the year 618.[8] Its peculiarity was that, when Zayd had some, ʿAmr could smell it. The perfume of the violet[9] clings only to men. The odours of acacia fruit[10] cling only to women, also sweet basil,[11] which is *rayḥān*, and called the basil flower.[12]

[88] *The names* of the people of this area are as follows: Ḥinkās, Yuʿfir/Yaʿfur, Ghasṭayṭ, Zibraqān, Zunqul, Diʿ, Maḥlas, Zubayr, Ḥimsīs, ʿAṭʿaṭ, Daʿdaʿ, ..., Jadīr, Māyis, Shiqdāf, ʿAṭūṭ, Daʿʿās, ..., Maṭʿūn, Maṭḥūn, Maḥmaṭah, ..., Ṭalilī, Ḍabīʿah, Sandaʿ, Qabīʿ, ʿArṭabīʿ, Bakmī, Jirbāḥ, Qaʿ, ..., ..., ..., Shamam, ʿAbūr, Mubdaʿ, al-Ḥabūb, Raʿbah, Ḥanbal, Qaḥīm, Jaḥūsh, Abjar, Quʿaysh, Saḥdar, Fashlā, Kaskāsh, Karkar, Fāwā, ..., Fakhm, Dankal, Kaʿdal, ..., Kalbī and Raqraq.[13]

[1] I.e. *barṭīkh*, not the normal *biṭṭīkh*.

[2] Arabic *qiththāʾ*.

[3] Arabic *shīḥ*, *Artemisia* sp. (Dimyāṭī, *Muʿjam*, p. 85; Hepper and Friis, *Plants*, p. 114).

[4] Arabic *ḥinnāʾ*, *Lawsonia inermis* L. (Wood, *Handbook*, p. 414). I am indebted to both FLS and DMV who provide me with information here and with the Wood reference. DMV adds that it is difficult to identify a species for that time.

[5] Arabic *ḥannūn*.

[6] Also Multān in Arabic. A town near Ghaznah on the Indus with a Muslim population (Yāqūt, *Muʿjam*, V, pp. 227–8; Le Strange, *Lands*, pp. 331, 333).

[7] Text al-Daybūl. A port on the NW coast of India, often in Arabic al-Dābūl, at the principal mouth of the Indus, about 95 miles S of Bombay (Le Strange, *Lands*, p. 331; Serjeant, *Portuguese*, map opposite p. 64; *EI*, 'Daybul').

[8] Begins 25 February 1221.

[9] Text *banafsaj*, *Viola odorata* L. (Dimyāṭī, *Muʿjam*, p. 25; Varisco, *Agriculture*, p. 198).

[10] Arabic *baram* which does not occur in the botanical sources. Lane, *Lexicon* (I, p. 195) says it is the fruit of any thorn tree or bush at its last stage of development, more specifically the fruit of the *talḥ*, *Acacia gummifera*.

[11] Arabic *ḥibāq*, plur. of *ḥabaq*, *Ocimum basilicum* L. (Dimyāṭī, *Muʿjam*, p. 39, *ḥabaq nabaṭī*; Varisco, *Agriculture*, p. 198).

[12] Arabic *ḥamāḥim* which Dimyāṭī (*Muʿjam*, p. 45) confirms is another name for *ḥabaq nabaṭī*.

[13] These names, some extremely unusual, I have vocalized with the kind assistance of FLS who collected them in person from the late Muḥammad al-Shamīrī.

The people of this area place *hā'* before *wāw* in the alphabetical order of the dictionary, as opposed to what everyone else does, *wāw hā'*; [their order] is *hā' wāw*. Muḥammad b. Abī Sa'īd al-Qāḍī al-Rāzī informed me as follows: In some parts I heard youths giving the order of the letters in this way and we agree with this. Their doing so is the correct [order]. I asked him why. He quoted as follows, 'He is God, One, the God, the Eternal.'[1] He continued, 'Our letter order is the correct one. "And he is God in the heavens and on earth; he knows what you keep secret and what you say out loud and he knows what you gain."'[2]

The majority of the town follows the law school of Sirāj al-Ummah Abū Ḥanīfah al-Nu'mān b. Thābit al-Kūfī al-Tābi'ī[3] – God be pleased with him. The cloth market in this town only opens up at siesta time after noon prayer. They all sell within the tribe. One of them will come in bringing something which he intends to sell. When he sells it and its price is reached, noon will have already drawn near and he will have his lunch and come back to the market [to complete the sale]. All heads of houses hoard[4] cereal crops like millet, sorghum and *juljulān*, which is sesame.

[89] During the season of grain crops, they deal in the Janad [*zabadī*][5] with an interest rate of fifteen to ten for a period of six months. Grain crops are measured in *mudd*, which is thirty-two *thumn*.[6] Each *thumn* is thirty-two *zabadī* and each *zabadī* is a *mann*, each *mann* two *raṭl* and each *raṭl* 120 dirhams. Each dirham is thirteen carats. The Egyptian dinar is worth four and a half *malakī* dinars. The dinar is four dirhams, each quarter being three *jā'iz*, each *jā'iz* eight *fals* and each *fals* four *dāris*.

The first person to strike the 'large' dirham was al-Malik al-Mu'izz Ismā'īl b. Ṭughtakīn, its weight being thirteen carats.[7] At first the weight of the Abbasid dirham, and after it the Sayfī,[8] was four carats and a *ḥabbah*.

Sesame oil is sold by the jar, whereas ghee is sold by the bowl,[9] each bowl being five *mann*. A *mann* of silk is 260 dirhams and a *mann* of meat 400. Fruit juice, cotton, myrtle[10]

[1] Quran 112:1 and reading *qultu* for *qāla*.

[2] Quran 6:3. The previous Quranic quotation begins '*huwa*', i.e. *hā'* then *wāw*. The second begins with the words '*wa-hwa*', i.e. *wāw* then *hā'*.

[3] The eponym of the Ḥanafī law school in orthodox Islam. He died in 150/767 (*SEI*, 'Abū Ḥanīfa').

[4] Arabic *ḥakkārīn* (Dozy, *Supplément*, I, p. 309; Kazimirski, *Dictionnaire*, I, p. 470).

[5] The text has only 'al-Janad' and I tentatively go along with Löfgren's suggestion that it should read *zabadī al-Janad*, *zabadī* being a measure of grain presumably originating in Zabīd (Dozy, *Supplément*, I, p. 578; Löfgren, *Texte*, I, p. 65 and II, p. 37; Varisco, *Agriculture*, pp. 164–5).

[6] See Hinz, *Masse*, pp. 45–7, 52.

[7] For the 'large' dirham, see Serjeant, *Portuguese*, pp. 146–9. Al-Malik al-Mu'izz was Ayyubid ruler of the Yemen between 593–8/1197–1201 and some of the dirhams struck in his name in Ta'izz and Zabīd have been published (Miles, 'Ayyūbid Dynasty', pp. 64–5; Balog, 'Dirhems Ayoubites', pp. 350–53).

[8] I assume the Sayfī to be the dirham struck by the father of al-Mu'izz Ismā'īl, al-'Azīz Ṭughtakīn (d. 593/1197) who had the honorific title Sayf al-Islām. There is a possibility, however, that it was the dirham struck in the Yemen in the name of al-'Ādil Abū Bakr who had the same title and, although never travelling to the Yemen, did have dirhams struck in his name there even after his death in 615/1218 (Miles, 'Ayyūbid Dynasty', pp. 82–3, 89).

[9] Arabic *jamanah* (Landberg, *Glossaire daṯînois*, I, 300).

[10] Arabic *hadas*, *Myrtus communis* L. (Dimyāṭī, *Mu'jam*, pp. 8, 155, *hadas* = *ās*; Kazimirski, *Dictionnaire*, II, p. 1400).

and *shaydhar* stone[1] are sold by the *mudd*, which is five *mann*, using the 'large' type. The stone weight used in Aden is a little more than that of Zabīd. Cloaks are produced in Zabīd, eight 'hand' cubits,[2] and a load of it, comprising 122, is bundled up in the same way as in al-Shiḥr. The length of silk and white cloths is twenty *ḥadīd* cubits.[3] The length of Persian cotton cloth[4] is six cubits and the loincloth[5] seven, the latter being of two kinds: one pure silk and the other of silk and linen mixture four cubits wide. [There are] also striped cotton cloth,[6] Djerba wool[7] and Sousse waist-wrappers.[8]

Preserved ginger is of two kinds: that cut, with a little honey, and that ground, which is excellent. The best tamarind is that which causes vomit.[9] Pelts are sold by numbers. The income of the tannery is 13,000 dinars. Dates, millet and sorghum are exported to the Hejaz and ten-year-old slave girls and beads are brought in from Abyssinia.[10] The town's income, [from] fishing boats, poll-tax, vegetables and herbs, bought with cereals and the [90] imports which pass through the gate, [amounts to] 90,000 *malakī* dinars. The income of the mint is 13,000 dinars and the wine house 12,000 dinars. The date-palm income is 100,000 dinars. God knows best and is most wise.

From al-Mahjam to Zabīd. To al-Kadrā' five parasangs.

Al-Mughallaf and al-Usaykhilah. There are two villages in the region of al-Jaththah,[11] one called al-Mughallaf and the other al-Usaykhilah. The people lived out their lives, the men ploughing, the women spinning, the donkeys braying at one another and the dogs barking at one another, when [on one occasion] in 564[12] they rose from the ground into the air, men and women, and disappeared from sight until the Day of Resurrection. No one knows what had befallen them, nor what had happened to them, nor indeed what they had done. They remain an example until the Day of Religion. It is said, 'The lightning of al-Mughallaf and al-Usaykhilah has flown off with you!' The village of the Amālik in the region of al-Ashʿūb south of Ṣanʿā' sank into the ground in

[1] FLS kindly quotes from her field notes where the information is that *shaydhar* is 'something hard and black made of stone' which is ground, mixed with oil and used to decorate the hands of women. FLS also directs me to Piamenta (*Dictionary*, I, p. 249) who has *shādhar*, 'dissolved sal ammoniac' and to Schönig, 'Cosmetics', p. 136, who agrees with Piamenta, but says it is a white stone. The word also means 'striped plaid' from the Persian *chādar* (Landberg, *Glossaire daṯînois*, III, p. 2032; Steingass, *Dictionary*, pp. 383–4), though it must be admitted that such a commodity would scarcely have been sold by the *mudd*.

[2] Arabic *thamāniyah adhruʿ bi-al-yad* (Hinz, *Masse*, p. 61, *dhirāʿ al-yad*).

[3] Arabic *ʿishrūn dhirāʿan bi-al-ḥadīd* (Hinz, *Masse*, p. 58; Serjeant, *Portuguese*, pp. 160, 162, *dhirāʿ al-ḥadīd*).

[4] Text *bayram* (Dozy, *Supplément*, I, p. 133; Steingass, *Dictionary*, p. 219).

[5] Arabic *subāʿiyyah* (Landberg, *Glossaire daṯînois*, III, p. 1894; Smith, 'Maritime Trade', pp. 132, 137).

[6] Arabic *milāyah* for *mulā'ah* (Dozy, *Supplément*, II, p. 609).

[7] Arabic perhaps *jirāb*, plur. of *jarbī* (Dozy, *Supplément*, I, 180; cf. OL's apparatus, n. 8). It may of course simple mean 'bag', 'receptacle' (Lane, *Lexicon*, II, 403), though this seems less in keeping with the context.

[8] Arabic *fuwaṭ*, plur. of *fūṭah* (Smith, 'Maritime Trade', p. 132).

[9] DMV convinces me that *al-muqallis* should be read here. Tamarind is certainly a laxative and here seems to be used to induce vomitting.

[10] The text actually seems to read 'wa-yu'khadhu ilā al-Ḥabashah al-jawārī al-ʿushāriyyah'. This would make little practical sense and OL is probably right to suggest 'wa-tudkhalu min al-Ḥabashah al-jawārī' etc.

[11] Maqḥafī (*Muʿjam*, p. 111) places the town between al-Mahjam and al-Kadrā'. FLS (unpublished notes) locates it W of Bājil, 1503 4314. See also Stone, 'Gazetteer', pp. 398–400.

[12] Begins 5 October 1168.

465.[1] When morning came, no one could be found who knew anything about the village, its inhabitants and their animals. 'So learn by example, O you who have eyes!'[2]

To al-Mahjam six parasangs. There is leprosy in the legs of the Yemenis because of the following: they eat too much sour milk with fish and the humidity gets the better of them and [the disease] attacks them. More accurately, they do not take care very much in certain matters because they leave bread and seasoning uncovered. The country is hot and there are many lizards and when the top is left off a vessel or food is not covered up, the lizards eat it and a trace of their saliva remains on it, so that whoever eats it, is afflicted with leprosy. It is also said that when a flying creature like a mosquito,[3] yellow in colour, and called [91] *b.rrah*,[4] bites someone on an empty stomach, this harmful disease afflicts him. It is also said that elephantiasis afflicts him. God knows best.

From Zabīd to Aden by way of the sea shore. From Zabīd to al-Muzayḥifah a parasang.[5] Al-Muzayḥifah is known by this name simply because there was nearby a small village of Arabs who were living in tents. They moved from the small village to this place, so the place became known as al-Muzayḥifah; as is said, 'So-and-so marched[6] to so-and-so', i.e. he moved. Mūsā b. al-Jabalī built a mosque there of baked bricks and gypsum. There is no place among emigrants better than it is, not [even] in Wādī Zabīd. The trees there are black myrobalan.[7]

To al-Suḥārī three parasangs.[8] ... which are three hills with trees and arak. Al-Suḥārī is on the coast with tall palm trees.

Selling the date palms. These palms were planted by Abū al-Qāsim and Yaʿqūb, the sons of Qūn.f.r. They grew and acquired a good reputation. Atābak Sunqur heard of them and said to his governors,[9] 'Impose a tax on [the owners] according to the number [of palms] and cheat them [when you calculate] this tax on them.' When the governors did this to [the owners], they asked for help against this practice. Atābak Sunqur said to them, 'Sell [them] to me and give yourselves relief from oppression!' They replied, 'Buy them all from us.' He asked if they would sell them at the price of a dirham for every palm. They replied they would. He asked all those present to witness that he had bought them from them. He ordered that the palms be counted and their correct total was 2,000 trees, so he gave them 500 dinars. Now the palm grove is two parcels of land [92], one of which was called al-Fāzah and the other al-Qubbah. When [Sunqur's]

[1] Begins 17 September 1072. This must be a reference to the earthquake of that year whose epicentre was probably NE of Zabīd (Ambraseys, *Seismicity*, pp. 33, 101).

[2] Quran 59:2.

[3] Arabic *nāmis*, a common S Arabian form of *nāmūs* (Piamenta, *Dictionary*, II, p. 498).

[4] Unidentified.

[5] A village of Wādī Zabīd, now ruined (Sharjī, *Ṭabaqāt*, p. 150; Maqḥafī, *Muʿjam*, p. 589).

[6] Arabic *ZaḤaFa*.

[7] Arabic *ihlīlaj*. DMV draws my attention to Wood, *Handbook*, p. 174 which lists *Terminalia brownii* Fresen. He adds that there is a similar tree which is more common, *Combretum molle* R. Br. ex G. Dor.

[8] Between Ḥays and al-Khawkhah, according to Maqḥafī (*Muʿjam*, p. 305). Hamdānī (*Ṣifah*, p. 75) has al-Ṣuḥārī, undoubtedly the same place. See also Kay, *Yaman*, end map. FLS has suggested that it is now called Abū Zahr at 1350 4315.

[9] The atabeg was in control of much of the Yemen in the name of the Ayyubids in the absence of a member of the ruling house between 598–609/1201–12 (Smith, 'Political History', p. 138–9; Appendix B.8 below).

amir[1] seized them, [the two original owners] regretted what they had done and sought to call off the deal. However, he refused. When one of them saw the cheating for what it was, he attacked the amir and pierced him in the heart and he died. But the palm grove has remained in [the Ayyubid] sultan's possession until now and no date palm is allowed [to be picked of its fruit] until after his [permission has been given]. In all these regions there is nothing better and more soundly planted and cultivated than these date palms. It is said that Sayf al-Dīn Sunqur only behaved oppressively towards the salt workers in Aden and the owners of these palms of Widn al-Khalq.[2]

To al-Khawihah half a parasang.[3] There there is a square mosque built by al-Ḥusayn b. Salāmah. In the courtyard of the mosque is a square rock, on which is the footprint of the she-camel of Muʿādh b. Jabal – God be pleased with him. There is also a great secret in the mosque: if there is some fear in the village, the people throw the property and furniture which they have into the mosque and escape with their lives. If evil people enter the mosque, no property is taken and God makes them blind. It is also said that the mosque disappears from sight. If a man sleeps in it and he does not have a good reason and is not innocent of any wrong-doing, he is thrown down at the well outside the mosque. A tax is levied [in al-Khawihah], a sixth on every load, together with the tax collected on fishing boats, seventy dinars a month.

To Mawshij one parasang, a village of lofty palms.[4] To al-Ḥalīlah[5] two parasangs among sand, stones and trees. *Qilā* is made there, which is potash,[6] and it is taken to all provinces of the Yemen. There are pretty girls there and beautiful women, some evil, some good who do not show their affection, [even when] it is permitted. [The poet] has recited as follows:

> There is beauty in Wāḥijah
> and in the regions of am-Ḥadūn;
> Most of it is in al-Ḥalīlah,
> but they are shy![7]

[93] I asked its inhabitants about the man who built it and they replied, 'We don't know, but our ancestors were bedouin folk who came into the village and found it empty of people. When they found it pleasant, they settled down to live here.'

[1] By amir, Ibn al-Mujāwir must mean one of the governors of Atabeg Sunqur. Sunqur himself died in Taʿizz in 609/1212, apparently of natural causes (Ibn Ḥātim, *Simṭ*, p. 147).

[2] Kay (*Yaman*, end map) has al-Khauhah, although his location is accurate, 1348 4315. It is today known as al-Khawkhah (Stone, 'Gazetteer', pp. 449–50).

[3] Unidentified, but cf. Kay (*Yaman*, end map) has al-Khauhah, although his location is accurate, 1348 4315. It is today known as al-Khawkhah (Stone, 'Gazetteer', pp. 449–50). Ḥāfat al-Widn to the SE of the town, Tabula III. DMV adds that *widn* in the Yemen is a large field (Hamdānī, *Ṣifah*, p. 199; Landberg, *Etudes*, I, pp. 324, 725; Landberg, *Glossaire daṯînois*, III, p. 2913).

[4] Maqḥafī (*Muʿjam*, p. 646) says it is 11 km S of al-Khawkhah on the coast. See also Niebuhr, *Description*, p. 196 and Tab. XX and Stone, 'Gazetteer', pp. 170–71.

[5] Unidentified.

[6] Arabic *ḥuṭum* (Piamenta, *Dictionary*, I, p. 98).

[7] I propose the reading *yakhjalūna*, which makes much more sense than the *yuʿajjilūna* of the text. I can only identify one of the three place names found in this little ditty. FLS (unpublished notes) is of the opinion that al-Ḥadūn is correct (*am-> al-*, as in many parts of South Arabia) and tentatively places it at 1333 4330. See also Stone, 'Gazetteer', p. 269.

To Mawzaʿ three parasangs.[1] This is Muhalhil and Kulayb territory and there the war of Basūs took place. In previous times, these regions belonged to B. Majīd who built al-Qulayʿah there.[2] This place fell into ruins because its inhabitants had differences. After them, it was inhabited by a group of the people of the island of Farasān in the last days of Sayf al-Islām Ṭughtakīn b. Ayyūb[3] and it has remained in their possession till now. A tax was levied there, on every load an eighth …

To al-ʿUmriyyah three parasangs.[4] There are two excavations in a wadi and this wadi has become famous by this name, according to Ghazzī b. Abī Bakr al-Ḥijāzī, because a woman came to this wadi called ʿUmriyyah, afflicted by a violent thirst. She climbed up to the top of this mountain following a flood which was flowing after rains, thinking it was water. But when she reached it, she was so dehydrated that she died as a result of her raging thirst. Both the wadi and the mountain were known by this name, ʿUmriyyah. The well was dug out after her death and given the same name as the mountain. The poet has recited as follows:

> I hesitated – I am indeed emaciated –
> turning round every possible idea, but I still do not know:
> Shall I be resolute like other people and show patience without them
> or am I content to turn away with a quick glance?
> May I ransom you! I have no patience, but I do have a stratagem to deal with you,
> but despair summoned me from you to patience.
> Defeated, I became patient, though I am indeed in pain,
> just as the thirsty one is patient in a waterless land.

[94] Rūbah al-Nakabī recited as follows [in Persian]:

> You pass before me; I look at your face which has plundered my heart,
> [with a look] just like Ḥusayn b. ʿAlī's thirsty gaze at the water in the plain of Karbalā.[5]

The interpretation of these two lines in Arabic is as follows: You pass me by, as I look into your face, I with plundered heart, just as al-Ḥusayn b. ʿAlī was looking at Karbalā in his thirst for water.

To ʿIbrah three parasangs,[6] a well dug out in the bottom of a wadi from where one can see the sea. It was given this name because its water is like human tears in purity.[7] Another version is that it is a crossing which caravans make.[8] Another thing was, according to Ghazzī b. Abī Bakr al-Ḥijāzī's story, that its people were proud. An example of their pride was that, when anyone of them was short of sustenence because he was wretched, exhausted and in need, he would not approve of begging from anyone, nor humiliate himself by seeking help from anyone. So he would dig a huge hole and

[1] Inland due E from Mocha, 1316 4330 (Kay, *Yaman*, end map; FLS, unpublished notes).

[2] Originally perhaps what its name implies, a small fortress. Unidentified.

[3] He died in 593/1197.

[4] Kay (*Yaman*, end map) has 'Al ʿUmayrah' in about the right location, but there is no further information. Otherwise unidentified. FLS kindly adds: The wadi name no longer exists. But today's Jabal al-ʿUmarī 1259 4328 – 1301 4328 and Biʾr al-ʿUmarī 1303 4328 locate Ibn al-Mujāwir's al-ʿUmariyyah.

[5] The poet is unidentified. A reference to the martyrdom of the son of ʿAlī b. Abī Ṭālib in 61/680.

[6] Maqḥafī (*Muʿjam*, p. 425) does not care to vocalize, but says the place is between Zabīd and Aden near the coast. See Stone, 'Gazetteer', pp. 365–66.

[7] If this is the true etymology, it must be ʿAbrah, 'tear'.

[8] This would also make the correct vocalization ʿAbrah, 'crossing'.

get into it with his family and they would all die, so that no rejoicing enemy, nor any concerned friend would know what happened to them. It has been recited as follows:

> Many's the handsome youth we've seen,
> going morning and evening, owning not a single dirham!
> He watches the night stars because of his afflictions
> and is found in the morning laughing and smiling.
> He would not ask his brethren for what they have,
> even if he were to die of hunger, through his self-restraint and false pride.

The graves of the people remain, with the space of a great building between each one of them. So it was called al-ʿIbrah, 'so learn by example, o you who have eyes!'[1] It could not be verified by Ibn al-Mujāwir whether they were Muslims or of some other religion. Traces of wells[2] remain, with stones in them.

[95] *Section*. I was informed by a local bedouin in this spot in 619[3] that a stranger passed by this well and asked him about Jabal al-Ḥāyilah, Nawjān and al-Nājiyah.[4] He said he told the stranger about the three mountains, saying, 'Why are you asking about these mountains?' He replied, 'I read in a book that no one will be saved at the end of time except those living on these three mountains.' The bedouin asked which of the mountains they were [in the book] and he replied, 'Nawjān, a mountain on which the fortress of ʿAzzān was built, and the two other mountains in its vicinity.' God knows best.

Description of Bāb al-Mandab. This was not sea in ancient times, i.e. the Red Sea, for it is a new sea, opened up by Dhū al-Qarnayn – another version is by one of the tubbaʿs. The reason is, according to what was mentioned by a number of local people including Amir Abū al-Ṭāmī Jayyāsh b. Najāḥ in his book *Kitāb al-Mufīd fī akhbār Zabīd*, as follows. When Dhū al-Qarnayn reached this wadi,[5] he looked around. He found it oppressively hot, so he opened it up, i.e. he dug out the end of the wadi. The sea poured out and a branch of it poured out as far as Suez and stopped there. It is said that Abyssinia was attached to the Arabian Peninsula. Dhū al-Qarnayn declared, 'We want to separate the two areas so that each one knows its lord, each one takes possession of its land and territory and there is an end among the people of domination and hostility.' When the sea was opened up, the two areas were separated, each one on its own. But the Abyssinians would wade across the sea, both on horseback and on foot, to raid the land of the Arabs. One of the Arabs therefore built a fortress on Jabal al-Mandab called Biʿidd and he extended a chain on the Arabian side opposite Abyssinia.[6] Any ship [96]

[1] Arabic *ʿibrah*, 'example', 'warning'. Quran 59:2.

[2] Arabic *khusuf*, plur. of *khasīf* (Lane, *Lexicon*, II, p. 739).

[3] Begins 15 February 1222.

[4] FLS suggests these names are corrupt and I have corrected the second from 'Najwān' at her suggestion. She places Nawjān at 1304 4340 and adds that N of it is a mountain today called Jabal ʿUzzān.

[5] I take this to mean Wādī al-ʿUmriyyah.

[6] Biʿidd is taken from the L MS. The word is without dots and vowels in the I MS and OL leaves it thus. A great deal of ink has now been spilt on this passage in general and on this sentence in particular (Beeston, 'Two Inscriptions', pp. 50–51 and a personal communication of about the same time; Beeston, 'Chain', pp. 1–2; FLS, personal communication, 4 December 2000). Briefly, Beeston's view was that the chain was real and stretched across the entrance to the anchorage of Khor Ghurayra on the Arabian side opposite the Abyssinian coast (Beeston, 'Chain', p. 6 and map, p. 4). I now, however, after reference to FLS's letter which

arriving would pass along side the chain until dues were paid from it and it would then journey in whichever direction it wished. The fortress remained as it was until the tubbaʿs, rulers of the mountain (another version is B. Zurayʿ, rulers of Aden[1]), but the most accurate version is the Abyssinians, rulers of Zabīd, destroyed it and the chain was removed. A trace of the fortress[2] has remained until now. It is said that at that time the sailor had passage only at Bāb al-Mandab,[3] because it was the point best placed to provide provisions[4] on the route. But there remained reefs,[5] [invisible and] visible,[6] hollows[7] and winds stirring up the water.[8] Now ships sail on the seaward side [of Perim]. Here there is deep sea, long and wide, because there is so much water.[9] We shall mention the remainder when we reach Aden. There is ambergris on the beaches of al-Mandab, more often than not found by fishermen.

The Hollows.[10] Towards the end of the wadi bottom, i.e. al-ʿUmriyyah, are three mounds of pebbles, the distance between each one being at least thirty cubits. I asked about them and a cameleer told me that these mounds mark three hollows dug by one of the pre-Islamic tyrants. There is a mound of pebbles on each hollow so that it can be recognised. They are real wonders. There is a tribal frontier[11] between al-Maʾjiliyyah and al-Suqyā.[12] This arid scrub is called Miṭār because its inhabitants can only irrigate it at times of rain.[13] At the spring of al-Darb[14] is the trace of a mosque in which is the mark of the she-camel of Muʿādh b. Jabal – God be pleased with him. It is an excellent place. To al-ʿĀrah three parasangs.[15]

---

brought about a rethinking of the problem in my mind, would like to consider we interpret this sentence as follows: a chain was put in place across from the Arabian mainland to the island of Perim, a two-mile stretch of water.

[1] Between 473–561/1047–1166 (Smith, 'Political History', p. 138).

[2] Reading *atharu-hu*, i.e. referring to the *ḥiṣn*, rather than *atharu-hā*, to the *silsilah*.

[3] I.e. between the Arabian coast and Perim, two miles across, the Small Strait (*Western Arabia*, p. 139).

[4] Arabic *aghzar mawḍiʿ*.

[5] Arabic *afshāt*, plur. of *fisht/fusht* (Tibbetts, *Navigation*, p. 537), meaning here reefs not visible above the surface of the water, as opposed to those which could be seen (see n. 6 below).

[6] Arabic *waḍaḥ* (Kazimirski, *Dictionnaire*, II, p. 1553).

[7] Arabic *buṭūn*, sing. *baṭn*, which could also mean 'bay', 'leeward side' (Tibbetts, *Navigation*, p. 515), but we are clearly seeking an additional danger here.

[8] I am tentatively reading *al-aryāḥ*, 'winds', for *al-awlād*, 'boys', which makes no sense.

[9] Arabic *min warāʾ ẓuhri-hi* (Tibbetts, *Navigation*, p. 534). To sum up this difficult and partly corrupt passage: previously, ships would pass through the two-mile stretch of water between the Arabian coast and Perim, despite its often hidden dangers and the dues to be paid at the chain, in order to take on provisions and water; now ships take the safer route, the twelve-mile stretch between Perim and the African coast, thus forgoing the opportunity to take on provisions.

[10] Arabic *fuqarāt*, sing. *fuqrah*; I take it as a name.

[11] FLS tells me that such tribal borders exist today on Tihāmah marked out by pillars made of rubble core and plaster.This is perhaps the border lines of the Ṣubayḥah tribe (*EI*, 'Ṣubayḥī').

[12] Al-Maʾjiliyyah is mentioned by Hamdānī (*Ṣifah*, p. 188). Al-Suqyā is modern-day al-Suqayyah, the most westerly settlement of the Ṣubayḥah tribe (FLS, unpublished notes; Kay, *Yaman*, p. 11 and end map).

[13] Arabic *ayyām al-miṭārāt* (Piamenta, II, p. 468).

[14] A common place name, not identified.

[15] About 35 miles E of al-Mandab along the coast (Kay, *Yaman*, end map; Maqḥafī, *Muʿjam*, p. 418; FLS, unpublished notes).

[97] *The building of al-Muzdawiyah al-Murrah.* When the nejus was killed in Abyssinia and some people escaped the killing and settled this area, it was called al-Muzdawiyah because they fled for their lives[1] lest they perish like their master, while the safety of his servants was guaranteed[, as long as they took flight].[2] Ibn al-Mujāwir said: It was called al-Murrah [bitter] because their lives had become bitter since they were scattered far and wide away from their lands and homes, their families and children separated from one another.

When this community died out, some Arabs called al-Marabūn[3] settled the land and lived there until it became isolated and some were lost. They left. I was told by Rayḥān, the client of ʿAlī b. Masʿūd b. ʿAlī[4] as follows. They settled in East Africa[5] and its regions and their offspring remained in Africa,[6] known as al-Marabūn, and they are now organized in tribes and families.

After they had gone, the Arabs built the town of al-Akhḍarayn above al-ʿĀrah.[7] I was informed by Yūsuf b. Ḥumaysīs[?] b. Abī Bakr that it was a fisherman's settlement, an indication of that being that they still find fish bones [there].

I was informed by Mūsā b. Dayfal[?] that rather it was a large town. When it fell into ruin, the Sīrāfī Persian immigrants to al-Mundhiriyyah built it below al-ʿĀrah on the sea. There are there traces of two large Friday mosques, other mosques, grain mills and acacia leaf mills which can be seen among arak trees. Ibn al-Mujāwir added that every town built by the Persians from Sīrāf had tanneries constructed in them. There they worked acacia leaf mills and there is no doubt that the people were tanners.

A wise man once said, 'Only fools, monkey trainers or tanners ever came out of the Yemen!' My brother, Aḥmad b. Muḥammad b. Masʿūd,[8] asked me why this was. I replied, 'They used to tan leather and it was brought to them from above Mecca and Najrān as far as Oman, from Ḥaly of B. Zuhrah[9] as far as [98] Kirmān, from Kīs, Jannābah and Fārs, from B. Makramān[?], from Zaylaʿ, Rahayto and al-Mundhiriyyah of Aden as far as Mecca.[10] All this [tanned] leather was taken to Iraq,

1 Arabic *iZDaWaw bi-arwāḥi-him.*

2 A tentative translation of the Arabic *dūn al-ghayr.*

3 The MSS have no dots and I tentatively follow OL's first suggestion, 'al-Marabūn', with a reference to Hamdānī (*Ṣifah*, p. 53). They claim descent from Aaron and hail from the region of Aden.

4 The uncle of Ibn al-Mujāwir (Smith, 'Eastern Connection', pp. 78, 81). Rayḥān is mentioned several times (ibid., p. 81).

5 Arabic Barbarah (Yāqūt, *Muʿjam*, I, p. 369–70).

6 Arabic Barr al-Sūdān.

7 About 35 miles E of al-Mandab, a little inland off the southern coast of Arabia and about 70 miles W of Aden (Kay, *Yaman*, end map). Al-Akhḍarayn is unidentified elsewhere.

8 See Smith, 'Eastern Connection', p. 81.

9 I think there is something wrong here. I can find no trace of a Ḥaly belonging to a B. Zuhrah. Kaḥḥālah (*Muʿjam*, II, p. 482) mentions a Qaḥṭānī tribe, Zuhrah b. Yazīd, but whether this is the tribe in question and where it is to be found is in doubt.

10 Kirmān is well-known, an enormous province E of Fārs and the capital in the N of the province (Le Strange, *Lands*, map VI). Kīs is in all probability the Gulf island of Kīsh in the Strait of Hurmuz. Although OL gives us Jannānah after reference to the L MS, I have corrected to Jannābah, a town on the coast of Fārs province, S of Sīnīz (Le Strange, map VI). I wonder if Makrān should follow Fārs, a province SE of Kirmān, S of Sijistān (Le Strange, map VII). Zaylaʿ and Rahayto are on the African coast opposite Bāb al-Mandab. The former occurs on Tibbetts' Red Sea and Gulf of Aden end map (*Navigation*) which, I note, also has 'Raḥaita' opposite Mocha, presumably the 'Raheita' of *Western Arabia*, p. 125. I take Rahayto from the Arabian Peninsula map situated right on the present-day Djibouti-Ethiopia border on the Red Sea coast.

Khurasan, Kirmān, Transoxania, Khwārazm and Hajar[1] and it was dispersed far and near. But less noticeable is how it is exported now because of the long distance between all places, whether by land or by sea, as far as India. All this had no effect there; as the saying goes, "Don't look at how tall the minaret is; rather look at the mosque itself!""

The shame of the inhabitants of al-Mundhiriyyah. I was told by a Hejazi as follows. The Persians from Sīrāf used to eat seer-fish.[2] In some seasons there is none and [once] when this happened two young slaves went to two merchants to buy seer-fish. When the fishermen [finally] brought in some seer-fish, the two slaves bid against one other for it until they pushed the price up to a thousand dirhams, when one of them bought it. When the slave brought the fish back to his master, [the latter] approved of what he had done, setting him free and providing him with one thousand dirhams on which to live. As for the other slave, his master was so angry with him that he treated him with extreme contempt, a contempt commensurate with the cunning employed by Zayd's slave[3] when he got the better of him.

I was informed by Aḥmad b. Sulṭān al-Majīdī as follows.[4] ʿAlī b. Mahdī demolished al-Mundhiriyyah in 554.[5] It is said that B. Majīd built the town and thus they remained until the area suffered drought and the people went hungry. It is said they scattered all over the place and [only] ruins remained. The Hejazis came and borrowed the land from B. Majīd. Now this place was agreeable to the Hejazis and they strengthened their hold over it when it became fertile and the people were no longer hungry. B. Majīd returned to their land [99] and to their native settlements, so the Hejazis fought them off, denied them their right to return and drove them from their houses against their will. As B. Majīd were powerless to get their own back, they divided into three groups: one group settled in Zaylaʿ, a second in Ẓafār,[6] and a third settled in Mogadishu. A rump of them remained in al-Jābiyah.[7]

The poet recited as follows:

> Men gave their lives to love her, but got nothing.

The following is a poem by a slave of Āl ʿĀmir:

> Oh, I have a debt from the days of him suffering hardship,
> and a debt from the days of al-Ḥusayn and I affirm [it].
> In addition I ask for my debt to be repaid;
> but the first denies that he owes me, just as the other one does.[8]

[1] This may be the chief town of medieval Baḥrayn, in this context not just the island but also much of what is now the eastern side of Saudi Arabia. However there are several Hajars (Yāqūt, *Muʿjam*, V, p. 393).

[2] Arabic *ḍayrāk* (Hunter, *Aden*, p. 22), i.e. species of the genus *Cybium* (Yule and Burrell, *Hobson-Jobson*, p. 808, who use the hyphen and suggest an etymology of the Portuguese *serra*).

[3] Ibn al-Mujāwir's way of saying 'the other slave'.

[4] Ibn al-Mujāwir's informant is from the tribe of B. Majīd.

[5] Begins 23 January 1159.

[6] I take this to be the Ẓafār on the Indian Ocean coast of present-day Oman, now in ruins and called al-Balīd, just 2 or 3 miles E of Ṣalālah (Costa, 'Ẓafār', *passim*; Smith, 'Rasulids in Dhofar', pp. 26 ff.).

[7] Close to al-ʿĀrah on the route to Aden (see al-ʿĀrah-Aden route below). Not otherwise identified.

[8] Difficult to interpret out of context as it is.

The inhabitants of [al-Mundhiriyyah] are fishermen and donkey men, good, trustworthy folk, their men outstanding.[1] They eat fish and nothing else. All the Arabs of these regions, mountains and plains as far as the Hejaz, none of them accepts judgement by the *sharīʿah*, but rather they approve of *manʿ* judgement,[2] which is, there is no doubt, a pre-Islamic judgement, by means of which they used to settle their cases with *kāhins* and Yamāmah al-Zarqāʾ. It is said that Yamāmah lived before Islam.[3] When the shaykh gave a judgement according to *manʿ* against an Arab that his head be cut off, he could not flee and, even if he wanted to escape, he would have been able to do nothing but stretch out his neck and accept the legal decision. When someone had served his punishment, the call would go out among the rest of the Arabs at every gathering, 'Now surely so-and-so has done as well as the Arabs!'[4] Anyone hearing it would reply, 'The young man is smart!'[5]

One eighth[6] of the *ʿushr* tax was taken on every load in al-ʿĀrah and on fishing boats and caravans coming in from Aden to Zabīd and going out from Zabīd to Aden, while ships of Zaylaʿīs arriving from Abyssinia [were charged] 1,200 dinars per annum. All [the dues] we have mentioned were removed in 627[7] but this tax was restored in [100] 624[8] and it went up to 1,700 dinars. The first person to work for a village tax was ʿAbdallāh b. Abī Bakr al-Aḥwarī,[9] but he remained corrupt[10] until the Day of Religion.

The following is a poem by Sharīf al-Raḍī[11] about something similar:

> He whose lineage is not good,
> no good will come out of him.
> Every man's deeds please him,
> Often he brings out what is inside him.

From al-ʿĀrah to al-Ḥalīlah on the return journey via Darb al-Kudayḥā.[12] From al-ʿĀrah to ʿAthr[13] three parasangs, a village on the sea shore. There is here what cannot be found in Mawzaʿ and [then] you cross to Mocha, a sheltered anchorage.[14] Its name with the

[1] Arabic *rijāl fuḥūl.*

[2] '... competence to defend oneself and protect others and that branch of customary law covering not only maintenance of security in inter-tribal anarchy, but the closely allied business of personal honour.' (Serjeant, 'Customary Law', p. 270; also 'Sunnah', p. 45; 'Zinā', p. 146; 'Interplay', p. 43).

[3] Usually called Zarqāʾ al-Yamāmah, a Nejdi woman in pre-Islamic times famed for her prodigious eyesight. Iṣfahānī (*Aghānī*, II, p. 33, IX, p. 175) relates the anecdote of the war of Ṭasm and Jadīs in which she figures. See also Nicholson, *History*, p. 25. Ibn al-Mujāwir believes her to be a priestly arbitrator (*kāhinah*).

[4] Arabic 'alā inna fulān bn fulān ṭāb bi-ṭīb al-ʿArab' (Wright, *Grammar*, I, p. 284, II, p. 310). We might say today, 'He has paid his debt to society.'

[5] Arabic *ḥādda al-fatā*. Or possibly, *jāda al-fatā*, 'the young man has done well' (OL's apparatus, n. 9).

[6] Reading *niṣf rubʿ* (OL's apparatus, n. 10).

[7] Begins 4 February 1223.

[8] Begins 22 December 1226.

[9] The man is from Aḥwar, a town about 120 miles E of Aden along the coast (Serjeant, *Portuguese*, end map).

[10] Reading *baqiya yukhnā* (OL's apparatus, n. 2).

[11] A writer, scholar and poet who died in 406/1016 (*EI*, 'al-S̲h̲arif al-Raḍī').

[12] Unidentified. For the whole itinerary, see Sprenger, *Reiserrouten*, p. 150.

[13] ʿUmārah (Kay, *Yaman*, p. 11) says ʿAthr is between al-ʿĀrah and al-Suqyā.

[14] Reading with OL (n. 9) *wa-taʿburu*. I am very grateful to FLS for drawing my attention to Lane, *Lexicon*, III, p. 889, where the word *dif* is defined 'shelter ... from the wind'.

Arabs is derived [from] bone marrow because one does not chew it, as bone marrow is not chewed.[1] It is the original road and on it in ancient times depended the flow of caravan traffic, since it was the nearest and coolest route because of the coastal and sea air. To al-Ḥalīlah three parasangs. It is [also] known as Bi'r ... and al-Muḥammadiyyah[2] and it is situated at the crossroads.

From al-ʿĀrah to al-Mafālīs. From al-ʿĀrah to Taran three parasangs.[3]

Taran.[4] The people of Taran are descended from a woman called al-Fāliqah who came out of the sea. She settled on land [101] and married a prominent Arab who took her to live in the area of Taran. Children were born to her, both male and female. The Arabs declared, 'The inhabitants of Taran are from the offspring of the Arab and the woman', meaning al-Fāliqah. When a great flood came down on them and turned away from its [usual] path so that an area other [than the agricultural land] was irrigated, she would sit in the bottom of the wadi and block it with her enormous bulk and the water would return to [its] normal course so that the [agricultural] land would be watered from its flow. There she would remain until all the land had been watered for the people. When the land was irrigated and the people had no [further] use of the flood water, then she would get up from where she was sitting and the excess flood water would run into the sea. It is said that she was a sorceress. I asked ʿAmr b. ʿAlī b. Muqbil, 'What on earth happened to Fāliqah?'[5] He replied that she was still alive. 'Where does she live?', I asked. 'In Wādī Qaṭīnah',[6] he replied. I asked where the wadi was. He said, 'In the regions of Taran. And she will not die until the Day of Resurrection.' I asked if anyone ever saw her. He replied, 'Yes, everyone approaching the end of his life-span.' I asked why this land was called Taran. He replied, 'Because people were amazed at her enormous shape, so Zayd used to say to ʿAmr, "You will indeed see!",[7] i.e. "you will see her." So the land was known by this name.' For this reason, people usually say, 'I am a Taranī.'

An Arab tribal group lived in the land of Taran. There is no doubt that they were B. Majīd, arable and stock farmers. When they grew rich and were comfortably off, they attacked some Hejazis unawares, killed some of them, after taking all their belongings and wealth, and returned victorious. The Hejazis remained troubled and exhausted for a whole year. Then a great horde of them together with some Sakāsik[8] and so-and-so

[1] This is a strange and difficult sentence and undoubtedly corrupt. The Arabic roots *m kh w/y* and *m kh kh* are both, particularly in certain noun forms (*makhā* – *mukhkh*) and the verb form V (*tamakhkhā* – *tamakhkhakha*), used to mean 'marrow', 'suck out the marrow from a bone'. The point appears to be that marrow is sucked out and not chewed as meat would be, yet it is hard to imagine how all this gives the port of Mocha (al-Makhā) its name! (Kazimirski, *Dictionnaire*, II, pp. 1071, 1075, 1119).

[2] See above p. 117, n. 5.

[3] Yāqūt (*Muʿjam*, II, p. 27) says that Taran is near Mawzaʿ and the fifth stopping place on the Aden pilgrim route.

[4] See Smith, 'Magic', p. 9.

[5] Arabic *mā faʿala Allāh bi-Fāliqah*.

[6] Unidentified; it might be Quṭaynah.

[7] Arabic *taran*, 2nd pers., sing., masc. of the so-called energetic (*al-nūn al-muʾakkidah*) of *raʾā* (Wright, *Grammar*, I, p. 61), making a strong future statement (Wright, II, p. 24).

[8] Originally a Ḥaḍramī tribe of Kindah who scattered quite widely throughout the south of the Peninsula (Kaḥḥālah, *Muʿjam*, II, p. 527; Caskel, *Ǧamharat an-nasab*, I, Tafeln 233, 243).

and so-and-so of those well known attacked[1] the inhabitants of Taran in 560.[2] So it became the general custom, when any of them was asked his name, he would reply, 'I am a Taranī', meaning from the descendants of those [102] who were present at the battle. The Hejazis have had possession of the land of Taran until the present time and all their crops are there. It has become their refuge and their property. To al-Nukhaylah three parasangs.[3] To al-Mafālīs three parasangs.

From al-ʿĀrah to Taʿizz.[4] From al-ʿĀrah to Shaʿb four parasangs.[5] To al-Niyyah three parasangs.[6] To al-Maḥjāṭ three parasangs.[7] To al-Ḥuṣayn two parasangs.[8] To al-ʿArīsh three parasangs[9] and to Taʿizz two parasangs.

From al-ʿĀrah to Aden. From al-ʿĀrah to al-Jābiyah a parasang. It is said that it is of the district of Taran and that the latter is of the regions of al-ʿĀrah. To Biʾr al-Ṣaḥbah three parasangs,[10] a well dug out at the end of the Mahdid dynasty.[11] There is also the tribal boundary of al-ʿUrf, al-Ḥarājirah, al-Jaḥf, al-Quʿayʿā[?] and ʿUwayd.[12] Opposite a pretty well on the left of the track is Jabal Ḥirz [talisman], which is also called Ḥarīz. It is known by this [former] name simply because it is used to achieve something.[13] It is called Ḥirz and also Jabal Ḥarīz, which means 'fortified'. God knows best what is correct.

Description of Jabal Ḥarīz. It is a lofty mountain, high in the air. Near to it is a mountain which has ..., i.e. which has a top upon which is built a fortress called al-Jāhilī.[14] [There is another one] called al-Azālī [eternal][15] because of its great antiquity, where people climb up. Only the pious and saints climb the other one. I was informed by ʿAlī b. Ṣabīḥ al-ʿUqūlī that Solomon [103] the son of David – peace be upon them both – built three [other] fortresses in the province of the Yemen: Baynūn, Ghumdān and Salḥīn.[16] [Then he also constructed] this [fourth] one, al-Qāʿidah, which is the best built. This was when Solomon – peace be upon him – married Bilqīs in the land of the Yemen.

[1] Arabic *kabasa ʿalā* (Dozy, *Supplément*, II, p. 438).

[2] Begins 18 November 1164.

[3] Unidentified.

[4] I.e. due N as the crow flies. We are particularly badly served by our geographical sources for this SW area of Arabia; Sprenger (*Reiserouten*, pp. 150–51) relies entirely on Ibn al-Mujāwir.

[5] Unidentified.

[6] Unidentified.

[7] Unidentified.

[8] Unidentified.

[9] Unidentified.

[10] Unidentified. Vocalization tentative, perhaps al-Ṣaḥiyyah.

[11] A Tihāmī dynasty destroyed by the Ayyubids after their conquest of the southern highlands and Tihāmah in 569/1173 (Appendix B.7 below).

[12] All unidentified.

[13] Reading *yatasabbabu*; i.e. it was used as a talisman.

[14] There are several fortresses of this name in the Yemen, but this one is unidentified.

[15] Unidentified.

[16] Baynūn, one of the wonders of pre-Islamic Yemen, was in the district of Dhamār, about 60 miles S of Ṣanʿāʾ (Hamdānī, *Ṣifah*, pp. 3, 104). There are more details in Hamdānī's *Iklīl*, VIII, p. 40. Ghumdān was an enormous building within the city of Ṣanʿāʾ near where the Great Mosque stands (Smith, *Ayyubids*, I, p. 153 and see below p. 180). Salḥīn was an ancient fortress in Mārib, supposedly built by the jinn in 70 years (Hamdānī, *Ṣifah*, p. 203; *Iklīl*, VIII, pp. 21, 36, 37).

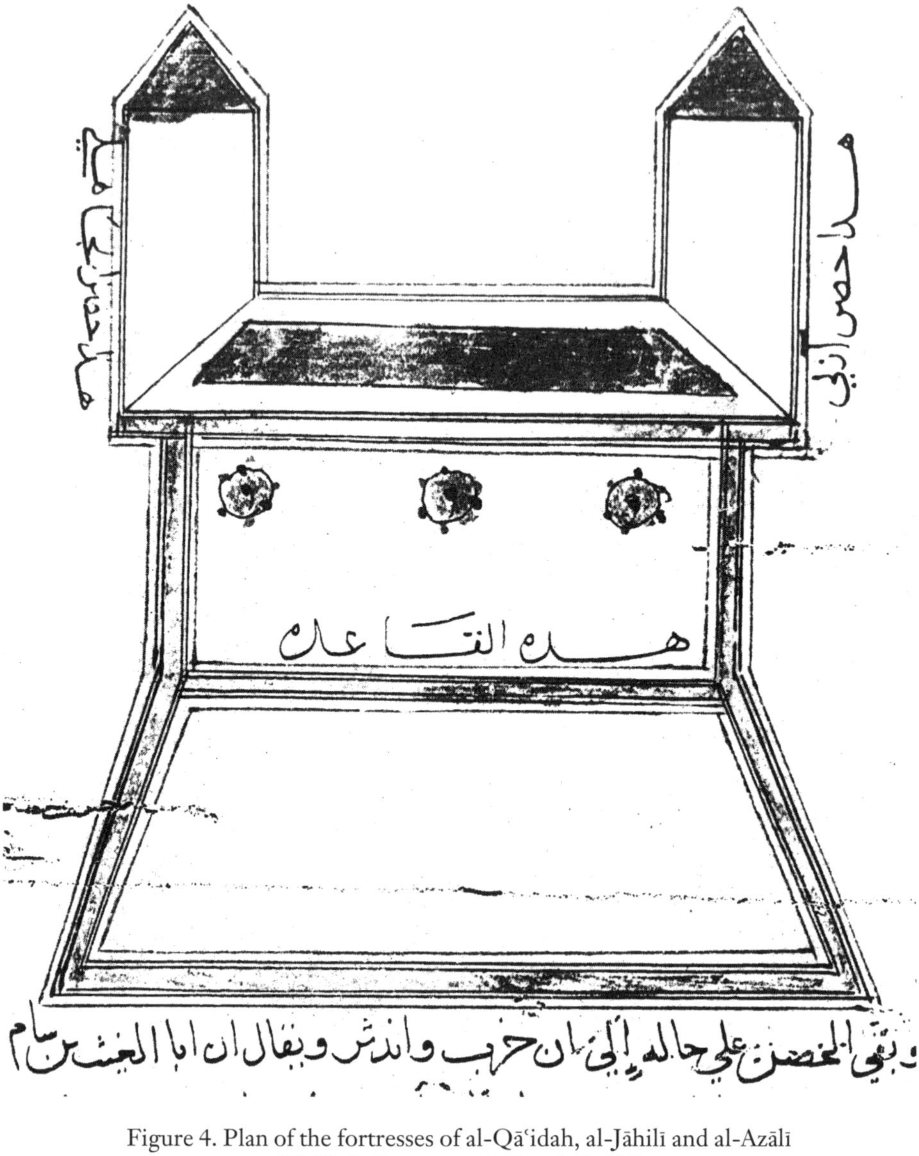

Figure 4. Plan of the fortresses of al-Qāʿidah, al-Jāhilī and al-Azālī
(I MS, f. 42a, text, p. 103, tabula IV)

According to the text, the three fortresses are situated on Jabal Ḥarīz. Of the two tower-like structures in the plan, the one on the right is marked Azālī and that on the left al-Jāhilī. The rectangle in the centre is labelled al-Qāʿidah.

He commanded the jinn to build all these fortresses in the following way: diagram (a diagram of its construction is as follows: as you can see on the following page [see Fig. 4]). God – praise to Him and He is ever almighty – knows best what is hidden and He is most wise.

[104] [Al-Qāʿidah] fortress[1] remained as it was until it fell into ruins and was covered in dust. It is said that Abū al-Ghayth Ibn Sāmir intended to renovate this fort during the reign of al-Ḥurrah al-Sayyidah bint Aḥmad b. Jaʿfar b. Yaʿqūb b. Mūsā al-Ṣulayḥī[2] after [the latter] had provided him with the wherewithal to build it and his ambition was fulfilled. He started to build, but hordes of jinn came up and killed everyone there. After his death, Dāʿī Saba' b. Aḥmad b. al-Muẓaffar al-Ṣulayḥī intended to renovate this fort.[3] Another version is that it was Dāʿī Saba' b. Abī al-Suʿūd b. al-Zurayʿ b. al-ʿAbbās b. al-Mukarram, the governor of Aden on behalf of the Fatimid dynasty.[4] But the jinn did not allow him. After the death [of the Zurayʿids], Sayf al-Islām al-Malik al-Muʿizz Ismāʿīl b. Ṭughtakīn b. Ayyūb intended to renovate it during the reign of al-Malik al-Nāṣir Ayyūb b. Ṭughtakīn b. Ayyūb b. Shādhī.[5] But a certain erudite man advised him to abandon it.

I asked ʿAmr b. ʿAlī b. Muqbil if there was a building on its summit. He replied, 'No one lived there except those who were in fear. There are there traces of walls which are covered in dust, irrigation dams which have been destroyed, cisterns in ruins and terraces which have been removed.' 'Was there a wall around it?' I asked. 'The mountain', he replied, 'was itself a wall. When the Arabs here at this time experienced fear or any act of tyranny from the ruler, they climbed up al-Qāʿidah with their livestock and their riding animals and stayed there until the land was at peace. Then they would reclaim the land. When its inhabitants were short of water, i.e. from the cisterns there which were in ruins, water was brought up from the foot of the mountain from three wells, one Bi'r ʿAbdal overlooking the track, the second Bi'r Yaʿūm and the third Bi'r Thaniyyah.' I asked if these wells were dug by the ancients, but he replied that, on the contrary, they were newly dug at this present time.

Description of Wādī ʿAbrah.[6] The fortress overlooks the sea. A prominent mountain, ..., projects from the sea, the distance [105] of a parasang [from the fortress], along a line [as straight as] the equator.[7] It is said that the builder [renovating] the fortress intended

[1] I am assuming al-Qāʿidah is meant; it is the last fortress mentioned. It is unidentified.

[2] The famous Sulayhid queen, reg. 467 or 479–532/1072 or 1086–1138 (Smith, 'Political History', p. 138; Appendix B.5 below). I am not sure where the 'Yaʿqūb' comes from and there is a difference of opinion concerning her pedigree. Hamdānī (*Ṣulayḥiyyūn*, p. 142, n. 1) finally settles for Aḥmad b. Muḥammad b. al-Qāsim after reference to a primary Ismāʿīlī source which even quotes her will (*Ṣulayḥiyyūn*, p. 323, appendix 9).

[3] From Bayt B. al-Muẓaffar of the Sulayhid house (Hamdānī, *al-Ṣulayḥiyyūn*, p. 335).

[4] D. 533/1138 (Hamdānī, *al-Ṣulayḥiyyūn*, p. 345). It would have been more accurate for Ibn al-Mujāwir to have said 'on behalf of the Sulayhid dynasty', although it is of course true that the Sulayhids were the close religious and political allies of the Fatimids in Egypt.

[5] Al-Malik al-Muʿizz Ismāʿīl could not possibly have been so involved 'during the reign of al-Malik al-Nāṣir Ayyūb'; the former was murdered in 598/1201 (Ibn Ḥātim, *Simṭ*, p. 81) and the latter reigned between 609–11/1212–4 (Smith, 'Political History', p. 139; Appendix B.8 below)! Perhaps what Ibn al-Mujāwir means is 'After the death [of the Zurayʿids], Sayf al-Islām al-Malik al-Muʿizz Ismāʿīl ... intended to renovate it, [but was murdered. There was another attempt to renovate it] during the reign of al-Malik al-Nāṣir Ayyūb ... .'

[6] There is no mention of a Wādī ʿAbrah in this section.

to break down the door[1] on the eastern side towards the sea and get inside it, but he could not because the rock was too hard. His aim was to prevent ships from passing through, because, if he were to connect the two, [the mountain and the fortress], together, he would be in a position[2] to capture the ships, since he had the advantage of a high position, whereas the ships remained below. When, however, he could not accomplish this, he declared that he was abandoning [the idea]. Now it is a good pearl-fishing area. Bi'r ʿAbdal along with Jabal al-Raddādīn has remained of the wells. There it was that the battle of Arabs against Arabs took place, a famous battle in the year 575.[3] [There is also] Bi'r Abī Bakr Shanlū[?] al-ʿAqrabī. At the well he built a mosque in 622.[4]

To al-Marjaḥiyyah three parasangs.[5] It is a brackish well in the territory of some Arabs called al-ʿAqārib.[6] To al-Bayḍā' two parasangs and it is known as Sabkhat al-Ghurāb [crow's salt pan] and also called Qāʿ al-Ghurāb [plain of the crow].[7] There used to be on the coast on the left of the track a well called al-Makhnaq, built by Commander Ḥusayn b. Salāmah. There is not in the whole of the known world anything sweeter and lighter for the heart than its water. The passage of caravans is along the sea-shore.

To Rubāk two parasangs.[8] This is a village which used to be inhabited. Amir Nāṣir al-Dīn [Ibn] Fārūt[9] produced a fine plot of cultivated land, where he excavated water channels and planted oranges, citrons, bananas and coconuts. Nākhūdhah ʿUmar al-Āmidī planted jack-trees,[10] which produces fruit from its trunk unlike other trees. These he planted in 625.[11] He also dug out cisterns there and there was an excavation called Ḥufrat al-Asad in former times, to which people from Abyan, Lahej and surrounding villages used to perform a pilgrimage on the first of the month of Rajab.[12]

[1] Reading '... *an yakhriba al-bāb*'. The idea was to establish control of the passage between the fortress and the mountain.

[2] Arabic *istaẓhara ʿalā* (Dozy, *Supplément*, II, p. 87).

[3] Begins 8 June 1179. The mountain is unidentified and I am not able to trace any record of a 'famous battle' at this location six years after the Ayyubid conquest of the S of the Yemen when the area under Ayyubid control was in the hands of various governors. It was perhaps no more than a local inter-tribal battle.

[4] Begins 13 January 1225.

[5] Unidentified.

[6] It seems to me quite a find that the ʿAqrabīs were known at this early date and mention here in a 7th/13th-century text probably makes them one the oldest tribal groups to survive in the form of a state until the 20th century. Until 1967 when the British left Aden, they formed a small sheikhdom with their capital in Bīr Aḥmad, just 5 miles west of Sheikh Othman, a town then within the colony of Aden. Their territory in the 20th century stretched along the coast from the creek of Bīr Aḥmad to Rās ʿImrān, the promontory about 10 miles W of Little Aden. Originally a sub-tribe of the ʿAbādil, the rulers of Lahej, the ʿAqārib threw off their allegiance about 1770. (Bombay, *Arab Tribes*, pp. 27–31; Aden Geography Board, *ʿAdan*, pp. 69–70; *Western Arabia*, p. 362; Kaḥḥālah, *Muʿjam*, II, p. 796).

[7] Unidentified.

[8] See Löfgren, *Texte*, I, pp. 20–21, quoting Abū Makhramah and confirming the spelling and the agricultural importance of the place.

[9] I have amended the name. See above p. 77, n. 5.

[10] The *nākhūdhah* is perhaps the father of ʿUthmān (see p. 160 below). Jack-tree, Arabic *shakī barkī*, *Artocarpus integrifolia* L. (Ibn Baṭṭūṭah, *Travels*, III, p. 609 and IV, p. 876; Löfgren, *Texte*, I, p. 20 and II, p. 24, 42–3; Dozy, *Supplément*, I, pp. 76, 780).

[11] Begins 12 December 1227.

[12] In medieval times, Abyan and Lahej often formed a joint fief and comprised the area to the immediate NW, N and NE of Aden, the former E of an imaginary line drawn due N of Aden, the latter W (*EI*, 'Laḥdj').

To al-Maksar a parasang,[1] a bridge built on seven columns by the Persians who ruled over Aden.[2] It is also said [106] Shaddād b. ʿĀd originally built it. I was informed by Yaḥyā b. Yaḥyā b. ʿAlī b. ʿAbd al-Raḥmān al-Zarrād as follows. It was built by a man from the mountains in 500.[3] It is also called al-Mazaff [place of hurrying/processing]. At first, people could only cross over by *ṣanbūq*, likewise water and firewood.

To Jabal Ḥadīd half a parasang.[4] It is said that a certain knowledgeable man came and founded two *buhār* and a half of iron from this mountain, but the mine has disappeared from sight. It is said that the founder was killed because of his founding the iron. At the foot of the mountain a mosque was built of stone and gypsum. To al-Mabāh a quarter of a parasang.[5] To Aden a quarter of a parasang.

What Aden was like in olden times.[6] From Suez to Aden, to beyond the mountain of Socotra, all of this was one stretch of land with no body of sea[7] at all. Dhū al-Qarnayn arrived during [one of] his tours and came to this very place. By digging out, he opened up an expanse of water[8] into [what became] the sea which then flowed until it stopped at the mountain of Bāb al-Mandab. So Aden remained in the sea, completely surrounded by it. Only the tops of the mountains could be seen in Aden like islands. One clear indication that what we are saying [is fact] is that traces of the sea and the waves can still be seen on the summits of Jabal al-ʿUrr and of the mountain on the top of which Ḥuṣn al-Taʿkar was built, and also of Jabal al-Akhḍar.[9]

The second indication [of the truth of the matter] is that Shaddād b. ʿĀd built Iram Dhāt al-ʿImād[10] between al-Lakhabah[11] and Lahej on the one hand and al-Maghāwī[12] on the other which is on the road to al-Mafālīs and this was the [stretch of] sand which

[1] This must be a bridge built across Khormaksar, the area of the isthmus connecting the Aden peninsula with the mainland, presumably across the creek (*khawr*) itself (Serjeant, 'Yemeni Merchants', p. 62). See also Löfgren, *Texte*, I, p. 19, who vocalizes the name according to its usual classical pattern, *maksir* (cf. Landberg, *Glossaire daṯînois*, III, p. 2574 'grande échancrure'). In the same passage, Abū Makhramah quotes mainly from Ibn al-Mujāwir, but adds that the bridge was '300 cubits and 60 paces'.

[2] Presumably a reference to the Persian invasion of the Yemen in AD 575 and the subsequent occupation (Smith, 'Political History', p. 129).

[3] Begins 2 September 1106.

[4] Right in the S of the isthmus, opposite the Maʿallā pier, the site of an iron mine (Löfgren, *Texte*, I, p. 18; Aden Geography Board, *ʿAdan*, map opposite p. 35).

[5] A place of some importance in its time and where people travelling out of Aden on foot would assemble to form a group and where incoming caravans would stop prior to entry into the town (Löfgren, *Texte*, I, pp. 18–9).

[6] See also Miles in Hunter, *Aden*, pp. 183–96 (an unreliable translation); Löfgren, *Texte*, I, pp. 24–70; Mermier, 'Fondations', p. 135; Smith, 'Magic', p. 15.

[7] Arabic *bāḥah*.

[8] Arabic *khalīj*.

[9] *ʿUrr* is a Sabaic word meaning 'mountain', 'bedrock' (Beeston, *Sabaic Dictionary*, p. 20). Hamdānī's description of the mountain (*Ṣifah*, p. 67) as 'a mountain surrounded by the sea' suggests that it is what is now known as Jabal Shamsān (*shams*, plus Sabaic nunation?), the massive range in the midst of the Aden peninsula, W of Aden town (Crater) (Landberg, *Etudes*, II, p. 1149). The other peaks are commonly mentioned in the text, but do not figure on modern maps of Aden.

[10] See Quran 89:7. Quranic exegetes took 'she of the columns' literally, whereas Ibn Khaldūn (*Muqaddimah*, I, pp. 26–8), after much argument, declares the phrase to mean 'she of the tent poles'. See also, *EI*, 'Iram'.

[11] According to Abū Makhramah (Löfgren, *Texte*, I, pp. 21–2), a village on the road to al-Mafālīs, 1¾ parasangs from Aden, a source of baked bricks and glass, inhabited by Arabs, including ʿAqrabīs.

[12] See below p. 164.

[reaches] as far as Jabal Dār Zīnah.[1] He built it only in the midst of the best and purest of lands and climate, far from the sea. Now the sea has reached[2] the borders of the territory of Iram Dhāt al-ʿImād [107] and carried some of it away. There was no sea in this area [previously] – it was created new by Dhū al-Qarnayn's opening up [the expanse of water]. It stretched from the island of Socotra and was one great flood until it came to a stop at the last part of al-Mandab.

The third indication [of the truth of the matter] is that the sea between al-Sirrayn and Jeddah is called Maṭārid al-Khayl [hunting grounds of horses] and Marābiṭ al-Khayl [tethering places of horses]. The origin of this is that the Arabs used to tether their horses in this area. The most accurate [version of the story, however,] is that they used to hunt horses there when there was no sea and the sea was dry land. When Dhū al-Qarnayn opened up Bāb al-Mandab, all the lands were drowned and their high lands became islands in the sea which was given the original name of Maṭārid al-Khayl.

One of the things mentioned by Amir Abū al-Ṭāmī Jayyāsh b. Najāḥ in his book *al-Mufīd fī akhbār Zabīd*, the first one (there are two books [called] *al-Mufīd*, the first composed by Amir Jayyāsh, the second by Fakhr al-Dīn Abū ʿAlī ʿUmārah b. Muḥammad b. ʿUmārah), is that the sea was [shallow enough to be] a ford because there was so little water in it and thus the Abyssinians conquered the Arabian Peninsula and ruled over Ṣanʿāʾ as far as the region of al-ʿAwāhil.[3] They remained before Islam and into the period of Islam until ʿAlī b. Mahdī destroyed them in 554.[4] During his time they became extinct and their state disappeared despite their strength.

We can now return to the subject of Dhū al-Qarnayn. The sea so remained until Dhū al-Qarnayn opened up Bāb al-Mandab. The sea flowed into [what was previously dry land] and only stopped at Suez; it was long, broad, abundant, spread out and extensive, so the land of Aden could be seen.

One of the things mentioned by Abū ʿAbdallāh Muḥammad b. ʿAbdallāh al-Kaysānī in his *Tafsīr* is as follows.[5] When Shaddād b. Ād left the land of the Yemen, making for Ḥaḍramawt, and arrived in Lahej, he looked at the hugeness of Jabal al-ʿUrr from afar and said to his assistants, 'Go and take a look at this mountain and what lies before it.' When they had examined the place, they returned and said, 'This place is a wadi [108] and in its bed are trees with large vipers in them and [the mountain] overlooks the briny sea.' When he heard what they had to say, he went down to Lahej and gave orders for wells to be dug from which the inhabitants of Aden now drink. He also gave orders for an entrance to be hewn out in the facing part of the wadi.

Description of the hewing out of an entrance and the excavation of a water channel. Two men took on the task of the excavation of the water channel and hewing out of the entrance

[1] It is not clear where this is, though there is a Jabal Dār Zīnah belonging to Āl ʿAzab in Bā Kāzim territory, i.e. in lower ʿAwlaqī country about 150 miles E of Aden (Ibn Rasūl, *Ṭurfah*, p. 144; Landberg, *Etudes*, II, pp. 1127–8; Löfgren, *Texte*, I, p. 25).

[2] Arabic 'wa-al-ān rajaʿa al-baḥr fī aṭrāf bilād Iram Dhāt al-ʿImād'. *Rajaʿa* is to be taken in its usual sense in *Tārīkh al-Mustabṣir*: i.e. this is happening for the first time.

[3] Hamdānī (*Ṣifah*, p. 81) mentions two wadis in the east of Mikhlāf Khawlān al-ʿĀliyah, al-ʿAwhal al-Aʿlā and al-Asfal.

[4] Begins 23 January 1159.

[5] Unidentified.

[of accommodation within the mountain].[1] Indian sages have said they were jinn,[2] one of them continuing to hew out the mountain and the other beginning to excavate the water channel at the top of [Jabal] Socotra in the region of Lahej.[3] The men remained at work hewing and excavating until only a small amount remained to them. The stone hewer said, 'I shall finish my work tomorrow, God willing.' The digger said, 'I shall bring water into Aden tomorrow, whether God is willing or not.' But parts of the channel were cut off from others, the source of the water became blocked, some parts of what he had built became stopped up, nothing was as planned, none of its shape remained and it had no real benefit. In his excavation, the digger reached beneath Jabal al-Ḥadīd and there it came to a halt.

Ibn al-Mujāwir said as follows. I saw the traces of this very channel built in stone and gypsum, a strong, solid structure, a cubit wide across the water to Jabal al-Ḥadīd. The sea had covered it over and it was not visible to the human eye except when the sea laid it bare, as it stretched out into the sea as straight as the line of the equator. He continued as follows. The next morning, the hewing out of the entrance was completed by the stone mason and its opening achieved what he had intended. It is said that he had been hewing out for a period of seventy years until he completed it. When much time had passed, Shaddād b. ʿĀd began sending all those who had to be imprisoned to this place; he would imprison them there and it remained a prison as [109] it was until the last part of the dynasty of the pharoahs who were the rulers of Egypt. After their demise, the place fell into ruin.

The towns which were prisons for rulers. Kashmir was the prison of Solomon, son of David – peace be upon them both. Ḥuṣn Dhī al-Qarnayn was the prison of Dhū al-Qarnayn.[4] Tirmidh was the prison of Alexander.[5] Mūltān was the prison of al-Ḍaḥḥāk al-Sāḥir.[6] Āmul and Sārī of Kai Kavūs, son of Kai Kavād, was the prison of the Greeks.[7] Ḥiṣiār Ṭāq was the prison of Bardsiyār.[8] Old Cairo was the prison of the Commander of the Faithful Abū Muḥammad Hārūn al-Rashīd. Merv was the prison of the Commander of the Faithful ʿAbdallāh al-Maʾmūn.[9] Damascus was the prison of Imam al-Nāṣir li-

[1] This section is corrupt and difficult to interpret. It is a question of two building works here: 1) a water channel bringing water into Aden from the Lahej area; and 2) hewing out accommodation inside Jabal al-Ḥadīd. It is tempting to suggest that the former is part of the elaborate system of channels and tanks found in Aden and studied by Norris and Penhey (*Survey*, *passim*).

[2] Arabic *ʿifrītayn min al-jinn*.

[3] This must be an error as there is certainly no mountain in the Lahej area with the name Socotra!

[4] Following Löfgren's apparatus and *Texte*, I, p. 27.

[5] Just N of the Oxus about 30 miles from Balkh to the SW (Le Strange, *Lands*, pp. 439–40 and map IX).

[6] This person is unidentified.

[7] Āmul was the capital of Ṭabaristān under the later Abbasids. Sāriyah, later Sārī, was an earlier capital and about 40 miles E of Āmul. Both lie S of the Caspian Sea (Le Strange, *Lands*, map V, p. 370). Ibn al-Mujāwir means Kai Kāvūs, the legendary Kayanian king. *Kai* is the sing. of *kayān* and means 'king', 'prince' (*CHIr*, III(1), pp. 374 ff., 436).

[8] This is probably Ḥiṣn Ṭāq, N of Zaranj, E of Lake Zarah in western Sijistān (Le Strange, *Lands*, p. 343 and map VIII). There is a second Ṭāq on the Ṭabaristān-Daylam border, S of the Caspian (Le Strange, map V). Löfgren (*Texte*, I, p. 27) suggests Bardashīr or (apparatus, n. 7) Farrukhsiyār.

[9] Presumably Great Merv, Marw al-Shāhijān, in the N of Khurasan on the Murghāb river (Le Strange, *Lands*, pp. 397–8 and map VIII).

Dīn Allāh[1] and it is said that there was a dungeon in it. When the Tigris overflowed, it filled up and the prisoners remained standing in water until it fell. From the wetness and brackishness of the water and the dampness of the earth, the skin of the prisoners split and the most a prisoner survived there was a month. Nehavand was the prison of Sultan Muʿizz al-Dīn Muḥammad b. Sām.[2] Lūḥak Ḥawrān was the prison of Sultan Bahrām Shāh.[3] The castle of Lahore was the prison of Khusrau Malik b. Khusrau Shāh.[4] Barʿad was the prison of Tāj al-Dīn Yïldïz al-Sulṭānī.[5] Kawālīwar was the prison of al-Malik Quṭb al-Dīn Abū al-Fawāris Aybak al-Āmulī.[6] ʿIwaḍ was the prison of Sultan Shams al-Dīn Iltutmish.[7] Herat was the prison of Sultan Ghiyāth al-Dīn Muḥammad b. Sām.[8] The fortress of Hazārasb [110] was the prison of Sultan Abū al-Fatḥ Muḥammad b. Tekish.[9] Kūshak Sanah Jawāhrān was the prison of Ṭoghrïlbeg Shāh b. Muḥammad.[10] Dahlak was the prison of ʿAbdallāh b. Marwān.[11] ʿAydhāb was the prison of the Fatimid caliphs. Taʿizz was the prison of the rulers of the Yemen. Qawārīr was the prison of the Mahdids. Jibāl Buraʿ was the prison of al-Malik al-Aʿazz ʿAlī b. Muḥammad al-Ṣulayḥī. Sīrāf was the prison of Sultan Maḥmūd b. Muḥammad b. Sām.[12] Aden was the prison of the pharoahs and became one of the prisons of the Fatimids.

The Indians have reported as follows. Aden was the prison of Das Sir, the name of a jinni who had ten heads, one of them al-Ghazāl Darsīr.[13] He used to live on Jabal

[1] Strangely Ibn al-Mujāwir gives Dijlah (Tigris) the definite article in the text and seems to think the Tigris could flood a prison in Damascus, which he calls al-Shām. If the latter means Syria, part of it could certainly be flooded by the Euphrates. I am puzzled by a reference to an Imam al-Nāṣir li-Dīn Allāh.

[2] Ghurid ruler in Ghaznah between 569–99/1173–1203 and supreme sultan in Ghūr and India during the last year (Bosworth, *Islamic Dynasties*, p. 298). The town is about 40 miles S of Hamadhān in Jibāl province (Le Strange, *Lands*, pp. 196–7 and map V; Ṭabarī, *History*, XIV, p. 2).

[3] The place is unidentified. Bahrām Shāh is perhaps Bahrām Shāh b. Masʿūd III, ruler of Ghaznah, c. 547–52/1152–7 (Bosworth, *Islamic Dynasties*, p. 296).

[4] Perhaps Qalʿat Lahūr (= Lāhawur?). Abū al-Muẓaffar Tāj al-Dawlah Khusrau Malik b. Khusrau Shāh, reg. 555–82/1160–86, in NW India. He was killed in 587/1191 (Bosworth, *Islamic Dynasties*, p. 296).

[5] The place is unidentified. This must be Tāj al-Dīn Yïldïz Muʿizzī, the governor in Ghaznah for the Ghurid Maḥmūd Ghiyāth al-Dīn (602–11/1206–15) (Bosworth, *Islamic Dynasties*, p. 298).

[6] The place is unidentified. Quṭb al-Dīn Aybak, the Ghurid ruler of Hindustan in Lahore, reg. 602–7/1206–10 (Bosworth, *Islamic Dynasties*, p. 300).

[7] 'A far-off land in the middle of India' (Yāqūt, *Muʿjam*, IV, p. 168)? Shams al-Dīn Iltutmish b. Ilam Khān, sultan in Delhi, 607–33/1211–36 (Bosworth, *Islamic Dynasties*, p. 300).

[8] Ghurid supreme sultan in Fīrūzkūh, 558–69/1163–73 (Bosworth, *Islamic Dynasties*, p. 298).

[9] I follow OL's corrected text and Yāqūt (*Muʿjam*, V, p. 404), who reminds us that the place name means 'a thousand horse' in Persian and tells us that it is a fine town with a well fortified castle in the regions of Khwārazm. This is the Khaljī sultan (Lane-Poole, *Dynasties*, pp. 297, 299).

[10] Le Strange (*Lands*, pp. 205, 412) lists two Kūshaks: one of the quarters of Iṣfahān, and a town in the Asfuzār region of Khurasan S of Herat. The other two words of the text remain a mystery. This must be either Ṭoghrïl Beg Muḥammad, the supreme sultan of the Seljuks who died in 455/1063 or Ṭoghrïl II b. Muḥammad, ruler of Iraq and western Persia, 526–9/1132–4 (Bosworth, *Islamic Dynasties*, p. 185).

[11] The son of the last Umayyad caliph, Marwān II b. Muḥammad (reg. 127–32/744–50). Both ʿAbdallāh and his brother, ʿUbayd Allāh, fought prominently in their father's cause against the Abbasids. During the last struggle against the latter in 132/750, both fled to Abyssinia. ʿUbayd Allāh was killed and ʿAbdallāh had to flee again. ʿAbdallāh was perhaps imprisoned on Dahlak island by the Abyssinians, although I can find no precise reference to this, nor indeed to his death (Ṭabarī, *History*, XXVII, p. 170).

[12] The Ghurid ruler Ghiyāth al-Dīn, 602–9/1206–12 (Bosworth, *Islamic Dynasties*, p. 298).

[13] The name means 'ten heads'.

al-Manẓar and take a walk on the sands of Ḥuqqāt.[1] After his death Hanūman[2] lived in Ḥuqqāt. It was Solomon, son of David – peace be upon him – who drove them out when he arrived in the land of the Yemen for Bilqīs, since these people mentioned above were spirits.

Aden was only given that name [ʿAdan] by ʿAdnān who, when he built it, called it after his son, ʿAdan. But Aden is simply derived from ʿĀd. It is said that the first person imprisoned there was a man called ʿAdan, so the place was called after him.

Ibn al-Mujāwir said as follows.The name of Aden [ʿAdan] is simply derived from the mine [*maʿdin*], i.e. Maʿdin al-Ḥadīd. It was called Ākhuri Sangīn by the Persians,[3] Samrān by the Indians,[4] ... by the blacks and Yaʾkul Ṣayda-h by the merchants.[5] It is also called Ḥabs Firʿawn [pharoah's prison], Muqām al-Jinn [abode of jinn] and Sāḥil al-Baḥr [sea shore]. It is called Hatām by the Indians and Sandās [rubbish dump] by the refined because everything thrown into the wind, the contrary wind brings back ...[6] It is also called the customs house[7] of the Yemen and among the people Dār al-Saʿādah [abode of happiness] after a building built by Sayf al-Islām Ṭughtakīn opposite the port. [111] It is also called al-Dār al-Ṭawīlah [long building] after a building built by Ibn al-Khāʾin opposite the customs house.[8] It is also called al-Manẓar after a building built by al-Malik al-Muʿizz Ismāʿīl b. Ṭughtakīn on Jabal Ḥuqqāt.[9] By the merchants it is also called Ṣīrah and Ḥayrah.[10]

[1] This particular mountain does not occur on modern maps of Aden. Ḥuqqāt is a bay in the E of the peninsula between Ṣīrah island in the N and Rās Marshag in the S and was the medieval port of Aden. The mountain may be one of the peaks to the S of Crater, some of which reach 500 m or so (Hunter, *Account*, plan of Aden; *Western Arabia*, map opposite p. 554). Abū Makhramah mentions a Dār al-Manẓar which was built 'on Jabal Ḥuqqāt' (Löfgren, *Texte*, I, p. 12). See frontispiece.

[2] De Goeje suggests plausibly that this is Hanūman and I follow this and correct here and below ('Communication', p. 31). He was the incarnation of Vagu, god of the wind and the general of the monkey king (Garrett, *Dictionary*, pp. 237–42).

[3] '... an empty, or rather, stony cratch', i.e. an unprofitable situation (Steingass, *Dictionary*, p. 25; OL's apparatus, n. 12, *Texte*, I, p. 29, n. 1).

[4] I have corrected from the text's Sīrān after reference to OL's apparatus, n. 13, and Muqaddasī, *Aḥsan*, p. 30.

[5] The lacuna is in the MSS. I am not happy with OL's suggestion (apparatus, n. 15), *maʾkal aydi-h*, 'place where he eats his fish', despite his lexicographical references, when the MSS clearly read *yaʾkulu ayda-h*, 'he eats his fish'! With fish aplenty in Aden, I see no reason the merchants would not jocularly refer to the town thus.

[6] Arabic *sandās* (Kazimirski, *Dictionnaire*, I, p. 1151). Despite the technical meaning of *azyab* (see Serjeant, *Portuguese*, p. 186; Tibbetts, *Navigation*, p. 513; Varisco, *Agriculture*, pp. 113–14 etc.), I take it here simply in its '(east) wind' meaning. Similarly *kaws* (Tibbetts, *Navigation*, p. 540; Serjeant, 'Socotra', p. 172); Löfgren's 'Gegenwind' (*Texte*, II, p. 56) fits the context admirably.

[7] Arabic *furḍah*. Connected with the verb *faraḍa ʿalā* 'impose a payment on', it is strictly speaking the place ashore where goods are stacked and where customs dues are paid. Landberg (*Etudes*, I, pp. 673–5) is right, of course, that originally this would be done on the beach without fear of theft. Since, however, we know that at the time of Ibn al-Mujāwir there was an agency house, *dār al-wakālah*, and a *zakāh*-house, *dār al-zakāh* (below, pp. 159–60), I would argue that we may safely translate *furḍah* 'customs house'.

[8] Perhaps a nickname, 'son of the traitor'. This seems the most likely reading from all the MSS of *Tārīkh al-Mustabṣir* and those of Abū Makhramah used by Löfgren in his *Texte*, I, p. 11.

[9] See n. 1 above.

[10] I.e. after the island to the E of the Aden peninsula. See n. 1 above. Muqaddasī (*Aḥsan*, p. 85) says Aden is like a sheep pen (*ṣīrah*), surrounded by mountain and sea, the latter in the east.

Jabal Ṣīrah. It is a lofty mountain in the sea opposite Aden and Jabal al-Manẓar; it is said it is part of the latter.[1] Muḥammad b. ʿAbdallāh al-Kaysānī has said in his *Tafsīr* that on the day of Resurrection a fire will come forth from Ṣīrat ʿAdan driving people to the Meeting Point. An illustration of that is that in the mountain a well, called Anbār and called by the Indian sages Fī Bar, was turned upside down and it continually puts out smoke. It is now called Biʾr al-Harāmisah.[2] No one can look into it because it is too hot, of difficult access and dark. There are broken stones around the well, also sleeping vipers and snakes rearing up. The Indians said that Hanūman i.e. the spirit mentioned above, dug this well. It is not [really] a well, but rather an underground passage leading under the sea to the town of Ujjainī Vikramāditya, the seat of the king of Malva in India.[3]

Section. I was informed by Mubārak al-Sharʿabī, the client of my father,[4] Muḥammd b. Masʿūd as follows: The reason for [112] the digging of the well of Fī Bar was that a spirit, ...,[5] stole Sita the wife of Ramacandra[6] from the regions of Ayodhya,[7] took her off and settled with her on the summit of Jabal Ṣīrah. He said he wanted to change her human shape into that of a jinni. While they were engaged in argument,[8] Hanūman heard of what was going on, he being another spirit in the shape of a monkey. So he dug this underground passage from the middle of the town of Ujjainī Vikramāditya beneath the sea. The end of the excavation reached the middle of Jabal Ṣīrah and he did all this in one night. He left the hole and found her asleep on the summit of the mountain under a thorn tree. He picked her up on his back and took her down the underground passage, journeying by night with her until he reached Ujjainī Vikramāditya. As dawn shone brightly, he handed her over to her husband Ramacandra. She bore him two male children, one called Lava and the other Kusā.[9] There is a long story, full of incident, attached to her, the telling of which would take too long, but the underground passage has remained until now.

In the same way, Kai Kavūs, son of Kai Kavād[10] dug an underground passage from al-Rayy to Māzandarān, a distance of thirty-six parasangs.[11] A certain Indian dug an underground passage in Devalvara in the regions of al-Sūmanāt,[12] the end of which led

[1] According to the plan of Aden (*Western Arabia*, fig. 40, opposite p. 554), the mountain on Ṣīrah rises to about 100 m. It is certainly opposite Aden town (Crater), but there is no high ground on the peninsula itself across from the island and I cannot see how the mountain on Ṣīrah could be part of Jabal al-Manẓar.

[2] Well of the Astronomers (Dozy, *Supplément*, II, p. 755).

[3] Ibn al-Mujāwir has only a vague notion of India! Ujjainī is the ancient capital of Malva, although Vikramāditya is a person's name, the founder of a dynasty in Ujjainī (Dey, *Dictionary*, pp. 122, 209).

[4] Reading *wālidī* (Smith, 'Eastern Connection', p. 81).

[5] The name of the spirit is not decipherable from *ḥ.ʾ.d.ḥ.ḥ.r.*

[6] In Indian tradition this story unfolds in Lanka (Garrett, *Dictionary*, pp. 239–42, 500–502, 585–86; Löfgren, *Texte*, I, pp. 30–31, notes 14 and 15).

[7] The kingdom of Rama (Dey, *Dictionary*, p. 14; Löfgren, *Texte*, I, p. 31).

[8] Arabic *fa-bayna-mā humā fī lā wa-naʿam idh*... A neat idiom! (Smith, 'Language', p. 331).

[9] The twin sons of Rama (Garrett, *Dictionary*, pp. 354, 360; OL's apparatus, n. 13 and *Texte*, I, p. 14).

[10] See p. 131, n. 7 above.

[11] Māzandarān is the name of the province which had earlier been called Ṭabaristān, S of the Caspian Sea. Al-Rayy is in the NE of the Jibāl privince to the S of Māzandarān (Le Strange, *Lands*, p. 368 ff. and map V).

[12] See Abū Makhramah in Löfgren, *Texte*, I, p. 31.

to …[1] in the regions of Devagiri,[2] the first part of the borders of which are Malva.[3] It ran also under sea and sand and it is said it was the work of the jinn – and there can be no doubt about that.

The chiefs of Hamadhān dug in the midst of their properties [113] an underground passage leading to Rūdhrāwar, a journey of three days.[4] Karshāsb b. Athraṭ b. Rustum[5] dug an underground passage in the middle of his palace in the fortress of Arāk in Sīstān, the end of which led into the middle of Ḥiṣār Ṭāq, a distance of twelve parasangs.[6] He also dug Biʾr al-Jubb in the environs of Mosul.[7] The Christians have said that, when he killed Sanḥārīb, his son,[8] who was being held hostage,[9] he threw him down into a hole which was near by. An underground passage was also dug out leading to the Zāb, a distance of four parasangs.[10] The Christians have also said that he lived as a hostage after the death [of his son], understanding what had happened in the past [to his son] and living until now in these parts.

A certain Indian tunnel digger dug an underground passage in the town of Barhank, a distance of four parasangs with a road [through it].[11] What was reported as follows by Abū Ṭālib b. Abī Bakr b. Abī Ṭālib al-Ḥaddānī, known as Ibn al-Suwaydāʾī, was his reason [for doing this]. He fell madly in love with the daughter of the king, so he dug an underground passage from his own house to that of the girl. He would go to her and she come to him along this route as long as they lived. When Sultan Niẓām al-Dīn Maḥmūd b. Sebüktegīn[12] laid waste the land, the underground passage remained as it was. There also remained on the road to Mecca a mountain called al-Makhrūq,[13] with a hole in it connecting the foot with the summit – it has been mentioned above.[14]

In the environs of Mosul, there is a village called al-Nāʿūr [waterwheel],[15] a place belonging to Arabs from the time of the Prophet – God bless him and grant him peace. The water of the waterwheel swirled so violently that an underground passage was dug out, stretching all the way from the waterwheel to the Tigris, a distance of five parasangs.

[1] Not decipherable from ḥ.ʾ.ḥ.h.n.

[2] See Löfgren, *Texte*, I, p. 31.

[3] Ibid., quoting Dey (*Dictionary*, p. 54) says Devagiri is a hill between Ujjain and Mandasor in the centre of Malva, which makes the reading *awwal ḥudūd-h Mālwā* difficult to interpret.

[4] Rūdhrāwar is an area famed for it saffron about halfway between Hamadhān and Nehavand in Jibāl province (Le Strange, *Lands*, p. 197 and map V).

[5] Persian Garshāsb, a legendary hero and dragon slayer. There is no Rustum in the long Ṭabarī genealogy (*History*, III, p. 115–16), but cf. Steingass (*Dictionary*, p. 1082), 'ancestor of Rustam'.

[6] There appears to be no Arāk in Sīstān/Sijistān, nor indeed Arrān (well-known as an area of Gīlān, W of the Caspian). Ḥiṣār Ṭāq is in Sīstān; see above p. 131, n. 8.

[7] OL suggests with the reading Dayr al-Jubb, but I take the *b r* of the L MS to read 'Biʾr'.

[8] See n. 2 above.

[9] Reading *murtahan*.

[10] There are two tributaries of the Tigris named Zāb, the Upper, which pours in the Tigris about 30 miles S of Mosul, and the Lower, about 40 miles S of that (Le Strange, *Lands*, p. 87 and map II).

[11] Edmund Bosworth suggests to me that this might be an error for Bihank and connected to the river of that name which rises in Assam and flows into the Bay of Bengal (Ahmad, *India*, 110–11). I am grateful to him for this suggestion and for the reference above.

[12] I.e. the third Ghaznavid ruler, Maḥmūd b. Sebüktegīn, reg. 388–421/998–1030 (*EI*, 'Ghaznawids').

[13] Unidentified.

[14] Reading *min liḥfi-h* with OL. Ibn al-Mujāwir has not in fact mentioned this mountain.

[15] The name does not seem to be known, but it must be al-Nāʿūr; the village is called after the waterwheel.

In the fortress of Nishapur Shāh Būr b. Irdshīr Bābkān dug an underground passage for a distance of five parasangs, leading into a desert area.[1] He did this simply to make the fortress secure [114] and to prevent the shedding of the blood of the people. As one says: Escape at the right time is victory.

We return to what we were saying at first.[2] When the ships are delayed from coming up with the trade-fleet of Aden port, seven head of cattle are taken to Jabal Ṣīrah at sunset. The cattle remain where they are until midnight. After the passing of the time limit, six head of them are brought back to Aden, while one head remains there in its place. Early next morning, it is slaughtered where it is. This slaughtered animal is called 'the slaughtered animal of the mountain'. When this action is performed, the ships proceed and catch up with one another. This has become the practice from the olden days of the Zurayʿid dynasty and other Arab dynasties, but it has been abandoned in these present times.

Section. When a ship is opposite the town of Socotra, [Sūq],[3] or Jabal Kudummul, the fact that she is opposite is called 'safety'.[4] An earthenware pot is taken on which is set a sail and rudder of all the ship's gear. In it is placed some food stuffs consisting of a little coconut, salt and ashes[5] and it is thrown into the sea of terrifying waves. People of experience who have tried it out say that it reaches the side of the mountain in safety.

In the time of the Copts and Greeks, when the Nile was rising, the most beautiful virgin would be decked out as decoratively as possible, dressed in jewellery and dresses and brought in front of witnesses with a drum and fife. They would set her afloat into the Nile. This practice was done away with in the time of the Commander of the Faithful, ʿUmar b. al-Khaṭṭāb.[6]

In Atchin[7] and all the regions of India and Sind, when anyone plants sugar cane, he dedicates it to an idol. When his cane grows well, he sacrifices a human being, for when his cane is healthy, he tricks some young person and kills him, sprinkling his blood on the roots [115] of the sugar cane on their feast day called al-Dīwānī.[8] When the Sind river rises, taking over from the tide and passing its usual limit, a young gazelle dressed in a red garment, perfumed and fumigated, is taken and released in the deepest part of the water and where the current is strongest and most violent. Then the water recedes with the help of God – He is ever almighty. We only mention this as a proof of what we say and what we said above. God knows best.

[1] Nishapur was one of the quarters of Khurasan. The town lies in the W of the province (Le Strange, *Lands*, p. 382 ff. and map VIII). The person is unidentifed. *Barriyyah* might be a place name here.

[2] In dealing with the following passage, I have lent heavily on the notes of RBS.

[3] RBS suggests that the town of Sūq is meant here, perhaps because of its importance as a medieval port. (Al-)Sūq is about 4 miles E of Hadibo, the capital of Socotra on the N coast of the island (Socotra map, Suk; Doe, *Socotra*, p. 13 and map, pp. 110–11; Smith, 'Dhofar and Socotra', p. 86).

[4] Arabic *fawlah* (more literally, 'good omen'). The practice is merely an offering after a safe arrival to appease evil forces such as the jinn. RBS has found modern equivalents ('Maritime Customary Law', p. 199).

[5] RBS notes that ashes are often used against the jinn.

[6] The second Orthodox caliph, reg. 13–23/634–44.

[7] Arabic Ajah. See Löfgren, *Texte*, I, p. 34.

[8] I can only think the well-known Hindu festival Diwali is meant. Edmund Bosworth directs me towards Yule and Burnell, *Hobson-Jobson*, pp. 308-09. I take the anglicized version of the name from the *Hobson-Jobson* reference.

Al-Muʿajjalayn.[1] This is a cistern at the end of Jabal Ḥuqqāt and Jabal Ṣīrah, on the summit of which al-Manẓar palace was built.[2] God only knows who created the cistern between Jabal Ḥuqqāt and Jabal Ṣīrah, with its many deep, terrible waves.

I was informed by Manṣūr b. Muqarrib b. ʿAlī al-Dimashqī as follows. When the water is cold in the cistern, the year will be hard for anyone travelling through an east wind. I asked him why. He said it was because the waves were so many and the sea so swollen. When the water in the cistern is tepid, the year will be good and of great ease for one travelling. This is proven by experience.

I asked Rayḥān, the client of ʿAlī b. Masʿūd b. ʿAlī b. Aḥmad,[3] why this place was called al-Muʿajjalayn and he replied that it was because only two out of four people return there.

Buḥayrat al-Aʿājim. It has been reported as follows. When Dhū al-Qarnayn released the sea from Jabal Bāb al-Mandab and it flowed out, all the area around Aden dried up. The half of Aden on the Jabal al-ʿUrr side from near to Ṣīrah lay exposed and that near to al-Mabāh and as far as Jabal ʿImrān[4] was dry. When the Persian rulers took over Aden they saw this exposed area and were afraid for the town, that someone coming to conquer might lay siege to it. [116] Then they made an opening on the side near to Jabal ʿImrān and released the sea over it. The sea poured forth, descending until it drowned the whole exposed area around Aden. Aden became an island. Anyone intending to journey in any direction would load his wares into *ṣanbūq*s, travelling on the original sea and onwards across[5] the [new area of] sea. The camel caravans arrived, picking up the goods from al-Maksar and journeying on with them. When they saw how tired the people were of all this, al-Maksar was built, which was a bridge built on seven columns, so the people began to use it on their beasts of burden etc. The new-made sea was called Buḥayrat al-Aʿājim[6] and was known by their name for all times.

The building of Aden. When the dynasty of the pharoahs came to an end, the place fell into ruins as their dynasty disappeared. A group of fishermen settled the island, fishing there. They remained a long time thus, provided with God's sustenance and a livelihood, until some Madagascans[7] arrived in ships with lots of people and took control of the island after chasing out the fishermen by force. They settled the summit of al-Jabal al-Aḥmar,[8] Ḥuqqāt and Jabal al-Manẓar, a mountain overlooking the

[1] I.e. 'the cistern of the two who died before their time'. See the final sentence of the section below at p. 138.

[2] It is impossible to understand the location of the cistern. Ṣīrah is an island and there is no mountain in the region of Ḥuqqāt.

[3] I.e. the author's uncle.

[4] Not marked on modern maps of Aden.

[5] Arabic *yuʿaddī* (Dozy, *Supplément*, II, p. 105). This is before the building of the bridge al-Maksar between Aden and the mainland.

[6] 'Lake of the Persians'. Abū Makhramah (Löfgren, *Texte*, I, p. 22) writes that B al-A was the sea stretching from al-Mabāh as far as Rubāk and as far as Jabal ʿImrān.

[7] Arabic *ahl al-Qumr* (Tibbetts, *Navigation*, p. 69). I leave the translation thus, although FLS suggests that Tibbetts' explanation might be too simplified. She further suggests that they could be the inhabitants of the Comoros.

[8] Not found on modern maps. See Norris and Penhey, *Tanks*, p. 6, the epigraph, thus linking this sentence with the building of the Aden tanks.

boatyards.[1] Traces of them still exist and their building remains in stone and gypsum, brought from these wadis and mountains. The poet recited as follows:

> I shed tears in large drops since the encampments are empty.
> He, urging on their reddish camels, travelled on, so the nightingales were disturbed.
> I stopped at their abodes, chattering on about them and asking,
> 'O abode, is there any news?' The answer came back quickly to me;]
> [117] Someone answered me with a shout from the encampments,
> 'Weep blood, o you who are unaware; the caravans have already departed.'
> I have a real temptress among them, naturally slender,
> in her cheek a rose and in her figure a lean branch.

They used to come up from Madagascar, taking in Aden in one go in one monsoon. Ibn al-Mujāwir said as follows. These communities with these rulers died out and this route fell in disuse. There is no one left in our time who knows what happened to them, nor how many they were, nor how they were.[2]

Section. Ibn al-Mujāwir said as follows. From Aden to Mogadishu is one monsoon, from Mogadishu to Kilwah a second and from Kilwah to Madagascar a third. But [some] people would turn the three monsoons into one: in 626[3] a ship sailed from Madagascar to Aden in this way, setting sail from Madagascar, making for Kilwah, but dropping anchor in Aden. Their ships have paddles[4] on account of the narrowness, rockiness and shallowness of their seas. When these people became weak and the East Africans got the better of them, they forced them out and took over the land and settled the wadi, a place which is now inhabited [by people] in reed huts.[5] They were the first to build reed huts in Aden. When they had gone, the place fell into ruin and remained thus until the inhabitants of Sīrāf moved out [and settled there]. They have been mentioned above.

Sulṭān Shāh b. Jamshīd b. Asʿad b. Qayṣar[6] came to Aden. He stopped and settled there and the place became repopulated. Drinking water was brought to them from Zaylaʿ, but when the long distance became too much for them, they built a tank for rain water and building clay was transported from around Abyan.[7] It is also said it was from Zaylaʿ. When there were many people in Aden, they built baths. One was constructed at Ḥabs al-Dam, a flow of water was provided and in 622[8] it [also] watered the land. They [also] built the Friday mosque, this at [118] the bathhouse

[1] Arabic *ṣināʿah* (Dozy, *Supplément*, I, p. 848).

[2] Arabic … 'wa-lā kam kayf kānat aḥwālu-hum wa-umūru-hum' (Smith, 'Language', p. 331).

[3] Begins 30 November 1228.

[4] I am grateful to Dionisius Agius and to FLS for their comments on the meaning of *ajniḥah*.

[5] Arabic *ṣarīfah, ṣarāʾif*, 'palm or reed huts' (Landberg, *Glossaire daṯînois*, III, p. 2127; Löfgren, *Texte*, II, p. 43).

[6] This and other members of the Qayṣarī house mentioned below do not figure in the historical sources at my disposal. The pre-Zurayʿid history of Aden is of course little documented and therefore little known and, given the lack of corroboration from other sources, we should treat this material with great caution. The editor of *Chronicle*, Yajima, mentions the name (p. 10) and would seem to have written of the family. I regret I have no access to his Tokyo publications.

[7] See Norris and Penhey, *Tanks*, p. 25.

[8] Begins 15 January 1225.

of al-Muʿtamid Raḍī al-Dīn ʿAlī b. Muḥammad al-Tikrītī.[1] He made Marbaṭ al-Saylah[2] in 625.[3] It filled the side of al-Jabal al-Akhḍar completely. When he saw this, he appointed himself sultan.

The honorific titles of the Persians who ruled over Aden. Our lord, the benefactor, mine of nobility, the learned ruler, the just, strengthened from heaven, granted victory over his enemies, crowned with glory and splendour, the revered shahanshah, controller of the community, lord of the sultans of the Arabs and Persians, preserver of God's servants, guard over God's land, valuing the friends of God, humiliating God's enemies, succour of this world and of the Faith, support of Islam and the Muslims, crown of the rulers of mankind, overpowerer of tyrants and polytheists, giving aid to the conquering state, destroying unbelieving communities, reviving brilliant practices, expanding justice and compassion, helper of the sultanate and the caliphate, pillar of the states of this world, rendering victorious God's highest word, providing well-being to all creation through your just treatment, destroyer of tyranny and deviousness, undertaking to strengthen the truth, bringing about man's righteousness, God's shadow on earth, reviver of religious custom and duty, sultan of land and sea, ruler of east and west, Atā Sultan Shāh b. Jamshīd b. Asʿad b. Qayṣar, Commander of the Faithful.

Another [was as follows]: Our lord, the benefactor, magnificence of the state and the Faith, glory of Islam and the Muslims, helper of rulers and sultans, succour of the armies of mankind, killer of Kharijites and polytheists, the prop of religion, order of the community, leader of the state, valuing the sultanate, implement of the caliphate, chief[4] of Iran and Turkistan, Abū Sinān Sayāwush b. Asʿad b. Qayṣar,[5] partner of the Commander of the Faithful.

Another [was as follows]: Our lord, the benefactor, partner in the Faith, oath of Islam, finely tempered sword of the state, prop of religious custom, aid of rulers, magnificence of amirs, Kurdū [119] Abū al-Muẓaffar Asʿad b. Qayṣar,[6] proof of the Commander of the Faithful.

Another [was as follows]: Our lord, the benefactor, glory of state and Faith, giving aid to Islam and the Muslims, valuing rulers and sultans, sword of religious custom, magnificence of religion, crown of the community, order of the state, assisting the caliphate, pride of amirs Munīr Bāyak Abū Shujāʿ Nāmshād b. Asʿad b. Qayṣar,[7] aid of the Commander of the Faithful.

Another [was as follows]: Our lord, the benefactor, the loyal, the most glorious, strengthened, helper of the Faith, pillar of Islam, the nobility of Turkistan, sharp sword of religious custom, glory of rulers, help of amirs, Zindeh Abū al-Fatḥ Kai Kuvād b. Muḥammad b. Qayṣar,[8] who values the Commander of the Faithful.

[1] The name and the following date indicate that he was in the train of the Ayyubids, but I find no reference to him in the sources.

[2] The open place in Aden where animals coming into the town were tethered (Landberg, *Glossaire daṯînois*, II, p. 1071).

[3] Begins 12 December 1227.

[4] Reading *bahlūl*.

[5] See above, p. 138, n. 6.

[6] Unidentified.

[7] Unidentified.

[8] Unidentified.

Another [was as follows]: The lord, reviver of the Faith, valuing Islam and stay of the state, strength of rulers, supporter of amirs, Abū Saʿīd Qayar b. Rustum b. Qayṣar,[1] support of the Commander of the Faithful.

Another [was as follows]: The lord, sword of the dynasty and the Faith, succour of Islam and the Muslims, crown of rulers and sultans, helper of religious custom, order of religion, pillar of the community, support of the rule, help of the caliphate, giving assistance to amirs, ruler of Arabs and Persians, Abū al-Ṣamṣām ʿĀd b. Shaddād b. Jamshīd b. Asʿad b. Qayṣar,[2] oath of the Commander of the Faithful.

Another [was as follows]: The lord, crown of the Faith, helper of Islam and the Muslims, glory of rulers and sultans, valuing religious custom, reviver of religion, succour of the community, stay of the rule, oath of the caliphate, glory of amirs, ruler of India and the Yemen, father of King Tāj al-Dīn Jamshīd b. Asʿad b. Qayṣar,[3] backbone of the Commander of the Faithful.

Another [was as follows]: The lord, pillar of the state and of the Faith, reviver of Islam and the Muslims, backbone of rulers and sultans, order of religion, rendering victorious religious custom, goodness of rulers, valuing amirs, Abū al-Wafāʾ Kadhār Shāh b. Hazārāsb,[4] oath of the Commander of the Faithful.

Another [was as follows]: The lord, valuing the state and the Faith, crown of Islam [120] and the Muslims, stay of rulers and sultans, prop of religious custom, support of the community, helper of the rule, reviver of the community, pillar of the caliphate, glory of amirs, Abū al-Barakāt al-Ḥārith Hazārāsb b. Jamshīd b. Asʿad,[5] sharp sword of the Commander of the Faithful. These are the Persian rulers of Aden.

Building the Friday mosque. One of the matters reported by ʿUmārah b. Muḥammad b. ʿUmārah in *Kitāb al-Mufīd fī akhbār madīnat Zabīd* was as follows.[6] The Friday mosque of Aden was built by ʿUmar b. ʿAbd al-ʿAzīz[7] and renovated by al-Ḥusayn b. Salāmah. But the most accurate version [of the story] is that the mosque was built by the Persians. The reason for its construction was that in their time they found a fine, large piece of ambergris which was brought to the lord of Aden. He asked them, 'What can I do with it? Sell it and build a Friday mosque using the money raised. In my opinion no dirham would be more legitimate[ly raised], nor spent in a better way, than this.' So they sold the ambergris and used the price raised from it to build the Friday mosque of Aden on the edge of the town. If someone asks why it was not built in the centre of town, I say, 'Because in the centre of town there is a spring of water stretching from the sea as far as al-Mimlāḥ. We have an illustration of what we are saying in that from the remains of the spring there is a salt pan where salt is made into blocks at al-Mimlāḥ.'

Ibn al-Mujāwir said as follows. I noticed behind the bathhouse of al-Muʿtamid Raḍī al-Dīn Muḥammad b. ʿAlī al-Tikrītī that a great flood watered the wadi land, so several tanneries appeared there dating from the time of the Persians. Because of the long period of time [since then], earth has covered them over.

1 Unidentified.
2 Unidentified.
3 Unidentified.
4 Unidentified.
5 Unidentified.
6 See Kay, *Yaman*, p. 9.
7 The 5th Marwanid Umayyad caliph, reg. 99–101/717–20 (Bosworth, *Islamic Dynasties*, p. 3).

I was informed by Rayḥān, the client of ʿAlī b. Masʿūd b. ʿAlī as follows. A great big bathhouse appeared at Ḥabs al-Dam near Jabal Ḥuqqāt, long and wide, which had been covered over by earth from the construction work carried out by the Persians. During the period of the Persian state, people used to find a great deal of ambergris towards Bāb al-Mandab. The fishermen too used to find it and when [121] a ship or merchant passed by, they would say, 'Buy our sea grass!', meaning ambergris. It is said that Shaykh Shubayr al-Ṣayyād found a piece of ambergris and did not know what it was. He took it home and, having no firewood, used it as fuel under his cooking-pot instead of firewood. People got to hear about this, so he was known as the man who stokes up the fire with ambergris. All this has stopped at this present time because of our being under suspicion and our evil deeds.[1] 'He whom God guides is indeed guided; he who leads astray will never find a guiding friend.'[2] When the days of the Persians came to an end, the Arabs ruled over [Aden].

History of the family of Zurayʿ b. al-ʿAbbās b. al-Mukarram, rulers of Aden.[3] Their pedigree is from Hamdān, then from Jusham b. Yām b. Aṣbā.[4] There was in their grandfather, al-ʿAbbās b. al-Mukarram b. al-Dhiʾb, a commendable precedent in raising the Mutanṣirī mission[5] along with Dāʿī ʿAlī b. Muḥammad al-Ṣulayḥī, then with his son al-Mukarram, when he went down from Ṣanʿāʾ to Zabīd and when his mother, Asmāʾ bint Shihāb b. Asʿad, was captured by al-Aḥwal Saʿīd b. Najāḥ.[6] The reason for their ruling over Aden was that, when al-Ṣulayḥī conquered it, when B. Maʿn were there, he left it in their hands. When al-Ṣulayḥī was killed,[7] B. Maʿn only pretended to continue their loyalty in Aden. So al-Mukarram sent Aḥmad b. ʿAlī against them.[8] He conquered it, did away with B. Maʿn and appointed as governors al-ʿAbbās and Masʿūd, the sons of al-Mukarram. He made al-Taʿkar in Aden the seat of al-ʿAbbās, this including the mainland and the gate. He made Ḥuṣn al-Khaḍrāʾ over to Masʿūd, this including the coastal area and shipping. He made them swear an oath to al-Ḥurrah al-Sayyidah, the daughter of al-Malik Aḥmad, since al-Ṣulayḥī had given Aden as a dowry when he married her to his son, al-Mukarram, in [122] 461.[9] The taxes of Aden continued to come to her, amounting to at least 100,000 dinars, until al-Mukarram Aḥmad died. After al-Mukarram's death, al-ʿAbbās and Masʿūd, his sons, kept their oath to her. When they died, Zurayʿ b. al-ʿAbbās and Abū al-Ghārāt b. Masʿūd took possession of Aden, so al-Mufaḍḍal b. Abī al-Barakāt[10] marched there and

[1] Since these are Ibn al-Mujāwir's own words, I have to wonder whether he is referring to some kind of anti-Persian feeling on the part of the local Arabs.

[2] Quran 18:17. Ibn al-Mujāwir misquotes here: *man yahdī* for *man yahdi*.

[3] 473–561/1080–1166. The pedigree is correct, although ʿUmārah (Kay, *Yaman*, 64) and Hamdānī (*al-Ṣulayḥiyyūn*, p. 345, tree 7; Appendix B.1 below) prefer al-Karam. This account is essentially ʿUmārah's (p. 64 ff.).

[4] Ibn al-Mujāwir is correct here and ʿUmārah (Kay, *Yaman*, p. 64), Aṣghā, wrong (Nashwān, *Shams*, VI, p. 3654; Caskel, *Ğamharat an-nasab*, I, Tafel 229).

[5] I.e. the *daʿwah* of the 8th Fatimid caliph, reg. 427–87/1036–94 (Hamdānī, *al-Ṣulayḥiyyūn*, p. 343, tree 7; Appendix B.1 below; Bosworth, *Islamic Dynasties*, p. 63).

[6] In c. 473/1080. For a brief survey of the event, see Smith, 'Political History', pp. 131.

[7] In 473/1080 (ibid., p. 133).

[8] The two were brothers, the date 473/1080 (ibid., p. 138).

[9] Begins 31 October 1068.

[10] Queen Arwā's (al-Ḥurrah) trusty lieutenant, lord of al-Taʿkar, overlooking Dhū Jiblah, the capital of the Sulayhids (ibid., p. 132).

battles took place between him and the [two Zurayʿids]. The last of these brought peace on the basis of half of the tax of Aden [being handed over to the Sulayhids]. When al-Mufaḍḍal died, the inhabitants of Aden seized the remaining half [of tax revenue], so Asʿad b. Abī al-Futūḥ, the cousin of al-Mufaḍḍal, marched on the [Zurayʿids] and made peace with them on the basis that a quarter of the tax revenue be handed over to al-Ḥurrah. When the B. al-Zarr[1] rose up in al-Taʿkar, the inhabitants of Aden seized the quarter assigned to al-Ḥurrah and she no longer had anything in Aden because of the death of her followers. ʿAlī b. Ibrāhīm b. Najīb al-Dawlah[2] could do nothing about all this. God knows best and is most wise.

What happened between them.[3] Al-Mufaḍḍal b. Abī al-Barakāt went down to Zabīd in the course of one of his raiding expeditions, accompanied by Zurayʿ b. al-ʿAbbās and [the latter's] uncle, Masʿūd b. al-Mukarram, [they being the lords of Aden at that time].[4] But they were both killed at the gate of Zabīd. After them in Aden, Abū al-Suʿūd b. Zurayʿ and Abū al-Ghārāt b. Masʿūd took over the reins of government, then after them Amir Dāʿī Sabaʾ b. Abī al-Suʿūd and Muḥammad b. Abī al-Ghārāt.[5] [There followed] then his son, ʿAlī al-Aʿazz, then ʿAlī b. Abī al-Ghārāt, then Dāʿī Muḥammad b. Sabaʾ,[6] then his son, ʿImrān. After his death, [Aden] remained completely devoted to the Zurayʿids, Muḥammad and Abū al-Suʿūd, ʿImrān's sons, who were children. God knows best and is most wise.

[123] *The reason for the fall of the rule of ʿAlī b. Abī al-Ghārāt and [Aden's] falling into the hands of Dāʿī Sabaʾ.* Muḥammad b. al-Jazarī was the deputy of ʿAlī b. Abī al-Ghārāt for half of Aden, while Aḥmad b. Ghiyāth[7] was the deputy of Sabaʾ in the [other] half. Ibn al-Jazarī shared with Aḥmad b. Ghiyāth in the portion of the tax revenue, but the followers of ʿAlī b. Abī al-Ghārāt began to indulge in oppression among the people: they did mischief, were corrupt and freely spoke ill of Dāʿī Sabaʾ. Then Commander Bilāl b. Jarīr al-Muḥammadī[8] rose against the governors of Aden, Dāʿī Sabaʾ already having commanded him to take up arms against the people and stir up fighting in Aden. Bilāl did this and great battles took place between them in Lahej, the last of which [ended in] the killing there by Dāʿī Sabaʾ b. Abī al-Suʿūd of ʿAlī b. Abī al-Ghārāt in 545.[9]

[1] This must be the correct reading. They are mentioned by ʿUmārah (Kay, *Yaman*, p. 66) and must have inhabited the area of Dhū Jiblah.

[2] The son of another of Arwā's supporters. His father eventually turned against her, was sent off back to Egypt and died at sea in c. 519/1125. If this information is true, his son must have been in Arwā's service and may even have remained after his father's death (Smith, 'Political History', p. 132).

[3] The following passage can be understood better after reference to Hamdānī (*al-Ṣulayḥiyyūn*, p. 345, tree 7, B. al-Karam). The tree is copied below as Appendix B.1.

[4] This last circumstantial clause is taken from ʿUmārah (Kay, *Yaman*, p. 49), since *wa-la-humā yawmaʾidhin ṣabiyyān/ṣibyān fī ʿAdan* in the text makes no sense.

[5] OL adds unnecessarily 'b. Abī Bakr'; Muḥammad's father was Abū al-Ghārāt (Hamdānī, *al-Ṣulayḥiyyūn*, p. 345, tree 7; Appendix B.1 below).

[6] The Zurayʿid ruler, 534–48/1139–53 (Smith, ' Political History', p. 138; Appendix B.6 below). I have ignored the phrase after 'Muḥammad b. Saba''. The text reads 'wa-hwa ākhir B. Dāʾūd!' ʿUmārah (Kay, *Yaman*, pp. 67/49 [Arabic], 270, n. 59) has *wa-hwa ākhir B. Zurayʿ* and is equally mistaken. Kay (p. 67/49) eventually follows al-Janadī, 'wa-hwa ākhir B. Masʿūd', though that is also inaccurate.

[7] ʿUmārah (Kay, *Yaman*, p. 68) calls his father ʿAttāb.

[8] See above p. 87, n. 6.

[9] Begins 30 April 1150.

[The former] bequeathed power to his son, ʿAlī al-Aʿazz,[1] who resided in al-Dumluwah. He planned to kill Bilāl in Aden. But ʿAlī al-Aʿazz died,[2] having bequeathed power to his children, Ḥātim, ʿAbbās and Manṣūr. They were minors, so he put them under the protection of Anīs, an Abyssinian slave. Now Muḥammad b. Sabaʾ[3] had fled from his brother and sought the protection of Amir Manṣūr b. Mufaḍḍal b. Abī al-Barakāt. He duly offered him this protection. When ʿAlī al-Aʿazz died in al-Dumluwah, Bilāl despatched some Hamdānīs and they snatched Muḥammad b. Sabaʾ away from al-Manṣūr b. al-Mufaḍḍal. They went back down to Aden and Bilāl made him ruler, making the people swear an oath to him and marrying him to his daughter. He prepared him to lead an army and he besieged Anīs and Yaḥyā, the governor in al-Dumluwah. He took control of the latter and the whole country obeyed him. Then he died in 548.[4] His son, ʿImrān b. Muḥammad, became ruler after him, then he died in 560,[5] leaving behind two sons, Muḥammad and Abū al-Suʿūd. Abū al-Nadā Bilāl b. Jarīr al-Muḥammadī became governor in [5]34[6] and died in 577,[7] leaving adult sons, including Mudāfiʿ and Yāsir, the last members of the dynasty.

[124] There is also another version of the story as follows. After their death, Sabaʾ b. Abī al-Suʿūd and Muḥammad b. Abī al-Ghārāt, the Zurayʿids, ruled over Aden, one collecting the tax on imports on land and the other on maritime imports. The area was divided equally between them, each one taking his due of taxes. A great dispute occurred among the people on the question of water and firewood and heavy fighting concerning income and expenditure and this was at the Sāʾilah.[8] Thus they remained until the ruler of the island of Qays[9] prepared *dūnījs*, *burmahs* like *bārīkhī burmahs* and *ṣanbūqs* in order to take Aden from its lords.[10] When the *dūnījs* arrived, they anchored under Jabal Ṣīrah.

[1] See Hamdānī's family tree (*al-Ṣulayḥiyyūn*, p. 345, tree 7; Appendix B.1 below).

[2] In 534/1139 (ibid.).

[3] Brother of ʿAlī, d. 548/1153 (ibid.).

[4] Begins 27 March 1153.

[5] Begins 18 November 1164.

[6] Begins 28 August 1139.

[7] Begins 17 May 1181.

[8] Does Ibn al-Mujāwir mean, or was this the same as, the Saylah?

[9] See Löfgren's long note (*Texte*, I, 43, n. 12). Qays is undoubtedly the island about 150 miles almost due N of Abu Dhabi in the Gulf, only about 10 miles from the Iranian coast (Lorimer. *Gazetteer*, IIB, pp. 1471–4 and map; Arabian Peninsula map; *Iraq*, p. 161; *EI*, 'Ḳays'). Despite Löfgren's note and Ibn al-Mujāwir's clear understanding to the contrary, Ibn Baṭṭūṭah (*Travels*, IV, p. 848) correctly takes Qays and Kīsh/Kis as two different islands, the latter being Kishm/Qeshm, the large island sitting in the straits of Hurmuz (*Iraq*, p. 158, 160, figs 42, 43). Le Strange (*Land*, pp. 6, 257, 261, 296) also muddies the water somewhat, particularly p. 257.

[10] I leave technical ship terms in their text original, since they vary so much in meaning chronologically and geographically and are difficult to translate precisely. These are ships coming from the Gulf to Aden: *dawānīj*, sing. *dūnīj*, perhaps the same as the Persian *dūnī* and *dūngī* (= dinghy) and the south Indian, Sri Lankan and Maldivian *dōni* (Muqaddasī, *Aḥsan*, p. 32; Kindermann, *Schiff*, p. 28; Steingass, *Dictionary*, p. 547; Yule and Burnell, *Hobson-Jobson*, p. 323; Tibbetts, *Navigation*, p. 56; Qanāʿī and Khuṣūṣī, *Tārīkh*, p. 352; Grosset-Grange, *Glossaire*, p. 110); perhaps *buramāt/abrām*, sing. *burmah* (not *būmah* which is a modern word) (Muqaddasī, p. 32; Kindermann, p. 7; Nukhaylī, *al-Sufun*, p. 13; Agius, *Dhow*, p. 202); Dionisius Agius informs me that the *burmah* is 'a medieval round ship of the Indian Ocean' which he discusses in a forthcoming book, *Classic Ships of Islam*; I tentatively read *bārīkhī* after reference to Kindermann, p. 5, *bārīkhah* which must be some sort of tug; I prefer RBS's reading *sanābīq* here, rather than *nahābīq*, although this is usually a small boat used to convey men and goods from roadstead to shore. It has come into Arabic through Persian from Sanskrit (*śambūka*) and has several spellings, *sīn* and *ṣād*, *qāf* and *kāf*, etc. (Yule and Burnell, *Hobson-Jobson*, p. 788; Agius, 'Vessel-types', p. 179; *Dhow*, pp. 218, 83–6).

They sent their messengers to the Zurayʿids, lords of al-Taʿkar and al-Khaḍrāʾ and they said to them, 'You should know that the ruler of Kis has sent us to take Aden. If you accept peace, it will be fine; if not, we shall move against you in conquest and this will be less pleasant.' The lord of Ḥuṣn al-Khaḍrāʾ told them, 'I am with you; the town is your town; put in charge here whomsoever you will!' When the [Qaysī] forces heard these words, they disembarked from the *dūnījs* and the *burmahs* on to the sea shore, their hearts at peace [at the thought of] security and obedience. The lord of the Ḥuṣn al-Khaḍrāʾ sent them every possible form of hospitality, despatching for them flour, sheep and goats and date wine. So the invaders made bread and cooked their meals and bowls were passed around everyone. When the chief of the Jāshū[1] saw the behaviour of his men, he said to them, 'Stop what you are doing! It must be a plot hatched against you, you ignoramuses!' So he defrayed the expenses of bread, meat and date wine for them and they choked back their tears[2] as he recited as follows:

> Four things were imposed upon me as a trial – they were forced on me
> only to destroy me or to bring disaster and wretchness on me:
> Anxiety, giving in to worldly things, indulging myself and my desires.
> How can I escape from the hands of my enemies?

[125] *Section*. When the Jāshū dropped anchor in the anchorage of Aden, the lord of al-Taʿkar sent a message to his cousin, the lord of al-Khaḍrāʾ, saying, 'What are you doing? This enemy has overwhelmed us!' He replied, 'We've gone too far and things are out of control! You do as you think fit!' [The lord of al-Taʿkar] said, 'Come down from al-Khaḍrāʾ and I shall be able to deal for you with the evil they are bringing, for misfortune has dropped [on us] like a thousand bowel movements!' So he handed over the fortress to his cousin. Al-Manṣūr b. Ismāʿīl[3] recited as follows:

> These people are [like] a deep sea
> and [you need] a ship to distance yourself from them!
> I have given you good advice, so see to
> yourself, you poor wretch!

I was informed by Shaykh Bilāl b. Jarīr al-Muḥammadī as follows. When Ḥuṣn al-Khaḍrāʾ in Aden was possessed and al-Ḥurrah Bahjah, mother of ʿAlī b. Abī al-Ghārāt, was taken, unique treasures were found to be hers and the whole of Aden was in my hands for a long period. Bilāl [also] said, 'Between Aden and Lahej is a journey of one night. I recall that I wrote from Aden giving news of the conquest and the capture of al-Khaḍrāʾ and I despatched someone to give the good tidings to our lord, Dāʿī Sabaʾ b. Abī al-Suʿūd. On the same day as the conquest of al-Khaḍrāʾ took place, our lord took the town of al-Raʿāriʿ.[4] My messenger and his messenger met with the good news in 545[5]

[1] I.e. the forces from Qays. This is probably no more than the colloquial Persian *chāshū*, 'sailors' (Löfgren, *Texte*, I, 44, n. 3; II, p. 25). Ibn al-Mujāwir's own amusing etymology can be found in the text below, pp. 284 ff. See also Smith, 'Wondrous', p. 117.

[2] Arabic *jāshū*, a very neat pun!

[3] I have had to omit the *nisbah* which follows, al-ʾ.?.z.y.

[4] This is the correct version of the name (cf. Yāqūt, *Muʿjam*, III, pp. 140–41; Kay, *Yaman*, pp. 270–71, al-Zaʿāziʿ). It is the old capital of the province of Lahej lying to the N of Aden (Hamdānī, *Ṣifah* [Müller], pp. 77, 97; [Akwaʿ], p. 145, n. 4; ʿAbdalī, *Hadiyyah*, pp. 10–11).

[5] Begins 30 April 1150.

and this was the most amazing coincidence. The Jāshū were busy eating and drinking and there were drunks everywhere. Their chief began to call out to his men, 'Stop what you are doing!' But only those with intelligence and understanding heard him, while the rest continued until the lord of Ḥuṣn al-Taʿkar with a force of men attacked and put the Jāshū to the sword. No one survived except the elderly and their skulls [126] filled the whole area. When an Adeni was in doubt about a place, he would say, 'Where is it in relation to the skulls?' So the place became known as al-Jamājim,[1] i.e. the skulls of the Jāshū.

When the Zurayʿids won this victory, they came down from their fortresses and settled in the wadi. They built some marvellous houses. They were the first to build houses in Aden in stone and gypsum. The stone was brought for building to Aden from the regions of Abyan. Only Abū al-Ḥasan ʿAlī b. al-Ḍaḥḥāk al-Kūfī revealed the stone quarry to the inhabitants of Aden. When he had settled in Aden, he bought black slaves to cut the stone from the mountains of Aden and slave girls used to carry them on their backs. From that time on, they cut stone there and each quarry became known by its owner: ʿAlī al-Ankī quarry, Yūsuf al-Ardabīlī quarry, ... al-Baḥḥār[2] quarry, Ismāʿīl al-Salāmī quarry, Ḥamīd b. Ḥamāsah quarry, ʿAbd al-Wāḥid b. Maymūn quarry and Abū al-Ḥasan b. al-Dūrī quarry. They seized them and they became their property and source of profit.

Section. Shams al-Dawlah Tūrān Shāh b. Ayyūb b. Shādhī seized ʿAbd al-Nabī b. ʿAlī b. Mahdī,[3] the last of the Arab rulers of the Zabīd area and took him chained to Aden. He also seized Yāsir b. Bilāl b. Jarīr al-Muḥammadī, client of Dāʿī Muḥammad b. Abī al-Suʿūd b. Zurayʿ, the last dāʿī ruler. He sat them both down in a tent alone. ʿAbd al-Nabī turned round, saw Yāsir b. Bilāl glancing furtively at him, and said, 'You evil slave! Are you not looking at a lion shackled with an iron shackle and chained with an iron chain?'

The Zurayʿids used to pay tribute[4] to the Fatimid caliphs because [127] of [their common] religious leanings, for these [Zurayʿids] were Ismāʿīlīs and each one of them who ruled over the Yemen was called dāʿī, i.e. he summons[5] people to the cause. The heretics[6] who are rulers of Girdkūh and Alamūt,[7] two fortresses on a mountain on isolated mounds[8] belonging to them, i.e. the heretics, used to take taxes from Jabal

[1] Elsewhere al-Jamājimī, al-Ḥumāḥim(ī) (Löfgren, *Texte*, I, p. 45, n. 11; Muqaddasī, *Aḥsan*, p. 102; Nashwān, *Shams*, III, p. 1280; Hamdānī, *Ṣifah*, p. 53).

[2] The MSS are illegible: r.?.t. h. Al-Baḥḥār is a tentative reading.

[3] Both Mahdid brothers, ʿAbd al-Nabī and Aḥmad, were seized by the conquering Ayyubids in Zabīd as the latter moved S down Tihāmah soon after their landing in the N in about 569/1173. The Mahdids were both put to death by strangulation in 571/1176. Yāsir was put to death in the same year (Ibn Ḥātim, *Simṭ*, p. 20; Smith, ' Political History', p. 134).

[4] Arabic *kharāj*.

[5] Arabic *yaDʿū*.

[6] Arabic *malāḥidah*, presumably the Assassins (see below n. 7).

[7] I vocalize the former after reference to Steingass (*Dictionary*, pp. 1022, 1080 [Girdkoh]) and Le Strange, *Lands*, p. 221, n. 1). The geographers do not appear to know it, but Steingass says it is a mountain in Māzandarān/Ṭabaristān. Alamūt is better known and is situated less than 20 miles N of Qazvīn, just within Jibāl province, S of Māzandarān (Le Strange, *Lands*, p. 221 and map V). Alamūt was built by the Shīʿī, Ḥasan al-Dāʿī ilā al-Ḥaqq in 246/860. It later passed to Ḥasan Ṣabāḥ, 'the Old Man of the Mountains', the leader of the renegade Assassins. All these fortresses were destroyed by the Mongols in the 7th/13th century (Le Strange, *Lands*, p. 221; *EI*, 'Alamūt').

[8] Reading *ʿalā mudūr la-hum*, sing. *madarah* (Dozy, *Supplément*, II, p. 575).

al-Summāq[1] which was theirs in the regions of Syria, from the Qarāmiṭah[2] in Sind and from the Tawrsanā[3] who were in the regions of Najrān. Even if they are unbelievers, they all follow the same belief.

After them, the Ghuzz[4] ruled over the town [of Aden] and built al-Manẓar on Jabal Ḥuqqāt, after Shams al-Dawlah Tūrān Shāh b. Ayyūb had returned to Egypt from the Yemen.[5] He handed over Aden to ʿUthmān b. ʿAlī al-Zinjibīlī al-Tikrītī.[6]

Building of the wall of Aden.[7] I was informed as follows by ʿAbdallāh b. Muḥammad b. Yaḥyā. A ship [coming] from the west to Aden anchored at night. The *nākhūdhah*[8] disembarked from the ship and made a tour of Aden. All at once he came upon a lofty house, with lit candles and burning aloes wood.[9] He knocked at the door and a servant came down and opened up for him, saying to him, 'Is there anything I can do for you?' The merchant replied, 'Yes', so the servant gave him permission to enter and the owner of the house invited him up. Up he went and each greeted the other without being aware of who the other was. The conversation flowed and eventually the *nākhūdhah* said, 'I have come tonight from the west and am wanting, if you, sir, will be so kind, to hide some of my precious commodities with you.' The owner of the house asked him why. He replied, 'Out of fear of the dāʿī!'[10] The owner of the house said, 'Come,[11] do not be afraid of tyrants! Transport all you have to such-and-such a house.' The merchant left the house and the mariners began to put the goods from the ship into chests [and transport them] to the house [indicated by the owner of the house he had visited] until they had cleared out two thirds of the contents of the ship. In the morning the *nākhūdhah* discovered that his host of the previous evening was none other than the dāʿī himself! He said to himself, 'There was I afraid [128] of the rain and I fell under the drain-pipe!' He became perplexed and felt ashamed. The dāʿī summoned him and said, 'I was your host last night, but today I am the dāʿī, ruler of Aden. Don't worry! Relax! The customs tax[12] of your ship is my gift to you along with the house to which you came. Here are a thousand dinars which you can spend while you are in our town. It would be wrong for me to take anything from you, either by way of a gift or in the

[1] A great mountain region in the district of western Ḥalab which was covered with Ismāʿīlī settlements (Le Strange, *Palestine*, p. 81).

[2] A branch of the Ismāʿīliyyah (*EI*, 'Ḳarmaṭī').

[3] An unrecognizable corruption.

[4] I.e. the Ayyubids.

[5] Tūrānshāh left the Yemen for Egypt in 571/1176 (Abū Makhramah in Löfgren, *Texte*, II, p. 131).

[6] Ibn Ḥātim (*Simṭ*, p. 20) calls him ʿUthmān al-Sinjārī or al-Zinjārī. Abū Makhramah (in Löfgren, *Texte*, II, p. 131) calls him Abū ʿAmr ʿUthmān b. ʿAlī al-Zinjīlī, ʿIzz al-Dīn. I have deleted Ibn al-Mujāwir's 'Fakhr al-Dīn Abū ʿUthmān' and corrected Löfgren' s insertion "ʿUmar b. ʿUthmān'. There is no evidence that he had connections with Tikrīt in Iraq, rather they were with Damascus where he died in 583/1187.

[7] See also Abū Makhramah's version (in Löfgren, *Texte*, I, p. 13).

[8] I.e. 'owner-captain', 'supercargo', Persian *nā-khūda* (Landberg, *Glossaire daṯînois*, III, 2729–30; Yule and Burnell, *Hobson-Jobson*, pp. 612–13, 'nacoda/nacoder'; Löfgren, *Texte*, II, pp. 58–9; Steingass, *Dictionary*, p. 1368).

[9] See above p. 52, n. 1.

[10] I.e. one of the Zurayʿid rulers (473–ca. 561/1080–1166). See Appendix B.6 below.

[11] Reading *aqbil*. It might also read *aqbalu*, ' I accept'.

[12] Ibn al-Mujāwir uses the word *ʿashūr*, a singular word (plur. *ʿashūrāt*) and not *ʿusūr*, the plural of *ʿushr* (See Smith, ' Trade', pp. 131, 135, n. 18, with all relevant references).

process of buying and selling.' The *nākhūdah* asked, ' Why are you doing all this?' The dāʿī replied, 'Because you came into our house yesterday at midnight.'[1]

[The dāʿī] ordered a wall to be extended from al-Ḥuṣn al-Akhḍar as far as Jabal Ḥuqqāt. A weak wall was thrown around, one part inserted into another. Through the constant [pounding] of the waves against it, it fell into ruin. Then a second wall was put round, made of intertwined reeds. This remained in place until ʿUthmān b. ʿAlī al-Zinjibīlī[2] built a wall on Jabal al-Manẓar as far as the end of Jabal al-ʿUrr. He put the Ḥuqqāt gate in it.[3] He put another wall on al-Jabal al-Akhḍar, the extent of which was from Ḥuṣn al-Akhḍar as far as al-Taʿkar over the tops of the mountains. He built a wall around the shore area from the shipyard as far as Jabal Ḥuqqāt. He put six gates in it: Shipyard gate, Ḥawmah gate, al-Saylah gate, two gates through which the flood went out when there was rain in Aden, Customs House gate, through which goods entered and left, a gate overlooking [the road], left open for incoming and outgoing customs fees, Ḥuyyaq gate and Land gate, mentioned above. He built the wall of Aden with stone and gypsum and the customs house with two doors.[4]

Section. Ibn al-Mujāwir said as follows. A man landing from the sea is like one coming out of the grave. The customs house is like the Meeting Place[5] where there are disputes, accounting, weighing and calculating. If anyone is in profit, he feels [129. Plan of Aden, see Fig. 5] [130] good, but if he is losing, he gets worried. If anyone travels in from the land, he belongs to those on the right; but if he comes in by sea, he belongs to those on the left.[6] If this is the state of a creature in the world of reality and corruption along with a creature of such-and-such, then what is the state of a creature before the Creator on the morrow in the gravest terror of being revealed? O God, do not dispute with us, O noble one.

Ibn al-Zinjibīlī built the grand market place[7] of al-ʿAtīqah, souks, shops and houses made of stone. In his time, Aden became great again. When Sayf al-Islām entered Aden, Ibn al-Zinjibīlī transferred the pious endowments of all the properties to Mecca in 575.[8] Al-Malik al-Muʿizz Ismāʿīl b. Ṭughtakīn b. Ayyūb built buildings, a new market place, the whole of which was lock-up shops for perfumers.[9] Then al-Muʿtamid Raḍī al-Dīn

[1] This remark of the dāʿī I interpret to refer to the fact that the *nākhūdhah* was his guest the previous night and the law of hospitality obliged him to treat the *nākhūdhah* in this way.

[2] Once again I have corrected the text by deleting 'Abū 'Uthmān 'Umar b.'.

[3] See Löfgren, *Texte*, I, p. 14.

[4] Ibid.

[5] Arabic *al-Maḥshar*, used as a euphemism for the Day of Judgement.

[6] The comparison between the customs house and the scene on the Day of Judgement continues, the left and the right bringing to mind the pans of the balance. This is also perhaps a reference to the two doors of the customs house.

[7] Arabic *qayṣāriyyah* (Dozy, *Supplément*, II, p. 432; *EI*, 'Ḳaysāriyya', '... large system of public buildings laid out in the form of cloisters with shops, workshops, warehouses and frequently also living-rooms ... from the Greek' "imperial" (Serjeant, 'Yemeni Merchants', pp. 634).

[8] Begins 8 June 1179.

[9] Arabic 'wa-banā al-Muʿizz ... bunyan (*sic* for bunan) jamīʿ-hā dakākīn bi-al-bāb wa-al-qufl lil-ʿaṭṭārīn qayṣāriyyah jadīdah', a difficult sentence. Serjeant tries ('Yemeni Merchants', pp. 65–6)) '... a block of houses, all of which was shops at al-Bāb and al-Qufl (Bāb al-Qufl?) for the *ʿaṭṭārūn* ..., a new *qayṣāriyyah*.' 'Ṭ built for the *ʿaṭṭārūn* a new *qayṣāriyyah*, all of it shops, with a gate (*bāb*) locked at night.' (ibid., p. 64). The former seems to me unlikely and I gloss the rather strange '*bi-al-bāb wa-al-qufl* ', 'with door and lock'. OL's n. 5 in his apparatus, suggesting *wa-alqā* for *al-qufl*, is also unsatisfactory.

Figure 5. Plan of Aden (I MS, f. 53a, text, p. 129, tabula V)

This is a complicated plan in which the mountains appear to be shown in white, though the written notes may refer to the black areas. Points of the compass are not given. 'The town of Aden' is marked in the centre of the circle. The sea would appear to be all round the lower half of the circle and the small circle at the bottom within the large town one is marked 'balance', perhaps the weighing house. Above that on the straight horizontal line is written 'customs house'. To the left of the customs house it is indicated that there is a place built by Sayf al-Islām, i.e. Ṭughtakīn b. Ayyūb, on the peak of Jabal Ḥuqqāt from where the ships of the Kārim merchants arriving from Egypt can be seen. To the right of the customs house is the fortress of al-Akhḍar. Jabal al-Manẓar is situated above the 'town of Aden' label and Jabal al-Aḥmar is above that to the right.

Muḥammad b. ʿAlī al-Tikrītī rebuilt it in the name of al-Malik al-Masʿūd Yūsuf b. Muḥammad b. Abī Bakr. The population increased there and they built houses and properties, settled by a group of Arabs 'from every remote ravine'.[1] Al-Muʿtamid Muḥammad b. ʿAlī also built a fine bathhouse. Wells were dug there, mosques too and *minbars* established; it became a fine place. The most accurate information is that it thrived only after the ruin of the port of Abyan and Haram.[2] The merchants moved from these two towns and settled in Qalhāt[3] and Mogadishu. So the three towns then flourished. God knows best.

Description of Aden. The town is built in a wadi, with the sea all around it. Its air is stifling, but it makes the wine ferment in the period of ten days. Its water comes from wells, but some of it is brought in from a distance of two parasangs. God knows best.

[131] *The sweet wells*. Inside Aden there are Ḥalqam ʿAwd well, belonging to the sultan, the well of ʿAlī b. Abī al-Barakāt Ibn al-Kātib, which is old, the well of Aḥmad b. al-Musayyab, the well of Ibn Abī al-Ghārāt,[4] which is near the gate of Aden and old, al-Muqaddam well, which is old, three wells belonging to Dāʾūd b. Maḍmūn al-Yahūdī, three wells belonging to Shaykh ʿUmar b. al-Ḥusayn, a well belonging to ʿAlī b. al-Ḥusayn al-Azraq, the well of Jaʿfar, which is old and forty cubits deep and the well of Zaʿfarān, bought during his lifetime and made into a pious endowment for the Muslims.

Section. I was informed by ʿAbdallāh b. Muḥammad b. Yaḥyā as follows. The water of the well of Zaʿfarān was transported to the whole of the Yemen. He added that this was because Sayf al-Dīn Atābak Sunqur, client of al-Malik al-Muʿizz Ismāʿīl b. Ṭughtakīn, drank some wine at the house of al-Muʿtamid Muḥammad b. ʿAlī al-Tikrītī, the taste of which pleased him and said to him, 'What did you make this wine of?' He replied, 'Of Zaʿfarān water. When St John's wort[5] is released into this water and left in the sun, it becomes wine and there is no need of honey, nor of anything else' (i.e. he actually put [the St John's wort] into [the water]). From that time on, this water was transported to al-Janad, Taʿizz, Ṣanʿāʾ and Zabīd, from which they would make wine. More accurately it is *tarib* water.[6] It is also said that originally it was extremely sweet, but now the salinity has got somewhat high because of the people's misdeeds.

The well of al-Salāmī was dug by Shaykh Ismāʿīl b. ʿAbd al-Raḥmān al-Salāmī. The well of Rawḥ is old, also that of ʿAwd. There are also the well of Ibn al-Dhuʾayb, son-in-law of Shaykh Muʿammar b. Jurayj, the well of al-Ḥammām, dug by Muḥammad b. ʿAlī

[1] Quran 22:27.

[2] The port of Abyan is presumably Shuqrā (Serjeant, *Portuguese*, end map). Haram (vocalization?) is a complete mystery.

[3] Now a ruined site, less than 80 miles S of Muscat, about 20 miles N of Ṣūr on the Gulf of Oman coast. It was an important medieval port (see below, pp. 279–80; Wilkinson, *Imamate*, p. 386, map 1; Smith, '"Anthropological" Passages', 167–8; Agius, 'Medieval Qalhat', *passim*).

[4] Presumably the Zurayʿid, ʿAlī b. Abī al-Ghārāt, who died in 545/1150 (Hamdānī, *al-Ṣulayḥiyyūn*, p. 345, tree 7; Appendices B.1 and B.6 below).

[5] Arabic *dādhī/dhādhī*, *Hypericum perforatum* L (Dimyāṭī, *Muʿjam*, p. 60).

[6] I think, however one reads *t.r.b* of the text, some botanical term is in question and I find *taribah* in Aṣmaʿī (*al-Nabāt*, p. 88). DMV points out to me that my original identification, *Garcinia mangostana*, is not found in the Yemen.

al-Tikrītī, the second well of al-Ḥammām, which is old, the well of Mawr, which is old, the well of Jallād, which is old, and the well of al-Khaḍḍāmī, also old.

[132] *Section.* I was informed by Muḥammad b. Zankal b. al-Ḥasan al-Kirmānī on the authority of an Adeni as follows. I was informed by ʿAbdallāh b. Muḥammad al-Isḥāqī, the Dāʿī, that there were within Aden 180 sweet wells, but they are not accessible [to everyone].[1] God knows best.

The brackish wells in Aden. There are the well of Waḍḍāḥ, which is old, with another well by the side of it, two wells at Marābiṭ al-Khayl, the well of Umm Ḥasan, which is old, the well of Qandalah on the road to the gate, the well of Sunbul near the bathhouse, the well of Sālim, the well of Ḥandūd, the well of Faraj, the well of al-Zunūj, the well of al-Afyilah, dug in 620,[2] the well of Raʾīs al-Shawānī,[3] a well near Dār al-Quṭayʿī al-Salāṭah, and the well of al-Sharīʿah.

Wells the water of which is the sea of Aden. There are a well in the Danākilah quarter, a well near a broken gate, three wells belonging to the Somalis, a well at the Friday mosque, a well at the Abān mosque, the well of the Mālikiyyah mosque, the well of Ḥabs al-Qāḍī, the well of Abū Niʿmah, the well of al-Jamājim, the well of al-Ṣanāʿinah, the well of the pottery souk, three wells at the house of Ibn So-and-so, the well of Sunbul, two wells at the mosque of the Prophet, the well of the learned Ẓafr, the well of Ḥuqqāt, two wells of Ḥasās and the well of al-Jarāʾihī. There is also the cistern at the well of Zaʿfarān, built by the Persians, a second built by the Zurayʿids on the Zaʿfarān road to the right of al-Darb at the side of Jabal al-Aḥmar. When it rains, the flood turns towards it for two days and it is guaranteed every [133] year 700 dinars [for its upkeep]. Ibn al-Mujāwir said that someone gave a guarantee for this of 1,300 dinars in the middle of Rabīʿ II 622.[4]

I tell the following story which was the subject of my conversation with al-Kirmānī, the well-digger. He said, 'Perhaps it's made up!' I replied, 'An indication [of the accuracy of it] is that clouds and the sun are still high above it and the less the sun the sweeter [the water].' He replied, 'Does the sun not take the lightness from the water?' I said, 'There is nothing lighter than salty water, nor heavier than sweet water.' He replied that he would like some proof of this. I continued, 'If the sea water were not light, it would stink; and if it stank, no one would travel across it. Because it is light, it settles down as it is and [this is] the fourth point.'

I was informed as follows by ʿAbdallāh b. Muslim, who lived in al-Mabāh, ʿAbdallāh b. Yazīd al-Ḥijāzī, Ghazzī b. Abī Bakr and ʿAmr b. ʿAlī b. Muqbil, all of them together. Behind Jabal al-ʿUrr is an open space, upon which is a round mountain with the sea all around it. At the beginning of the wadi, i.e. at the side of the mountain, there emerges a spring of sweet water which takes over the wadi. Because of the wetness of this spring, arak, *tanḍub*[5] and French cotton trees[6] have grown up and it will perhaps become a

[1] Tentatively reading *māniʿah*, i.e. privately owned?

[2] Begins 4 February 1223.

[3] 'The captain of the galleys'; see below p. 156 ff.

[4] April 1225.

[5] *Capparis decidua* Pax. (Dīnawarī, *Plants*, p. 24; Dimyāṭī, *Muʿjam*, pp. 28–9; Wood, *Handbook*, p. 122).

[6] Arabic *ʿushar*, *Calotropis procera* Willd. R. Br. (Dīnawarī, *Plants*, p. 44; Dimyāṭī, *Muʿjam*, p. 102; Varisco, *Agriculture*, p. 137).

forest. I asked, 'Why don't the inhabitants of Aden drink from it?' [Al-Kirmānī] replied, 'There is no way up there, nor is there [even] a pedestrian path clinging to the side of the mountain.' I asked how he had come to know this. He replied, 'One year Aden was in conflict and its gates closed. We were in al-Mabāh, but we fled with our camels into this wadi.' He continued, 'Then Ibn al-Maʿalā became hot and thirsty and this was the origin of ...[1] However, he was immediately safe.'

The sweet wells outside Aden. There are the well of Aḥmad al-ʿAshīrī, which is old but with good water, the well of Aḥmad b. al-Musayyab, dug in [134] 614,[2] the well of al-ʿAqlānī, dug in 615,[3] the well of Khayṭ, which is ancient and the well of ʿAqāb, which is also called the Kilāb well. It is said that dogs dug up the earth in this particular place, so this man ʿAqāb dug a well there which became known as the well of al-Kilāb [the dogs]. Aḥmad al-ʿAshīrī renovated the structure in 602.[4] There are also the well of al-Jadīdah, dug in 621,[5] the well of al-Salāmī, dug in 617,[6] the wells which are on the Lakhabah road, the Lakhabah wells, the well of al-Sammākīn on the road near the mosque, dug in 616,[7] the well of al-Muwaḥḥidīn on the first part of the beach of al-Lakhabah, the well of the Builders, dug in 614[8] to make unbaked bricks, the well of Shaykh ʿAlī b. ʿUbayd in the centre of al-Lakhabah, dug in 610,[9] the well of al-Saʿafah, dug on the road to al-Mafālīs, which is old and only drunk from when water is expensive in Aden and the well of al-ʿImād on the Abyan road, which is old and drawn from during the monsoon.

Most of the inhabitants of the town [of Aden] are Arabs, brought together from Alexandria, Egypt, the countryside, as well as East Africans, Persians, Ḥaḍramīs, Mogadishans, mountain folk, Dhubḥānīs,[10] Zaylaʿīs, ... and Abyssinians. They have come together here from all corners of the earth and have become rich and well-to-do. The majority of the inhabitants are Abyssinians and Somalis. There is no one in the known world, on land or sea, more amazing and more shameless than Somali women. God knows best.

A word on the shamelessness of Somali women.[11] When a Somali woman is quarrelling with another, she removes all her clothes, slaps her breast, claps, jumps up and down and her eyes stare piercingly into the face of the other. Both of them are now [as if] sleeping, then bending over; now laughing and crying; then scowling and repressing [their feelings].[12] She plucks out [135] her pubic hair, sprinkling it into the air. She puts her finger

[1] Reading the verb *ḥarra* for the *ḥabara* of the text. The whole sentence is corrupt and the translation tentative.
[2] Begins 10 April 1217.
[3] Begins 30 March 1218.
[4] Begins 18 August 1205.
[5] Begins 24 January 1224.
[6] Begins 8 March 1220.
[7] Begins 19 March 1219.
[8] Begins 10 April 1217.
[9] Begins 23 May 1213.
[10] Dhubḥān is an area of al-Maʿāfir (today al-Ḥujariyyah), the mountainous area S of Taʿizz (Hamdānī, *Ṣifah*, pp. 67, 71, 74; Maqḥafī, *Muʿjam*, pp. 248–9).
[11] See Smith, '"Anthropological" Passages', pp. 165–7.
[12] Reading *takḥimu* with OL.

into her vagina and makes the other lick her vaginal juices.[1] Or she pushes her finger into her anus and makes her adversary smell the excrement. Whatever one does, the other does also. I have never seen [anyone] more shameless, dirtier and more immodest than the Somalis – may God grant them no good for their being Muslims. The Prophet – God bless him and grant him peace! – said, 'Modesty is part of the faith.' Some wise man said, 'If you show no modesty, then do what you want.' A certain Persian recited the following verse in this regard [in Persian]:

> What a bon mot! Chosroes said to the soldier,
> 'If you have no shame, go, do whatever you want!'[2]

Section. When a wife of the picture sellers in Mosul[3] and a woman naphta seller in Baghdad quarrel with one another, she climbs up on to the roof naked, stands on the edge and strikes her hand on her vulva, saying, 'Make unbaked bricks from my shit and straw of my pubic hair!'[4]

Women brought up in the caravanserais are called *kām-sarwānī*[5] by the Persians. When one of them quarrels with another, she puts her finger in her excrement[6] and makes her adversary smell it. When one of the women of the Sanākimah[7] in the Yemen quarrels with another, she raises her skirt, kneels on all fours and says to the one she is confronting, '[Come on,] my girl, have a good look at my crescent moon which has just risen and my cut parsley!'[8]

The women of Sīwistān[9] take off their clothes and go down into the flood water to swim naked. When the women of the Qarāmiṭah squat down to relieve themselves, they cover up their face, but they remove all their clothing! The women of al-Nahrawān[10] stand up straight in front of the barber who cuts their pubic hair for them. If one wants him to cut the hairs around her anus, the barber inserts into her anus a small ball [136] to which is [attached] a long thread. The woman collects her hair over the ball, while the barber pulls out the thread with his left hand, and as the hair emerges, cuts the hair with his right hand. Men do the same. Byzantine women go into the baths with men

[1] Arabic *min raḥim-hā*.

[2] The translation of this Persian line is that of Dr Charles Melville to whom I am extremely grateful for his help. The line is from Gurgānī's *Vis* (Morrison, *Vis*, p. 89).

[3] RBS agreed with my reading *nisā' min al-ṣūriyyīn* and the latter could be picture-makers. 'In the considerably earlier Zaydī manual of Uṭrūsh (Serjeant, 'Zaidī Manual', *passim*), there is reference to pictures etc. and how they should be mutilated and this is fairly near Mosul relatively.' (RBS)

[4] Arabic 'iḍribī min khurī libn / wa-min shiʿratī tibn' – a vulgar little ditty!

[5] *Kām* means 'desire' in Persian and OL suggests reading, *kām-rawā'ī*, 'gratification'. However, the *kām sarwānī* of the text would seem to mean 'cameleer gratification'! (Steingass, *Dictionary*, pp. 679, 1009).

[6] Arabic *jaṣ* for *jaʿs*.

[7] '... a very low grade group who eat carrion etc. I think they are like the *akhdām* [the black low class who clean the streets etc. today], or probably are *akhdām*.' (RBS)

[8] Arabic
> *bi-llāh yā sittī abṣirī al-hilāl qad ṭalaʿ*
> *wa-al-ḥazā qad inqaṭaʿ*!

Ḥazā, identified by Lewin, the editor of Dīnawarī (*Plants*, p. 28), as *Anethum graveolens*, dill. But DMV writes: 'al-Bīrūnī ... discusses [the word] as a parsley-like plant eaten raw ... It was used by the Arabs to keep out evil spirits in a house and used in amulets ....'

[9] A large region of Sind where it borders on India (Yāqūt, *Muʿjam*, III, p. 301).

[10] A town N, slightly E, of Baghdad on the canal of that same name (Yāqūt, *Muʿjam*, V, pp. 324 ff.; Le Strange, *Lands*, map II).

and the woman enters naked with her husband. When one of the fishwives of Daybul quarrels with another, she puts a fish into her vagina; the women who sell vegetables put a radish into their vagina.

Their clothes are linen and [they have] turbans with a glossy finish.[1] The Persians put on their turbans, leaving one end of the turban outside, and they push it back into the turban.[2] The followers of Shaykh ʿAdī in Mosul[3] are the same. Each one of them wears on his shoulder a piece of linen [used as] a prayer-mat or an embroidered cloth.[4] When one of them is told, 'Come with me to see so-and-so', he replies, 'I'm naked!' 'Do you have no clothes on?' 'You're right; [I do have clothes on,] but I have no *k.r.w.*'[5] Their womenfolk wear silver anklets called *ḥijl*,[6] necklaces[7] – called ...[8] among the Persians – and bracelets.[9]

An [Adeni] recited as follows on the subject of the jewellery of the Yemenis.

O completely full moon risen!
O dawn's light dispersed!
O smooth, soft branch
on a sand hill abounding in herbage!
O you flashing from the front tooth of one
my heart desires, as it glistens!
O you gazelle who passed me by
one late afternoon dragging along your robes,
Bedecked with anklets, bracelets
and necklaces, plump-faced,[10]
Courageous, elegant,
wearing a neck-ring and a bonnet,
With fulsome ankles,[11] with their anklets,
wearing kohl and made-up,[12]
Endowed with divine favours, perfumed,
benevolent, wearing ornaments.

[137] The original population [of Aden] was from India, Sind, Abyssinia and Egypt. Their food consists of bread and their relish is fish. The limit of their women's handiwork is baskets made of date-palm leaves.[13] Their menfolk sell perfume and coir.[14]

[1] Arabic *amlas*.

[2] This difficult, corrupt sentence reads 'wa-ammā al-ʿAjam fa-tataʿammamu bi-dhuʾābah barr al-dhuʾābah fa-tagharrazu-hā fī al-ʿimāmah thāniyah'.

[3] I.e. Shaykh ʿAdī b. Musāfir al-Ḥakkārī who settled in Mosul where he founded the Sufi order called al-ʿAdawiyyah. He was put to death in 557/1162 (*EI*, "Adī b. Musāfir').

[4] RBS writes, 'I can only suggest *kirbās muṣallā*, a piece of muslin or linen used as a prayer carpet.'

[5] I can make nothing of *k.r.w*, but it must be synonymous with *kirbās* (see above n. 4).

[6] Or *ḥajl*. Ibn al-Mujāwir glosses with the word *khalkhāl*.

[7] I read *ḥarrāq* rather than *ḥ.rāf* (Piamenta, *Dictionary*, I, p. 90, *ḥarrāqah*, quoting a Yemenite Jewish source).

[8] In the I MS *m.s.?.h*; in the L MS *m.sh.j.h*.

[9] Arabic *dumluj/dumlaj*.

[10] Arabic *mumaljaʿ* (Piamenta, *Dictionary*, II, p. 471).

[11] Arabic *muʿabbal* (Kazimirski, *Dictionnaire*, II, p. 159, *ʿablat al-khalkhāl*, 'femme qui a les jambes très-grasses à l'endroit où se portent les *khalkhāl*').

[12] Arabic *musharraʿ* (Piamenta, *Dictionary*, I, p. 252).

[13] Arabic *qifāʿ*, plur. of *qafʿah* (Kazimirski, *Dictionnaire*, II, p. 790; Löfgren, *Texte*, II, p. 53).

[14] Arabic *qunbār*, which might also mean 'crayfish' (Ital. 'gambaro', 'gambero') (Dozy, *Supplément*, II, p. 408).

Their houses are built square, each one standing alone, with two storeys, the lower of which are stores and the upper reception rooms. They are built of stones, gypsum and wood, with a salt and gypsum mix.[1]

Section. Dogs hide away there during the daytime, because one particular dog with rabies bit one of the Somali children. The Somali woman asked the help of Raḍī al-Dīn al-Muʿtamid Muḥammad b. ʿAlī al-Tikrītī. He gaves orders that every dog in Aden should be killed. Twenty-five were killed in one day and the rest fled to the mountain tops and into the wadi bottoms. There they stayed all day, but they would come out at night and roam round the town. This was in 592.[2] They would eat what they could find thrown away on rubbish dumps, because they were [everywhere] on the ground. Ibn ʿAbbād al-Rūmī[3] recited as follows:

> [The women] bring up cats without [any other] use [than]
> to eat what they cast down, stillborn babies.
> These [women] are the graves of bastards;
> when they give birth to them, they feed [their] cats.

There are no dogs in evidence in Mecca during the day, but they take refuge in the mountains. In Kufa they take refuge in the palm groves and in Mogadishu in the cemeteries. In Aden, we have recourse to God against the dogs biting us, since they resist a liquid poison because they drink so little water. When they do have water, it is the most salty it could possibly be.

[138] *The arrival of ships in Aden.*[4] When a ship arrives in Aden and those looking on and the look-out[5] on a mountain spot it, he shouts at the top of his voice, '*Hīriyā*!'[6] This is [from] the top of Jabal al-Akhḍar on which was built al-Ḥuṣn al-Akhḍar. It was originally called Sīrsiyah. The look-out can only look out at sunrise and sunset, since then the sun's rays are on the surface of the sea, so whatever there is can be seen even at great distance. Now the look-out will have in front of him a piece of wood and when something appears to him on the sea, he aims at this particular thing with the stick. If it is a

[1] I had originally thought that 'salt' must be an error here and that this is the last thing to be included in a list of building materials. However, a very reliable Najrānī source tells me that salt and gypsum are commonly mixed together with water to make either paint, or, as is the case here, plaster. Salt is also mixed with lime in Najrān to whitewash buildings.

[2] Begins 6 December 1195.

[3] Al-Ṣāḥib Ibn al-ʿAbbād and Ibn al-ʿAbbād al-Kātib are one and the same, the Buyid man of letters and vizier who died in 385/995 (Iṣfahānī, *Aghānī*, VI, pp. 15–16; *EI*, 'Ibn ʿAbbād'). I cannot trace the lines in question in context and the translation is very tentative. The cats are used by the women to eat their stillborn babies and thus hide their fornication.

[4] See Hunter, *Aden*, p. 191; Landberg, *Etudes*, II, p. 1324; Löfgren, *Texte*, I, p. 56; Serjeant, 'Ports', p. 215; Smith, 'Trade', p. 129.

[5] Arabic *nāṭūr*. The root has more the meaning of guarding a vineyard, palm grove etc., but is also used of the matelot charged with look-out duties in the crow's nest (Dozy, *Supplément*, II, p. 683; Kazimirski, *Dictionnaire*, II, p. 1283).

[6] Landberg (*Etudes*, II, p. 1324) proposes *hūriyāh*, deriving it from the south Arabian and Gulf *hūrī*, a small boat, usually a dug-out, used for inshore activities, which he says is a Javanese word. See also Kindermann, *Schiff*, pp. 106–7 (with a Hindustani etymology); Grosset-Grange, *Glossaire*, p. 111. The word, not surprisingly, has passed into Mehri (Johnstone, *Lexicon*, p. 162, *hāwri*). I leave *hīriyā* and take it simply as a traditional cry from the professional look-out.

bird or some such thing, it moves to the right or the left, or it rises or descends, so he knows that it is nothing [important]. But if the image is straight along the stick, he is sure that it is a ship. He makes a sign to his colleague, as he shouts out '*Hīriyā*!' His colleague in turn makes a sign to his companion who informs a courier[1] that there is a ship. Then the courier takes news of ships to the governor of the town. When he has left the governor, he informs the officials in the customs house. After them, he shouts as loud as he can from the mountain top, '*Hīriyā, hīriyā, hīriyā*!' When the general public hear the voice, everyone climbs a mountain, or goes up to a roof to look out right and left. If what the look-out has said is accurate, he is given a *malakī* dinar for every ship and this [comes] from [the budget] of the customs house. If, however, he is not accurate, he is given ten strokes of the cane.

When the ship draws near, messengers[2] embark in *ṣanbūq*s to meet the ship. When they come along side the ship, they embark and greet the *nākhūdhah*. They ask him where he has come from and the *nākhūdhah* asks them about the town [139], who the governor is and about the price of goods. All those on board with family in the town or acquaintances send through him either their congratulations or their condolences. A messenger comes forward[3] and writes down the name of the *nākhūdhah* and those of the merchants. The ship's clerk[4] will have already written down everything in the hold of the ship, goods and cloths, and hands a chitty to the messengers. They all disembark into *ṣanbūq*s to return to town, straight to see the governor. They give him the clerk's chitty along with the name of the merchants listed and they chat with him about the ship, where she has come from and what goods are on board. The messengers leave him and tour the town to give news to the families of those who have arrived to be reunited with them. Each one then takes his payment.[5]

When the ship arrives at anchorage and drops anchor, the deputy sultan arrives and the inspector embarks to search them all one by one;[6] the search covers the turban, hair, sleeves and trouser belt and under the arms and he taps the man's pocket with his hand, inserts his hand between his buttocks and goes to great pains to smell him. In the same way an old woman searches the women, passing her hand over their buttocks and private parts. The merchants disembark into town and bring down their baggage the next day. After three days, the cloths and goods are off-loaded into the customs house and unbound piece by piece[7] and counted cloth by cloth. If spices are part of the merchandise, they are weighed on a steelyard. An estimation is made of everything the weight of which is doubtful, so that nothing is left. They have already sworn an oath by God before the officials that they will do all in their power [to act honestly]. Ibn

[1] OL's *jurāb* makes no sense to me (Kindermann, *Schiff*, p. 16; Löfgren, *Texte*, II, p. 25). I much prefer Landberg's *khabbār* (*Etudes*, II, p. 1325) or, even better, *jarrāy*.

[2] Arabic sing. *mubashshir*, literally 'bearer of good news' (*bushr* or *bushrā*).

[3] Reading Landberg's and OL' s *mubashshir naḥw al-nākhūdhah*.

[4] Text *karrānī*, from the Sanskrit *karana*, entering south Arabian Arabic through Hindi and also used as the name of one of the mixed castes of Hindus (hence Portuguese, *canarim*, 'half-breed') who were writers and accountants. The Anglo-Indian word is 'cranny'. *Karrānī* was still commonly used in British South Arabia up to the 1960s (Yule and Burnell, *Hobson-Jobson*, pp. 273–4; Löfgren, *Texte*, II, p. 55; Ibn Baṭṭūṭah, *Travels*, II, p. 383).

[5] I.e. the *mubashshir* is paid in tips from those to whom he brings news. The payment is called *bishārah*.

[6] See Serjeant, '"Interlopers"', p. 90.

[7] Arabic *shaddatan shaddatan* (Dozy, *Supplément*, I, p. 736).

al-Mujāwir remarked as follows. Then misfortune overcomes the merchant, sadness overwhelms him and he remains in the wadi of evil fate because of what they do to him to drive away good luck and happiness![1]

[140] *Customs dues*,[2] followed by taxes and regulations, which were instituted during the time of the Zurayʿids. It is said that the first man to institute customs dues was someone called al-Yahūdī. Another version was that he was called Khalaf al-Yahūdī al-Nihāwandī. The people have continued to follow their [taxation] rules and taxes, [and will do so] until the Day of the Faith.[3]

Eight dinars customs dues and one dinar galley-tax[4] is levied on a *buhār* of pepper, and another two dinars as it is exported.

On a piece of indigo, four dinars galley-tax and a quarter as it leaves the customs house.

On a *buhār* of assa gum,[5] which is [also called] *ḥiltīt*,[6] eight dinars.

On a *buhār* of perfumed cherry bark,[7] three and a half dinars.

On a *buhār* of sugar of bamboo,[8] twenty-one, minus one third, dinars[9] [customs dues] and a dinar galley-tax.

On a stick of *dafwāʾ* tree,[10] a half of the whole.[11]

On a *farāsilah* of camphor,[12] twenty-five, plus a half, plus a sixth, dinars.[13]

On a *buhār* of cardamom,[14] seven dinars.

On a *farāsilah* of cloves,[15] ten dinars and a dinar galley-tax.

(There are ten *mann* to a *farāsilah* and twenty *raṭl*).[16]

[1] I suppose Ibn al-Mujāwir is trying to say that these searches and weighing practices were a prelude to the demand for customs dues.

[2] Arabic *ʿashūr*. For this passage, see Smith, ' Maritime Trade', p. 132–3, where the list of commodities and payments is given in full in tabular form.

[3] I.e. these rules and taxes, originated by the Zurayʿids, have continued under the Ayyubids.

[4] Arabic *ʿashūr al-shawānī*. *Tārīkh al-Mustabṣir* does not have the singular of this latter word, but the following are listed: *shawnah* (Fīrūzābādī, *Qāmūs*, IV, p. 243); *shāniyah*, *shawnah*, *shīnī*, *shīniy(y)ah*, *shānī* (Dozy, *Supplément*, I, p. 793); *shāniyah* (Kazimirski, *Dictionnaire*, I, p. 1278); *shīn* (Lane, *Lexicon*, IV, p. 1635). See also Kindermann, *Schiff*, pp. 53–4; Löfgren, *Texte*, I, p. 59, II, p. 43; Smith, *Ayyubids*, II, pp. 124–5 and Idrīsī, *Opus*, I, p. 72.

[5] Text *ankuzah*, Persian *anguzhad*, *Ferula assa foetida* L. (Dīnawarī, *Plants*, p. 28; Dimyāṭī, *Muʿjam*, p. 142; Löfgren, *Texte*, II, p. 44).

[6] See Lane, *Lexicon*, II, p. 626, an Aramaic word.

[7] Arabic *maḥlab*, *Prunus mahaleb* L. (Löfgren, *Texte*, II, p. 29; Dimyāṭī, *Muʿjam*, p. 142).

[8] Text *ṭabāshīr*, Sanskrit *tvakshira*, Persian *tabāshīr* (Yule and Burnell, *Hobson-Jobson*, p. 887; Löfgren, *Texte*, II, p. 44). The word might also mean 'chalk' and both would have been imported from India for medicinal purposes.

[9] I.e. twenty and two-thirds.

[10] Ibn Manẓūr (*Lisān*, XIV, p. 264) and L (III, p. 895) mention a *shajarah dafwāʾ*, a 'great, inclining, shady tree', but I cannot identify it further. See also Löfgren, *Texte*, II, p. 33.

[11] Such an expression presumably indicates payment of *ʿashūr* in kind.

[12] Text *kāfūr*. A *farāsilah* is the weight of 20–35 *raṭl* (Hunter, *Aden*, p. 74; Serjeant, *Portuguese*, p. 151; Yule and Burnell, *Hobson-Jobson*, p. 358–9 [from Vulgar Latin *particella*, English 'parcel'?]; Rossi, *L'Arabo*, p. 152; Löfgren, *Texte*, II, p. 49).

[13] I.e. twenty-five and two-thirds.

[14] Arabic *hayl*.

[15] Text *qaranful* (Greek καρυόφυλλον).

[16] Are these equivalent weights provided by Ibn al-Mujāwir meant to refer only to cloves? See Yule and Burnell, *Hobson-Jobson*, pp. 563–4; Hinz, *Masse*, pp. 16–23; Mortel, 'Weights', pp. 180–81.

On a *farāsilah* of saffron,[1] three and a third dinars.

On a *buhār* of flax,[2] seven and a half dinars.

When [the contents of] a ship are sold, ten dinars are levied on the vendor per hundred [dinars raised by him].[3]

A half is levied on iron as customs dues.[4] (This was instituted during the rule of Sayf al-Islām Ṭughtakīn b. Ayyūb.The first man from whom it was levied was Abū al-Ḥasan al-Baghdādī in 598.[5] Another version is it was someone called al-Farwānī.)

On lac-dye, either a quarter, or a third, of the whole,[6] plus two dinars as security.[7]

On a *buhār* of madder[8] twelve dinars, the new rate brought in during the time of al-Malik al-Muʿizz Ismāʿīl b. Ṭughtakīn,[9] and previously it was two or three dinars.

On a *buhār* of tamarind,[10] three *jāʾiz*.

On ten flax cloths,[11] two and a half dinars.

On ten silk cloths,[12] three quarters of a *jāʾiz*.

On [141] a head of sheep, a quarter [of a *jāʾiz*].

On a head of horse, when it is imported into the town, fifty dinars, instituted during the rule of al-Malik al-Nāṣir Ayyūb b. Ṭughtakīn b. Ayyūb,[13] and when it is exported, seventy dinars are levied.

On slaves, per head, two dinars and half a dinar when he is exported.

On a Goanese slave,[14] eight dinars and a dinar galley-tax. Half a dinar, this going to the man in charge of the winery tax,[15] is levied on the slave on export.

On pieces of Zabīd silk[16] are levied half a dinar and a *jāʾiz*.

On a Ẓafārī garment, a quarter [of a dinar] and a *jāʾiz*.

On a piece of white cloth, an eight [of a dinar].

On Sousse linen, three carats.[17]

On Sousse waist-wrappers,[18] a quarter [of a dinar] and a *jāʾiz*.

[1] Text *zaʿfarān*.

[2] Or 'linen', *kattān*.

[3] Presumably this is over and above the charges on individual items. As FLS kindly points out to me, it is possible that the ship itself is being sold, though my feeling is that he is talking of the contents thereof.

[4] I.e. payment in kind.

[5] Begins 1 October 1201.

[6] *Lāk*, used as a dark red dye. From the Sanskrit *lākshā*, Hindi *lākh* (Yule and Burnell, *Hobson-Jobson*, pp. 499–500; Steingass, *Dictionary*, p. 1112; Serjeant, *Textiles*, p. 171).

[7] Arabic *istiẓhāran*; perhaps the two dinars' worth of lac is a minimum and two dinars had to be handed over if the dues did not reach that amount.

[8] Arabic *fuwwah*, *Rubia tinctorum* L.; the root is used as a red dye (Hunter, *Aden*, p. 105; Dimyāṭī, *Muʿjam*, p. 120; Löfgren, *Texte*, II, p. 51).

[9] The third Ayyubid sultan in the Yemen (reg. 593–98/1197–1201). See Appendix B.8 below.

[10] Arabic *ḥumar*, *Tamarindus indica* L.

[11] Arabic *maqāṭiʿ*, probably of flax (Dozy, *Supplément*, II, p. 374; Serjeant, *Textiles*, pp. 152, 176).

[12] Arabic *ʿuqudāt*, probably of silk (Dozy, *Supplément*, II, p. 150; Serjeant, *Textiles*, p. 176; Piamenta, *Dictionary*, II, p. 334, *ʿaqdah*).

[13] The fourth Ayyubid sultan in the Yemen (reg. 609–11/1212–14). See Appendix B.8 below.

[14] Arabic *ʿawīlī*. The tentative translation follows Löfgren (*Texte*, II, p. 48), relying on Dozy, *Supplément*, (II, p. 191).

[15] Arabic *ḍāmin dār al-nabīdh*.

[16] Arabic *shiqaq al-ḥarīr min ʿamal Zabīd*.

[17] Arabic *sūsī*, i.e. made in Sousse (Sūsah) in Tunisia (Löfgren, *Texte*, II, pp. 40–41; Serjeant, *Textiles*, p. 130).

[18] Arabic *fuwaṭ al-sūsī*.

On a score of bed covers,[1] four dinars.
On a score of woven fabrics,[2] two and a half dinars.
The same for loincloths.[3]
On a score of calico garments,[4] two and a half dinars.
On large Sousse linen,[5] two *jā'iz* and a carat.
On small Sousse linen, two *jā'iz* and two *fals*.
On every basket[6] of sorghum, an eighth [of a *jā'iz*].
Almighty God – praise to Him – knows best.

The imposition of the galley-tax.[7] The Zuray'id rulers had no knowledge of galleys and remained [ignorant of them] until Shams al-Dawlah Tūrān Shāh b. Ayyūb arrived [in Aden] together with a whole fleet of them.[8] The governor, 'Uthmān b. 'Alī al-Zinjibīlī al-Tikrītī, left Aden, but the galleys remained there when he fled. Sayf al-Islām Ṭughtakīn b. Ayyūb entered the Yemen.[9] An intelligent man gave him some advice, saying, 'How can you consider the levy of customs dues from merchants lawful?' Ṭughtakīn replied, 'I shall continue as the Ayyubid rulers did in days gone by.' The man said to him, 'They used to seize from people by force; but you, take this in a way which will make you the object of gratitude among the people.' He asked what it was [he was advising]. He continued, 'Send [142] these galleys to sea to protect the merchants from pirates and they will be doing something useful for them, rather than their sitting idly [in port], rotting in the sun.'[10] 'You have certainly come up with a good idea', Ṭughtakīn exclaimed. So he sent the galleys to India where they were stationed before the landfalls,[11] protecting the merchant shipping from attack by pirates.

Thus they continued until the year 613.[12] An important figure came and said, 'God make the rule of our lord, the sultan, last for ever. Every year 50,000 or 60,000 dinars are spent to no avail from our lord's coffers on the galleys. If our lord takes this amount from the merchants, it will do them no harm.' He asked what he should do. 'For every thousand dinars raised from customs dues,' he replied, 'a hundred should be taken for the galleys. It will be collected for our lord, so will not be noticed by the merchants!'

[1] Text *kawrajat al-maḥābis*, the former word of Indian origin, but whose exact etymology is uncertain. It is the Portuguese *corjá* and the Anglo-Indian 'corge' (Löfgren, *Texte*, II, p. 27, but cf. Serjeant, *Textiles*, p. 130, n. 64).

[2] Arabic *aḥwāk*, plur. of *ḥawk/ḥawkah*.

[3] Arabic sing. *subā'ī*.

[4] Arabic *khām Hindī* (Löfgren, *Texte*, II, p. 31).

[5] Arabic *sawāsī al-kattān al-kibār.*

[6] Arabic *qafah*. But DMV tells me that he has met the word *qufā* in an early Rasuid administrative text meaning a large measure in Abyan, = 2 Laḥjī *mudd*.

[7] See Smith, 'Maritime Trade', pp. 131–2.

[8] In 569/1173.

[9] This sentence is corrupt and can only be understood after careful reading of the historical texts. I have corrected from the following Arabic: 'fa-lamā kharaja walī 'Uthmān b. 'Alī al-Zinjibīlī al-Tikrītī 'Adan wa-baqiyat 'inda-h al-shawānī ilā an haraba dakhala Sayf al-Islām Ṭughtakīn b. Ayyūb al-Yaman'. 'Uthmān fled from the Yemen to Iraq as soon as he heard of the arrival in the Yemen of Ṭughtakīn in 579/1183 (Ibn Ḥātim, *Simṭ*, p. 24).

[10] Arabic '*... baṭṭālah taqra'u-hā al-shumūs*'!

[11] Arabic *manādikh*, plur. of *mandakh* (Löfgren, *Texte*, II, p. 59; Serjeant, *Portuguese*, p. 192; Tibbetts, *Navigation*, p. 542).

[12] Begins 20 April 1216.

This [arrangement] was brought in during the rule of al-Malik al-Masʿūd Yūsuf b. Muḥammad b. Abī Bakr b. Ayyūb[1] and remained in force until 625.[2] The sharif[3] wrote as follows to al-Malik al-Masʿūd, 'Income from the galleys comes in whether they are at sea or not.' So al-Malik al-Masʿūd said, 'If what he says is correct, abolish it.' So the galley-tax was abolished, but his customs dues were henceforth levied [and will continue thus] until the Day of Resurrection including the galley-tax in them.[4] God knows best.

Commodities for which no customs dues are taken.[5] Imported from Egypt: wheat, flour, sugar, rice, soap from al-Raqqah,[6] saltwort,[7] syrup,[8] olive oil, flax oil,[9] salted olives, everything connected with sweetmeats[10] (in small quantities) and honey (in small quantities).

Imported from India: everything for re-export,[11] preserved myrobolan,[12] turban linen,[13] cushions, grape baskets,[14] circular leathers,[15] rice, kedgeree,[16] which is mixed rice and mung beans,[17] sesame and soap. [143] Other commodities include: incense from Kalah,[18] *nasham* wood,[19] clove firewood and garments made in Bhatticala.[20]

[1] The sixth and last Ayyubid sultan in the Yemen, (reg. 612–26/1215–28). See Appendix B.8 below.

[2] Begins 12 December 1227.

[3] This sharif is still as much a mystery now as it was when I wrote 'Maritime Trade' in 1996, including a long n. 30 (p. 136) on the subject. In theory, the sharif might be: a) the sharif of Mecca; b) the Sulaymānī sharif of Jīzān; or c) one of the Zaydī sharifs. On further reflection none is likely to have had any influence over the Ayyubid sultan in Aden. Perhaps Ibn al-Mujāwir means *baʿḍ min al-ashrāf*, 'a certain sharif', in the technical sense of a descendant of the Prophet.

[4] In fact, the galley-tax was reinstated in Aden by the later Rasulids (628–c. 845/1230–1441) and levied regularly along with *ʿushr* (tithe) and *dilālah* (broker's fee) (Smith, 'Port Practices', p. 211).

[5] See Löfgren, *Texte*, I, p. 63 and Smith, 'Maritime Trade', p. 133.

[6] The well-known town on the Euphrates where olive oil and pens were produced, as well as soap (Muqaddasī, *Aḥsan*, p. 145; Yāqūt, *Muʿjam*, III, pp. 58–60; Le Strange, *Lands*, p. 102).

[7] Arabic *ushnān*, *Salsola kali* L., for washing clothes (Löfgren, *Texte*, II, p. 22; Dimyāṭī, *Muʿjam*, p. 12; Hepper and Friis, *Plants*, p. 107).

[8] Arabic *quṭārah* (Löfgren, *Texte*, II, p. 52).

[9] Arabic *zayt al-ḥārr* (Dozy, *Supplément*, I, p. 616; Löfgren, *Texte*, II, p. 28).

[10] Arabic *nuql/naql*. I choose a general term for what might well be dried fruits or nuts (Löfgren, *Texte*, I, p. 62, n. 8; Dozy, *Supplément*, II, p. 717, *nuqalī*, 'vendeur de fruits'; Piamenta, *Dictionary*, II, p. 495, *naqīlah*, plur, *anqul*, 'candy and dried fruits').

[11] Arabic *kull mā yursalu* (rather than the *Tārīkh al-Mustabṣir* text's *yurāsalu*) *fī al-baḥr*.

[12] Text *al-halīlaj al-murabbā*, dried fruits and kernels exported from India and used in medicine (Yule and Burnell, *Hobson-Jobson*, pp. 607–9; Löfgren, *Texte*, II, p. 60).

[13] Arabic *akrār*, plur.of *karr* which means also 'prayer mat' (Kazimirski, *Dictionnaire*, II, p. 879; Dozy, *Supplément*, II, p. 452).

[14] Arabic *masāwir*, plur. of *maswarah* (Dozy, *Supplément*, I, p. 701).

[15] Arabic *anṭāʿ*, plur. of *naṭʿ/naṭaʿ* (Dozy, *Supplément*, II, p. 683; Serjeant, *Textiles*, index p. 226; Piamenta, *Dictionary*, II, p. 488).

[16] Text *kijrī*, Hindi *khichrī*, still found today in our cookery books. See Yule and Burnell, *Hobson-Jobson*, p. 476.

[17] Arabic *māsh* (Varisco, 'Crop Register', p. 17 and *Agriculture*, p. 181).

[18] Arabic *mughr kalāhī*. *Mughr* is *Boswellia carteri*, according to *GD* (III, p. 2710) and Löfgren (*Texte*, II, p. 57), *Boswellia sacra*, according to Groom (*Frankincense*, pp. 106–7). Kalah must be in the vicinity of the Malacca Peninsula, although there are different theories about its exact location (Smith, 'Maritime Trade', p. 138, n. K).

[19] A wood of the *Grewia* species, used in the manufacture of bows (Dīnawarī, *Plants*, p. 51; Aṣmaʿī, *Nabāt*, p. 36; Dimyāṭī, *Muʿjam*, p. 151; Hepper and Friis, *Plants*, p. 237, 'nescham', 'neschamm').

[20] On the Malabar coast (Löfgren, *Texte*, I, p. 63, n. 1; Serjeant, *Portuguese*, p. 64, map 2).

From the region of al-Shiḥr: stoned dates, i.e. with their stones removed, salted fish without heads (if they have heads, a levy is made), thongless Indian sandals (if they have thongs, a levy is made).

There is no levy on he-goats and she-goats. The reason for this is that some Abyssinian traders[1] arrived, bringing sheep and goats to be counted. When the [customs-]tellers[2] were busy with their calculations, a he-goat got up, breaking with the flock and went and sat down right behind Yāsir b. Bilāl b. Jarīr al-Muḥammadī – or more correctly behind Dāʿī ʿImrān b. Sabaʾ.[3] When they had finished counting, they made to include the he-goat with the [rest of the] flock, but the dāʿī said, 'God forbid that we take any [customs dues] on him. He has sought my protection!' So he exempted him from the dues. The more correct version of the story is that he saw the he-goat's beard and said, 'God forbid that any customs dues be levied on his beard!'

There are also beads imported from Daybul and young ... slaves from India.[4]

What was instituted in Aden,[5] an agency tax[6] and a *zakāh*-house.[7] In Jumādā I in the year 624,[8] or more accurately, 625,[9] an agency-house was set up in Aden and on every commodity on which no customs dues were levied *zakāh* was taken. Five [different] dues[10] are now taken in one go: an old fee[11] which goes into the customs house coffers; a galley-tax;[12] an agency-house tax (a carat on every dinar); a *zakāh*-house tax; and a broker's fee.[13]

[144] *Section*. Nakhudhah ʿUthmān b. ʿUmar al-Āmidī arrived from his home town and two *mann* of aloes wood of inferior quality were found on him which they confiscated from him. When the time came to make the calculations, the price of the *mann* of aloes wood was fixed at six dinars, his outgoings in customs dues being one and a half dinar, in galley-tax three quarters [of a dinar]. The cost [of one *mann*] in the agency-house was fixed at twenty-five dinars, of which the agency tax came to eight dinars and two *dānaq* [of aloes], plus *zakāh*, a dinar and a quarter and a broker's fee of half a dinar. The total came to fifteen dinars. The price of the aloes, six dinars, was subtracted from the total taxes, leaving him nine dinars to pay. Nakhudhah ʿUthmān b. ʿUmar al-Āmidī swore an oath by the great God that he would not pay a single *fals*. He added, 'What is quite enough is that you are taking the two *mann* of aloes away from me, without [my getting] anything [in return] and you are demanding nine more dinars from me!'

1 Arabic *saffārah*. See also Smith, 'Wondrous', p. 111.

2 Arabic *ʿaddādīn*.

3 Ibn al-Mujāwir may mean the Zurayʿid ʿImrān b. Muḥammad b. Sabaʾ who died in 560/1165. Whichever version of the story is correct, the anecdote dates back to the Zurayʿids in Aden.

4 Arabic *ghilmān ḥ.w.d.r*.

5 See Löfgren, *Texte*, I, p. 63; Smith, 'Maritime Trade', p. 134, 'Port Practices', p. 209.

6 Arabic *wakālah*.

7 Arabic *dār al-zakāh*.

8 May 1227.

9 May 1228.

10 Arabic *ʿashūrāt*.

11 Arabic *ʿashūr qadīm*.

12 Arabic *ʿashūr al-shawānī*.

13 Arabic *dilālah*.

Now Amir Nāṣir al-Dīn Nāṣir b. Fārūt and others got involved in this matter. They said to [the officials involved], 'He is a man who frequently visits Aden, and we are taking too much from him.' A mediator became involved and finally [a solution was found in which] there was no gain or loss on either side.[1]

Everything in Aden, except fish and water (nothing else), was included and a sixth of a *buhār* was added in [weighing by] steelyard over and above what it had been in the first place. All the measures of the Yemen were changed and they made them all according to the standard measure of al-Janad. They also changed all the tariffs[2] in 625.[3] The customs house worked on trust with the people and it is said that one ship paid a total of 80,000 dinars in taxes.

Every year about seventy or eighty ships anchored beneath Jabal Ṣīrah.[4] Every year too four lots of treasury funds were sent up to Taʿizz: the income of ships coming from India, the entry of madder into Aden, the export of horses from Aden to India and the income of ships travelling to India. Each of these lots of funds [145] totalled about 150,000 dinars. This practice came to an end in our time, in 625.[5]

The commercial dealings of Aden during the Zurayʿid period were in ...[6] gold according to the Bisṭāmī standard,[7] but less than it. The currency in the town was *malakī* gold, the Egyptian dinar equivalent to four and a half *malakī*, the dinar made up of four quarters, each quarter three *jāʾiz*, each *jāʾiz* eight *fals*, each *fals* two *bayḍah*.[8] It is said that the first person to strike *malakī* dinars was Aḥmad b. ʿAlī al-Ṣulayḥī in Ṣanʿāʾ.[9] Rosī cloth[10] is sold by the *qaṣabah*,[11] the length of each *qaṣabah* being four *ḥadīd* cubits. Teak planks are sold by the *ḥadīd* cubit. Everything which is sold by the market salesman is taxed on the basis of trust. Anyone who pushes up the price is taxed at a higher rate.[12] Thus it is with slaves and slave girls.

[1] Arabic *rās bi-rās* (Dozy, *Supplément*, I, p. 494).

[2] Arabic *waʿd*. Dr Fatima al-Muhairi suggests this translation to me. See also Dozy, *Supplément*, II, p. 822, 'convention'.

[3] Begins 12 December 1227.

[4] See Serjeant, 'Yemeni Coast', p. 189. It is worthy of note that the modern port of Aden is situated in the NW of the peninsula at Steamer Point, set up in the 1870s by the British. In the early 1840s, Haines, the Indian Navy officer who took Aden for the British in 1839, reported that the Front Bay harbour, as he called the bay, was silting up and no longer suitable for the larger 19th-century ships (Gavin, *British Rule*, pp. 103–6). Jabal Ṣīrah is on the eastern side and presumably these ships are anchored in Ḥuqqāt Bay, clearly the site of the medieval port (see frontispiece). Varisco (*Agriculture*, p. 218) thinks 70–80 ships a year a low figure, but one must remember this is Zurayʿid and Ayyubid, not Rasulid, Aden under discussion here and it seems a reasonable figure to me (Smith, Review Varisco, *Agriculture*, p. 12).

[5] Begins 12 December 1227. Evidently about the time Ibn al-Mujāwir was writing *Tārīkh al-Mustabṣir*.

[6] I can make nothing of *al-s.?.ʿā?.y*.

[7] Bisṭām is the second town of the province of Qūmis, S of Māzandarān and Jurjān. There was a gold mine in the hills near the first town of Dāmghān, about 40 miles SW of Bisṭām (Yāqūt, *Muʿjam*, I, p. 421; Ibn Baṭṭūṭah, *Travels*, III, p. 585; Le Strange, *Lands*, pp. 365–6 and map V).

[8] A very small copper coin, possibly from the Hindi *paisā* (Löfgren, *Texte*, II, p. 24; Yule and Burnell, *Hobson-Jobson*, pp. 703–4; Piamenta, *Dictionary*, I, p. 46).

[9] Reg. 460–67 or –79/1068–74 or –86. ʿUmārah (Kay, *Yaman*, p. 37) gives the precise date of the first striking of the *malakī* dinar, 479/1086. See also Lowick, 'Unpublished Dinars', pp. 263–70 and plates.

[10] Persian, '... kind of stuff' (Dozy, *Vêtements*, p. 188; Steingass, *Dictionary*, p. 595).

[11] Measure of length, nearly 4 m (Dozy, *Supplément*, II, p. 353; Hinz, *Masse*, p. 63).

[12] A tentative translation of the corrupt 'wa-kull mā yubāʿu fī al-munādī kharaj[?] wa-amāmah wa-man zāda rakiba!'

Selling slave girls.[1] The slave girl is fumigated with an aromatic smoke, perfumed, adorned and a waist-wrapper fastened round her middle. The seller[2] takes her by the hand and walks around the souk with her; he calls out that she is for sale. The wicked merchants appear, examining her hands, feet, calves, thighs, navel, chest and breasts. He examines her back and measures her buttocks in spans.[3] He examines her tongue, teeth, hair and spares no effort. If she is wearing clothes, he takes them off; he examines and looks. Finally he casts a direct eye over her vagina and anus, without her having on any covering or veil. When he has examined, expressed his approval and bought the slave girl, she remains with him for about ten days. When he has taken care of her, had his fill, become bored and tired of her and got what he wanted from her, his lust is at an end. Zayd, the buyer, says to ʿAmr, the vendor, 'Indeed, sir, we have a case to settle in court!'[4] So they attend in front of the judge and one makes a claim against the other, [suggesting there is] a defect [in the slave girl].

[146] *Sale and defect.*[5] I was informed by al-Ḥasan b. ʿAlī Ḥazawwar al-Fīrūzkūhī as follows. I sold an Indian slave girl in Aden to an Alexandrian and she remained with him for seven days. When he had had his fill of her, a claim was made that she had a defect. So he summoned me before the judge and formally made the claim against me that she had a defect. The judge asked what her defect was. He declared, 'She has a wide and soft vagina'. I said to him, 'If your penis is too small and you cannot stimulate much virginal juice in the slave girl, what can her fine, plump, white, plucked vagina do?!' When the judge had heard her, he told those present to dismiss them. We left, I went to my work and the slave girl remained part of his property and I do not know what happened to the pair of them.

If Zayd buys a garment, then thinks it expensive and [sees that] it is thin at the edge, he returns it to its [previous] owner because it is clearly defective, but the broker still takes his broker's fee [if necessary] in the presence of the qadi [who gives his judgement] vigorously and forcefully. The judge makes a judgement in his favour, two *fals* brokerage fee for every two dinars [of the price]. If he [arranges] a sale in your shop, he gets one *fals* for every dinar [of the price]. If he [arranges] a bulk sale, he gets a dinar on every hundred dinars [of the price]. They get a quarter for every piece of indigo.

When anyone wants to leave [Aden] through the gate to bid farewell to a traveller, he cannot, unless he has written permission and a guarantor for everything which might later appear as his debt, money or taxes, and the governor's logo is included on the document. If all that is arranged, then he may leave. If he has no guarantor, then someone will call out in the souk, 'So-and-so is leaving through the gate. Anyone owed anything by him should claim it!' If any debt is discovered against him, God is sufficient [to prevent] the Believers fighting [among themselves].[6] If no debt is discovered against him, he goes wherever he wants. There is the following maxim: The man with no money is in God's keeping![7] A poet has recited as follows:

[1] See Löfgren, *Texte*, I, p. 66; Smith, 'Maritime Trade', p. 130.

[2] Arabic *munādī*, literally 'someone who calls out [that there is something for sale]'.

[3] Arabic *yasburu*.

[4] A loose translation of 'bi-ism Allāh yā khwājā baynī wa-bayna-k sharʿ Muḥammad b. ʿAbdallāh'.

[5] See Löfgren, *Texte*, I, p. 66; Serjeant, 'Forms of Plea', p. 13.

[6] I.e. he pays up and the matter is closed.

[7] Akwaʿ (*Amthāl*, II, p. 1150, no. 4973) glosses, '... fears no one because he has no money and nothing which makes him afraid.' The compiler also quotes the verse.

No child dies when he has few cares,
nor is there anything he fears that will come to pass.
He enjoyed his youth and benefited from knowledge,
but his ultimate wish is to be alone and keep silent.

[147] *The downfall of Aden.*[1] The sea overflowed, so the whole area was flooded. The town became part of the sea. It was mentioned in 'The Beginning of Creation' that ships were passing the town fleetingly as they got under sail. The crews would say among themselves, 'We have heard that in ancient times there was a great, thriving town in this ocean, permanent, flat, healthy for its inhabitants, a noble place.' One says, 'What was it called?' But the reply is, 'Its name eludes me.' After its downfall, the port of Ghulāfiqah – or more accurately al-Ahwāb – thrived until it became better than Aden.

I was informed as follows by Aḥmad b. ʿAbdallāh b. ʿAlī al-Ḥammāmī al-Wāsiṭī. Only a little of the building of Aden is left. I asked why. He replied, 'I read in some book [that Aden was destroyed] when its buildings reached as far as its gate.' Ibn al-Mujāwir said, 'Some of the buildings did reach as far as the gate.'

Others have said: Aden's downfall came in 627.[2] What points to the truthfulness of this statement is the arrival in Aden of Nūr al-Dīn ʿUmar b. ʿAlī b. al-Rasūl on Wednesday, 26 Rajab, 624.[3] On Monday, 2 Shaʿbān, he imposed a purchase price[4] for madder on everyone in Aden, foreigner or local, strong or weak, man or woman, chaste[5] or fornicator, on the price of one *buhār* 200 dinars and eighty *malakī* [dinars]. He imposed a tax for the people on firewood. The days were like those of the Assembly,[6] all those gathering together crying out, 'Where can we escape?'[7] In 625,[8] he confiscated all the merchants' pepper, all footwear, copper and rare commodities.[9] The price of a *buhār* of pepper was forty dinars. He imposed a purchase price for pepper of sixty dinars on the Karimi merchants. He took brass from them at a price per *buhār* of sixty dinars and imposed its purchase price on the footwear merchants of eighty [148] dinars. He offered the pepper merchants madder at the price per *buhār* of eighty-four dinars, taking a *buhār* and a quarter for each *buhār*, but when he sold it, he handed over three-quarters of a *buhār* for a *buhār*. After all this, the following had to be paid out on imported goods: customs dues, galley-tax, agency tax, *zakāh* and a broker's fee, leaving an excess with the merchant of precisely nothing![10] He adds up the total bill and experiences [nothing but] regret and nothing to be pleased

[1] See Löfgren, *Texte*, I, p. 68.

[2] Begins 20 November 1229. This is the latest date found in *Tārīkh al-Mustabṣir*.

[3] The date is the equivalent of 12 July 1227. Nūr al-Dīn ʿUmar became the first Rasulid sultan in the Yemen in c. 628/1230, ruling until 647/1249. For the historical background to Nūr al-Dīn's visit to Aden, see Ibn Ḥātim, *Simṭ*, p. 194, and Smith, 'Ayyubids and Rasulids', pp. 5–10, especially p. 8.

[4] Arabic *ṭaraḥa ʿalā* (Dozy, *Supplément*, II, p. 31, '*imposer* une denrée à un homme, le forcer de l'acquérir à un prix excessif que l'on a fixé soi-même'; Löfgren, *Texte*, II, p. 45).

[5] Arabic *ḥurrah* (Dozy, *Supplément*, I, p. 263).

[6] I.e. on the Day of Resurrection.

[7] Quran 75:10.

[8] Begins 12 December 1227.

[9] Text *barbahār* (Löfgren, *Texte*, II, p. 23). Dionisius Agius has kindly supplied a list from Iṣṭakhrī (Leiden, 1870, pp. 34. 127) as follows: aloes, camphor, precious gems, bamboos, ivory, ebony, sandalwood, perfumes, drugs and condiments.

[10] Arabic 'yafḍulu maʿ al-tājir lāsh lāsh'.

about.[1] Nūr al-Dīn ʿUmar confiscated all the cotton of those arriving from India with the merchants, squandering it all for himself, [not allowing others to] sell or buy. The steelyard was taxed at the rate of 20,000 dinars per annum. Oil [was taxed] up to five dinars each *buhār*. The vegetable souk, slave girls, ripe dates, meat and all riding beasts [were taxed] to produce 11,000 dinars. Absolutely everything had a tax upon it, except water and fish.[2]

From Aden to al-Mafālīs.[3] From Aden to al-Mabāh a quarter of a parasang. To al-Mazaff a parasang, its length being 300 cubits and sixty paces. It was built by Shaddād b. ʿĀd when he built Aden. Another version is that it was built by the Persians when they released the sea over al-Mabāh until all the lands around Aden were flooded. Shaykh ʿAbdallāh b. Yūsuf b. Muḥammad al-Musulmānī, the perfumer, renovated the buildings and assigned certain crops in Aden as a pious endowment for them.

To al-Mimlāḥ a quarter of a parasang, a place where salt is made up into blocks. It used to be exempted, but now there is a tax on it. It is said that some of it was assigned to the sultan, since Atābak Sayf al-Dīn Sunqur bought half of it for 1,000 dinars.

To al-Majdūlī a quarter of a parasang.[4] To al-Lakhabah a quarter of a parasang, from where baked bricks and glass are transported to Aden. It was built by Abū ʿAmr ʿUthmān b. ʿAlī al-Zinjibīlī. To al-Ḥajar al-ʿUrr a parasang[5] and it is the distance of a hundred stones laid out to the right of a tower-house.[6]

To the well of al-Rajʿ two parasangs, crossing some sand called al-Maghāwī.[7] As for Wādī al-Rajāʿ, it is an [149] unspoiled wadi and called al-Ḥirdah[8] by the Arabs, [lying] among tamarisk[9] and arak trees. A fine mosque has been built at the well.

I was informed by al-Ḥasan b. Muḥammad b. al-Ḥasan b. ʿAlī b. al-Ḥusayn al-Maḥfanī as follows. The mosque and well in al-Rajāʿ was built by Ẓafr b. Muḥammad b. Ẓafr, the man of letters. The locals who are ʿAqrabīs say that the water of al-Ḥirdah does not go together with food,[10] i.e. the eating of bread and the drinking of the water of the well of al-Rajāʿ do not go together, because this water makes eating food superfluous.

To Nuwayʿim two parasangs.[11] Al-Nuwayʿim is an unspoiled wadi, palm groves and *sidr* trees. I was informed as follows by some of its inhabitants that there were two wadis, one of them al-Nuwayʿim and the other Wādī Marḥab, both of them being situated where the last part of the plain [joins with] the beginning of the mountains.

[1] Reading with OL 'yajidu nadaman wa-lā riḍan'.

[2] Arabic 'wa-lam yabqa shayʾ yadūru ʿalay-h ism wa-ḥarf illā wa-qad rajaʿa fī-h ḍamān mā khalā al-māʾ wa-al-samak'.

[3] See Sprenger, *Reiserouten*, p. 151, and Löfgren, *Texte*, I, p. 69.

[4] Unidentified.

[5] Unidentified.

[6] Arabic *al-darb*, which could be a place name.

[7] Both unidentified. Al-Rajʿ and al-Rajāʿ would appear to be one and the same.

[8] I take the vocalization from Hamdānī (*Ṣifah*, pp. 52, 120), but this is not the place described by him.

[9] Arabic *athl*, *Tamarix orientalis* Forssk. See above p. 74, n. 9.

[10] Arabic *ʿaysh* (Landberg, *Glossaire daṯînois*, III, p. 2346).

[11] Unidentified.

To al-Mafālīs two parasangs, a simple[1] town built on the pass of a triangular mountain. Sayf al-Islām[2] built a simple fortress on the summit of this mountain, called al-Maṣāniʿ, said also to have been built in ancient times. It is solid and strong. The inhabitants of al-Mafālīs only buy and sell on certain appointed days, on no others.

The Building of al-Jubb. The Arabs of this area are Arabs of the Tihāmah regions from Mawzaʿ as far as the regions of Abyan, called B. al-Ḥārith[3] and who claim a love of God and [do anything] in His cause. If any of them finds a dead gazelle, he takes it, washes it, puts a shroud on it and buries it. Mourning for the gazelle lasts seven days among all the tribes [of the area]; they rip their clothes, pull out their hair, sprinkling dust over the parting of their hair. They were asked about their practices and they replied, 'We adhere to the root and confess to having abandoned the branch!.' As Qays b. al-Mulawwaḥ has recited:[4]

> Your eyes are her eyes, your neck her neck,
> but your leg bone is delicate.

[150] No one of this tribe eats bread, nor drinks with a woman, even if he were to die of hunger and thirst. Similarly camels are not used, while donkeys are ridden at the front. The name al-Mafālīs is simply derived from lack of money.[5] As Abū Nuwās has recited:[6]

> I want a piece of paper, for I have none,
> while the majority of those with me are people with paper.
> God curse them for their friendship and knowledge;
> those of them well-to-do are like bankrupts.[7]

From al-Mafālīs to Taʿizz.[8] From al-Mafālīs to the mountain pass[9] of al-Ḥumar a parasang and a half.[10] It was built by Shaykh Aḥmad b. al-Junayd b. Baṭṭāl. I was informed by Yaḥyā b. ʿAbd al-Raḥmān al-Zarrād[11] as follows: Muḥammad b. Sulaymān b. Baṭṭāl built it. It is said that there were 360 bends[12] – i.e. *farkah*[13] – and at every bend

[1] Arabic *mukhtaṣir* (Dozy, *Supplément*, I, p. 376).

[2] I.e.Ṭughtakīn b. Ayyūb, the second Ayyubid sultan in the Yemen, reg. 579–93/1183–97. See Appendix I below.

[3] Perhaps Bal-Ḥārith; see Kaḥḥālah, *Muʿjam*, I, p. 102.

[4] See above p. 54, n. 14.

[5] Arabic *iflās*.

[6] The renowned Abū Nuwās al-Ḥasan b. Hāniʾ al-Ḥakamī, famous in particular for his songs of wine, hunting and young boys, who died c. 198–200/813–15 (*EI*, 'Abū Nuwās'). See his *Dīwān* [Ṭabbāʿ], pp. 355–6.

[7] Arabic *mafālīs*.

[8] See Sprenger, *Reiserouten*, p. 151.

[9] Arabic *naqīl* (Landberg, *Glossaire daṯînois*, III, p. 2816; Goitein, *Travels*, p. 95; Smith, *Ayyubids*, II, p. 128).

[10] I vocalize tentatively after reference to Maqḥafī (*Muʿjam*, p. 191) who says there is a Ḥumar (without the article) in the district of Taʿizz. It must be said, however, that the L MS variant, 'al-Ḥamrā', can also be found among Maqḥafī's list, 'a thriving village E of al-Janad'. See also Abū Makhramah in Löfgren, *Texte*, II, p. 225.

[11] 'The Strangler'! I am not sure that this is correct. There is a 'Raddād', the intensive form of *rādd*, 'repellent', on p. 167 below.

[12] See Serjeant, 'Tower-house', p. 276, for the whole of this passage concerning the building of the mountain pass.

[13] Arabic *farkah* (I take a chance on the vocalization [the noun of unity of the *maṣdar fark*] which RBS leaves *frkah*). The basic meaning of the root is one of 'rubbing and pressing' (Lane, *Lexicon*, VI, p. 2387). Since it has the specific meaning of 'rubbing and pressing an ear of corn to remove the husk from the kernel', I wonder if it is derived from the process involving the wheat mentioned in the text. The sacrifice is to propitiate the jinn.

a head of cattle was slaughtered as a sacrifice and there were also six loads of wheat and the expenditure of 300 dinars. It is also said that the expenditure of each bend was 1,000 dinars. At each bend, he built a watering place and a mosque. When he had finished it, his wife claimed her dowry from him. He asked her what she wanted. She replied, 'I want you to give me a garment that you have made and you are released from [your obligation to provide] a dowry.' So he gave her a garment which he had made. It was completed in 420.[1] Another version is that it was in 520.[2] It is a fine, amazing building.

The stones on the mountain pass. On the pass there are two stones with the shape of the vaginas of two women in them. I asked the donkey driver about them and he replied. 'They were two women who have been transformed into stones, one of them can be seen on the peak of a mountain [151], while the second has been broken up and scattered over some of the terrace structures.' Between the one stone and the other was a space of ten cubits. They menstruate every month, but another version is every year.

Ibn al-Mujāwir said: I saw something like blood on it, but I am not sure whether it was blood or something else. I was informed as follows by Aḥmad b. al-Muhannā al-Ṣaffār al-Ḥallī al-Qudsī: This blood might indicate humans, because what indicates humans is the basic fact that [although] it is made of stone, it [still] flows [with blood]. One of them said, 'There is an offensive odour which can be smelt from the stone.' I smelt it, but experienced something different from what they had mentioned. The stones are at bend 230, on the right as you go up from al-Mafālīs to al-Juwwah[3] and on the left as you go down from al-Juwwah to al-Mafālīs, a distance of 130 bends. Their distinguishing feature is that on the top of one stone two acacia trees[4] have grown and their shadow reaches the second stone which is part of the same construction. The mountain pass remained as it was until Shams al-Dawlah Tūrān Shāh b. Ayyūb entered the Yemen.[5] The Arabs destroyed some of the pass so that none of the Ghuzz[6] could pass along it. It remained destroyed until Sayf al-Islām Ṭughtakīn b. Ayyūb became ruler.[7] He repaired it from his own money. The most accurate account is that he ordered the builder to be given the honorific title of Jalāl al-Dīn. This was before Shaykh Muḥammad b. Sulaymān b. Baṭṭāl al-Rakbī built this pass on the Ḥirz road. This was because he was leaving Lahej, entering a wadi and continuing to walk to al-Juwwah through side-wadis, wadis and a plain for a short distance. People made the journey along the Ḥirz road in great fear, [but] since the traveller on it is [now] protected,[8] it was called the Ḥirz [protection] road. We shall mention it [again] under the heading of the regions of al-Juwwah.

Down to the lower mountain pass is two parasangs. There there is a place on a slope called al-Majriyyah[9] about which one of them recited as follows:

[1] Begins 20 January 1029.
[2] Begins 27 January 1126.
[3] Both this town and al-Dumluwah are about 20 miles W of al-Janad and about 25 miles NW of Ta'izz (Kay, *Yaman*, end map; Smith, *Ayyubids*, II, pp. 167–8).
[4] Arabic *salam*. See p. 43, n. 3 above.
[5] I.e. in 569/1173.
[6] I.e. the non-Arab Ayyubids whose upper echelons were Kurds and Turks and an ethnic mix of both.
[7] I.e. in 579/1183.
[8] Reading with OL *yaḥruzu*.
[9] Unidentified.

We passed through al-Ḥamrāʾ[1] and al-Majriyyah
among [all] these mountains and wadis.

[152] To al-Ḥanashayn half a parasang.[2] They are two white lines, straight along the side of the mountain. It is said that they were two snakes[3] meeting together; they were struck by lightning and turned into two white lines. To al-Ḥ.wāḍ a parasang,[4] a plain full of great fear. To al-Juwwah half a parasang, in the district of al-Dumluwah. To al-Dumluwah a parasang. God knows best.

[153] *The building of the fortress of al-Dumluwah.* I was informed as follows by Yaḥyā b. ʿAlī b. Aḥmad al-Raddād: A bedouin woman, an owner of livestock, was oppressed by the deputies.[5] When she saw for herself that people were bold enough to take her livestock, she drove what remained of them and climbed up al-Dumluwah, where she settled. When the time came for the livestock taxman[6] to take from the livestock, she refused to pay what she was obliged, both genuine [taxes] and not, and she remained where she was. When they saw her great courage and strong sense of honour, some people climbed up to her, but she made it impossible for them to do so. They surrounded her and lay siege to her, but nothing else was done about her. When the governor of the time heard news of the woman and her refusal to pay what well-known taxes she should and carry out her obligations [dating from] ancient [times] and they saw how strong her position was, he sent to her, [offering] her and her followers protection and that taxes be removed from her and her livestock and she feel secure. So the woman came down and the governor built an impregnable fortress at the place, which was in itself strong and solid. Because of the long delay suffered by those beneath it who were seeking to take it, it was called al-Dumluwah.[7] Muḥammad b. Ziyād al-Māzinī recited as follows, eulogizing Abū al-Suʿūd b. Zurayʿ:[8]

O you watching, tell me you see him as he is;
I reckon he has materialized in a pearl.
I saw no one rising up on high,
until I saw you, [Abū al-Suʿūd b. Zurayʿ,] sitting in [defence of] al-Dumluwah.

None of the Arabs was able to take it except Sayf al-Islām Ṭughtakīn b. Ayyūb after he besieged it for six years.[9] In the end, he bought it from Commander Kāfūr, client of the dāʿī,

[1] See p. 165, n. 10 above.

[2] Unidentified.

[3] Arabic *ḥanashayn*.

[4] Unidentified.

[5] I.e. the Ayyubid deputies who ruled over lower Yemen and Tihāmah in the period between the departure of al-Muʿaẓẓam Ṭūrānshāh and the arrival of al-ʿAzīz Ṭughṭakīn, 571–9/1175–83 (Smith, 'Political History', p. 138; Appendix B.8 below).

[6] Arabic *al-rāʿī*. It seems to me that this was an official whose job was to administer a tax on livestock which was paid in kind.

[7] Arabic 'li-dawām makth ṭālibī-h taḥta-h ʿalā akhḍi-h'; i.e. the letters of the name of the fortress are derived from the *dāl* of *dawām*, the *mīm* of *makth* and the *lām* of *ṭālibī-h*!

[8] The son of the founder of the Zurayʿid dynasty whose date of death is unknown (Kay, *Yaman*, pp. 307–8; Hamdānī, *Ṣulayḥiyyūn*, table 7, p. 345; Smith, 'Political History', p. 136; Appendix B.1 below). The poetry is also quoted by Yāqūt (*Maʿjam*, II, p. 471).

[9] Ṭughtakīn was not an Arab by Ibn al-Mujāwir's usual definition; he was of the Ghuzz. He ruled during the period 579–93/1173–97, although there are no accounts of dramatic sieges during this time in the Ayyubid sources.

for 100,000 dinars, on the understanding that Kāfūr take everything in it away and hand over the fortress with nothing [154] in it.[1] Kāfūr was an Abyssinian. When he had taken the total sum, he took the dāʿī's wife and all the contents of the fortress to al-ʿĀrah and put in charge of al-Dumluwah Muʿallim Aḥmad al-Ṣulwī,[2] a slave girl, and, it is said, an Abyssinian slave. Kāfūr embarked on board ship and crossed over to Abyssinia. He sent his seal to Sayf al-Islām and he in turn sent it to Muʿallim Aḥmad al-Ṣulwī [with the command] to hand over the fortress. But Aḥmad al-Ṣulwī declared, 'I shall neither listen to, nor obey, Sayf al-Islām or Commander Kāfūr; today I am ruler, [the one] to take possession of this fortress.' So Sayf al-Islām gave his reply and attacked the fortress. He besieged it for another six months, but could not get the better of the muʿallim. When the siege was pressed hard, he bought the fortress for the second time, [this time] from the muʿallim for 60,000 dinars. He took possession of it and demolished it, rebuilding it. He put six gates into it, including al-Dhirāʿ gate, Nabhān gate, al-Asad gate and al-Ghazāl gate. He dug three cisterns in it, one in the sun under the mountain and the other two in the shade. He planted there a fine cultivated area and built a square. He went to extremes to fortify it.

The last person to buy al-Dumluwah was a cavalryman of Jawzā, the wife of Atābak Sayf al-Dīn Sunqur,[3] for a total price of 20,000 dinars after he had besieged it for a whole year during the rule of al-Malik al-Masʿūd Yūsuf b. Muḥammad b. Abī Bakr.[4] When it was completely in his possession, he built a second wall around the whole fortress, in 614,[5] to render it impregnable. Sayf al-Islām had planted a cultivated area, called either al-Jinān or al-Jannāt,[6] beneath the fortress, in which there were all kinds of fruits. Citrons used to grow there, each one weighing ten *mann*.[7]

[155] *From al-Juwwah to Aden* returning via the Ḥirz road. From al-Juwwah to al-ʿĀyirayn two parasangs.[8] To the mountain pass of Ḥirz a parasang. It was only known by this name because, when someone goes along it, he is protected[9] against being seized. It was the ruler who made this facility.

To al-Māʾ al-Ḥārr half a parasang.[10] It is a spring from whose source hot [water] comes and the place is known by this name. A number of screw-pine trees have grown up on the spot, belonging to God and [to be used] in God['s cause].

To al-Daʿīs four parasangs,[11] which is in the area of Lahej. The regions of Lahej [extend] far and wide. They stretch a distance of twenty parasangs and there are large

[1] Arabic *shibh jawf ḥimār*, 'like the belly of an ass'. The 'dāʿī' is presumably one of the Zurayʿid rulers.

[2] *Muʿallim* is certainly a title in this context and it may well be that al-Ṣulwī, or one of his ancestors, had nautical connections. For *muʿallim* = 'captain', 'pilot', see Tibbetts, *Navigation*, pp. 58, 535.

[3] Reg. 598–609/1201–12. His wife is not mentioned in the Ayyubid historical sources.

[4] Reg. 612–26/1215–28. I cannot trace the incident in the Ayyubid histories.

[5] Begins 10 April 1217.

[6] See Smith, *Ayyubids*, II, pp. 166–7.

[7] Text *utrunjah*, *Citrus limonum* Risso (Dimyāṭī, *Muʿjam*, p. 9; Varisco, *Agriculture*, p. 182). Since a *mann* is a weight somewhere between 0.8 and 3 k (Hinz, *Masse*, pp. 16–23), we are talking of some remarkable citrons here!

[8] Unidentified.

[9] Arabic *yuḤRaZu*.

[10] See Löfgren, *Texte*, I, p. 146; Smith, *Ayyubids*, p. 174.

[11] Abū Makhramah (in Löfgren, *Texte*, I, p. 73; II, p. 182) says the place is 'in the region of Abyan' and 'near Abyan'. Abyan and Lahej formed one fief in Ayyubid times which stretched over the whole area N of Aden, Abyan to the E of an imaginary line drawn due N from Aden, Lahej to the W (*EI*, 'Laḥdj'). Since there is doubt here whether al-Daʿīs falls into one or the other, one might assume that that it is about due N of Aden.

villages, including al-Raʿāriʿ,[1] about which ʿAlī b. al-Ḥusayn al-Aʿraj recites as follows:[2]

> Al-Raʿāriʿ is empty of the sons of Masʿūd;[3]
> lions have taken over from monkeys!

But Dāʿī Sabaʾ b. Abī al-Suʿūd[4] told him: It was rather 'lions have taken over from lions', meaning Muḥammad b. Manīʿ b. Masʿūd b. al-Mukarram who was lord of Lahej.[5] It was conquered by Sabaʾ b. Abī al-Suʿūd b. Zurayʿ b. al-ʿAbbās b. al-Mukarram. As for the hills[6] of al-Daʿīs, there is no honour there. 1,000 *malakī* dinars are sent up from there to the treasury every year. Nāṣir al-Dīn Muḥammad b. ʿUmar b. al-Mahdī al-Rāzī[7] took control of it and destroyed it. He plundered its inhabitants and burned it on 1 Shawwāl, 624.[8] They all moved to Aden, while its bedouins scattered in the Tihāmah regions of the Yemen. To Aden four parasangs.

From al-Juwwah to Taʿizz. To Wādī Warazān a parasang,[9] a river which marks the boundaries of three regions: al-Juwwah [156], al-Janadiyyah and Taʿizz. To Akamat Hamdān a parasang.[10] To al-Ḥamrāʾ half a parasang.[11] To al-Ḥawbān half a parasang,[12] where Atābak Sunqur built a square cistern. To Taʿizz a quarter of a parasang. These regions are called Ḥayyiz al-Akhḍar[13] because there are so much grass, water and greenness.

Description of the fortress of Taʿizz. It is a fortress built on the road to Jabaʾ;[14] the mountain is called al-Akhḍar.[15] [The fortress] is solid and strong, [made of] gypsum and stone, with gates and firm walls and inhabited. There is no fortress in the whole of the Yemen more auspicious than this, because it is the seat of rule and the fortress of rulers. Ibn

[1] See above p. 144, n. 4.

[2] An unidentified poet who must have supported the Abbasid line of the Zurayʿids (Hamdānī, *Ṣulayḥiyyūn*, p. 345, table 7; Appendix B.1 below).

[3] I.e. Muḥammad b. Mānīʿ and his kinsmen, the Masʿudid line of the Zurayʿids in fact; see previous note and below n. 5.

[4] The Abbasid Zurayʿid who died in 533/1138 (see above n. 2). He is here protesting that all Zurayʿids are strong and courageous, not just his own, Abbasid, line.

[5] D. 545/1150, killed by Muḥammad b. Sabaʾ in Lahej (Kay, *Yaman*, p. 68–79; ʿAbdalī, *Hadiyyah*, pp. 56–63, with a different version of the verse in question which, he says, was composed by ʿAlī b. Ziyād al-Māzinī).

[6] Arabic *qūr* (*al-Daʿīs*), plur. of *qārah* is my tentative reading here.

[7] Neither the individual, nor the event can be found in the Ayyubid sources.

[8] 14 September 1227.

[9] This wadi can be clearly seen on Kay's *Yaman* end map, although, if its upper reaches fall between al-Juwwah and Taʿizz, as the text indicates, its exact location here may need correction.

[10] Unidentified.

[11] See p. 165, n. 10 above.

[12] Area of plain and some hills NE of Taʿizz (Ḥajarī, *Majmūʿ*, II, p. 299; Maqḥafī, *Muʿjam*, p. 198).

[13] Ḥayyiz is suggested by Sprenger (*Reiserouten*, p. 152) and accepted in the text by OL. Its meaning is 'tract', 'region'.

[14] A little SW of Taʿizz itself, W of Jabal Ṣabir (Kay, *Yaman*, end map; Smith, *Ayyubids*, II, p. 164 and map I; Ḥajarī, *Majmūʿ*, I, p. 172; Maqḥafī, *Muʿjam*, p. 105). This must be the fortress of al-Qāhirah, situated between the town and Jabal Ṣabir (Niebuhr, *Voyage*, I, figs LXVI and LXVII, between pp. 300–301, 'Kähhre').

[15] The former Jewish quarter (RBS) which is marked as such on Niebuhr's fig. LXVI (*Voyage*, I, between pp. 300 and 301).

al-Mujāwir said: I saw in a dream someone who was saying to me, 'The fortress of Ta'izz is called Tall al-Dhahab [hill of gold].' Or he said, 'Jabal al-Dhahab [mountain of gold].' I thought over carefully what he said and found it to be true, since the wealth of the whole of the Yemen is amassed in it. A wise man said: It is a stronghold placed between two towns, one al-Maghribah,[1] and the second on the side of Jabal Ṣabir as follows. Its plan is as follows [see Fig. 6].

Description of Jabal Ṣabir. It is a circular mountain, its circumference being three days['s walk]. I have referred to it as being long and wide, with a vast array of villages, fortresses, cultivated areas, vines and crops on it. It has four passages, al-Khashabah, Birdād, 'Atdān and Jaba'.[2] Only these tracks can be traversed by pedestrian and rider alike because it is so rugged and rough, but it is a pleasant mountain. Shams al-Nahār, the daughter of either Aḥmad b. Saba' b. Abī al-Su'ūd or Saba' b. Sulaymān[3] has recited as follows, [157 – plan of the fortress of Ta'izz] [158] criticizing me:

> How can being apart be good for you, when you left your native land?
> The lover abandons his love and seeks to stay in Aden.
> You have substituted hunting ships' masters for hunting gazelles;
> you have substituted Ṣīrah for Ṣabir, sultan of the mountains of the Yemen.[4]

In one of the caves of Ṣabir were the people of the cave and al-Raqīm, they about whom God – He is mighty and glorious – has said, 'They remained in their cave for three hundred years and they added nine [more].'[5] Their names were Maksalimīnā, Yamlīkhā, Marṭūnus, Akfīshiṭnūnus, Furūrus and ... The name of the dog was Dīr, or, it is said, Qiṭmīr, or Ḥamrān, Anṭbīs, or al-Ḥāyin.[6] Others have said: ..., ..., ..., ..., ... and ...[7] 'Their dog was stretching out his paws on the threshold.'[8] Near the door of the cave is a mosque and at the door of the mosque a spring called 'Ayn al-Kawthar. This is an excellent place to which visitations are made on 10 Rajab. If anyone says that they were not in this region, we say they were, for Decius is the ruler who founded the town of al-Kadrā' and settled in al-Janad. The inhabitants were

[1] Part of the Ṣabir range.

[2] The first of these passages is unidentified elsewhere. Birdād is the passage between Ṣabir and Dhakhir (Hamdānī, *Ṣifah*, pp. 67, 74, corrected from Yazdād; Maqḥafī, *Mu'jam*, pp. 68–9). 'Atbān is E of Ṣabir (Hamdānī, *Ṣifah*, p. 77). Jaba' is probably SW of Ta'izz, close by, between Ṣabir and Dhakhir, a village of al-Ma'āfir (Hamdānī, *Ṣifah*, pp. 54, 99; Kay, *Yaman*, end map; Smith, *Ayyubids*, II, p. 164; Maqḥafī, *Mu'jam*, p. 105).

[3] I cannot trace a member of the Zuray'id dynasty bearing the name Saba' b. Sulaymān.

[4] Ṣīrah being the port of Aden. You have abandoned your mountains around Ta'izz for the sea and the port of Aden. This makes the 1st pers. pronoun 'me' puzzling. If the poet is addressing Ibn al-Mujāwir, the latter must have spent some time in Ta'izz and regarded it as home, and then left it for Aden. He must also have been personally acquainted with one of the Zuray'id family, Saba' b. Sulaymān in the later part of the 6th/12th century. If the former, Aḥmad b. Saba', is correct and he were the brother of Muḥammad b. Saba', this would be too early for any personal contact with Ibn al-Mujāwir.

[5] Quran 18:25. Al-Raqīm is either the name of the dog, or the tablet which contains the story of the youths involved. The Arab geographers generally regard it, however, as the name of a place (*SEI*, 'Aṣḥāb al-Kahf'; *EI*, 'Aṣḥāb al-Kahf'). RBS reports on a Masjid Ahl al-Kahf in Sa'dī territory in Yāfi' and mentions the Ta'izz connection also ('Yāfi', Zaydīs etc.' p. 92).

[6] The names are tentative and illegible.

[7] The names are illegible.

[8] Quran 18:18.

[157]

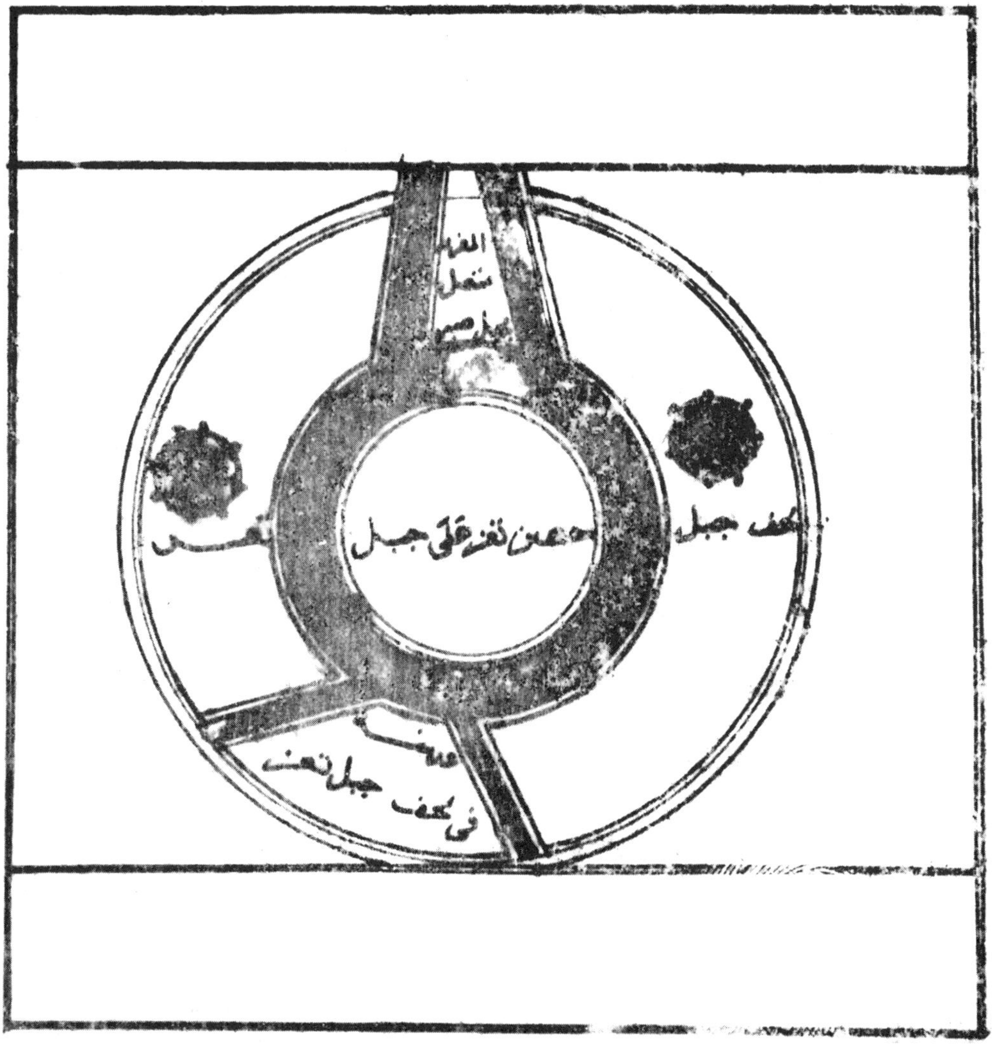

Figure 6. Plan of Taʿizz (I MS, f. 64b, text, p. 157, tabula VI)

The smaller centre circle contains the label 'the fortress of Taʿizz on a mountain'. To the left is the single word 'Taʿizz' and to the right, 'slope of a mountain'. At the bottom at about seven o'clock are the words, 'a town on the slope of the mountain of Taʿizz'. The note at the top reads, 'al-Maghribah, connecting with Jabal Ṣabir'. The top of the circle must therefore be S.

from the people of Ephesus.[1] When everything was finished and they had left their town, they climbed up Jabal Ṣabir, took refuge in a cave and we know what happened to them and their dog with them. As God – He is ever almighty – has said, 'And their dog was stretching out his paws on the threshold. If you had observed closely, you would have turned away from them in flight and would have been filled with awe of them.'[2] As a poet has recited:

Doubt and differences of opinion have become too much, as each one
seeks success on the straight path;
My belief is that there is no god but He,
then there is my love for Aḥmad and ʿAlī.
A dog was triumphant through his love for the people in a cave;
how could he bring wretchedness with his love of the family of the Prophet?

[159] Diʿbil b. ʿAlī al-Khuzāʿī has recited as follows:[3]

The Abbasid rulers are seven in the books;[4]
the books do not tell us of an eighth.
So too the people of the cave were seven in the cave,
noble; when they were counted, [they were seven] and a dog their eighth.

The water of Taʿizz comes down from Jabal Ṣabir. Sayf al-Islām Ṭughtakīn bought it for 10,000 dinars from its people [specifically] for this water. He assigned all the profit made from it to be employed in the way of God. The water is called al-Khashabah and is light, wholesome and healthy. It is said there is a broken spring which produces a great deal of water: half of it is directed towards Taʿizz and half descends to the town of Jabaʾ, this latter being more healthy and better than the water of al-Khashabah which is directed towards Taʿizz. Now the inhabitants of Jabaʾ only take kindly to strangers by drinking this water, not by any other means, because of its goodness. All Ṣabir fruits, firewood and wood for building sag because the branch is pliable, and the clouds bring heavy rain. From the time when someone enters al-Durayʿāʾ until he drops down to the mountain pass of al-Ḥamrāʾ,[5] cold air blows every late afternoon, reviving the spirit and thereafter the horizon is crowned with clouds and the rain comes down for just one passing hour, then it clears up. The weather remains like this for a period of six months during the summer.

Section. When you see the crescent moon in water inclining to a red colour, it indicates the wind will blow; when you see blackness in the middle of it, it indicates rain. When you see the eye of the sun as it is rising with some cloud in the middle of it, it indicates rain and brightness together. When you see the sun set with bits of cloud on it and around it, it indicates rain. When you see clouds dispersed, it indicates rain. When the crescent moon is two or three nights old and if [160] you see on its horns as if it is dark and stained with blood, it indicates winter and much rain.

[1] The text has al-Ufsūs. The tradition in the West is that the seven sleepers were from Ephesus (*SEI*, 'Aṣḥāb al-Kahf'; Cross, *Oxford Dictionary*, 'Seven Sleepers', p. 1246; *EI*, 'Aṣḥāb al-Kahf').

[2] Quran 18.18.

[3] Well-known Abbasid poet, 148–246/765–860 (Iṣfahānī, *Aghānī*, IX, p. 67; Brockelmann, *Geschichte*, Sup. I, pp. 121–2; Zolondek, *Diʿbil*, pp. 3, 6).

[4] See Zolondek, *Diʿbil*, pp. 13, 94.

[5] They must be a village and mountain pass on Jabal Ṣabir. For the latter, see p. 165, n. 10 above.

Countries where it rains a lot. Rain comes down constantly in the regions of Mārdān;[1] in the regions of Kilāb[2] for ten months. In the territory of B. Sayf[3] in the province of the Yemen, [it rains] for forty days then it is dry two months. Thus it is called Peeing-it-down![4] In the area of al-Maynāw,[5] [it rains] for a period of four months. In Sumatra the rain comes down from the clouds as if [from] the mouths of waterskins. Sailors only find their way to Sumatra by the great amount of lightning flashing. In Khawr Fawfal,[6] [it rains] for four months. In al-ʿAynayn,[7] fine date-juice falls constantly like milk [poured out].[8] In Pemba and the island of Mombasa,[9] it falls constantly; in Sind for a period of forty days. Throughout India there is sometimes a cloudless period, sometimes rain as many as ten times in one day. Also it rains on one house, but not on another. It is said that it sometimes rains on one of an ox's horns, but not on the other! Rain falls in the mountains of the Yemen for six months between noon and late afternoon.

Water and winds and things associated with each star and sign of the zodiac.[10] The period of Aries and Libra are the blazing fires.[11] Gemini is the good winds and the south wind.[12] Cancer is sweet water and rain, moving constantly, and what descends from the sky.[13] Leo is the fires which smoke in stoves and knowledge of the air and the fires which are in stones.[14] Virgo, whenever it conforms with Libra, is the winds which [161] pollinate the trees by blowing on them, make the fruit plump and they indicate good weather.[15] Scorpio is the flowing water into which [the water of] such as cisterns, floods, shallow wells[16] and soaked clay comes down in stages.[17] Sagittarius is the rivers and natural fires in the bodies of animals.[18] Aquarius is running water, the seas and storm

[1] This might well be Mādīn, a fortress in the Jazīrah, stronghold of the Ḥamdān amirs (Yāqūt, *Muʿjam*, V, p. 39; Le Strange, *Lands*, p. 96 and map III).

[2] I take this to be Kilāb b. Rabīʿah, who occupied vast areas of the northern Arabian Peninsula and parts of Syria (Kaḥḥālah, *Muʿjam*, III, p. 989; Caskel, *Ǧamharat an-nasab*, I, Tafeln 92, 93).

[3] Of Murād, living N of Taʿizz and between it and Zabīd (Ibn Rasūl, *Ṭurfah*, p. 36). Part of this passage is translated in Smith, 'Wondrous', p. 112.

[4] This is the best I can do with al-Bawwālah!

[5] Ibn al-Mujāwir is here ranging far and wide, so could this be Yāqūt's 'town in Sicily' (*Muʿjam*, V, p. 245)?

[6] Unidentified.

[7] There are several candidates for this place: a hill in the Uḥud range near Medina; two mountains in the same range; even Uḥud itself; a water source in Bahrain; a mountain in the Yemen only three miles from the ancient fortress in Ṣanʿāʾ called Ghumdān (all the above without the article) (Yāqūt, *Muʿjam*, IV, pp. 173–4, 180).

[8] Arabic *ṣimāq*, plur. of *ṣamqah*, strictly speaking 'lait qui a perdu son goût' (Kazimirski, *Dictionnaire*, I, p. 1372). Since K also defines the word 'grande cruche', I suppose one might stretch the meaning here to 'like [pouring out] pitchers [of it]'.

[9] I read Mombasa here with RBS, rather than OL's Manfiyyah which Yāqūt (*Muʿjam*, V, p. 215) suggests is 'a well-known place on the Zanj coast'. FLS also suggests Mafia.

[10] Arabic *burj* (Varisco, *Agriculture*, p. 85).

[11] Varisco (*Agriculture*, p. 86) lays out neatly the signs of the zodiac and their associations with the humours, the elements and the planets in Islamic tradition. Aries is associated with fire.

[12] Gemini is associated with air (Varisco, p. 86).

[13] Cancer is associated with water (Varisco, p. 86).

[14] Leo is associated with fire (Varisco, p. 86).

[15] Libra is associated with air, though Virgo with night and the earth (Varisco, p. 86).

[16] Arabic *qarab* (Zabīdī, *Tāj*, IV, p. 10; Kazimirski, *Dictionnaire*, II, p. 704).

[17] Arabic *bi-al-marāqī*, plur. of *marqan*, *marqāh* or *mirqāh* (Lane, *Lexicon*, III, p. 1141). The sentence is a problematic one. Scorpio is associated with water (Varisco, p. 86).

[18] Sagittarius is associated with fire (Varisco, p. 86).

winds which bring about the uprooting of trees and spoil plants.[1] Pisces is stagnant water and sea water and it indicates trees of medium height.[2]

The regions of the communities of Taʿizz are called al-Shaʿbāniyyāt[3] and its borders [extend] as far as Wādī Warazān and the cistern of al-Ḥawbān.[4] There Sulaymān Shāh b. Shāhanshāh b. Shādhī[5] used to recite as follows:

> I was afflicted by her to the exclusion of [other] beautiful women; my life blood
> melts away and I feel anxious inside, being pulled apart by separation.
> I remained in the shelter of al-Ḥuayb and in the morning
> she was in the fortress of Taʿizz. This being apart is a real killer![6]

From Taʿizz to al-Janad. From Taʿizz to Birkat al-Ḥawbān a quarter of a parasang.[7] To Wādī al-Samkar a quarter of a parasang. Al-Samkar was a Jew killed by ʿAlī b. Abī Ṭālib – God be pleased with him. In this place are lands overcome by water, one of which ...[8] To al-Janad half a parasang. God knows best and is wisest.

The building of al-Janad. The ancients planted palm groves in the large open space of al-Janad and they bore fruit. As time went by, they became full of vegetation. The palms remained as they were until King Decius appeared and cut them down. He built in the open space of al-Janad a huge town which he called Ephesus. There the event took place between the people of the cave and King Decius. God knows best. The plan of al-Janad is in the following form: [162. Plan of al-Janad, see Fig. 7]

[163] It is said that the people in one of the caves of Jabal Ṣabir are still asleep. They are those about whom God – He is mighty and glorious – has said,[9] '[Some] will say, guessing at random at what is secret,[10] "They were three and their dog the fourth." [Others] will also say, "They were five and their dog the sixth." [Yet others] will say, "They were seven and their dog was the eighth." Say, "My Lord knows best their number; only a few know them."' Mention has already been made of them in Ephesus ...[11] inhabited until a brother, al-Muʿizz b. Maʿn b. Zāʾidah al-Shaybānī, became ruler of the Yemen.[12]

[1] Aquarius is traditionally associated only with air, it would seem (Varisco, p. 86).

[2] Pisces is associated with water (Varisco, p. 86).

[3] Maqḥafī (*Muʿjam*, p. 357) mentions the name, then in the singular, though he says there is a Upper Shaʿbāniyyah and a Lower Shaʿbāniyyah, a vast area around Taʿizz. Varisco (*Agriculture*, p. 309) places it N of Taʿizz.

[4] A plain and hills between Taʿizz and al-Janad, i.e. to the N of the former in Upper Shaʿbāniyyah (Ḥajarī, *Majmūʿ*, p. 299; Maqḥafī, *Muʿjam*, p. 198). The distance from Taʿizz to the cistern is a quarter of a parasang (see below).

[5] Perhaps the Seljuk Sulaymān Shāh b. Muḥammad (reg. 555–6/1160–61) (Bosworth, *Islamic Dynasties*, 186).

[6] Al-Ḥuṣayb is Zabīd. The lines are difficult, being as they are out of context.

[7] Ḥajarī (*Majmūʿ*, II, p. 432) and Maqḥafī (*Muʿjam*, p. 325) confirm the existence of a village of al-Janad by this name, though they give no details.

[8] Unidentified place name. The Jew and his killing at the hand of ʿAlī do not seem to figure in the relevant histories. There is a lacuna at the end of the sentence in the text.

[9] Quran 18:22. See also Cross, *Oxford Dictionary*, p. 1246.

[10] Arabic *rajman bi-al-ghayb* (Penrice, *Dictionary*, p. 56).

[11] A lacuna in the text.

[12] The passage is corrupt. There is no mention of one al-Muʿizz, a son of Maʿn b. Zāʾidah, in the sources at my disposal and indeed the word looks decidedly strange as an *ism*. Maʿn is not universally accepted as the ancestor of B. Maʿn who ruled Aden prior to the Zurayʿids, until 473/1080 to be precise (Ibn Khaldūn in Kay, *Yaman*, pp. 159, 243; Smith, 'Political History', p. 133).

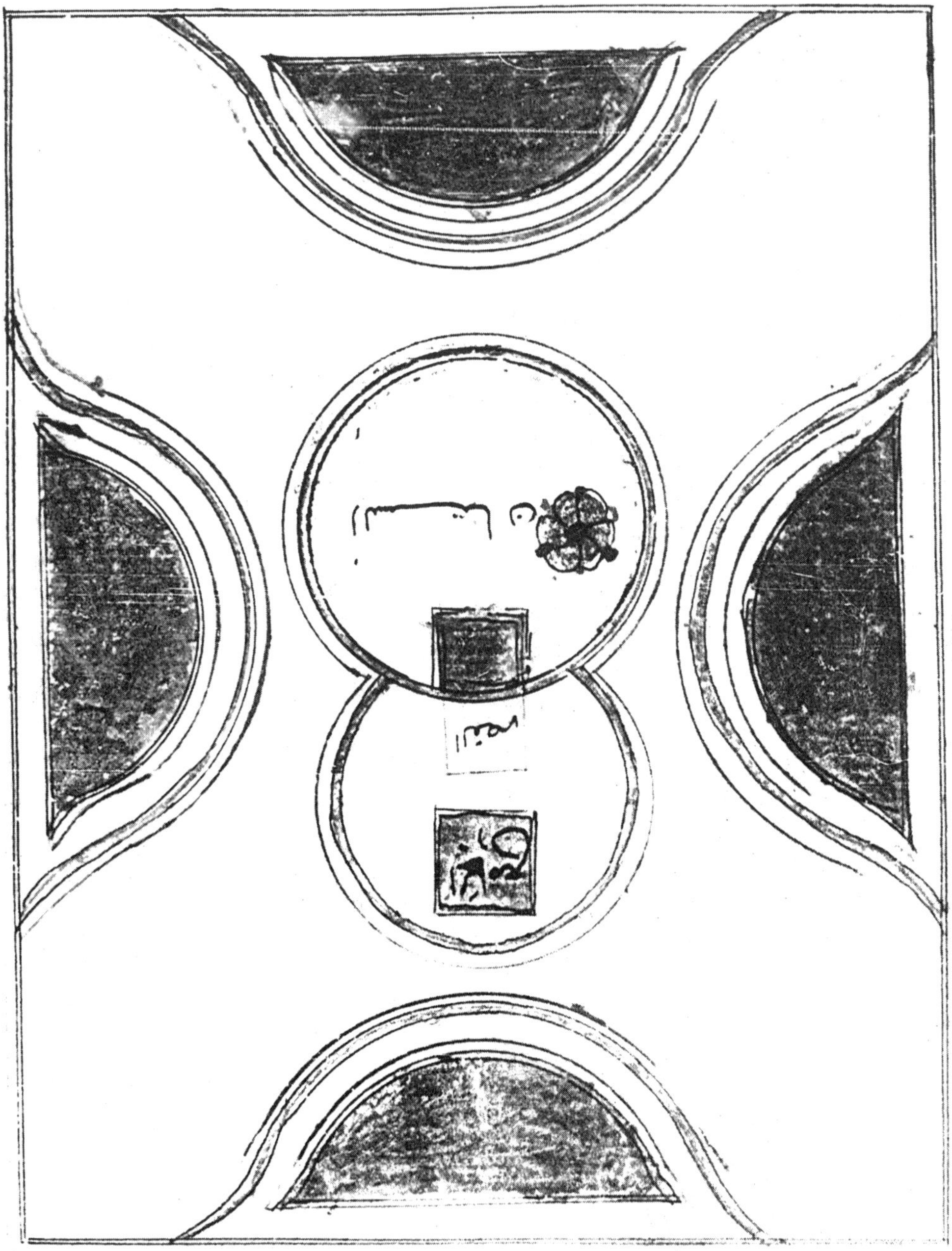

Figure 7. Plan of al-Janad (I MS, f. 66a, text, p. 162, tabula VII)
The town is surrounded by four mountains protruding in black into the rectangular plan: at the top, the E, the bottom, Jabal al-Samīʿ, W, right Jabal Ṣabir, S, and left Jabal al-Taʿkar, N. The upper circle contains the Friday mosque (presumably that of Muʿādh b. Jabal) and the citadel (*qaṣr*) and the lower a cultivated area (*bustān*).

The ruler began to appropriate wealth and take women captive with his foul deeds, giving them [only] vile hope. When the Arabs saw his behaviour, they killed him and rebelled throughout the land. His brother, Maʿn b. Zāʾidah al-Shaybānī,[1] heard the news, mounted up, came at the head of horse and infantry and took control of the Yemen, after he had put its people to the sword and laid al-Janad in ruin. He blocked three hundred *ghayls*, i.e. sweet springs.[2] It is said that one of the *ghayls* was blocked with salt, so its water became brackish. [There was so much salt in it that] it could be taken away from [the stream] in these extreme amounts.[3]

When Muʿādh b. Jabal became governor of the Yemen on behalf of the Prophet[4] – God bless him and grant him peace – he built it as a town called after himself, Jabal. However, the builders changed the *lām* to a *dāl*.[5] Then it was called al-Janad, because it was the army barracks.[6]

I was informed as follows by ʿAbdallāh b. Muḥammad b. Yaḥyā: Originally it was called Qāriʿ al-Ajnād[7] because its inhabitants were the troops of the Yemen. But none of them heard what the other was saying, nor approved of the authority of one of them over another. So when the prattle became too much between ʿAmr and Zayd, Naṣr and Jaʿfar left to go to the Prophet – God bless him and grant him peace – with the approval of Khālid and Zubayr,[8] seeking from him someone to whom they could pay *zakāh*, teach them the holy law and to whom they could appeal for a judgement. The Prophet – God bless him and grant him peace – sent Muʿādh b. Jabal. I said to him,[9] 'I want some proof of this.' He replied, quoting the following poetry: [164]

[164] O B. Masʿūd, tether the horses from Qāriʿ al-Ajnād!
What are you doing, o clients, about the barking dogs in the wadi?[10]

I was informed as follows by one of them that everything that was dug out in the *ghayl* was of no account. … i.e. …[11] he used to give him a loaf of bread and a bone, or a piece of meat and some dirhams, or some dinars, it was also said. It continued in this way until the water from the ghayl flowed and [the land] became luxuriant. The building remained as it was until Sayf al-Islām Ṭughtakīn b. Ayyūb[12] took control. He built a wall around it made of stones and gypsum. He raised it up with earth and unburned

[1] The ruler now appears as Maʿn's brother! See p. 174, n. 12 above.

[2] A *ghayl* is a permanent flow of water (Landberg, *Glossaire daṯînois*, III, p. 2389).

[3] I translate tentatively thus, although the Arabic reads 'wa-ṣāra yaḥmilu min-hu milḥan ilā hādhih al-ghāyah', which makes no apparent sense. I am reading '… yuḥmalu min-h milḥ …'

[4] See Smith, 'Early and Medieval History', p. 53, and Madʿaj, *Yemen*, p. 13. Madʿaj refers to him as a 'representative' of the Prophet 'for religious affairs'.

[5] I.e. al-Jabad from al-Jabal.

[6] Arabic *maskan al-JuND*.

[7] Perhaps Qāʿ al-Ajnād, the latter the plural of *jund*?

[8] I take all these names as imaginary characters.

[9] I.e. Ibn al-Mujāwir questions his informant who then quotes this doggerel which happens to mention Qāriʿ/Qāʿ al-Ajnād.

[10] The metre of the second hemistich of the first line is faulty, whichever version of the place name one tries to read! Who B. Masʿūd and the 'clients' (*mawālī*) are is a mystery.

[11] Arabic *ḥabaṭ … zabadī/zubdī turāb ay mann turāb* seems to me to be corrupt. *zabadī/zubdī* is a measure, as is *mann* (Dozy, *Supplément*, I, p. 578; Löfgren, *Texte*, II, p. 37; Hinz, *Masse*, pp. 16 ff.). I read *aw qiṭʿat laḥm* for *ay* … in the following sentence.

[12] The second Ayyubid sultan in the Yemen, reg. 579–93/1183–97 (Smith, 'Political History', p. 138; Appendix B.8 below).

bricks in [5]97,[1] or more accurately 593.[2] He put five gates into the wall: al-Manṣūrah gate, al-Ḥadīd gate (built by al-Malik al-Masʿūd Yūsuf b. Muḥammad b. Abī Bakr),[3] al-Aqṭaʿ gate and al-Sirr gate which leads to Bustān al-Sulṭān.

Description of Jabal al-Baqar:[4] These are [in fact] two mountains behind al-Janad at a distance a quarter of a parasang. The Arabs built two fortresses there and all the people became the fighting force, morning and evening, night and day. The inhabitants of al-Janad remained with them in a state of hardship and exhaustion until it was taken over from the Arab rulers, razed and its wells stopped up.[5] Now two mountains remain, standing, but [their structures] in ruins. No one calls out on them and no one answers!

Description of Akamat Sulaymān[6] and Biʾr al-Nakhr.[7] There was near the mountain an impregnable fortress called Akamat Sulaymān, [165] built by Solomon, son of David – peace be upon him. When the Arabs rebelled against Maʿn b. Zāʾidah al-Shaybānī, they fortified themselves in the fortress and fighting between the two sides went on for some days. On the sea side there was beneath the fortress a deep, wide, long well. At the top of the castle[8] were stairs down to the bottom of this well where horses and men went down. The well was shared between two parties, the town's inhabitants, who drank there secretly, and the troops of Maʿn b. Zāʾidah, who drank openly. One day, a rider went down with his horse to the bottom of the well to water it. When the horse had drunk at the trough, it snorted[9] because the water was so deep. So the well was called Biʾr al-Nakhr. When Maʿn b. Zāʾidah got to know of the sharing of the well between them, he released some naphtha into the water and anyone who drank from it died. So the fortress was handed over to him and when he had taken possession, he demolished it and the well, both together.

Description of the Friday Mosque.[10] The first person to build the Friday mosque was Muʿādh b. Jabal together with the inhabitants of al-Janad and the villages around. Commander al-Ḥusayn b. Salāmah rebuilt it and Amir al-Mufaḍḍal b. Abī al-Barakāt b. al-Walīd renovated it in chiselled stone and square unbaked bricks in 480.[11] ʿAlī b. al-Mahdī[12] burnt it in 554.[13] It is said that people interceded energetically to get him to

[1] Begins 12 October 1200.

[2] Begins 24 November 1196; Ibn al-Mujāwir is correct here and the 597 date must be erroneous.

[3] The sixth and last Ayyubid sultan in the Yemen, reg. 612–26/1215–28 (Smith, 'Political History', p. 139; Appendix B.8 below).

[4] Unidentified.

[5] Arabic ... *ilā an mulikat min mulūk al-ʿArab* which OL suspects is a dubious reading although his suggested correction seems unlikely. I am unable to relate this to any actual historical event.

[6] Unidentified.

[7] Unidentified. 'The snorting well', see below.

[8] Reading *ʿalā dhurwat al-qalʿah* with OL.

[9] Arabic *nakhara*.

[10] For a detailed description of the mosque, see Costa, 'Mosque', pp. 43–67.

[11] Begins 8 April 1087. See also Kay's translation of Janadī's account of the reconstruction and subsequent burning (*Yaman*, pp. 258–60).

[12] The first Mahdid ruler in Tihāmah, reg. 531–54/1136–59 (Smith, 'Political History', p. 138; Appendix B.7 below). See also Kay, *Yaman*, p. 260, quoting Janadī who says it was ʿAlī's son, Mahdī, who burned the mosque down.

[13] Begins 23 January 1159.

keep it, but he said, 'It deserves to be put to the fire.' 'Why?', he was asked. 'Because the Ismāʿīlī *khuṭbah* has been proclaimed from its *minbar*,' he replied, referring to the Zurayʿid rulers, governors of Aden. 'They are unclean and the mosque is sullied by their being mentioned [in the *khuṭbah*]. Everything which is unclean is purified and we have purified it with fire.'

[Al-Malik al-ʿAzīz Ṭughtakīn] Sayf al-Islām[1] rebuilt it and in addition raised its roofs with baked brick and gypsum after he had gilded it.[2] He executed [designs] in it [166] in lapis lazuli in 603[3] during the rule of al-Malik al-Nāṣir b. Ṭughtakīn b. Ayyūb.[4] One wise man said, 'Take the *minbar* from the Friday mosque of Taʿizz and the roof from the Friday mosque of al-Janad!'

On the first Friday in Rajab [people] from all around pray in the mosque of al-Janad and on that day everyone pays what he can afford, a dirham or a dinar, in order to pray two Friday *rakʿahs*. That day is indeed a memorable one. The inhabitants of al-Janad and the surrounding villages tell stories of the excellence of this mosque [and] concerning paying a visitation to it on the first Friday in Rajab that it is equivalent to a lesser pilgrimage – others say [even] to the full pilgrimage. People continued to visit it every year on the first [Friday] of Rajab until immediately after ...[5] [ʿAlī b. Ḥātim b. Aḥmad b. Ḥātim] used to until he poisoned [Sayf al-Islām] with a melon.[6] It is said that he took a poisoned needle threaded it with a poisoned thread, sticking the needle into the side of the melon and dragging the thread through it. He brought it to Sayf al-Islām, as he was engaged in the building of al-Manṣūrah.[7] He [also] revealed a knife [which ʿAlī held] over the melon so that he could eat some of it. Sayf al-Islām accepted the melon from him, cut it, ate it and thereby felt ill. He said to ʿAlī b. Ḥātim,[8] 'God's help is to be sought against what you describe!' He replied, 'Eat, my lord; it is nothing but good.' Shaykh [ʿAlī b.] Ḥātim b. Aḥmad[9] immediately left. [Sayf al-Islām's] heart pained him and he died – God have mercy upon him.

[1] The second Ayyubid sultan in the Yemen, reg. 579–93/1183–97 (Smith, 'Political History', p. 138; Appendix B.8 below).

[2] See Costa, 'Mosque', *passim*, for details of the construction and renovations.

[3] Begins 8 August 1206. This date is too late, for Sayf al-Islām Ṭughtakīn died in 593/1197 and was buried in Taʿizz (Ibn Ḥātim, *Simṭ*, p. 40, and n. 1 above).

[4] Al-Malik al-Nāṣir ruled in fact between 609–11/1212–14 (Smith, 'Political History', p. 138; Appendix B.8 below). I think Ibn al-Mujāwir is getting confused between Sayf al-Islām Ṭughtakīn, reg. 579–93/1183–97, and Sayf al-Dīn Sunqur, the Ayyubid atabeg, reg. 598–609/1201–09 (Smith, 'Political History', p. 138).

[5] There is a lacuna here in the text which makes the following sentence problematic.

[6] The name given in the text, Ṣafī al-Dīn Ḥātim b. ʿAlī b. Muḥammad b. al-Muʿallim, does not figure in the relevant sources at my disposal, nor does it tally with the name given below, p. 167 of the Arabic text, seemingly the same man (see n. 8 below). The individual, whose name I have tentatively provided, was the second sultan of the dynasty I call B. Ḥātim (II) (Smith, *Ayyubids*, pp. 68) and who held power in Ṣanʿāʾ and the north at the time of the Ayyubid conquest in 569/1173 (Smith, *Ayyubids*, pp. 73–5). However, ʿAlī b. Ḥātim certainly did not poison Sayf al-Islām who died in his bed in 593/1197. Only al-Nāṣir Ayyūb, the fourth Ayyubid sultan, was poisoned, and that was in 611/1214 by one Ghāzī b. Jibrīl (Ibn Ḥātim, *Simṭ*, p. 152).

[7] A fortress at the southern foot of the mountains of al-Dumluwah, built a little before Sayf al-Islām's death in 593/1197 (Ibn Ḥātim, *Simṭ*, p. 39).

[8] See above n. 6.

[9] I have corrected the name, as this must be the murderer, not, as the text would have it, his father.

I was informed by ʿAbdallāh b. Muḥammad that he used to recite as follows on the subject of expropriation:[1] 'My wealth has availed me nought. My power has gone from me. Take him and shackle him, then cause him to burn in hell, then cause him to enter a chain seventy cubits long ...' to the end of the verse.

I was informed as follows by a mountain man of the Sulayhid family: He said that he recited,[2] 'He who has amassed wealth and prepared it thinks his wealth makes him immortal. Nay, he will surely be flung into hell! What will make you know what hell is, the fire of God kindled, which looks down [167] on the hearts [of men]. It is covered over them in outstretched columns.' He kept on reciting this until he died – God have mercy upon him.

The building remained as it was until al-Malik al-Muʿizz Ismāʿīl b. Ṭughtakīn b. Ayyūb[3] died and the lands reverted to their owners. It is also said that they did not revert [to their owners] until Shaykh ʿAlī b. Ḥātim b. Aḥmad b. Ḥātim b. Aḥmad b. ʿImrān[4] carried out his poisoning in Zabīd. It is also said that Ibn al-Muʿallim only made Sayf al-Islām Ṭughtakīn drink [the poison] to take revenge on him after he killed al-Malik al-Muʿizz in Zabīd.[5]

Section. It used [to be said][6] in the time of Sayf al-Islām Ṭughtakīn b. Ayyūb that he would not die until he had taken control of Constantinople and made it prosper. So for a long time his hopes were for this lower world and its embellishment. Al-Manṣūrah was founded and while the workmen were digging the foundations a stone emerged on which the following was written: 'So-and-so, son of So-and-so, the wretch, built the city of Constantinople', continuing that he died and was buried on a particular date of the month and year. He asked what its original name was and was told it was called Constantinople. He exclaimed, 'May we die, by the Lord of the Kaʿbah !' He was given [poison] to drink, died and was buried in al-Maghribah in Taʿizz. His only intention in building this [latter] town was to store all the mountain crop revenues there, as has already been mentioned.[7]

Section. The noble amir, ʿAlī b. Muḥammad al-Ṣulayḥī,[8] settled in a village in the regions of al-Mahjam called Umm al-Duhaym and Biʾr Maʿbad.[9] Saʿīd b.

[1] Quran 69: 28–32.

[2] Quran 104: 2–9.

[3] The third Ayyubid sultan in the Yemen who died in 598/1201 (Smith, "Political History', p. 138; Appendix B.8 below).

[4] I correct from ʿAlī b. Ḥātim b. ʿAlī b. Ḥātim b. ʿAlī b. Muḥammad b. al-Muʿallim. He was actually killed in al-Qawz, a little to the north of Zabīd, and Sunqur appears to have been involved, though not as the actual murderer (Ibn Ḥātim, *Simṭ*, pp. 81–2). See also p. 178, n. 4 above.

[5] Ibn al-Mujāwir is clearly confused here: my reading here is for the 'Sayf al-Dīn Sunqur' of the text. Sayf al-Islām Ṭughtakīn, however, had nothing to do with the murder of al-Muʿizz Ismāʿīl. This whole passage reminds us of Ibn al-Mujāwir's carelessness in reporting historical events. For the translation 'take revenge on', see Lane, *Lexicon*, III, p. 873.

[6] Adding *yuqālu* with OL (apparatus, n. 4).

[7] Ibn al-Mujāwir mentions him in the context of Taʿizz (above p. 172) and says (on p. 161), 'Every year too four lots of treasury funds were sent up to Taʿizz ...'

[8] The first Sulayhid leader (reg. 439–59 or –73/1047–66 or –80) (Hamdānī, *Ṣulayḥiyyūn*, p. 335, table 2; Smith, 'Political History', p. 138; Appendix B.5 below).

[9] FLS ('Gazetteer', p. 241 with all relevant references) tells this story and has full accounts of both Umm al-Duhaym and Biʾr (Umm) Maʿbad.

Najāḥ[1] said, 'When we entered al-Mahjam, only ʿAbdallāh b. Muḥammad b. ʿAlī[2] realized. He rode off and told his brother, "Our lord, ride, for this is indeed al-Aḥwal b. Najāḥ!"[3] ʿAlī replied to his brother, "I shall only die in al-Duhaym and Umm [168] Maʿbad." (It was thought that [he would die in] the Umm Maʿbad where the Prophet – God bless him and grant him peace – stopped when he was migrating accompanied by Abū Bakr.[4]) Someone said to ʿAlī, "Fight for your life, for this is Biʾr al-Duhaym b. ʿAbs. This mosque is [on the site of] the tent of Umm Maʿbad, daughter of al-Ḥārith al-ʿAbsī."[5] ʿAlī was killed there.'

It was in the horoscope of al-Malik al-Muʿizz that he would only be killed in Iraq after his taking possession of it and [that] an Umayyad would destroy the dynasty of the Abbasids.[6] It was after he had become convinced of this that he was killed in Wādī al-ʿIrq of Zabīd.[7] Al-Muḥannanī[8] recited as follows about him:

Death, every time it comes,[9] unfolds the shroud,
while we are heedless of what is wanted of us.
Do not feel confident of the lower world and its embellishment,
even if you put on one of its fine garments.
Where are those dear to us and under our protection? What have they done?
Where are those who were our succour there?
Death has given them to drink from an impure cup
which made them hostages for the layers of the earth.

To the castle of Ḍirās half a parasang.[10] To Wādī Warazān half a parasang. To Dhū Jiblah half a parasang.[11] The mountain pass of Dhū Jiblah, called al-Naqīlayn,[12] can be climbed. There are two mountains, one of them called Naqīl Nadrān[13] and the other Naqīl al-ʿAkāʾif.[14] This name came into general use only because there were some obsessed[15] old women there. God knows best.

[1] The second Najahid ruler, reg. c. 452–81/ca. 1060–88 (Smith, 'Political History', p. 138; *EI*, 'Na<u>dj</u>āḥid'; Appendix B.4 below).

[2] I.e. ʿAlī's brother who died in 459/1066 also (Hamdānī, *Ṣulayḥiyyūn*, p. 335, table 2).

[3] Saʿīd's nickname, 'the squint-eyed'.

[4] I.e. during the *hijrah* from Mecca to Medina.

[5] FLS (Gazetteer, p. 241) says the tribe is still known in the area of Sihām, S of al-Mahjam which is on the Wādī Surdud.

[6] Arabic, perhaps corruptly, [*wa-*]*umawī muzīl dawlat Banī al-ʿAbbās*, emended to form a *ḥāl* clause by OL. Needless to say, this prophecy did not come true either!

[7] See FLS ('Gazetteer', p. 371) suggests that it is the modern-day ʿUkāsh, whose coordinates she provides.

[8] Unidentified and vocalized thus by OL.

[9] Arabic *ḥayn*, 'time of death', or *ḥīn*, 'time'.

[10] Ḥajarī (*Majmūʿ*, III, p. 552) has Ḍarās, a village in the district of Dhū al-Sufāl, i.e. near Wādī Nakhlah (see Kay, *Yaman*, end map). Maqḥafī (*Maʿjam*, pp. 395–6) has Ḍirās and includes a village in the area of Nakhlān.

[11] Often abbreviated to Jiblah, this beautiful town lies a few miles W of Ibb, N of al-Taʿkar and E of Jabal Baʿdān. It still contains the mosque in which Queen Arwā, the Sulayhid ruler, lies buried (Smith, *Ayyubids*, II, p. 149, with references; Lewcock and Smith, 'Two Early Mosques', pp. 125–30; Smith, *Lightning*, p. 7, map 2).

[12] Strictly speaking 'the two mountain passes', mentioned by both Ḥajarī, *Majmūʿ*, IV, p. 744, and Maqḥafī, *Muʿjam*, p. 665, in the area of Dhū Jiblah and Ibb.

[13] Tentative reading from the L MS and unidentified.

[14] Unidentified.

[15] Arabic *muʿtaKiFāt*.

The building of Dhū Jiblah.[1] Dhū Jiblah is in Mikhlāf Jaʿfar. Jiblah was a Jew who sold pottery in the place where Dār al-ʿIzz[2] was built and the town was called after him. The person first to found Dhū Jiblah was ʿAbdallāh b. Muḥammad al-Ṣulayḥī who was killed at the hand of Saʿīd al-Aḥwal b. Najāḥ, together with [169] his brother, Dāʿī ʿAlī b. Muḥammad b. ʿAlī, on the day of al-Mahjam.[3] His brother had made him governor of the fortress of al-Taʿkar, this being a stronghold looking down on Dhū Jiblah, the latter at its foot. It is a town between two rivers which flow [summer and winter alike].[4] It was founded by ʿAbdallāh b. Muḥammad in 458.[5] Al-Ḥurrah al-Malikah al-Sayyidah, the daughter of Aḥmad b. Jaʿfar b. Mūsā al-Ṣulayḥī, used to live there.[6]

Section. In the year 547,[7] Dāʿī Muḥammad b. Sabaʾ[8] bought all the strongholds belonging to the Sulayhids, numbering twenty-eight, from Amir Manṣūr b. Mufaḍḍal,[9] also some towns, including Dhū Jiblah. He bought them at the cost of 100,000 dinars. Amir Manṣūr b. Mufaḍḍal settled in his two fortresses, Ṣabir and Taʿizz, and divorced his Sulayhid wife, the daughter of ʿAlī b. ʿAbdallāh b. Muḥammad al-Ṣulayḥī.[10] The dāʿī went up to al-Mikhlāf, settled in Dhū Jiblah and married the wife of Amir Manṣūr b. Mufaḍḍal. Poets have offered congratulations on many occasions and praised him both for the strongholds and for the 'pearl' mentioned above.[11] He was beside himself with joy at what happened to him and stretched out his hand [to distribute] gifts. God knows best.

The mikhlāf of the Yemen is said to be like the district.[12] One says, [for example], Mikhlāf Taʿkar and Mikhlāf Jaʿfar, i.e. the districts of Taʿkar and those of Jaʿfar. The *mikhlāf* is the region of each fortress itself which has a way up to it. [170] These districts belong to

[1] Ibn al-Mujāwir takes this passage from ʿUmārah (Kay, *Yaman*, p. 29/40).

[2] A palace erected by the Sulayhids in 481/1088 (Kay, *Yaman*, p. 41; *EI*, 'Ṣulayḥids').

[3] See above p. 180, n. 2.

[4] Added from ʿUmārah (Kay, *Yaman*, p. 29/40).

[5] Begins 3 December 1065.

[6] She is usually called Arwā bint Aḥmad in the Ismāʿīlī sources, though her pedigree beyond her father has produced some dispute. ʿUmārah (Kay, *Yaman*, p. 38/28) gives Aḥmad b. Jaʿfar b. Mūsā and this has been copied by Ibn al-Mujāwir here. However, Hamdānī (*Ṣulayḥiyyūn*, p. 142, n. 1) gives the name of her father from his Ismāʿīlī source which has the text of her will (Hamdānī, *Ṣulayḥiyyūn*, p. 323, appendix 9): Aḥmad b. Muḥammad b. al-Qāsim. The Sulayhid administration was moved from Ṣanʿāʾ to Dhū Jiblah in c. 480/1087 (Smith, 'Political History', p. 132).

[7] Begins 8 April 1152.

[8] See p. 142, n. 6 above.

[9] Sulayhid amir and vizier of Queen Arwā, who died in c. 540/1145 (Kay, *Yaman*, p. 267; Smith, 'Thaʿbāt', p. 120).

[10] The Sulayhid wife is Arwā, who was in fact the daughter of ʿAlī b. ʿAbdallāh b. Muḥammad, though not Queen Arwā (see above n. 6), whose father was Aḥmad. I have corrected the "Abdallāh b. ʿAbdallāh' of the text. (Kay, *Yaman*, p. 76; Hamdānī, *Ṣulayḥiyyūn*, p. 335, table 2).

[11] Arabic *wa-al-ʿaqīlah al-madhkūrayn* (read *al-madhkūrah*?) (Kazimirski, *Dictionnaire*, II, p. 322) which is grammatically incorrect and makes no sense in this context. Ibn al-Mujāwir has taken this inaccurately from ʿUmārah (Kay, *Yaman*, p. 56) who speaks of two women. The 'pearl' is Arwā bint ʿAlī.

[12] Reading as a heading *yuqālu mikhlāf al-Yaman* with OL (apparatus, n. 10). This is an extremely important passage which appears to define very specifically the Yemeni *mikhlāf*. 'Districts' is the translation of the Arabic *aʿmāl*. For a comprehensive discussion of the word *mikhlāf*, see Matsumoto, 'Regional Divisions', pp. 104–58, especially p. 105.

this fortress.[1] All the environs of every fortress, its villages and agricultural lands, constitute its *mikhlāf*. *Mikhlāf* to the Yemenis carries the meaning of an extensive area.[2] *Mikhlāfs* are only known in the mountains of the Yemen; they are not known at all in the Red Sea coastal regions. God knows best.

Jurists taking control in the fortress of al-Taʿkar.[3] When al-Manṣūr b. Jayyāsh b, Najāḥ[4] was removed from Zabīd by this brother, ʿAbd al-Wāḥid b. Jayyāsh,[5] he and his slaves took refuge with al-Malik al-Mufaḍḍal b. Abī al-Barakāt[6] and pledged themselves to [hand over] a quarter of the land to him in return for his help. Al-Mufaḍḍal marched with them, expelled ʿAbd al-Wāḥid and put them back in control. Then he decided to doublecross them and take Zabīd for himself. Al-Taʿkar was free [of Mufaḍḍal's presence], [but ʿAbd al-Wāḥid and his slaves] all remained in Tihāmah for a long time. In al-Taʿkar there was Mufaḍḍal's deputy called al-Jamal,[7] who was strongly attached to the [Sunnī] cause.[8] So seven of his brethren who were jurists went up to join him in al-Taʿkar; they included Muḥammad b. Qays al-Wuḥāẓī, ʿAbdallāh b. Yaḥyā and Ibrāhīm b. Zaydān[9] and they gave the latter the oath of allegiance. They took over the fortress from al-Jamal. Now their subjects had asked the jurists, when they were at the summit of the fortress, to light a fire and this was done at night. In the morning, there were 20,000 with them at the top of the fortress. The jurists took possession of this [place] which they had previously not known. News reached al-Mufaḍḍal in Tihāmah, so he marched with the speed of a gazelle, turning aside to no one until [he arrived] in al-Taʿkar. Khawlān[10] rose up to aid the jurists and al-Mufaḍḍal set up a siege against them. When this had gone on for a long time, Ibrāhīm b. Zaydān declared, 'I shall not die until I kill al-Mufaḍḍal. After that, death is welcome!' He went off to al-Mufaḍḍal's concubines

[1] A corrupt passage reading, 'wa-al-mikhlāf aʿmāl kull ḥiṣn bi-dhāti-h yakūnu ṣaʿūdan udkhilat tilk al-aʿmāl ilā al-ḥiṣn'. The translation is tentative.

[2] Arabic *quṭr*.

[3] It is important to realize that these 'jurists' are Sunnīs, as opposed to the Sulayhid Shīʿīs.

[4] One of Jayyāsh's five sons, listed by ʿUmārah (Kay, *Yaman*, p. 93). Jayyāsh, the last effective ruler of the Najahids in Tihāmah, died in 498/1103–4 or 500/1105–6 and these events presumably take place soon after.

[5] Another son of Jayyāsh listed by ʿUmārah (Kay, *Yaman*, p. 93).

[6] A Ḥimyarī amir appointed by Arwā's husband, al-Mukarram, over al-Taʿkar and a confidant of the queen. ʿUmārah (Kay, *Yaman*, pp. 49–54, 149–50, 258–58) says much of his services to the Sulayhids.

[7] This is a more likely form of the name than al-Ḥ.m.l, though the more reliable ʿUmārah gives the latter (Kay, *Yaman*, p. 53, al-Ḥamal), while Ibn Khaldūn, not the best of sources on the Yemen, provides al-Jamal (Kay, *Yaman*, p. 150).

[8] See n. 3 above. The point is of sufficient importance to supply 'Sunnī' here.

[9] I opt for Muḥammad b. Qays al-Wuḥāẓī, the form provided by ʿUmārah (Kay, *Yaman*, p. 53) in preference to Ibn al-Mujāwir's 'al-Zujjājī'. He would thus be of the Wuḥāẓah/Uḥāẓah tribe of Sabaʾ al-Aṣghar of al-Kilāʿ of Ḥimyar (Ibn Rasūl, *Ṭurfah*, p. 54), which name also indicates an area to the N of Ibb. It is possible that ʿAbdallāh b. Yaḥyā is the jurist listed by Ibn Samurah (*Ṭabaqāt*, p. 215), '... b. Muḥammad b. Abī ʿImrān' who died in 554/1159. ʿUmārah calls Ibrāhīm '... b. Muḥammad Zaydān' (Kay, *Yaman*, p. 55) and he was, according to ʿUmārah and Ibn Khaldūn (Kay, *Yaman*, pp. 53, 150, 169), the former's paternal uncle.

[10] A large tribal group of great antiquity whose original territory had lain between Ṣanʿāʾ and Mārib in pre-Islamic times. A large section of the tribe had settled in Mikhlāf Jaʿfar before the events in question (Caskel, *Ǧamharah*, I, Taflen 176, 243; Ibn Rasūl, *Ṭurfah*, pp. 13–14; Kay, *Yaman*, pp. 54–5).

[171], brought them out in their finest, most beautiful attire, put tabors in their hands and took them up to the roofs of the palace where al-Mufaḍḍal and all his followers could see them and hear their voices. Now al-Mufaḍḍal was the most jealous and proudest of men and it was said that he died on that very night.

Others have reported as follows: al-Mufaḍḍal sucked on a ring which had been prepared for him and in the morning he was dead with the ring in his mouth. He died in Ramaḍān 504.[1] When he died, al-Ḥurrah went up from Dhū Jiblah and encamped at the gate of al-Taʿkar. She corresponded with the jurists and treated them with courtesy, writing a letter to them granting them all the safe-conduct and wealth they had suggested [she should grant them]. They laid down the condition that she should leave, together with her throng, but send them anyone of whom she approved as governor. Our lord, Commander Fatḥ, son of Commander Miftāḥ, became governor.[2]

I was informed as follows by Sultan Nāṣir b. Manṣūr:[3] I was informed by Ibrāhīm b. Zaydān that his share of the money was 55,000, i.e. dinars, when they brought him down from the fortress of al-Taʿkar.[4]

The description of the building of Dhū Jiblah. It is said that al-Ṣulayḥī built it in Mikhlāf Jaʿfar.[5] [The latter's] borders stretch in length from Naqīl Ṣayd[6] as far as Maṣābiḥ[7]. In width, they are from Sūq Waṣafāt[8] as far as Ḥuṣn al-Ṭarīmah[9] and to Dhū al-Usūd[10] in the borders of Mikhlāf Ḥabb. Qalʿat al-Nahrayn is so called because Jabal al-Taʿkar lies between the south and the north of the town.[11] The confluence of the two rivers is within the bounds of the town at

[1] April 1111.

[2] I have corrected from the text's 'Fatḥ b. Fatḥ'. He is described by ʿUmārah (Kay, *Yaman*, p. 54) as Arwā's client (*mawlā*).

[3] Ibn al-Mujāwir quotes from ʿUmārah (Kay, *Yaman*, p. 54) as if this were his own informant rather than the latter's.

[4] I follow OL's *nazzalū-h* (apparatus, n. 10) rather than Ibn al-Mujāwir's *tarakū-h* which makes no sense (cf. Kay, *Yaman*, p. 40 [Arabic]).

[5] I.e. ʿAbdallāh b. Muḥammad, brother of the first Sulayhid ruler, ʿAlī, in 458/1066. ʿAbdallāh died in 459/1067 (Kay, *Yaman*, p. 40; Hamdānī, *Ṣulayḥiyyūn*, p. 335, table 2).

[6] The mountain road due N of Ibb and S of Yarīm, the modern-day Sumārah pass (Smith, *Ayyubids*, II, p. 199 and map I; Kay, *Yaman*, end map).

[7] This word carries no dots in the MSS and I spell it tentatively thus. Naqīl Ṣayd is N of Dhū Jiblah, so this must be the southern limit of Mikhlāf Jaʿfar.

[8] Thus in the MSS and my spelling is tentative. Unidentified. Presumably the western border of Mikhlāf Jaʿfar.

[9] I tentatively spell the name thus, as the MSS have no dots. It might of course be al-Ṭuraymah, or indeed be spelt in Arabic with *ẓāʾ* and/or a *zāy*. Unidentified. Presumably a fortress within Sūq Waṣafāt.

[10] Unidentified and of course it might read 'al-Aswad'.

[11] Ḥabb fortress is well known. These are thus the E/W borders of Mikhlāf Jaʿfar. I take Qalʿat al-Nahrayn (castle of the two rivers) to be another name for Dhū Jiblah, the castle being Dār al-ʿIzz, and the two rivers mentioned in Ḥajarī (*Majmūʿ*, I, pp. 34–6) and Maqḥafī (*Muʿjam*, pp. 108–9). See also Yemen map. This description of the position of al-Taʿkar is difficult to understand. The mountain dominates the town from the direction of the S and SE, as the poem belows confirms. See also Smith, *Lightning*, p. 7, map 2.

a place called Wādī Maytam.[1] Al-Māzinī[2] has recited as follows in one of his poems:

[172] Neither Cairo, nor Baghdad, nor Tabaristan,
Is like a town possessed by the two rivers.
Khadid is to its north and Ḥabb to its east;
likewise its lofty Taʿkar is to the south.

The following by him is also recited:

Al-Khawarnaq and al-Sadīr and Bāriq are not like ...[3]
No indeed, neither is al-Nuʿmān like al-D..., ...[4]

Muḍṭabiʿ al-Dawlah Mawāhib b. Jadīd al-Muqriʾ[5] recited as follows, eulogizing al-Malik al-Mufaḍḍal b. Abī al-Barakāt b. ʿAlāʾ al-Ḥimyarī:

So I abandoned it in my yearning for Dhū Jiblah
and left it to the rulers of the easterners.[6]

Wonders and strange things about the Yemen. These include Ḥuṣn Ashyaḥ.[7] Some of the things mentioned by ʿUmārah b. Muḥammad b. ʿUmārah in his book, *al-Mufīd fī akhbār Zabīd*, are as follows: al-Muqriʾ Sulaymān b. Yāsīn, a follower of Abū Ḥanīfah,[8] told me, 'I often spent the night in Ḥuṣn Ashyaḥ, when I would see the sun rising at dawn in the east and without any light at all in it. When I looked towards Tihāmah, I could see a night mist, [so thick that it] prevented anyone walking from recognizing his companion close at hand. I used to think that this was clouds and smoke, but it was in reality the last traces of night.[9] I swore that I would only pray the morning prayer in accordance with the Shāfiʿī rite.' The followers of Abū Ḥanīfah delay [173] the morning prayer until the sun is almost rising over the lowlands of Tihāmah. The reason for this is simply that the

[1] OL's readings *ākhar* or *ḥadd* are both possible, for the confluence is on the outskirts of the town, though within its confines. Maytam is a wadi which seems to be made up from those of Dhū Jiblah and Jabal Baʿdān and which ultimately flows into Wādī Tuban and down to Lahej. I would suggest Ibn al-Mujāwir indicates here that the name Wādī Maytam begins in Dhū Jiblah (Hamdānī, *Ṣifah*, p. 75; Waysī, *al-Yaman*, p. 42; Kay, *Yaman*, pp. 264–5 and end map; Smith, *Lightning*, p. 7, map 2). The course of Wādī Maytam can be traced on the Yemen map, from Dhū Jiblah down into Wādī Tuban.

[2] I assume this to be Bakr b. Muḥammad al-Māzinī who died in 249/863 and who was renowned as a grammarian and the teacher of al-Mubarrad (Carter, 'Grammar', p. 125).

[3] The first two are ancient palaces near al-Ḥīrah, S of Kufa (Yāqūt, *Muʿjam*, II, pp. 401–3, III, pp. 201–2; Le Strange, *Lands*, pp. 75–6 and map II; Ibn Baṭṭūṭah, *Travels*, II, p. 271, Gibb's n. 3). Bāriq is featured in Yāqūt (*Muʿjam*, I, pp. 319) as a watering place between al-Qādisiyyah and Basra and a poem is quoted linking it with the other two palaces. I can make nothing of the final word of the first hemistitch, but take the initial *kāf* as the preposition *ka-*, particularly in view of the *mithla* in the second.

[4] The second name of this hemistitch is uncertain, if indeed it is a name. Without the context, I exclude from the translation *h.ṭ.l al-yadayn*, literally 'with weak/stiff/exhausted hands' (Landberg, *Glossaire daṯînois*, III, p. 2873, reading the plur. *huṭl*; Kazimirski, *Dictionnaire*, II, p. 1428, reading *hiṭl*).

[5] Hamdānī (*Ṣulayḥiyyūn*, p. 165) calls him Mawāhib b. Ḥadīd al-Maghribī.

[6] The two pronouns perhaps require a plural meaning, 'them'. I am not sure what is meant by '*mulūk ahl al-mashriq*', but perhaps the eastern regions of the Yemen are in question.

[7] See p. 99, n. 19 above.

[8] I.e. a follower of the Ḥanafī school of law. Their founder died in 150/767 (*SEI*, 'Abū Ḥanīfa'; *EI*, 'Abū Ḥanīfa'; *SEI*, 'Ḥanafites'; *EI*, 'Ḥanafiyya').

[9] Reading *ʿaqābil* for *ʿaqābīl*, plur. of *ʿuqbūl/ʿuqbūlah*, 'reste', 'dernières traces' (Kazimirski, *Dictionnaire*, II, p. 311).

east [as observed from] Ashyaḥ is unimpeded by mountains and its summit is high. It is the seat of Dāʿī Saba' b. Aḥmad b. ʿAlī al-Ṣulayḥī about whom ʿAbdallāh b. al-Ḥasan b. ʿAlī b. al-Qumm[1] recites as follows:

> When I eulogized the strong, elegant horseman, Ibn Aḥmad,[2]
> he rewarded me and requited me praise for praise.
> He gave me poetry in exchange for my poetry and added for me
> gifts, the latter my capital, the former my profit.
> I opened a way to him through the throng until I saw him;
> I was like one who had opened a way through darkness into morning's light.
> Time when there was no Ibn Aḥmad was deemed repugnant,
> while time when he was there was deemed unblemished.

Najd al-Ḥanashayn, in the territory of the Najahids.[3] These areas in ancient times were called the regions of Najd and were only known as al-Ḥanashayn when its two lords fought and wounded each other. While they were fighting, a flash of lightning fell upon them and burnt them. Another version is that the ground gave way under them and they sank into a hole. The hole remains, but in the shape of a great, bottomless well. It was known as al-Najd in al-Ḥanashayn and also Najd al-Ḥanashayn in the regions of al-Ḥaql and al-Kafl.[4]

Ḥuṣn Tharayd.[5] It was built by Solomon, son of David – peace be upon him – in the territory of B. Sayf. There is a circular wall on the hump of a lofty mountain, high in the air. In the middle of the fortress is an ancient bottomless lake created by God on the ridge of the mountain. It is sweet water and sometimes fish are seen in it [174], as well as sea beasts, and there are terrifying waves. The wall has been built on its shore, encircling the lake.[6] Inside the wall three houses have been built, no more, in one of which three men live, in the second four and the third five. The number adds up to twelve men, [stationed] there as a garrison.[7] None of the Ghuzz rulers[8] could take it from its owners, B. Sayf. It is said that there is a tree there whose height is only three cubits and no bird can perch in it without immediately falling off dead. There are still dead birds of every kind under it.

I was informed as follows by Aḥmad b. Muḥammad b. al-Muhannā al-Ṣaffār: I saw in the land of the Somalis trees under which there were dead monkeys. I asked one of them about what happened to the monkeys and he replied, 'This is a poisonous tree.

[1] ʿUmārah (Kay, *Yaman*, p. 43) calls him "Aly ibn al-Ḳumm' and Hamdānī (*Ṣulayḥiyyūn*, p. 161, where the verses are quoted with one or two minor variants) al-Ḥusayn al-Qummī.

[2] I prefer to read *al-hibrizī* with OL (apparatus, n. 4) and translate it after reference to Steingass (*Dictionary*, p. 1488) and K (II, p. 1381). The text has *al-hayzarī* (also ʿUmārah [Kay, *Yaman*, p. 43]). Hamdānī and his original Ismāʿīlī source have *al-hizbarī* (*Ṣulayḥiyyūn*, p. 161). The man in question is the Sulayhid amir from Bayt B. al-Muẓaffar, the subject of n. 19 on p. 99 above. See also Hamdānī, *Ṣulayḥiyyūn*, p. 335, table 2.

[3] Literally, 'Najd of the two snakes' and unidentified, although Ibn al-Mujāwir must here be discussing territory in the region N of Dhū Jiblah. As for the Najahids, they ruled from Tihāmah between 412–98/1021–1104 (Smith, 'Political History', pp. 131–2, 138; *EI*, 'Nadjāḥids'; Appendix B.4 below).

[4] There are dozens of Ḥaqls in the Yemen, though none in the sources appears to fit this general locality. Al-Kafl, if that is indeed the correct vocalization, is unidentified.

[5] A wadi and fortress somewhere E of Naqil Ṣayd in the region of Damt (Hamdānī, *Ṣifah*, p. 101; Ḥajarī, *Majmūʿ*, I, p. 165; Maqḥafī, *Muʿjam*, p. 97).

[6] This must be what is meant by *mustadār bi-al-buḥayrah*. I wonder if the 'lake' is a hot-water spring pool like those in abundance near Ḥammām Damt.

[7] Arabic *rutbah* (Löfgren, *Texte*, II, p. 35).

[8] I.e. the non-Arab Ayyubids.

When[1] its wood becomes hot, poison is given off from it. They put it on their arrows and anyone hit by the arrows who does not scoop out the flesh and the wound together, dies immediately. The monkeys come to eat its fruit because it is sweet and they die as you can see.'

Ibn al-Mujāwir said: The only monkeys who die are those with a wound or some illness inside their belly. The tree's poison reaches the wound, mixing with the blood and he dies. As a result, he is thrown down like the trunk of a date-palm which has been cut down. This tree is without any doubt poisonous.

Ibn al-Mujāwir said: I saw in a dream on the night of 22 Ramaḍān 620[2] someone saying, 'In the land of Zanzibar, there is a tree called fire; anyone who touches it gets burnt immediately.'

The etymology of Ḥuṣn Tharayd is simply the *tharīd* of bread and meat.[3] That is, for everyone who rules over this fortress, the Yemen remains in front of him like a bowl of *tharīd*. He eats what he wants, i.e. he rules over what he desires.

In 615,[4] all [175] the mountains of the Yemen were planted with madder. They stopped planting other crops, because some were planting wheat and barley and each *jarīb*[5] produced only five *malakī* dinars. So they planted madder and a *jarīb* produced sixty dinars for them. In 622,[6] a *buhār* of madder in Aden sold at seventy-six dinars. When people saw what was happening, they cried out, 'We're abandoning everything except madder; we'll plant that!' They [all] planted it, even slaves, slave girls, women, the tribal shaykhs and the very rich.[7] They continued [doing this] until al-Malik al-Mas'ūd Yūsuf b. Muḥammad from Egypt took over control [again].[8] He seized all the madder, not allowing anyone even a single ounce. All this [had in the past been] permitted, [but it was] wasteful. This was in 624.[9]

Mathābah, including Badr al-Fiḍḍah.[10] Its inhabitants are a tribe called B. Nihm.[11] In the markets[12] of Ṣa'dah, there were easy sales, even if it were the man himself who was [for

[1] Reading *idhā* with OL (apparatus, n. 8) instead of the *alladhī* of the MSS and text.

[2] 20 August 1223.

[3] A dish of sopped bread, meat broth and bread (Varisco, *Agriculture*, p. 209, n. 10).

[4] Begins 30 March 1218.

[5] A land measurement, about a hectare (Hinz, *Masse*, pp. 65–6; Pellat, *Avares*, p. 315; Serjeant, *Misers*, p. 26).

[6] Begins 13 January 1225.

[7] Arabic *ghanī*, although OL (apparatus, n. 3) suggests the word might be read more appropriately in the context *fatā*, 'young'/'young man'.

[8] He arrived first in the Yemen from Egypt in 612/1215. He returned to the Yemen from a trip to Egypt in 624/1227, hence my addition of 'again', and died on his way N in Mecca in 626/1228 (Smith, 'Political History', p. 136).

[9] Begins 22 December 1226.

[10] I think this is a rogue passage and the heading is missing from the L MS. If the reading is Mathābah, as OL suggests (apparatus, n. 5), one has recourse only to Hamdānī (*Ṣifah*, p. 128), al-Mathābah al-Musharrafah, with no clear indication where the place is. Badr al-Fiḍḍah does not figure in the geographical sources at my disposal, although Ḥajarī (*Majmū'*, p. 105) and Maqḥafī (*Mu'jam*, p. 65) both list a Badr in the region of Ṣa'dah and this is where the anecdote of the text takes place.

[11] Hamdānī (Löfgren, *Muštabih*, p. 46) lists the following Yemeni tribal names: Nihm, Nuham and Nuhm. The first, the largest tribe of the three, is of Bakīl of Hamdān and located in the Jawf region, NE of Ṣan'ā' (Hamdānī, *Ṣifah*, p. 81; Ḥajarī, *Majmū'*, IV, p. 746–7; Maqḥafī, *Mu'jam*, p. 666–7) and this is the vocalization I use here. None, however, appears entirely appropriate, if we are talking of an incident in Ṣa'dah.

[12] Reading *aswāq* with Löfgren (apparatus n. 7).

sale].[1] It is said that Zayd brought a slave, intending to sell him in the souk. The slave said to his master, Zayd, 'Get up on this stone and call out that Zayd is for sale.'[2] When he had got up [on it], the slave called out that Zayd was for sale, 'Who will buy this slave?' So he was bought from the slave; the slave sold Zayd and took the price and went on his way!

From Dhū Jiblah to Ṣanʿāʾ.[3] From Dhū Jiblah to al-Qurayn[4] a parasang. To al-Saḥūl two parasangs and this is where Saḥūlī clothes are woven. The Prophet was shrouded in two cloths from here. This is the wadi belonging to B. Abaḥ, the tribe of Faqīh Abū ʿAbdallāh Mālik b. Anas al-Abaḥī, imam of Dār al-Hijrah.[5] To Dhirāʿ al-Kalb a parasang.[6] To the castle of Ibb two parasangs.[7] To al-Maghribah two parasangs,[8] built [176] by al-Malik al-Muʿizz Ismāʿīl b. Ṭughtakīn.[9] To al-Maʿbar a parasang.[10] To Ḥuṣn Samāwā a parasang.[11] To the stone enclosure[12] of Naqīl Ṣayd a parasang. This is terraced, built by al-Malik al-Agharr ʿAlī b. Muḥammad al-Ṣulayḥī,[13] who recited as follows:

> I settled the best of my people in Iraq
> and the Nabataeans in the villages of Qatāb.[14]

Qatāb is part of al-Ḥaql and al-Ḥaql is part of Wādī Ṣayd. A flow of spring water descends from the summit of the mountain pass, called al-Jabal, as far as a cistern. In the cistern is a small trough, in which there is a hole. The water goes down into it and no one knows where it flows.

[1] This is the best I can do with this corrupt sentence which is in fact omitted in the L MS.

[2] The whole passage smacks of oral information and this is a wonderful example of the non-classical Arabic features of Middle Arabic (see Introduction above, 'The Text, language'), in both its syntax (asyndeton) and morphology (*nādī* for *nādi*): *iṣʿad ʿalā hādhā al-ḥajar nādī ʿalā Zayd.*

[3] I.e. a route due N.

[4] I vocalize the name thus. It might well of course be al-Qarīn.

[5] It is well known that the tribe (also al-Aṣābiḥ, Dhū al-Aṣbaḥ) inhabited Wādī al-Saḥūl, among other places, and reckoned the founder of the Mālikī school of law, Mālik b. Anas (d. 179/795), among its sons. He is known frequently as the imam of Dār al-Hijrah, i.e. Medina, where he was born and died. It is a tribe of Ḥimyar (Kay, *Yaman*, pp. 17 [ʿUmārah], 176 [Ibn Khaldūn], 245; Kaḥḥālah, *Muʿjam*, I, p. 32; Ḥajarī, *Majmūʿ*, I, pp. 82–4; Maqḥafī, *Muʿjam*, pp. 34–5; *SEI*, 'Mālik b. Anas'; *EI*, 'Mālik b. Anas'; *EI*, 'Mālikiyya').

[6] Three stages from Dhamār, a rugged place, half-way to Ṣanʿāʾ, according to Nahrawālī (Smith, *Lightning*, p. 66, also p. 203, n. 18), though clearly in between Dhū Jiblah and Ibb.

[7] Ibb is now a large town just a few miles to the E of Dhū Jiblah on the Taʿizz-Ṣanʿāʾ main road. Waysī (*al-Yaman*, p. 26) has a map of the area, with photographs of the town on pp. 40, 294. See also Smith, *Lightning*, p. 7, map 2.

[8] There are several places of this name in the Yemen, though this one is unidentified.

[9] The third Ayyubid ruler in the Yemen, reg. 593–98/1197–1201 (Smith, 'Political History', p. 138; Appendix B.8 below).

[10] The article is crucial here to distinguish this place from the well-known Maʿbar on the Jahrān plain further N. It is in all probability the one described by Ḥajarī (*Majmūʿ*, IV, p. 712) and Maqḥafī (*Muʿjam*, p. 609) as belonging to a district (*ʿuzlah*) of the Yāfiʿ in Mikhlāf al-Shawāfī in the regions (*aʿmāl*) of Ibb.

[11] Unidentified and vocalized in the L MS.

[12] Arabic *jadarah*.

[13] 'The fair, noble ruler', the first Sulayhid, reg. 439–59 or –73/1047–66 or –80 (Smith, 'Political History', p. 138; Appendix B.5 below).

[14] The verse is found in Hamdānī (*Ṣifah*, p. 104) with some minor variant readings, composed, he says, by a tubbaʿ, a pre-Islamic ruler of the Yemen. Qatāb is called Ḥaql Qatāb by Hamdānī (in loco). I choose the spelling after reference to Maqḥafī (*Muʿjam*, p. 506), although Ḥajarī (*Majmūʿ*, IV, p. 646) is careful not to vocalize. Presumably, the Nabataeans are meant here, though their being settled in the Yemen at this time can be nothing but poetic hyperbole!

To Ḍarbat ʿAmr a parasang.[1] This is [a reference to] the blow dealt by ʿAmr b. ʿAbd Wadd al-ʿĀmirī[2] into a rock into the heart of which his sword plunged as a knife plunges through a piece of fresh cheese. The reason for his striking the stone was that he was followed by some Arabs (more accurately, by Sayf b. Dhī Yazan;[3] another version is by some Abyssinians). When he became exasperated by them, he struck the rock once. The Abyssinians saw this and were driven back whence they came. Another version is that when Sayf b. Dhī Yazan saw the blow, he knew that he could only achieve anything there by force, so he left for Iraq to seek the help of the emperor. The latter gave him an army by means of which he took over the Yemen. When Sayf b. Dhī Yazan was in firm control of the Yemen, ʿAmr b. ʿAbd Wadd, left for the Hejaz. It was he against whom the Commander of the Faithful ʿAlī b. Abī Ṭālib – God's approval be upon him – went forth to fight. The Prophet – God bless him and grant him peace – cried out 'Allāhu akbar!' three times and said, 'The whole faith has gone out to fight the whole of polytheism.' ʿAmr was killed at the hand of the Commander of the Faithful ʿAlī b. Abī Ṭālib in the fight. The following was recited:

> Be the son of whomsoever you will and behave with decency,
> whether you are an Arab or a non-Arab.
> The youthful [hero] is he who says, 'Here I am.'
> He is not the one who says, 'My father was [so-and-so].'[4]

[177] To Manzil al-Aṣamm a parasang.[5] It is only known by this name because a deaf man arrived at this place and could hear the sound of water flowing below ground. He dug wells – it is also said, channels – and settled there and it became known by this name.

To Dār al-Ḍayf a parasang.[6] A bedouin lived here and wrote in a rock near its gate as follows:

> Oh, whoever comes to Dār will never leave,
> because there is a man in Dār who provides lunch![7]

Ibn al-Mujāwir said: I was surprised that he did not write as follows:

> Oh, whoever comes to Dār will never go on his way,
> because there is a man in Dār who provides dinner![8]

The writing is still there now as it was.

[1] Unidentified. The meaning is 'the blow of ʿAmr'.

[2] A Qurashī who strongly opposed the Prophet and who was finally killed by ʿAlī b. Abī Ṭālib at the famous incident of the Ditch (5/626). The happening described here is not documented in the early historical sources and I am tempted to speculate that the 'Blow of ʿAmr' might have been the blow dealt by ʿAlī to kill this infidel (Guillaume, *Life*, pp. 454–5; Ṭabarī, *History*, VIII, pp. 18–19; Wāqidī, *Maghāzī*, pp. 470–71).

[3] Pre-Islamic Yemeni hero-king who, in his attempt to rid the country of its Abysssinian conquerors, summoned help from the Persian emperor, Anūshirwān in AD 575. He was killed by the Abyssinians in Ṣanʿāʾ soon after (Rāzī, *Ṣanʿāʾ*, pp. 298, 558; Wahb, *Tījān*, pp. 317–21; Smith, 'Early and Medieval History', p. 51).

[4] I.e. act yourself, do not stand by and boast of your lineage.

[5] 'Deaf man's abode'. Both Ḥajarī (*Majmūʿ*, IV, p. 721) and Maqḥafī (*Muʿjam*, p. 633) know of this place and say it is called after an Abyssinian military commander (*qāʾid*) who was deaf.

[6] Unidentifed.

[7] Arabic *yuʿaddī* rhymes with *yughaddī*.

[8] Ibn al-Mujāwir's humour provides this doggerel, *yumashshī* rhyming with *yuʿashshī*.

Apropos, Abū Firās b. Ḥamdān recited as follows:[1]

> My fire is an honourable one, blazing up for guests travelling by night.
> O fire, if you do not attract a guest, you are not my fire!

Description of Jabal ...[2] Sulṭān al-Aʿẓam Bahrām b. Shāh b. Masʿūd[3] never gave money to anyone unless he gave up along with it people whom it was deemed necessary to kill. When he was asked about this, he replied, 'Money is something which has no value, no worth and no place with me, unless you are to give up souls.' On this subject is what al-...[4] has recited:

> Everything which has a price can be sold at a like price,
> except souls which have no price.

[178] The wise Naṣr Allāh al-Ghaznawī[5] has taken up this topic as follows [in Persian]:

> Since the beginning of the world's creation until the time of the king,
> there has been pardon on the part of dignitaries and sin on the part of underlings,
> Especially in the period of that king because of whose justice
> amber does not have the power to push around straw.
>
> I who had been struck by arrows aimed [to kill me] by the machinations of my enemies,
> have remained alive till the Day of Assembly through the auspicious fortune of the king.
>
> My soul is the gift of a king in whose time there are several [other]
> crown-bestowing monarchs and justice-seeking amirs;
> There must be a monarch of the planets to return these six lines
> with pointed arrows, on to the face of the moon,
> So that kings who dole out gold and silver can learn from
> Bahrām Shāh, sultan of the faith, the manner of bestowing souls.

To al-Malāwī three parasangs.[6] To al-Ḥizyaz two parasangs.[7] To Madārah a parasang.[8] To Naqīl Aslaḥ two parasangs, going up.[9] To Ḥadārān a parasang, going

[1] Usually called Abū Firās al-Ḥamdānī. He was an extremely well-known poet who died in 357/968 (Tayib, 'Abū Firās al-Ḥamdānī', *CHAL*, pp. 315–27; *EI*, 'Abū Firās al-Ḥamdānī').

[2] This is clearly a heading in the I MS, though Löfgren does not take it as such in the printed text. The unpointed word which follows I tentatively accept as *jabal*, although one would have expected the name of the mountain to follow immediately. There is no lacuna in the MSS however and the text is clearly corrupt.

[3] This is Abū al-Muẓaffar Bahrām Shāh b. Masʿūd who ruled twice for the Ghaznavids in the east and north-western India, from 511/1117 and c. 547–52/1152–57 (Bosworth, *Islamic Dynasties*, p. 296).

[4] I cannot unravel al-?ār.k.l, the first two letters of which after the article are doubtful.

[5] Löfgren's apparatus n. 1 points out that his true name is Naṣr Allāh, the 6th/12th-century translator into Persian of *Kalīlah wa-Dimnah*. Bahrām Shāh is the Ghaznavid sultan (510–52/1117–57) (Browne, *Literary History*, II, pp. 299, 349; Rypka, *History*, pp. 222 ff.; *EI*, 'Naṣr Allāh b. Muḥammad', 'Bahrām Shāh').

[6] Unidentified.

[7] A village about 7 km SE of Ṣanʿāʾ where Imam Yaḥyā and his minister, ʿAbdallāh al-ʿAmrī, were murdered in 1948 (Rāzī, *Ṣanʿāʾ*, p. 625; Serjeant and Lewcock, *Ṣanʿāʾ*, pp. 43, 229, 432), so there is something wrong here. Ibn al-Mujāwir perhaps has this in the wrong sequence and it may have been the nearest point to Ghayl al-Barmakī (see p. 190, n. 3 below).

[8] Unidentified.

[9] I leave the spelling as it is in the text, although RBS indicates that this is the mountain road of Yasliḥ. I take the vocalization of the latter from Maqḥafī (*Muʿjam*, p. 712), although the editor of Hamdānī (*Ṣifah*, p. 190) inserts a *ḍammah* over the letter *yāʾ*. The former says it is 45 km from Ṣanʿāʾ and the latter makes it clear that it is the road up due N out of the Jahrān plain.

down.[1] To Ḥabārā a parasang.[2] To Ghayl al-Barmakī two parasangs.[3] [This is] flowing water. When Imam Abū Muḥammad Hārūn al-Rashīd had killed all the Barmecides,[4] one of them fled and settled in Ṣanʿāʾ. When he discovered there was so little water for its inhabitants, he bought some land of Qāʿ ʿAbbād b. al-Ghamr[5] and dug a great channel there. It is said that the source [179] of the channel was in Iraq. When the flow of the *ghayl* was fully accomplished, he gave it as a *waqf* for the weak[6] of Ṣanʿāʾ and the *ghayl* became known as al-Barmakī. It is also said that it was dug by Barmak al-Dhahab, i.e. he was not found wanting in acquiring gold to dig it.[7] To Ṣanʿāʾ two parasangs.

The building of Ṣanʿāʾ. I was informed as follows by Yaḥyā b. ʿAlī b. ʿAbd al-Raḥmān al-Zarrād:[8] Seth, son of Adam – peace be upon him – built the town of Ṣanʿāʾ and planted two gardens outside it, one to the right of al-Darb,[9] the other to the left. They were in length [the distance] from Ṣanʿāʾ to Iraq, seven days' journey.

I was informed as follows by Sultan Jamīl: It was built by Shem, son of Noah – peace be upon him – since he took control of the place.[10] [Before this] he could not stay in any one town, so he used to move around the world, seeking an airy place with light water, a temperate land as far as health goes, so that the pain he felt would be relieved. He found a place which suited his nature, for when he settled in Ṣanʿāʾ, the pain left him. Then he went up to Jabal Nuqum[11] where he settled, saying to his family and all his followers, 'Let each one of you inhabit a place where he can settle down.' So the people made settlements and it became a town, seven parasangs long by seven wide. Its regions went as far as Basra and the road remained in use and thriving until sand covered it and cut it.

Hūd – peace be upon him – built a well inside its mosque, the first well dug in the existing and vanishing world. Al-Malik al-Agharr ʿAlī b. Muḥammad b. ʿAlī al-Muʿallim al-Ṣulayḥī[12] built the wall round it with stones and gypsum, putting seven gates in it:

[1] Spelling tentative and unidentified.

[2] Spelling tentative and unidentified.

[3] See p. 189, n. 7 above. Ghayl al-Barmakī is named after Muḥammad b. Khālid al-Barmakī of the famous Barmecide family of Persian origin who was sent to Ṣanʿāʾ as governor under the Abbasids in 183/799. It surfaces – and this may be the location Ibn al-Mujāwir has in mind – a few miles to the SE of the city, S of Jabal Nuqum. The most detailed account of the *ghayl* is in Serjeant and Lewcock, *Ṣanʿāʾ*, pp. 19–23. See also Rāzī, *Tārīkh*, p. 106–7; Abū Makhramah in Löfgren, *Texte*, p. 214; Amri, 'Document', p. 30 and *passim*).

[4] The famous fifth Abbasid caliph, reg. 170–93/786–813 (Bosworth, *Islamic Dynasties*, p. 6). This is a slightly different version of events which is unlikely. The downfall of the Barmecides happened in Muḥarram 187/January 803 (Sourdel, "Abbāsid Caliphate', p. 116; *EI*, 'al-Barāmika').

[5] I correct after reference to a n. of RBS and his '*Ghayls*', p. 22. See also Hamdānī, *Iklīl*, I, pp. 414–15. It is not clear where precisely this land is.

[6] Arabic *ḍuʿafāʾ*, probably meaning those not bearing arms (Serjeant, '*Ghayls*', p. 22).

[7] A fanciful alternative version. Is there some reference here to the word *barmakī* in Persian in the sense of 'noble', 'liberal' (Steingass, *Dictionary*, p. 179)?

[8] It is not clear why Löfgren settles on this name, when the MSS have al-Zawwād and al-Raddād.

[9] This could mean 'tower-house', or even 'citadel', perhaps 'wall' also.

[10] See also Rāzī (*Tārīkh*, pp. 20–22, 180–83) and Serjeant and Lewcock (*Ṣanʿāʾ*, pp. 122, 128, 131) on his role in the early development of Ṣanʿāʾ.

[11] The large and imposing mountain to the E of the city.

[12] The founder of the Sulayhid dynasty who died in 459/1066 or 473/1080 (Smith, 'Political History', p. 138; Appendix B.5 below).

Ghumdān gate, leading to the south, Damascus gate, leading to Mecca, al-Sabaḥah gate,[1] leading to Maḥallat al-Sabaḥah, these [three] being dressed [with gypsum],[2] Upper Khandaq gate, through which the flood enters, Lower Khandaq gate [180], through which the flood pours out to water the land,[3] al-Naṣr gate, leading to Jabal Nuqum and Birāsh[4] and Sharʿah gate, leading to Bustān al-Sirr.[5] God knows best.

The palace of Ghumdān. The first person to begin building it was Shem, son of Noah – peace be upon him – when he built Ṣanʿāʾ.[6] Another version is that it was Solomon, son of David – peace be upon them both – when he entered the Yemen and married Bilqīs.[7] The tubbaʿs among the rulers of the Yemen had a unswerving desire and lofty ambition to build it and all their rulers used to put one palace on top of another until these palaces reached a height of seventy-two storeys, or it is said, ninety-three storeys. The last one to build there was Asʿad al-Kāmil (another version of the name is Asʿad al-Khuzāʿī),[8] [who built] a glass palace and this was the last. ʿAbdallāh b. Dārī b. Abī Bakr al-ʿAnbarī recited the following to me on the eve of Sunday, 5 Ṣafar 623:[9]

> Only someone like Ibn Dhī Yazan takes vengeance,
> since he was made to go to sea for years because of his enemies.
> He came to Hericles, having fled in fear,
> but found no help from him when he asked.
> He turned to Khusrau after seven
> years, reckoning his life and wealth of little importance.
> He came with the Persians, bringing them forward,
> imagining them mountains over the surface of the earth.
> [They were] great leaders, pure chiefs,
> lions who train their young in the thicket.
> What a noble band came out!
> I have never seen the likes of them among men.
> You sent lions against black dogs,
> whose fleeing band were defeated throughout the land.
> Cling to musk when they flee in fear,[10]

[1] I have corrected Löfgren's al-Sh.y.khah (Serjeant and Lewcock, *Ṣanʿāʾ*, p. 131).

[2] RBS (*Ṣanʿāʾ*, p. 131) suggests the *makhdūmīn* of the text is the same as *makhtūmīn*.

[3] RBS (*Ṣanʿāʾ*, p. 131) thinks the two Khandaq gates are in the openings (*manāshir*) under the walls across the Sāʾilah.

[4] A place to the E of the city near Nuqum (Kay, *Yaman*, end map; Smith, *Ayyubids*, II, p. 142).

[5] The vocalization of the gate is doubtful. RBS points out (*Ṣanʿāʾ*, p. 131) that, if the road leads to Wādī al-Sirr, it should be placed E of Dimashq gate.

[6] Ghumdān is situated on the eastern side of the Great Mosque and there are several legends attached to it (Rāzī, *Tārīkh*, pp. 20–24; Faris, *Antiquities*, pp. 8–9, 13–17; Serjeant and Lewcock, *Ṣanʿāʾ*, pp. 36, 37, 38, 40, 44 ff).

[7] The legendary pre-Islamic figure, the 'Queen of Sheba'. The Old Testament version of the story is in 1 Kings:10.

[8] Tubbaʿ Abū Karib Asʿad, c. AD 385–420, a well-known king of Ḥimyar who figures prominently in later Islamic writings (Faris, *Antiquities*, p. 16).

[9] 5 February 1226. The original poem was composed by Abū al-Ṣalt b. Abī Rabīʿah al-Thaqafī according to Ibn Isḥāq, and Umayyah b. Abī al-Ṣalt according to Ibn Hishām (*Sīrah*, I, pp. 65–66; Guillaume, *Life*, p. 32). Ibn al-Mujāwir's text version differs in both the order of some lines and in certain readings. The name in the text is Sayf b. Dhī Yazan.

[10] The black dogs are the occupying Abyssinians. The *Sīrah* version reads, '*fa-'shrab hanīʾan*', 'drink your fill'.

and let your garments fall loose today.
[181] Drink your fill, wearing your crown, reclining
in your abode where people stay at the top of Ghumdān.
These are noble deeds, not two pails of milk
mixed with water which later becomes urine!

I was informed by the qadi of the highlands from the Sulayhid family that he was told by a man who heard Abū Muḥammad ʿAbdallāh b. Ḥamzah al-Ḥasanī speak as follows: The last traces of the shadow cast by the palace of Ghumdān reached as far as Wādī al-Ẓahr.[1] I asked him what the distance was between them. He replied, 'Like from Zabīd to al-Zarībah.'[2] Now from Zabīd to al-Zarībah is a distance of a parasang, more or less. Ibn al-Mujāwir said: There is no doubt that the shadow cast by the palace reached as far as Wādī al-Ẓahr when the sun was close to setting, since at such a time the shade and shadow is enough to appear like something three or four times bigger than the building itself. But rather the light from its lamps could be seen from al-Madāʾin,[3] and it was also said, as far as Medina.

The palace remained as it was until the period of the caliphate of the Commander of the Faithful ʿUmar b. al-Khaṭṭāb – God be pleased with him. One night he sat outside Medina when he saw something shining in the sky like a brilliant star. He asked about it and someone present with him among his servants said, 'This is the light of a candle burning at the top of Ghumdān palace in Ṣanʿāʾ.' So he gave orders for it to be destroyed and it was. Now there remains a huge mound and on the spot of the palace Badr al-Dīn Ḥasan b. ʿAlī b. Rasūl built another palace, a massive structure, in 618.[4]

I was informed as follows by Yaḥyā b. ʿAlī b. ʿAbd al-Raḥmān al-Zarrād: The palace of Ghumdān was built by a woman called al-Zabbāʾ[5] who gave instructions that a tall palace be placed on top of every other palace, each palace being forty cubits (using the ʿUmarī measurement),[6] the same in width and the same in height.

Imam Abū Bakr Muḥammad b. al-Ḥasan b. Durayd al-Lughawī al-Azdī recited as follows on this subject:[7]

[1] A beautiful wadi about 7 miles to the NW of Ṣanʿāʾ, long a place of relaxation away from the city. Much of it is narrow and it waters much agriculture and horticulture, including grapes (Smith, *Ayyubids*, II, pp. 217–18, with full references; Wilson, *Gazetteer*, 221, s.v. Ẓahr).

[2] A village in Wādī Zabīd mentioned by Redhouse (Khazrajī, *ʿUqūd*, III, p. 214, n. 1566, 'Zerebiyya'), Ḥajarī (*Majmūʿ*, II, p. 395, with vocalization) and Maqḥafī (*Muʿjam*, p. 290, al-Zuraybah). FLS ('Gazetteer' with full references) finally goes for al-Zarībah on the grounds that the diminuative form is not found today.

[3] The Sasanian capital in Iraq, 7 leagues below Baghdad and occupying both banks of the Tigris, originally Ctesiphon and Seleucia (Yāqūt, *Muʿjam*, V, pp. 74–5; Le Strange, *Lands*, p. 33).

[4] Brother of the first Rasulid sultan, al-Manṣūr ʿUmar, an amir of some influence in the Yemen during the Ayyubid period. In 626/1228, he was exiled to Egypt by al-Masʿūd Yūsuf, the last Ayyubid ruler of the Yemen, the latter fearing his strong personality and his ambition. 618 begins 25 February 1221.

[5] The Arabic name, 'the hairy one', or Zenobia or Bath-Zabbay, queen of Palmyra. She is also reputed to have built castles on both banks of the Euphrates (*EI*, 'al-Zabbāʾ').

[6] Despite the fact that Amīn and Ibrāhīm (*Muṣṭalaḥāt*, p. 51) assert that the *dhirāʿ* originated with the Umayyads and do not list the *ʿumariyyah*, it is to be associated with the second caliph (Hinz, *Masse*, p. 60, who gives the precise measurement 72.815 cm).

[7] The famous lexicographer and poet who died in 321/993, author of the lexicon *al-Jamharah fī al-lughah* and *Kitāb al-Ishtiqāq* (Carter, 'Lexicography', pp. 111–12; Nicholson, *History*, p. 343; *EI*, 'Ibn Durayd').

[182] He lodged al-Zabbā' in a palace, she being
an eagle of the air, soaring up high.
[She is] a sword by means of which his determination increased
until he shot to the furthest limit possible.
[The sword] gave the Abysinnians poison to drink, quenching their thirst;[1]
and occupied the sitting-place of the images of Ghumdān.[2]

It is mentioned by al-Mas'ūdī in *Kitāb Murūj al-dhahab* that the palace of Ghumdān was built for a second time better than it was originally.[3]

Section. I was informed as follows by Salāmah b. Muḥammad b. Ḥajjāj al-Madhḥijī: The ancients built a palace in Bayt Bi'r Fās al-'Awāmil[4] and raised it up seventy storeys in stone, white marble. A certain Abyssinian made a fire in it and burnt it. He destroyed it and parts of it fell on top of others and it became like a huge wall. Mecca could be seen from it. Imam Abū Ja'far al-Manṣūr[5] built the green dome in Baghdad seven storeys high, each one a vault so that the wind could not cast them down from their high place and it could be seen from Hīt and Tikrīt.[6]

The Persian rulers built Khusrau's estrade in al-Madā'in and one could see as far as Ḥulwān from it.[7] There is also mentioned Iram al-'Imādiyyah[8] whose description is well known, otherwise we would have mentioned it in complete detail.

Al-Kawālī built the palace of Adūr Ḥ.w.r.h.r in the fortress of Gwaliyar up to nine storeys.[9] A distance of ten days can be seen from it and it is still standing and inhabited until now.

In olden days, there was a pearl on the top of the dome of al-Masjid al-Aqṣā. When it was dark, the women of Ḥawrān[10] carried out some delicate spinning by the light of the pearl. It was built by Solomon, son of David – peace be upon him. It was destroyed by Nebuchanezzar of Babylon and a distance of ten days could be seen from it.

The fortress of Māridīn can be seen from the Euphrates, [183] seven days' distance.[11] Kuwārā is a pre-Islamic fortress built by an Indian virgin.[12] Between it and Sind

[1] A reference to the conquering Abysinnians who occupied the Yemen between the years AD 525 and 575 (Smith, 'Early and Medieval History', p. 51).

[2] Arabic '... *min Ghumdāna miḥrāba 'l-dumā'* which RBS translates (Serjeant, '*Miḥrāb*', p. 452), 'In Ghumdān (castle) [he came to] the *miḥrāb* of the statues'. He then suggests it is the place in the palace where the women are to be found. I.e. al-Zabbā' joined the women of the palace.

[3] See *Murūj*, II, 206, para. 1022, 382, para. 1376. Mas'ūdī does not support Ibn al-Mujāwir's statement in so many words.

[4] Unidentified.

[5] 'Abdallāh b. Muḥammad, the second Abbasid caliph, 136–58/754–75 (Bosworth, *Islamic Dynasties*, p. 6).

[6] The former is on the Euphrates about 90 miles from Baghdad, as the crow flies, to the NW. The latter is N of Baghdad about 95 miles away on the Tigris (Yāqūt, *Mu'jam*, II, pp. 38–39, V, pp. 420–21; Le Strange, *Lands*, pp. 25, 65 and Map II).

[7] Just over 100 miles to the NE of al-Madā'in (Yāqūt, *Mu'jam*, II, pp. 29–93; Le Strange, *Lands*, pp. 191–2 and Map II).

[8] I.e. Iram Dhāt al-'Imād. I follow RBS's reading rather than the text or Löfgren's apparatus.

[9] Formerly capital of the Sindhia state of the same name and now a place in Madhya Pradesh (*EI*, 'Gwāliyār').

[10] Al-Masjid al-Aqṣā is the mosque in Jerusalem. Ḥawrān is a large area, part of the province of Damascus, about 120 miles to the NE of Jerusalem (Le Strange, *Palestine*, pp. 33–5, map opposite p. 14).

[11] About 90 miles from the nearest point on the river. The town is about 140 miles NW of Mosul (Yāqūt, *Mu'jam*, V, p. 39; Le Strange, *Lands*, p. 96 and Map III [Mārdīn]).

[12] I am unable to identify the place and the person.

is ...[1] Rāwāstān can be seen from Tūrān, and beyond right down to the coast of Sind for a distance of fifteen days.[2] Mahrāst b. Arjāsb built Wajmat Tūl Adr in Balkh during the period of Darst the Wise.[3] He erected a green way-mark on the dome of al-Wajmah, but the violent wind blew it away, casting it down on the ground at a distance of twenty-five parasangs, and this was because it was so high.

Description of Jabal al-Mudhaykhirah.[4] I heard that it was in height about twenty parasangs. Its environs were agricultural fields and water supplies, where Flemingia grows like saffron.[5] It can only be approached along one road. Dāʿī ʿAlī b. al-Faḍl[6] was known as the shaykh of Lāʿah, this being the Lāʿah, a pleasant village beside it, called ʿAdan Lāʿah.[7] This is not the Aden of Abyan on the coast. ʿUmārah b. Muḥammad b. ʿUmārah said that he had actually been into this ʿAdan Lāʿah; it was the first place where the Alawite mission[8] in the Yemen had appeared. From it [came] Manṣūr al-Yaman and Dāʿī ʿAlī b. al-Faḍl.[9] The following dāʿī of the Fatimid state reached ʿAdan Lāʿah: Abū ʿAbdallāh al-Ḥusayn b. Aḥmad al-Shāfiʿī al-Shīʿī al-Kūfī, lord of the Alawite mission in North Africa.[10] ʿAlī b. Muḥammad b. ʿAlī al-Muʿallim al-Ṣulayḥī[11] studied there as a boy [184] and it was a mission headquarters in the Yemen. Now this Dāʿī ʿAlī b. al-Faḍl had conquered[12] Jabal al-Mudhaykhirah and had the *khuṭbah* recited in the name of the Alawite mission in 304.[13] Then the men of Asʿad b. Yuʿfir,[14] lord of Ṣanʿāʾ, took it back from him.

[1] There is a lacuna in the text and the MSS.

[2] Yāqūt (*Muʿjam*, III, p. 19) reads Rāwasān and says it is a village of Nishapur. Tūrān is an area of Makrān centered on Quṣdār (Kuzdar) (Le Strange, *Lands*, 331–32 and Map VII), the latter being about another 170 miles from the coast as the crow flies. The reading of the verb *y.?.dī/ā* is tentatve and clearly not fully understood by Löfgren.

[3] The person and place are unidentified.

[4] For the location, see p. 94, n. 8 above. Ibn al-Mujāwir takes this passage from ʿUmārah (Kay, *Yaman*, p. 6/Arabic p. 5).

[5] Dr Jenny Balfour-Paul informs me (personal communication, 14 August 1997) that, contrary to widespread belief, *wars* is not *Memecylon tinctorium* (Kay, *Yaman*, p. 6; Varisco, *Agriculture*, p. 157 and note), but rather *Flemingia grahamiana* or *F. macrophylla*. It is used as an orange dye (Lemmens and Wulijarni-Soetjipito, *Plant Resources*, p. 16).

[6] I have corrected his and his father's name. ʿUmārah and Ibn al-Mujāwir have 'Muḥammad' and the latter 'b. al-Mufaḍḍal'. Two dāʿīs, ʿAlī and Manṣūr al-Yaman left Kufa in 267/881 for the Yemen in order to take the mission there (see Geddes, 'Apostasy', p. 80 and *passim*).

[7] S of and in the region of Ḥajjah and J. Miswar, the wadi being a tributary of Mawr (see Kay, *Yaman*, pp. 232–3; Werdecker, 'Contribution', pp. 37, 40, 55, 56 and end map; Wilson, *Gazetteer*, p. 235).

[8] I.e. the Ismāʿīlī *daʿwah*.

[9] See above p. 94, n. 6.

[10] I have corrected the text's 'al-Ḥasan'. I am at a loss to know where 'al-Shāfiʿī' comes from. The man was either a Ṣanʿānī or a Kufan. The date of his arrival in North Africa is in doubt, but he was killed in Raqqādah in 299/911 (Nuʿmān, *Iftitāḥ*, pp. 58–64 and *passim*; Kay, *Yaman*, pp. 324–25; Abun-Nasr, *History*, pp. 80–82; Daftary, *Ismaʿili History*, pp. 99–100; *EI*, 'Abū ʿAbd Allāh al-S̲h̲īʿī').

[11] The first Sulayhid ruler in the Yemen, 439–459 or 473/1047–1066 or 1080 (Smith, 'Political History', p. 138; Appendix B.5 below).

[12] Reading *ghalaba* with Löfgren's apparatus. Again I correct the name, "Alī' for the 'Muḥammad' of the text.

[13] Begins 5 July 916.

[14] See p. 95, n. 2 above.

Description of Shibām.[1] This is very well fortified, a valuable region[2] with villages, agricultural lands and a large Friday mosque. Cornelium and onyx are extracted from it, they being stones which are hard[3] and when worked their real essence appears. One of the governors of Abū al-Jaysh Isḥāq b. Ziyād[4] who acted against it was Sulaymān b. Ṭarf, lord of ʿAththar,[5] one of the rulers of Tihāmah. His domains [stretched] for a distance of ten days, by two days in width, that is from al-Sharjah[6] as far as Ḥaly.

Its annual revenues amounted to 500,000 ʿAththarī dinars.[7] Although he refused to visit Abū al-Jaysh Isḥāq b. Ziyād, Sulaymān used to recite the *khuṭbah* in his name and strike coins in his name. He also used to have wealth and gifts carried to him every year whose amount is not known. [That part] of the Yemen which remained intact under Ibn Ziyād when he was advanced in age was from al-Sharjah as far as Aden in length and from Ghulāfiqah as far as Ṣanʿāʾ in width. I saw the total amount of the revenues of the territories of Ibn Ziyād after deductions for the year 366[8] was 1,000,000 ʿAththarī dinars, leaving aside [taxes] from Indian ships, various types of wood, musk, camphor, sandalwood, China, ambergris on the coasts at Bāb [185] al-Mandab, Aden, Abyan, al-Shiḥr, pearl fishing, taxes levied on the island of Dahlak, including, among others, 1,000 slaves, 500 of them male slaves and 500 Nubian slave girls.

The Abyssinian rulers from beyond the sea used to exchange gifts with him and sought to be in communication with him. This Abū al-Jaysh died in 371,[9] leaving a child whose name was ʿAbdallāh (or, it was said, Ibrāhīm, or Ziyād). His sister, Hind, daughter of Abū al-Jaysh, together with his Abyssinian slave, a major-domo called Rashīd, was his guardian.[10] One of Rashīd's slaves of Nubian stock was Ḥusayn Ibn Salāmah. The latter was his mother, and he was known by her name. This Ḥusayn grew up to be clever and upright. When his master Rashīd died, he became vizier to the son of Abū al-Jaysh and to his sister, Hind. But the outlying regions of their state declined and the governors of the fortresses and mountains took possession of all that had been theirs. Al-Ḥusayn Ibn Salāmah made war on the mountain people until they submitted.

[1] A settlement of some antiquity and the seat of the first native Yemeni dynasty in Islam, the Yuʿfirids. It is about 25 miles NW of Ṣanʿāʾ as the crow flies and is variously called Shibām-Kawkabān, Shibām Ḥimyar and Shibām Aqyān (Kay, *Yaman*, end map; Werdecker, 'Contribution', pp. 3–36 and end map; Smith, *Ayyubids*, II, p. 203; Wilson, *Gazetteer*, pp. 198–9).

[2] ʿUmārah (Kay, *Yaman*, p. 5) reads *ʿamal mustaqill bi-nafsi-h*, 'an independent area'.

[3] Following ʿUmārah's *muʿassāh*.

[4] The Ziyadids are badly documented, but this is in all probability Isḥāq b. Ibrāhīm b. Muḥammad, the last of the line, 299–371/911–81 (Kay, *Yaman*, pp. 8, 291–2; Smith, 'Political History', pp. 130, 138; Appendix B.3 below).

[5] This appears to be the Ḥakamī who gave his name to al-Mikhlāf al-Sulaymānī in northern Tihāmah (Smith, *Ayyubids*, II, p. 53; Stone, 'Gazetteer', pp. 164–5).

[6] This may be the Wādī Zabīd Sharjah and the other is near Ḥaraḍ. It is close to Ḥays and called Sharjat Ḥays to distinguish it from Sharjat Ḥaraḍ (Ḥajarī, *Majmūʿ*, III, p. 449; Maqḥafī, *Muʿjam*, p. 349). FLS is right to point out to me that Ibn al-Mujāwir's description of the borders of al-Mikhlāf al-Sulaymānī is exaggerated and refers me to Kay, *Yaman*, p. 7, where ʿUmārah says it was seven days in length. She prefers the identification of Sharjat Ḥaraḍ.

[7] Some of these have been published (Darley-Doran, 'Examples', pp. 184, 201), and date from 375/985 and 393/1003.

[8] Begins 30 August 976. The 1st person pronoun is presumably a transmitter used by ʿUmārah.

[9] Begins 7 July 981.

[10] Arabic *tawallat kifālata-h* (Dozy, *Supplément*, II, p. 478).

Sulaymān b. Ṭarf and Ibn al-Ḥarāmī[1] also submitted and the area of control of Ibn Ziyād was as extensive[2] as it had been originally.

Description of Ṣanʿāʾ. The inhabitants of Ṣanʿāʾ drink from Ghayl al-Barmakī, which has already been mentioned. It is beneficial to all those who drink it. Its air is cold like that of Khurasan. It is conducive to the production of all kinds of goods and is totally without harm. Saffron in particular remains there in some quantity. All kinds of fruits exist there: apples, apricots,[3] peaches,[4] plums,[5] quinces,[6] grapes,[7] figs[8] and pears.[9] There are also roses, narcissi[10] and jasmine and all sorts of odoriferous and aromatic plants and vegetables.[11]

[186] I was informed by Qayar, the client of Jamāl al-Dīn wa-al-Dawlah Jawhar[12] that radishes[13] are sold cut into four. I asked him why this was and he replied that a woman was found using one in her vagina and the governor of the town knew exactly what she was up to, so he ordered that radishes should only be sold when they had been cut [into four]. They actually established this as a regular practice.

Water freezes in Ṣanʿāʾ. I was informed as follows by Sulaymān b. Manṣūr: Water freezes over geese and cranes[14] and of their bodies only their heads can be seen. Then a fox[15] comes upon the ice and takes off the heads of the birds. Ibn al-Mujāwir said: This is impossible, since every body has the breath of life in it and nothing can become frozen over because the natural heat overcomes the cold. Water can only freeze over something which has died, because life is naturally hot and soft, while the nature of death is cold and dry. When this matter was under discussion, what he said was incorrect and what the fox is supposed to have done cannot have happened.

The inhabitants of Ṣanʿāʾ are of Persian descent. The Persians were released from prisons and shackles during the rule of Yazdgird b. Shahriyār b. Bahrām[16] (another version of the story is during that of Khusrau b. Kavād,[17] along with Sayf b. Dhī Yazan) in order to take the Yemen from the Abyssinians.[18] Their story is well known and set down in writing.

There is no town in the whole of the Yemen larger, more agreeable and worthy than Ṣanʿāʾ. It is a town absolutely the same [all over] and has such a moderate climate that no

[1] An amir of Ḥaly (ʿUmārah in Kay, *Yaman*, p. 7).
[2] Reading with Löfgren *wa-istawsaʿat*.
[3] Text *mishmish* (Varisco, *Agriculture*, p. 190).
[4] Text *khawkh* (ibid., p. 189).
[5] Text *injāṣ* (ibid., p. 186).
[6] Text *safarjal* (ibid., p. 195).
[7] Text *ʿinab* (ibid., p. 186).
[8] Text *tīn* (ibid., p. 196).
[9] Text *kummathrā* (ibid., p. 182, *kumathrā*).
[10] Text *narjis*. See above p. 53, n. 3.
[11] Text *al-mashmūmāt wa-al-rayāḥīn wa-al-buqūl* (Varisco, *Agriculture*, p. 198).
[12] See Landberg, *Etudes*, II, pp. 940–41.
[13] Text *fijl*. See above p. 36, n. 8.
[14] Reading with Löfgren *al-wuzz wa-al-karākī*.
[15] Text *darīn* which Ibn al-Mujāwir feels necessary to gloss (Dozy, *Supplément*, I, p. 438).
[16] The last Sasanian emperor, reg. AD 632 or 633–31/651 (*CHIr*, III(1), pp. 170 ff.; *EI*, 'Yazdadjird III')
[17] Sasanian emperor Khusrau I Anūshīrvān b. Kavād, d. AD 579 (*CHIr*, III(1), pp. 64, 151–62).
[18] In AD 575 (Smith, 'Early and Medieval History', p. 51).

one moves from one place the whole of his life, summer and winter. [Daylight] hours are nearly the same in both winter and summer. Ṣan'ā' has a huge ruined building.

Section.[1] In the time of Sa'd al-Khuzā'ī,[2] one of the tubba's, some Yemenis left to conquer North Africa, including the town of the Ṣinhājah.[3] When they had conquered it, they thought it a good idea to settle there.

When [187] the Prophet – God bless him and grant him peace – broke the Ka'bah idols, B. Muqbil[4] stole that belonging to Manāh[5] and took it to India. They scattered throughout the regions of the land and settled there.

B. Jafnah[6] became Christians in the days of the Commander of the Faithful 'Umar b. al-Khaṭṭāb – God be pleased with him – because of some upheaval;[7] some of them went to Constantinople and to the land of al-Ad'awān,[8] raging[9] against the population of North Africa. Abū Tammām said of them, 'When Isaac, son of Abraham – peace be upon him – called upon his son, Jacob, to accept the prophethood, the whole race became angry and entered the territory[10] of the Franks, together with a group of Israelites, they settled there, including the offspring of the Franks.'

B. 'Ijl were ejected by Rabī'ah (or more accurately al-M.r.q.'ah)[11] and the latter settled them in Khurasan.

The ruler of Khūzistān[12] moved against his subjects and they moved to the regions of al-Kurr[13] where they settled.

[1] In this untitled section, Ibn al-Mujāwir lists early emigrations of Yemenis and others.

[2] I can find no trace of this man. The tubba's' conquest of North Africa is associated with one Afrīqus/Ifrīqīs b. Qays b. Ṣayfī (Ibn Ḥazm, *Jamharah*, p. 439; Ibn Khaldūn, *Muqaddimah*, I, p. 21, also Rosenthal's n. 54), though both the above reject the idea that the pre-Islamic rulers of the Yemen could have marched into North Africa in this way.

[3] A Berber tribe, thought by some (though this is rejected by Ibn Khaldūn, *Muqaddimah*, I, 22) to be the descendants of the tubba's in North Africa.

[4] It is not clear which of the two Muqbils is meant here: Muqbil b. 'Awf, or Muqbil of Thaqīf (Caskel, *Ǧamharah*, I, Tafel 101; Kaḥḥālah, *Mu'jam*, III, p. 1131). In any case, this anecdote does not figure in the *sīrah* literature and there is no telling how Ibn al-Mujāwir came by it.

[5] An ancient goddess whose idol had been erected on the coast at al-Mushallal between Mecca and Medina. Ibn al-Kalbī (*al-Aṣnām*, p. 13–15) says it was destroyed by 'Alī b. Abī Ṭālib, whereas Wāqidī (*Maghāzī*, II, p. 870) reports that Sa'd b. Zayd al-Ashhalī was sent to destroy it.

[6] Jafnah b. 'Amr of Ghassān of al-Azd, or Jafnah b. 'Awf of Khuzā'ah of al-Azd (Caskel, *Ǧamharah*, I, Tafeln 176, 196; Kaḥḥālah, *Mu'jam*, I, p. 197)? In any case, this is an unlikely story which finds no support elsewhere.

[7] Arabic *laṭmah*, literally 'slap in the face' (Kazimirski, *Dictionnaire*, II, p. 997; Piamenta, *Dictionary*, II, 449, 'fighting').

[8] Unidentified.

[9] Arabic *munāḥimīn* (?).

[10] Reading with Löfgren *ḥawzah*.

[11] Perhaps 'Ijl b. Lujaym of Bakr b. Wā'il is meant here, a tribe originating in al-Yamāmah, though with later connections with the Euphrates, Kufa and Persia (Caskel, *Ǧamharah*, I, p. 353, II, Tafel, 141; Kaḥḥālah, *Mu'jam*, II, 757). The single name 'Rabī'ah' is not sufficient to identify this tribe and the alternative given by Ibn al-Mujāwir is unidentified.

[12] The small province sandwiched between Jazīrah in the W and Fārs in the E, with Jibāl to the N. Its capital was al-Ahwāz (Yāqūt, *Mu'jam*, II, pp. 404–6; Le Strange, *Lands*, pp. 232–47 and Map I).

[13] There are two rivers named Kur/al-Kurr, the Cyrus, one in Arrān to the W of the Caspian, and one in Fārs, near Iṣṭakhr. It is not possible to say which is meant here (Idrīsī, *Opus*, I, p. 423, the latter; Ibn Khurdādhbah, *al-Masālīk*, p. 175, the former; Le Strange, *Lands*, pp. 177–81, 275–7).

An Arab force of B. Tamīm in the days of ʿUmar b. ʿAbd al-ʿAzīz b. Marwān went and conquered Sind.[1] When they found it pleasing, they settled there and al-Kawkar, al-Ḥ.m.t, al-... and Ḥājir appeared from them.[2]

An army left Antioch[3] in the days of ʿAbd al-Malik b. Marwān for North Africa. When they found it pleasing, they settled there and the 'Veiled Ones'[4] appeared from them.

It is said in the *Tarjamah* that some from the offspring of Maẓlūm b. al-Ṣaḥāḥ b. Jandab al-Kilābī,[5] the best, those influential in Khwārazm, were taken by Sultan Maḥmūd b. Sebüktigin[6] and expelled to India. When they found it pleasing, they settled there.

When the Ibāḍiyyah[7] rebelled against ʿAlī b. Abī Ṭālib in the Yemen from the regions of Iraq, they turned their backs, keeping the sword behind them until he forced them across the sea and they settled the province of Oman.

The people of Tripoli in North Africa moved during the caliphate of ʿUthmān b. ʿAffān – God be pleased with him – to Bārī and Tūliyah.[8]

B. Kinānah expelled the Franks from Ascalon and settled it.[9] When it fell into ruins, they scattered all over the land.

B. Ḥayyah[10] left Syria during the time of the rule of Imam Abū ʿAbdallāh Jaʿfar al-Manṣūr [188] and settled in North Africa.

When Nebuchanezzer raided the Israelites of Syria, the Jews settled Nahr al-Sabt near the mountain range of the Hejaz.

When the tyranny of Sultan Muʿizz al-Dunyā wa-al-Dīn Abū al-Muẓaffar Muḥammad b. Sālim[11] was at its height against the Khwārazmiyyah,[12] he sent down from

[1] The Umayyad caliph, 99–101/717–20. I can find no reference to such military activity at this time.

[2] I translate literally and these names may indicate places or tribes.

[3] Anṭākiyyah, capital of the ʿAwāsim province in the N of Syria (Le Strange, *Palestine*, pp. 36–9 and map opposite p. 14). The date must have been between 65–86/685–705, the regnal years of ʿAbd al-Malik. Perhaps the reference here is to Zuhayr b. Qays, whose Arab army defeated the Berbers in 67/686. Alternatively, Ḥasan b. al-Nuʿmān, the Arab commander in North Africa, was sent reinforcements by ʿAbd al-Malik in 79/698 (Abun-Nasr, *History*, pp. 69–70).

[4] Perhaps a reference to the Tuaregs.

[5] Unidentified.

[6] I.e. the Ghaznavid, reg. 388–421/998–1030 (Bosworth, *Islamic Dynasties*, p. 296).

[7] For the Ibāḍiyyah, see *EI*, 'Ibāḍiyya' and Rawas, *Oman*, pp. 80–81, who sums up neatly their dogmas and their political theory, placing them on the less extreme wing of the Khawārij. I think this is a reference to the events following the Ṣiffīn arbitration between ʿAlī and the Umayyad contender, Muʿāwiyah b. Abī Sufyān, in 38/657. The use of the term Ibāḍiyyah is an anachronism here, as the movement was only established a few years later. Many of ʿAlī's followers later turned against him, including Omanis (Rawas, *Oman*, pp. 53).

[8] I.e. between the years 23–35/644–56. Bārī is a village of the south-eastern district of Baghdad, Kalwādhā (Yāqūt, *Muʿjam*, I, 321; Le Strange, *Lands*, pp. 31–2). Tūliyah is mentioned by Ibn Khurdādhbah (*Masālik*, p. 93), a town on a lake behind al-Ṣaqālibah(?).

[9] Presumably Kinānah b. Khuzaymah of ʿAdnān, from the area of Mecca and in 6th/12th century some migrated into Egypt (Caskel, *Ǧamharah*, I, Tafel 3; Kaḥḥālah, *Muʿjam*, III, pp. 996–7). Ascalon ('Asqalān), the well-known coastal town, W, slightly S, of Jerusalem (Le Strange, *Palestine*, pp. 400–402 and map opposite p. 14), had been finally captured by the Franks under Baldwin III in 548/1143 (Holt, *Age*, p. 44; *EI*, 'Kināna').

[10] Unidentified. A dubious reading. The date must have been about 136–58/754–75, the regnal years of the 2nd Abbasid caliph, ʿAbdallāh al-Manṣūr.

[11] I would have thought that Ibn al-Mujāwir is referring to one of the Khwārazm shahs, though there is none of that name.

[12] Holt (*Age*, pp. 65–6) calls the Khwarazmians freebooting warriors recruited from the Kıpchak Turks in Central Asia by the Khwārazm shahs in the early 7th/13th century.

Nishapur a thousand men, their hands tied behind their backs, bareheaded, barefooted and bound with mangonel ropes. He broke them up and tore them apart all over the furthest reaches of India.

When the might of Sultan ʿAlāʾ al-Dīn Abū al-Fatḥ Muḥammad b. Tekish[1] was great against al-Khiṭā and the Tatars, he drove out those of them he wished and settled them in the regions of K.r.m.s.l.[2]

When the might of the Turks was great against Sultan ʿAlāʾ al-Dīn Muḥammad, they moved the Muslims from Khurasan to Baghdad, Awrāq al-Shajar and al-Qaṣrān and pushed them across the Sayḥūn.[3]

There is the following poetry:

> My two friends, my sleep is absent from my eyelids
> and I cannot endure and I cannot even pretend to endure now they have gone.
> My heart accepts no comfort for [past] loves
> and my eyelid is scarred with tears and without sleep.
> I am sad whenever mention of you passes [over me];
> part of me is with you, while part of me apart.
> If nights bring you and me together,
> the time of being together returns, made happy by our being together.
> I fast my time away, seeking God's face voluntarily
> and I join my face to the dust, as I prostrate myself.

Some of the people of Ṣanʿāʾ and all the people of the east follow the Zaydī rites, that is the school of Imam Zayd b. ʿAlī b. al-Ḥusayn b. ʿAlī b. Abī Ṭālib, abandoning the contrived, newfangled Zaydiyyah, those called the Ṣāliḥiyyah and the Jārūdiyyah.[4] They wear untanned leather because of the cold country. Their young folk wear the *futūḥī*.[5]

[189] *A detailed description of the futūḥī*. An old woman took Abū Saʿīd b. al-Ḥusayn b. Aḥmad b. Bahrām al-...,[6] or more accurately ʿAlī b. al-Faḍl,[7] to a tailor to teach him tailoring. The young lad used to take a garment in pieces from his teacher the tailor and sew it somewhere his teacher could not see. When this had gone on for a long time, the tailor asked him about his absence all alone. ʿAlī b. al-Faḍl told him, 'I take the garment from you and climb up to the highest point of Nuqum where I sew it, looking down and thinking, if I ruled Ṣanʿāʾ, by which gate I would enter the town.' When the tailor heard

[1] 596–617/1200–1220, one of the later Khwārazm shahs, of the line of Anūshtigin Shiḥnah (Bosworth, *Islamic Dynasties*, p. 179).

[2] The Tatars were a Mongolic tribal grouping (*EI*, 'Tatar'). The place name is unidentified.

[3] Awrāq al-Shajar is unidentified. Al-Qaṣrān is another name for Sīrjān, the second city of Kirmān (Le Strange, *Lands*, p. 301 and Map VI). The Sayḥūn is the River Jaxartes (Yāqūt, *Muʿjam*, III, p. 294; Le Strange, *Lands*, p. 476 and Map IX).

[4] The Ṣāliḥiyyah (identical to the Batriyyah) accept the first two Orthodox caliphs and the first six years of the caliphate of ʿUthmān. Their founder was the 2nd/8th-century al-Ḥasan b. Ṣāliḥ b. Ḥayy al-Kūfī. I am very grateful to Bernard Haykel who provided this information for me and directed me to *EI*, 'al-Ḥasan b. Ṣāliḥ b. Ḥayy al-Kūfī'. The Jārūdiyyah is listed as a branch of the Zaydiyyah whose members accepted any Fatimid Alid as imam. The name comes from Abū al-Jārūd Ziyād al-Surḥūb (*EI*, 'al-D̲j̲ārūdiyya').

[5] Clearly a voluminous woman's garment with ample sleeves (see the following section).

[6] The I MS has al-Ḥ.?āhī, the L MS al-Ḥā.ī.

[7] See p. 194, n. 6 above. ʿAlī later turned against the Ismāʿīlīs and was killed by their imam, al-Mahdī, in 303/915 (Geddes, 'Apostasy', p. 84).

what ʿAlī b. Faḍl had to say, he replied, 'Come on, let's settle on Jabal Nuqum!' So there we settled.

Now all those who killed, or were fleeing from a debt or some injustice, would climb up to join them and would be safe. Thus they continued where they were until a group of people had assembled and attached themselves to them, rebels on the mountain. This military force[1] began concentrating all its efforts against Ṣanʿāʾ and when ʿAlī b. al-Faḍl had become powerful and the governors of Ṣanʿāʾ weak, he took control of the town and established himself as ruler.

Now he was a follower of the Qarmaṭī rite[2] and was a great lover of women, explaining in full to them the *futūḥī* garment. He used to stand them in a circle and he would enter throught the sleeve of one of them. He would take pleasure in fondling her breasts, the creases of her belly and [all] her nooks and crannies, holding on to the material [of her garment] and leaving through one sleeve into the sleeve of her neighbour [in the circle]. He would carry on until he had done the complete round [of the women]. None was uncovered and each one experienced exactly what her neighbour experienced, distracted in her joy!

The *futūḥī* was so called because he conquered[3] Ṣanʿāʾ, or, it is also said, because he opened up [the skill of] tailoring.[4]

The women of Baghdad used to wear it until the last period of the rule of Imam Abū Muḥammad al-Ḥasan al-Mustaḍīʾ bi-Nūr Allāh, Commander of the Faithful,[5] but it was [entirely] replaced in the time of the rule of Abū al-ʿAbbās Aḥmad al-Nāṣir li-Dīn Allāh, Commander of the Faithful.[6] All Arab, Turkomen, Kurdish and Baluch[7] women [190] and those of Sīstān wear it until now.

One exclaims in Ṣanʿāʾ: Abū Ḥassān! I was informed as follows by Yaḥyā b. ʿAbdallāh al-Khayyāṭ:[8] Asʿad al-Ṣanʿānī planted some barley on a plot of land he had. When it was ready to harvest, he said to the harvesters, 'Come on, anyone who wants to harvest wheat!' So a group joined him, but when they reached the crop, it was barley! The harvesters shouted out one to the other, 'Abū Ḥassān!', meaning the owner of the crop, since his *kunyah* was Abū Ḥassān, and implying that Abū Ḥassān had lied. From that time, the year 622,[9] it was said in Persian, 'who shows wheat and sells barley', i.e. he is proclaiming this very crop to be wheat, while he was actually producing barley for sale. This is a tremendous disgrace!

For such occasions, one says, 'Ṣanʿāʾ is under siege!'[10] Sulaymān b. Manṣūr informed me as follows: If something falls into the beard of an Arab, i.e. [for example] like bread

[1] Arabic *sariyyah*.

[2] Branch of the Ismāʿīliyyah, named after Ḥamdān Qarmaṭ, who refused to accept Fatimid claims to the imamate (*EI*, 'Ḳarmaṭī').

[3] Arabic *istiFTāḤa*.

[4] Reading with the I MS *al-khiyāṭah*; i.e. it became a popular pastime.

[5] The Abbasid caliph, 566–75/1170–80 (Bosworth, *Islamic Dynasties*, p. 6).

[6] Successor of the above, 575–622/1180–1225 (Bosworth, *Islamic Dynasties*, p. 7).

[7] The text reads erroneously 'wa-al-Bādh.j'.

[8] See Smith, 'Wondrous and Humorous', p. 112. Perhaps the name of his informant, 'the tailor', reminds Ibn al-Mujāwir of this particular anecdote.

[9] Begins 13 January 1225. Persian *gandum-namāʾi jau-farosh*.

[10] Arabic *Ṣanʿāʾ muḥāṣarah*. Discussing this passage with a group of Ṣanʿānīs, I discovered that to this day anyone noticing a foreign body in the beard of a fellow-eater will say, '*Aḍ-ḍabi fī al-bustān*', to which the response is, '*Bi-al-khams niṣṭādu-h*'! ('There's a gazelle in the garden!' 'We'll hunt him down with our five fingers!')

crumbs, some husk or something which should not be there, ʿAmr says to Zayd, 'Ṣanʿāʾ is under siege!' So Zayd will clutch his beard and shake it, so that the object falls out, saying, 'Far be it from Ṣanʿāʾ to be under siege, as long as this beard remains!' This is a signal among people.

The following poetry was recited:

> I kept on traversing one vast desert after another
> in sorrow until I came upon Ṣanʿāʾ.

In Syria one says, 'Aleppo is under siege!'

The wonders of Dhamār.[1] There are no snakes, nor scorpions in Dhamār.[2] If anyone brings a snake into Dhamār, as he goes through the gate, the snake dies. If any of the soil of Dhamār is removed and sprinkled over the snake-charmer's basket, it will kill all his snakes. This is the most amazing phenomenon there is! It is said that the region of Dhamār is sulphurous. Nothing [191] harmful remains there that is not destroyed. Sulphur is taken from Dhamār to every area of the Yemen. Their wells are [only] three cubits deep.

Description of Jabal Usī.[3] This is the mountain where vitriol stones are found.[4] In the eastern regions of Dhamār two parasangs distant is a mountain called Usī. All its rocks and clay, its right and left and north and south are one piece, enormous.[5] In one of its obstructions, i.e. [like] a molar tooth, is a cave and in the cave a sea of boiling hot water. Anyone in the area who falls sick takes it as a cure. Each one according to his means cuts [the throat of an animal][6] at the mouth of the cave and goes down inside. Then he swims in the water and when he comes out is cured. Above [ground] there is a circular town hewn out from its mountains and called al-Maʿdin and al-Maqarr.[7] In the areas east of Ṣanʿāʾ is Jabal al-Lawz[8] and a seat of government, a prosperous town. Beyond it is M…h,[9] a long, wide town. Throughout this mountain almonds[10] and nothing else grow.

[1] See Smith, 'Wondrous and Humorous', p. 114.

[2] A well-known town about 50 miles due S of Ṣanʿāʾ, traditionally regarded as the most southerly boundary of Zaydī Islam (Harris, *Journey*, pp. 257–72; Smith, *Ayyubids*, II, p. 147). From Qadi Ismāʿīl al-Akwaʿ, Serjeant reports that Dhamārīs believe that, because of the sacred area (*ḥawṭah*) called after Imām Yaḥyā b. Ḥamzah (614/1217 [Bosworth, *Islamic Dynasties*, p. 96] – though Serjeant's note reads '8th cent. H') in which there are the graves of 31 imams, there are no snakes in the town!

[3] The text reads L.sh.y which cannot be correct. My reading here represents the original name without the article (Hamdānī, *Ṣifah*, p. 104), although today it is called al-Lisī (Waysī, *al-Yaman al-kubrā*, p. 54; Maqḥafī, *Muʿjam*, p. 549). It is interesting that Harris (*Journey*, p. 258) in the late 19th century calls it 'Issi'. The shift to the more modern al-Lisī is understandable (Usī/Isī> al-Isī> al-Lisī) and not without parallels. It is about 20 km E of Dhamār and an important source of sulphur.

[4] Arabic *shabb*. The stones, called *shabb yamānī*, are glistening white and from them are extracted vitriol and alum (Lane, *Lexicon*, IV, p. 1493, III, p. 1266, *zāj*; Varisco, *Agriculture*, p. 173).

[5] Reading *lakht* (Kazimirski, *Dictionnaire*, II, p. 980) for the *l.ḥ.b* of the text.

[6] Reading *yafrī/yufrī* with RBS.

[7] I.e. the ruins can be seen. 'The mine' and 'the settlement'.

[8] Reading *mashāriq Ṣanʿāʾ*. Löfgren wants to read *maghārib*, but this makes no geographical sense. I am extremely grateful to Clive Smith for pointing this point out to me. Maqḥafī (*Muʿjam*, p. 552) says that J. al-Lawz is one of the mountains of Khawlān. See also Smith, *Lightning*, pp. 139–45.

[9] Unidentified.

[10] Arabic *lawz*.

Description of marriage among the people of these regions.[1] When Zayd seeks the hand of ʿAmr's daughter and he responds favourably to him in this request, Zayd says to ʿAmr, 'I want to see the beauty of your daughter for myself.' So ʿAmr will say to him, 'Go to such and such a market, for she goes there every week.[2] See her[3] for yourself buying and selling and also [see] her beauty.' Zayd goes off to the market which ʿAmr has indicated to him and sits down on the busy main route.[4] Along comes his fiancée with a bundle on her back. She puts down in the market what she has been able to carry. She sells what she brings and buys what she requires. She puts her bundle back [192] on her back. Her fiancé follows her and watches her crossing mountains, wadis, side wadis, plains, [more] mountains, easy-going terrain and hard-going. During all this time, she does not drop the bundle from her back, nor take a rest. If her appearance, her beauty, her carrying, her selling, her buying and the strength of her resolve to carry a heavy load please the man, then he will take her and consummate the marriage and she will remain at her work until she dies.

The following is the appearance of the bedouin and desert folk. They dress in untanned leather[5] because the area is so cold. It is said that a man said, 'In Aden I have a craving before God – He is ever mighty and glorious – for the waters of Ṣanʿāʾ and in Ṣanʿāʾ for the firewood of Aden. Both are my property.'

Its inhabitants do not know how to light a lamp.[6] I was informed by Muḥammad b. Manṣūr b. Muḥammad al-Wāsiṭī as follows: Trees called *shawḥaṭ*[7] grow in the regions of Taʿizz and Ṣanʿāʾ. When the top of the tree is set alight, it burns like a candle. In other areas only *shawḥaṭ* has ever [been used to] produce light, nothing else, instead of a lamp and wicks.

They eat wheat, fenugreek and meat and, weak and strong, they continue to drink through both summer and winter. They journey to Aden to buy cotton, perfume and Indian swords.[8] The limit of their studies is in [seeking] knowledge of precious stones and alchemy, astrology, grammar, logic, philosophy, astronomy, geometry, arithmetic and calculating by means of the letters of the alphabet.[9] Some claim 'wisdom and decisive judgement'[10] for themselves.

They build with old stone, digging out ancient foundations and taking out blocks four cubits in length and the same in width. These stones are broken up, worked and used for building. They build according to the features of Baghdad in their incising and gilding.

[1] See Landberg, *Etudes*, II, pp. 864–6 and Smith, 'Wondrous and Humorous', p. 120.

[2] Arabic *tatawaʿʿadu*. For *waʿd* = week, see Rossi, *L'Arabo*, p. 237 and Landberg, *Glossaire daṯînois*, III, p. 2928.

[3] The *shāhid-hā* reading of the text may be retained (cf. Landberg's MS reading *tushāhid-hā*) and taken as an asyndetic imperative, very common in Middle Arabic (Smith, 'Language', pp. 343–4).

[4] Arabic *qāriʿat al-ṭarīq* (Dozy, *Supplément*, II, p. 333).

[5] Arabic *khām*.

[6] See Landberg, *Etudes*, II, p. 999.

[7] Landberg's *Grewia populifolia* Vahl (*Etudes*, II, p. 999) was correct. DMV tells me that this has now been replaced taxonomically by *G. tenax* (Forssk.) Fiori (Wood, *Handbook*, p. 100). He adds that today *shawḥaṭ* is used for *Grewia tembensis* Fresen. The tree, as well as possessing the qualities described, is used for producing bows and also called *sharyān* and *nabʿ* (Dimyāṭī, *Muʿjam*, pp. 81, 84, 149; Dīnawarī, *Plants*, p. 41; Hepper and Friis, *Plants*, p. 236).

[8] Text *hunduwān* (Dozy, *Supplément*, II, p. 766).

[9] Arabic *jummal/jumal* (Lane, *Lexicon*, II, p. 461).

[10] Quran 38:20 (Penrice, *Dictionary*, p. 43).

[193] *Description of Wādī al-Ẓahr.*[1] I was informed as follows by the agency official,[2] ʿAbdallāh b. Muslim al-Zabīdī: In the regions of Ṣanʿāʾ is a wadi called Wādī al-Ẓahr. One year there was productive rain, scattered far and wide and ample[3] and from it the wadis flowed, the land was watered and the thirst of God's servants was quenched. The last parts [of the flood] flowed into the wadi and because of its vehement flow, washed the land clean of earth and pebbles. As a result, a large rock appeared in the bottom of the wadi and the following was written on it:

> I am the one made to bring the plague upon Thamūd
> and ʿĀd, then other people.
> He who does some evil or some good
> because of [this deed], finds it written down on record.

The rock remained in the bottom of the wadi, read by any Zayd and ʿAmr and the lesson learnt from it for some months by every Qayṣar and Jaʿfar.[4] After this a flood greater than the first came down and engulfed the rock in pebbles and earth. Everything returned as it had been and it is not known till now where the site was.

From Ṣanʿāʾ to al-Maḥālib on the return journey.[5] From Ṣanʿāʾ to the fortress of Thulā three parasangs,[6] built by B. M...[7] shaykhs. I was informed as follows by Manṣūr b. Muqarrib b. ʿAlī al-Dimashqī: A tubbaʿ built seven fortresses, including Kawkabān,[8] Ḥabb, Jabaʾ, Bukūr,[9] Ṣ.ḥ.m[10] ʿAzzān[11] and Thulā.

To ʿAzzān a parasang and a half, built by Amir ʿImād al-Dīn Yaḥyā b. Ḥamzah al-Ḥasanī.[12] To Misk four parasangs.[13] To Ḥajjah two parasangs.[14] Now the province of Ḥajjah is long and wide and includes 230 fortresses. [Among them] are those called

[1] A tributary of Wādī al-Khārid, often erroneously spelt Ḍahr, situated at its nearest point about 7 miles NW of Ṣanʿāʾ (Smith, *Ayyubids*, II, pp. 217–18 with full references).

[2] Arabic *wakīl*, i.e. he was an official of the *dār al-wakālah*, the state office administrating the agency tax, introduced into the Yemen in late Ayyubid times (See p. 60, n. 6 above; Smith, 'Maritime Trade', pp. 130, 134; 'Port Practices', pp. 209, 211–12, 215, both with references).

[3] Arabic *ghayth ṭiḥṭāḥ raḥrāḥ* (Lane, *Lexicon*, III, p. 1050–51; V, p. 1830).

[4] 'Every Tom, Dick and Harry'!

[5] I.e. to the NW and then the W (p. 79, n. 2 above). See Sprenger, *Reiserouten*, p. 153.

[6] About 40 km NW of Ṣanʿāʾ (Werdecker, 'Contribution', pp. 38–40 and map; Smith, *Ayyubids*, II, p. 211; Wilson, *Gazetteer*, p.111; Golvin and Fromont, *Thula*, *passim*; *EI*, 'T͟hulā').

[7] The text is illegible.

[8] About 36 km NW of Ṣanʿāʾ, above Shibām (Werdecker, 'Contribution', pp. 30–32, 34–6 and map; Smith, *Ayyubids*, II, pp. 168–69; C. Smith, 'Kawkabān', *passim*; Wilson, *Gazetteer*, p. 284, who mentions other Kawkabāns).

[9] The first letter is not vocalized in the MSS and the text. I think it is the fortress which Werdecker ('Contribution', p. 122) places at 1533 4347, i.e. about 11 km W of Kawkabān. See also Smith, *Lightning*, p. 8, map 3.

[10] I am unsure of the correct spelling of this fortress which is unidentified.

[11] There must be dozens of ʿAzzāns in southern Arabia. This one would appear to be near Thulā, if it is the same ʿAzzān as that described below as being a parasang and a half distant. See also p. 99, n. 10 above.

[12] The Zaydī imam. See p. 201, n. 2 above. I have corrected the 'al-Ḥusyanī' of the text.

[13] Unidentified.

[14] A town and area about 36 km NW of Thulā. It was clearly a whole area in Ibn al-Mujāwir's experience (Werdecker, 'Contribution', map; Smith, *Ayyubids*, II, p. 156, 'al-Bilād al-Ḥajjiyyah'; Wilson, *Gazetteer*, p. 129).

al-Maqṭūʿah,[1] al-Jāhilī,[2] al-Aghrābī,[3] Qarn [194] ʿIshār,[4] al-Sharafah,[5] al-Qaṭīʿ,[6] Jabal ʿAmr,[7] al-Ẓafīn,[8] al-Rahbah[9] and al-ʿIyār.[10]

I was informed as follows by Sulaymān b. Manṣūr: All of the above mentioned fortresses are well fortified and were given by al-Malik al-Masʿūd Abū al-Muẓaffar Yūsuf b. Muḥammad b. Abī Bakr,[11] together with 30,000 dinars, when they surrended Ḥuṣn Bukūr to him in 616.[12] To al-Dhanāʾib five parasangs.[13]

In these regions,[14] one side of a litter[15]can be hired, that on the mountain side for a dirham, that on the wadi side for a dinar. I asked why. [My informant] said, 'Because there are many lions in these parts. The lion will lie in wait on a rocky mountain ledge overhanging the road. One feels nothing until he is seized by the lion with contempt, [staring at him], eyeball to eyeball. The one on the wadi side, however, is free from fear of the lion, for he is sitting in a safe place.'[16] It is said that the 'lions' of this area [only] behave like lions, i.e. they are sorcerers, turning their appearance into that of a lion.

I was informed as follows by ʿAlī b. Muʿālī al-Dallāl: The lions of this area do not kill donkeys, cows or sheep; they only go for human beings. If one reaches a tree, the lion remains beneath it, staying for a period of three or four days, waiting for the man until he gets tired and climbs down, so the lion eats him. One can find men saying to the lion, 'Oh, please, please spare my life!'[17] – while the lion [merely] wants to get him down and is drumming his forepaws, while the person [is trying to] get him to swear by Him who is worshipped until he can run away from him.

I asked what the reason was for people behaving like lions, for is anything to be gained from oppressing one's fellow human beings? He replied, 'They teach one another sorcery and a man becomes a lion and does all in his power to bring harm to his fellow humans in the most savage manner possible. Throughout their lives, they are the subject of long, involved stories'[18] The Prophet – God bless him and grant him peace – has said, 'Poverty is all but unbelief.' To al-Maḥālib five parasangs.

[1] Unidentified.

[2] See Smith, *Ayyubids*, II, p. 165.

[3] The spelling is tentative and it is unidentified.

[4] Unidentified.

[5] Unidentified.

[6] Unidentified.

[7] One or two km SW of Ẓafīr Ḥajjah, i.e. about 8 km N of the town of Ḥajjah (Werdecker, 'Contribution', pp. 52, 53 and map; Wilson, *Gazetteer*, p. 252).

[8] Or al-Ẓufayn. Unidentified.

[9] The vocalization is in doubt and it is unidentified.

[10] Unidentified.

[11] The last Ayyubid ruler of the Yemen, reg. 612–26/1215–28 (Smith, 'Political History', p. 139; Appendix B.8 below).

[12] Begins 19 March 1219.

[13] Wilson (*Gazetteer*, p. 168) suggests that this is a low-lying area below and just to the W of al-Dhanūb (Werdecker, 'Contribution', p. 53 and map); i.e. about 8 km NW of Ḥajjah town.

[14] See Smith, 'Magic', pp. 9–10.

[15] Reading '*shuqqat/shiqqat al-shuqduf*', rather than the text '*al-shuqqah al-shuqduf*'. See also Dozy, *Supplément*, I, p. 774.

[16] Arabic *ʿalā tall al-salāmah*.

[17] Arabic 'bi-Allāh ʿalay-k alā mā ʿafawt ʿannī'!

[18] The text is corrupt and should perhaps read 'wa-inna-hum ṭūl ḥayāti-him fī-him ḥikāyāt ṭawīlah ʿarīḍah', rather than the meaningless 'wa-inna-hum ṭūl ḥayāti-him bayt-hā ḥikāyah ṭawīlah ʿarīḍah'.

[195] *From Ṣan'ā' to Mārib*. I was informed as follows by Salāmah b. Muḥammad b. al-Ḥadhjāj al-Madhḥijī: From Ṣan'ā' to Miswar four parasangs, the territory of B. Bāhish.[1] To Wādī Jannāt four parasangs.[2] To al-Ma'zimayn four parasangs.[3]

Destruction of the dam of al-Ma'zimayn. I was informed as follows by Muḥammad b. Salāmah b. Ḥajjāj:[4] The people of Shaddād and 'Ād[5] filled in the gap between two mountains with rocks and stones,[6] building them up until they were level with the top of the mountains. The floods began to come up against it,[7] as the water collected, becoming [like] a sea dammed up. They would water their lands and livestock from it and it is said they used to water cultivated areas full of grapes, date palms and agriculture almost as far as Syria and there were villages joined one to another.

The area remained a thriving one until God destroyed it. The reason for this, according to what al-Rāzī has mentioned,[8] is that a caravan set out from Syria and a rat had jumped up from the ground on to the back of one of the camels in the caravan. The rat moved from one camel to another and [the caravan] crossed over from place to place until it reached the town of Mārib. The rat jumped down from the camel and got inside the dam, where it began to do its work. It is said that one day al-Nu'mān[9] went out and began to hunt. He found the rat with its iron canine teeth undermining the dam. When he returned to his father, al-Mundhir, he told him the story of the rat and described its teeth made of iron, as it undermined the dam. [196] Al-Mundhir told him, 'What we have discovered in books, namely that only a rat with iron teeth can destroy the Mārib dam, is accurate, my son. I want you, when we enter the monastery and churches on Sunday, with all the people assembled there, to come over to me, pick a quarrel with me over some matter and be rude to me. When you think it has gone on long enough, come and slap my face with the palm of your hand.' Al-Nu'mān asked how he could do such a thing. His father said, 'Do what I have asked you to do, son, because I have a plan and you will benefit from it.' So the boy did as his father told him. When he slapped the old man, the latter (ever since known as al-Malṭūm [the slapped one]) became angry. He rose up among the host of people, saying, 'O Arab notables, I can no longer live among you.' They all

[1] Since this route runs to the E from Ṣan'ā', this Miswar cannot be the famous mountain to the NW of the city. The Bāhish of the text, completed from the L MS, and the Yāhish of Sprenger (*Reiserouten*, p. 153) look doubtful and I find the names nowhere in the sources available to me.

[2] Unidentified.

[3] *Ma'zim* means 'narrow', 'strait' in Arabic and this is the name of the two mountains either side of Wādī Adhanah between which the Mārib dam was built (Hamdānī, *Ṣifah*, p. 80; *EI*, 'Mārib').

[4] See *Nūr*, p. 71.

[5] The people of 'Ād were the rebellious folk to whom Hūd was sent to turn them from their idolatry (Quran 7:65).

[6] Arabic *raṣāṣ*. See p. 29, n. 4 above.

[7] Reading *taqallabu* for *tataqallabu* with the *Nūr*, rather than the *t.f.l.t* of the text.

[8] One might have expected Ibn al-Mujāwir's informant here, al-Rāzī, to be Aḥmad b. 'Abdallāh b. Muḥammad al-Rāzī (d. 460/1068), the author of the famous *Tārīkh Madīnat Ṣan'ā'*. He does mention the dam several times in his work, although the story of the rat does not appear.

[9] He is the son of the famous al-Mundhir IV and was the last of the Lakhmid kings of al-Ḥīrah in southern Iraq in the 6th century AD. The Lakhmids conquered far and wide within the Arabian Peninsula, although they have never elsewhere to my knowledge been directly associated in this way with Mārib. Their participation in the actual event of the destruction of the dam, which took place in the 6th century AD, does of course add spice to the story. The Lakhmids became Christians, hence the reference to monasteries and churches (*EI*, 'al-Ḥīra', 'Lakhmids'; Shahîd, *Martyrs*, pp. 266–72).

asked him why. He replied, 'A mere lad has caused me distress and broken my respect and honour.' He immediately cried out that the dam was for sale, so the Arab tribesmen all flocked around him to buy it. 'How much?' they cried. 'Cover this sword of mine to the hilt!', he exclaimed, as he plunged the tip of his sword[1] into the ground. The Arabs began to bring gold, silver and jewels to him, continuing to pour gold up to the hilt of his sword. The old man took the wealth and went up the mountain, where they settled opposite the dam. The mountain was called Jabal Ḥifā.[2] He and his family waited for the destruction of the dam. When the rat had firmly established itself in the dam and breached it, the flood water poundered against it and destroyed it. I was informed as follows by Salāmah b. Muḥammad b. Ḥajjāj that, when the dam burst,[3] the water carried away among other things a thousand beardless youths mounted on piebald horses, apart from the greys, sorrels, blacks and chestnuts. The following has been recited:

> The dam of al-Maʾzimayn was demolished and
> time passed, while the water is led away all over.

[197] To Mārib four parasangs, also called al-Ḥunayn. From this town the jinn carried off the throne of Bilqīs to Persia in the time of Solomon, son of David – peace upon both of them. As God – He is ever mighty and glorious – has said,[4] 'Is your throne thus?' She replied, 'It is as if it is the very one.' The following has been recited:

> Our lady, lady of a people who
> surpassed, just as Bilqīs surpassed, [others of] high rank.

The litterateur, al-Ṣābir, has recited as follows in praise of Sultan Atsiz b. Alap Arslan, chamberlain of al-Sinjarī [in Persian]:[5] ...

When the dam broke, the water took Mārib along with everything else. When the evil and harm wrought by the dam had ceased, the people surrounded two places still intact, together with two walls,[6] one place called the Upper Quarter and the other the Lower Quarter. In the Upper Quarter is a route called al-Fuḍūl road. Those striking one another, behaving badly, the one beaten or the beater, have nothing taken for them, nor is anything rightfully theirs taken away from them. But if anyone is not on the road, everyone has a right to take and to give back.

I was informed as follows by a Maghribī: Ḥusām al-Dīn ʿAlī Luʾluʾ[7] was a governor in Ṣanʿāʾ and called governor of al-Fuḍūl. From everyone who was dependent on him for

[1] Reading *dhubāb sayfi-h* with the *Nūr*, rather than the *dhuʾāb sayfi-h* of the text.

[2] Ḥ.fā is not vocalized in the text and the MSS and indeed the *fāʾ* is only certain from the diagram of Mārib (text p. 198). I vocalize after Yāqūt (*Muʿjam*, II, p. 274), who says it is a place and a mountain, although he does not say where.

[3] Reading *waqaʿa* with the *Nūr*, rather than the *dafaʿa* of the text.

[4] Quran 27:42.

[5] The poet is Ṣābir b. Ismāʿīl al-Tirmidhī, the 6th/12th-century poet often called Adīb Ṣābir, who wrote panegyrics praising the Seljuk supreme sultan, Aḥmad Sanjar (511–52/1118–57) (*EI*, 'Ṣābir'; Bosworth, *Islamic Dynasties*, p. 185). The poetry itself is too corrupt to attempt to translate.

[6] Reading *sūrayn* for *ṣūrayn*. For *darb* = quarter, see Landberg, *Glossaire daṯînois*, I, p. 731.

[7] The son of Luʾluʾ, a mamluk of the last Ayyubid ruler in the Yemen, al-Masʿūd Yūsuf, he left the Yemen with his master in 626/1228 (Smith, 'Ayyubids and Rasulids', pp. 6–9)? Perhaps this is an error and Ḥusām al-Dīn Luʾluʾ himself is meant. He returned later to the Yemen and under the second Rasulid ruler, al-Muẓaffar Yūsuf, he commanded the coastal force which was despatched to conquer Dhofar in 678/1279, where he remained for a time with the new Rasulid governor, Sayf al-Dīn Sunqur (Smith, 'Rasulids in Dhofar', pp. 30–31). See also Ibn Ḥātim, *Simṭ*, I, pp. 176–96, 514–29.

[198]

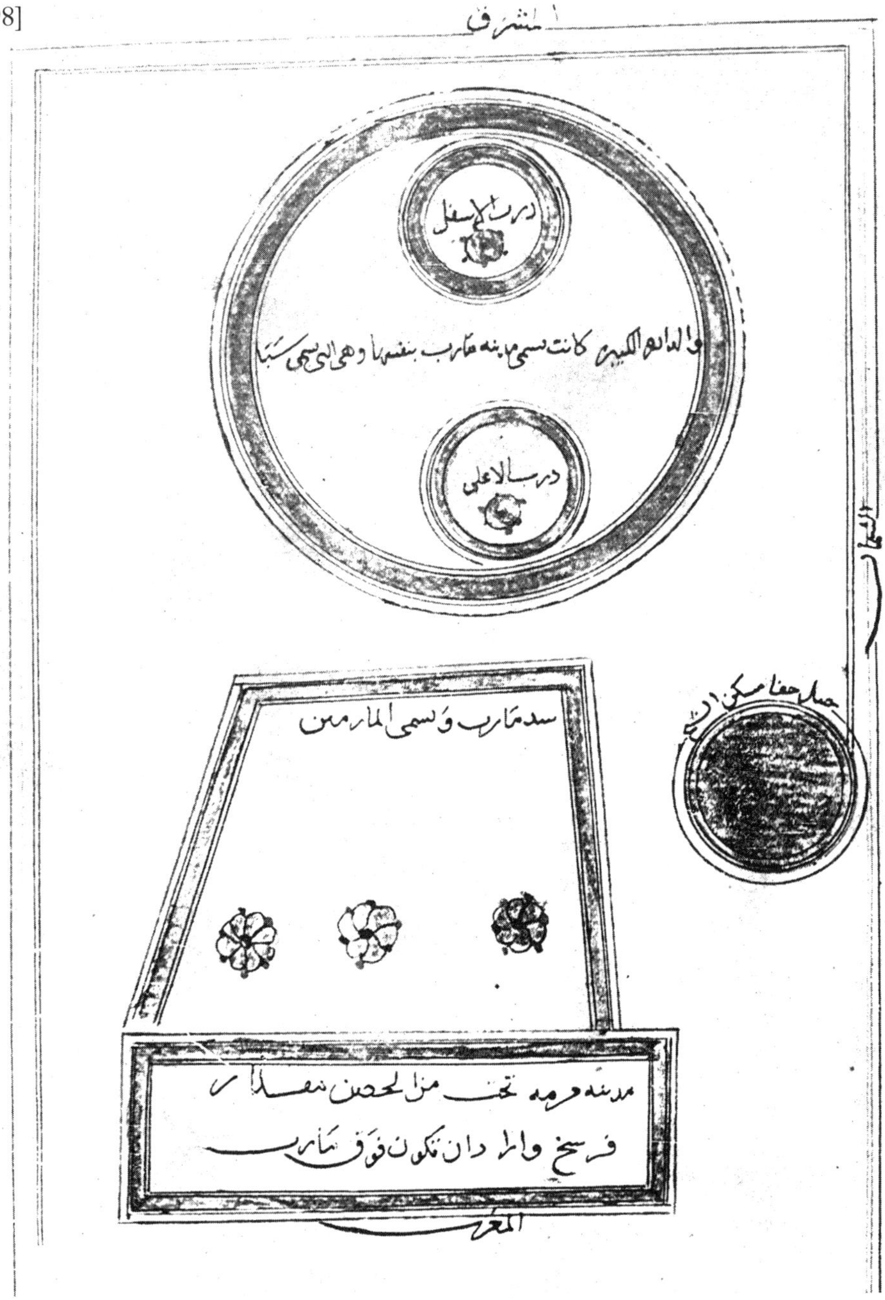

Figure 8. Plan of Mārib (I MS, f. 79b, text, p. 198, tabula VIII)

The town is situated within the large circle at the top of the plan in the E and the note tells us that the town is also called Sabaʾ. There are two small walled off areas (sing. *darb*) within the town, an upper in the W and a lower in the E. The N is on the right, the W at the bottom and the S on the left. The small circle on the right is labelled at the top Jabal Ḥifā and below the shaykh's dwelling place. The dam, called al-Maʾzimayn, is indicated at the top of the structure surmounting the rectangle at the bottom, i.e. S of Jabal Ḥifā. The note within the rectangle is garbled and corrupt.

[performing] the pilgrimage, he would take a dinar. It is in the following form: [198. Plan of Mārib, see Fig. 8]

[199] It is said the town of Mārib was built by Saba' b. Yashjub b. Ya'rub b. Qaḥṭān.[1] It is also said it was 'Ābir, who was Hūd – peace be upon him. It is said that it is called the Mārib dam simply because, when God gave power to 'the destroying wind'[2] over the people of 'Ād, every day so-and-so used to stand at the dam in order to repel affliction from his family. The wind would knock them together, just as God – He is ever mighty and glorious – has said, 'It left nothing, but came upon it and made it old and decayed.'[3] They built the dam to repel the power of the water from themselves. When this community left,[4] the flood collected there and the water increased. So it remained a flow of water, upon which villages, buildings and agricultural lands were built as far as the borders of Syria and all this was watered from it.

Section. A boy was born in Mārib to Ḥaṣīṣ b. Ḥiṣn,[5] news of whom reached Ḥaḍramawt in the evening, a distance of eight days, because all the agricultural look outs passed on the news until it reached Ḥaḍramawt.[6] This was because the country was built up and the inhabitants numerous.

In the regions of al-'Awāhil[7] is a mountain called al-Ma'din,[8] a silver mine, and a mountain called Sirwāḥ,[9] a gold mine, whose soil was yellow like arsenic. People nowadays do not know what it was for. It is said that the people of 'Ād, when they were in this area, used to extract the gold and silver from these two mines.

Between the area of al-'Awāhil and Wādī Bayḥān is a salt mountain. The Arabs of Madhḥij, the bedouin and the local [people] get their lump salt only from it. It is said, however, that the Arabs of Najd and the bedouin in the environs take a certain measure of it [also]. Ostriches, cheetahs, gazelles and oryxes[10] can be found in these lands. All the building of the inhabitants is in marble, dressed [200] and carved. In ancient times, it used to be brought from Jabal Yām[11] near to Barāqish,[12] four parasangs away, a white fortress.

[1] Qaḥṭān was the son of Hūd (Ibn Rasūl, *Ṭurfah*, p. 11). For the genealogy of Qaḥṭān, see Caskel, *Ǧamharah*, I, Tafel 176.

[2] Ibn al-Mujāwir is suggesting that *ma'rib* is an Arabic word which may mean something like 'time of want/need/hardship', if one takes it as the *ism al-makān wa-al-zamān* from *ariba*, or 'time/place of striking' from *araba* (Kazimirski, *Dictionnaire*, I, p. 22). It is in all probability a Sabaic word and occurs in the pre-Islamic inscriptions as both M R B and M R Y B (*EI*, 'Mārib'). See Quran 51:41 and Penrice, *Dictionary*, p. 99.

[3] Quran 51:42.

[4] Reading *ghadat* with the *Nūr* rather than the *'adhdhaba* of the text.

[5] Perhaps Ḥuṣayṣ.

[6] Reading with the *Nūr*, *ḥattā ittaṣala*, rather than the text *ammā al-khabar*, which makes no sense.

[7] There are two mountains, al-'Awhal al-A'lā and al-'Awhal al-Asfal, to the N of Mārib between the latter and Wādī al-Jawf and these are probably meant here (Hamdānī, *Ṣifah*, pp. 81, 102, [ed. al-Akwa'], p. 154 and n. 1; Maqḥafī, *Mu'jam*, p. 473).

[8] The famous silver mine and village is mentioned by Hamdānī (*Ṣifah*, 81).

[9] Or Sirwāj, unidentified.

[10] Arabic *ayāyil* for *ayā'il*, plural of *iyyal*, *uyyal* or *ayyil* and the translation provided would seem to fit into the list of fauna in the text. It might, however, rather indicate a mountain goat (= *wa'l*).

[11] The tribe is Ismā'īlī, of Ḥāshid of Hamdān, later inhabiting the area of Najrān. They originate from Jabal Yām which overlooks Wādī al-Jawf from the W (Hamdānī, *Ṣifah*, p. 81; Waysī, *al-Yaman al-kubrā*, p. 772; Ḥajarī, *Majmū'*, IV, pp. 774–5; Maqḥafī, *Mu'jam*, p. 706; Smith, *Ayyubids*, II, p. 239).

[12] The town of pre-Islamic Yathil, capital of Ma'īn, situated in Wādī al-Jawf (Habshush, *Travels*, pp. 48–53; Smith, *Ayyubids*, II, p. 139; Maqḥafī, *Mu'jam*, p. 67).

From Mārib to al-Jawf.[1] From Mārib to Warsān four parasangs,[2] a small well built by the people of ʿĀd. To Barāqish four parasangs, in the region of al-Jawf. To Maʿīn a parasang.[3] To Haram a parasang.[4] About the latter the following has been recited:

Between Maʿīn and Haram
are seventy wells belonging to Ibn Lakhm,[5]
cased in teak from top to bottom.
Lakhm are still ... Lakhm,[6]
conquered by Hudhayl, ʿAqīl[7] and Jusham.

To upper al-Jawf four parasangs, territory of B. Duʿām.[8] There there are of the populated Adite villages, Darb al-Ẓālim, al-Sūq, Dār ʿAyyah, Waḥsān, Saʿmūm and Ṣahīd.[9] The plain is sown with wheat and cumin[10] and each one of these villages is flourishing with its own inhabitants. But there is still constant fighting between them and the local shaykhs leave their wealth to their own families, while the weak sow and reap. Those places empty of inhabitants are al-Sawdāʾ, Ḥurāḍah, Darb B. M.ḥ.r.m and al-ʿĀṣ?ah.[11] In al-Jawf are al-Sawdāʾ, al-Bayḍāʾ, Maʿīn, Haram, Sarāl, Barāqish, Darb Aqā, Maqʿad al-Fīl, al-Jār, Bardā, Ḥamiḍah, Ḥamiḍ and al-Hujayrah.[12] God knows best.

Description of these regions, the dwelling places of Shaddād and ʿĀd and the haughty tubbaʿs. Their buildings in rock, marble and stone, some [201] cut out of the mountains. God – He is mighty and glorious – has said, '...while you hew out houses from the mountains', ' feeling safe.'[13] It is said that the stone was easy to work for them for the period of a month every year (or more accurately, for ten days). During this time

[1] I.e. in a northerly, north-westerly direction. See Sprenger, *Reiserouten*, p. 154.

[2] Unidentified.

[3] 5 km SE of al-Ḥazm, the latter now the chief town of Wādī al-Jawf, in its upper reaches. It was known in pre-Islamic times as Qarnaw (Hamdānī, *Ṣifah*, p. 167; Habshush, *Travels*, pp. 46–7; Maqḥafī, *Muʿjam*, pp. 613–14).

[4] 2 km only from al-Ḥazm in Wādī al-Jawf and also called Kharibat Āl ʿAlī (Habshush, *Travels*, p. 50 [Haram = al-Farʿ]; Fakhry, *Journey*, I, pp. 141, 143, especially n. 1, 146, III, Pl. LXI, where he describes al-Ḥazm as 'the site of ancient Harim'; Maqḥafī, *Muʿjam*, p. 678).

[5] Presumably a member of Lakhm b. ʿAdī of Kahlān of Qaḥṭān, the ancient tribe of Yemeni origin scattered throughout much of the Middle East (Caskel, *Ǧamharah*, I, Tafeln 176, 246; Kaḥḥālah, *Muʿjam*, III, pp. 1011–12; *EI*, 'La<u>kh</u>m').

[6] There is corruption in these verses and it is not even possible to be sure of the metre. A tentative rendering of the Arabic *min jawf al-qadam*. The second hemistitch is particularly corrupt; Arabic 'mā bariḥat Lakhmu ḥā? Lakhmi'.

[7] I leave this tribal name spelt thus, as the I MS appears to indicate this vocalization, rather than ʿUqayl. There is a number of tribes called by both forms of the word and it is impossible to identify which is intended.

[8] A division (*baṭn*) of Bakīl of Hamdān (Caskel, *Ǧamharah*, I, Tafeln 230, 231; Ibn Rasūl, *Ṭurfah*, p. 7; Kaḥḥālah, *Muʿjam*, I, p. 380).

[9] These places are unidentified. ʿAṣiyyah might be ʿUṣayyah. The final one might be Ṣuhayd or even Ṣahyad.

[10] Arabic *kammūn*, *Cuminum cyminum* L. (Dimyāṭī, *Muʿjam*, p. 136; Varisco, *Agriculture*, p. 182; 'Agriculture', p. 346).

[11] Al-Sawdāʾ is the ancient NŠQ of the pre-Islamic inscriptions, only 15 km to the E of al-Bayḍāʾ, with some of its wall still standing (Hamdānī, *Ṣifah*, p. 167; Maqḥafī, *Muʿjam*, p. 332; Fakhry, *Journey*, I, pp. 140, 147). For al-Bayḍāʾ, see Fakhry, ibid. I vocalize Ḥurāḍah after Hamdānī (*Ṣifah*, p. 160), though this is not the place in question in the text. The last two are unidentified.

[12] All the places not already dealt with above are unidentified.

[13] There are two quotations run together here: Quran 26:149 and 15:82.

they used to work it as they wanted. When they denied God's favour – He is mighty and glorious – they were swallowed up and scattered to the furthest ends of the earth and the lowest depths of the sea, east, west, north and south. On this subject, Abū Nuwās al-Ḥasan b. Hāni', known as al-Madhḥijī has recited as follows:[1]

With some young blades
in the prime of their youth, adorned by culture;
When Time caused doubt and suspicion, they divided
in the land and scattered far and wide.[2]
Fate will never bring back the likes of them
to me; far from it! They were marvels.
When I was certain that their spirit
would not return as long as I live,
I displayed a patience not displayed by anyone
and different desires shared me among themselves.

So the houses became graves and the abodes abodes collapsing one on the other. The date palms and trees were uprooted and in their place Dead Sea apple[3] and arak grew up. The bedouin settled in their hair tents and the camels began to pasture among the ruins. The gazelles drank from the dew and the drains. 'What awful drinking and bad the resting place!'[4] One of them composed as follows on this subject:

My two friends, stop the mount for a while;
the sick of the encampment will be cured of their thirst.
These are their traces. [The women folk] have prolonged my desire
and left my heart as [mere] traces on my [otherwise] vacant land.
If their abodes are empty of them,
they have left my heart in torment.
Were it not for the fact that their reddish white camels on the morn of their departure
had been loaded up with my passion, I would not have been able to depart.
[202] The women on the day of separation
left my anguish and crying there for me.
Of every white gazelle, one to whose beauty there is no equal
departed – they were all sick to my heart –
Her face is like a full moon, the sides of her neck a gazelle;
her buttocks are like sand hills and her slimness a reed.

It is recited as follows by another:

O heart, are you consoled, when you forget,
or are you troubled in the agonies of love?
Indeed, no life [previously] pleasing to me is [now] good
until my people are back as they were.
Far from it! They were separated. So no, indeed, there was no desire
in my soul to be near them after they had left.

[1] See *Dīwān* [Wagner], p. 30, [Ṭabbā'], p. 50, See also Nicholson, *Translations*, pp. 31–2 and *EI*, 'Abū Nuwās'.

[2] Arabic *fa-iqtasamū aydī Sabā*, a reference to the scattering of Saba' after the destruction of the Mārib dam (Lane, *Lexicon*, IV, p. 1287).

[3] Arabic *'ushar*.

[4] Quran 18:29.

How wretched is my life! I used to be at ease with it
in the days I had desires and places to call home.
I took an oath – no one pleased my heart after they had gone,
nor did anyone appear to anyone else.

This area is called al-ʿAwāhil and in length is from Najrān to Bayḥān and in width is from Rawḍat Nasr to Ḥaḍramawt.[1]

From Mārib to Ṣanʿāʾ on the return journey. From Mārib to Biʾr Mawhal two parasangs.[2] To Ḥarratayn two parasangs.[3] To Ṭabāl al-ʿĀshir two parasangs.[4] To al-Raḥabah two parasangs.[5] To Ṣanʿāʾ two parasangs.

From Ṣanʿāʾ to Ṣaʿdah, on the ancient route. Ibn al-Mujāwir said: In pre-Islamic times, this road was used, but when Islam triumphed, it fell into disuse. From Ṣanʿāʾ to Marmal three parasangs,[6] the seat of authority of the regions of al-Khashab,[7] which is where Thamūd settled, or more accurately the tubbaʿs. Everything built is in stone [203] and gypsum, both towns and villages. The length of each block of stone is about ten cubits. All of this which was built is now in ruins.

To Tharayd three parasangs, part of the regions of Bawnayn, two wadis.[8] To the top of Naqīl ʿAjīb three parasangs,[9] terraced by Asʿad al-Kāmil. To Naqīl al-Faqʿ a parasang.[10] To al-Muṣayriʿ a parasang,[11] where the Commander of the Faithful ʿAlī b. Abī Ṭālib cast down[12] the unbelievers. One of those Arabs cast down recited as follows:

Devour us, you beasts of prey, and drink us down!
You beasts of prey, you will indeed miss us!
We are wearing our helmets and carrying our Yemeni shields,
and swords dragged along, while you make your excuses.

To Najd Farsh two parasangs, a terraced mountain pass.[13] To al-ʿAmashiyyah three parasangs.[14] To al-Darb two parasangs.[15] To Ṣaʿdah two parasangs. God knows best.

[1] See above p. 208, n. 4. Maqḥafī (*Muʿjam*, pp. 276–7) lists several places of the name al-Rawḍah, though none Rawḍat Nasr. One or two, however, are in the general area of Mārib and al-Bayḍāʾ.

[2] Unidentified.

[3] I tentatively suggest this reading, although there are no dots provided and it is unidentified.

[4] The reading is tentative (or Ṭiyāl with the L MS?) and the place unidentified.

[5] Just N of Ṣanʿāʾ, the site of the present-day international airport (Akwaʿ, *al-Buldān*, p. 118).

[6] This is probably Jabal Ḍīn, about 30 km due N of Ṣanʿāʾ, the *qiblah* of the city (Rāzī, *Tārīkh*, p. 82; Akwaʿ, *al-Buldān*, pp. 176, 257; Serjeant and Lewcock, *Ṣanʿāʾ*, p. 277; Thenayian, *Study*, pp. 79, 135 and map 4).

[7] I vocalize this place name after reference to the Yemeni geographies, although this particular one does not find a place in them.

[8] I correct from T.w.?.? n in the text after reference to RBS's note. The two Bawns are al-Asfal and al-Aʿlā. Qāʿ al-Bawn is marked on Thenayian's map, N of ʿAmrān (*Study*, p. 80 and map 4).

[9] The mountain of ʿAjīb is about 22 km N of ʿAmrān (Thenayian, *Study*, pp. 80–81, with full references).

[10] Just over 30 km on from ʿAjīb, now called al-Ḥamūdī (Thenayian, *Study*, pp. 72–3, plate IIIB, map 4).

[11] Unidentified.

[12] Arabic *ṣarraʿa*.

[13] Unidentified.

[14] Corrected from al-ʿAmīshah/ʿUmayshah of the text. About 58 km north of al-Faqʿ on the pilgrim route and the name also of the extensive plain (Hamdānī, *Ṣifah*, p. 186; Thenayian, *Study*, pp. 63, 63, 75–6, 83 and map 4).

[15] See Thenayian, *Study*, p. 83.

The ruins of ancient Ṣaʿdah. When something happened to Dhāt al-Niḥyayn and ʿAmr b. Maʿdī Karib al-Zubaydī[1] realized what had befallen her, he loaded up some camels with sand and set out with them in the morning to Ṣaʿdah. He said to his family, 'When you enter Ṣaʿdah, block off [the way][2] with the camel loads of sand between the two leaves of the gate.'[3] So they did what he commanded them to do and filled the leaves of the gate with sand. The bedouin found out, so he ordered the gate to be closed. When it was closed, the bags of sand did not ... between the leaves of the gate.[4] Then ʿAmr b. Maʿdī Karib al-Zubaydī went to the Hejaz, followed by a bedouin. When he came upon him unawares, ʿAmr drew his sword and struck the rock which has already [204] been mentioned. It became known as Ḍarbat ʿAmr.[5] When the man saw the blow, he left him alone. ʿAmr continued to rely on his strength until he left for the Hejaz and became a Muslim at the hand of the Prophet – God bless him and grant him peace. Another version is that it was at the hand of one of the caliphs. He set out with Saʿd b. Abī Waqqāṣ[6] to conquer the Persians and was killed in the regions of Nehavand in the province of Iraq.

When something happened to the people of Ṣaʿdah, they withdrew from 'every remote ravine'.[7] Each one settled in his own abode and his own area. Because of this, there are five [interior] walls.[8] It is said that ancient Ṣaʿdah was in the beginning at Ḥuṣn Tulammuṣ.[9] After the ruin of Ṣaʿdah and its high places, al-Hādī Yaḥyā b. al-Ḥusayn rebuilt it.[10]

[1] 'She of the two ghee-skins', a lady of the tribe of Taym Allāh b. Thaʿlabah and the subject of the proverb 'more preoccupied than Dhāt al-Niḥyayn'. In pre-Islamic times, she was selling ghee and was approached by Khawwāt b. Jubayr al-Anṣārī, he apparently wishing to buy. She untied one of her full ghee-skins and he told her to hold it to allow him to look at another skin. He untied another skin and asked her to hold that also. With both her hands thus occupied and unwilling to lose her precious ghee, she was forced to give in to his evil advances (Ibn Manẓūr, *Lisān*, XV, pp. 311–12)! ʿAmr, Yemeni warrior/poet, died, it is elsewhere reported, in 16/637 or 21/641, the latter more likely, as he was indeed involved at Nehavand where he may have been killed (see below n. 6). He had accepted Islam with his tribe, B. Zubayd, in 9–10/630–31, 'the year of the delegations', though apostatized after the death of the Prophet, only then to rejoin later (Ibn Hishām, *Sīrah*, II, p. 583, Ṭabarī, *History*, IX, p. 90, XIII, 27, 29, 201, 202, 205, XIV, p. 12; *EI*, "Amr b. Maʿdīkarib').

[2] Arabic *usfuqū*.

[3] This and the following sentences are strange, possibly corrupt and require a little imagination to unravel. The text reads 'usfuqū al-zawāmil (sing. *zāmilah*, Dozy, *Supplément*, I, p. 604) al-raml bayn durūqay al-bāb'. The singular is *daraqah* (Dozy, *Supplément*, I, p. 435). A plural form *durūq* has here been given a dual ending.

[4] Arabic 'lam yajī' [*sic*] maʿa-hum al-akyās al-raml bayn durūqay al-bāb'.

[5] I.e. ʿAmr's blow.

[6] Renowned Muslim general and hero of the defeats of the Persians at al-Qādisiyyah (16/637–38) and Nehavand (21/641). He died between 50–58/670–78 (Ṭabarī, *History*, XIV, pp. xiv–xv; *EI*, 'Saʿd b. Abī Waqqāṣ'). See also above n. 1.

[7] Quran 22:27.

[8] Arabic *darb*, plur. *durūb*, i.e. the interior walls of the town which demarcate the quarters of the town (Landberg, *Glossaire datînois*, I, pp. 730–31).

[9] The Yemeni writers al-Akwaʿ (*al-Buldān*, p. 57) and Maqḥafī (*Muʿjam*, p. 93) confirm the correct spelling of this place name. It is one mile and a half SW of present-day Ṣaʿdah. See also Smith, *Ayyubids*, II, p. 209.

[10] The first Zaydī imam in the Yemen who died in 298/910. He was a Ḥasanī sharif who arrived in Ṣaʿdah in 284/897 from where he promulgated his Zaydī mission (ʿAlī b. Muḥammad, *Sīrah*, passim; van Arendonk, *Débuts*, *passim*; Smith, *Ayyubids*, II, pp. 76–7).

The rebuilding of Ṣaʿdah, built by the sharifs.[1] It was built during the rule of Imam Abū Mūsā Muḥammad al-Amīn bi-Allāh, Commander of the Faithful.[2] Another version of the story is that it was built of old, in pre-Islamic times. The most accurate report is that it was built at the same time as the building of Ṣanʿāʾ and it was, without doubt, built by Shem, the son of Noah – peace be upon him.

When ancient Ṣaʿdah fell into ruins and something happened to its inhabitants, Yaḥyā al-Hādī b. al-Ḥusayn intended to build a mosque in the area. A merchant approached him and said, 'Appoint me as your agent to build it.' He did so and the merchant built the mosque. When its building was complete, al-Hādī said to the merchant, 'Have you reckoned up how much has been spent?' 'God forbid,' exclaimed the merchant, 'that I take any fee for building God's house!' Al-Hādī settled in the mosque where it was and the people settled there with him.

The communities became numerous and built a town, markets, houses and other properties.[3] When they realized what was happening, they threw around four [interior] walls as follows: al-ʿAtīq wall, al-Qāḍī wall, al-Ghuzz wall, built in the time of Sayf al-Islām Ṭughtakīn b. Ayyūb,[4] and al-Qāḍī Ibn Zaydān wall. These four [interior] walls were included within one [other] wall, the [main town] wall.[5] Built [205. Diagram of Ṣaʿdah, see Fig. 9] [206] into the main wall was al-ʿAtīq wall gate, ʿAlī b. Qāsim gate, al-Ghuzz wall gate, al-Qāḍī Ibn Zaydān wall gate, Ḥūth gate and al-Imām wall gate.[6] As for the latter, it is a fortress built by Muḥammad b. ʿAbdallāh b. Ḥamzah[7] in an isolated position, north-east of the town with nothing at all near by. Only the imam and his offspring lived in it. A diagram of how the town looks on the following page.

As for the town, it is thriving, has a large population and wealthy, with the means of supporting itself. The inhabitants' drinking water is from channels and springs and their crops are wheat and barley. There are trees and water channels. They wear silk and cotton, as outside the town it is extremely hot and moderately hot inside.[8] They are good people, laying claim to wisdom, a knowledge of precious stones and the religious sciences. They all follow the rite of Imam Zayd b. ʿAlī b. al-Ḥusayn b. ʿAlī b. Abī Ṭālib and are the driving force within the rite.

Section. I was informed as follows by ʿAlī b. Muḥsin al-Jabalī: The Abbasids feared none save the Zaydīs. I asked why this was and he replied, 'Because the *sunnah* and the feeling

[1] I take this as the plur. of *sharīf* here and there is no further mention of it. It should be said, however, that there is one place, al-Sharaf, in the Ṣaʿdah area.

[2] The sixth Abbasid caliph, 193–98/809–13 (Bosworth, *Islamic Dynasties*, p. 6).

[3] See also Landberg, *Glossaire datînois*, I, p. 730.

[4] The second Ayyubid ruler of the Yemen (reg. 579–93/1183–97) (Smith, 'Political History', p. 138; Appendix B.8 below). 'Ghuzz' means the non-Arab Ayyubids, and is clearly the required reading, rather than that of the text, al-f/q.r.

[5] Arabic *sūr*. The interior walls divide off the quarters of the town.

[6] The plan indicates that al-ʿAtīq was the gate in the E, al-Ghuzz in the W, Ibn Zaydān in the S and al-Imām outside the town to the NE. Ḥūth is a town about 80 km S of Ṣaʿdah (Smith, *Ayyubids*, pp. 163–4) and therefore the Ḥūth gate was also in the S.

[7] Although the text reads 'Abū Muḥammad', I am convinced that this is the son of the famous Zaydī imam, ʿAbdallāh b. Ḥamzah, who rose in 614/1217 and died in 623/1226 in Ḥūth (Ibn al-Ḥusayn, *Ghāyah*, pp. 407, 416; Lane-Poole, *Dynasties*, p. 102; Bosworth, *Islamic Dynasties*, p. 96).

[8] Arabic '... li-anna al-bilād ẓāhiru-hā ḥārr bi-al-marrah wa-bāṭinu-hā ḥārr layyin'.

[205]

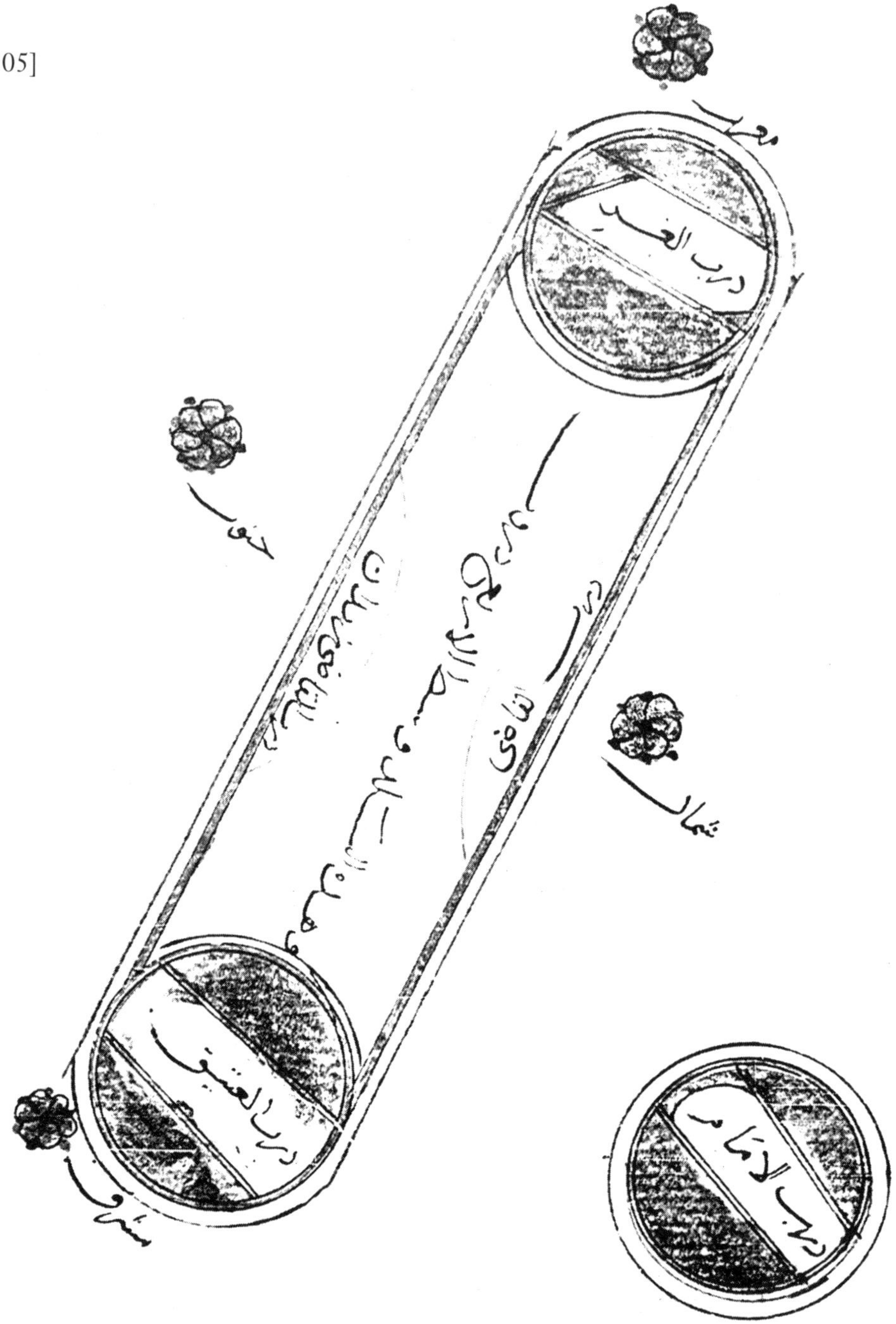

Figure 9. Plan of Ṣaʿdah (I MS, f. 82b, text, p. 205, tabula IX)
The points of the compass are marked as follows: N on the right side, S on the left, W at the top and E at the bottom. The note in the centre of the plan proclaims that this area is in the middle of four quarters (the word *darb* is used here and in the text, literally an inner wall, dividing off the quarters of the town). The top quarter in the W is labelled 'al-Ghuzz', in the N on the right, 'al-Qāḍī', in the E at the bottom, 'al-ʿAtīq' and in the S on the left, 'al-Qāḍī Zaydān'. The small circle N of the town in the lower right hand corner represents the quarter, 'al-Imām'.

of community[1] are derived from the party of the Abbasid imams, [whereas] the Shīʿah Imāmiyyah[2] say, "There is no imam but he who brings unity." Moreover, they are waiting for the emergence [from seclusion] of the Awaited Imam Muḥammad b. al-Ḥasan.[3] They are now separate from the two factions.'

The real force of the area [of Ṣaʿdah] is the Zaydīs, since in their view anyone who is righteous, obedient to the Faith, a sharif of the family of al-Ḥasan b. ʿAlī b. Abī Ṭālib and has five [specific] qualities is an imam who must be obeyed. Anyone of this description who rises up, the Zaydīs rise up with him and fight before him.

Aḥmad b. ʿAbdallāh b. Ḥamzah[4] came upon a store of weapons[5] in [207] the environs of Ṣaʿdah. There came to light among other things four hundred Dāʾūdī instruments for making chain-mail,[6] as well as weapons and military equipment and they made a [successful] quest for gold. However, none of this worked out well for them, because there was a talisman set upon it and they were not able to gain access to it in 624.[7]

From Ṣaʿdah to Dhahbān.[8] From Ṣaʿdah to al-Ḥawānīt four parasangs,[9] built by Asʿad al-Kāmil in Wādī Sajʿ.[10] He built this place, al-Ḥawānīt, when he decided that ...[11]

To Khaṭm al-Bakarāt two parasangs.[12] It is said that this place was known by this name only because a jinni[13] said to the poet Ramīm b. Jābir, 'You recite a line to me and I shall recite one like it to you until the one who beats his opponent is pronounced victorious. [This is] on the condition that you do not mention a cock in your poetry.' He agreed and one continued to recite a verse and his opponent to recite one like it until Ramīm b. Jābir was unable [to keep to the condition] and recited as follows:

> A red cock of Solomon,[14] no jinni can be found
> in his neighbourhood, nor is that where one can be heard.

[1] Arabic *jamāʿah*.

[2] I have been able to discuss this complex passage with Bernard Heykal. His ideas are reflected in the translation and in the following note. I am extremely grateful to him for sharing his views with me. The Sunnīs are the Abbasids. The Imāmiyyah are the Twelver Shīʿīs. Their brand of Shīʿism was adopted later by the Safavids (907–1135/1501–1722) as their official religion (*SEI*, 'Shīʿa'; *EI*, 'Imāmiyya'; Daftary, 'Ḥasan-i Ṣabbāḥ', p. 182). Heykal would prefer to read 'al-Shīʿah al-Imāmiyyah' and omit the *wa-* of the printed text. The Shīʿah are divided into those who are waiting for the Mahdī (they are not feared because they are docile) and those who have real applicants for the imamate. The Zaydīs represent a potential ideological and military threat to the Abbasids because they claim the imamate and the leadership of the Muslim community.

[3] Cousin of ʿUbayd Allāh/ʿAbdallāh al-Mahdī, the first Fatimid caliph, he went into seclusion in 260/873 (Hamdānī, *al-Ṣulayḥiyyūn*, p. 343, table 7).

[4] Another of the sons of the Zaydī imam, ʿAbdallāh b. Ḥamzah (d. 623/1226) (Ibn al-Ḥusayn, *Ghāyah*, p. 406; see also p. 213, n. 7 above).

[5] Reading Löfgren's *silāḥ*, rather than the *sāj/sāḥ* of the MSS.

[6] Text *zaradiyyah* (Dozy, *Supplément*, I, p. 585). I am not sure of the implication of 'Dāʾūdī'.

[7] Begins 22 December 1226.

[8] See Sprenger, *Reiserouten*, p. 155. For Dhahbān in the N of Tihāmah, see p. 65, n. 11 above.

[9] Unidentified.

[10] Now known as Shajʿ, due N of Ṣaʿdah (Thenayian, *Study*, pp. 99, 102 and map 13.1).

[11] Arabic *an yaʿmura ?.?.l. r.f al-ʿ.rāq*.

[12] Unidentified. For this anecdote, see Smith, 'Magic', p. 12.

[13] Arabic *ʿifrīt min al-jinn*.

[14] The full meaning is difficult to grasp. Solomon in Arab tradition has authority over nature and is associated with magic and the supernatural (*EI*, 'Sulaymān ibn Dāwūd'; Thackston, *Tales*, p. 301).

When the jinni heard this, he flew up into the air and landed to take hold of Ṣaydaḥ, a young she-camel of Ramīm b. Jābir, and tear her limb from limb.[1] When Ramīm saw what had happened, he grieved for his she-camel and began to weep and to inscribe her picture on [all] the rocks. In these parts, there was not a single rock on which there was no picture of the she-camel, so the place became known as Khiyam al-Rukkāb.[2] About this he would recite:

> There is no young girl like Mayyā,
> nor any slim beast like Ṣaydaḥ.

[208] He also recited the following:

> I was sitting on one side of the debate,
> while Ṣaydaḥ was pasturing among strong reddish-white she-camels.

To al-Qadīm two parasangs, an inhabited place.[3] The following was recited:

> ... ... and Karīm left me.
> The light of Yām has returned ... I can see al-Qadīm.[4]

This is Yām b. Abā[5] whose settlement is in Wādī al-Khāniq and al-Ḥuqqah.[6]

To Multaqā al-Awdiyah a parasang.[7] To Ghasl Julājil two parasangs.[8] To al-Mukhtalaf two parasangs, an inhabited place.[9] To al-Barah a parasang.[10] To Wādī Tafūṣ two parasangs.[11] To al-Jabal al-Aswad a parasang.[12] To al-Sarawāt two parasangs.[13] To Rufaydah two parasangs.[14] To Ṭarīb two parasangs.[15] To Dhahbān two parasangs. These regions are called Bīshat al-ʿAbbās b. Mālik b. ʿAmr b. Wāʾil, going back to Nizār.[16]

[1] Arabic *ṣayyaḥa qiṭaʿ qiṭaʿ* (Lane, *Lexicon*, IV, p. 1752).

[2] Ibn al-Mujāwir seems to forget that the name the derivation of which he is clarifying is originally given as Khaṭm al-Bakarāt ('muzzle of the young she-camels'). He now provides a new version. The place name, 'tents of the riders', does not fit in with the origin of the place name at all!

[3] Unidentified.

[4] The first hemistitch is corrupt and unintelligible. The second hemistitch is also corrupt and may read *wa-ʿāda sanā Yāmin ...*

[5] An Ismāʿīlī tribe still known in the area of Najrān (Hamdānī, *Ṣifah*, pp. 115, 136; Caskel, *Ǧamharah*, I, Tafel 229; Ibn Rasūl, *Ṭurfah*, p. 117; Kaḥḥālah, *Muʿjam*, III, p. 1259; *EI*, 'Yām').

[6] One of the wadis of Ṣaʿdah according to Hamdānī (*Ṣifah*, p. 114), it flows also through the area of Najrān N of the town (Thenayian, *Study*, p. 84). Ḥuqqah, if this is indeed the correct spelling, is unidentified.

[7] Literally, 'the confluence of the two wadis', but I take it as a place name.

[8] Just S of Wādī al-Mukhtalaf, about 100 km N of Ṣaʿdah (Thenayian, *Study*, map 13.1).

[9] Unidentified.

[10] Unidentified.

[11] Unidentified.

[12] Unidentified.

[13] This is the name of the whole mountain range running N–S in western Arabia, although this must refer to some precise location which is unidentified.

[14] Zulfa ('Communities', p. 78) says Bilād Rufaydah is 70 km SW of Abhā, the provincial capital of ʿAsīr in present-day Saudi Arabia.

[15] Hamdānī (*Ṣifah*, p. 116) says it belongs to B. Nahd and 'a place of Ṭayy'' (p. 253).

[16] The town of Bīshah is about 230 km N of Abhā and still today the extensive region around is called after the town (Farsi, *Guide*, map 35; Thenayian, *Study*, pp. 117–18, map 13). I cannot trace the line right back to Nizār, but see Caskel, *Ǧamharah*, I, Tafel 212.

From Ṣaʿdah to Najrān. From Ṣaʿdah to Zahrān three parasangs,[1] belonging to the son of a ruler of the family of ʿAbdallāh b. Ḥamzah,[2] since he bought the lands of Zahrān from their owners in a deal he made with them.[3] Ra's al-Rakb belonged to a people called al-Aqshūr.[4] To al-Ḥadd three parasangs.[5] To al-Rakb three parasangs, a large wadi, running with clear water.[6] To al-Khāniq three parasangs, [where there are] palm groves and running water, the first part of which runs out of al-Rakb.

To Kawkabān two parasangs,[7] from where one heads out into Najd. This [209] fortress was placed between Najd and the mountains of the Yemen. It is well fortified and the seat of the ruler of Najrān.

To al-Ḥuqqah a quarter of a parasang, the original town of Najrān which had the main function of buying and selling.[8] Its inhabitants are divided into three religions: a third Jews, a third Christians and a third Muslims. The Muslims there are themselves divided into three rites: a third Shāfiʿīs, a third Zaydīs and a third Mālikīs.[9] It is the town which belonged to the people of al-Ukhdūd,[10] about whom God – He is mighty and glorious – has said,[11] 'Those of the pit were killed, of the fire fed with fuel, when they sat by it.'

To Qābil a quarter of a parasang.[12] To Ḥabawnā four parasangs.[13] To Qarqar four parasangs.[14] God knows best.

Description of the town of Qarqar. I was told by an informant that Qarqar used to be a flourishing town with three hundred places to stay there and three hundred horsemen. It fell into ruin because the communities had differences of opinion.

Section. Zayd al-Badawī met ʿAmr al-Qarqarī who was living and settled in the Najd desert with the bedouins. Zayd said to ʿAmr, 'How come I find you in southern Najd after you were within the confines of Qarqar with a thousand milch-camels you

[1] Unidentified.

[2] The reference is to the Zaydī imam, d. 614/1217. See Appendix B.2 below.

[3] Arabic *bayʿ wa-shirā*, omitted from the L MS.

[4] Both the place and the tribe are unidentified.

[5] Unidentified.

[6] A tentative translation of 'yajrī ʿalā ṣafā'.

[7] Not, of course, *the* Kawkabān, NW of Ṣanʿāʾ. Unidentified.

[8] Arabic 'wa-ʿalay-hā al-muʿawwal fī al-bayʿ wa-al-shirā'? See Lane, *Lexicon*, V, pp. 2200–2202.

[9] Serjeant ('Saint Sergius', p. 575) poses the interesting question whether Ibn al-Mujāwir here is writing of his contemporary findings or quoting from an earlier source. 'A survival', writes Serjeant in 1959, 'of the Christian community into the Middle Ages is a little unexpected, but the Jewish community, ..., survived up till its final exodus a few years ago.'

[10] Arabic *aṣḥāb al-ukhdūd* (Penrice, *Dictionary*, p. 41).

[11] Quran 85:4–6.

[12] Hamdānī (*Ṣifah*, p. 115) mentions Qābil Najrān. Farsi (*Guide*, map 10) has al-Qābil on the southern edge of the Najrān oasis, a little to the SW of the town.

[13] Usually spelt with *alif maqṣūrah*, Hamdānī's (*Ṣifah*, p. 188) Ḥabawnan on the 'Ḥaḍramawt lower road', also a wadi inhabited by Yām. See also Akwaʿ, *Buldān*, p. 81 and Ḥajarī, *Majmūʿ*, II, p. 228.

[14] Mentioned incidentally by Hamdānī (*Ṣifah*, p. 169) and Yāqūt (*Muʿjam*, IV, p. 326) says it is beside a place called al-Qurayyah, which itself is between al-Falaj and Najrān.

pastured in the morning?[1] Now I find you warding off fear.' So ʿAmr al-Qarqarī recited as follows:[2]

I want to enter among the houses of Qarqar,
but I have a heavy debt which prevents me.
If my debt had been paid off, I would have done just that,
but the debt of al-Qarqarī [makes me] a victim.

[210] A market called al-ʿAmidayn took place beside Qarqar. This market was so called simply because the Arab shaykhs used to set up one column of gold and one of silver and the market was called after these two columns.[3] It has now become a market for the produce of desert lands where they are sown and ploughed. The original form has gone, but the name remains.

Their rulers are a people called B. ʿAbd al-Madān,[4] the people of the amenable and excellent Shaddād b. ʿĀd. An Arab recited as follows about them:

Were it not for B. ʿAbd al-Madān and their horse,
Certain [other] tribes would have taken up residence in you, Najrān.

Another poet has recited as follows:

... do you not know that my heart
loves you, O lightning over the Yemen![5]
If I kill you vilely,
then no shaykh creeps along on the tips of his toes.
If I am killed, then it is destiny and ...
and among my people on the saddle of a horse.
If I am killed, then Quraysh have been already killed
and B. ʿAbd al-Madān have already been killed.

These tribesmen do not accept non-Arab, nor [even] Arab rulers.[6] The last person to be ruler of the B. ʿAbd al-Madān were two brothers called Qadi ... and the other, Qadi ...[7] During their time, the hand of Amir Muḥammad b. ʿAbdallāh b. Ḥamzah came upon them and he took from them half of the income of the land, because Amir Muḥammad b. ʿAbdallāh and his brother, Aḥmad, sons of ʿAbdallāh b. Ḥamzah, married the sisters of Qadi ... and Qadi ..., sons of Ṣuʿayb b. ʿAdnān b. ʿAbd al-Madān in 623.[8]

[1] A corrupt passage, reading '... bi-alf ghazūr ghadawt al-ān arā-k radd al-shard', translated tentatively. I suppose it means he was in good circumstances in Qarqar, but was now living in fear.

[2] The name is of one of Ibn al-Mujāwir's imaginary characters and I cannot trace the poetry elsewhere. The second hemistitch of the first line quoted is reminiscent of a hemistitch of the Abbasid poet, Yaḥyā b. Ṭālib al-Ḥanafī (quoted in Noeldeke, *Delectus*, p. 26, line 3).

[3] Hamdānī (*Ṣifah*, p. 84) has ʿAmidān with no article. Ibn al-Mujāwir uses *ʿāmūd*, meaning 'column' for the more usual *ʿimād* and *ʿamūd* (Dozy, *Supplément*, II, p. 170).

[4] Of Madhḥij of B. al-Ḥārith b. Kaʿb (Caskel, *Ǧamharah*, I, Tafel 259; Ibn Rasūl, *Ṭurfah*, p. 35; Kaḥḥālah, *Muʿjam*, II, p. 734 (erroneously ʿAbd al-Maddān).

[5] I.e. heralding rain!

[6] Arabic 'wa-al-qawm lā yuṭīʿūna li-mulk al-Ghuzz [i.e. the Ayyubids] wa-lā li-salāṭīn al-ʿArab'.

[7] The names of both are omitted without a lacuna.

[8] Begins 2 January 1226. The whole passage is corrupt and the translation tentative.

[211] *Description of Bi'r al-Ṣufr.*[1] The Commander of the Faithful ʿUmar b. al-Khaṭṭāb[2] – God be pleased with him – ordered a well to be dug in one of the regions of Qarqar which was very deep and wide and that it be cased with coated brass like baked brick and with some lead cast in among it. So the well was built as mentioned above and it remains as it is. Another version is that it was built by a prominent Arab before Islam. After a long time, it became effaced and hidden. The Commander of the Faithful ʿUmar b. al-Khaṭṭāb – God be pleased with him – again gave orders for its rebuilding, so it remained as mentioned above. The well is indeed a wonder!

Description of Najrān in Tihāmah.[3] From Ḥaraḍ to Qarār three parasangs.[4] To Najrān two parasangs, a simple village whose inhabitants live in anxiety, unlike others. They are grief-stricken, repressing their rage and reciting stories.[5] To al-Ḥāwah three parasangs.[6] To Ḥadab four parasangs.[7]

If someone asks how one can distinguish between the two names [of Najrān], I reply that this one is a simple village in Tihāmat al-Yaman, in ruins, whereas the other is an extensive and broad province, flourishing and [stretching] from the north of Najd al-Yaman and the seat of its rule. One is the young slave, the other the sultan; one is the ball, the other the playing field! The province of Najrān is called Wādī Sawḥān.[8]

Ibn al-Mujāwir said: What illustrates that this province was built by the Persians is that there is a building of Bahman b. Isfandiyār which is a citadel in the regions of al-Madāʾin called Dār Rayḥān.[9] There is no doubt that it is he who built this wadi and it was given the same name mentioned above in the regions of al-Madāʾin, Sawḥān. Ramīm b. Jābir has recited the following about it:

[212] I compare it to a bow of the *shiryān* tree,[10] cut down,
in that the archer finds pleasure in it and makes it sweet.
I compare it to a virgin filly with anklets,
as I ride her out among kings on a day of battle.
I compare it to a small valley[11] where the breeze inclines.
Is the fine rain from above it, as the river gives it to drink?

There is also Wādī al-ʿAlāʾim.[12] As one of them said, 'In Najrān are Wādīs al-Khasf and al-ʿAlāʾim.' Ibn al-Mujāwir said: The name al-Khasf is simply derived from [the

[1] Literally 'well of brass'.

[2] The second Orthodox caliph, reg. 13–23/634–44.

[3] Unidentified.

[4] Unidentified.

[5] A possibly corrupt passage: *wa-yaskunu ahlū-hā fī ighṣāṣ bi-ʿaks baʿḍ wa-hum fī al-taghaṣṣuṣ yatajarraʿūna al-ghuṣaṣ wa-yaqirrūna al-qiṣaṣ.*

[6] Unidentified.

[7] Unidentified.

[8] Unidentified.

[9] This ancient Iranian king, the Kaysinian father of Sāsān, is not associated elsewhere with al-Madāʾin, nor can I trace a building of this name connected to the king or to the place. Perhaps Ibn al-Mujāwir is thinking of Khusrau I Anūshirvān (Le Strange, *Lands*, pp. 33–5, 208, 337; *CHIr*, III(1), p. 377; III(2), p. 710 [where there is mention of Khusrau's palace in Ctesiphon]; *EIr*, 'Bahman (son of Estandīār)').

[10] *Sharyān* or *shiryān* is *Grewia populifolia* Vahl., a mountain tree with a sweet yellow berry, used for making bows (Aṣmaʿī, *al-Nabāt*, p. 24; Dimyāṭī, *Muʿjam*, p. 81; Hepper and Friis, *Plants*, p. 236).

[11] Arabic *jawnah* (Dozy, *Supplément*, I, p. 236).

[12] Unidentified.

word for] fertility.[1] By this he meant Wādī al-Rifā'[2] where the wind of the *ṭarf* star[3] blows for a period of twelve nights and destroys the agriculture and the vines. A certain bedouin recites as follows about it:

> Najrān survived during the *ṭarf* and still
> in Baḥrān[4] there are a dome and thrones.

One of them recites as follows by Ramīm b. Jābir:

> Many a night during the nights of the *ṭarf*, dark,
> black and wintry[5] have I spent, going on all night!

Section. Abū Bakr [Ibn al-Mujāwir][6] said: Baḥrān is simply derived from people saying, 'I split[7] the she-camel's ears,' with the meaning of 'cutting' her ears. The word *baḥīrah* means 'she-camel with split ears'.[8] There is also what God – He is ever almighty – has said,[9] 'God has not made anything of a *baḥīrah*, nor the mother of a *baḥīrah*',[10] which is a she-camel which has produced ten offspring left alone to pasture at will.[11] They are not ridden, nor is their fur clipped, 'nor a *waṣīlah*',[12] which is an ewe when she has produced six offspring, two she-kids by two she-kids, and which has brought forth [213] for the seventh time a she-kid and a billy kid. It is said that she has 'joined'[13] her brother. They milk her milk for men [only], to the exclusion of women. And 'nor a *ḥāmin*',[14] a stallion camel whose own offspring has produced his offspring, so he is not ridden, nor his fur clipped, and he is allowed to pasture at will. God knows best.

A word on the disappearance of the rule of the family of Ḥamzah and its happening to B. al-Hādī ...[15]

Section. A stallion camel with pustules is said to be *'ārr*.[16] His treatment, when some part is paining him, or he is in rut or has some disease which requires cauterization, is that

[1] Arabic *khiṣb*.

[2] Unidentified.

[3] The name of two stars according to Lane (V, p. 1843), the two eyes of Leo and one of the Mansions of the Moon. See also Varisco, *Agriculture*, *passim*, e.g. pp. 25, 29, 103, 110.

[4] This must be another name for Najrān, not just a misreading (see next section), though not mentioned in the sources at my disposal.

[5] Arabic *laylah jumādiyyah*, the latter derived from the Jumādā months (Lane, *Lexicon*, II, p. 452; Varisco, *Agriculture*, pp. 118–19, 124).

[6] This is the only occasion in the whole of the text on which what is presumably Ibn al-Mujāwir's given name is used by him.

[7] Arabic *baḥartu* (Lane, *Lexicon*, I, pp. 156–7).

[8] Arabic *baḥīrah* (ibid.).

[9] Quran 5:103.

[10] Arabic *sā'ibah* (Lane, *Lexicon*, I, p. 157).

[11] Arabic *suyyibat*.

[12] See Kazimirski, *Dictionnaire*, II, p. 1550.

[13] Arabic *waṣalat*.

[14] Arabic *ḥāmin* (Lane, *Lexicon*, II, p. 652).

[15] This is a passage abruptly abandoned in all the MSS. It presumably concerns a family of the Zaydīs imams, al-Hādī being the first (284–98/897–911), and Ḥamzah may be the father of 'Abdallāh, the imam between 583–614/1187–1217.

[16] The text actually has *'urr* which is the disease itself. *'Arr* would be incorrect here, since its meaning is 'mange', a disease not treated with cauterization (Lane, *Lexicon*, V, p. 1990).

another [healthy] stallion is taken, cauterized upwind and the one with pustules will have been placed in line downwind, with the result that the smell of cauterization burning will reach the one with pustules. Then he will recover from his disease and become well. Al-Nābighah has recited as follows:[1]

> You charged me with the offence of [another] man and left him
> like the one with pustules, while another is cauterized as he pastures.

Why is butter not made from the milk of camels? I was informed as follows by Fāṭimah, daughter of ʿAlī b. Masʿūd:[2] I asked a Yemeni woman who had lots of camels[3] about this and her reply was that the ancients used to extract butter from camel's milk, but then they announced that they would abandon this practice. [This was] because a woman quarrelled with her son, the son took a sling[4] and hurled a stone in the direction of his mother. She had in her hand a ball of camel-milk butter. She hit her son with it and the rock-hard ball of butter fell upon a vital part of the lad's body and he died. When this happened, the Arab shaykhs announced [214] among their tribes that the churning of camel milk [for butter] was to be abandoned altogether. They added, 'We still do not follow this practice.'

A wise man has said: If Zayd greases his hair with camel oil, nothing can pull it out. Hair is only clean, when it is shaved [close], since, [when it is not], it is very thick.

Ṭarīq al-Raḍrāḍ.[5] Ṭarīq al-Raḍrāḍ ran from Najrān[6] to Basra, the distance between the two towns being seven days. At the end of each parasang of the road a stone has been erected, made of baked brick and gypsum. It was built by ʿAmr b. Maʿdī Karib al-Zubaydī. More accurately, it was one of the constructions of al-Nuʿmān b. al-Mundhir,[7] when he left the Yemen making for Iraq. [Even] more accurately it was built by Sayf b. Dhī Yazan, when he left in the direction of Iraq. He asked for the assistance of[8] Khusrau b. Kavād b. Yazdagird b. Hurmuz, a ruler of the Persians. The most accurate version of the story is that it was built by pre-Islamic Arabs, when they settled the land of Najd, because in those areas they were like worms and mosquitoes!

The watering places in the different locations were dug in ancient times. The builders constructed large buildings from the gate of Ṣanʿāʾ to Iraq, one on the edge of [the territory of] another. When there was fear or joy in the Yemen, [lamps] were lit on

[1] Al-Nābighah al-Dhubyānī, Ziyād b. Muʿāwiyah, pre-Islamic poet, friend and client of the Lakhmid king of al-Ḥīrah, al-Nuʿmān b. al-Mundhir, during the latter half of the century before Islam. The late flowering of his poetic talent provided the nickname *nābighah*, 'gushing forth with vigour and in abundance' (Lane, *Lexicon*, V, p. 1990; Nicholson, *Literary History*, p. 122–3; Tayib, 'Pre-Islamic Poetry', pp. 30, 38, 44, 47, 49, 57, 103 [where this line is translated], 110; *EI*, 'al-Nābighah al-Dhubyānī').

[2] If Ibn al-Mujāwir's name is Abū Bakr b. Muḥammad b. Masʿūd, this might well be his cousin (Smith, 'Eastern Connection', p. 80).

[3] Reading with Löfgren *muʿabbalah*.

[4] Arabic *khadhf* for *mikhdhafah* (Lane, *Lexicon*, II, p. 713).

[5] I.e. 'crushed pebbles', 'hard stones' (Lane, *Lexicon*, III, 1095).

[6] I.e. the well-known Najrān, now situated just N of the Saudi-Yemeni border.

[7] Al-Nuʿmān III, the last of the famous Christian Lakhmid kings (AD 554–602) (Shahîd, *Martyrs*, p. 269, 271–2; *EI*, 'al-Nuʿmān (III) b. al-Mundhir').

[8] The translation follows the text *wa-istanjada bi-Kisrā* …, although I am forced to wonder if we should read *wa-istajadda Kisrā* …, 'It was renovated by Khusrau …'.

the very top of each building and they could see [a light] in a lamp[1] at the top of each building, a wonderful sign.[2] They could see the same thing in the fortress of Qarn al-Jund,[3] through which one entered Najd. Also in Najd a building had been built near Qaṣr Waliʿān[4] and in al-Ṣaʿīd[5] in the regions of Ṣaʿdah. A light was lit in Waliʿān which could be seen in a building above al-Khabt,[6] through which one [also] entered Najd. Another building was built near to yet another in the regions of Iraq. So when [215] morning came, news, good or evil, of benefit or harm, would be with the Iraqis. As the poet has recited:

> The voice crying out [with the news] reaches Iraq in one day
> and the sudden raider makes good progress in the period of one night.

The closure of Ṭarīq al-Raḍrāḍ. I was informed as follows by Muḥammad b. Salāmah b. Muḥammad b. Ḥajjāj:[7] A bedouin woman set off – it is also said it was the daughter of ʿAmr b. Maʿdī Karib – riding a she-ass and carrying two ghee-skins,[8] i.e. two vessels.[9] While she was going through the desert, she came upon a wayfarer who tried to seduce her. However, she refused to do what he wanted. He said to her, 'If this is the case, then give me some of your ghee.' She replied, 'You are welcome; have a drink.' She got the two vessels down and opened the top of one of them. The man drank from it, but insisted that it was not good ghee. She opened the second for him and he drank what he wanted. Then he told her to take hold and she took the two pots. Then he exposed her from behind and had sexual intercourse with her, she all the time afraid that she would allow the butter to spill over![10] Thus they continued until he had finished with her. She tied up the top of the two skins, put them up on the she-ass and went about her work. He also went on his way and finished his journey.

Her father, ʿAmr b. Maʿdī Karib – it is also said it was her brother – learned what had happened. He came and filled in the wells and demolished the milestones. He also destroyed the buildings to stop traffic along the road. When the wells became choked up and the sand dispersed, the remains [of the wells only] appeared [on the surface]. The road closed. It was also known as Dhāt al-Niḥyayn [she of the two ghee-skins], i.e. the woman with the two vessels. God knows best and is most wise.

[216] *Al-Fayḍ*.[11] This is sand like white wheat flour[12] on this side of the regions of al-Tanʿīm[13] near to the high mountains of the Yemen. No one can cross al-Tanʿīm because

[1] Reading *fānūs* with Löfgren.

[2] Reading *tafʿīl ʿajīb* with Löfgren.

[3] Unidentified.

[4] There is a mountain of this name 20 km N of Ṣaʿdah (Maqḥafī, *Muʿjam*, p. 702, with no vocalization). The vocalization is that of Löfgren in the text.

[5] An extensive fertile agricultural area S of Ṣaʿdah (Maqḥafī, *Muʿjam*, p. 382).

[6] Unidentified.

[7] This anecdote is told in its true context above (p. 212, n. 1), where the woman is named Dhāt al-Niḥyayn.

[8] Arabic *niḥy*, strictly speaking a skin used for churning butter.

[9] Arabic *ḥarf*, strictly speaking a clay vessel.

[10] Arabic *yatabaddadu* (Dozy, *Supplément*, I, p. 55).

[11] The place is marked by Farsi (*National Guide*, map C11) about 75 km NW of Najrān. The word means any river full of water, here used figuratively, a river of sand.

[12] Arabic *daqīq al-samīdh*.

[13] Unidentified.

it is too high. Walking through this sand takes a whole month, but it is also said that it takes only some days. It is what is called accumulated sand and this is the sand which is on the edge of Ṭarīq al-Raḍrāḍ – it cut the road after [previously] protecting it. It is said that Sayf b. Dhī Yazan went along it to Iraq and returned to the Yemen with Persian troops on the edge of it, the journey between these two provinces being seven days, or alternatively ten days, as we have mentioned above.

There is another version of the story that ʿAmr b. Maʿdī Karib was beyond the desert with his womenfolk.[1] When he filled in the wells, the dust poured down and their remains were covered up. The ruler of Ṣaʿdah came at the head of a large group of men after he had destroyed it – its destruction has been mentioned above. When the town fell into ruin, the people built in the exact spot of the ruins, or, it is said, near to it. The most accurate version is that there was building in the middle of the ruins and they said that they were abandoning the outskirts. It is said that the people were only prepared for war by a bedouin from Dhāt al-Akīk and Dhāt al-Ḥarmal.[2] On this subject, ʿAntarah used to recite as follows:

> It was a long stay at the remains of the abode
> between al-Akīk and Dhāt al-Ḥarmal.

When the bedouin was at his wit's end and the earth poured down into their houses, he left for the Hejaz and was killed at the hand of the Commander of the Faithful ʿAlī b. Abī Ṭālib – God honour him.

It is said that a man only moves from where he is for four reasons: because of sustenance of which he can have his full share; because of a death which might make it necessary; because of some good fortune which comes to him; and because of some misfortune which overwhelms him.

I was informed as follows by Hishām b. Masʿūd al-Najrānī in the residence of the amir: [217] This road leads to Kufa – or to Basra. The Yemenis used to travel along it twice a year with their donkeys, bearing hides to one of these two towns. I asked what places they passed through and he replied al-Yamāmah, al-Ḥasā'[3] and Basra. I asked him when he came to know that it was in use and he replied that it was in the year 520.[4]

The following has been recited:

> When I realized my neglect [and that I was] without direction,
> and that the sharpness of my blade was impaired,
> I gave my obedience to you against my will,
> so that God might accomplish something which was to be done.

Someone else recited as follows:

[1] Arabic *ḥuʿun*, plur. of *ḥaʿīnah*.

[2] Unidentified.

[3] For al-Aḥsā', which is the plur. of *ḥisy*, 'water which the earth imbibes from sand [above it]', 'small quantity of water' (Lane, *Lexicon*, II, pp. 572–3). Originally it was a famous town in al-Baḥrayn, i.e. the eastern coastal strip of Arabia from the Qaṭar peninsula N in the direction of Kuwait (Yāqūt, *Muʿjam*, I, p. 112). A small town still exists a few miles to the SE of the large town of al-Hufūf and it also gives its name to the area of eastern Saudi Arabia opposite the island of Bahrain (Farsi, *National Guide*, map A2).

[4] Begins 27 January 1126.

I asked people about complete friendship,
but they said there was no way to achieve it.
Hold fast to your love of a freeman, if you have it,
for a freeman is rare in this lower world.

Description of the area of Najd. Najd is a high land, with pleasant hills, good, pure earth,[1] with a moderate climate, agreeable to those who live there and to those who enter it. The ancients built forty palaces there, altogether, or more accurately, near one to the other. In Iraq, they are called the palaces of Najd. By the local people they are called al-Sakīt, and, another version, Maʿāṣim.[2] They were built in stone and gypsum, on hills and solid, belonging to al-Rabīʿ b. Zuhayr,[3] ʿAmr b. Maʿdī Karib and ʿAntar b. ʿAmr b. Shaddād.

My informant told me as follows: I used to travel around the desert of Najd with the bedouins and we would find arak trees and wells cased with stones and gypsum and into some buildings were put planks of teak. We used to find vines bearing grapes of different varieties and date palms bearing *khalāl* dates,[4] also figs, peaches, plums and all kinds of fruits. There can be no doubt that this [218] province was flourishing and cultivated areas thrived there on well irrigation. All this was found in the land of Najd and the close proximity, as we have mentioned. God – He is ever mighty and glorious – is most wise.

Description of the water of al-Habāʾah.[5] Originally, according to what my informant has mentioned, al-Habāʾah was a long, wide, deep pool. No one can find the bottom of it because the flood flows so strongly, pouring down from the huge, high mountains. Someone recited as follows about it:

O mountains of the north, what lofty peaks!
My ewes are barren;[6] God put you to the test!

The water flows from the pool into a wadi as far as the land and, because it flows so vehemently together with its long range, it digs out the earth as far as the houses. Many floods flow into it and it is filled with water, thus becoming a lake never lacking in water. If the bedouins were to ladle out from it, irrigate and ask that their wealth and livestock be watered from it, the water would [still] not be lacking and not one finger's measure [of difference] would be noticed.

[1] Arabic *ḥurrat al-arḍ* (Lane, *Lexicon*, II, p. 538, *arḍ ḥurrah*, 'land in which is no salt earth').

[2] Literally 'defended places'.

[3] Unidentified, but presumably an ancient pre-Islamic figure and I wonder if Ibn al-Mujāwir means Qays b. Zuhayr (see p. 225, n. 1 below).

[4] Lane, *Lexicon* (II, p. 780) says that they are in a state in which they are termed *balaḥ*. This latter is the penultimate stage in the ripening process, that before the final stage termed *busr*. The fresh ripe date is called *ruṭab* (Varisco, *Agriculture*, p. 193; Kazimirski, *Dictionnaire*, I, p. 608). DMV confirms to me that the above is correct, although the final stage seems to differ in terminology. I am very grateful too to him for the following references: Sijistānī, *Nakhl*, p. 113; Saʿīdān, *Mawsūʿah*, I, p. 518; *Western Arabia*, pp. 488–9.

[5] Yāqūt (*Muʿjam*, V, p. 389) does not explain where this place is, but he tells us that it is in Ghaṭafān territory where Ḥudhayfah and Ḥamal were killed by Qays. He also quotes this and other poetry concerning the incident.

[6] Arabic *qawṭ*, plur. *aqwāṭ*, 'troupeau de brebis' (Kazimirski, *Dictionnaire*, II, p. 835) and *maḥl*, 'stérilité' (Kazimirski, *Dictionnaire*, II, p. 1069).

Qays b. Zuhayr b. Jadhīmah b. Abī Sufyān killed his kinsmen here.[1] He came to them and found them swimming, so he put them to the sword, saying, 'The water of al-Habā'ah has bequeathed me humility. May I depart oppressing or oppressed!' He also recited as follows:

> I cured my soul of Ḥamal b. Badr
> and my sword has cured me of Ḥudhayfah.
> If through them I have cured my thirst for revenge,
> yet I have through them only cut off my own fingers!

There it was where ʿAntar b. Zabībah[2] killed forty prominent Arab horsemen. This water is the assembly place for the tribes and their dissensions. In these places ʿAntar b. Zabībah, Qays b. Zuhayr, ʿAmr b. Maʿdī Karib and other Arab leaders, shaykhs and heads live.

My informant has reported as follows: [219] We find in the desert of Najd, where there is no building and no settlement, graves have been built in baked brick and gypsum, thousands of them. People nowadays do not know to whom they belong. I have been informed as follows by Muḥammad b. Abī Ḥāmid who said that the poet, Abū Bakr, had told him that he read the following on a grave:

> Death brought me forth from my residence,
> for the earth is where I lie after having enjoyed a pleasant life.
> What a fine man who has seen my grave and it made him sad
> and who was in fear of what vicissitudes Fate would bring him!
> This is the destiny of those in this lower world; if they assemble
> therein, the uncertainty of delay deceives them.
> I ask God's forgiveness against my willfulness and error
> and ask Him for pardon on the day I stand before Him for His judgement.

Of the palaces is Ḥajar ʿAbdallāh,[3] a palace built on a high hill in stone and gypsum and baked bricks and gypsum. After that is the palace of ʿAntar, built in stone and gypsum and baked brick and gypsum, a solid, well made structure, and then Bi'r al-ʿĀṣimiyyah.[4]

A description of Bi'r al-ʿĀṣimiyyah. It was built on twenty-four columns, six columns opposite another six, and square.[5] It was cased on the outside with marble, the length of each slab twenty cubits, and gypsum, in steps, the way down to it being by a flight of stairs. From the time it was built until now,[6] it has not dried up, nor has a bottom been discovered. It is an amazing construction, the heart of the regions of ...[7] Then there is

[1] A chief of ʿAbs of Ghaṭafān. 'His kinsmen' were Ḥudhayfah and Ḥamal of Dhubyān of Ghaṭafān. The story of the feud and the killings is told in Nicholson, *Literary History*, pp. 60–61 and there is also a translation in verse of the poetry found there.

[2] See p. 54, n. 9 above.

[3] Unidentified.

[4] Unidentified.

[5] Six columns opposite another six would give 22 in all in a square structure. It is difficult to imagine exactly how this well structure would look.

[6] Reading with the L MS *al-ān*, rather than *hādhih al-ghāyah*.

[7] ?.?.lāt, perhaps for Tathlīth? See p. 266, n. 1 below and Farsi, *National Guide*, map 24.

the ruined town of al-Hujayrah.[1] The castle in its midst remained inhabited with people living in it and a well was dug also in the middle from which the Arabs watered their camels and their riding camels.

To the east of al-ʿĀṣimiyyah is Qaṣr al-Ḍabyah.[2] There are date palms [220] all around the castles, [which were] for the purpose of dwelling and also to store their goods, ghee and dried curd, whenever a flood reached them. The place has the following appearance and God knows best. [plan – see Fig. 10]

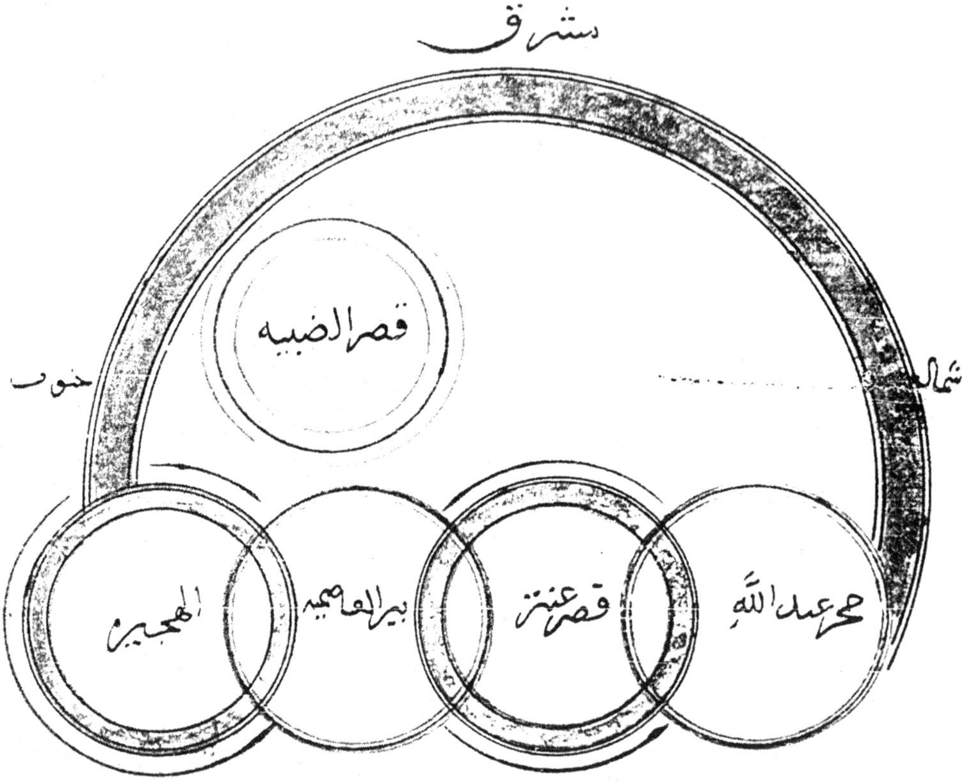

Figure 10. Plan of Biʾr al-ʿĀṣimiyyah (I MS, f. 88a, text, p. 220, tabula X)
Three points of the compass are marked: E at the top, N on the right and S on the left. Biʾr al-ʿĀṣimiyyah is represented by the second circle from the left and the other circles are the castles around it from right to left: Ḥajar ʿAbdallāh, ʿAntar and (on the left of Biʾr al-ʿĀṣimiyyah) al-Hujayrah. The circle made up of three concentric rings due E of Biʾr al-ʿĀṣimiyyah represents the castle of al-Ḍabyah.

The wadis of Najd. Al-Ḥasā, al-Yamāmah and below it al-Akīk and Dhāt al-Ḥarmal, these places are wadis which can be looked down on. Also al-ʿAwāhil, al-ʿUwayhil …,[3] Sahl,

[1] Al-Hamdānī mentions al-Hujayrah on several occasions (*Ṣifah*, pp. 27, 51, 116, 119, 186, 189) often in association with Tathlīth and clearly between Najrān and Bīshah. This is, I think, the correct reading here rather than al-Hijrah.

[2] For al-Ẓabyah, rather than al-Ṣabiyyah, although it is unidentified.

[3] Unidentified. The dots represent a second word, ḥ.ḥ.mn.

Jāsh and ʿIshrūn,[1] the sand between Najrān and al-Hujayrah and a place[2] between al-Hujayrah and Mecca. In the rainy season, the wadis and the floods flow. In a period of little rain, a man can dig with his hands and the water will gush out. He can drink [221] and water his riding camels, whilst everyone seeks his own land and his own desert area during the misfortunes of famine.[3] On this subject, the following is recited:

> Were it not for her curing him wearing the garb of our time
> and bearing misfortunes, he who comes would be hunted down.

Another has recited as follows:[4]

> Were it not for hardship, everyone would be master over [such] liberality
> [as] makes poor, with bravery [in battle] the [only real] killer.

These ten wadis flow through the desert of Najd when it rains and as they come to an end reach the sea.

Generosity. A wise man said: Generosity is a dinar and twenty carats[5] to the Arabs and four carats throughout the rest of the world. Miserliness is a dinar and twenty carats[6] among the Byzantines (and it is also said, among the Indians), or more accurately among the North Africans, and four carats throughout the rest of the world.

It is said that the first person to feed [the poor] was Abraham the Friend – peace be upon him – and this was his practice. It is also said that there were three, 'those of the Heights':[7] Abū Ṭālib because he raised the Prophet – God bless him and grant him peace,[8] Anūshirvān because he was just[9] and Ḥātim because he was generous.[10]

It is said that a certain Arab began to feed [the poor], wanting to be the equal of Ḥātim in his own time. A poor man came to him, asking for something. So he gave him what he had asked for. The beggar returned to him, and a third time, and a fourth and a fifth. So the man claiming [to be like Ḥātim] said, 'Leave me alone, my friend; you are lacking in good faith and very rude. This is the fifth or sixth time you've come!' The beggar replied, 'If he is Ḥātim, he will build a castle and open up four hundred windows in it. Indeed, I used to enter [222] every window every day, four hundred, [in Ḥātim's

[1] All unidentified.

[2] Reading *mawḍiʿ* with the L MS, or a place called W.ḍ.ʿ.

[3] Arabic *bi-razāyā al-maḥlah*. The following line of poetry may be corrupt and I translate very tentatively.

[4] I translate this difficult line which is out of context tentatively.

[5] I have translated thus, as in the following line, although the text has no '*wa-*'. See following note.

[6] It is Löfgren who adds plausibly *wa-* … to *ʿishrūna qīrāṭan*, thus giving the meaning 'and 24 carats'. See previous note.

[7] *Aṣḥāb al-aʿrāf*. See Quran 7:46, 'On the heights are men who know each one by their sign.' The word *aʿrāf* which gives its name to this chapter of the Quran is used of the wall which divides paradise from hell (Lane, *Lexicon*, V, p. 2015; Penrice, *Dictionary*, p. 96).

[8] The father of ʿAlī b. Abī Ṭālib and paternal uncle of Muḥammad who, after the death of ʿAbd al-Muṭṭalib, the Prophet's grandfather, took Muḥammad into his care. Muḥammad's father, ʿAbdallāh, had died probably before Muḥammad was born (Guillaume, *Life*, p. 79; Watt, *Mecca*, pp. 32–3).

[9] I.e. Khusrau I, son of Kavād, the Sasanian king, reg. AD 531–78 (*CHIr*, III(1), pp. 153, 600ff.). See n. 2002 above.

[10] A legendary pre-Islamic figure who personifies generosity and hospitality in Arab tradition. The story of his slaughtering of all his father's camels in order to give hospitality to complete strangers appears in Iṣfahānī, *Aghānī* (XVI, p. 100) and is translated by Nicholson (*Literary History*, pp. 85–6).

castle], without any hindrance. I was among the first like [one of] his retinue.'[1] The following was recited:

> Jamīl has given generously time after time;
> generosity is nought but a habit to Jamīl.

When the man claiming [to be like Ḥātim] heard what the beggar said, he declared that he would stop rendering[2] with gypsum in his building.

When Ḥātim of Ṭayy' put provisions in front of his guests and there was something left over, he would not take it back to his encampment, but he would leave it where it was. He recited as follows:

> We went on our way, but left our provisions behind us on the ground;
> a share of the provisions of the generous belongs to the birds.

The desert Arabs always eat lunch around noon and dinner around midnight. They will only delay their lunch and their dinner for a guest who comes to them. Whenever a caravan arrives at the encampment of Arabs, the people go out to the caravan and each one takes hold of three or four persons of those in the caravan. It is the same for those women, old women and children in the tent. But all those who are less mobile shout out at the top of their voices, '[Come] to me, you worthy Arabs – God bless you', indicating with their hand the person concerned. When someone of high standing comes to them, a camel is slaughtered for him. If it is a wayfarer, an ewe is slaughtered for him. If it is a group and the hospitality is to be for just one of the people, the owner of the tent puts in front of the person the brisket and rump [of the ewe], indicating to those who have arrived that the invitation is for one man and the rest are not invited and will not attend. The owner of the tent takes a loaf which he breaks into three or four pieces, throwing it in front of the person for whom the invitation is meant. He boils the meat in salt water and crumbles bread for the *tharīd*,[3] [223] over which he pours a large helping of ghee. He soaks the meat in gravy and scatters all the meat over the *tharīd*. This is a speciality of the Arabs which they call *'arabiyyah*.[4]

Section. A group of poets alighted at a bedouin in the waterless desert and he butchered one of his stallion camels for them. That night he entertained them. When they were all contently engaged in conversation, the poets asked the bedouin, 'Where do you come from? How many is your family? How much wealth do you have?' The bedouin replied to them, 'I am a stranger, camped in this place. My only family is an old woman and I have no wealth apart from the camel which I slaughtered for you.' The following was recited:[5]

> Generosity is my natural inclination, but I have no wealth;
> what else can one do who manages his food well?
> Follow my example[6] until the time of ease comes, a debt which I bear, while I [also] have hopes in the [future] unknown.[7]

[1] Arabic *sāqah*.
[2] The *assasa* of the text makes no sense here. With OL, I read *aṣṣaṣa*, literally 'make solid'.
[3] I take the L MS reading, *yathrudu*, to be better here. The text has *yattaridu*. For *tharīd*, see Serjeant, *Misers*, p. 47, n. 221.
[4] Ibn al-Mujāwir thus explains this adaptation of *tharīd* to his reader.
[5] The poet is unidentified.
[6] Arabic *fa-hā-ka khaṭṭī* (Wright, *Grammar*, I, p. 296).
[7] Arabic 'daynan 'alay-ya wa-lī fī al-ghaybi āmālu'.

A story. On the authority of Abū ʿAmr al-Dimashqī there is the following: We set off for Mecca with Abū ʿAbdallāh Ibn al-Jalāl, but we found nothing [on the way] to eat. So we went up to an encampment in the desert and there was there a bedouin woman who had an ewe. We asked her how much she wanted for the ewe and she replied, 'Fifty dirhams'. We said to her, 'Do us a favour!' so she replied, 'Five dirhams.' 'You're driving us away!',[1] we exclaimed, but she replied, 'No, indeed! You asked me to do you a favour. If it had been at all possible, I wouldn't have charged anything!' Abū ʿAbdallāh Ibn al-Jalāl intervened [and addressing the group], said, 'What [224] do you have?' They admitted they had six hundred dirhams. 'Give them to her and leave the ewe with her!', he said. We never made a better journey than this! God knows best.

Protection arrangements[2] *among the Arabs.* [In the case] when an Arab apprehends a robber, or a prisoner,[3] or anyone who has committed murder, if the prisoner eats dates or meat in the house of his captor, he will kill him after two days and two nights, or, alternatively, after three days, or after seven days. If he eats bread, he will kill him after two days and one night, or two days and two nights, or after seven days. If he drinks water in his house, it will be after one day, or after one hour. If he drinks milk, he is immune from being killed until after three days with the same number of nights. It is said that survival lies in the prisoner's protection arrangement until each one leaves his captor. Once his captor has offered him hospitality, the former's [full] rights no longer exist and the latter is safe from anything which he does not like.

It has been asked why this is. The reply is that meat remains in one's stomach for two days and two nights, while bread remains one day and one night and water one day. Being safe from punishment can mean something which is invisible and a sense of honour does not demand that you kill someone when your bread is still in his stomach.

Section. Diʿbil b. ʿAlī al-Khuzāʿī had satirized al-Muṭṭalib b. ʿUbayd Allāh al-Khuzāʿī[4] and the two met up on the road. The latter said, 'Come to my home with me.' So he went with him. When Diʿbil entered, al-Muṭṭalib said to him, 'I shall certainly kill you in an evil manner!' Diʿbil replied, 'Do not kill me while I am hungry. Give me a good meal and then do what you will. You will find me, God willing, "one of the patient".'[5] Al-Muṭṭalib said to him, 'You have found a good way out! If I feed you, I shall have to spare your life; and if I do not feed you, I shall be a real miser!' Diʿbil replied, 'Indeed, [225] may I never speak ill of you again!' So al-Muṭṭalib let him go and gave him a good reward.

If anyone whose blood can be spilt bites the hem of a woman or child, [punishment for] the transgression of the guilty man is unlawful to the one seeking to kill him. When anyone whose blood can be spilt flees to someone's house, he will ask for his protection and if the owner of the house pardons him for what passed between them ...[6]

[1] Arabic *tanharīna, tanharīna*!

[2] Arabic *dhimām*, plur. of *dhimmah*.

[3] Arabic *rabīṭ* (Dozy, *Supplément*, I, p. 502).

[4] For Diʿbil, see p. 172, n. 3 above. His satire of al-Muṭṭalib can be found in Iṣfahānī (*Aghānī*, XVIII, pp. 44, 49). Diʿbil also wrote an elegy on his death (Iṣfahānī, *Aghānī*, XVIII, p. 34).

[5] Quran 37:102.

[6] There is a lacuna in the text, not shown in the MSS.

There is the story that some people asked for protection from Ḥujr b. Muhalhil. He gave them protection against the elements and built a wall of stone and gypsum for them, setting up leather awnings, not allowing them to be exposed to the wind.

Section. A water carrier [once] went down a well on the road to Mecca, for water could [not] be taken[1] from it by bucket because there was so little in it. The pilgrims moved off unaware [that he was still down the well]. The water carrier remained where he was for three days and three nights. At the end of this period of time, an Arab came along, put his bucket down and saw the water carrier at the bottom. [The former] drew the water, watered his horse and drank. He pulled the water carrier up from the well and put him behind him on his horse. He took him a short distance and arrived at some desert lowland where there was none of God's creatures except one lone encampment, that is a hair tent belonging to him. In the tent there was one woman, the man's wife. She got up and washed the hands and feet of the water carrier with hot water and she warmed him up. The water carrier slept and rested; he woke up to find a hot meal and he ate his supper. He ate his fill and the owner of the tent and his wife slept until morning. Then the owner of the tent went out, saddled, bridled, then mounted his horse and went off to hunt. The water carrier remained with the woman who was concerned about his condition and looked after him until he recovered and felt well. When his circulation was flowing as normal, he opened his eyes. At sunset, the owner of the tent returned [226] and brought before him what God – praise to Him – had provided in the way of game for a meal. They both ate together.[2] The water carrier remained as he was for three days and on the fourth ate his fill, felt better and took his rest. He gazed at the woman and found her a pleasing image. Despite his weakness, he felt strong enough[3] in this situation to try to seduce her on different occasions, but she stopped him, though he did not give up. No matter how hard he tried, she resisted to the end.[4] When the chaste wife saw the real truth [that he would not give up], she seized him, tying him up around his shoulders near to a dog which she had.

> Among [women] is she who is equal to eighty young she-camels;
> among them is she who is equal to a stallion camel's hobble rope;
> Among them too is she – may God not blanch her face –
> who, when she sits with a visiting male, is still among women.[5]

When her husband returned, he could see that the situation had changed. He got up, went over to him and untied his bonds. He brought him what there was [to eat]. But he continued to try to seduce her for three consecutive days, while she treated him with honour.[6]

[1] The text reads 'yubraḥu min-h al-māʾ fī al-dilāʾ'. Löfgren in his apparatus suggests *y.n.z.ḥ*, though it is my feeling that the text is sound and perfect sense is achieved with the addition of a negative.

[2] The text reads 'wa-aḥḍara … ṭabkhan aw aklan jamīʿan'. I prefer '… ṭabkhan wa-akalā jamīʿan'.

[3] Arabic *fa-ṭālat yadu-h* (Dozy, *Supplément*, II, p. 72, 'il devint puissant').

[4] Arabic perhaps 'fa-qāma maʿa-hā bi-al-kulliyyah wa-qāmat maʿa-h bi-al-maniyyah'. Löfgren wishes to read *bi-al-munyah*.

[5] A difficult piece quoted out of context which I translate tentatively. I use 'visiting male' for the Arabic *zīr* (Lane, *Lexicon*, III, p. 1269).

[6] Text *wa-tafʿalu bi-h al-dast*.

Ibn al-Mujāwir said: There is no doubt that this woman's star sign was Virgo. As Abū al-Rayḥān Muḥammad b. Aḥmad al-Bīrūnī has stated in his *Kitāb al-Tafhīm fī 'ilm al-tanjīm*:[1] [Those under] Aries, Taurus, Leo, Capricorn and Pisces[2] all lust after sexual intercourse. Those under Libra and Sagittarius have a little of that. In women's matters, those under Taurus, Leo, Scorpio and Aquarius show signs of chastity, while those under Aries, Cancer and Libra show signs of being corrupt. Those under Gemini, Virgo and Pisces take the middle ground among them. Those under Virgo are the most chaste.

When things got out of control,[3] the bedouin asked the water carrier where he wanted him to take him. 'To Kufa', he replied. So he saddled his horse,[4] equipped himself and mounted, [227] placing the water carrier behind him in the saddle. He journeyed with him for two days and one night until he looked over high ground [above] Kufa. When he had set the water carrier down from his horse, each one bade the other farewell. Then the bedouin said, 'Please don't tell anyone what has happened and don't tell me further what took place – God prepare a good reward for you.' As has been recited:

> Do not destroy a good deed; you will destroy it,
> if you choose a man who commits errors and transgressions.
> If you were to water a thorn with rose water ...
> ... and the carob tree bears fruit.[5]

Someone else recited as follows:

> A noble man is not one who, when his friend slips,
> divulges what he knew of his secrets.
> A noble man is one whose friendship endures
> and who keeps a secret, whether his friend acts with purity of mind, or does wrong.

Yet another recited as follows:

> Do not keep company with a fool, for he
> will take away your virtue with his corrupt ways.
> I have taken possession of a hair tent of which spoke
> a certain cultured bedouin.
> Being near a sound she-camel does not benefit the mangy
> – rather the sound camel herself becomes mangy!

Why is the statement made that a Najdī locust does not eat grass, but sniffs the best air, drinks the best water, grows up in the best places and becomes a cure for every ill? It is said that they appear in Najd in regions called al-Dahnā',[6] this place being east of the sea.[7] Someone else has said: Rather they come from the sea with the permission of God

[1] See Bīrūnī, *Instruction*, para. 355.

[2] For a convenient list of the signs of the zodiac, see Varisco, *Agriculture*, p. 86.

[3] A tentative translation of 'fa-lammā 'azza al-ḥadd 'an al-ḥadd'.

[4] Reading *fa-shadda ḥiṣāna-h*.

[5] These two lines are irretrievably corrupt. The text has *khurnūb/kharnūb = kharrūb* in the final hemistich. This is *Ceratonia Siliqua* L. and Dimyāṭī (*Mu'jam*, p. 51) indicates it is the carob tree. See also Dīnawarī, *Plants*, p. 31. Its grain was used as a weight (Hinz, *Masse*, p. 14).

[6] The desert area N of the Rub' al-Khālī (Farsi, *National Guide*, p. 120).

[7] The Dahnā' is an extensive area about equidistant from the Red Sea and the Gulf. The description is therefore a strange one. Löfgren's suggestion in his apparatus is no less unlikely: *mushrif al-jabal*, 'overlooking the mountain'.

– He is ever mighty and glorious. Ibn al-Mujāwir has said: They are close to manna and quails, descending on to olive trees [228] in the mountains of the Byzantines and in other places. The quail is a bird which arrives at Damietta[1] on the ground and has been mentioned above.[2] It is not known whence it comes. The locust is the same; it comes God only knows from where. When locusts swarm[3] on the ground in the desert, they are called 'foot soldiers'.[4] But when they are scattered and creep on the ground, they are called *dabbā'*.[5] When they fly, they are called *jarād*. A Quranic exegete has said: Written on their wings is the name of God, the greatest, and for this reason they can fly and have the ability to eat crops etc., because they are the troops of God – He is ever mighty and glorious – and He has given them authority over His land and His servants.

Section. Some locusts alighted near the tribe of Zayd, as some also alighted near that of 'Amr. Zayd's tribe said to 'Amr's, 'Here we are killing locusts protected by you.' When 'Amr's tribe heard this, they said, 'We won't do as you say! We won't allow you to kill what we protect.' So fighting broke out between the two tribes and continued until they were both wiped out. One of 'Amr's tribe recited as follows:

> Some of us have given protection to the locusts of Najd
> and have made them forbidden to those who would kill them.

Section. Zayd fell gravely ill, so ill that the physicians were not able to treat him because of the scarcity of the drugs required to treat the disease. When he was on the point of death, the physician said to his relatives, 'Feed him whatever he wants, [229] for he is about to die.' The sick man began to eat what he wanted until one day locusts came to his mind, so he bought some and ate nothing else. When he had eaten many, he was cured of his illness. The physician saw him and said, 'Please tell me what electuaries you have taken, what you have drunk and eaten!' He replied that he had had locusts. The physician told him, 'You're right, for locusts will have been sitting on herbs and eating them. Their benefit has not yet reached man's ken, but the special properties of these herbs have been just right to deal with your illness. You have recovered! The locusts were the means of your recovery. I have indeed looked in all the medical text books in order to find a medicine for your illness. However, there was no successful outcome for me so I told you to eat whatever you wanted!'[6] God knows best.

Marriage among the Najdīs.[7] I was informed as follows by Sulaymān b. Manṣūr: All [those] in the mountain and desert regions, the bedouins, [the people of] Tihāmah and Najd marry off their daughters without allowing the girl any inheritance. But if the girl is a virgin, she is fitted out and married off at the expense of her father. If the girl has a

[1] In the Nile delta about 200 km E of Alexandria.

[2] It has not in fact been mentioned elsewhere.

[3] Reading with Löfgren *'arasha*.

[4] Arabic *'arjal* (Kazimirski, *Dictionnaire*, II, p. 211, 'nombreuse troupe d'hommes à pied').

[5] Or perhaps *dabbāb* (Dozy, *Supplément*, I, p. 421).

[6] Arabic 'fa-qultu bi-tark al-ḥimyah la-k'. For *ḥimyah*, 'abstaining from things injurious in a case of sickness', see Lane, *Lexicon*, II, p. 652.

[7] See Landberg, *Etudes*, II, p. 862 and Smith, 'Some "Anthropological" Passages', p. 167.

family, no one will seek to reprove her.[1] But any woman who has [only] a small family and tribal group is not frequently asked for in marriage. If she cannot support [the cost of] her herds, her wealth and her servants, on a pre-arranged occasion she rides out in a high litter and her herds are driven to market. Someone makes the announcement for her, 'Does anyone want a bride and a few animals?'[2] [230] But if she is a divorced or widowed woman, he would shout out, 'Come now, who wants to marry an experienced woman and [to take possession of] her wealth?'[3] So anyone who desires her and her wealth marries her. Then her father, or her brother, or her cousin or one of her relatives says to the man, 'Marry her, my fine Arab![4] If you are not too keen on her, then you are her marriage agent; marry her off to whomsoever you wish.'

One of them recited as follows:

> You should [marry] stubborn women and don't trample
> on someone down-trodden who has been humiliated.
> If you treat her well, she will say, 'I have been well treated before.'
> If you humiliate her, she will say, 'My shoe slipped!'

Another recited as follows:

> O you giving me good news! ... O spouse returning to her family!
> I gave you the good news of loss from a day returning.

When the woman enters her husband's house,[5] her female neighbours come two by two to congratulate her on her complete joy. Each one brings with her a bag full of white flour, or parched barley meal, or some dried grapes. Then the woman is given a hundred full bags[6] from which she can provide for herself for some months and days. If any of the women attending the wedding has a wedding of her own, that woman returns [231] the bag full, just as it was. These are their customs.

The women of these parts spin cotton, just as animal hair is spun very thick according to regulation.[7] Something like Sousse cloths,[8] like woollen garments called al-Hujayrah clothes, are woven from it and worn by slaves, slave girls and non-tribesmen. It is said that there are sixty weavers with their dependants[9] in this area.

The people know no faith except that Zayd draws a circle on the ground and says to ʿAmr with whom he has a dispute, 'Step inside.' When he does so, he tells him to raise his head to God. When he raises his head to the sky, Zayd says, 'God is sufficient as our lord; get on your way, my good man – God bless you!' This is the people's faith.

[1] The text reads 'fa-qad istarāḥat ʿawādhilī min ʿitābī', with 1st pers. pronouns and Landberg simply glosses, '... elle trouve par cela facilement à se marier.'

[2] Arabic *dhawd* (Lane, *Lexicon*, III, pp. 987–8). Landberg prefers to read *wadūd*, 'a loving bride'!

[3] The text is extremely corrupt and the above is a tentative and plausible reconstruction. It reads: 'fa-in kānat rājiʿan (Lane, *Lexicon*, III, p. 1041, i.e. 'returning to her family') yunādī ʿalay-hā alā wa-man yaṭlubu ... hiya al-marʾah al-thayyib wa-al-dwd (read dhawbah?) māl-hā wa-naʿam-hā min ... (lacuna) wa-amānāt'.

[4] Arabic *yā wajh al-ʿArab*.

[5] See Landberg, *Etudes*, II, p. 861.

[6] Reading *ṭaraf* (Landberg, *Glossaire daṯînois*, III, p. 2203, 'poche'; Landberg, *Etudes*, p. 862, 'trousses'). Synonymous with *jarāb* below.

[7] Arabic '... ka-mā yughzalu al-wabar bi-al-qānūn ghalīḥ marrah'.

[8] Arabic *siyāsāt*.

[9] Reading *wa-dajāj*.

The wealth of this area comes in two kinds: sheep on the one hand, and some camels and horses on the other. Some people called al-Shāwiriyyah[1] take exclusive care of the camels and the sheep, while some of the camels and the horses are cared for by the Dawāsir.[2] They know nothing else other than this wealth, for example goats, cattle, oxen, donkeys and mules. Now the bedouin settle among residences in their hair tents with their horses, camels and sheep; they are people who give generously.

Their food is camel meat, their drink milk and they ride horses. They buy and sell horses and camels and wear unbleached cloth. They are strong people and speak correct Arabic. They wonder round the desert with their livestock and do not pay any levy, nor do they even know about taxes. Ibn al-Mujāwir said: No bedouin takes refuge under a roof, nor pays any levy; they are of the children of Ishmael, son of Abraham the Friend – peace be upon him – there is no difference of opinion about this, nor any doubt. God knows best.

The borders of Najd[3] are the territory from al-Yamāmah almost to Medina, back over the Basra desert until it stretches over Bahrain to the sea. This is the extent of Najd.

[232] *From Ṣaʿdah to Ṣanʿāʾ returning on the new road.*[4] Ibn al-Mujāwir said: I was informed as follows by al-Ḥasan b. ʿAlī b. Muḥammad al-Tūlī al-Ṣaʿdī: When God – He is ever mighty and glorious – brought about the success of Islam, they followed the road as given below. From Ṣaʿdah to al-Khiyām three parasangs, also called al-Durūb.[5] To al-ʿAyn a parasang.[6] To al-ʿAmashiyyah four parasangs.

Within these boundaries is a town called Khaywān and there is also Wādī Khayrān.[7] It is a town situated on the side of a mountain. One of the pieces of information about it is that there were 600 streets there and through each street would emerge 600 horsemen. A dam like al-Maʾzimayn in Mārib mentioned above[8] had been built for this town. When the dam was destroyed, the town was destroyed. Now it is the property of Aḥmad and Muḥammad, sons of ʿAbdallāh b. Ḥamzah.[9] They bought its lands with large quantities of gold, arable and stock farm land. It was called Khayrān in pre-Islamic times because the people there were so good.[10]

To Ḥūth five parasangs. To Jaḥdam four parasangs.[11] To Ṣanʿāʾ two parasangs.

[1] I cannot trace any reference to these people.

[2] The text reads al-Dawāshir. However, this would seem to be a reference to the large tribal group whose area spreads from Wādī al-Dawāsir to just S of Riyadh in Najd (Kaḥḥālah, *Muʿjam*, I, pp. 392–3).

[3] See Ibn Ḥawqal, *Ṣūrah*, p. 19.

[4] See Sprenger, *Reiserouten*, p. 156.

[5] Hamdānī (*Ṣifah*, p. 246) says al-Khiyām is a village ʻheavy with reeds (*asal*)ʼ. It is situated in Wādī Asal (Thenayian, *Study*, p. 83 and map 4). Al-Durūb is unidentified.

[6] Theniyian (*Study*, p. 76) says this is the same as al-Aʿyun (Hamdānī, *Ṣifah*, p. 245; Ḥarbī, *Manāsik*, p. 643). There is a cistern, a *ghayl*, an aquaduct and a mosque, according to Thenayian's observations (*Study*, pp. 76–7 and map 4).

[7] Thenayian (*Study*, p. 82) tells us of the town and the wadi about 140 km N of Ṣanʿāʾ and provides full references. I am inclined to read Wādī Khaywān too despite Ibn al-Mujāwir's derivation below, perhaps calling it Khayrān in error and coming up with a rather colourful etymology. Thenayian (*in loco*) mentions the fanciful description of the town.

[8] See p. 205 above.

[9] I.e. the Zaydī imam, reg. 583–614/1187–1217. His son Muḥammad, mentioned here, was imam between the years 614–23/1217–26 and Aḥmad from 623/1226 (Kay, *Yaman*, p. 319; Lane-Poole, *Dynasties*, p. 102; Smith, *Ayyubids*, II, p. 77; Bosworth, *Islamic Dynasties*, p. 96).

[10] See n. 7 above. Khayrān must be meant here which Ibn al-Mujāwir is associating with *khayr*, ʻgoodnessʼ.

[11] Unidentified.

The dream. Ibn al-Mujāwir said: I had a dream and it was as if I was in an inhabited town, whose buildings were in carved stone, the length of each one five cubits and each in a different colour. It had a Friday mosque and other mosques, religious hostels,[1] caravanserais[2] and places of learning, together with markets and shops.[3] It was a place of recreation between two high mountains, with abundant water, water channels, trees and cultivated areas. One of the mountains of the wadi was situated exactly opposite[4] the other standing on the edge of it. The souk had been rendered with gypsum from top to bottom. If an ant were to crawl over the surface of any place of the mountain which had been filled in, anyone at a distance would appear the same size as it [from the top].

It was as if I was saying to one of them, 'What do you call this [233] town?' He replied it was Ḥajb. When I asked the meaning of this name, he said it was [so called] because it had vanished[5] from the sight of those who were looking. I further asked to which district it was thought to belong and he replied it belonged to the district of Ṣanʿāʾ in the Yemen. This was on the eve of Friday, 6 Ramaḍān 624.[6]

From Taʿizz to Zabīd on the return journey.[7] From Taʿizz to ʿUdaynah[8] a quarter of a parasang, a village at the foot of the fortress. The poet has recited the following about it:

> When lightning flashed from ʿUdaynah, I
> cried out, 'How about our loved ones who are far away?'

To al-Dumaynah a quarter of a parasang,[9] where pottery is made. To Wādī Ḥadhrār a quarter of a parasang.[10] To Biʾr Māhūt a quarter of a parasang.[11] It is also called al-Ajnās, where Nūr al-Dīn ʿUmar b. ʿAlī b. Rasūl built a mosque with three domes in 623.[12]

To Biʾr al-Ṣadʿ a parasang.[13] To Wādī al-Nakhl a parasang.[14] To Wādī al-Ḥinnāʾ a parasang.[15] All its planted crops are henna[16] and it has many monkeys. To al-Shiyālayn a

[1] Arabic *khānqāt*.

[2] Arabic *rubuṭ*, plur. of *ribāṭ*.

[3] Ibn al-Mujāwir mentions both *dakākīn* and *ḥawānīt*.

[4] Reading *ṭabbaqa* (Lane, *Lexicon*, V, p. 1825).

[5] Arabic *iḤtaJaBat*.

[6] 12 September 1226.

[7] See Sprenger, *Reiserouten*, p. 156.

[8] I take the diminutive form from Niebuhr (*Voyage*, III, p. 211), 'Oddene'. He adds that it is near the Qāhirah citadel of Taʿizz, which fits in well with Ibn al-Mujāwir's description. See also Smith, *Ayyubids*, II, p. 212.

[9] The vocalization is taken from Hamdānī (*Ṣifah*, pp. 99, 204) who talks simply of a village of the Maʿāfir.

[10] I retain the I MS spelling after Maqḥafī (*Muʿjam*, p. 163), although this is not the place in question.

[11] Unidentified.

[12] Al-Ajnās/-sh is unidentified. Nūr al-Dīn ʿUmar, who entered the Yemen with the early Ayyubids, was the first Rasulid sultan of the Yemen, reg. 628–47/1230–49 (Smith, 'Political History', p. 139).

[13] Unidentified.

[14] This is a common place name of course. I wonder if the well-known Wādī Nakhlah near Ḥays is meant here; see p. 90, n. 6 above.

[15] Unidentified.

[16] Arabic *ḥinnāʾ*.

parasang.[1] To 'Uqdat Maj'ar a parasang.[2] To al-Kadaḥah a parasang.[3] To Ḥudaylah a parasang, also called Sarādīb al-Nīl.[4] To al-Duray'ā' half a parasang.[5] God – praise to Him and He is ever almighty – knows best.

The Dalanqūq bird. [It is] a black and white[6] bird which resembles ...[7] This [species is found] in Iraq with a long bill [and it also] inhabits these mountains.[8] A feature of its behaviour is that, when it sings, it dances. Al-Jammāl informed me as follows: It sings and dances a lot only in the rainy season and in winter. This [234] is the most amazing thing the author has ever seen.

In the Yemen, there is a bird called a *jawlab*[9] which is larger than is usual.[10] Its wings are red and it has two bills! Someone said of its cooing that it is [like saying], 'My master, answer my mistress!'[11] Someone else said of its singing, 'They are drumming the napes of the necks of black men!'

In these mountains is a bird which roars like a rutting camel. Birds like *ṭīṭawiyyah*[12] come to Zabīd every sunrise. This is in winter. They are called hoverers and are carried on camels,[13] circling the town four times, then returning. No one knows where they come from, where they go to in the evening, nor where they hasten [at night].[14] They are one of the wonders.

Wild basil[15] grows in these mountains, called in Tihāmah *ḥabaq*[16] and in Zabīd they call it *naḥālah* ...[17] This place was the extremity of Abyssinian territory when they were governors of Zabīd.[18]

[1] Tentatively from Sprenger, otherwise unidentified.

[2] Unidentified.

[3] Maqḥafī (*Mu'jam*, p. 535) mentions a wadi to the W of lower Wuṣāb, which would however appear to be too far N for this route.

[4] Unidentified. The second name means 'indigo vaults'.

[5] A different place from that mentioned above (p. 172, n. 5).

[6] Arabic *ablaq*, 'piebald', usually used of the horse. Perhaps the bird in question is the sacred ibis, *Threskiornis Aethiopicus* (Stone, *Tihāmah*, p. 19). See Smith, 'Wondrous and Humorous', p. 114.

[7] The MSS and text are unclear at this point.

[8] I.e. between Ta'izz and Zabīd.

[9] Probably a dove of some kind. Both Rossi (*L'Arabo*, p. 162) and Varisco ('Production of Sorghum', p. 81) have *jawlabī* which DMV tells me is a Ṣan'ānī dialect word. The latter adds that *jawlab* is used for the palm dove (*Streptopelia senegalensis*) and the red-eyed dove (*S. semitroquata*) among other species.

[10] Arabic *akbar min al-qasm* (Kazimirski, *Dictionnaire*, II, p. 738).

[11] Arabic *sayyidī ajib sittī*.

[12] Kazimirski, *Dictionnaire* (II, p. 130) gives a singular *ṭayṭawā*. The family Scolopacidae are called *ṭīṭawiyyah/ṭayṭawiyyah* in Arabic (al-Lūs, *al-Ṭuyūr*, II, p. 67 ff.). This includes the woodcock, the snipes, the curlews, the godwits, the sandpipers etc.

[13] Arabic *ḥawwāmāt*. FLS suggests to me that they might be cattle egrets, *Bulbucus ibis*. See also Stone, *Tihāmah*, p. 19.

[14] Arabic *yakūrūna* (Kazimirski, *Dictionnaire*, II, p. 942).

[15] Arabic *barrī*.

[16] Arabic *ḥabaq*, *Ocimum basilicum* L.

[17] The first word is dubious and only vocalized in the L MS and the second is unclear.

[18] Ibn al-Mujāwir means the Najahids (412–551/1021–1156) (Smith, 'Political History', pp. 131–32; *EI*, 'Nadjāḥids'; Appendix B.4 below).

To al-Sāsah a parasang.[1] To al-Mukhayshīb a parasang,[2] the end of the mountain regions. To al-Q.w.b.zayn a parasang.[3] To Ḥasib al-Dīn half a parasang.[4] They were two important thriving settlements. One indication of their size was the fact that four hundred horse would ride out from them. God imposed upon them a beast which the Yemenis call a chameleon,[5] which bit them and they all died. The Khurasanis call it 'sun worshipper';[6] in Zābulistān[7] it is called *sikand*[8] and Ibn al-Mujāwir has recited the following about it:

[235] Hey, fearful Time, what have you done
that you have constantly made [the world] the colour of the *sikand*?
Sometimes it is yellow-faced, sometimes green, sometimes the hand of a friend, sometimes a fetter on the foot.[9]

The people Nehavand call it *r.k.t. r.l.h*, while the Hejazis call it *umm ḥubayn*,[10] since each one has a tongue longer than a hundred cubits. The people of Abyan call it *fukhākh*,[11] but the Arabs who speak pure Arabic call it *ḥirbā'*. Ka'b b. Zuhayr has recited as follows:[12]

On a day when the chameleon remains standing erect towards the sun,[13]
as if his side exposed to the sun is baked on the fire.

To al-Salāmah half a parasang.[14] Whenever there is fear in this area, the people of Shamīr[15] raid them, since the village is at its foot.

[1] Stone ('Gazetteer') has found only this reference to the place.

[2] The place is still known to this day. It is also mentioned by Ibn Ḥātim (*Simṭ*, I, p. 283), *Chronicle* (p. 33) and Khazrajī (*'Uqūd*, II, p. 130). FLS mentions the place in an unpublished report of May 1993 on the Zabīd–Ta'izz road.

[3] Unclear in all MSS and the text and I spell after reference to Stone ('Gazetteer'). See also *Chronicle* (pp. 88, 143, 169).

[4] I accept FLS's vocalization ('Gazetteer'). The place was known as Ḥaṣibah in the 12th/18th century (Niebuhr map).

[5] Arabic *ḥirbā'*.

[6] Persian *āftāb parast* (Steingass, *Dictionary*, p. 79).

[7] The text has Zāwulistān. Ibn al-Mujāwir must mean Zābulistān (*EI*, 'Zābul, Zābulistān') which is the northern area of Sijistān, 'the highland of Ḳandahâr country, along the upper waters of the Helmund' (Le Strange, *Lands*, p. 334 and map VIII).

[8] See Steingass, *Dictionary*, p. 689.

[9] I.e. sometimes helpful and sometimes a bind.

[10] See Lane, *Lexicon*, II, p. 507.

[11] See Landberg, *Glossaire daṯînois*, III, p. 2402.

[12] Al-Muzanī, a well-known poet who attacked Muḥammad in his verses, but who later composed this panegyric of him and was received by him in Medina (Iṣfahānī, *Aghānī*, XV, pp. 147–51; *EI*, 'Ka'b b. Zuhayr'; Tayib 'Pre-Islamic Poetry', p. 41).

[13] Text *muṭakhiban* (cf. Nöldeke, *Delectus*, p. 112, line 29, *murtabi'an*, 'on the look out').

[14] Still found today (FLS). The place is mentioned in several sources, notably Ibn Ḥātim (*Simṭ*, I, p. 283, 286); Smith (*Ayyubids*, II, p. 197); *Chronicle* (p. 98); Khazrajī (*'Uqūd*, I, p. 140; II, pp. 22, 27, 32 etc.); Sharjī (*Ṭabaqāt*, pp. 24. 68, 85 etc.) and Ibn al-Dayba' (*Qurrah*, I, p. 123, Salāmat Ḥays). See Stone, 'Gazetteer'.

[15] Large massif S of Ḥays (Stone, 'Gazetteer'). Ḥajarī (*Majmū'*, III, p. 457) says it is a part of Maqbanah. Maqḥafī (*Mu'jam*, p. 622), however, states that Shamīr is the ancient name for the later Maqbanah, a huge area to the NW of Ta'izz.

To Ḥays half a parasang.[1] It was built by Amir Jayyāsh b. Najāḥ,[2] the ancestor of the rulers of Zabīd who controled Zabīd and the Tihāmah area. When he became ruler, he built Ḥays. He then sent for his family and relatives, [asking them] to move from Abyssinia and settle in Ḥays. It is said there is not a single house of Arabs there, all of them being the offspring of blacks. The Yemenis have coined a story as follows. Zayd says to ʿAmr, 'Good heavens, you're only harming a billy-goat!' ʿAmr replies, 'Why?' Zayd says, 'Just as Ḥabb has been handed over, [236] Ḥays has been taken [in return.][3] The reason for this was what Yaḥyā b. ʿAlī b. ʿAbd al-Raḥmān al-Zarrād mentioned, namely that ... Ḥabb means the fortress of Ḥabb.[4] Sayf al-Dīn Sunqur granted him Ḥays, but took Ḥabb from him. So this has remained a saying among the general public in Zabīd. In the same way, one of the rulers of Mosul handed over a castle and took Sinjār.[5]

To al-Dawāmil a parasang.[6] To al-Sardāb a parasang.[7] To al-Qurtub half a parasang. To Zabīd half a parasang.

From Zabīd to Ḥajjah. From Zabīd to al-Qaḥmah three parasangs. To al-Kadrāʾ two parasangs. To the edge of al-Ghānimiyyah three parasangs.[8] To al-ʿAmd three parasangs[9] at the promontory of Wādī Liʿsān.[10] To Asḥar three parasangs.[11] To Ḥarāz, the preserved, three parasangs.[12]

The building of Ḥuṣn Masār.[13] In the year 429[14] al-Ṣulayḥī[15] arose[16] on the top of Masār, the highest peak in the Ḥarāz mountains. There were with him seventy who had given him the oath of allegiance[17] in Mecca during the pilgrimage season in 426,[18] [vowing to

[1] A town still to be found in Tihāmah, famed for its ceramics industry. It is about 40 km S, slightly E, of Zabīd (Stone, 'Gazetteer', pp. 312–13, with an excellent historical and geographical entry with full references).

[2] See Smith, 'Wondrous and Humorous', p. 115. The 4th Najahid ruler, reg. 482–98/1089–1104 (Smith, 'Political History', p. 138; *EI*, 'Na<u>dj</u>āḥids'; Appendix B.4 below).

[3] The two parts of the conversation make up the following doggerel:

wa-allāhi mā taḍīr illā tays / ka-mā uʿṭiy ḥabb wa-ukhidh ḥays.

The implication is that we have in reality gained nothing. We might have got a dish of pâté (*ḥays*), but we have given up our basic food, namely our grain (*ḥabb*). So, Ibn al-Mujāwir is suggesting, the town became known as Ḥays.

[4] This sentence is badly corrupt and the translation tentative.

[5] A town and plain in the Jazīrah, a little to the N of the Tharthār river, about 55 miles W, slightly S, of Mosul (Le Strange, *Lands*, pp. 98 and maps II and III).

[6] Unidentified.

[7] I think FLS's suggestion that this is a corrupt form of al-Suradāt is an attractive one (Stone, 'Gazetteer'), though for the time being I leave the name as I find it in the text and the MSS.

[8] The I MS reads 'al-ʿAnamiyyah', the L MS reads 'al-Ghunaymah'. I correct after consulting FLS

[9] Unidentified.

[10] Extending to the western slopes of Ḥarāz (Hamdānī, *Ṣifah*, p. 105; Kay, *Yaman*, p. 248 and end map).

[11] Unidentified.

[12] See p. 100, n. 2 above.

[13] See Kay, *Yaman*, p. 23, ʿUmārah's text, p. 17.

[14] Begins 14 October 1037.

[15] I.e. ʿAlī b. Muḥammad (p. 100, n. 2 above).

[16] Reading *thāra* with ʿUmārah, rather than the text *banā*.

[17] Reading *qad bāyaʿū-hu* rather than the text *qad bāyaʿa-hum*. ʿUmārah reads *qad ḥālafa-hum*.

[18] Begins 16 November 1034.

stand by him] to the death and to support the mission, all of them being of his people and his families, powerful and in large numbers. There was no building at the top of the mountain, but it was a solid peak and inaccessible. When he took control of it, before noon of the day following the night on which he did so, twenty thousand swordsmen had surrounded him, laid siege to the place and shouted abuse at him, saying, 'Either you come down or we fight you and your followers with hunger!' He replied, 'I have done all this simply [237] out of fear for your lives, lest this mountain be taken over [and used] against us and against you. If you leave me, I will guard it for you; if not, I shall come down to you.' So they departed and left him. Within six months he had built the fortress and fortified it to perfection. Al-Ṣulayḥī remained on Masār, his cause growing, from the year 429.[1]

He lived in fear of Najāḥ, lord of Tihāmah, and humoured him and submitted to his will. However, al-Ṣulayḥī acted against Najāḥ and murdered him by poison with the help of a beautiful slave girl whom he had sent to him as a gift. The death of Najāḥ happened in al-Kadrā' in 452.[2]

In [4]53,[3] al-Ṣulayḥī wrote to Imam al-Mustanṣir bi-Allāh,[4] consulting him on the question of an open proclamation of the mission. His reply came back giving him his permission. At this, he took possession of the land, conquering [highland] fortresses and the Tihāmah area. Before the end of [4]55,[5] no plain, no rugged terrain, no land and no sea of the Yemen remained unconquered by him. This was something unknown both in pre-Islamic and Islamic times.

[Ibn al-Mujāwir] said: Ḥuṣn Masār can be seen from Zabīd, to the north-east[6] on the summit of the mountain like a lofty hill overlooking the Tihāmah regions. In 625,[7] it was taken by Sharif 'Imād al-Dīn Yaḥyā b. Ḥamzah[8] and it is still now in his possession and at his disposal.

To al-Jabalayn three parasangs.[9] To Sūq al-Qibāb three parasangs in the middle of Wādī Sāri'.[10] I was informed by Sulaymān b. Manṣūr as follows: The inhabitants of Masār wrote on the door of their mosque, 'If anyone comes to our mosque in the evening, this is fine, but he should expect no dinner from us!'

Section. Yūsuf b. Yaḥyā related on the authority of his father on the authority of Ghassān on the authority of Abū 'Ubaydah b. Jahīm b. Khalaf who said: We came to al-Yamāmah and stopped with Marwān b. Abī Ḥafah. He fed us dates and sent [238] his servant boy

[1] Begins 14 October 1037.

[2] Begins 6 February 1060.

[3] Begins 26 January 1061.

[4] The Sulayhids were Ismā'īlīs and were here consulting the Fatimid caliph in Egypt Ma'add b. Ismā'īl (reg. 427–87/1036–94) (Bosworth, *Islamic Dynasties*, p. 63).

[5] Begins 4 January 1063.

[6] Arabic *yamīn al-qiblah*. From Zabīd, the *qiblah* is about due N, so right of the *qiblah* will mean NE.

[7] Begins 12 December 1227.

[8] The brother of the Zaydī imam, 'Abdallāh b. Ḥamzah (Kay, *Yaman*, table opposite p. 302; Lane-Poole, *Dynasties*, table facing p. 102).

[9] Unidentified.

[10] I find no mention of a wadi in the sources, although Sāri' is described as a well-known territory in the region of al-Maḥwīt, S of Ḥajjah (Ḥajarī, *Majmū'*, p. 410), and an extensive area NW of Shibām Kawkabān (Maqḥafī, *Mu'jam*, p. 297).

with a *fals* and a bowl[1] to buy some oil for him. When he brought the oil to him, he said, 'You've cheated me out of a *fals*!' The servant asked how and Marwān replied, 'You have taken the *fals* for yourself and cadged the oil! You really are the stingiest person!' He recited the following about the incident:

> Marwān has no concern for a *ghirsh*,
> but he certainly does for a *fals*!

To the edge of Niẓār three parasangs.[2] To Rabḍ four parasangs.[3] To Lāʿah four parasangs. To al-Mikhlāfah two parasangs.[4] To Ḥajjah four parasangs.

I was informed as follows by Yaḥyā b. ʿAlī b. ʿAbd al-Raḥmān al-Zarrād: There are some mountains in the highlands whose edges were struck by lightning and [each one] has become a prominent peak with a well fortified fortress resting on it, like al-Dumluwah, Ḥabb, al-Taʿkar and Bukūr. Lightning does not strike an inhabited fortress without destroying it, reducing its surrounding area to ruins and reducing it to nothing, razing it to the ground. When local bedouins pass over one of these mountains, Zayd says to ʿAmr, 'This is the fortress of Naṣr b. Jaʿfar and this is the abode of Khālid b. al-Walīd.[5] It was destroyed in such and such a year.' Only continuous lightning shatters and obliterates the mountains of the Yemen and this is the most amazing thing there is.

From Zabīd to Ghulāfiqah. From Zabīd to al-Qurashiyyah a parasang.[6] It was from here that Abū Mūsā al-Ashʿarī[7] came – God be pleased with him – one of the great Companions and one of the two arbitrators appointed by Commander of the Faithful ʿAlī b. Abī Ṭālib and Muʿāwiyah b. Abī Sufyān – God be pleased with both of them.[8]

[239] *Section.* In the villages of al-Zabībah, al-ʿAnbarah,[9] al-Harmah[10] and al-Qurashiyyah, no local girl appears until her marriage contract has been concluded, her dowry fixed and the payment made. Only then does the girl appear with a drum and a pipe for all the world to see with enthusiastic guests,[11] receptions, marriage money and the handing over ceremonies.[12] Someone asked about what they do. They replied, 'We are afraid to bring out a little girl. When she reaches maturity, she notices that she has grown up and that her cheeks, her figure, her breasts and the creases of her belly are

[1] Arabic *sukurrujah/sukurrajah*, from the Persian *sukrachah* (Steingass, *Dictionary*, p. 688).

[2] Unidentified.

[3] Unidentified.

[4] The area to the S and SW of Ḥajjah (Wilson, *Gazetteer*, p. 296).

[5] The latter was a famous military commander, hero of the early Islamic conquests, but I take these names simply to indicate 'so-and-so'.

[6] The home of the Qurashiyyīn, a tribal group of the Ashāʿir (Maqḥafī, *Muʿjam*, pp. 511–12). The direction from Zabīd is about due N.

[7] Abū Mūsā was appointed ʿAlī's arbitrator at Ṣiffīn (*EI*, 'al-Ash͟ʿarī, Abū Mūsā' and n. 8 below).

[8] The reference is to Ṣiffīn and the arbitration between ʿAlī and Muʿāwiyah in 37/657 (*EI*, 'Ṣiffīn').

[9] There are two places of this name and the exact location of this one is not known. See Stone, 'Gazetteer', p. 143, for a full discussion and references.

[10] Mentioned by both Ḥajarī (*Majmūʿ*, IV, p. 751) and Maqḥafī (*Muʿjam*, p. 678), though with nothing more than the comment 'a village in Zabīd'.

[11] This is the tentative translation of what appears to be *muhāmīn*.

[12] Arabic *taslīm*, i.e. handing the bride over to her husband.

comely and she is pleased by her beauty. So she feels the need to step out on a different path. Yet we keep her as she is. When she notices that her vagina[1] is deep, messy,[2] soft, emitting a bad odour and of ugly[3] appearance, her fire goes out and her suitors are few because of her deep vagina.[4] It is only when he hands her her dowry, she appears and is brought all simple and nice[5] to her husband's house.' The length and breath of the country north of Zabīd follow this practice and aim.

To Khabt Nafḥān two parasangs,[6] in the regions of al-Maḥālib. There is nothing in these lands which glistens more than this. To Ghulāfiqah two parasangs.

The building of Ghulāfiqah. There was between Ghulāfiqah and al-Makīnah[7] a town called al-Zibr.[8] The name al-Zibr is simply derived from the Psalms,[9] the Psalms of David – peace be upon him. It is said that [it is alternatively derived] from a piece of iron.[10] It has been covered over by the dusty wind and become sand hills. Ibn al-Mujāwir said: In this place I found a grave on the sea shore. The sand had been turned[11] into stone and the bones of the dead had become fixed into solid rock. God – He is mighty and glorious – knows best.

[240] *Section*. When a thousand years have passed over dust, it becomes sand. And when a thousand years have passed over sand, it becomes stone. And when a thousand years have passed over stone, it becomes dust! So according to this theory, there can be no doubt that the grave was three thousand years old, since it had been covered over three times, once with dust, once with sand and once with stone.

When al-Zibr fell into ruin, a woman called Bint Isrāʾīl (no doubt the daughter of Jacob, son of Isaac, son of Abraham – peace be upon him) built Ghulāfiqah. With the passage of time and the turning of the celestial bodies, it fell into ruin and [only] traces and remains were left until it was renovated by some Persians, more precisely from Sīrāf, called Awlād Ibn al-Qushayrī.[12] It is also said that they were people from those who had left Jeddah because of what happened between them and Amir Shukr b. Abī al-Futūḥ in 495.[13] There is complete and precise mention of this above under the area of Jeddah.[14] When the people settled there, they built a handsome minaret. After a long time, it disintegrated and its teak columns were taken to the Masjid

[1] The text's *falq* or *falaq* is a possible, though perhaps unlikely, euphemism, = *farj*. I prefer the *qulfah* of the L MS (Lane, *Lexicon*, VIII, p. 2992). See below n. 4.

[2] Perhaps reading *wasikhah*.

[3] Arabic *waḥsh* (Dozy, *Supplément*, II, p. 788).

[4] Reading with the L MS *qulfah*. See above n. 1.

[5] Arabic *hayn layn* (Wehr, *Dictionary*, p. 1039).

[6] FLS places at 1428 4329.

[7] Unidentified.

[8] Unidentified.

[9] Arabic *zabūr*, synonymous with *zibr*.

[10] Arabic *zubrah*.

[11] Reading *juʿila* with Löfgren.

[12] I cannot trace such a name in medieval Sīrāf.

[13] Begins 26 October 1101. There is an error here. Shukr died in 453/1061 (p. 46, n. 12 and p. 74, n. 3 above). Also I find no reference to Ibn al-Mujāwir's mention of Shukr and the Persians in Jeddah.

[14] See above p. 74, n. 3.

al-Ashā'ir[1] in Zabīd which was being built there. It is said that this mosque was built by Commander Ḥusayn Ibn Salāmah. They also built fine houses and mosques with courtyards,[2] made from *kāshūr* stone,[3] which is stone extracted from the bottom of the sea.

Section. I was informed as follows by Yūsuf b. Aḥmad b. Ya'īsh: When the people of Ghulāfiqah fasted the month of Ramaḍān, Zayd, the leader from Awlād al-Qushayrī, said, 'God bear witness against anyone of the populace who has sold or is selling [241] firewood to my brother 'Amr.' He sent a message to the assistants and followers of his brother 'Amr, saying to them, 'Not a single one of you will bring firewood to 'Amr's house, or I'll do such and such to him! I am banning anyone from bringing firewood into his house!' On the eve of the festival, 'Amr gave instructions to his family to prepare a cooked meal with a roast. But they said, 'How can we cook, when your brother Zayd has banned us from bringing in firewood?' So he produced some coarse flax clothes soaked in ghee and set them alight under the cooking pots. On festival day, when prayers had been said, 'Amr spoke up before his brother Zayd and said, 'Come to my house, friends and family – God bless you.' So they all went to his house to eat different foods, drinks and roasts, more than usual. Zayd stood up and said to his brother 'Amr, 'Where did you get firewood?' 'Amr replied, 'Because of your stinginess, I was prevented from using firewood, so I set light to some flax clothes soaked in a large quantity of butter.' Thereupon his brother Zayd grew tired of his brother's high-mindedness and [offered to] feed all the people of Ghulāfiqah from his house, but they took only 'Amr's food. Zayd was amazed at what he had done and his high-mindedness and said, 'Abū Muḥammad, your foot is in a salty place, but the tree has a surplus of leaves in your hand. As for miserliness, when it does not hear you, it disappears into thin air. You are like the sea, while your hand in giving is a shore.' Zakrī b. Sakīlā b. 'Abdallāh al-Buḥturī[4] recited the following to me in praise of Jayyāsh b. Najāḥ:[5]

> He it is who buys garments of praise at the price of what has been collected
> by his hands and protects them from being bought [by anyone else].
> He it is who lights two fires: one of war
> which is never extinguished and one of hospitality.

[242] *Section.* Satan was asked, 'Whom do you love most of mankind?' He replied, 'A stingy worshipper!' He was also asked, 'Whom do you hate most of mankind?' 'A generous sinner!' 'How come?', he was asked. 'Because I hope God will not accept the worship of the miser and I am aware that no good will come to him because of his stinginess. Also I do not believe that God will come upon a sinning servant, see his generosity, save him and have mercy on him because of it!'

[1] Ḥaḍramī (*Jāmi'at al-Ashā'ir*, p. 25) lists 4 stages in the building of the mosque complex: the foundation by Abū Mūsā al-Ash'arī and his descendants, 1st and 2nd centuries of Islam until 204/819–20, further development under the Ziyadids and Najahids until 551/1156–7, during the Ayyubid period until 625/1227–8 and finally work under the Rasulids. Noha Sadek tells me that there has been no specific study of the beams of the mosque and frankly the whole paragraph inspires very little historical confidence.

[2] Reading *bi-al-ṣāḥ*.

[3] Although I can find no trace of this word in the lexicographical works, it must surely be coral.

[4] Unidentified.

[5] See p. 238, n. 2 above.

Section. Abū Dulaf al-Qāsim b. ʿĪsā al-ʿIjlī[1] had a neighbour who had been wealthy, but who had been dispossessed, so he eventually had to sell his house. Haggling went on over it and he stated a price of 1,500 dinars. But the reply was that his house was only worth 1,000 dinars. His reply to this was that his having Abū Dulaf as a neighbour was worth 500 dinars! Abū Dulaf heard about this, asked him to come to see him and gave instructions for him to receive 1,000 dinars, saying, 'Absolve us from blame in this matter. Don't move from our neighbourhood.' The blind ʿAlī b. Jabalah al-Ḍarīr used to recite as follows on this subject:[2]

This lower world and Abū Dulaf are the same,
both desert and settled [lands].
When Abū Dulaf turns away,
the lower world turns away immediately after.

We all settled in the place until they died out – almighty God have mercy upon them. The following was recited.

Fie to this lower world!
It has made deeds and intentions vile.
The whole of life is a worry,
whose outcome is death.

[243] *Biʾr al-Rubāniyyah*.[3] I was informed as follows by Rayḥān, client of ʿAlī b. Masʿūd b. ʿAlī:[4] The first one to starting digging the well was an ape, i.e. a monkey.[5] He dug out the earth with his hand until sweet water gushed out around ʿAql al-…,[6] its true depth being about four cubits. When the Persians saw it, they threw a wall around it[7] made of stones and gypsum. It was but a short distance from the town among tall, lofty palms. It has remained the watering place of the inhabitants of Ghulāfiqah. Also the crews of ships coming in or going out who reached its water find it plentiful. The well was known as al-Biʾr al-Rubbāniyyah, after the monkey which first dug it. Another version of the story is that al-Rubbāḥ was the name of a man and it was not a monkey.

This town is the port of the Kārim merchants[8] when they arrive from Egypt. Herbs[9] and palm leaf baskets are distributed from it, also fish as follows: mullet,[10] sardine,[11]

[1] Abbasid poet and military commander who died c. 225–8/840–43 (Iṣfahānī, *Aghānī*, VII, pp. 153–64, XVIII, pp. 101–5; *EI*, 'al-Ḳāsim b. ʿĪsā').

[2] See Iṣfahānī, *Aghānī*, XVIII, pp. 101–5.

[3] Unidentified.

[4] The client of the uncle of Ibn al-Mujāwir. See Smith, 'Eastern Connection', p. 81.

[5] Ibn al-Mujāwir uses the word *rubbāḥ* which he then glosses as *qird*. Lane, *Lexicon* (III, p. 1009) says *rubbāḥ* is a Yemeni word. See also Nashwān, *Shams*, IV, p. 2380; Landberg, *Glossaire daṯînois*, II, pp. 1062–5; Iryānī, *Fī al-lughah*, p. 340).

[6] Unidentified.

[7] Reading *sawwarat-hu* for the *ṣawwarat-hu* of the text.

[8] A family of spice (particularly pepper) merchants and bankers (Dozy, *Supplément*, II, p. 460; Ayalon, 'Kārimī', *passim*; Goitein, 'New Light', *passim*; Serjeant, 'Fragments', p. 113; Cahen and Serjeant, 'Fiscal Survey', p. 27; Serjeant, 'Yemeni Merchants', pp. 68–71; Allouche, *Mamluk Economics*, p. 16; Varisco, *Agriculture*, p. 227; *EI*, 'Kārimī').

[9] Arabic *al-ḥashīsh al-akhḍar*.

[10] Arabic *al-samak al-ʿarabī* (Hunter, *Account*, p. 23).

[11] Reading *wa-ʿaydah* with Löfgren (Landberg, *Glossaire daṯînois*, III, p. 2345).

seer-fish,[1] *ra'īd*,[2] *marāwiḥ*,[3] *fār al-baḥr*,[4] shark,[5] catfish,[6] eel,[7] *farā*,[8] *safiyyah/safīh*[9] and *ṭawīlah*.[10] The latter has a vagina which looks like that of a woman and it is never bought from a fisherman until he swears an oath that he has not used it for sexual intercourse. Its flesh is sold for medicinal purposes by weighing it on a balance. The *safiyyah/safīh* has a shell, jaw bones[11] and is very spritely.[12] All these fish are taken up to Zabīd which they call al-Multaḥḥ.[13] The taxes of the fish souk in Zabīd are thirteen *malakī* dinars a day. Almighty God – praise be to Him – knows best.

[244] *The island of Farasān*.[14] Between Dahlak and Ḥaly Ibn Ya'qūb. There are two inhabited towns on it, one Sūr and the other Juddah,[15] built by the Persians, or more accurately by Mālik b. Zuhayr.[16] The inhabitants of the island are devout and God-fearing. Between the two parts [of the island] runs a large, wide river, with pure, sweet, light, health-giving water, which begins with a spring. It is called Mā' Turāb. Trees, vegetables and herbs of all kinds have grown up on the bank of the river and all sorts of grain crops and vegetables are cultivated there. They have all the domesticated animals, like cattle, goats, sheep, camels and riding animals. All kinds of fish and sea creatures are found with them. Almighty God – praise to Him – has singled out the inhabitants of this island. When the sun rises a fathom, the air reverberates and then all of those in the village go outside and stand in rows on the sea shore. After a while birds like buntings[17] or, it is also said, like quail,[18] a hundred thousand of them come down. When they get to the shore, not one of them can fly away, so everyone eats his fill, having killed them and cooked them. There is nothing else on them except meat and fat and they are the people's staple diet throughout time. No one gets tired of eating them despite the fact that they continue [to be available], since the meat is light, pleasant to the taste and healthy. I asked what the birds are called and he replied that they are quail,[19] which is the bird

[1] Arabic *ḍayrāk*.
[2] Unidentified. It could also be *ru'ayd*.
[3] Unidentified.
[4] Reading with Löfgren *fār al-baḥr*, *Pastinaca marina* (Dozy, *Supplément*, II, p. 235).
[5] Arabic *qirsh* (Dozy, *Supplément*, II, p. 327).
[6] Reading *al-bayāḍ* (Kazimirski, *Dictionnaire*, I, p. 184; Hunter, *Account*, p. 23).
[7] Arabic *mukhnif* (Hunter, *Account*, p. 23).
[8] Unidentified.
[9] Unidentified.
[10] Unidentified.
[11] Arabic *ṣadaf*. *Ṣabāyā* might also mean 'pupils of the eye'. For the anatomical meanings of *ṣabiyyah*, see Lane, *Lexicon* (IV, p. 1650).
[12] Arabic *dhāt … al-maraḥ*.
[13] I find no reference to this name elsewhere.
[14] See above p. 73, n. 8.
[15] I cannot trace any reference to these places on any of the islands in the material available to me. They are in fact several and directly opposite Jāzān/Jīzān on the Arabian coast about 50 km at their nearest point.
[16] Mālik b. Zuhayr b. 'Amr b. Fahm, great-grandson of Fahm, the father of the other famous Mālik. They were Tihāmīs by origin, according to Ṭabarī (*Tārīkh*, I, 609; *History*, IV, pp. 128–9), who migrated to Bahrain in pre-Islamic times and joined allied Arab tribes to become Tanūkh.
[17] Probably *Emberiza calandra*, common or corn-buntings (Viré, *Traité*, p. 274).
[18] The text has *summān* (Dozy, *Supplément*, I, p. 687). It is undoubtedly the *sumānā*, *Coturnix coturnix* (Viré, *Traité*, p. 133; Varisco, *Agriculture*, p. 76, *simmān*).
[19] Arabic *salwā*.

about which God – He is ever mighty and glorious – said,[1] 'We have sent down manna and quails to you.' I also asked my informant what the circumference of the island is. He replied that it is the journey round of a whole day for a man who is running. It was Badr, the client of Bishr al-Ṣūfī, who informed me of all this.

The island of al-Ghanam.[2] This is an island, part of the land of the Sudan between ʿAydhāb and Baḥrah, called Jazīrat al-Ghanam. [245] There are one hundred thousand head of sheep and goats on it, even more, and all of them are wild. The reason for this is what Rayḥān, client of ʿAlī b. Masʿūd b. ʿAlī al-Mujāwir, has already mentioned,[3] namely that a ship arrived from a certain town of the Sudan,[4] whose cargo was sheep and rams. They dropped anchor at this island as the head wind was strongly against them. When they had been forced to stay there for a long time, they let out the sheep on to the island in order to pasture. Suddenly the wind was favourable to them, so they drove the rams on board the ships, but forgot eight or nine head of sheep on the island. Because the captain[5] was impatient to be off, they could not move around to find the sheep. The crew set sail and off they went in safety. The young sheep and goats remained on the island and mated with one another, producing offspring over a long period of time. They became numerous and took over the island. So the island was called after them. Now when a ship drops anchor, the crew can only hunt any of these sheep and goats after much exertion, using bows and arrows. Sometimes they get nothing because they have become feral and run faster than gazelle. They fill the whole island until now. God knows best what is correct.

Jazīrat al-Nāmūs.[6] Jazīrat al-Nāmūs is as follows. I was informed by Rayḥān, client of ʿAlī b. Masʿūd b. ʿAlī, that it is between Dahlak and ʿAqīq,[7] an island full of mosquitoes.[8] No human can cross it, nor settle it because there are so many mosquitoes there. God knows best!

[246] *From Zabīd to al-Ahwāb*.[9] From Zabīd to al-Musallab a parasang.[10] It is said that al-Musallab was given that name because its women plundered[11] [men's] minds with their excellence, their beauty and their elegance. As the poet has recited:

[1] Quran 7:160.

[2] Literally the 'Island of Sheep and Goats'.

[3] See p. 121 above.

[4] The text and MSS read al-W.ddān and I follow Löfgren's plausible suggestion.

[5] Arabic *rubbān* which must here mean 'captain', rather than 'navigator' or 'helmsman' (Landberg, *Glossaire datînois*, II, p. 1059; Serjeant, *Portuguese*, p. 195; Tibbetts, *Navigation*, p. 60).

[6] In parts of South Arabia, *nāmūs* (usual meaning 'honour' = *sharaf*) means the same as *nāmis*, and this is the case here (Nashwān, *Shams*, X, p. 6758, interestingly the only lexicographical source for this second meaning that I can locate). Punning with the word is frequent in my experience and the anecdote of the British colonial official who tells a gathering of tribesmen that, thanks be to God, they have no *nāmūs* is one I have heard more than once!

[7] FLS has found ʿAqīq (*Red Sea Pilot*, 1932, p. 203: 1813 3814, gulf, port and islands).

[8] The text here has the word *nāmis*. See above n. 6.

[9] See Sprenger, *Reiserouten*, p. 157.

[10] There is little information on this place other than that it is near Zabīd (Akwaʿ, *Madāris*, p. 171; Maqḥafī, *Muʿjam*, p. 592). FLS places it at 1409 4315.

[11] Arabic *yusallibūn*, a masc. plur. verb after a fem. plur. subject, quite common in Middle Arabic.

God give the ladies to drink and the abode of al-Ḥuṣayb!
Its abodes have nothing but beauty!

Ibn al-Mujāwir said: [I swear] by God, the Compassionate, the Merciful, that I have never seen in the whole of the Yemen, mountain and plain, a beautiful face upon which the gaze can rest; there is no elegance, no charm, no grace and no sweetness among them, nothing but a name without substance. All you see are evil old hags, with vile bodies, ill-mannered, full of deceit, foul-mouthed and dirty eaters. As al-Ẓahīrī[1] has recited:

Touch not wine, for it is all blood
that has dripped, drop by drop, from the heart of the grape.
In the morning, it will be as clear as daylight to you
with whom you have been disporting in the dark night.[2]

When Ṣalāḥ al-Dīn Yūsuf b. Ayyūb made certain pious endowments in Egypt, mentioned above under the regions of Jeddah,[3] Tūrān Shāh b. Ayyūb, or more accurately Ṭughtakīn b. Ayyūb al-Muʿizz, made as pious endowments Wādī al-Jurayb, al-Ḥarb[4] and al-Musallab. Their income continued to be sent up to Mecca, until in 615[5] al-Malik al-Masʿūd [Yūsuf] b. Muḥammad b. Abī Bakr[6] withheld[7] their endowment and the income of these villages continued to be assigned to [Yemeni] state coffers.[8] Moreover, Ṭughtakīn b. Ayyūb had made as a pious endowment the town of Umm al-Dajjāj[9] to Medina together with all of its lands, [247] [entrusting it to] Qāḍī ʿAlī b. al-Ḥusayn b. Wuhayb. When Amir Qāsim b. al-Muhannā b. Jammāz, lord of Medina, conquered Mecca in 622[10] [however], their income remained assigned to the state coffers [in Mecca]. In 625,[11] al-Malik al-Masʿūd Yūsuf returned Umm al-Dajjāj to Amir Shīḥah and its income came to Medina as it had previously done.

To al-Ahwāb two parasangs through lofty palms.

The building of al-Ahwāb. [Al-Ahwāb was built][12] by Abū al-Qāsim al-Rāmisht b. Shīrawayh b. al-Ḥusayn b. Jaʿfar al-Fārsī[13] in 532,[14] an excellent town, when he came

[1] Ẓāhīr al-Dīn Fāryābī, a Khurasani poet of the late Seljuk period, d. 598/1201 (Browne, *Literary History*, II, pp. 412–25).

[2] I am grateful to Charles Melville for his rendering of this poem.

[3] See above pp. 76–7.

[4] I cannot trace a wadi of the name al-Jurayb, though several places are known, the most famous being in the Ḥajūr region to the W of Ḥūth (Hamdānī, *Ṣifah*, pp. 69, 113; Kay, *Yaman*, p. 281; Maqḥafī, *Muʿjam*, pp. 119–20). The second place name I read very tentatively.

[5] Begins 30 March 1218.

[6] The 6th and final Ayyubid ruler in the Yemen, reg. 612–26/1215–28 (Smith, 'Political History', p. 139; Appendix B.8 below).

[7] Reading *khabala* with the text, though Löfgren's *ḥawwala*, 'changed' is possible.

[8] Text *dīwān*.

[9] Unidentified.

[10] Begins 13 January 1225.

[11] Begins 12 December 1227.

[12] Löfgren has correctly filled in *buniya al-Ahwāb*.

[13] A tycoon who died in 534/1140 and whose centre of operations was Sīrāf (Stern, 'Rāmisht', *passim*; *EI*, 'Sīrāf').

[14] Begins 19 September 1137.

from India on his way to the pilgrimage. It had souks, a Friday mosque and shops, he having brought teak there from India. When the Abyssinian state came to an end and ʿAlī b. al-Mahdī took control,[1] he destroyed the mosque of al-Ahwāb. He took the wood from the mosque to the tomb which he erected in Zabīd in 555.[2]

It is the port for those ships arriving from Aden. The valley bottom of al-Ahwāb is related in meaning to the word *ahwāl*[3] because it is at the furthest point of the bottom of al-Suḥārī,[4] a place of dread because it is open country.[5] One of the Zaylaʿīs who brought safe-conducts to Jibrīl b. Zayd b. Fāris[6] said, 'Take away the burden of our customs dues for ten years and I shall construct the anchorage of al-Ahwāb for you.' He asked him how he would do this and he replied, 'I shall load ships with stones and earth and cast them lengthways opposite the anchorage to shelter it from the strong waves and the wind.' This was indeed something of importance to Jibrīl.

My informant said: There are four towns on the Sudan coast opposite four towns on the Arabian side: ʿAydhāb is opposite Jeddah – or more accurately [248] ʿAydhāb is opposite al-Jār, the anchorage of Yanbuʿ, Dahlak is opposite al-Sirrayn, Zaylaʿ is opposite al-ʿĀrah and ʿAwān[7] is opposite al-Ahwāb.

From Aden to Shibām.[8] From Aden to al-Raʿāriʿ four parasangs. On top of the well are two crows which have been there throughout time. It is part of the regions of Lahej and ʿAlī b. Ziyād al-Māzinī recites as follows about it:[9]

> Al-Raʿāriʿ is free of the Masʿūdīs,
> so their commitments there are not like commitments.
> Āl al-Zurayʿ have settled there and it is a case of
> lions having settled in place of other lions.

To Abyan four parasangs, a group of villages built by Hejazis. It is also said that they were built by B. ʿĀmir of the Hejaz who settled in the houses, built the villages, ploughed the fields, planted the crops and raised their families there. The area remained in their hands until the end of the Abyssinian state.[10] In these regions are

[1] Najahid rule came to an end in Tihāmah at the end of the 5th/12th century. ʿAlī b. al-Mahdī took control in 531/1136 (Smith, 'Political History', p. 138).

[2] Begins 12 January 1160. Since he died in 554/1159 soon after his entry into Zabīd, I take the word *mashhad* here as translated. Ibn al-Mujāwir seems to be telling us that he built his tomb in Zabīd from the teak taken from the mosque soon after entering the town.

[3] Plur. of *hawl*, 'terror'. Ibn al-Mujāwir is suggesting that the roots *h y/w b* and *h w l* have the same meaning, 'fear', 'dread'.

[4] See p. 116, n. 8 above.

[5] A tentative translation of the rather strange *mawḍiʿ hawl li-kawni-h kashfan*.

[6] Presumably a local Tihāmī governor whom I am unable to identify.

[7] Mentioned incidentally in Garcin, *Centre musulman*, p. 223, 'Celui qui veut se rendre dans l'Amhara part de la ville de ʿAwan qui se trouve sur la côte du pays des Abyssins.'

[8] The second Shibām mentioned in the text (see p. 195, n. 1 above) at the western end of Wādī Ḥaḍramawt about 18km W of Sayʾūn (Smith, *Ayyubids*, II, p. 204).

[9] These verses are quoted in Yāqūt (*Muʿjam*, III, pp. 140–41) and ʿAbdalī (*Hadiyyah*, p. 6). See also p. 144, n. 4 above.

[10] The Najahids whose rule petered out in the last few years of the 5th/very early 12th century (Smith, 'Political History', p. 138; Appendix B.4 below).

Khanfar,[1] al-Ṭariyyah,[2] Jabnūn,[3] al-Maḥall,[4] al-Salāmah[5] and Masjid al-Ribāṭ[6] In this area is the tomb of the prophet Ṣāliḥ[7] and a righteous saint. All the women of these parts are sorcerers.

Description of a ʿafw.[8] When a woman wants to learn definitive sorcery,[9] she takes a human and roasts him until he dissolves and is rendered down into grease. He cools down and when he has done so, she drinks all [the fat] from which she becomes pregnant. After seven months, she gives birth to a wild human like a cat in length and breath, called a *ʿafw*. It is said that he has on him a penis the same size as that of a large young ass.[10] The sorcerer continues to [249] go round with him and bring him up until he grows up and becomes strong. When he reaches sexual maturity, the *ʿafw* has intercourse with his mother. When he has intercourse with her and if she were to ...[11] No one can actually see the *ʿafw* except his mother, who is his spouse – no one but she can look upon him. Ibn al-Mujāwir said: He is called a young ass [*ʿafw*] simply because he forces his penis upon her and she cannot bear it. It is also said that he does not learn sorcery, nor does she teach him. It is said the *ʿafw* is like something which figured in the following poem:[12]

> When the *ʿafw* attacks ...
> ...
> ...
> and he shouts with a weapon.

The women of these regions were originally of the following kind. One would walk to al-Maʿbar[13] and return in one night. I was informed as follows by Muḥammad b. Zankal b. al-Ḥasan al-Kirmānī,[14] head of Kirmān, living in Masjid al-Ribāṭ: They turn men into donkeys and oxen by whatever means they wish.

To Dār Zīnah nine parasangs,[15] a mountain overlooking the sea, inhabited by al-Jaḥāfil,[16] an Arab tribal group. The mountain is known by this name simply because,

[1] A large town in Abyan in Hamdānī's day (4th/10th century) (*Ṣifah*, pp. 53, 97). In more recent times, it has become the name specifically of a large rock in the Abyan town of Jaʿār.

[2] A village inhabited by ʿĀmiriyyūn, according to Hamdānī (*Ṣifah*, p. 97). See also Ḥajarī (*Majmūʿ*, III, p. 558 and Maqḥafī (*Muʿjam*, p. 403).

[3] Unidentified.

[4] This would appear to be Hamdānī's (*Ṣifah*, p. 97) Maḥall Ḥamīd/Ḥumayd, a village in Abyan.

[5] Unidentified.

[6] RBS mentions a *ribāṭ* in Abyan which gives its names to a place ('White Dune', pp. 74–7).

[7] The prophet sent by God to Thamūd (Quran 7:73). The text includes the abbreviated form of the pious utterance which is usually reserved for the Prophet Muḥammad and which I have omitted in translation.

[8] See Smith, 'Magic', p. 10. This word may be read *ʿafw*, *ʿifw* or *ʿufw*.

[9] Arabic 'al-siḥr al-tāmm lā qabla-h wa-lā baʿda-h'.

[10] Arabic *al-ʿafw al-kabīr* (Lane, *Lexicon*, V, p. 2094).

[11] The corrupt Arabic appears to read 'fa-idhā jāmaʿa-hā fa-law rakibat al-marʾah jarrah ... (illegible imperf. verb) bi-hā al-jarrah ʿan-hā'.

[12] There follow two lines of poetry too corrupt to interpret.

[13] Between Dhū Jiblah and Ṣanʿāʾ (p. 187, n. 10 above).

[14] Unidentified.

[15] Unidentified. The name means 'adornment'.

[16] A tribe of Madhḥij in Lahej, though there are many also in Ḥaḍramawt (Ibn Rasūl, *Ṭurfah*, pp. 36, 143, 145; Kaḥḥālah, *Muʿjam*, I, p. 168; ʿAbdalī, *Hadiyyah*, pp. 44, 168; Maqḥafī, *Muʿjam*, p. 112).

when ships from other provinces arrive, it appears adorned because it is the shortest distance from Aden. The seat of rule in these parts is a town called Dathīnah.[1]

To Bayḥān seven parasangs, a long, wide wadi where there are villages and date palms. Mention of its inhabitants and their descent into the territory of Bilqīs has already been dealt with above in the first part.[2]

To Wādī Ḥarīb four parasangs.[3] To ʿĀzib six parasangs.[4] It fell into ruins with one single flood of water.

Ibn al-Mujāwir said: A rat destroyed three different regions: the village of Mukhāshin,[5] built by Abū Bakr b. Manṣūr b. al-ʿAṭṭār al-Ḥirrānī[6] in the districts of Ṣarṣar[7] in [250] the time of the rule of Imam Abū Muḥammad al-Ḥasan al-Mustaḍīʾ bi-Nūr Allāh, Commander of the Faithful.[8] The rat prevailed against Dabālī,[9] an area of forty villages (or more accurately four hundred villages) in the region of Baghdad. The rat excavated its lands and the Euphrates rose, the water entering underground passages. When the water rose, it carried off villages and agricultural lands in one go. Then there is the Mārib dam mentioned above.[10]

To ʿAybar twelve parasangs,[11] the settlement of Eber,[12] son of Shem, son of Noah – peace be upon him. It is said that laterns were lit from Sabaʾ[13] to ʿAybar. It was also said that it was a flourishing place, peaceful and calm, but now it has become desert and sandy plain, perilous places.

To Shibām nine parasangs.

The building of Shibām. When Solomon, son of David – peace be upon them both – married Bilqīs, her sister, Nuʿm, bought some she- and other camels and settled with her wealth and livestock on some land. When the livestock ate the sweet herbage, the lands became wet with their urine. She ordered the herdsmen to put earth over the dampness to keep harm from the livestock. This they continued to do until it became a huge mound high in the air. She put around it a wall and settled within, putting into the wall three gates: Zabīd gate through which the livestock entered and went out. ʿAlī b.

[1] This is the name of a whole region in later times. It may of course have been a town in Ibn al-Mujāwir's time – or he may be in error. The area of Dathīnah as we know it would certainly be on the way from Aden to Shibām in Wādī Ḥaḍramawt between Abyan and Bayḥān (von Wissman map, inset 'Dathīnah'; *EI*, 'Da<u>th</u>īna').

[2] Despite this statement, Ibn al-Mujāwir has not mentioned the inhabitants of Bayḥān specifically.

[3] The text reads 'Jarīb' which I tentatively amend. The town of Ḥarīb is about 23 km NW of Bayḥān and the wadi is to the N and NE of the town, S and SW of Mārib (Yemen map).

[4] Unidentified, although the Yemen map has an ʿĀrin in the Ramlat al-Sabʿatayn about 50 km NW of Shabwah and the two could easily be confused.

[5] I go tentatively with Löfgren's suggestion, although the text and MSS have Maḥāsin (Yāqūt, *Muʿjam*, V, p. 67).

[6] Unidentified.

[7] Just a short distance due S of Baghdad on the Kufa road (Le Strange, *Lands*, p. 32 and map II).

[8] The Abbasid caliph, reg. 566–75/1170–80 (Bosworth, *Islamic Dynasties*, p. 6).

[9] Unidentified.

[10] See above pp. 205ff.

[11] Unidentified.

[12] Arabic ʿAybar, Hebrew ʿĒber, '... Shem also, the father of all the children of Eber ...' (Genesis 10:21); Brown, Driver and Briggs, *Lexicon*, p. 720).

[13] Presumably the Sabaean capital, Mārib.

al-Mahdī[1] has now built a strong fortress and he settled in the town. It is said that when ʿAlī b. al-Mahdī built this fortress, he named it Zabīd after the town of al-Ḥuṣayb[2] in the Yemen. There was also al-Ibil gate through which the camels went out to pasture; Masīlat Aʿwāmm al-Khalq gate,[3] which is also called Ridfayn gate.[4] When she had finished building it, she called it Dhū Manākh, ʿAdhbah and Shibām.[5] It is said that Shibām is the name of a woman, so the building was known by her name. God knows best.

[251] *Shibām.* How many Shibāms are there? One is Shibām Ḍamarmar, a ruin which was set out and built at the bottom of Ḥuṣn Ḍamarmar.[6] There is nothing left of the whole of this site except the Friday mosque which is still in use. Then there is Shibām Kawkabān in the mountains, still inhabited. Finally there is Shibām in Ḥaḍramawt and this is the one in question.

Description of al-Dawār.[7] When Nuʿm settled in the town, she built in its midst a palace called al-Dawār, long, wide and high. The early sages said: The bedouins will certainly triumph over three things ending up with al-Dawār. The sword will not sleep and will perhaps be drawn[8] on both sides. They took the palace al-Dawār when it was still inhabited. It is said that she built Shibām by oppression since she forced her way on to the people's lands. When she had finished building it, ʿUthmān[9] took control of it. It is also said that ʿUthmān seized it from her. Its [Ayyubid] rulers continued to control it until the last of them, ʿUmar b. Mahdī,[10] took it by the sword, renovated the fortress, strengthening it in the extreme, and made it the seat of his rule, after building its walls, ditches and gates. When God's command came, his work was of no use whatsoever, as ʿAbd al-Nabī b. ʿAlī b. Mahdī[11] recited when he became ruler of al-Ḥuṣayb:

[1] The first Mahdid ruler (531–54/1136–59) based in Tihāmah. Despite some exaggerated accounts of the territory of the Mahdids by ʿUmārah (Kay, *Yaman*, pp. 129–32), there seems to be no evidence that the Mahdids were directly involved in the Ḥaḍramawt.

[2] I.e. Zabīd.

[3] The vocalization is tentative and the text reads Masīlat al-Aʿwāmm al-Ḥ.l.q.

[4] Vocalization uncertain.

[5] I find no mention of these alternative names in the sources available to me.

[6] This is undoubtedly the mountain Dhamarmar/Dhū Marmar and the Shibām at its foot is today called Shibām Ghirās. It is situated a few miles from Ṣanʿāʾ in the direction of the NE (Smith, *Ayyubids*, II, p. 147, with full references). Ibn al-Mujāwir's spelling mistake here would seem to indicate that the passage somewhere along the line has been dictated and the *ḍād* confused with the *dhāl*.

[7] The text and the MSS read 'al-Dawr' in this heading, though it seems clear that the palace is called al-Dawār.

[8] Reading *yajlū* for the *yakhlū* of the text. Ibn al-Mujāwir is saying there will be three armed struggles for the castle.

[9] This is ʿUthmān al-Sinjārī/al-Zinjārī/al-Zinjibīlī, appointed deputy over Aden and its environs in 571/1175 when the 1st Ayyubid sultan, al-Muʿaẓẓam Tūrānshāh, the brother of Saladin, returned to Egypt. Taking the coastal road via Aḥwar, ʿUthmān did march on Ḥaḍramawt in about 575/1179 and conquer the whole of it (Ibn Ḥātim, *Simṭ*, I, pp. 20, 23; Shāṭirī, *Adwār*, pp. 177–9; Kindī, *Tārīkh*, I, pp. 70–71; ʿAlawī, *Tārīkh*, II, pp. 404, 425, 430).

[10] An Ayyubid amir holding Ḥaḍramawt and al-Shiḥr as a fief and killed in 623/1226 by his own deputy, according to Ibn Ḥātim (*Simṭ*, I, pp. 189, 192), the date perhaps being erroneous. The work was carried out in 618/1221 and he was killed in 621/1224 according to Shāṭirī (*Adwār*, p. 180) and ʿAlawī (*Tārīkh*, p. 495).

[11] In 554/1159, the 2nd Mahdid ruler in Tihāmah (Smith, 'Political History', p. 138; Appendix B.7 below).

We took[1] it with our horse at its Sahām gate
and they did not neglect to pass by al-Shuwāriq gate.
We put a ditch around the citadel of al-Ḥuṣayb;
God's command will not induce [us] to dig ditches.

It was said the Arabs conquered the whole of Ḥaḍramawt in 621.[2] [252] Their ruler was [in power] for four years and left things behind like a hundred *buhār* of silver coin, apart from implements, equipment, horses and goods. His son, Nāṣir al-Dīn Muḥammad b. Mālik[3] subjugated some of Ḥaḍramawt in 624[4] and he is its ruler until now. God knows best.

Description of Shibām, the seat of rule in Ḥaḍramawt. This province is where Ḥaḍramawt b. Qaḥṭān b. ʿAybar b. Shālikh b. Arfkhashd b. Sām b. Nūḥ – peace be upon him – settled. Biʾr Barhūt[5] is the well where the souls of the occupants of hell are assembled – we take refuge with God from them. He whom God guides has no one to lead him astray. 'He whom God guides, he is rightly guided; he whom He leads astray will find no guiding friend.'[6] And fire continues to come forth from it through all time. My father, Muḥammad b. Masʿūd b. ʿAlī b. Aḥmad Ibn al-Mujāwir al-Baghdādī al-Naysābūrī,[7] wrote to Jaʿfar b. ʿAbd al-Malik b. ʿAbdallāh b. Yūnis al-Khazrajī al-Jurjānī, threatening and filling him with dread, 'I am the man of Barhūt; I am the stairway to hell!' There is no one in the real and corrupt world worse than its people, no one with more evil and less goodness. They are much given to blaming one another, little given to protecting those who seek their protection and spilling much of the blood of those killed. Zayd abuses ʿAmr; ʿAmr flogs Zayd; Naṣr regards ʿAmr's wealth as public property; Jaʿfar spars with Khālid; Walīd picks quarrels with his neighbour; this one strikes[8] that one; this one bites that one. They are there, backs turned, ill-fated, luckless and bankrupt.[9] As Abū Nuwās – God have mercy upon him – has recited:[10]

[253] They said, 'You have remembered the encampment of Asad –
may your wealth be little! Tell me who B. Asad are.
Who are Tamīm? Who are Qays and their family?
The Arabs of the desert are nobodies to God.'

[1] Reading *akhadhnā* for the *akhathnā* of the text. An error of dictation?

[2] Begins 24 January 1224. This would seem to indicate the recapture of their land by the Arab Ḥaḍramīs from the Kurdish Ayyubids. This date in Shāṭirī (*Adwār*, p. 180) is given as the death of ʿUmar b. Mahdī (see p. 250, n. 10 above).

[3] This character appears nowhere in the Ḥaḍramī sources.

[4] Begins 22 December 1226. It would appear from the text to have been only shortly after this date that *Tārīkh al-Mustabṣir* was composed.

[5] Probably to be spelt thus by analogy with the common South Arabian pattern, *faʿlūt* (Sayhūt, Raysūt, Rakhyūt etc.), though see Landberg, *Etudes*, I, p. 483) for possible variants. Yāqūt (*Muʿjam*, I, pp. 405–6) confirms its position in Wādī Ḥaḍramawt and lists its traditional features according to several Arab writers.

[6] Quran 18:17.

[7] The mention of Ibn al-Mujāwir's father by name here is of great interest (see above, 'Introduction, The Author').

[8] Reading the more appropriate *yantishu* of Landberg (*Etudes*, I, p. 483), rather than the *yanbushu* of the text.

[9] Arabic ʿadbār madābīr anḥās manāḥīs mafālīs'.

[10] *Dīwān* [Wagner], p. 110; [Ṭabbāʿ], p. 172.

He also recited as follows:

Leave the traces covered with dust by the south wind;
The vicissitudes of time wear away their newness.
Leave some [desert] land to the rider of the robust she-camel,
where the noble stallion and she-camel can travel at a good pace.[1]
[It is] a land whose vegetation is Dead Sea apple[2] and acacia,
most of its quarry being the hyena and wolf.
Do not deprive the bedouin of their amusement,
nor their livelihood – their livelihood is barren.
Leave the milk drunk by men
among whom gracious living is strange.
Better than it is pure wine;[3]
with the cup of it a well-mannered cup-bearer goes round.

Thus the area of Ḥaḍramawt was called 'the beguiled wadi'.[4] God gave it the name al-Aḥqāf,[5] as He said – He is ever mighty and glorious – in the story of the prophet, Hūd – peace be upon him[6] – '... when he warned his people among the sands.' Al-Aḥqāf is precisely this place and its lands.

Their food is sardines, which are small fish, together with oil cake[7] and milk the colour of mustard. Men's clothes are blue, they have bare heads and feet; women's clothes are the *futūḥī*[8] and the garment is dyed with vitriol, when it becomes neither green nor blue, rather a strange colour. The women plait their hair in the middle of their head, so it is like a hoopoe bird which they call *ṭurṭur*.[9] They are dirty, weak and evil,[10] with ample plaits,[11] drinkers,[12] honey makers, bulky and over-worked.[13]

[254] Men's names are in [the form] of a *kunyah*.[14] Some of them are as follows: Abā Lālakah,[15] Abā Hālikah,[16] Abā Madās,[17] Abā Fāris,[18] Abā Ra's,[19] Abā 'Ury,[20] Abā Ḥaṣā,[21]

[1] Reading *takhubbu* with the *Dīwān* [Wagner], p. 43; [Ṭabbā'], p. 53.
[2] Arabic *'ushar*, *Calotropis procera* R. Br.
[3] *Dīwān* [Wagner], p. 44; [Ṭabbā'], p. 54, reading *shamūlun*.
[4] Arabic *al-wādī al-maftūn*. This might also mean 'tormented', 'tortured'.
[5] See above p. 56, n. 16.
[6] Quran 46:21.
[7] Arabic *kusb* (Kazimirski, *Dictionnaire*, II, p. 893, *kuzb*).
[8] See above pp. 199–200.
[9] *ṭurṭur* is a bonnet (Dozy, *Vêtements*, pp. 262–78, *ṭurṭūr*; Dozy, *Supplément*, II, p. 36).
[10] This whole passage is corrupt. Reading here *wasikhāt rahikāt qadhirāt* with Löfgren.
[11] Reading *al-ḍāfīn al-ḍafā'ir* with Löfgren.
[12] Reading *shāribīn* with Löfgren.
[13] Arabic *'asāsīl maqdūdīn makdūdīn*?
[14] The Arabic name made up usually of 'Abū', 'father of ...'. In Ḥaḍramawt, 'Abā', as here, is more likely and most commonly in the form 'Bā'. It is frequently used to form a nickname, e.g. 'Abā Lālakah', 'Abā Hālikah', 'Abā Madās' below.
[15] Presumably meaning 'not for you'!
[16] 'Loser', fem.
[17] 'Shoe', 'sandal', though D (I, p. 475), has also '*sole* (poisson)'.
[18] 'Rider', 'horseman'.
[19] 'Head'.
[20] '[Horse] without a saddle'.
[21] 'Pebbles', 'small stones'.

Abā Kharā,[1] Abā ʿAwf,[2] Abā Bawl,[3] Abā Faqūq,[4] Abā Daqūq,[5] Abā Khall,[6] Abā Ḥabl,[7] Abā Fīl,[8] Abā …,[9] Abā Rīq,[10] Abā Barīq,[11] Abā Ḥayf,[12] Abā Dalīf[13] and Abā Kanīf.[14] Whatever [name] comes to their tongue, they always use the *kunyah* form and they do not turn their noses up at such names. It is the same with the Danākil,[15] the people of Mosul, some of the Arabs, the people of Nehavand, some parts of the Yemen and the people of ʿUsfān.[16]

Section. In the time of Sayf al-Islām Ṭughtakīn b. Ayyūb,[17] ships from al-Shiḥr and Ḥaḍramawt arrived in Aden and the customs officials began to question the crew of one of them about their names. The reply came back as follows: '[There is] Abā Ḥajr,[18] Abā Kharā,[19] Abā Kuwwah,[20] Abā Faswah[21] and Abā Shaʿrah.[22] But the customs officials refused to write their names in the registers. All the cloth in the customs post was dealt with except those of the Ḥaḍramīs which remained there trodden under foot. When things had gone on for some time and more and more difficulties were arising, word reached Sayf al-Islām and he summoned the officials and asked them about the delay in finishing with the Ḥaḍramīs once and for all.[23] The officials replied, 'We cannot register the names of these people in the official register.' He asked why. They continued, 'Because their names are disgusting!'[24] Sayf al-Islām told them, 'If you do not want to write down their names, how can I take customs dues from them?' So he released them and let them go on their way.

1 Arabic *kharā* for *kharāʾ*, 'shit'.

2 *Abū ʿAwf* is the male locust, but for all the other meanings of *ʿawf*, see Lane, *Lexicon* (V, p. 2198).

3 'Urine'.

4 Perhaps *faqāq*, 'stupid'.

5 'Eye medicine'.

6 Arabic *ḥall* and *jull* are also possible, but perhaps *khall*, 'vinegar', is meant.

7 'Rope'.

8 'Elephant'.

9 Illegible.

10 'Saliva'.

11 'Brilliance', 'splendour'.

12 'Tyranny'. *jiyaf* might be meant here, 'corpses'.

13 'Gentle stroll'.

14 'Latrine'.

15 A tribe inhabiting the African Red Sea coastal area and inland as far as the main escarpment of Ethiopia (*EI*, 'Danḳalī).

16 A wadi in the vicinity of Mecca where there are situated small agricultural villages. Its precise distance from Mecca varies with every geographer one reads: Idrīsī (*Opus*, I, p. 141), Yāqūt (*Muʿjam*, IV, pp. 121–2), Ḥarbī (*Manāsik*, pp. 463–4) and Ibn Baṭṭūṭah (*Travels*, I, p. 187 [Gibb's n. 124]). Wohaibi (*Northern Hijaz*, pp. 284–9 and map) places ʿUsfān NW of Mecca on the Syrian pilgrim route, though he does not attempt to solve the issue and explain the discrepancies.

17 Brother of Saladin and 1st Ayyubid ruler in the Yemen, 569–71/1173–5 (Smith, 'Political History', p. 138; *EI*, 'Tūrānshāh b. Ayyūb'). This anecdote is referred to in Serjeant, 'Ḥaḍramī Network', p. 148.

18 Male and female 'private parts'.

19 See above n. 1.

20 Or *kawwah*. Löfgren suggests *kiswah*, 'cloth', 'garment', but we are surely looking for something obscene here! *Kuwwah*/*kawwah* means 'hole', 'aperture' and I take it as a reference to the vagina.

21 'Noiseless fart'.

22 'Pubic hair'.

23 Reading 'al-takhalluṣ wa-al-tamalluṣ (with the L MS) wa-al-tajammuṣ min al-Ḥaḍārim'.

24 Arabic *li-anna asmāʾa-hum dūnah*.

[255] *Section.* A certain weaver was told, 'You have produced a son, so choose a name[1] for him.' [My informant] said: They chose as a name for him ʿAbd Rabb al-Samāwāt al-Sabʿ wa-Rabb al-ʿArsh al-ʿAẓīm.[2] Someone asked whose son he was and the reply was that he was the son of ʿAbd al-Karīmi Alladhī Yumsiku al-Samā'a an Taqaʿa ʿalā al-Arḍi illā bi-Idhni-h.[3] [To the boy concerned] he called, 'Hello there, half of the Quran!'

Even more amazing than this is [the story] that a Persian who lived in Azerbaijan called his son ʿAbd Man al-Arḍu Qabḍatu-hu Yawma al-Qiyāmati wa-al-Samāwāti Maṭwiyyātun bi-Yamīni-h.[4]

I was informed as follows by Manṣūr b. al-Muqarrib b. ʿAlī al-Dimashqī: By origin the Ḥaḍramīs were slaves and clients, so they are stupid and outwardly arrogant. In the whole of the inhabited world there is no one more greedy and less determined than they. They have scattered themselves along the coastal areas and dispersed near and far throughout the earth, to the left and right, as a poet has recited: [in Persian]

> A person whose affairs are disorganized and chaotic
> In his own house is patient and enduring when in exile

Description of Qarn Abā Ibrāhīm.[5] This is a spring which flows in the area of Dawʿān.[6] When a Ḥimyarī passes along the wadi, the spring flows. It is also said, however, that [all] its rain falls on one single day and from it the Ḥimyarī, no one else, can drink. ʿAlī b. Muḥammad b. Aḥmad al-Sibāʿī informed me that there is a jinni who has been put in charge of the wadi. If a Ḥimyarī passes through, the jinni releases the water along the wadi so that the Ḥimyarī or a group [of Ḥimyar] can drink. If a Khawlānī stretches out his hand to the water, [256] it disappears into the sand. Thus there is a second spring belonging to Khawlān called ʿAmal. Only a Khawlānī can drink from it, and no Ḥimyarī can, as has already been described above. This is the most amazing thing there is. Ḥimyar cry, 'We come first!' Khawlān reply, 'You come first in the wages you receive for tilling the soil;[7] we come first in meeting our foes in battle!'

Section. I was informed as follows by ʿAbdallāh b. Muḥammad b. Yaḥyā al-Ḥā'ik:[8] Spinning among the women of the Yemen is of two types, the Fārsī and Ḥimyarī. I asked for further details. He replied, 'The Ḥimyarī method is the one when the spinner puts out her middle finger over her thumb as she is spinning; the Fārsī method is the one when the spinner puts her thumb in over the middle finger from above the thread.'

[1] Ibn al-Mujāwir uses the word *kunyah*, strictly speaking not the word for a given name which is *ism*.

[2] 'Servant of the Lord of the Seven Heavens and Lord of the Great Throne'. Quran 23:86.

[3] 'Servant of the Noble One Who Holds Back Heaven From Falling Upon Earth, Unless By His Leave'. Quran 22:65.

[4] 'Servant of Him Whose Grasp Is The Earth On the Day of Resurrection And By Whose Right Hand The Heavens Are Rolled Out'. Quran 39:67.

[5] See Smith, 'Wondrous and Humorous', p. 114. RBS drew my attention to his *Prose and Poetry*, p. 16, n. 44, in which he reports the tradition in Wādī Dawʿan that there is a spring there called Shājī Mājī (*sa-ajī mā ajī*, 'I'll come, I won't come'!) and this may be the spring in question here.

[6] Spelt thus here and on p. 258 of the text below. It is often found in the form Dawʿan. The wadi is a continuation of Wādī al-Ḥajarayn, becoming Dawʿān S of the town of the same name. It flows S-N into Wādī al-Hajarayn and on into Wādī Ḥaḍramawt. Its main towns are Sīf and al-Khuraybah (von Wissmann map; Ingrams, *Arabia*, especially pp. 159–66 and map).

[7] Reading *fī ajr al-ḥirāthah*.

[8] I.e. the weaver.

From Shibām to Ẓafār.[1] From Shibām to Tarīm seven parasangs.[2] In the midst of the mountain there is a solid peak protruding into the air like a minaret. A fortress has been built on it called al-Mashriq. The following has been recited:

> My lover came early one morning
> from the west on a grey steed.
> I exclaimed, 'Praise to you, you on high;
> the sun has risen in the west!'

Section. Amir Fahd b. ʿAbdallāh b. Rāshid[3] sat looking out on a seat in this fortress commanding a view, when he saw two men going along in the early morning off the road. He sent after them and brought them before [257] him. They turned out to be Arabs and he asked them whence they had come. They replied they had come from Basra in Iraq. He asked how long it took them and they replied it was between three and seven days. He asked them all about themselves. They told him as follows: We are bedouin inhabiting Iraq and Basra. A shaykh noticed two men riding cross-breed horses coming one morning after us through the desert. The shaykh told us to see what these two men were up to. So this friend of mine and I set off to follow their tracks until it began to get dark. When it was dark, we lost track of them. We ended up climbing hills and dropping down into wadis, through sand and stones. This went on for a long time and we wanted to get back to our families, but did not know the way. We kept walking on until we came out above this town. 'What is this province?', they asked. He replied, 'This is Tarīm in the district of Ḥaḍramawt. Welcome, God bless you.'

The town is built around the fortress and one ruler built a Friday mosque there in Tarīm. When its construction was complete, he said to the architect, 'Can you build anything better than this?' He said that he could, so the ruler immediately struck off his head for fear that he would build something better in some other place.

Among the masterpieces of Commander Ḥusayn b. Salāmah[4] is the construction of large Friday mosques and tall minarets from Ḥaḍramawt to Mecca – almighty God protect the town. The distance [in which he built is sixty days and he dug wells for irrigation and channels running with water in isolated deserts and erected milestones and signs marking parasangs and postal stages along the roads.][5] Of these I have seen some, both inhabited and no longer in use. There are also those which people have described to me comprehensively. The first of these was the Friday mosque of Shibām and Tarīm, two towns in Ḥaḍramawt. The building of mosques reached from these as far as Aden.

[1] See Sprenger, *Reiserouten*, p. 142.

[2] About 25 miles E of Shibām in Wādī Ḥaḍramawt, an ancient centre of learning (von Wissmann map; *EI*, 'Tarīm'). If Ibn al-Mujāwir's parasang is the distance one can walk in one hour, 7 hours to walk the 25 miles from Shibām, presumably in the easy-going wadi bottom, is about what one would expect.

[3] Described as the sultan of Ḥaḍramawt below (p. 268 below). An energetic member of the Āl Rāshid of Ḥimyar, rulers of Ḥaḍramawt from Tarīm between about 400–700/1009–1300. He flourished in the late 6th/12th century, though his date of death does not seem to have been recorded (ʿAlawī, *Tārīkh*, *passim*, especially pp, 415–16; Shāṭirī, *Adwār*, pp. 168 ff.).

[4] See ʿUmārah in Kay, *Yaman*, p. 9/Arabic, p. 7.

[5] I have added between square brackets the missing words from ʿUmārah's text which are to be found in Löfgren's apparatus, n. 13.

To Qabr al-Nabī Hūd – peace be upon him – eight parasangs.[1] The length of the tomb is seventy cubits. [258] In these districts also is the tomb of Daniel[2] – peace by upon him – descendant of Hūd, which is forty cubits long. I was informed as follows by ʿAlī b. Muḥammad b. Aḥmad al-Sibāʿī: The tomb of Daniel, descendant of Hūd – peace by upon them both – is in the village of Hudūn, built by Hūd in the district of Dawʿān.[3] Ibn al-Mujāwir said: It is possible that the prophet Hūd had two sons, Rūniyā and Daniel.

The tomb of the son of Dhū al-Qarnayn is thirty-five cubits long and that of Ezra[4] – peace be upon him – twenty-eight cubits. Ibn al-Mujāwir said: I do not think that these people were as tall as this, but they simply made their graves long.

To Maḍī five parasangs.[5] To Khalkhalīj ten parasangs.[6] To Ẓuhūr ten parasangs.[7] To Mahrūt seven parasangs.[8] To Kadnūb five parasangs,[9] a place with date palms. To Mārib twenty parasangs,[10] also with date palms, half way.

I was informed in 621[11] as follows by one of their officials in the emirate office in Mecca: These lands, mountains and side-wadis were the settlements of the people of Shaddād b. ʿĀd. During the spring they would amuse themselves there and had erected on the tops of the mountains and down in the wadi bottoms benches made of stone and gypsum and flat-topped piles of earth[12] where they would stay in spring to relax. Someone else told me: These benches and piles were made there only after they began to suffer from ants, for they experienced great pain from them. Then they left the settlements and took their families to live on the mountains

[1] The tomb is about 33 miles E of Tarīm in Wādī Ḥaḍramawt which becomes somewhere E of the town Wādī al-Masīlah (von Wissmann map). RBS has described in detail the pilgrimage to the tomb and includes a plan (Serjeant, 'Pre-Islamic Prophets', pp. 121–79, p. 152, fig. 2; Landberg, *Etudes*, I, pp. 432 ff.; Ingrams, *Arabia*, photos between pp. 272–3). The 8 parasangs distance is from Tarīm.

[2] Known as Bin Hūd, whose sanctuary lies in Wādī Hadā, W of Saʿīd Bā Qādir in Wāḥidī country at Qabr Bin Hūd (von Wissmann map). Ibn al-Mujāwir is therefore mistaken to locate his tomb in Ḥaḍramawt. He was supposed to be Dhāniyāl b. Hādūn b. Hūd b. Dhāniyāl b. Hūd and to have originated in Ḥaḍramawt (Serjeant, 'Pre-Islamic Prophets', pp. 166–73).

[3] RBS says the tomb of another descendant of Hūd, Hādūn b. Hūd, is at Balad Hudūn 'on the right side of the Wādī Dawʿan travelling northwards' (Serjeant, 'Pre-Islamic Prophets', p. 166). This may be what Ibn al-Mujāwir is calling to mind. A Hadūn is marked in Wādī Dawʿan on the von Wissmann map.

[4] Ibn al-Mujāwir has al-ʿUzayr, although Arabic ʿUzayr is without the article (Quran 9:30; *SEI*, "Uzair'; *EI*, "Uzayr').

[5] Unidentified. It may be Maḍā.

[6] Unidentified.

[7] Unidentified.

[8] Unidentified.

[9] Unidentified.

[10] Unidentified.

[11] Begins 24 January 1224.

[12] It seems clear to me from what Ibn al-Mujāwir says that these are the meanings of *dikāk* and *maṣāṭib*. Sprenger's (*Reiserouten*, p. 143) 'Terrassen' must be discounted. Landberg's 'magasins pour l'encens et la myrrhe' (*Glossaire daṯînois*, I, p. 829) is equally improbable. In any case classical Arabic allows such meanings as 'an elevated place, a flat-topped structure upon which one sits', 'kind of wide bench of stone or brick' (Lane, *Lexicon*, III, p. 899, plur. of *dakkah*), i.e. a permanent structure. *Miṣṭabah*, on the other hand, is 'a square, flat-topped pile of earth, raised for the purpose of passing the night upon it', seemingly not finished with stone etc. (Lane, *Lexicon*, IV, p. 1686).

and in the side-wadis and wadis. They made these benches scattered around the bottom of the wadis and on the top of the mountains. When the ants became too much for them, they lit fires around the benches so that the ants could not climb up to them. God [259] – who is ever almighty – has said,[1] 'So we sent down upon them the flood, locusts, lice, frogs and blood' to the end of the verse. The benches are there until now despite the length of time which has elapsed; the places where the fires were lit also. The benches appear in the following form: [plan]

Traces of the abode remain in ruins;
every lover wanders around within them.
...
...[2]
The lovers departed and left me behind
at night, like an ewe with her slaughterer.
He spent his evening time in a tribe's encampment.
When the lovers depart, he is [still] there in the morning.

[260] Abū Tammām Ḥabīb b. Aws al-Ṭā'ī has recited as follows:

We question her about which abodes remained
and which encampments are still in place;
and what would she do if she were to say farewell and wave
to us with her hand and make a sign.
It is only a question of being absent from her if I turn my back on her
and the solace of my heart turns away when she turns her back.
Lovers' eyes are hot,
while those of the gloating are cool.
When separation summoned me, I turned my back;
when it summoned her, she obeyed.
I have never seen anyone like myself who better cared for a covenant of protection,
nor anyone like her who did not keep to her agreement with me and the convenant of protection she had with me.

The area of the mounds is part of the region of Ḥaḍramawt as far as the furthest reaches of Oman with all the coastal plains and their highlands.

To Ḥabarūt four parasangs.[3] To al-Tahūdī four parasangs.[4] To al-Shiʿb seven parasangs, a source of the ben-oil tree.[5] To Ḥalūf five parasangs.[6] To al-Ghayl eight parasangs,[7] three springs which emerge from a mountain track (called Jabal al-Asfal), which is indeed a mountain road. To Ẓafār four parasangs. All these places are abundant in water and side-wadis full of water, not built upon, except in some places. God knows best and is most wise.

[1] Quran 7:133.
[2] Corrupt and with lacunae.
[3] Situated right on the Yemen-Oman border as it is at present about 50 miles inland from Ghubbat al-Qamr (Arabian Peninsula map).
[4] Unidentified.
[5] Unidentified. Arabic *bān*.
[6] Unidentified.
[7] Unidentified.

The destruction of Ẓafār.[1] Ẓafār was destroyed in the year 618[2] by Aḥmad [b. Muḥammad b.] ʿAbdallāh b. Mazrūʿ al-Ḥabūḍī[3] in fear of al-Malik al-Masʿūd Yūsuf b. Muḥammad b. Abī Bakr b. Ayyūb.[4] The former built al-Manṣūrah and named it al-Qāhirah. It became inhabited in 620.[5] [261] The name by which it is known is Ẓafār and it is on the sea shore. A wall made of stone and gypsum (or baked brick and gypsum) was built around it. Four gates were put into the wall: the sea gate which leads to the sea called al-Sāḥil gate. On the land side there are two, both called by the names of the gates of Ẓafār [previously] demolished: one in the east called Ḥarqah gate,[6] leading to ʿAyn Farḍ;[7] the second in the west called al-Ḥarjāʾ gate, leading to al-Ḥarjāʾ.[8] Al-Ḥarjāʾ is a [262] pleasant town, situated on the sea shore near to the settlement [of Ẓafār]. [Aḥmad b. Muḥammad] only built al-Manṣūrah to fortify the area for fear of people [attacking from without]. But when he had built al-Manṣūrah, al-Malik al-Masʿūd paid him no heed; nor did he censure him for what he had done. 'The command of God is ever a certain destiny.'[9] The following is a plan of al-Manṣūrah as it was laid out [plan of Ẓafār, see Fig. 11].

Towns destroyed in fear of enemies who then did not show up. In the region of Sind, Sultan Nāṣir al-Dīn Abū al-Fatḥ Qubāchah[10] destroyed the castle of Kalūr W.s.b[11] at the furthest extent of his territory in 612,[12] fearing al-Sulṭān al-Aʿẓam ʿAlāʾ al-Dīn Abū al-Fatḥ Muḥammad b. Tekish.[13] He also destroyed the following in Sind in 622:[14] Ahrāwat, Sātar, ..., ..., ..., Urwahām Rā... S.r.w.r, ..., ..., Darharūt, Shāhakā, Rāḥ ... and ...[15] All these, fearing Sultan Jalāl al-Dīn Mank Bartī b. Muḥammad b. Tekish.[16]

[1] See Smith, 'Dhofar and Socotra', p. 83, Costa, 'Study', pp. 11–50, a complete study of the medieval site, and Guest, 'Ẓufar', pp. 402–10.

[2] Begins 25 February 1221.

[3] The early history of the Ḥabūḍī/Ḥabūẓī family before the Rasulid conquest in 678/1279 is obscure. They presumably came from the Ḥaḍramī town of Ḥabūḍah/Ḥabūẓah near Shibām. Ibn Khaldūn (Kay, *Yaman*, pp. 121, 182, 311), an unlikely source in this case, tells us that Aḥmad b. Muḥammad al-Ḥabūḍī, nicknamed al-Nakhūdah, was a rich merchant so in favour with the ruler of Ẓafār that the latter made him vizier. Upon the latter's death, Aḥmad took control of the town.

[4] Ibn al-Mujāwir erroneously calls al-Masʿūd 'father of al-Muẓaffar Yūsuf b. Muḥammad b. Abī Bakr b. Ayyūb. Al-Masʿūd *was* Yūsuf b. Muḥammad etc., the 6th and final Ayyubid ruler of the Yemen (reg. 612–26/1215–28) and I have corrected the text.

[5] Begins 4 February 1223.

[6] I was informed by Shaykh ʿAbd al-Qādir Sālim al-Ghassānī in 1977 that the word *ḥarqah* in Omani Arabic means 'kiln'. See also Johnstone, *Jibbāli Lexicon*, p. 115, where Ḥarḳem is listed as the name of the site of al-Balīd (i.e. medieval Ẓafār) among Jibbāli speakers.

[7] Unidentified.

[8] Known to this day, a hamlet immediately to the W of al-Balīd where fish for cattle fodder is dried under trees. See also Tabula XII, p. 261 of the text where al-Ḥarjāʾ should be read.

[9] Quran 33:38.

[10] Muʿizzī governor of Sind at the time of the conquest by the dynasty of Slave Kings in 602/1206 (Lane-Poole, *Dynasties*, pp. 294–5; Bosworth, *Islamic Dynasties*, p. 302; *EI*, 'Sind').

[11] Unidentified.

[12] Begins 2 May 1215.

[13] The Khwārazm shah, reg. 596–617/1200–1220 (*EI*, 'Kh̲wārazm-Sh̲āhs').

[14] Begins 13 January 1225.

[15] Unidentified and illegible.

[16] The Khwārazm shah called Mingburnu (reg. 617–28/1220–31), son of Muḥammad b. Tekish (*EI*, 'Kh̲wārazm-Sh̲āhs').

[261]

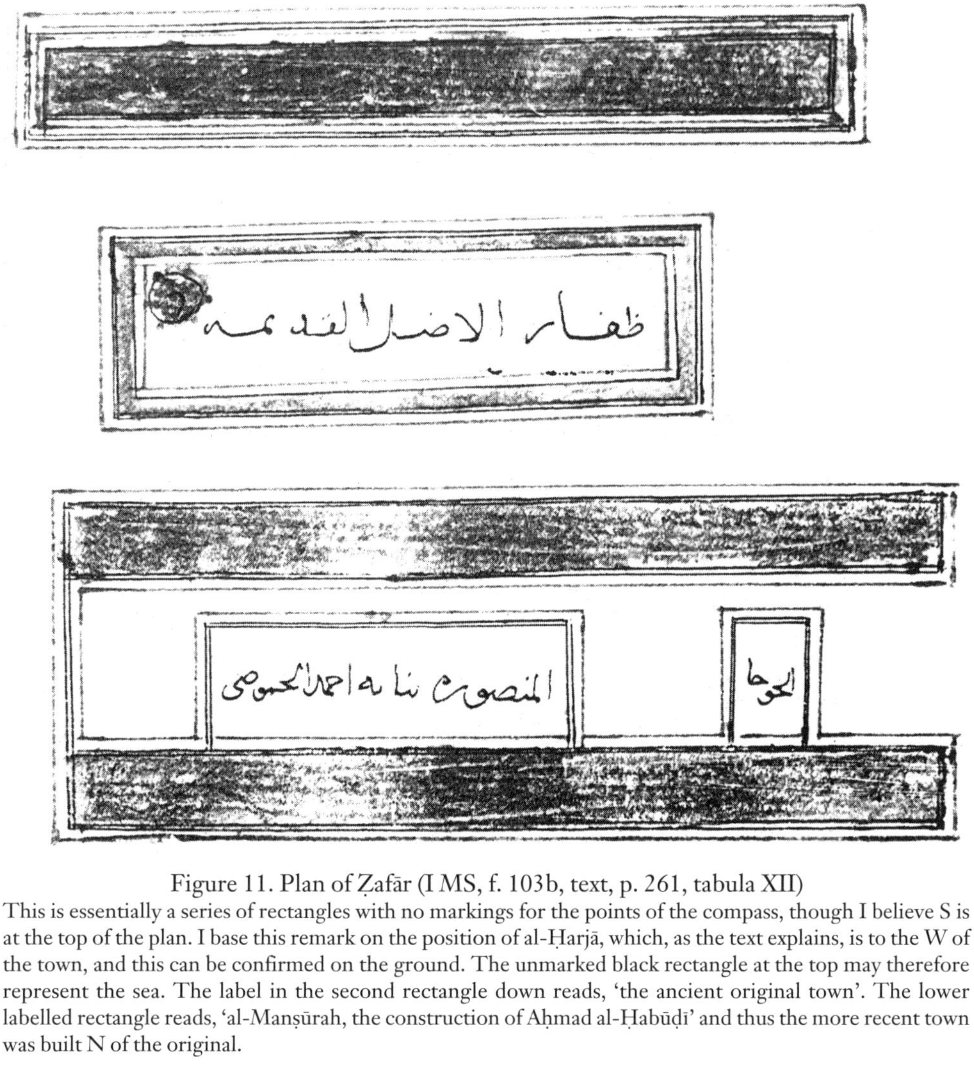

Figure 11. Plan of Ẓafār (I MS, f. 103b, text, p. 261, tabula XII)

This is essentially a series of rectangles with no markings for the points of the compass, though I believe S is at the top of the plan. I base this remark on the position of al-Ḥarjā, which, as the text explains, is to the W of the town, and this can be confirmed on the ground. The unmarked black rectangle at the top may therefore represent the sea. The label in the second rectangle down reads, 'the ancient original town'. The lower labelled rectangle reads, 'al-Manṣūrah, the construction of Aḥmad al-Ḥabūḍī' and thus the more recent town was built N of the original.

In 570[1] Ṣalāḥ al-Dīn Yūsuf b. Ayyūb destroyed Ascalan, Gaza and al-Dārūm in the coastal area [of Palestine] and Rastan, Qalʿat al-Afḍal and al-ʿAbbāsiyyah, fearing the Franks.[2]

Sultan ʿAlāʾ al-Dunyā wa-al-Dīn Abū al-Fatḥ Muḥammad b. Tekish destroyed Qalʿat Marwrrūdh and Rusūm and in Sind Badwūb, Ḥāmā, Hāsūrā, ..., Mank Rāwar Qaṣr Ayyūb, [263] Kūb, ..., ... and ..., fearing their vassal rulers.[3] That was in 564.[4] He left the towns, but destroyed the fortresses because every village in this territory had a strong fortress built by the Indians of a bygone age.

Al-Malik al-Muʿaẓẓam ʿĪsā b. Abī Bakr b. Ayyūb[5] in 624[6] destroyed al-Karak, al-Shawbak, Jerusalem, Eilat and Latikiya in Greater Syria ...,[7] fearing the Franks.

The Muʿizzī king,[8] who took over the rule of Sultan Sanjar[9] of Khurasan, destroyed Merv, Sarakhs,[10] Nishapur in Iraq and al-Rayy and Hamadhān and in Kirmān Ḥ..., Bam and Kārī,[11] in Zābulistān Ḥawr,[12] fearing Sultan ʿAlāʾ al-Dīn Ḥusayn Lank al-Ghūrī.[13] This was in 540.[14]

[1] Begins 2 August 1174.

[2] In medieval times, Gaza was a coastal town which belonged to Palestine, one of the last towns towards Egypt (Le Strange, *Palestine*, pp. 441–3). Al-Darūm, ancient Daroma, modern Dayrān, is the territory of Bayt Jibrīn/Jibrīl, between Jerusalem, Ascalan and Gaza (Le Strange, pp. 412–13 and map). Rastan, ancient Arethusa, is on the Orontes a little south of Ḥamāh (Le Strange, pp. 519–20 and map). The last two are unidentified and I can find no specific reference to the destruction of these places as described.

[3] Only Marw al-Rūd/Marrūd is identifiable here. It is the so-called Little Merv, on the river about 150 miles S, slightly E, of Merv, about 100 miles N, slightly E of Herat (Le Strange, *Lands*, p. 400, map I). The Sindi names are unidentified. The end of the sentence reads perhaps the Arabic *amlāk-hā al-mahanah*.

[4] Begins 5 October 1168.

[5] Ayyubid intellectual and ruler of Damascus who died in 624/1227 (Zabīdī, *Tarwīḥ*, p. 63; Runciman, *Crusades*, III, Appendix III, Table 5).

[6] Begins 22 December 1226.

[7] Al-Karak is the well-known crusader fortress at the southern end of the Dead Sea (Le Strange, *Palestine*, pp. 479–80). Al-Shawbak is a fortified castle near al-Karak, between Amman and Eilat (Le Strange, p. 536). Latikiya is well known on the N Syrian coast in the province of Homs (Le Strange, pp. 490–92 and map). The passage omitted in translation, found only in the margin of the I MS, would appear to read *wa-hwa miʾatayn wa-sittīn* ...

[8] The Muʿizzī or Shamsī slave kings of northern India, not of Khurasan, ruled between 602–89/1206–90 and we must once again correct Ibn al-Mujāwir's historical observations (Bosworth, *Islamic Dynasties*, p. 300). See also n. 9 below.

[9] Abū al-Ḥārith Aḥmad Sanjar, Seljuk sultan was ruler of Khurasan 490–552/1097–1157 (and after 511/1118 supreme sultan of the Seljuks). He could not have been succeeded by a 'Muʿizzī king'. In 552/1157, Khurasan was seized by Turkish slaves (*CHIr*, V, pp. 135 ff.; Bosworth, *Islamic Dynasties*, p. 185; *EI*, 'San<u>dj</u>ar'). If the 540/1145 date below is correct, it must have been Sanjar himself who carried out the destruction.

[10] A town on the River Herat in Khurasan, situated about 100 miles E of Nishapur (Yāqūt, *Muʿjam*, III, pp. 208–9; Le Strange, *Lands*, pp. 395 ff. and map VIII).

[11] The first of the three is illegible. Bam is one of the five districts of Kirmān and the chief town of the district (Le Strange, *Lands*, p. 312 and map VI). Kārī is unidentified.

[12] Again Ibn al-Mujāwir's Zāwulistān would seem to be Zābulistān. The actual place is unidentified.

[13] There are two Ghurid Ḥusayns, I, ʿIzz al-Dīn (reg. 493–540/1100–1046), and II, his son, ʿAlāʾ al-Dīn (reg. 544–56/1149–61). Ibn al-Mujāwir seems to have confused the two and ʿIzz al-Dīn must be meant here (Bosworth, *Islamic Dynasties*, p. 298).

[14] Begins 24 June 1145.

Khan al-Ḥusayn b. ʿAlī al-Khaljī[1] destroyed Daybul in 619,[2] fearing Nāṣir al Dīn Qubāchah.

In 620,[3] al-H… destroyed Qalʿat al-Islām,[4] fearing the Khalj.[5]

In 610,[6] … Khān … destroyed all the Persians, fearing the Muslims.

In 618,[7] Aḥmad b. Muḥammad b. ʿAbdallāh al-Ḥabūḍī destroyed Ẓafār, fearing al-Malik al-Masʿūd Yūsuf b. Muḥammad.

The old route.[8] From Baghdad to Ẓafār and Mirbāṭ, the route used to be safe. The [Iraqi] bedouins used to travel along it twice a year, bringing horses and in exchange taking away perfume and cloths[9] to return to Iraq. [264] When Aḥmad b. Muḥammad [first] defeated these [local] people, they denounced[10] [what he had done] within the territory and conflict[11] arose in the area. The roads were cut and obliterated. When, however, Aḥmad b. Muḥammad b. ʿAbdallāh b. Mazrūʿ al-Ḥabūḍī [more effectively] assumed control and settled down in power there, the people felt secure and the country [once again] flourished. The bedouins ventured in person[12] along the old road, using the direct route to Ẓafār with their horses and they bought and sold. When they were intending to return, they were asked by Aḥmad b. Muḥammad how they knew the road. One of the bedouins replied that he had travelled on that road once as a child with his father. Now he had simply followed the road applying the full knowledge [which he had acquired of it]. God had decreed their safety and they had reached their destination. Aḥmad b. Muḥammad asked them from where they had set out. They replied they had come from the place of martyrdom of al-Ḥusayn b. ʿAlī b. Abī Ṭālib – God be pleased with both of them. When they reached such-and-such a halting-place, the road divided into two, one leading to al-Ḥasā and al-Qaṭīf,[13] the other to Mirbāṭ and Ẓafār. Aḥmad b. Muḥammad said to them, 'God is a witness that any bedouin who travels this road again has no one but himself to blame.' They asked why and he replied, 'We were afraid that the road would disappear with the frequent passage of travellers and that the cavalry of the Commander of the Faithful[14] attack us in this region. I, moreover, have destroyed the town and built al-Manṣūrah in order to ward off evil from myself.' So the bedouins left the area of Ẓafār[15] and never returned. The route there was closed off in 616.[16]

[1] Unidentified.

[2] Begins 15 February 1222.

[3] Begins 4 February 1223.

[4] Unidentified.

[5] See n. 1 above.

[6] Begins 10 May 1213.

[7] Begins 25 February 1221.

[8] See Sprenger, *Reiserouten*, p. 146, and Smith, 'Dhofar and Socotra', pp. 84–5.

[9] Reading Arabic *bazz*, rather than the more unlikely *burr*, 'wheat'.

[10] I have amended the *fataḥū* of the text to read *qabbaḥū*.

[11] Reading *khilāf* for *kh.l.f.*

[12] Arabic *ʿalā ruʾūsi-him* (Dozy, *Supplément*, I, p. 495).

[13] A large town on the Arabian coast of the Gulf, a little N of al-Dammām (Farsi, *Guide*, p. 120, map 106).

[14] I.e. the Abbasid caliph in Baghdad.

[15] This must be what 'fa-dakhalat al-bidwān min balad Ẓafār' means.

[16] Begins 19 March 1219.

The winds can be given three epithets. There is a wind which is stormy, destructive and very strong.[1] When it blows, dust blocks up all the windows of the houses and the openings in the walls. It is said that, when it blows, [265] it is so strong that stones tumble down from the top of the mountain so that they now bring the mountain right to the sea, even though [originally] it was a whole day's journey between the mountain and the sea. Its origin stemmed from the fact that almighty God – praise to Him – destroyed the people of ʿĀd by means of this wind. It is indeed 'the destroying wind'.[2] The names for it are three derived from the distress [it brings].

I was informed by a ship's captain in Aden that there is a wind, the *azyab*, the south wind,[3] and which blows from Rās Fartak[4] as far as Mirbāṭ. The poet, al-Ghaznawī,[5] has recited as follows [in Persian]:[6]

> Then you will be brought down and let to settle in a place where
> Divine Wrath serves you as archers [defending you] and Adversity, the dagger drawn [ready to defend you][7]
> When the mettle of man's courage is strewn on iron oxide, it bursts into fire;[8]
> When the loins of a strong man's courage are rubbed into sulphuric acid, they are dissolved away like kidney beans![9]

Description of al-Manṣūrah.[10] Its climate is good and its atmosphere agreeable. Its water is from a good, sweet river.[11] Fruits of all varieties are produced there: from India, betel nut[12] and coconut;[13] coastal fruits [include] sugar cane and bananas; from Iraq, pomegranates, grapes and many date palms; from Egypt, lemons,[14] citrons[15] and oranges;[16] from Sind, nabk;[17] from the Hejaz, doum, which is *muql*.[18]

[1] Arabic *ʿāṣif qāṣif dhāt shiddah wa-ṣalābah*.

[2] Quran 51:41.

[3] Tibbetts calls it the NE monsoon (*Navigation*, p. 368) and a SE dry wind halfway up the Red Sea (p. 369). See also Varisco, *Agriculture*, pp. 113–14.

[4] Just over 150 miles W of Ẓafār across Qamr Bay (Serjeant, *Portuguese*, end map; Arabian Peninsula map).

[5] I.e. Ḥasan Ghaznawī, the court poet of Ghaznah who died in 556/1160 (Rypka, *History*, p. 197).

[6] The lines presuppose something like 'If you follow the path of the Prophet in the manner so far described in the foregoing verses of the poem, as a consequence …'

[7] The idea is that God's wrath and adversity actually serve to defend you against all enemies, since these things are visited on your foes, not on yourself.

[8] I.e. his gall bladder is rent with fear. The term 'bursts into fire' can also be translated 'turns into a dried pomegranate grain'. The former is the correct translation and the latter a poetic image used as a *double entendre*, clearly complementing the kidney bean in the second hemistich.

[9] The smallness of the kidney bean is contrasted to the thickness of the sturdy strong back of the champion.

[10] See Smith, 'Dhofar and Socotra'. p. 85.

[11] Arabic *khalīj*.

[12] Text *fawfal/fūfal*, *Areca catechu* L. The seed of the areca palm (Dīnawarī, *Plants*, p. 47; Ibn Baṭṭūṭah, *Travels*, II, p. 387, *tānbūl*, with full references; Varisco, *Agriculture*, p. 182).

[13] Text *nārajīl*, *Cocos nucifera* L. (Dimyāṭī, *Muʿjam*, p. 149; Varisco, *Agriculture*, p. 182).

[14] Text *laymūn/līmūn*, *Citrus limonum* (Dimyāṭī, *Muʿjam*, p. 141; Varisco, *Agriculture*, p. 182).

[15] Text *utrunj*, *Citrus medica*.

[16] Text *nāranj*, *Citrus aurantium*.

[17] Arabic *nabq*.

[18] See p. 81, n. 6.

All its inhabitants are Ḥaḍramīs who have moved from their homes and settled there. Their food is fish, sorghum[1] and finger millet.[2] Their riding animals are fed on dried fish, sardines.[3] They fertilize their lands only with fish. It is said too that they thicken their *harīsah*[4] [266] only with fish, nothing else.

Their women are sorcerers who can walk from Ẓafār to the mainland of Java in one night.[5] [They are sorcerers] because they are close to the island of Socotra. The journey between them [and the island] is two days and one night by sea. The islanders [of Socotra] pay a levy[6] to Ibn al-Ḥabūḍī.

The isle of Socotra.[7] It is said that in ancient times this whole area[8] was sea, nothing else. Socotra was something between sea and land.[9] When God opened the mouth from opposite the mountain, [Socotra,] the sea flooded out as far as Bāb al-Mandab, between Aden and Zabīd, and the water stopped there.[10] [Later,] when Bāb al-Mandab was opened up, the water stopped at the furthest, [northern,] end of the Red Sea.[11] [Thus] the mountain of Socotra has now become an island in the ocean.[12]

The true circumference of the island is forty parasangs or more. Al-Ḥammāmī said, 'Its true circumference is eighty parasangs or more.'[13] In the whole of the ocean there is no island bigger, nor better than [Socotra]. It has date palms, cultivated areas[14] and fields of sorghum and wheat.[15] There are camels and cattle and thousands upon thousands of sheep. Water flows on the surface of the ground, sweet and fresh. It is a large river whose source gushes out, long and wide, from the mountains. More often than not [this river] provides an excess of fish for the sea.[16] Aloes[17] and dragon's blood[18] grow, watered by it. On the shores [of the island] there is much ambergris.

[1] Arabic *dhurah*.

[2] Arabic *kinab*. DMV informs me that this is finger millet, *Eleusine coracana* (Serjeant, 'Cereals', p. 55, one of the five species; cf. Löfgren, *Texte*, II, p. 55; Varisco, 'Agriculture', p. 331).

[3] Arabic *ʿayd*.

[4] A dish usually of boiled meat, but here fish, with wheat or rice (Arberry, 'Cookery-book', pp. 198–9, 'heat well and allow to set in a smooth paste'! Also Pellat, *Avares*, p. 316, 'mets fait de froment cuit et de viande en pâte').

[5] I read here al-Jāwah al-Mulā for al-Jāwah al-M.y.l, i.e. Mul Java, meaning Java proper (Ferrand, 'L'Elément persan', p. 229). See also Smith, 'Magic', p. 11.

[6] Arabic *qiṭʿah*.

[7] See Smith, 'Dhofar and Socotra', pp. 85–6 and 'Magic', p. 15. Cf. Serjeant, 'Coastal Population', p. 140. RBS has a different interpretation of this passage and writes of Ibn al-Mujāwir as if he died in the late 7th/13th century (Smith, review of Doe, *Socotra*, pp. 137–8).

[8] I.e. according to my own interpretation the area E of an imaginary line from Cape Gardafui to, say, Saihut, while all W of that line was *land*.

[9] I.e. at high tide it was covered completely, but at low tide its highest mountains could be seen above the surface of the sea.

[10] I.e. as far as Bāb al-Mandab, what was previously land was now flooded with water.

[11] I.e. the Red Sea (Baḥr al-Qulzum in the text) which did not previously exist was flooded in this second stage.

[12] I.e. since God had removed so much water in order to make the Gulf of Aden and the Red Sea.

[13] The island is about 150 miles in circumference, so the former would seem to be the correct measurement.

[14] Arabic *basātīn*.

[15] Arabic *ḥinṭah*.

[16] The text seems to be corrupt. I take this to mean that there were so many fish in the river that they got washed out into the sea.

[17] Arabic *ṣabir*.

[18] Arabic *dam al-akhawayn*, *Dracaena cinnabari* (Forbes, *Natural History*, pp. xl–xli, with photograph; Botting, *Island*, p. 208; *Western Arabia*, pp. 208, 611).

The inhabitants are Christians and sorcerers. One example of their sorcery is the following. Sayf al-Islām made ready against the island – or more correctly Sayf al-Dīn Sunqur, the client of Ismāʿīl b. Ṭughtakīn[1] – five galleys[2] to take the island. When the [Ayyubid] enemy approached the island, it disappeared from sight. They patrolled up and down, up and down, night and day [267] for several days and nights, but found no sign of the island, nor had any news of it at all. So they returned. It is said that it is written of the island, Socotra, in the works of the accursed Byzantines, 'The protected island is in the territory of the Arabs.'

The seven birds.[3] The author of *Kitāb al-Rahmānj*[4] writes as follows: If a traveller in this [Arabian] Sea sees seven birds right out to sea, he knows he is opposite the island of Socotra.[5] Anyone who travels in this sea and comes across the island, will see the seven birds, night or day, morning or evening. From whatever direction ships approach, the birds receive them. No one will find them turning away. This happens all the time. No one has the impression there are eight, nine or six, [for there are always] exactly seven. This is one of the wonders. How much thought scholars have devoted to them! However, their true *raison d'être* has never been discovered by any of them, nor indeed what information on them there really is and how they can be described.

Ibn al-Mujāwir said: I travelled from Daybul to Aden on board the ship of Nākhūdā Khwājah Najīb al-Dīn Maḥmūd b. Abī al-Qāsim al-Baghawī in partnership with Shaykh ʿAbd al-Ghanī b. Abī al-Faraj al-Baghdādī at the end of 618.[6] I saw the seven birds out at sea and in the morning we saw the island [of Socotra]. There are four large settlements on the island: al-Sūq,[7] Fātik,[8] Mūrī[9] and among their villages, Qaryah – how wonderful![10] It is an island with the mountain all over in a circle, its peak reaching up beyond the range of vision. The mountain is inhabited by a mountain folk who oppose the plain dwellers. The island has cultivated areas and buildings; also towns and villages, some unknown to others. Everyone hangs a cross around his neck, [268] each according to his rank.[11] Around

[1] Sayf al-Islām is Ṭughtakīn b. Ayyūb, the 2nd Ayyubid ruler of the Yemen (579–93/1183–97). Ismāʿīl was the 3rd Ayyubid ruler (593–8/1197–1201) (Smith, 'Political History', p. 138; Appendix B.8 below).

[2] Arabic *shawānī*.

[3] See Serjeant, 'Coastal Population', p. 140 and Smith, 'Dhofar and Socotra', p. 86.

[4] Persian *rahnāmaj* (Steingass, *Dictionary*, p. 600), 'route book', 'pilot guide'. See also Ferrand, 'Elément', p. 213.

[5] An obvious indication of a mariner's landfall.

[6] Early 1222.

[7] Just over 3 miles from the current chief town, Hadibo, on the N coast of the island in Tamrida Bay (Socotra map; Serjeant, *Portuguese*, end map).

[8] RBS suggests that this is Fatk which is Qalansiyyah, on the NW coast of the island (*Western Arabia*, map opposite p. 614; Socotra map; Serjeant, *Portuguese*, end map; Serjeant, 'Coastal Population', p. 141).

[9] A settlement which appears to be just in from the N coast in Qadhub/Kathub Bay, about 3 miles W of the village of that name (*Western Arabia*, map opposite p. 614; Socotra map).

[10] The Arabic reads '... wa-mā ḥawla-hā min al-qurā qaryah mā shāʾ Allāh'! Serjeant ('Coastal Population', p. 141) suggests this is the full name of the village: Qaryat Mā Shāʾ Allāh, and draws attention to the existence of Bandar Garrieh on the Socotra map, some 12 miles E of Hadibo. My own translation is based on the common Arabic expression *mā shāʾ Allāh*, an exclamation of approval and wonderment.

[11] Serjeant ('Coastal Population', p. 141) translates 'means'.

the edges of the island of Socotra are many landing places, like Bandar Mūsā[1] and Rās Mūmī.[2]

The life-style of the people of these coastal areas is [tied up] with pirates, since the latter come and stay with them for six months [at a time], selling them their loot. They eat and drink [with them] and have sexual relations with their wives. They are an artful, debauched lot,[3] procurers,[4] their old women more active in this than their men. But among their menfolk is one more of a procurer than a black man leading a rutting stallion camel [in search of a she]! As a poet has recited:

> Were [one of their] old women to be cast into the depths of the sea,
> she would come ashore leading a whale.
> By her cunning she can lead along a thousand mules,
> Even if they are led by a spider's thread![5]

The above is the description of the island of Socotra, while the sea and shipping [can be seen] as in the following plan. [Map of the island of Socotra, see Fig. 12]

The above is the side of the island of Socotra where one climbs up. This is the picture you see, if you are in the middle of the island and if you are facing it.[6] If you approach it from the sea, this picture will perhaps alter and you will see the island differently.

From al-Manṣūrah to Raysūt[7] three parasangs and you cross Jabal Rās al-Ḥimār[8] at the end of Ghubbat al-Qamr.[9] Raysūt used to be a great town and there was a road to it leading from Baghdad, paved[10] and plastered with gypsum and lime. Caravans would bring up goods[11] or footwear,[12] taking commodities down which had been brought in from[13] India like brass,[14] cinnabar,[15] rose-water and silver etc. But it was destroyed over a long period of time [by constant use].

To Dukhān three parasangs.[16] To Ḥārith [269. Map of the island of Socotra, see Fig. 12] [270] three parasangs.[17] To Marāwah three parasangs.[18] To Ḥalaqāt four parasangs.[19]

[1] E of Qalansiyyah, still said to be known (Serjeant, 'Coastal Population', p. 141).

[2] RBS amends the Rās Māfī of the text to read Rās Māmī and from there suggests (Coastal Population', p. 141) it is Rās Mūmī, the peninsula in the far E of the island (*Western Arabia*, map opposite p. 614; Socotra map).

[3] Arabic *julḥ*, plur. of *ajlaḥ* (Landberg, *Glossaire daṯînois*, I, p. 295).

[4] Arabic *qawwād*.

[5] Cf. RBS's more elegant poetic translation ('Coastal Population', p. 141; Smith, 'Serjeant', p. 451).

[6] Reading with Löfgren *wa-ḥādhayat-hā*.

[7] See Smith, 'Dhofar and Socotra', p. 87, and Sprenger, *Reiserouten*, p. 144. Raysūt is about 15 km across the bay from Ẓafār (al-Balīd), an excellent deep water harbour (Costa, 'Study', p. 111, fig. 1; Smith, 'Rasulids', p. 26).

[8] Unidentified.

[9] The text reads here and below Ghubb al-Qamr which I amend. *Ghubbah* means 'bay' (Tibbetts, *Navigation*, p. 536) and this bay is well known (Arabian Peninsula map; Serjeant, *Portuguese*, end map).

[10] Arabic *muṭabbaq*.

[11] Text *barbahār*.

[12] Arabic *khuff* (Löfgren, *Texte*, II, p. 32).

[13] Reading with Löfgren ... *tudhkhalu min* ...

[14] Arabic *ṣufr*.

[15] Text *zunjufr/zinjafr*.

[16] Unidentified.

[17] For what it is worth, I follow Sprenger's suggestion (*Reiserouten*, p. 144).

[18] Unidentified.

[19] Unidentified.

[269]

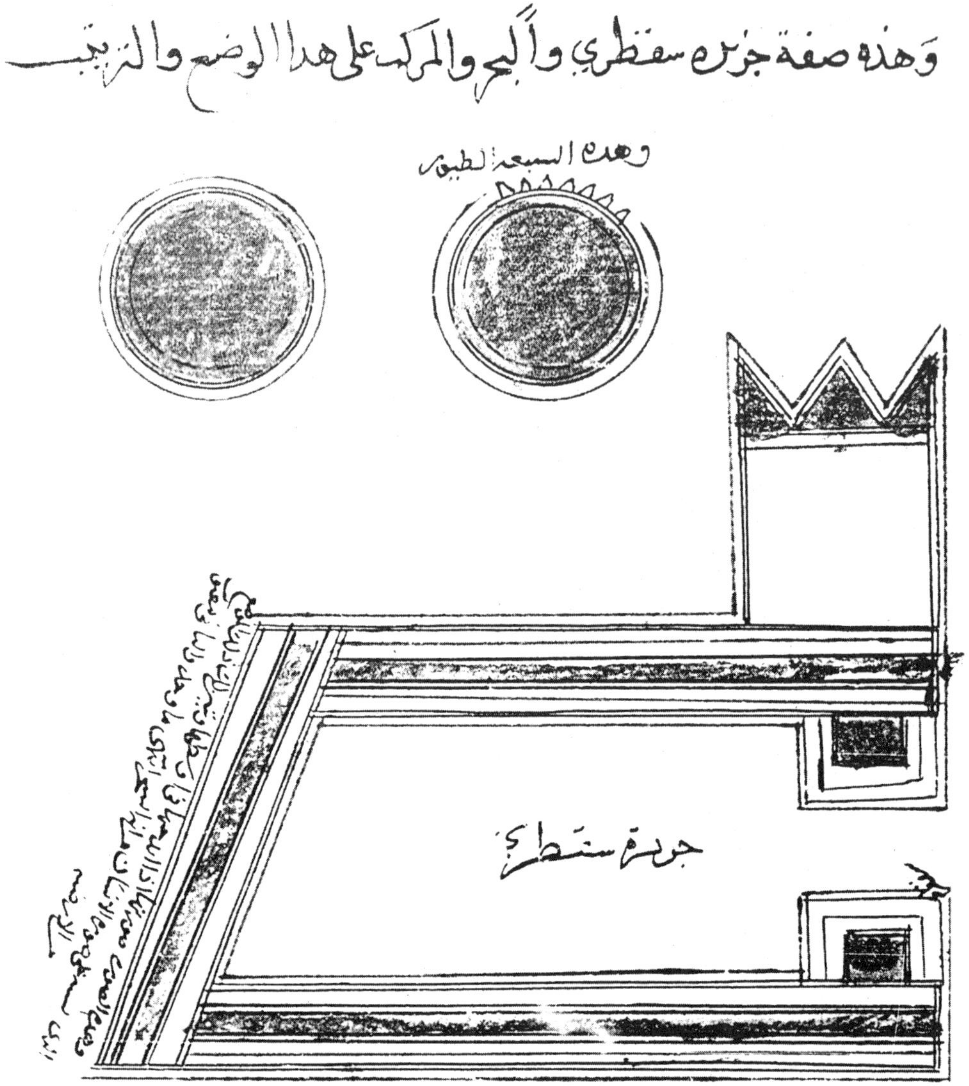
وهذه صفة جزيرة سقطري والبحر والمركب على هدا الوضع والترتيب
وهذه السبعة الطيور
جزيرة سقطرى

Figure 12. Map of the island of Socotra (I MS, f. 106b, text, p. 269, tabula XIII)
A strange map of the island. The seven birds are depicted as triangles at the top of the map. The only place labelled is Rās Māy ('Rās Māmī? 'Rās Mūmī?), i.e. the furthest point E of the island (see p. 265, n. 2). The top of the page must therefore be E. The 'Island of Socotra' is marked within the enclosure and the other label says simply, 'Socotra'.

You cross Jabal Fartak right at the beginning of Ghubbat al-Qamr and it is a landfall[1] for ships coming from India.

To Ḥawayl six parasangs.[2] To Ḥayrīj six parasangs.[3] In this area there are seven ransacked villages called by the Persians Hawaskān, i.e. disowned.[4]

I have been informed by Aḥmad b. ʿAlī b. ʿAbdallāh al-Ḥammāmī al-Wāsiṭī as follows: Between al-Shiḥr and Aḥwar[5] are seven 'black' villages, i.e. with blackened earth, ransacked by God – He is ever mighty and glorious – they being the villages of the Adites.

To al-Raydā' six parasangs.[6] To al-Shiḥr five parasangs, a good anchorage in the region of Ḥaḍramawt. To al-Shuḥayr four parasangs.[7] To Mukallā a parasang. To Bīr ʿAlī six parasangs.[8] To Lasʿā' five parasangs.[9] To Ḥuṣn al-Ghurāb four parasangs, the fortress of Samuel, son of ʿĀdiyā, the Jew.[10] To Majdāḥ four parasangs.[11] To al-Ḥawrā eight parasangs.[12] To Aḥwar eight parasangs. To Abyan six parasangs. To Lahej four parasangs and to Aden three parasangs.

From al-Manṣūrah to Qalhāt.[13] From al-Manṣūrah to Mirbāṭ four parasangs, built by Persians and is said to have been built because, and the name Mirbāṭ is derived from the fact that, it was the tethering place of the horses belonging to the Persians of Sīrāf.[14] The last people to rule over Sīrāf were Persians of Manjū.[15] [Mirbāṭ] was destroyed by Aḥmad b. Muḥammad b. ʿAbdallāh [271] b. Mazrūʿ al-Ḥabūḍī.

[1] Arabic *mandakh*.

[2] Corrected from al-Ḥuṣwayn after reference to Serjeant, *Portuguese*, p. 58 and n. 11. RBS then places it (*Portuguese*, end map) about 10 miles SW of Rās Fartak. See also Arabian Peninsula map.

[3] A port just to the W of Wādī al-Masīlah where it pours into the sea, about 15 miles W of Saihut (Serjeant, *Portuguese*, p. 54 and n. 5 and end map).

[4] I can throw no further light on this statement.

[5] About 130 miles E of Aden, a little inland (Arabian Peninsula map; Serjeant, *Portuguese*, end map).

[6] Unidentifed.

[7] This place, without the article, is on the Southern Arabia map, about 15 miles W of al-Shiḥr, a little inland on the E bank of Wādī Ḥuwayrah.

[8] Nearly 80 miles SW of Mukalla (Southern Arabia map; Serjeant, *Portuguese*, end map). Thought to be the site of the ancient frankincense port of Qana, it is described in detail by Lankester Harding (*Archaeology*, p. 46, with a frontispiece photograph) who says the promontory is about 4 km S of Bīr ʿAlī.

[9] Ibn al-Mujāwir (or his informant) here becomes confused and Ḥuṣn al-Ghurāb is very close to Bīr ʿAlī (n. 8 above). Lasʿā' is RBS's reading of a dubious text and is unidentified.

[10] 'An Arab of Jewish descent and Jew by religion' who is famed in Arab tradition for his loyalty and trustworthiness and whose pre-Islamic story is told by Iṣfahānī (*Aghānī*, XIX, pp. 98–9) and translated in full by Nicholson (*Literary History*, pp. 84–5). In the *Aghānī* version of his story he lived in a fortress called al-Ablaq at Taymā' in the NW of the Arabian Peninsula.

[11] Löfgren says (p. 270, n. 11 of the apparatus) this is now called Majdaḥā. The Southern Arabia map has a Majdaḥah about 5 miles E of Bīr ʿAlī and Ḥuṣn al-Ghurāb and Rās Majdaḥah protruding into the Indian Ocean opposite the island of Barrāqah, further proof that Ibn al-Mujāwir's route here is unreliable.

[12] About 55 miles W of Bīr ʿAlī, a little inland (Southern Arabia map).

[13] See Smith, 'Dhofar and Socotra', p. 87.

[14] See p. 71, n. 1 above.

[15] Little seems to be known of these Persians from a house called Āl Bulukh who ruled over the Omani Indian Ocean coastal region in the late 6th/12th century immediately before the Habudid dynasty. They seem to have been centered on Mirbāṭ and their last ruler, Muḥammad b. Aḥmad al-Akḥal died in 600/1203 (Abū Makhramah in Löfgren, *Texte*, II, p. 194–5).

To Arḥūb two parasangs.[1] To Kankarī four parasangs.[2] To al-Nūs three parasangs,[3] passing through high mountains. To Ḥāsik two parasangs,[4] which is opposite the Kuria Muria Islands, two islands out to sea.[5] To Madrakah four parasangs.[6] To Masira four parasangs,[7] passing through Ghubbat al-Ḥashīsh.[8] The people of the island [of Masira] are called the Mahrah.[9] God knows best.

The genealogy of the Mahriyyah.[10] I was informed as follows in al-Mafālīs by ʿAlī b. Muḥammad b. Aḥmad al-Sibāʿī,[11] who was informed by Fahd b. ʿAbdallāh b. Rāshid,[12] sultan of Ḥaḍramawt: The Mahrah originally come from the village of al-Dabādib[13] where prayer did not exist. This was because Abū Bakr al-Ṣiddīq – God be pleased with him – despatched an army into these regions,[14] but the inhabitants of the village resisted them. When they gained the upper hand over the inhabitants, they put them to the sword, continuing their killing among them until the blood congealed to the height of a standing man. Only three hundred virgins survived, all wearing anklets and bracelets and [elaborately] clothed.[15] They kept themselves to a mountain opposite. When the mountain dwellers saw what had happened, they provided them with dowries[16] and married them off. The Mahrah are of their progeny.

Aḥmad b. ʿAlī b. ʿAbdallāh al-Wāsiṭī informed me as follows: The Mahrah originated from the remnants of the people of ʿĀd. When God destroyed these [various]

[1] Tony Hazeldine informed me some years ago that in his opinion Sudḥ is meant here. Sudḥ is about 20 miles E of Mirbāṭ on the coast (Arabian Peninsula map).

[2] Tibbetts has Jinjarī (*Navigation*, p. 442); Qinqarī on the Lorimer map (*Gazetteer*) and perhaps Yāqūt's (*Muʿjam*, II, p. 168) Janjarah. See also Smith, 'Dhofar and Socotra', map p. 92.

[3] Lorimer and Tibbetts have Jabal Nūs without the article, a little to the S of Ḥāsik (map and *Navigation*, p. 442). The Arabian Peninsula map has Ra's Nuṣṣ a little S of Ḥāsik which may be one and the same.

[4] A well-known coastal settlement correctly placed by Ibn al-Mujāwir opposite the Kuria Muria Islands (Lorimer map; Arabian Peninsula map; Tibbetts, *Navigation*, p. 442; Smith, 'Kuria Muria Islands', p. 280).

[5] Ibn al-Mujāwir calls them Khūriyān Mūriyān and they in fact number five in all. They lie in the bay of the same name about 25 miles off the Arabian mainland. The closest island, Ḥāsikiyyah, is only 20 miles from Ḥāsik. The implication here is that Ibn al-Mujāwir did not visit them and the two he mentions may well have been Ḥallāniyyah and Sūdah/Sawdah (Smith, 'Kuria Muria Islands', p. 280).

[6] About 200 miles E of Ḥāsik as the crow flies (Lorimer map; Tibbetts, *Navigation*, pp. 357–8, 443–4; Arabian Peninsula map). So this is a gross underestimation, whether he travelled by land, in which case he would have had to go a considerable distance inland, or by sea. I am rather inclined to opt for the latter here, since he mentions no other place between Ḥāsik and Madrakah and in view of the difficulty of the land journey.

[7] I have anglicized the Arabic al-Maṣīrah. It is about 150 miles from Madrakah to the beginning of the Masira Channel which is situated between the island and the mainland and about 12 miles wide (Arabian Peninsula map). The island is about 40 miles long and 10 broad (De Gaury, 'Note', *passim* with map).

[8] The bay beyond Madrakah (Lorimer map), called on the Arabian Peninsula map Khalīj al-Maṣīrah (Tibbetts, *Navigation*, pp. 443–4).

[9] The people of Masira are in fact Arabs, Ḥikmān and Janabah (Tony Hazeldine). De Gaury ('Note', p. 499) confirms the language is Arabic, as are clearly for the most part the place names on his map. But perhaps Ibn al-Mujāwir met Mahrah seafarers there.

[10] See Smith, 'Wondrous and Humorous', p. 116.

[11] The MSS are unclear, but this same informant appears on p. 254 above.

[12] I have amended the 'Fahr' of the text. See above p. 255, n. 3.

[13] Unidentified.

[14] Presumably a reference to a campaign in the Riddah wars, the so-called wars of Apostasy.

[15] Arabic *mukhalkhalāt* ('wearing *khalākhīl*'), *mudamlajāt* ('wearing *damālīj*'), *mulabbasāt*.

[16] Arabic *aMHaRū-hum* (the masc. pronoun for *-hunna*), the same root letters as MaHRah.

communities,[1] these were saved and lived in the mountains of Ẓafār, on the island of Socotra and that of Masira. They are a tall, handsome folk, having their own language which none can understand but they. They are also called the Sorcerers,[2] [272] a name derived simply from sorcery,[3] since there is ignorance, as well as intelligence, and some madness in them. They eat God's bounties without praising Him or giving thanks.[4] They also worship other [gods]. In these parts they resemble animals, swarming across these plains like floods and these mountains like ghosts.[5] A poet has recited as follows of them:

> How you are warned! But warnings have no effect on you.
> The shepherd cries out to his lambs and [thus] are they driven on.
> You have become satisfied with [only] the appearance of real people,
> but you are cattle in the actions you perform.
> If you were really humans, the vicissitudes of time would make you aware;
> but you are nought but donkeys!

To Darb Jaʿlān three parasangs.[6] To Ṣūr four parasangs.[7] To al-ʿĀ?.b[8] two parasangs. To Qalhāt two parasangs.

The building of Qalhāt. The first persons to settle the coastal area at Qalhāt were fishermen, non-tribesmen,[9] dependent on God for their sustenance. When they had been there for some time, they were pleased with the place and other people joined them and were on friendly terms with them. They multiplied and became numerous. Then a certain Arab shaykh called Mālik b. Fahm[10] settled among these fishermen. In his desire to work [for the good] of the town, he would stand on the sea shore and any ship he saw sailing by out at sea he would shout to the crew, 'Tell [the captain]; bring [her in]!',[11] i.e. tell them to come into the town, meaning the crew. So the town was called Qulhāt.

But I was informed as follows by Aḥmad b. ʿAlī b. ʿAbdallāh al-Wāsiṭī: It was in ancient times called Hāt Qall. I asked him why. He replied that, when the army fled

[1] A clear reference to the 'punishment' stories of the Quran in which God wreaks His terrible pubishment on those who refuse to heed the warnings of His prophets.

[2] Arabic *al-saḥarah*, plur. of *sāḥir*. It might be of course that Ibn al-Mujāwir has heard of them also as al-Shaḥarah which in Arabic might refer to the Sḥeri (i.e. Jibbālī) speakers of the Omani highlands (Johnstone, *Jibbālī Lexicon*, p. xi).

[3] Arabic *siḥr*.

[4] By a simple change of punctuation (which, of course, does not exist in the MSS anyway), the following translation is also possible: '..., since there is ignorance in them, as well as intelligence. In their madness, they eat ...'

[5] Reading *al-khayāl* with Löfgren (p. 272, n. 1 of the apparatus).

[6] See Lorimer (*Gazetteer*, IIA, pp. 882–5 and map). Wilkinson (*Imamate*, p. 29) calls Jaʿlān a 'sub-region' of Oman, 'separated from the Sharqiya by the encroaching Wahiba sands...' It is thus the area between the Wahībah sands and the Gulf of Oman coast (Wilkinson, *Settlement*, p. 9, fig. 2; *Imamate*, map 1, p. 386). We must assume Darb Jaʿlān was a settlement in Jaʿlān.

[7] The well-known port and ship-building centre about 20 miles up the Gulf of Oman coast from the furthest point E, Rās al-Ḥadd, and about the same distance down the coast from Qalhāt (Lorimer, *Gazetteer*, IIB, pp. 1847–50 and map; Arabian Peninsula map; Agius, 'Medieval Qalhat', pp. 173, 175; *Dhow*, pp. 24, 120, 140).

[8] Unidentified.

[9] Arabic *ḍuʿafāʾ*.

[10] See p. 244, n. 16 above.

[11] The Arabic reads *qul hāt*.

from the battle of al-Nahrawān,[1] they settled in this coastal area [273. See Fig. 13] [274] and they used to say to their servants, 'Bring!',[2] i.e. the provisions, those which had come with them from Iraq. But when they were beginning to run low,[3] one of them said to his servant, 'Bring!', so he replied, 'They are running low.' So the place was called Hāt Qall. As time passed, the name was turned round and became Qalhāt.

The place flourished during the time there of Shaykh Mālik after he put a wall around it made of stone and gypsum in 615.[4] He was a just ruler there and ships from all directions, through every inlet, came. It became a great and respected town.

Section. Zayd came across 'Amr walking to his house and said to him, 'Why on earth are you walking backwards?' He replied, 'Since Fate has turned around, we should fit in with what she does!' A poet has recited as follows:

I had a place to stay among those departing;
it was far away and time destroyed it.
Those departing left sadness behind for me;
What a wretched friend is Sadness!

The town looks like the following: [See Fig. 13]

Jabal al-Sa'tarī.[5] [It is] a mountain the distance of a parasang from the town [of Qalhāt]. [There is also] a long road, wide enough to climb up and come down [at the same time]. Thyme[6] grows there all over it, from beginning to end, and on the summit of this mountain Noah's ark was made – peace be upon him. I was informed by 'Abd al-Ghanī b. Abī al-Faraj al-Baghdādī that it was made in iron, its true size that of a large house. Consequently, when the ark became grounded on the mountain, since the flood water had risen above all God's creation [275] the amount of seventeen cubits, they cast anchor. But the anchor caught on the rocks of the mountain and would not rise with them [as the ark rose]. The water flowed over [the side of] the ark, [so] the latter was cut [loose]. The anchor has remained where it was and can [still] be visited.[7] It is an excellent place. God knows best and is most wise.

The Ibāḍiyyah. Their origins are in the descendants of the man who claimed that 'Alī b. Abī Ṭālib – God be pleased with him – was divine. [Muḥammad, the Prophet] – God bless him and grant him peace – said to 'Alī, 'Two people will bring destruction on

[1] I have amended the 'al-Nahrayn' of the text. The town is about 20 miles NE of Baghdad along the great Khurasan road (Le Strange, *Lands*, p. 61 and map II). The famous battle took place there in 38/678. 'Alī b. Abī Ṭālib overtook those of his former followers who had objected to his having accepted arbitration at Ṣiffīn earlier in the year. Some were persuaded to rejoin him, while many were killed by his army (*CHIs*, I/A, p. 71; Shaban, *Islamic History*, II, pp. 76–7; *EI*, 'al-Nahrawān').

[2] Arabic *hāt*.

[3] Arabic *qall*.

[4] Begins 30 March 1218.

[5] Perhaps an error for Jabal al-Sa'tar; see n. 6 below.

[6] Arabic *sa'tar*, *Thymus serpyllum*, mother of thyme (Dimyāṭī, *Mu'jam*, p. 72; Hepper and Friis, *Plants*, p. 173). The form of the word is *ṣa'tar* in Aṣma'ī (*Nabāt*, p. 15, synonymous with *nabgh*) and Dīnawarī (*Plants*, pp. 41–2).

[7] This is a very tentative translation of a corrupt passage which reads as follows in Arabic: 'wa-ghamara al-riḥ (read *al-mā*?) quṭi'at al-safīnah al-a.r.?.h wa-baqiya al-anjar wa-al-a.ḥ.r.?.h mawḍi'-h yuzār'.

[273]

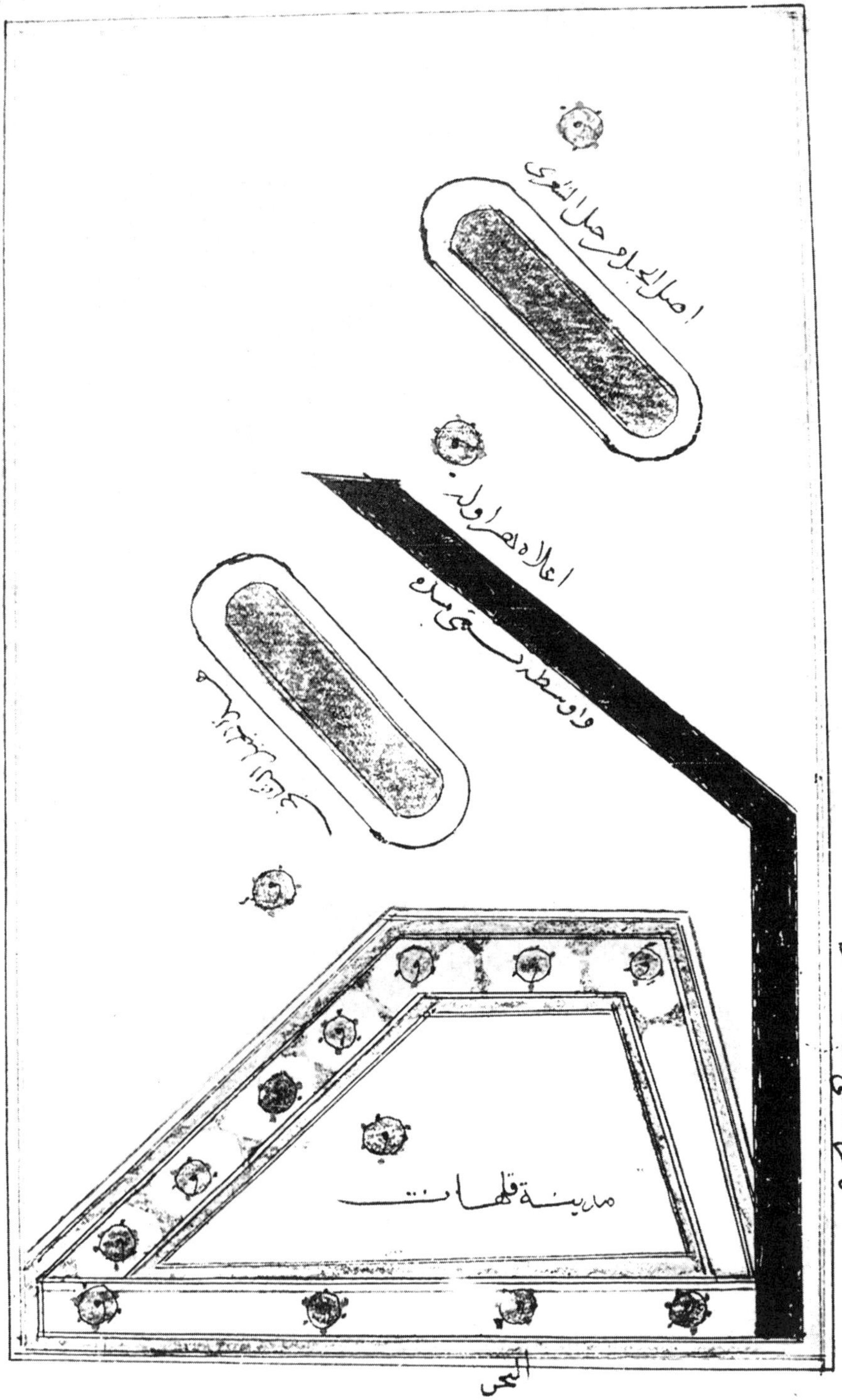

Figure 13. Plan of Qalhāt (I MS, f. 108a, text, p. 273, tabula XIV)
The sea is marked at the bottom of the plan with the town of Qalhāt above it inside the area of the plan and surrounded by fixed grey lines perhaps representing walls. The mountain furthest from the town is Jabal al-Saʿtar(ī). Other names are without dots.

account of you: a dear friend and a loathing enemy.' The first person to ascribe divinity to ʿAlī – God be pleased with him – was Abū al-Thadyān.[1] ʿAlī b. Abī Ṭālib said to him, 'Stop saying [such things]; keep yourself away from idle talk, for I eat, drink, sleep and marry. He who is distinguished by these qualities is excluded from worship. For God – His name is mighty and His praise glorious – is almighty and his qualities free from existing[, as humans exist] and from pleasures. How can this be so concerning [someone who] eats and sleeps as we have mentioned?'

When Abū al-Thadyān abandoned this previous belief of his, people began a new set of doctrines and some of them came out [in rebellion], settling in the area of the Great Marshes.[2] They still follow this set of beliefs until now ...[3]

From al-Manṣūrah to Aden on the return journey.[4] From al-Manṣūrah to Raysūt three parasangs, from where one crosses Jabal Rās al-Ḥimār ...[5] At that time the Commander of the Faithful ʿAlī b. Abī Ṭālib – God be pleased with him – went out [to do battle]. The enemy were arranged in ranks at al-Nahrawān,[6] but he broke them, putting them to the sword. He continued killing [276] them until he had annihilated them all. He returned the mule to the bridge, but it fell half way across. ʿAlī b. Abī Ṭālib – God be pleased with him – cried, 'Look out for those under the bridge!' And they were with Abū al-Thadyayn. The Commander of the Faithful ʿAlī b. Abī Ṭālib – God honour his face – said to him, 'The truth has come; falsehood has gone. Accept Islam and you will be spared.' He replied, 'How can I accept Islam, when the mule has knowledge of the unseen, namely that I was under the bridge?' Then ʿAlī unsheathed his sword and cut off his head. Those who had survived fled, but the sword continued to wreak its havoc among them[7] until he had pushed them back across the sea and they settled in these parts. So love was exchanged for hatred and among them were dear friends and loathing enemies, perishing both in their love and hatred.[8] As a poet has recited:

> There is both bitterness and sweetness in love;
> there is both unhappiness and happiness in love.

Another poet has recited as follows:

> Oh, alas for the pain of separation, alas!
> How bitter and how sweet is love!
> My tears have written a line on my cheek;
> God have mercy on one who approaches and receive him with hospitality!

[1] The reference here is to Dhū al-Thudayyah ('he of the little breast'), a man said to have had one deformed arm in the shape of a woman's breast and who was among those killed at al-Nahrawān by ʿAlī b. Abī Ṭālib (see above p. 270, n. 1). All the classical lexica have the story (e.g. Lane, *Lexicon*, I, pp. 333–4).

[2] Arabic *al-baṭāʾiḥ*, plur. of *baṭīḥah*, i.e. the area between Kufa and Basra in southern Iraq (Le Strange, *Lands*, pp. 26, 41, map II; Lassner, *ʿAbbāsid Rule*, p. 138).

[3] The end of the sentence is corrupt and unintelligible.

[4] I.e. from NE to SW.

[5] There must be a lacuna here, although it is not shown in the MSS.

[6] I have again (see p. 270, n. 1 above) amended from al-Nahrayn.

[7] I omit, with the L MS, *wa-warāʾ-hum min al-ghayb* which appears to me to have been included in error.

[8] The text as it is is corrupt and I am tentatively accepting the reading of the L MS from Löfgren's apparatus.

They call ʿAlī b. Abī Ṭālib Abū Turāb and they say that [Ibn Muljam][1] was a believer in his youth, but when he became adult, he denied his faith. They would recite the following in their own hearing:

> God bless the martyr of Ibn Muljam and grant him peace,
> who struck down polytheism with a sword until it was blunt.

They recite a line of poetry by Ibn Sukarrah:[2]

> They insulted ʿAlī, just as they insulted your old man,
> unbelief for unbelief and faith for faith.

[277] *Concealed knowledge and a hidden secret.*[3] When their ships are brought down [to the water] and launched,[4] they cannot be brought up or taken down until they all say with one voice, 'O ʿAlī!'[5] They claim that they can remain pulling their ships for a long time, becoming tired and exasperated. So they say to one another, 'Mention that man!', meaning ʿAlī b. ʿAbī Ṭālib – God be pleased with him. Their shaykhs say, 'Launch your ships, if you are going to!' They remain in difficulty and exhausted, with a headache and in distress, crying out and in uproar until they all say with one voice, 'O ʿAlī!' Then the ship runs more easily than a drink of cool water into the mouth of a thirsty man and thus the ship floats along[6] in the sea. A poet has recited as follows:

> There are things that I seek and you are my means [of help]
> [to reach] God, O my lord, Mūsā b. Jaʿfar.[7]
> If someone troubled comes to you asking for something,
> you give every pauper what he has been hoping for.

Another poet has recited as follows:

> When my enemies and those envious of me gang up on me
> without my being in the wrong, I make God my lord.
> And I cling to the *mīm* of Muḥammad, the *ʿayn* of ʿAlī, the two *ḥā*'s and the *fā'*.[8]

Maḥmūd has recited as follows:

> So by the right of the sanctity of five men,
> there is no one like them among men.
> ...[9]
> of this is Gabriel proud.

[1] He is ʿAbd al-Raḥmān b. Muljam who murdered ʿAlī in 40/661. The story of the conspiracy to kill all three principal players in the arbitration at Ṣiffīn and their actual murders is told is some detail in Mubarrad, *Kāmil*, III, pp. 196–200. See also *EI*, 'Ibn Muld̲j̲am'.

[2] The poet is unidentifed.

[3] Another disgression sparked off by mention of ʿAlī b. Abī Ṭālib.

[4] Arabic *aw* (for *wa-*?) *kawwarū* (Serjeant, *Portuguese*, p. 80).

[5] Arabic *yā la-ʿAlī*.

[6] Arabic 'fa-yaṣbī (Landberg, *Glossaire dat̲înois*, III, p. 2117) al-markab wa-yasbaḥu fī al-baḥr wa-yaʿūmu'. Tautology gone mad! See also Landberg, *Etudes*, I, p. 52.

[7] Mūsā al-Kāẓim, the Shīʿī imam who died in 83/702, son of Jaʿfar al-Ṣādiq (*EI*, 'Mūsā al-Kāẓim').

[8] Reading *wa-ʿayni ʿAliyyin* in the second hemistitch. I.e. I think of Muḥammad, the Prophet, ʿAlī, his nephew and son-in-law, Ḥasan and Ḥusayn, the two sons of ʿAlī, and Fāṭimah, Muḥammad's daughter and ʿAlī's wife.

[9] The first hemistitch is omitted.

[278] *The Ibāḍiyyah*. Any man who hates ʿAlī b. Abī Ṭālib – God be pleased with him – menstruates through his anus at the beginning of each month (it is also said that it is through his penis), just as a woman menstruates.

In the environs of Ṣanʿāʾ some of them call themselves al-Samārah.[1] Their distinguishing mark is that they hang a leather bag full of sand on their penis and when the sand is wet they change it for another. This bag is called a *miṭharah*.[2]

The Salaqlaqiyyah.[3] Any woman who hates ʿAlī b. Abī Ṭālib – God be pleased with him – menstruates through her anus. They are the Salaqlaqiyyah.

Ibn al-Mujāwir said: Any descendant of Abū al-Thadyān, man or woman, and those who were at al-Nahrawān,[4] the men are called the Ibāḍiyyah and the women the Salaqlaqiyyah. [This is] because they are well known for this particular defect. God knows best and is most wise.

The territory of the Khawārij[5] *and the Ibāḍiyyah*. I was informed as follows by al-Ṣaffār: All the people of Azerbaijan were ...[6] They all accepted Islam and followed the doctrine of Imam Abū ʿAbdallāh Muḥammad b. Idrīs al-Shāfiʿī – God be pleased with him.

Kilwah changed from being Shāfiʿī to Khārijī and they still until now follow this doctrine.

In the Maghreb, Nafūsā,[7] as also Rārah,[8] Tlemcen,[9] Rās [279] al-Makhbaz,[10] Tāhart,[11] Suwayqat Ibn Madkūl[12] and the mountains, Naṣīr[13] and Gibraltar,[14] these areas followed the Kharijite doctrine of old. Recent rulers of the Maghreb, Muḥammad b. al-Ḥasan b. Tūmart al-Barbarī and ʿAbd al-Muʾmin b. ʿAlī al-Kūmī pushed the people to the extremities of this doctrine. There are some in Egypt and in Syria, Damascus and Ḥarrān.

[1] I find no explanation of this name.

[2] Literally 'an instrument of purification'.

[3] Defined by Ibn Manẓūr (*Lisān*, X, p. 163) simply as 'a woman who menstruates through her anus', without any reference to the Ibāḍiyyah.

[4] Again I amend from the 'al-Nahrayn' of the text.

[5] Those supporters of ʿAlī who rebelled against him when he accepted the arbitration at Ṣiffīn in 37/657 (*EI*, 'Ṣiffīn).

[6] A lacuna in the MSS.

[7] Spelt invariably elsewhere Nafūsah, in North Africa. Idrīsī (*Opus*, I, pp. 229, 278–9) says it is a vast fertile mountain. See also Yāqūt, *Muʿjam*, V, pp. 296–7; *EI*, 'Nafūsa'.

[8] Reading doubtful and unidentified.

[9] Nine stages from Fez (Idrīsī, *Opus*, I, pp. 224, 249–50; Yāqūt, *Muʿjam*, II, p. 44). About 60 km from the Mediterranean and just over 100 km SW of Oran (Abun-Nasr, *History*, pp. 4–5 map). See also *EI*, 'Tilimsān'.

[10] Unidentified.

[11] Idrīsī (*Opus*, I, pp. 255–7) says that it is four stages from the sea, originally two large towns, the old one having a wall. Inhabited by Berbers, traders, agriculturalists, it is famous for horses, a good water supply, trees, fruits etc. Yāqūt (*Muʿjam*, II, pp. 7–9) says it is at the top of Jabal Jazzūl. See also *EI*, 'Tāhart'.

[12] Idrīsī (*Opus*, I, pp. 308, 309, 312) calls it Suwayqat Ibn Mathkūd. Yāqūt (*Muʿjam*, III, p. 288) has Suwayqat Ibn Maktūd.

[13] Unidentified. It might be Nuṣayr.

[14] Named after Ṭāriq b. Ziyād who landed there in 92/711 at the early stages of the Arab occupation of the Iberian Peninsula (*EI*, 'D̲j̲abal Ṭāriq').

[The territories of the Kharijites are as follows.] In Diyār Bakr,[1] Baghdad and in the Jazīrah ...[2] and Akhtārah,[3] together with the whole of the district of Mosul and the mountains of the Kurds, the Dabābilah[4] and all the followers of Shaykh ʿAdī.

In Baghdad, Bāb al-Barah,[5] al-Ḥarbiyyah,[6] Dār al-Qazz,[7] al-S.rẓah,[8] Bāb al-Azaj,[9] al-Ḥalbah,[10] al-Baṣaliyyah[11] and al-Ḥarīm[12] there are different people, but some of the people of Wāsiṭ al-Qaṣab [are Kharijites] and a village in Bahrain whose name escapes my informant.

In al-ʿIrāqayn,[13] Basra and Hamadhān.

In Arrān, Salmāst.[14]

In ...[15]

In Khurasan, Herat, Isrāsīr,[16] together with all the areas of Tīm ...,[17] including the areas of Ḥ.wād.r[18] ...[19] In Sīstān, as far as Wādī Sūl.[20] There there are more than ...[21] villages in a single line.

In the Yemen, Zabīd and its environs, Majhar.[22] In the highlands, [there is also] al-Sharaf, which is in the region of Zabīd opposite Qilḥāḥ. The inhabitants of al-Sharaf (meaning the sharifs) are not [in fact] people of noble descent. It is an area called al-Sharaf and it is simply a name. They pay a levy to the descendants of al-Ḥasan b. ʿAlī b. Abī Ṭālib. The whole of the Yemen became peaceful because of him ...[23] They

[1] The northern most and smallest of the three provinces of the Jazīrah in Iraq, named after the tribe Bakr b. Wāʾil, with Āmid its chief town, this latter sometime called Diyār Bakr, as it is today. The town is about 200 miles up the Tigris from Mosul (Yāqūt, *Muʿjam*, II, p. 494; Le Strange, *Lands*, pp. 108–9 and map III). It is strange that Ibn al-Mujāwir includes Baghdad in Diyār Bakr.

[2] An illegible place name.

[3] The L MS vocalizes thus, but the place is unidentified.

[4] Unidentified.

[5] Presumably the quarter near the Basra gate in the SE of the Round City (Lassner, *ʿAbbāsid Rule*, p. 190).

[6] The military quarter to the NW of the Round City (Lassner, *ʿAbbāsid Rule*, pp. 87, 186–7).

[7] Unidentified.

[8] Unidentified.

[9] Unidentified.

[10] Unidentified.

[11] Unidentified.

[12] Unidentified.

[13] Le Strange (*Lands*, p. 25, n. 1) explains exactly the meanings of al-ʿIrāqayn: the early capitals, Kufa and Basra; or Arabian and Persian Iraq, the latter being the Jibāl province. In view of the two towns mentioned, it is the second meaning which is required here.

[14] Arrān is the province hemmed in by the Kur and Aras rivers and sometimes called Bayn al-Nahrayn (Yāqūt, *Muʿjam*, I, p. 136; Le Strange, *Lands*, pp. 176–7 and map III). There is no place of the name Salmāst there, nor indeed to be found in all the sources available to me. I wonder if Ibn al-Mujāwir might be in error here for Salmās (Yāqūt, *Muʿjam*,III, pp. 238–9; Le Strange, *Lands*, p. 166 and map III), although the latter is in Azerbaijan.

[15] I omit the province and places mentioned here. The text is extremely corrupt and all are unrecognizable.

[16] Unidentified.

[17] Yāqūt (*Muʿjam*, II, p. 67) says Tīm is a village of Balkh in Khurasan and also a Soghdian village in Samarqand. The rest of the name is unrecognizable.

[18] Unidentified.

[19] I am obliged to omit an extremely corrupt passage here.

[20] The wadi is unidentified.

[21] There is a lacuna in the text.

[22] Unidentified.

[23] There is a lacuna in the text.

are Ḥanbalīs,[1] because they claim among themselves that no one is [280] truly a Ḥanbalī until he loathes ʿAlī. Of the other religions, the Jews are different from all faiths.

It is said that the first person to abuse Abū Turāb in Syria was Muʿāwiyah b. Abī Sufyān and this became an established practice among them which they continued down to the end of their dynasty.[2] The whole world abused him except Khwārazm, mentioned above.[3]

Section. It was said that al-Walīd b. ʿAbd al-Malik[4] was renowned for his ignorance. One day he mentioned ʿAlī b. Abī Ṭālib – God be pleased with him – from the *minbar*, but spoke ungrammatically. One of those who was there said, 'I do not know which of the two matters concerning him is more amazing, his bad grammar equalled by no one, or his assigning ʿAlī – God's pleasure be upon him – to the fraternity of thieves!'[5]

I have been informed as follows by Aḥmad b. ʿAlī b. ʿAbdallāh al-Wāsiṭī: ...[6] and put aside from all the imams Muʿāwiyah, Yazīd and ...[7] on Thursday, 22 Ramaḍān 625.[8] Muʿāwiyah b. Abī Sufyān, the scribe of God's revelation and the immediate successor of the Messenger of God – God bless him and grant him peace – was right. They were the first to abuse [ʿAlī] from the *minbars* of Islam.

Imām al-Ḥaramayn [Abū al-Maʿālī ʿAbd al-Malik] wrote as follows in *Kitāb al-Lumaʿ*:[9] Muʿāwiyah is wrong, while ʿAlī adheres to the truth.

[The territory of the Kharijites includes] the whole of Oman, Qalhāt, al-Furāt,[10] Ṭīwī[11] Muscat,[12] Ḥayy ʿĀṣim,[13] Sohar,[14] Khawr Fakkān,[15] Kumzār,[16]

[1] The followers of Aḥmad b. Muḥammad b. Ḥanbal who died in 241/855 in Baghdad. They show a particular reverence for the memory of Muʿāwiyah and for the Umayyad house and are therefore anti-ʿAlī (*SEI*, 'Aḥmad b. Muḥammad b. Ḥanbal').

[2] I.e. the Umayyad dynasty which gave way to the Abbasids in 132/750.

[3] Ibn al-Mujāwir does not in fact mention this elsewhere in the text.

[4] The 6th Umayyad caliph, reg. 86–96/705–15 (Bosworth, *Islamic Dynasties*, p. 3).

[5] Arabic *luṣūṣiyyah*. I am not sure that there is any deeper meaning than the one conveyed in the translation, though it should perhaps be pointed out that one encounters an amazing diversity of technical terms concerning all manner of underworld characters and their gangs (Serjeant, *Misers*, pp. 36 ff.; Bosworth, *Islamic Underworld*, I, pp. 1–48).

[6] The text is corrupt and appears to read 'kataba w.h.?.(?).? al-abnūs ʿalā faṣṣ khātami-h ... (lacuna) y'.

[7] Corrupt with lacuna.

[8] 26 August 1228.

[9] Abū al-Maʿālī ʿAbd al-Malik al-Juwaynī Imām al-Ḥaramayn died in 478/1085. He wrote among other things *Kitāb Lumaʿ al-adillah fī qawāʿid ʿaqāʾid ahl al-sunnah* (Brockelmann, *Geschichte*, I, pp. 484–6).

[10] Unidentified.

[11] A few miles N of Qalhāt (Lorimer map; Agius, *Dhow*, map 1). Löfgren vocalizes Ṭaywā.

[12] The present capital of the Sultanate of Oman about 80 miles up the Bāṭinah coast from Qalhāt (Arabian Peninsula map). Originally a mere anchorage (*marsā*) of the more important Sohar (see below n. 14), it came more into its own from the early 10th/16th century when the Portuguese arrived in the area (Smith, 'Masqaṭ', p. 147; *EI*, 'Maskaṭ').

[13] Unidentified.

[14] Arabic Ṣuḥār, about 130 miles up the Bāṭinah coast from Muscat. It was the major medieval port of Oman (Arabian Peninsula map; *EI*, 'Ṣuḥār').

[15] Coastal town still known to this day in the United Arab Emirate state of Sharjah. It is about 75 miles up the coast from Sohar (Lorimer, *Gazetteer*, IIA, p. 516 and map; Arabian Peninsula map).

[16] Coastal settlement right at the tip of the Musandam Peninsula projecting into the Strait of Hurmuz. It is about 75 miles N of Khawr Fakkān (Lorimer, *Gazetteer*, IIB, p. 1040 and map; Arabian Peninsula map).

and Julfār.[1] [There are also] those in the mountains, ...[2] and Tharwā Shamā'il.[3]

[281] *The conquest of Oman.* I read in the second book of *Masālik al-mamālik*[4] where it is mentioned that the majority of the regions of Oman were Ibāḍī until the battle took place between them and a group of B. Sāmah b. Lu'ayy b. Ghālib.[5] Muḥammad b. al-Qāsim al-Shāmī left [after the battle and went] to Imam Abū al-ʿAbbās Aḥmad al-Muʿtaḍid bi-Allāh b. Abī Aḥmad Muḥammad b. al-Muwaffaq (or, it was said, Ṭalḥah b. al-Mutawakkil – or, it was said, the son of al-Muwaffaq, Muḥammad b. Jaʿfar al-Mutawakkil),[6] seeking his help. So he despatched Abū al-Nūr[7] with him and he conquered Oman for al-Muʿtaḍid bi-Allāh and established the *khuṭbah* in his name there. The Ibāḍīs departed for the region of S.r.d.ḥ.ḥah[8] where they settled and have lived until now. But if we were to open this door, there would be too much to say. Brevity in such a matter is more proper and better. God knows best.

The Khwārazmian conquest of Qalhāt.[9] When Khwājah Raḍī al-Dīn Qiyām al-Mulk Abū Bakr al-Zūzanī[10] became governor of Kirmān, Makrān[11] and Fārs, he killed by the sword Sultan ʿAlā' al-Dīn Muḥammad b. Tekish, ruler of Qalhāt. It is said that Mālik b. Fahm died during the period of Raḍī al-Dīn Qiwām al-Mulk. ...[12] Raḍī al-Dīn Qiwām al-Mulk despatched ships and took over Qalhāt together with all the regions of Oman.

[1] An important port on the western coast of the UAE in the emirate of Ras-al-Khaimah, situated just N of the town of that name. Known from very early Islamic times and much used by the Umayyad and Abbasid caliphs to disembark armies engaged in campaigns against the Ibāḍīs in Oman, it has a fine natural harbour. It declined in the 11th/17th century (*EI*, 'Ra's al-Khayma').

[2] Illegible.

[3] Unidentified.

[4] Ibn al-Mujāwir has been reading Iṣṭakhrī (*Masālik*, p. 27), one of the number of works with this title.

[5] I.e. the battle of al-Qāʿ in 278/891 (see n. 6 below). B. Sāmah are a branch of Quraysh (Kaḥḥālah, *Muʿjam*, II, pp. 497–8; Caskel, *Gamharah*, I, Tefeln 4, 29). Rawas ('Oman', p. 251, map 3) places them in the S of what is now the UAE from Sohar in the E across to Abu Dhabi in the W, including the area of al-ʿAyn.

[6] Aḥmad is the Abbasid caliph, reg. 279–89/892–902, and this is the correct version (see below in this note); Ṭalḥah was not a caliph, but the son of al-Mutawakkil Jaʿfar, reg. 232–47/847–61; the third possiblity cited by Ibn al-Mujāwir is a puzzle: Muḥammad b. Jaʿfar al-Mutawakkil was the Abbasid caliph, reg. 247–8/861–2, but his cognomen was al-Muntaṣir (Bosworth, *Islamic Dynasties*, p. 6). In fact, this must be a reference to the battle of al-Qāʿ in 278/891 fought between the Ibāḍī Imam ʿAzzān and the Nizārīs of B. Sāmah. The latter were heavily defeated and two of their number, Muḥammad b. al-Qāsim and Bashīr b. Mundhir, went off to Bahrain where they asked for help firstly from the Abbasid governor of al-Muʿtaḍid Aḥmad, Muḥammad b. Nūr, and then Muḥammad b. al-Qāsim went on to Baghdad to appeal to the caliph in person. The resulting Abbasid invasion of Oman brought an end to the second Ibāḍī imamate in the country (Rawas, *Oman*, pp. 191–7).

[7] Ibn al-Mujāwir means Muḥammad b. Nūr, the Abbasid governor of Bahrain (n. 6 above).

[8] Doubtful and unidentified.

[9] I translate thus at the suggestion of Professor C. E. Bosworth.

[10] His *nisbah* may be spelt either way, though the name of the Qūhistān town is more often found as Zūzan (Yāqūt, *Muʿjam*, III, p. 158; Le Strange, *Lands*, p. 358 and Map VIII). He was governor under the Khwārazm shahs (Bosworth, *Islamic Dynasties*, pp. 178–9).

[11] The vast desert province wedged between Kirmān in the W, the Indian Ocean in the S and Sijistān in the E and N (Le Strange, *Lands*, pp. 329 ff., Maps I and VII).

[12] The Arabic text appears to read *fa-fī tilka ... wa-al-ʿurḍah*, for the latter word of which Löfgren suggests the reading *wa-al-furṣah*, but this makes no sense to me.

He had governors, administrators and deputies collecting income from the land and merchants' customs dues. [There were also other] taxes and administrative regulations. He himself used to send silk[1] from Kirmān and [his agents] would sell it, collect taxes for the territory and thereby buy Arabian horses which they would send to him, about five hundred at a time. He would use the inferior ones for riding and send on the Najdī horses to Khwārazm to be presented to the sultan.

After the death of Raḍī al-Dīn Qiwām [282] al-Mulk in Kirmān,[2] he left behind in Qalhāt 64,000 *mann* – it is also said 80,000 – of silk, together with five hundred horse. Qalhāt [was removed] from the hands of the Khwārazmiyyah, together with the horses and silk, in 615.[3] After his death, Qalhāt was taken over by Shaykh Mālik b. Fahm b. Mālik ...[4] [and] in 616[5] he built a wall round Qalhāt made of stone and gypsum.

Description of the sperm whale.[6] One day opposite the town, the inhabitants of Qalhāt discovered a large island. Shaykh Mālik b. Fahm told them to find out for him about the island and what it was. So the fishermen went off and returned to him and told him it was a whale floating on the surface of the sea. He told them to drag it into the town. So the fishermen boarded their fishing boats[7] and fastened their anchors[8] to the whale, dragged it back and landed it on the shore.The people began to examine it and its enormous form, but then it stank and became putrid.[9] Inside its belly appeared a piece of ambergris weighing three *buhār*. When the people got to know all about it, they cut the ambergris up and plundered it. It reached [the people of] the whole area, both weak and strong. When Shaykh Mālik b. Fahm acquired some in 610,[10] [it was] a *buhār* (using the 'large' weight)[11] out of a total of two hundred *mann*.

Section.[12] A sperm whale found a piece of ambergris floating on top of the sea and swallowed it. The piece settled in its intestines and its stomach was too weak to digest it. So it died and floated on the surface [283] of the sea. The waves pounded it and washed it up on the shore at Qalhāt and thereby some people became rich.

I was informed as follows by Muḥammad b. Bundār al-Jawzī: I bought some pieces of this ambergris, a *ḥiml*[13] at the lowest possible price. I took it and journeyed with it to

[1] The text has *ibrīsam/ibrīsum*, the Persian word *abrīsham/abrīshum* (Kazimirski, *Dictionnaire*, I, p. 4; Steingass, *Dictionary*, p. 8). D (I, p. 2) says it is 'soie mêlée de coton'.

[2] See p. 277, n. 10 above.

[3] Begins 30 March 1218.

[4] Text *min* followed by a lacuna.

[5] Begins 19 March 1219.

[6] Arabic *battān*, *Physeter polycyphus* (Landberg, *Glossaire daṯînois*, I, pp. 132–3). For this passage, see also Serjeant, 'Yemeni Coast', pp. 189, 191, n. 10.

[7] Text *ṣanābiq*.

[8] I had been prepared to accept *anjar* corrected from Landberg (*Glossaire daṯînois*, I, p. 133) at first instead of the *aḥribah* of the text. However, Dionisius Agius knows *aḥribah* (he gives no sing.) and says it is an old term for 'anchors'.

[9] Arabic *jāfa wa-khāsa* (Landberg, *Glossaire daṯînois*, I, p. 664; Piamenta, *Dictionary*, I, p. 141).

[10] Begins 23 May 1213.

[11] The *buhār* weight varied according to the article being weighed and this is how I interpret the 'large' weight here (Yule and Burnell, *Hobson-Jobson*, pp. 47–8; Hinz, *Masse*, pp. 9–10).

[12] See Landberg, *Glossaire daṯînois*, I, p. 133.

[13] A large weight, a camel load, over 240 kg.

Khwārazm where I sold it to Turkān Khātūn ...[1] 'Alā' al-Dīn Muḥammad b. Tekish, ten *mithqāl* for thirty dinars.

Description of Qalhāt.[2] Qalhāt is a place on the sea shore surrounded by mountains. It is said it is like Aden [in this regard]. Its water is good and is brought from ...[3] There there is the river of Socrates, the water of which is from the mountains, flowing among palm groves and cultivated areas, light, healthy and sweet to the taste. Linguists say that Oman[4] is called after 'Umān b. Na'sān, son of Abraham the Friend – peace be upon him – and that it is he who built it. [But] Ibn al-Mujāwir says that the region of Oman is so called because it has goodness everywhere.[5]

Their food is dates and fish. Their clothes are blue and they go bare-headed. Groups of seven men buy a slave girl. Whenever one of the seven goes in [to her], he takes off his shoes and leaves them at the door. If anyone of the seven comes, he sees the shoes and turns on his heels, knowing that one of his group is with the slave girl.

There is no one in the whole of the inhabited world more hostile to strangers than they are. Zayd says to 'Amr, 'Yes, by him who crushes[6] the stranger with stones,[7] attack him with a ...[8] and give him some more with a stick!' There is no one more cowardly than they. When they spot pirates at sea, one says to another, 'By your wealth, what shall we give him?[9] Hand it over [284] and you will survive!' So they surrender the ship to the pirates and leave empty handed.[10] There is no steelyard smaller than that of Qalhāt.

From Qalhāt to Muscat. From Qalhāt to Ṭīwī three parasangs. To Muscat[11] six parasangs. Its original name was Maskat.[12] It is said that, when the Companions arrived there, everyone in the town remained silent,[13] so it was called Maskat.[14] God knows best!

Description of a fish-trap.[15] There is a fish-trap in Maskat, with a look-out[16] who sits all the time at its mouth and when a shoal of fish enters the trap, the look-out knows how

[1] A lacuna in the text.
[2] See Smith, '"Anthropological" Passages', pp. 167–8.
[3] Text *m.?.d.h.*
[4] Arabic 'Umān.
[5] Arabic *ta'ummu bi-al-khayr.*
[6] Reading *bāziq* with Löfgren (Landberg, *Glossaire daṯînois*, III, p. 167).
[7] Arabic *jandal* which Ibn al-Mujāwir then glosses *ya'nī al-ḥajar* (Lane, *Lexicon*, II, p. 470).
[8] Text *r.w.?.r.*
[9] Arabic *iy bi-al-māl mā nu'ṭī-h.*
[10] The Arabic has the colourful expression *'arāyā al-astāh*, 'with bare buttocks'!
[11] Arabic Masqaṭ.
[12] See Smith, 'Masqaṭ', p. 147.
[13] Arabic *sakata.*
[14] I.e. 'place of silence'.
[15] Arabic *'innah*, classical Arabic *'unnah*. The classical Arabic meaning is 'enclosure (made of wood)', 'booth' (Nashwān, *Shams*, VII, p. 4279; Lane, *Lexicon*, V, p. 2165). See also Landberg, *Glossaire daṯînois*, II, p. 1396, III, p. 2332. Nowhere is the definition given of a fish-trap, although this is evidently what it means here. Ibn al-Mujāwir's *'innah* must be akin to Serjeant's Bahrain *ḥaḍrah* ('Fisher-folk', p. 489 and *passim*, and Khalifa, 'Fishing', p. 230) and would seem to be permanent.
[16] See above p. 154, n. 5.

many fish there are. He was asked about this and replied, 'When I see the first fish,[1] I know through long experience how many will follow it in.'

This town used to be the anchorage of the town of Sohar and it was here where ships coming from the ends ...[2] used to anchor. They would come up to Sohar with footwear and other commodities, buying and selling. From there the goods would go up to Kirmān and from Kirmān to Sijistān.[3] Then the goods would be divided up for Khurasan, Transoxania, Zābulistān, al-Ghūr and Karmīl.[4]

To Ḥayy ʿĀṣim six parasangs. To Asrār six parasangs.[5] To Sohar four parasangs.

Description of Sohar. I was informed as follows by Abū al-Majd b. Abī Muḥammad al-Kamāl b. al-Kamāl al-ʿAlawī al-Ḥusaynī: [285] Sohar was [made up of] 12,000 villages with 12,000 castles with 12,000 rivers and 12,000 mosques. Each *nākhūdhah* would live in his own castle and his family drink from his own river. On Friday, he would go to the mosque at the head of an assembly of ninety-nine of his servants, followers, relatives and helpers.

I was informed by one of them that after it was built there were 192 steelyards for weighing merchandise for the use of anyone seeking [to buy] and anyone who sought [to sell].

Description of Dār al-Khatmah. A certain *nākhūdhah* built a residence [in Sohar] and gave instructions for the Quran to be written in gold on it, or more precisely on the teak beams[6] of the residence. [The text was] carved and inserted in twelve writings. A complete recitation[7] was fitted into one row of the house and there was enough space for it. So the residence was called Dār al-Khatmah.

The people used to build in baked brick, gypsum and teak. But it all fell into ruins and the jinn began to settle around the buildings.

I was informed by Shaykh Abū Bakr al-Barī that these regions belonged to the Seljuk rulers of Kirmān. But they were all erased. The Ghuzz[8] conquered them and the region was abandoned. Then the Arabs assumed authority over the regions and destroyed them.

[1] Arabic *muqaddam al-asmāk*.

[2] A lacuna in the text.

[3] An earlier form of Sīstān, the province S of Khurasan (Le Strange, *Lands*, pp. 334 ff. and map VIII).

[4] Ibn al-Mujāwir's Zāwulistān must be Zābulistān as above. Ghūr (or Ghūristān), without the article, is a large area of southern Khurasan situated between Bāmiyān in the E and Herat in the W, N of the Herat river (Le Strange, *Lands*, p. 339 and map VIII). Karmīl (spelling?) is unidentified.

[5] About 15–20 miles N of Sohar (Lorimer map).

[6] I translate *tawāzīr* thus, presumably the plur. of *tawzīr*, and the MSS are clearly written and pointed. I use only the context, for I find nothing in the lexicographical literature on this word, although *w z r* in certain patterns has the idea of help and support. On this basis, I suppose it might refer to wooden pillars.

[7] Arabic *khatmah*, i.e. a complete recitation of the Quran from beginning to end (*SEI*, 'Khatm, khatma'; *EI*, 'Khatma, khitma').

[8] 440–c. 584/1048–1188. At about the latter date, the Turkish Oghuz tribesmen (the Ghuzz of the text used here, the word used more accurately than its usual vague reference to non-Arabs) within Seljuk lands revolted against them (Bosworth, *Islamic Dynasties*, pp. 186, 188).

Section. Zayd travelled away from his native land and then returned only to find that Baḥārah al-Ḥammāl[1] had become qadi of the district. The qadi, al-Ḥammāl, said to Zayd, 'Increase in number those first camels of good breeding,[2] for we are in a slump at present.'[3] Zayd asked, 'How [286] can this be – God keep our lord the qadi long in office and confirm his principles?' The qadi replied, 'Originally, our ancestors were of high standing until we began carrying[4] firewood for the community and now later generations have become their judge!'

Ibn al-Mujāwir said: In the days of our ancestors, they settled in these castles. We do not live in them now, but are satisfied with changing living quarters among the ruins. As a poet has recited:

> O you weeping after your dear ones [have gone]
> among the abodes and the remains,
> After they have gone,
> do you know what the taste of slumber [is like]?
> He replied to me, 'No, by Him with whom
> my heart is in pledge,
> How can calm [lead] to sleep,
> when my means of achieving rest are far away?
> When will the tears of him
> killed by Misfortune become cool?'

[There is also the following poem] by Qadi Abū Bakr al-Rāfiʿī[5]

> I ask God's forgiveness for him who bade farewell,
> while we were weeping altogether because we were about to be separated.
> He let fall tears from his eyelids,
> when he saw me doing the same.
> He said to me as we parted,
> 'How great and painful is separation!'

[There is a poem] as follows by al-Sayf al-Ḥakamī:[6]

> O doves of the tamarisk trees of Wādī al-Ḥimā,
> You have awakened and stirred up passionate love [within me]!
> My enemies, you and my weeping have no fear,
> and I see none of their tears.
> When doves coo, it fills me with longing
> and dark lips increase my longing all the more.

Another poet recited as follows:

> Every land where you stay longs for you;
> 'tis as if you are rain [falling on all] corners of the land.

[1] The first name is doubtful. Arabic *ḥammāl* means 'porter', 'carrier' and see n. 4 below.

[2] The text has *ubsuṭ mā kāna min al-ibil al-awāʾil min al-rifʿah*. Löfgren has suggested the exclusion of *al-ibil* by means of square brackets. I, however, prefer to leave the metaphor intact.

[3] Arabic 'wa-mā naḥnu al-ān fī-h min al-hubūṭ'. I.e. we were originally of high standing, fell on hard times, but now we have gained a high position and our fortunes have started to improve.

[4] Arabic *ḥammālīn* – how, we assume, the qadi got his name al-Ḥammāl.

[5] I cannot identify the poet in question.

[6] I cannot identify the poet in question.

[287] When Raysūt fell into ruin, Sohar flourished and when Sohar fell into ruin, al-Tīz[1] and Hurmuz[2] were built. When al-Tīz and Hurmuz fell into ruin, Aden was built.

To al-ʿAqr four parasangs.[3] To Kalbah four parasangs.[3] To[4] Khawr Fakkān four parasangs. To Dibā four parasangs.[5] To Līmah four parasangs.[6] To Kumzār three parasangs. To Ẓafār eight parasangs.[7] To Qays eight parasangs, a day and a night out to sea.

The building of Qays – settled by Magians.[8] How it all came about was as follows, as Saʿd b. Mālik b. Dāʾūd b. Sulaymān al-Anṣārī has reported: The Magians fled when the dynasty changed with the conquest of the Arabs over the Persians.[9] They settled on the island and, after a long time had passed, built good quality, high, lofty houses with baked bricks and gypsum. As times changed, bringing injustice with them, they left the island and it became a prison of the rulers of Persia. It was called in their time Zandān.[10] The rulers proceeded in accordance with their usual behaviour until Sīrāf was destroyed.[11]

Two Sīrāfīs turned up on the island and settled there. They were well pleased with the place and took control over the island where there were some fishermen. The two men from Sīrāf got the better of the fishermen and drove them out in humiliation. They ruled over the island and built solid houses there. It is said that they built them on the foundations of the [original] Magian buildings. They planted palm groves and settled there. I was informed by Yaḥyā b. ʿAlī b. ʿAbd al-Raḥmān al-Zarrād that it was 120 years since the island of Qays was built and this information was provided in 624.[12]

They fixed [a levy] of one dinar on every ship which passed through [288]. In the second and third years, they settled on three dirhams and they kept on raising [the levy] until it was fixed at ten and has remained so until now.

When the two men [from Sīrāf] became powerful and took over control, one of them claimed that he was sultan and this has been the established practice until now, though this is in name rather than in practice. He had the *khuṭbah* read on Friday from the *minbar* in the name of the sultan of the east and west, ruler of the land. One man

[1] Without the article. The important port of Makrān on the Persian side of the Gulf (Le Strange, *Lands*, pp. 329–30 and Map VII).

[2] This would be old Hurmuz at this time, situated in from the Kirmān coast and E of the island, at the head of a creek where ships entered from the sea. It is now known as Mināb (Le Strange, *Lands*, p. 318 and Map VI).

[3] I.e. from Sohar. About 15 miles N of Asrār (Lorimer map).

[4] About 20 miles N of al-ʿAqr, also called Ghāllah (Lorimer map).

[5] Situated about 20 miles N of Khawr Fakkān, now sitting on the UAE border with the Musandam enclave of Oman (Arabian Peninsula map).

[6] About 25 miles N of Dibā (Lorimer map; Arabian Peninusula map).

[7] Presumably on the western side of the present-day UAE coast and the port used for travel to Qays island.

[8] See p. 143, n. 9 above.

[9] Presumably after the Oghuz revolt c. 584/1188 against the Seljuks when the region was subsequently abandoned and taken over by 'the Arabs' (p. 280, n. 8 above). But see also p. 143, n. 9 below.

[10] I can find no mention of this alternative name elsewhere.

[11] I am convinced that Ibn al-Mujāwir is floundering in serious historical confusion here! The notable destruction of Sīrāf was by earthquake in 366 or 367/977 and this certainly does not fit into the historical pattern envisaged in my n. 9 above. Perhaps it is a different 'conquest of the Arabs over the Persians' and/or a different destruction of Sīrāf.

[12] Begins 22 December 1226.

suggested he was sultan of Ṭās ... and ruler of Ladūkrān,[1] these being two places at the ends of the island. The true circumference of the island is a parasang, but it is [also] said it is three days.

In Bahrain he had ships called *dūbah*[2] fashioned for him among the ...[3] The Arabs who are land owners in Bahrain pay 20,000 a year to make these *dūbah* in their land.

One night he got drunk and said to a stranger who was with them, 'I give you Safāhāt.'[4] The stranger accepted the gift, so in the morning the ruler told his vizier to write an order for so-and-so for his door-keeper to hand over Safāhāt to him. The official did as he was told. After some days, the ruler met the stranger by chance and said, 'Are you not yet ready to go to Safāhāt?' The stranger replied, 'God prolong the ruler's might, I want some money to get to Safāhāt.' 'Give him 500,000 dinars,' said the ruler. So the man took the money and returned to his home town.

Why the island of Qays was so called. Qays b. Zuhayr b. Jadhīmah b. Abī Sufyān the master of al-Dāḥis and al-Ghabrā', and Rabī' b. Sās, the owner of al-Khaṭṭār and al-Ḥanfā', laid a wager with each other [on the outcome of a horse race].[5] Now al-Khaṭṭār [289] and al-Dāḥis were stallions and al-Ghabrā' and al-Ḥanfā' mares. Al-Dāḥis beat al-Khaṭṭār and a dispute arose between the parties. So Qays b. Zuhayr, the master of al-Dāḥis departed for the region of Oman to extinguish the fire of evil. When he had settled down in Oman, he opened a shop and became a perfume dealer, remaining [there] buying and selling. Two of the amirs of Oman laid a wager between them, since there was a dispute about the race between al-Dāḥis and al-Khaṭṭār. The two amirs came to the old perfumer and asked him about the race and who won and who lost. The old man said to them, 'Are you really asking me?' 'Yes, indeed', they replied. 'Al-Dāḥis won', he told them. When the one who lost the wager heard this, he became angry. He reviled the old man and spat in his face. Then the latter shut his shop, went home, saddled and bridled al-Dāḥis and mounted, saying to his daughter, Yāqūtah, 'Go ahead of me to such-and-such a well and wait there.' The old man went to where the people had collected and proclaimed, 'I am Qays b. Zuhayr and this horse of mine is al-Dāḥis. Whoever did not know me [before], should [now] know who I am.' He attacked the man who had spat in his face[6] and cut his head off. He rode al-Dāḥis on to the well, mounted his daughter, Yāqūtah, behind him and rode the horse to the sea shore.[7] He spurred on the horse, but he would not go into the sea. So he put a cover over his eyes and the horse went into the water and swam right out to sea. But the horse tired and all three drowned.

[1] There is a brief description of the island in *Iraq*, p. 161. No place names are given, however, and I am unable to trace these names elsewhere.

[2] Dionisius Agius suggests this reading to me and directs me to his *Wake*, p. 87. It is a large double-ended cargo craft.

[3] Text Āl Ḥ.s.?.w.?.

[4] Unidentified.

[5] This is a variation on the famous story of the pre-Islamic war between 'Abs and Dhubyān, two branches of Ghaṭafān. Qays was a 'Absī chief and, traditionally, his antagonist Ḥudhayfah b. Badr. In the original story too al-Dāḥis is matched with the mare, al-Ghabrā'. For the full account of the original, see Nicholson, *Literary History*, pp. 61–2.

[6] Reading 'wa-ḥamala 'alā alladhī tafala ...' with the L MS.

[7] I follow the context here, perhaps *fa-rakiba al-khayl* for *fa-tabi'at-h al-khayl ilā al-sāḥil* which makes no sense to me.

The people of the island of Qays have reported as follows: The horse swam, carrying his two riders, until the island loomed up before them. So they settled there and the population of the island are descended from them. And thus their island is called Jazīrat Qays, since he, Qays b. Zuhayr b. Jadhīmah b. Abī Sufyān, was the father of its people.

It is also said that the island was ...[1] When Qays with Yāqūtah and al-Dāḥis arrived, the inhabitants of the island put him in complete charge of their everyday and financial affairs.[2] The descendants of the Jāshū intermarried with them and he married Yāqūtah to the most senior man on the island and he produced children by her who were the Persians. Until this day, the Persians have in their heads the stupidity of the Arabs!

I was informed as follows [290] by a Persian ...:[3] The Jāshū are from Daylam.[4] They used to live in the desert in Fārs and its environs, an area rich in horses, livestock and camels. After a long time, they kept to the mountains and built castles in which they lived. They became known as the Shabānkārah, meaning 'those who let down their hair' like the Kurds.[5] When they had constructed the fortresses and they were inhabited, building was increased. One of them settled on the island of Qays and the Jāshū grew out of his descendants. This latter is the accurate version.

The origin of the name Jāshū.[6] A certain king was attacked by pleurisy[7] and the omens indicated to him that, if he had intercourse every night with a virgin Nubian slave girl, his unfortunate illness would disappear. (Ibn al-Mujāwir comments, 'In all creation there is nothing as hot as the vagina of a Nubian slave girl. With that heat the pleurisy gradually dissolves, descending along with the sperm into the girl. When the woman stands up, she shakes out the sperm, now free of the ill effects of the disease, out of her vagina. No harm comes to the girl. But others say it does do her harm.') When the king heard this, he sent one of his viziers to the Sudan, commanding him to buy one hundred virgin Nubian slave girls. When the vizier was ready [to depart], he cut off his penis, put it into a box and handed it over to the king. He journeyed until he reached the Sudan, where he bought the virgin slave girls and took them back to the king. When the latter came to one, he found she was not a virgin – and the same with the second, the third, the tenth, right up to the hundreth! He found them all in the same condition.[8] When the vizier had entered into the presence of the king and his courtiers, [291] the king said to those present, 'There has been some poking!'[9] That is, he has been penetrating them, or he has deflowered them![10] The king added, 'There was indeed no

[1] There is a clear lacuna in the L MS.

[2] Arabic 'wallaw-hu ahl al-jazīrah 'alā arwāḥi-him wa-amwāli-him'.

[3] A lacuna in all the MSS.

[4] I.e. the highlands of Gīlān (*EI*, 'Daylam', 'Gīlān').

[5] I am grateful to Edmund Bosworth for his suggestion here that these are the people in question (*EI*, 'Kurds'). The word *s.wākārah* means nothing in Persian.

[6] The true etymology of *jāshū* may be nothing more than the colloquial Persian word *chāshū* (Löfgren, *Texte*, II, p. 25).

[7] Text *birsām*. The word might mean 'tumour' (Lane, *Lexicon*, I, p. 187), but the commoner meaning is that given and this would, in any case, seem to fit the context of the story better. It is made up of two Persian words: *barr*, 'breast', and *sām*, 'swelling' (Steingass, *Dictionary*, pp. 166, 643).

[8] Arabic *'alā nasaq wāḥid*.

[9] Arabic *jāshak* (= *jā' al-shakk*) which can also mean 'there was some doubt', hence the two glosses.

[10] Arabic *istafaḍḍa-hum* (for *istafaḍḍa-hunna*) (Landberg, *Glossaire daṯînois*, III, p. 2423).

doubt.'[1] That is, certainty has emerged out of doubt in the matter. So when the vizier realized what the king was saying, he called for the box, opened the lid and there was the penis inside. 'What made you do such a thing?' enquired the king. 'I was afraid of exactly what has happened', he replied. Then the king called all the slave girls and asked them what had happened. They replied, 'We stopped at such-and-such an island and swam in a spring of sweet water. We knew nothing of what happened to us, but each one of us was accompanied by a jinni who deflowered her.' The king ordered them to be returned to their island. So they dwelt on the island of Qays where they built houses. They multiplied and the inhabitants became many. They were called Jāshak because of the utterance made by the king. The expression remained with them and they became known as Jāshū.

Section. I was informed as follows by Abū al-Qāsim b. Ibrāhīm b. Muḥammad al-Murābiṭ: Something happened like this in the Maghreb. The king sent a vizier called ...[2] to the Sudan to buy some slave girls for himself. When the king approached the girls, he discovered they were not virgins.[3] 'They are fornicators!',[4] he exclaimed, thereby accusing the vizier of acting in a hostile manner against him. So their whole tribe was known as Zanātā; they are Berbers, one man and 50,000 swordsmiths.[5] Ibn al-Mujāwir said, 'What I think is that they divided into two groups, one settling in the Maghreb and known as Zanātā and the other on the island of Qays, known as the Jāshū.'

[292] *Pearls*. They come from an oyster which develops at the bottom of the salty sea. When rain falls during April,[6] the oyster comes up, some of it opening after it rises to the surface of the sea for the rain to collect. However many drops fall on one oyster, that oyster is united with these rain drops which sink to the bottom of the sea inside the oyster to make it grow. As a poet has recited:

> September[7] is my time with you; it does not leave me,
> while March[8] and April belong to someone else.

Anūshirvān the Just said to his vizier, Buzurgmihr,[9] 'How much is this crown of mine worth?' He replied, 'The income of a shower of rain in April.' 'What do you mean?' he

[1] 'There was indeed no doubt' begins the punning which is almost impossible to render into English and could mean either 'There was indeed no doubt' or 'There has not been any penetration'. In order to make anything of this in English, one has to assume that the meaning of *jāshak* has been taken to refer to 'doubt'; viz. 'there was indeed no doubt'.

[2] Lacuna followed by *b.'.'.y*.

[3] Text *wajada wisāʿan*. Löfgren suggests the reading *wa-wajada-hunna wisāʿan* or *wa-wajada ʿinda-hunna wasāʿan*. If we accept the former, *wisāʿ* should be taken as the plur. of *wāsiʿ* or *wasīʿ*, literally 'wide'. In the latter, *wasāʿ* would have to be taken as a noun, = *wasāʿah*, 'width'.

[4] Arabic *zanatā*, 'they (fem. plur.) have committed fornication'.

[5] Zanātah are indeed Berbers, one of the three major tribal groups, according to Ibn Khaldūn. They cooperated with the Arab invaders of the Maghreb and some of them claimed Arab descent (Ibn Khaldūn, *Muqaddimah*, I, p. 270 and *passim*; Abun-Nasr, *History*, pp. 8–9). This last sentence is doubtful and the meaning obscure.

[6] Arabic *Nīsān* (Varisco, *Agriculture*, pp. 31, 244–5).

[7] Arabic *Aylūl* (ibid., p. 38).

[8] Arabic *Ādhār* (ibid., p. 30).

[9] 'Steward of the royal palaces' (*CHIr*, III(2), p. 738).

asked. The vizier said, 'If it falls on land, you have wheat; if it falls out to sea, you have pearls.'[1]

Muḥammad b. Manṣūr b. Muḥammad al-Wāsiṭī recited the following to me:

He is noble, even if harm befalls him,
a man of virtue and pride.
The mean are not expected to bring honour,
since there are mixed qualities in them,
Like drops of rain: they are poison when they fall into the
mouth of a serpent, but a pearl when collected by an oyster.

I was informed as follows by Muḥammad b. Abī Sa'd al-Rāzī, the qadi: In al-Rayy, I heard directly from Abū 'Abdallāh Muḥammad b. 'Umar b. al-Ḥusayn, called Ibn Khaṭiyyah, as follows: The oyster only opens to receive the rain well out to sea beyond the real and corrupt world. When an abundance has entered into the oyster, the latter swims to the bottom of the sea, moving from place to place, until it settles in its pearl-fishing ground, Bahrain, Kīsh,[2] al-Ma'bar,[3] [293] Saylān[4] and various other places. Oyster fishing begins only on the day the palm puts out the spadix and closes on the day the raceme is cut.[5] This is because the sea is calm during this season.

The fishing ground at ...[6] is open to all; everyone dives as he wishes and takes his share of God's sustenance. Because they are so numerous, the pearls are [used as] ornaments for women, children and the shaykhs. It is a season like the crop season on land and everyone is able to enjoy them[7] only during this period. Then all of this comes to a stop and the fishermen begin to fish, with civil servants controlling them, as well as financial officials[8] and tax collecters[9] who take from them from first to last. If one single pearl were to be found in the possession of anyone, the official would seize everything he has.

Section. Jamāl al-Dīn Bukhtyār, the tax-collector,[10] sent someone with some capital amounting to 1,000 *mithqāl* to India. When he was half-way there, he was captured by pirates and he survived with his life and ten *mithqāl* in gold. He came back to Qays and while he was sitting in his house one day, two blacks came to him and offered him the opportunity to purchase a pearl from them. He indicated that he was willing and then one of them took out of his mouth a pearl larger than an sparrow's egg. When the man saw the pearl, he hesitated, turned round, put it in his mouth and swallowed it. 'Give it back!' they cried, so he admitted to them that he had left it in his mouth to see how pure it was and it had gone down into his gut. 'Then you should give us what it is worth', they insisted. He took out the ten *mithqāl* for them, swearing by the great God that he

[1] A piece of doggerel: Arabic *burr*, 'wheat', rhyming with *durr*, 'pearls'.
[2] The long island in the Strait of Hurmuz.
[3] Unidentified.
[4] Unidentifed.
[5] Arabic *ṭal'*, 'spadix', which appears on 29 October; the *'idhq*, 'raceme' is cut at harvest time, commencing 19 July (Varisco, *Agriculture*, pp. 158, 192, 194).
[6] A lacuna in the text.
[7] Reading with Löfgren *lam yaḥla-h*.
[8] Arabic *'ummāl*, plur. of *'āmil*.
[9] Arabic *qubbāḍ*, plur. of *qābiḍ* (Dozy, *Supplément*, II, p. 301).
[10] Here Ibn al-Mujāwir calls him *al-qābiḍ*, but see p. 287, n. 1 below.

possessed [294] nothing else. 'Take of it what you will', he said, 'and leave me with what you will.' So they counted out eight and gave him two back.

The man journeyed on in safety and reached Safāhāt, where he gave the pearl to Jamāl al-Dīn Bukhtyār, the qadi,[1] saying to him, 'Discharge me from the amount for which I was responsible to you.' He replied, 'You are discharged and I exonerate you from the amount of 1,000 *mithqāl*.' (Now the weight of each *mithqāl* is six *dānaq*, each *dānaq* being four *ṭaysūj*,[2] each *ṭaysūj* being four *sha'īrah*.[3]) He also gave him a hundred *mithqāl*, from which he might live and eat his daily bread.

News of the pearl reached Baghdad and Imam Abū al-'Abbās Aḥmad al-Nāṣir li-Dīn Allāh,[4] Commander of the Faithful, sent a message to Jamāl al-Dīn Bukhtyār to despatch the pearl to him. When it arrived and [he saw it] with his noble eye, he sent him the price of the pearl, 6,000 *mithqāl*. It is said that [its true value] was estimated at 24,000 dinars.

Section. There was a king of Kashk who died and who was succeeded by his son. The latter discovered some goods and offered them for sale. Merchants would come into different quarters [of the town],[5] each one buying what he wanted and what was profitable to him. Shaykh Abū Ṭālib b. 'Alī b. Suwayd (or, it is said, 'Abd al-Laṭīf, the son of Abū Ṭālib b. 'Alī b. Suwayd al-Tikrītī) came upon the indigo stores where there remained twelve pieces. He paid for them, took them and went on his way, taking them with him. God decreed a safe journey for him and he arrived in Tikrīt.

A Jewish dyer came to buy a piece from him. He took the piece in order to see the merchandise for himself, when suddenly [295] it transpired that the piece was full of pearls! When Shaykh Abū Ṭālib saw this, he said to the Jew, 'Pay me for the piece of indigo and the pearls have nothing to do with you. Don't tell what you have seen!' The Jew left with his possessions.

Shaykh Ibn Suwayd began to teach his son to perforate pearls. The son began perforating each pearl which was like a hen egg and the shaykh began to send out pearl necklaces from Tikrīt to Greater Constantinople, the furthest lands of the Maghreb, India and to the Turks and he is still selling these to this day.

Ibn al-Mujāwir said: The reason [for what happened] regarding this piece [of indigo] was as follows. The king used to keep pearls and any which were particularly expensive, large and beautiful he would leave in a bag until there were many of them. When they were numerous, he sewed up a bag, filled it with expensive pearls and again sewed it up in a canvas sack, inserting four loops into it and covering it with cattle hide, so it was like a piece of indigo. He put his mark on it so that he would recognize it and stuffed it among the indigo. When it appeared among the property of Ibn Suwayd, it was said that his wealth could not be measured and that there was no end to the blessings of this piece [of indigo]. It was recited as follows:

[1] He is here referred to as *al-qāḍī* (p. 286, n. 10 above).

[2] The arabized form of the Persian *tasū* (Steingass, *Dictionary*, p. 301, 'the weight of four barley corns'; Hinz, *Masse*, p. 34). It also occurs in Arabic in the form *ṭassūj* (Fīrūzābādī, *Qāmūs*, I, p. 205).

[3] Literally 'a barley corn' (Dozy, *Supplément*, I, p. 764, with a reference that 1 *dānaq* = 10 *sha'īrah*; Hinz, *Masse*, p. 34).

[4] The Abbasid caliph, reg. 575–622/1180–1225 (Bosworth, *Islamic Dynasties*, p. 6).

[5] Arabic *ḥuwaf*, plur. of *ḥāfah* (Landberg, *Etudes*, I, p. 558; Landberg, *Glossaire daṯînois*, I, p. 519; Löfgren, *Texte*, II, p. 30; Piamenta, *Dictionary*, I, p. 114).

Wealth eludes one who does not sleep in order to journey by night [to carry out his business],
while the living of another comes while he is asleep.

The island of Qays. [It is] an island whose circumference is three parasangs, the length and breadth being the same.[1] It has date palms and acacia leaves as an agricultural crop. The king's palms produce *sukhkhal* dates.[2] Sand can be dug out by hand and water of the sweetest kind gushes out. It is said that the cultivated area of the king has a ditch[3] running with water all round it. Successive kings in the early days dug out reservoirs and tanks and it remains flourishing to this day and has abundant spring and flood water.

The food of the inhabitants is fish and they make [296] their *harīsah* dishes of it and they are eaten with dates. The people of the island have no other food. They take their food only with the right hand and if anyone breaks [the food] with both hands, it is [regarded as] a major breach of etiquette.

The people build in stone and gypsum and their houses are very tall, one producing a building of seven storeys. Each house is like a fortress.

Trees are continually brought there from Basra and herbs and all sorts of vegetables are cultivated.

The inhabitants of the island show a natural inclination towards arrogance and also frivolity and madness. As the saying goes, 'Madness comes in many different varieties.'[4] They trace their ancestry back to Qays b. al-Mulawwaḥ, or, it is said, to Imru' al-Qays. But the correct genealogy goes back to Qays b. Zuhayr, the one mentioned above.

Their dress comes from the regions of al-Mahdiyyah in the Maghreb and they let the fringes[5] of their turban hang down long. They are real sea dogs. The lord of the island has neither horses nor soldiers, nothing but *dūnījs*,[6] *burmahs*[7] and *nuhbūghs*[8] like *qawārib*[9] but they are used at sea. The inhabitants became content to live in a certain place and settled there.

[1] Lorimer (*Gazetteer*, IIB, p. 1471) says 10 miles long and 4½ wide; *Iraq*, p. 161, 9½ miles long and 4½ miles wide.

[2] *Faute de mieux*, I read *sukhkhal* with Löfgren. However, such dates are usually of poor quality (Lane, *Lexicon*, IV, p. 1325; Kazimirski, *Dictionnaire*, I, p. 1066, plur. of *sākhil*).

[3] Text *kārīz*, a Persian word (Steingass, *Dictionary*, p. 1004).

[4] A well-known saying (Akwaʿ, *Amthāl*, I, p. 382).

[5] Arabic *hudabāt* or *hudubāt*, plur. of *hudbah* or *hudubah*. The usual plur. is *hudab* (Lane, *Lexicon*, VIII, p. 2884).

[6] The text has *al-nawā?.?.ḥ* and Löfgren proposes – all the more plausibly since Yāqūt (*Muʿjam*, IV, p. 422) mentions them in the specific context of Qays – *al-dawānīj*, sing. *dūnīj/dūnij* (Idrīsī, *Opus*, I, p. 388, mentioned in the context of pearling; Kindermann, *Schiff*, p. 29; Tibbetts, *Navigation*, p. 525, 'long boat'; Grosset-Grange, *Glossaire*, p. 110). I venture the reading *nawātī*, an Arabic plur. form of the Persian *nūtī*, 'sailor' (Steingass, *Dictionary*, p. 1432), although the list is more likely to be one of ships.

[7] The text has *būmah* which cannot be correct in a 7th/13th-century context.

[8] The text has *al-hā?.?.q* and Löfgren proposes *al-nahābīgh*, plur. of *nuhbūgh* (Kindermann, *Schiff*, p. 28; Nukhaylī, *Sufun*, p. 151, 'long and fast'). Dionisius Agius thinks this might be the *nūbiyyah/nūbah* (= *dūbah*) encountered above at p. 283, n. 3.

[9] The text has *al-ʿaqārib*, 'scorpions'. I read *qawārib*, 'boats', tentatively with Löfgren, but the picture of a ship with the profile of a scorpion is not difficult to visualize.

The women dress in black. When a man marries a woman, he gives her a hundred dinars; she gives him another hundred and writes him a guaranty of a fixed amount, two hundred dinars,[1] which falls due on a specific date. Whatever amount the man adds on to the dowry, the woman adds in cash. If the dowry falls short, the cash does also.

They are a people who have great esteem for strangers and take great care of them. The women dominate the men of these parts and a man can do nothing without the say-so of his wife, whether it is good or bad. This is contrary to what the Messenger of God – God bless him and grant him peace – said: Consult them and contradict them, for there is blessing in contradicting them![2]

The deputies of Qays used to hand over a levy to al-Sulṭān al-Aʿẓam Rukn al-Dunyā wa-al-Dīn Abū al-Fatḥ Malik Shāh b. Maḥmūd b. Alp Arslān.[3] But when he died and was succeeded after his death [297] by al-Sulṭān al-Aʿẓam Muʿizz al-Dunyā wa-al-Dīn Abū al-Ḥārith Sanjar b. Ayyūb Shāh,[4] who paid no heed to the poor because his rule was so extensive and because of his wealth, this [levy] was stopped, but later renewed by Imam Abū al-ʿAbbās Aḥmad al-Nāṣir li-Dīn Allāh, Commander of the Faithful – God's blessing be upon him.

The reason for this, according to his own statement, was that a certain Baghdadi merchant died on the island of Qays and left 30,000 dinars in gold which the king seized. The heir [to the wealth] produced a legal document, after establishing his case before a judge. But when the king was informed of the matter, he was too arrogant to pay and asserted his superiority over the heir. The latter referred[5] the document to Baghdad, explained to the imam[6] his circumstances and what had happened to him. The imam gave instructions to Amir ...,[7] lord of Basra, to suspend the resources of the inhabitants of the island and they were in straitened circumstances. When the king saw his circumstances getting worse, he decided of his own accord in 615[8] that the 30,000 dinars which belonged to the deceased [should go] to his heirs in Baghdad, together with a half of the income of the island of Qays for the caliph. On the island there is a financial official working for the caliph and another for the lord of Kīsh, as on the same island there is one working for the caliph and another for the king. A poet has recited as follows:

> O you killing me wrongfully, not in friendship,
> be careful! As you requite you shall be requited!

[1] Arabic 'wa-katabat ʿalay-h qabālat dayn ḥāll qārr bi-mablagh mi'atayn dīnār'.

[2] Arabic *shāwirū-hum* (read *-hunna*) *wa-khālifū-hum* (read *-hunna*), the masc. pronoun for the fem., common in Middle Arabic.

[3] I have left this name as Ibn al-Mujāwir has it, though this would seem to be Malik Shāh I, reg. 465–85/1073–92, one of the Great Seljuks of Persia and Iraq, who was in fact the son of Alp Arslān and Maḥmūd was one of his sons (Bosworth, *Islamic Dynasties*, p. 185).

[4] I have left this name as Ibn al-Mujāwir has it. Aḥmad Sanjar, son of Malik Shāh I, was ruler of Khurasan 490–552/1097–1157 and after 511/1118 supreme sultan of the Seljuks (Bosworth, *Islamic Dynasties*, p. 185).

[5] Arabic 'wa-radda al-wārith bi-kitāb al-ḥukm ilā ...'

[6] I.e. the Abbasid caliph.

[7] The text has ?ād.k.?.n.

[8] Begins 30 March 1218.

This island is well fortified, a good, decent place. Its people mostly travel by sea and sell their goods.[1] The only taxes they pay are ...,[2] but none of them can buy or sell stone pots[3] and spear shafts[4] except the king himself. If their owner does not sell these things [298] to the king, he will take them by force. It is said that he has stores of stone and earthenware pots,[5] also full of spear shafts.

No passport[6] is of any use to the traveller unless it has seventeen signatures of the king's deputies and the eighteenth of the king himself. I was informed as follows by Jawshan Bām b. Abī Bakr b. Sulaymān al-Jāshū: Whenever the king comes across a signed passport, he signs it again for the man concerned by means of a stick of wood made by himself which is in fact a toothpick with which one picks ones teeth when eating unlawful meat. If it is suitable [for the occasion], a young slave carries it, but the toothpick is not appropriate for anyone writing a note. I asked what the idea of the toothpick is and he replied, 'I don't know beyond the fact that these are practices which have taken place since ancient times.' I asked who made these toothpicks and he replied that it was the king personally.

What the island consists of on the ground, originally Dafā, Wādī al-Aḥjār, Ghaṭafān, Liwā, Ḥiwār, Ḥiwayn, M.ḥ.?.r.?ah, al-ʿAqr, Kaltā, Ṣāḥat, L.y.m?n, Karār, Ḥaṣab, Jarʿā and al-M.j.z.rah.[7] The Friday address is also given in the name of the ruler in Cambay, Sūmanāth and ?.d.r.?.s.r.[8] These areas are one country. When the ship of the ruler of Qays arrives, it is shown the utmost respect, since the people there choose the king from Qays because he is close to them. When the Friday address has been given in the name of the caliph, it is pronounced after this in the name of the lord of Kīsh.[9] Almighty God – praise be to Him – knows best.

What the lord of Qays did (he is also called lord of Kīsh) and what the lord of Makrān did with him. The king [of Makrān] sent Tāj al-Dīn Abū al-Makārim b. al-Ḥasan and Ibn al-Ḥusayn Kahrū with a large amount of wealth and they bought for him from Muscat a horse, valued at a thousand *mithqāl*. The horse was put on board ship by which it was brought over from the Arab side to [299] the Persian. The king of Qays heard all about the horse, so he sent some *dūnīj*s and *burmah*s and they cut the sea route and seized the horse. When Tāj al-Dīn Abū al-Makārim heard what had happened to the horse, he took some pirate ships and turned them towards the landfalls of the Qaysī [king]. He gave them instructions, 'Every ship you see belonging to the lord of Qays, seize it by force!' So they seized that monsoon season twelve ships laden with all kinds of wares,

[1] See p. 163, n. 9 above.

[2] I am mystified here. The text appears to read 'Abū Nuqtaḥ', which might be a coin of some description.

[3] Arabic *qudūr al-birām*, the latter being the plur. of *burmah* (Lane, *Lexicon*, I, p. 195).

[4] Arabic *qaṣab al-qanā*, the latter being the plur. of *qanāh* (Kazimirski, *Dictionnaire*, II, p. 826).

[5] Reading with Löfgren *wa-ghaḍā'ir*, meaning 'earthenware' (*ṭīn ḥurr*, as the lexica define *ghaḍīrah*).

[6] Arabic *fasḥ* (Lane, *Lexicon*, VI, p. 2395; Kazimirski, *Dictionnaire*, II, p. 592).

[7] These doubtful names I take to be those of settlements on Qays. All except Wādī al-Aḥjār, Ghaṭafān and Liwā are vocalized and spelt tentatively and I cannot further identify them. None figures in Lorimer's list of Qays villages (*Gazetteer*, IIB, pp. 1472–3).

[8] On the Indian coast at the head of the Gulf of Cambay near Gujerat. Sōmanāth is W of Diu and perhaps the third place is Madwara (Tibbetts, *Navigation*, p. 451 and end map India).

[9] Ibn al-Mujāwir is clearly using Qays and Kīsh interchangably.

gifts, rare presents and wealth. The lord of Kīsh sent a messenger to Tāj al-Dīn of Makrān,[1] saying, 'Tell me, praise be to God for his blessings; by God whose aid is to be sought against the people of this age, how have kings become pirates, cutting the sea routes against those travelling over it?' Tāj al-Dīn of Makrān told the messenger, 'It was indeed your king who informed me of the cutting of the route!' The messenger replied, speaking directly for his king, 'Someone like me is vying with someone like you in power!' 'You have no power,' retorted Tāj al-Dīn. The messenger replied, 'I myself know you full well!' Tāj al-Dīn said, 'Without any choice [on my part]!' The messenger said, 'I shall certainly redeem you according to what you deserve!' Tāj al-Dīn said, 'This is what I want!' The messenger said, 'I shall bring that about!' 'God willing', added Tāj al-Dīn.

> Indeed, I would never speak to him, even if
> he were the new moon, the sun or one content.
> I shall certainly bear with patience against the bitterness of his leaving,
> lest you see me as the rebuker and he is healed.
> Whose pact in love is strong before you,
> so that you are true, and who pays in full so that you do the same?

Another poet recited as follows:

> He who does not visit you, do not visit
> him and do not ...[2] generosity.
> Stretch forth to him the rope of loathing
> and dig a fathom down for him in the earth.
> If he is free of guilt and you meet him,
> forgiveness bestows upon him peace.
> When his days are over,
> you are free from blame.

[300] Another poet recited as follows:

> I shall don a new garment of patience
> and twist together a new rope against separation,
> perchance I, unwillingly not willingly,
> might free my heart little by little.

Al-Qālī. This is a source of tar which gushes up in the midst of the sea. When there is a lot of tar, the waves pound it piece by piece, the weight of each piece being about a thousand *mann*. I was informed as follows by Jawshan Bām b. Abī Bakr b. Sulaymān: When anyone dives to the right of the tar with a waterskin and puts the mouth of the waterskin down over the mouth of the spring, the waterskin is filled with sweet water, cool and easy to swallow.[3] I asked how this was. He replied, 'Since nothing emerges from the spring except together with the hot water. The water which emerges from the tar is sweet and healthy.' A wise man said: Nothing dissolves the tar at its source, nor links it together with the waves other than the hot water which dissolves it and pours

[1] The text reads 'b. Makrān' and I correct here and below.
[2] No lacuna is visible in the MSS.
[3] Arabic *shibb al-zulāl* (Lane, *Lexicon*, III, p. 1242; Kazimirski, *Dictionnaire*, I, p. 1003).

the water forth from beneath and it emerges on the surface of the earth and the sea. In this way can ambergris be measured.

Al-Qālī is a flowing spring in the seas of ruin where there is no building, nor any abode. It emerges exactly as the spring of tar does. Almighty God knows best,

Bahrain. This is an island in the Persian Gulf, just as Suez is in the Red Sea.[1] It is said that it is an island in a salt sea above a sweet water sea; thus it is called the Two Seas.[2] Some locals informed me, saying, 'If someone dives down between the two waters and drinks, he drinks sweet water, while that above is brackish, salt water.' He also said, 'Bahrain is only called thus because of the sea [on the one hand] and its inhabitants who are like the sea in their generosity [on the other]!' Thus it is a land called the Two Seas, one sea of water and another of [301] people.

The island is also called Uwāl[3] and has three hundred and sixty villages which all, bar one, follow the Imāmī[4] tenets of Islam. The food of the people is dates and fish, some sweet smelling honey and [other] putrid[5] food. Others have said that the island of Uwāl is in the middle of the pearl-fishing ground of Bahrain and there is nothing purer, more glistening than its pearls. It is an island in the midst of the gulf, surrounded by the Arab side and Fārs [on the other]. A poet has recited as follows [in Persian]:

> Your face is a pearl and my two eyes the sea;
> O pearl, far from the sea, how are things with you?[6]

[1] Interestingly named here Baḥr al-Ḥabashah.

[2] Arabic al-Baḥrayn.

[3] Idrīsī (*Opus*, I, p. 386) agrees with Ibn al-Mujāwir's statement, whereas Yāqūt (*Mu'jam*, I, p. 274) says only that it is an island 'in the region of Bahrain'. I take the vocalization from Yāqūt. See also Doy, 'Bahrain', pp. 158 ff.

[4] I.e. Shī'ī (Serjeant, 'Fisher-folk', p. 488).

[5] The text is difficult and corrupt: ... *min mādhī rā'iḥah wa-ṭu'm r.?.n.* I follow RBS and read the final word quoted *'afin*, rather than Löfgren's *r.f.n.*

[6] A line of poetry in Persian, the author of which is identified by Löfgren as Ḥasan Ghaznawī. See p. 262, n. 5 above.

APPENDIX A

The Routes of Ibn al-Mujāwir

The following is a comprehensive list of all forty-two routes provided by Ibn al-Mujāwir in *Tārkh al-Mustabṣir* and includes the places, the distance given and a page reference. All figures in square brackets are numbers of the pages of Löfgren's Arabic text. All other figures are parasangs, unless another measurement of distance is clearly indicated.

Route 1 from Mecca to Hajar
[14] To Wādī Marr 4
To al-Hadā/Hadah 4
To Burzah 4
To Shābah 4
To Medina 4
To Hajar 7

Route 2 from Medina?
[16] To al-Khaḍrā' 4
To ʿAyn al-Nabī 4
To (al-)ʿUmaq 4
To Najd 4
[17] To Bi'r ʿAlī b. Abī Ṭālib 4
To Qubā 4
To Medina 1

Route 3 from Mecca to al-Ḥajar [text al-Ṭā'if]
[17] To Minā 1
To al-Mashʿar al-Ḥarām 1
To Jabal ʿArafāt 1
To al-Burqah 3
To al-Marzah 4/6
To al-Ḥajar 2

Route 4 from al-Ṭā'if to Jabal B. Badr
[25] To al-Maʿdā 6
To Khabt ʿAntar 5
To Ḥaddān 6
To Karā 5
To al-Darb 2
To Nawā 1
[27] To al-Fardā' 6
To al-Malḥā' 6
[31] To Abīdah 1
To al-ʿAqīq 6
To Tabālah 8
To Jabal B. Badr 8

Route 5 from al-Ṭā'if to Ṣaʿdah
[37] To al-Maʿdin 4
To al-Rān 8
To al-Maḥrā 8
To al-Dawrah 4
To Yāfiʿ 8
To ʿAdā 8
To Rān Kīsah(?) 4
To Ṣafī 4
To Khafan 4
To Madar 4
To ʿAḍḍat ʿArīn 4
To Bilād B. Qarn 4
To Bilād B. ʿAbd al-Dār 20
To al-Dhahbān 7
[38] To Bilād Qaḥṭān 4
To Rāḥat B. Shurayf 2
To Ṣaʿdah 20

Route 6 from al-Ṭā'if to al-Ṭawd al-Aʿẓam
To Ḥadab al-Ranj 2
To al-Ṭawd al-Aʿam 3

Route 7 from Mecca to Jeddah
[40] To ʿAyn Abī Sulaymān 1

To Maqtalat al-Kilāb 1
[41] To al-Rikābiyyah 1
To Ḥaddah 1
To al-Qurayn 1
[42] To Kitānah 1
To al-Thadyayn 1 mile
To Wādī al-Sidrah 1
To al-Ghār ½
To al-Fajj al-Akhḍar ½
To al-Farʿ ½
To Mathwab ½
Abū al-Raḥim 1 mile
To al-Nuhūd 1 mile
To al-Mīnah/al-Ḥudaybiy(y)ah ½
To Jeddah ½

Route 8 from Mecca to Ṣaʿdah
[52] To al-Qurayn 1
To al-Bayḍāʾ 2
To Idām 3
To Wādī al-Muḥram 3
To Farʿ 5
[53] To al-Sirrayn 3
To Wādī al-Athalāt 3
To Ḥaṣārah 5
To Ḥaly 7
[54] To al-Dabsāʾ/Sharm al-Jāriyah 5
To Dhahbān/Wādī al-Dawm 4
[55] To Bayḍ 4
To al-Rāḥah/Rāḥat al-Muʾayyad 4
[56] To Hajar 4
To al-Hiliyyah 8
To al-Maḥālib 2
[57] To Ḥirdah 3
To al-Madārah 3
To Shamr 2
To Qalḥāḥ 1
To al-Afrūr 3
To al-Ẓuhayrah
[58] To Shaʿb 5
To Ḥūth 10
Ṣaʿdah 14

Route 9 from al-Maḥālib to Zabīd
[58] To al-Mahjam 3
[59] To al-Kadrāʾ 5
[62] To al-Qaḥmah/Dhuʾāl 1½
To Maḥall Ibrāhīm 3
To Safākā 3
To Zahrān ¼
[63] To Fashāl 4
To Wādī Rimaʿ ½
To Qūniṣ/Wādī al-ʿIrq ½
To Zabīd 4

Route 10 from al-Mahjam to Zabīd
[90] To al-Kadrāʾ 5
abandoned?
To al-Mahjam 6?

Route 11 from Zabīd to Aden
[91] To al-Muzayḥifah 1
To al-Suḥārī 3
[92] To al-Khawihah ½
To al-Mawshij 1
To al-Ḥalīlah/al-Ḥulaylah 2
[93] To Mawzaʿ 3
To al-ʿUmriyyah 3
[94] To ʿIbrah 3
abandoned?

Route 12 from al-ʿĀrah to al-Ḥalīlah (return)
[100] To ʿAthr 3
To al-Ḥalīlah/al-Muḥammadiyyah 3

Route 13 from al-ʿĀrah to al-Mafālīs
[100] To Taran 3
[102] To al-Nukhaylah 3
To al-Mafālīs 3

Route 14 from al-ʿĀrah to Taʿizz
[102] To Shaʿb 4
To al-Niyyah 3
To al-Maḥjāṭ 3
To al-Ḥusayn 2
To al-ʿArīsh 3
To Taʿizz 2

Route 15 from al-ʿĀrah to Aden
[102] To al-Jābiyah 1
To Biʾr al-Ṣaḥbah 3
[105] To al-Marjaḥiyyah 3
To al-Bayḍāʾ/Sabkhat al-Ghurāb 2

To Rubāk 2
To al-Maksar 1
[106] To Jabal Ḥadīd ½
To al-Mabāh ¼
To Aden ¼

Route 16 from Aden to al-Mafālīs
[148] To al-Mabāh ¼
To al-Mazaff 1
To al-Mimlāḥ ¼
To al-Majdūlī 1
To al-Lakhabah ¼
To al-Ḥajar al-ʿUrr 1
To al-Rajʿ(?)/al-Rajāʿ 2
To Nuwayʿim 2
To al-Mafālīs 2

Route 17 from al-Mafālīs to al-Dumluwah [text Taʿizz]
[150] To al-Ḥumar 1½
[151] To Lower al-Ḥumar 2
[152] To al-Ḥanashayn ½
To al-Ḥ wāḍ 1
To al-Juwwah ½
To al-Dumluwwah 1

Route 18 from al-Juwwah to Aden
[155] To al-ʿyirayn 2
To Ḥirz 1
To al-Māʾ al-Ḥārr 1
To al-Daʿīs 4
To Aden 4

Route 19 from al-Juwwah to Taʿizz
[155] To Wādī Warazān 1
To Akamat Hamdān 1
To al-Ḥamrāʾ ½
To al-Ḥawbān ½
To Taʿizz ¼

Route 20 from Taʿizz to al-Janad
[161] To Birkat al-Ḥawbān ¼
To Wādī al-Samkar ¼
To al-Janad ½

Route 21 from [al-Janad](?) to Dhū Jiblah
[168] To Ḍirās ½
To Wādī Warazān ½
To Dhū Jiblah ½

Route 22 from Dhū Jiblah to Ṣanʿāʾ
[175] al-Qurayn 1
To al-Saḥūl 2
To Dhirāʿ al-Kalb 1
To Ibb 2
To al-Maghribah 2
[176] To al-Maʿbar 1
To Ḥuṣn Samāwā 1
To Naqīl Ṣayd 1
To Ḍarbat ʿAmr 1
[177] To Manzil al-Aṣamm 1
To Dār al-ayf 1
[178] To al-Malāwī 3
To al-Ḥizyaz 2
To Madārah 1
To Naqīl Aslaḥ 2
To Ḥadarān 1
To Ḥabārā 1
To Ghayl al-Barmakī 2
[179] To Ṣanʿāʾ 2

Route 23 from Ṣanʿāʾ to al-Dhanāʾib [text al-Maḥālib]
[193] To Thulā 3
To ʿAzzān 1½
To Misk 4
To Ḥajjah 2
[194] To al-Dhanāʾib 5

Route 24 from Ṣanʿāʾ to Mārib
[195] To Miswar 4
To Wādī Jannāt 4
To al-Maʾzimayn 4
[197] To Mārib 4

Route 25 from Mārib to al-Jawf
[200] To Warsān 4
To Barāqish 4
To Maʿīn 1
To Haram 1
To upper al-Jawf 4

Route 26 from Mārib to Ṣanʿāʾ (return)
[202] To Biʾr Mawhal(?) 2

To al-Ḥarratayn 2
To Ṭabāl al-ʿĀshir 2
To al-Raḥabah 2
To Ṣanʿāʾ 2

Route 27 from Ṣanʿāʾ to Ṣaʿdah (ancient route)
[202] To Marmal 3
To Tharayd 3
To Naqīl ʿAjīb 3
To Naqīl al-Faqʿ 1
To al-Musayriʿ 1
To Najd Farsh 2
To al-ʿAmashiyyah 3
To al-Darb 2
To Ṣaʿdah 2

Route 28 from Ṣaʿdah to Dhahabān
[207] To al-Ḥawānīt 4
To Khatm al-Bakarāt 2
[208] To al-Qadīm 2
To Multaqā al-Awdiyah 1
To Ghasl Julājil 2
To al-Mukhtalaf 2
To al-Baṣrah 1
To Wādī Tafūṣ 2
To al-Jabal al-Aswad 1
To al-Sarawāt 2
To Rufaydah 2
To Ṭarīb 2
To Dhahabān 2

Route 29 from Ṣaʿdah to Qarqar [text Najrān]
[208] To Zahrān 3
To al-Ḥadd 3
To al-Rakb 3
To al-Khāniq 3
To Kawkabān 2
[209] To al-Ḥuqqah ¼
To Qābil ¼
To Ḥabawnā 4
To Qarqar 4

Route 30 from Ḥaraḍ to Ḥadab [text Najrān (Tihāmah)]
[211] To Qarār 3
To Najrān 2
To Ḥāwah 3
To Ḥadab 4

Route 31 from Ṣaʿdah to Ṣanʿāʾ (new route)
[232] To al-Khiyām/al-Durūb 3
To al-ʿAyn 1
To al-ʿAmashiyyah 4
To Ḥūth 5
To Jaḥḍam(?) 4
To Ṣanʿāʾ 2

Route 32 from Taʿizz to Zabīd (return)
[233] To ʿUdaynah ¼
To al-Dumaynah ¼
To Wādī Ḥadhrār ¼
To Biʾr Māhūt ¼
To Biʾr al-Ṣadʿ 1
To Wādī al-Nakhl 1
To Wādī al-Ḥinnāʾ 1
To al-Shiyālayn 1
To ʿUqdat Majʿar 1
To al-Kadaḥah 1
To Ḥudaylah/Sarādīb al-Nīl 1
To al-Durayʿāʾ ½
[234] To al-Sāsah 1
To al-Mukhaysīb 1
To al-Q w b zayn 1
To Ḥaṣīb al-Dīn ½
[235] To al-Salāmah ½
To Ḥays ½
[236] To al-Dawāmil 1
To al-Sardāb 1
To Qurtub ½
To Zabīd ½

Route 33 from Zabīd to Ḥajjah
[236] To al-Qaḥmah 3
To al-Kadrāʾ 2
To al-ʿAnamiyyah(?) 3
To al-ʿAmd 3
To Asḥar 3
To Ḥarāz 3
[237] To al-Jabalayn 3
To Sūq al-Qibāb 3
To Niẓār 3
To Rabḍ 4
To Lāʿah 4

To al-Mikhlāfah 2
To Ḥajjah 4

Route 34 from Zabīd to Ghulāfiqah
[238] To al-Qurashiyyah 1
[239] To Khabt Nafḥān 2
To Ghulāfiqah 2

Route 35 from Zabīd to al-Ahwāb
[246] To al-Musallab 1
[247] To al-Ahwāb 2

Route 36 from Aden to Shibām
[248] To al-Raʿāriʿ 4
To Abyan 4
[249] To Dār Zīnah 9
To Bayḥān 7
To Wādī Ḥarīb 4
To ʿĀzib 6
[250] To ʿAybar 12
To Shibām 9

Route 37 from Shibām to Ẓafār
[256] To Tarīm 7
[257] To Qabr al-Nabī Hūd 8
[258] To Maḍī/Maḍā 5
To Khalkhalīj 10
To Ẓuhūr 10
To Maharūt 7
To Kadnūb 5
To Mārib 20
[260] To Ḥabarūt 4
To al-Tahūdī 4
To al-Shiʿb 7
To Ḥalūf 5
To al-Ghayl 8
To Ẓafār 4

Route 38 from al-Manṣūrah [to Aden]
[268] To Raysūt 3
To Dukhān 3
To Ḥārith 3
[270] To Marāwah 3
To Ḥalaqāt 4
To Ḥaṣwayl 6
To Ḥayrīj 6
To al-Raydāʾ 6
To al-Shiḥr 5
To al-Shuḥayr 4
To Mukalla 1
To Bīr ʿAlī 6
To Lasʿāʾ 5
To Ḥuṣn al-Ghurāb 4
To Majdāḥ 4
To al-Ḥawrāʾ 8
To Aḥwar 8
To Abyan 6
To Lahej 4
To Aden 3

Route 39 from al-Manṣūrah to Qalhāt
[270] To Mirbāṭ 4
[271] To Arḥūb 2
To Kankarī 4
To al-Nūs 3
To Ḥāsik 2
To Madrakah 4
To Masira 4
[272] To Darb Jaʿlān 3
To Ṣūr 4
To al-ʿ.?.b 2
To Qalhāt 2

Route 40 from al-Manṣūrah to Aden (return)
[275] Raysūt 3
abandoned

Route 41 from Qalhāt to Muscat
[284] To Ṭīwī 3
To Muscat 6

Route 42 [from Muscat to Qays]
[284] To Ḥayy ʿĀṣim 6
To Asrār 6
To Sohar 4
[286] To al-ʿAqr 4
To Kalbah 4
To Khawr Fakkān 4
To Dibā 4
To Līmah 4
To Kumzār 3
To Ẓafār 8
To Qays 8

APPENDIX B

Genealogical and Dynastic Tables

1. Genealogical Table of B. Al-Karam/Al-Mukarram (Yemen)

al-Mukarram

- Masʿūd
  Māniʿ
  Muḥammad
- al-ʿAbbās
  Zurayʿ
  Abū al-Suʿūd
  Sabaʾ
  Muḥammad

2. The Zaydī Imams from the 5th to the 7th/13th Century (Yemen)*

Ḥamzah b. Abī Hāshim	d. 458/1065
al-Fāḍil b. Jaʿfar b. al-Qāsim	d. 460/1067
Muḥammad b. Jaʿfar	d. 478/1085
Jaʿfar b. Muḥammad b. Jaʿfar	478/1085 (oath of allegiance)
Yaḥyā b. Muḥammad	511/1117 (*daʿwah*)
ʿAlī b. Zayd b. Sulaymān	531/1136
al-Mutawakkil Aḥmad b. Sulaymān	532–66/1137–70
al-Manṣūr ʿAbdallāh b. Ḥamzah	583–614/1187–1217
al-Hādī Yaḥyā b. Ḥamzah	614/1217
al-Nāṣir Muḥammad b. ʿAbdallāh	614–23/1217–26
al-Mutawakkil Aḥmad b. ʿAbdallāh	623–56/1226–58(?)
al-Muʿtaḍid Yaḥyā b. Muḥsin	d. 636/1238(?)
al-Mahdī Aḥmad b. al-Ḥusayn	646–56/1248–58(?)

*It is not possible to give a comprehensive list of Zaydī imams and it is not always clear who the 'official' imam is when there is more than one claimant to the office. The above list was made up after reference to the following sources: Kay, *Yaman*, pp. 302–3; Wāsiʿī, *Tārīkh*, pp. 28–33; Smith, *Ayyubids*, II, pp. 76–7; Bosworth, *Islamic Dynasties*, p. 96.

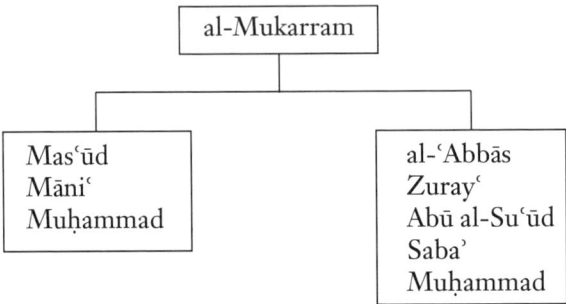

3. The Ziyadids (Yemen)

Muḥammad b. Ziyād	203–45/818–59
Ibrāhīm b. Muḥammad	245–83/859–96
Ziyād b. Ibrāhīm	283–9/896–902
(Ibn) Ziyād	289–99/902–11
Abū al-Jaysh	299–371/911–81(?)
(?)	(?)

4. The Najahids (Yemen)

Najāḥ	412–52/1021–60
Sa'īd b. Najāḥ	452(?)–81/1060(?)–88
Jayyāsh b. Najāḥ	482–98/1089–1104
Fātik I b. Jayyāsh	c. 500–503/1089–1109
Fātik II b. al-Manṣūr	503–31/1109–37
Fātik III b. Muḥammad	531–53/1137–58

5. The Sulayhids (Yemen)

'Alī b. Muḥammad	439–59 or –73/1047–66 or – 80
Aḥmad b. 'Alī	460–67 or –79/1068–74 or –86
Arwā bint Aḥmad	467 or 479–532/1074 or –86–1138

6. The Zuray'ids (Yemen)

al-'Abbās b. al-Mukarram/al-Mas'ūd b. al-Mukarram	473–7/1080–84
al-Mas'ūd b. al-Mukarram/Zuray' b. al-'Abbās	477–504/1080–1110
(?)	
'Alī b. Saba'	533–4/1138–39
Muḥammad b. Saba'	534–48/1139–53
'Imrān b. Muḥammad	548–61/1153–66
Various slave ministers	561–69/1166–73

7. The Mahdids (Yemen)

'Alī b. Mahdī	531–54/1136–59
'Abd al-Nabī b. 'Alī	554–69/1159–73

8. The Ayyubids (Yemen)

Tūrānshāh b. Ayyūb, al-Muʿaẓẓam	569–71/1173–75
Various deputies	571–79/1175–83
Ṭughtakīn b. Ayyūb, al-ʿAzīz	579–93/1183–97
Ismāʿīl b. Ṭughtakīn, al-Muʿizz	593–98/1197–1201
Interregnum of Atabeg Sunqur	598–609/1201–12
Ayyūb b. Ṭughtakīn, al-Nāṣir	609–11/1212–14
Sulaymān b. ʿUmar, al-Muaffar	611–12/1214–15
Yūsuf b. Muḥammad, al-Masʿūd	612–26/1215–28
Rasulid deputy	626–28/1228–30

9. The Musawids (Hejaz)

Jaʿfar	350s–370/960s–980
ʿĪsā b. Jaʿfar	370–84/980–94
Abū al-Futūḥ b. Jaʿfar	384–432/994–1039
Shukr b. Abī al-Futūḥ	432–53/1039–61

10. B. Hāshim (Hejaz)

Abū Hāshim Muḥammad	456–87/1064–94
Qāsim b. Muḥammad	487–518/1094–1124
Fulaytah b. Qāsim	518–27/1124–32
Hāshim b. Fulaytah	527–49/1132–54
Qāsim b. Hāshim	549–56/1154–61
ʿĪsā b. Fulaytah	557–70/1161–74
Dāʾūd b. ʿĪsā	570–89/1174–93
Mukthir b. ʿĪsā	589–99/1193–1202

11. B. Qatādah (Hejaz)

Qatādah b. Idrīs	597–617/1200–20
Ḥasan b. Qatādah	618–19/1220–22
Rājiḥ b. Qatādah	630–38/1232–40

APPENDIX C

List of Literary Works Quoted by Ibn al-Mujāwir in the Text

The numbers in the right-hand column refer to the page numbers above.

Kitāb Lumaʿ al-adillah	Imām al-Ḥaramayn	276
*Kitāb Maʿrifat al-adyān***	al-Rāzī	62
Kitāb al-Masālik wa-al-mamālik	al-Iṣṭakhrī	277
*Kitāb al-Mufīd fī akhbār Zabīd**	Jayyāsh b. Najāḥ	119, 130
*Kitāb al-Mufīd fī akhbār Zabīd**	ʿUmārah	87, 140, 184
Kitāb Murūj al-dhahab	al-Masʿūdī	33, 193
*Kitāb al-Rahmānj***	?	264
Kitāb al-Tafhīm fī ʿilm al-tanjīm	al-Bīrūnī	231
Kitāb al-Tafsīr	al-Kaysānī	130, 134
Tārīkh/Akhbār Makkah	al-Fākihī	32, 47, 70
*al-Tarjamah***	?	198

* known, but not extant ** not known

GLOSSARY

NB the numbers quoted after each entry refer to the pages of this volume.
The note at the foot of the page may provide an explanation of the word concerned and it will direct the reader to the word in the text itself.
Plurals where relevant follow the entry heading which is usually the singular form.
Abbreviations are as follows: capital Roman numerals indicate derived forms of verbs; plur – plural; v – verb.

ablaq black and white 236
'addā v II go across, leave 188
'addād customs teller 160
'afin putrid 292
āftāb; āftāb parast chameleon/sun-worshipper 237
'afw/'ifw/'ufw young ass 248
aḥmar; dīnār aḥmar gold dinar 36
ajlaḥ; julḥ debauched 265
ajnabī(?); *ajnāb* outsider 74
'alawī unit of currency 40, 69
alyah sheep's rump 40
amhara v IV provide with dowry 268
amlas glossy 153
'āmūd column 218
anjar anchor 78
ankuzah as(s)a gum 156
'aqqār; 'aqāqīr herbal medicine 56
'arabiyyah type of dish 228
'arasha v swarm 232
'arjal foot soldiers 232
arghada v IV have in plenty 31
'ārr with pustules 220
'arṣah stretch of land 78
'ashshā v II give dinner to 188
'ashūr; 'ashūrāt custom fee 146
'ashūr al-shawānī galley-tax 156
'āṣif stormy 262
aṣṣaṣa v II render solid 228
athlah/athl tamarisk 75
'awf male locust 232
'awīlī slave 157
'ayd/'aydah sardine 243
'aysh food 164
ayyil see *iyyal*
azyab (east) wind 262

bābūnaj camomile 53
bāḥah body of sea 129
baḥara v split 220
baḥīrah she-camel with split ears 220
bahlūl chief 139
ba'īd; ba'īd al-ghawr intellectual 29
balad ground floor 37
balaḥ at the stage of beginning to ripen (date) 105, 224
bakka v break 31
bān ben-tree 74
banafsaj violet 113
band; band al-sayf cross-belt 59
baram acacia fruit 113
barbahār rare commodities, medicinal drugs 163
barīq brilliance/splendour 253
barr; arḍ barrah good earth 96, 286
barṭīkh see *baṭṭīkh*
baṭn; buṭūn hollow 120
baṭṭāl lying idle (ship) 158
battān sperm whale 278
baṭṭīkh/biṭṭīkh melon 36, 113
bayāḍ catfish 243
bay'ah unit of weight 41

bayram cotton cloth 115
bayyata v II make a surprise attack by night 105
bāziq crushing 279
bazz cloth 261
birsām pleurisy/tumour 284
bishārah payment (to port messenger) 155
b.rrah type of flying insect 116
burj sign of the zodiac 173
burmah; birām round ship, stone pot 143, 288, 290
burr wheat 261

dabbāb locusts (on the ground) 232
dabbūqah tress 83
dādhī/dhādhī St John's wort 149
dafwā' species of tree 156
ḍa'īf; ḍu'afā' not bearing arms 190, 269
dajāj dependants 233
dakkah; dikāk bench 256
dalīf gentle stroll 253
dam; dam al-akhawayn dragon's blood tree 263
ḍamān tax 106
daqīq; daqīq al-samīd/al-samīdh white flour 222
daqūq eye medicine 253
dār; dār al-wakālah state office administering the agency tax; *dār al-zakāh* *zakāh*-house 160, 263
darīn fox 196
ḍaraba v *'alā* take 65
daraqah: durūq (*durūqayn*!) leaf (of door) 212
darb: durūb tower-house, wall 68, 107, 164, 190, 212
dāris: dawāris bronze coin 40
dawr wall 69
ḍayqah lack of water 71
ḍayrāk seer-fish 244
dhabīlah dhabā'il wick 53
dhādhī see *dādhī*
dhawd a few animals 233
dhirā': dhirā' al-yad hand cubit 40
dhirā' al-ḥadīd al-Miṣrī 41
dhirā' 'umariyyah 192
dhubāb tip (of sword) 206
dhurah sorghum 55
dībājah adornment 38
dilālah broker's fee 159
dūbah large double-ended cargo craft 283
dubbah pumpkin 83
dukhn millet 55
dumluj/dumlaj bracelet 153
dumyah: duman image/statue 193
dūnīj/dūnij: dawānīj type of ship 143, 288
durr pearls 286

faḥl fuḥūl: rijāl fuḥūl outstanding men 123
falq/falaq vagina 241
fals unit of currency 40, 77
fann: fann al-tārīkh historical geography/topography 29
faqāq stupid 253
fār: fār al-baḥr type of fish 244
farā type of fish 244
farā v cut the throat of 201
farāsilah unit of weight 156
farika v hate/divorce 111
farkah rubbing/pressing 165
fasḥ passport 290
faswah noiseless fart 258
faṭīr unleavened bread/fried dish 112
fawfal/fūfal betel nut 262
fawlah safety/good omen 136
fijl radish 36
fisht/fusht: afshāt reef 120
fukhākh chameleon 237
fūlādh purest iron 54
fūṭah: fuwaṭ waistwrapper 115
fuwaṭ al-sūsī Sousse waistwrappers 157
fuwwah madder 157

ghadā v leave 188
ghaddā v II give lunch to 188
ghaḍīrah: ghaḍā'ir good earth 290
gharab willow 63
ghawr low ground 66
ghayl permanent flow of water 176
ghimd scabbard 206

ghubbah bay 265

ḥabaq: ḥibāq sweet basil 113, 236
ḥabbah unit of currency 76
ḥādda v III be smart 123
hadas myrtle 114
ḥāfah: ḥuwaf quarter 287
ḥājah: ḥawā'ij spices/needs 96
ḥajl/ḥijl anklet 153
ḥajr private parts 253
ḥakkār hoarding/hoarder 114 n. 4
halīlaj myrobolan 159
ḥāmin stallion camel 220
ḥaml/ḥiml unit of weight 71
ḥammara v II give a red appearance 42
ḥannūn henna/henna flower 108
harīsah dish of meat or fish, set in a paste 263, 288
harj: wa-harj wa-marj having no worries 35, 71
ḥarqah kiln 258
ḥarrah: ḥirār lava field 43, 66
ḥarrāq necklace 153
ḥaṣā pebbles/small stones 233
ḥawālah credit slip 106
ḥawk/ḥawkah: aḥwāk handwoven fabric 158
ḥawwāmah type of bird 236
ḥawzah territory 197
ḥayf tyranny 253
hayl cardomom 156
hayn: hayn layn simple and nice 241
ḥayn time of death 180
ḥays date pâté 238
ḥazā parsley 152
ḥāzzah: ḥawāzz plot of land 91 n. 9
hibrizī strong, elegant horseman 185 n. 2
hilāl: ahillah double edge 59
ḥiltīt as(s)a gum 156
ḥimāḥim basil flower 236
ḥimyah abstaining from things injurious in a case of sickness 232
ḥīn time 180
ḥinnā' henna 235
ḥinṭah wheat 263
ḥirbā' chameleon 237
hudbah: hudabāt/hudubāt fringe 288 n. 5
ḥujzah waistband 66 n. 14
ḥumar tamarind 89, 157
hunduwān Indian swords 202
ḥuqb: aḥqāb age 57
ḥurr chaste 163
  ḥurrat al-arḍ pure earth 224
ḥuṭum potash 117

ibrīsam/ibrīsum silk 278
'idhq raceme 105
'ifw see *'afw*
iḥlīlaj myrobalan 116
iḥtajaba v VIII vanish 235
iḥtajaza v VIII surround/put on waistwrapper 66 n. 13
imtakka v VIII suckle 30
injāṣ plums 196
'innah/'unnah fish-trap 279
irtifā' revenue 98 n. 6
isḥil spinach 90
ishtahara v VIII become famous 85 n. 10
ist astāh see *'uryān*
istafaḍḍa v X deflower 284
istaẓhara v X be in a position to 128
istiftāḥ conquest 200
istihār: istihāran as security 157
iyyal/uyyal/ayyil oryx 208
izdawā v VIII: *izdawā bi-arwāḥi-h* flee 121 n. 1

jadarah enclosure 187
jāfa v become putrid/stink 287 n. 9
jamal: jamal aḥmar thoroughbred camel/anything highly prized 36
jamanah bowl 114
jamrah: jimār pebble 46
jandal stones 279
jarād locusts (flying) 232
jarbī: jirāb Djerba wool 115
jarīb measure of land/hectare 186
jariba v become rusty 58
jarīr cameleer 82
jarrāy courier 155
jāsha v choke back one's tears 144
jawhar grain 59
jawlab pigeon 236
jawr behaving badly 65

jināḥ: ajniḥah paddle/oar 138 n. 4
jizyah tax 75
juljulān sesame 114
jumādī wintry 220
jummal/jumal calculating by means of the letters of the alphabet 202

kabasa v *ʿalā* attack 125
khadhf sling 221
kādhī fragrant screw-pine 107
kaff scale (of balance)/palm (of hand) 70
kafīʾ equal 48
kāfūr camphor 51, 156
kaj ba-kaj in an unofficial way 41
kammūn cumin 209
kanib/kinab species of cereal 263
kanīf latrine 253
kāra v hasten 236
kārīz ditch 288
karr: akrār prayer mat/turban linen 159
kattān flax/linen 157
kaws contrary wind 133 n. 6
kawrajah score 158
kawsaj/kūsaj: kawāsij with scanty beard 110
kawwara v II launch 273
khabala v withhold 246
khabbār courier 155
khabt scrub 91
khaḍḍara v II give a dark green appearance 42
khafūsh dish 112
khalāl at the stage of beginning to ripen (date) 224
khalīj expanse of water, river 262
khaliq of sweet disposition 111
khalkhāl anklet 153
khām untanned leather 202
khām Hindī calico 158
khānqāh religious hostel 235 n. 2
kharā/kharāʾ shit 253
khardal mustard grain/unit of weight 57
kharrūb see *khurnūb*
khāsa v become putrid/stink 278
khasīf: khusuf well 119
khatmah recitation (of the Quran) 280
khawkh peaches 196
khayāl ghost 269
khilāf Egyptian willow 63
khiṣb fertility 220
khiyār cucumber 36, 108
khuff footwear 265
khulayṭ mulayṭ all mixed together 107
khurnūb/kharnūb carob tree 231
khuzāmā lavender 51
khwush/khwash good-quality 42
kijrī kedgeree 159
kīmukht grain (of leather) 41
kirbās: kirbās muṣallā piece of muslin/linen used as prayer carpet 153
kiyūrā keora 108
kuʿb: akʿāb small breast 112
kubān type of bread/soup 112
kummathrā/kumathrā pears 196
kūr: akwār: akwārāt bees' nest 43
kurkī: karākī crane 196 n. 14
kurrāth leeks 36
kusb oil cake 252
kuwwah/kawwah hole/vagina 253

laḥūḥ type of bread 112
lajūj unwelcome/quarrelsome 55
lāk dark red dye 157
lakht enormous 201
laqaḥ pollinating 105
laṭmah slap in the face/upheaval 197
lawz almonds 201
laymūn/līmūn lemons 262
laynūfar/līnūfar lotus 53, 108
lazima: lazima-h baṭnu-h need to eat 51

madarah mudūr mound 145
mādhī honey 292
mafrūk hated/divorced 111
maftūn beguiled/tormented 252
maḥābis plur bed covers 158
maḥaqa v burn up 55
maḥkūk smooth 102 n. 2
makhdūm dressed 191
makhṣūṣ especially endowed 29
makka v press 30, 124
makkah pressing hard 30, 32, 71
maks: mukūs: mukūsāt tax 77
maktūm type of date 36

malāḥidah plur heretics 145
malakī type of dinar 40, 78, 89
mandakh: manādikh landfall 158
mānī' not accessible 150
manqūsh dressed 49
manshūr official note 36
manthūr stock 52
maqāṭi' plur flax cloths 157
maqrāh cistern 32
maraḥ sprightliness 244
marāwiḥ(?) type of fish 244
marj see *harj*
markūb: al-markūb al-waṭī' footwear 96
marqan/marqāh/mirqāh stage/step 173
marrah: marrah/bi-al-marrah very 58 n. 11, 213 n. 8, 233 n. 7
māsh mung bean 159
mashmūm(ah) aromatic plant 196 n. 11
mashshā v II go on one's way 188
masīl wadi 85
masrūq hidden 44 n. 6
maṣrūr tied up 34
maswarah: masāwir grape basket 159
mawsim pilgrimage season 40
ma'zim narrow/strait 205
mihār levelling board 95
mikhlāf: makhālīf mountain district 67, 181
milāyah striped cotton cloth 115
miqra'ah whip/instrument of striking 77
mirzabah: marāzib groove 58
mishmish apricots 196
miṣr amṣār town 29
miṣṭabah: maṣāṭib mound of earth *256*
mu'abbal with many camels 153 n. 11
mu'abbal with fulsome ankles 153
mu'āmalah equivalent value 38
mu'arraḍ extended over 56
mu'assā hard 195 n. 3
mubashshir port messenger 155
mudamlaj wearing bracelets 268 n. 15
mudarraj built in layers 64
mudd unit of weight 41
mughr incense 159
mujabbanah cheese cake 40
mukassarah winding wadi in flood 54
mukhalkhal wearing anklets 268
mukhlif replacement husband 55
mukhnif eel 244
mukhtaṣir simple 165 n. 1
muktasī in full leaf 54
mulayṭ see *khulayṭ*
multaḥḥ type of dish 112
mulūkhiyyah plant used for soup 112
mumalja' plump-faced 153
munādī salesman 162
munāḥim raging against 197
muqābaḍah: muqābaḍatan by direct sale 41
muqaddam: muqaddam al-asmāk first fish (into the trap) 280
muqallis having a laxative effect 115
muql fruit of the doum palm 81
musharra' made-up 153 n. 1
muṣlābah hardness(?) 83
muṭabbaq paved 265
mu'takif obsessed 180
mutaqaddim infantry sword/of good quality 57

nabgh thyme 270
nabq nabk 54
naḥālah basil 236
nahara v drive away 229
nahd: nuhūd breast 70
najd highland 66
nakhara v snort 177
nākhūdhah owner-captain/supercargo 146
nāmis/nāmūs mosquito 116, 245
naqīl mountain pass 165
narājīl coconut 262
nāranj orange 52
narjis/nirjis narcissus 53, 196
nasaq: 'alā nasaq wāḥid in the same condition 284
naṣfiyyah: naṣāfī silk and linen cloth 34 n. 1
nasham species of tree 159
nashsha v drive out
naṭ' circular leather 159
natasha v strike 251
nāṭūr look-out 154
naynūfar/nawfar lotus 53 n. 1
niḥy ghee-skin 222

nuql/naql sweetmeats 159
nushshāb arrows 89

qabālah leasing contract 105
qabwah: qubā vault 45
qadhir evil 111
qaḍīb sharp 58
qafʿah: qifāʿ basket 153, 158
qarā v collect 32
qarab shallow well 173
qārah qūr hill 169
qaranful cloves 156
qāriʿah: qāriʿat al-ṭarīq main route 202
qaṣabah measure of length 161
qāṣif destructive 262
qaṭīb mixed milk/buttermilk 112
qawwād procurer 265
qawṭ: aqwāṭ ewe 224
qayṣariyyah market complex 147
qilā potash 117
qulqulah: qalāqil pellet drum, type of plant 107
qināʿ: qunūʿ bonnet 34
qirsh shark 244
qiṭʿah financial contribution/levy 35
qiththāʾ snake cucumber 36, 113
qulfah vagina 241
qunbār coir, crayfish 153
quṭārah syrup 159
quṭr/quṭur aloes, extensive area 52

rabʿ: al-rabʿ al-maskūn inhabited earth 57
rabīṭ prisoner 229
raḍrāḍ crushed pebbles/hard stones 221
raghad: raghadan in plenty 31
rahik weak 11
raḥmah rain/mercy 33
rahnāmaj route book/pilot guide 264
rāʿī livestock taxman 167
raʿīd/ruʿayd species of fish 244
raqīṣ dancer 92 n. 3
rās: rās bi-rās no gain on either side (in a transaction) 261
ʿalā ruʾūsi-him in person 261 n. 12
raṣāṣ archaeological remains, stones 29
rayḥānah bounty 49
raziyyah/razīʾah: razāyā misfortune 227
ribāṭ: rubuṭ hospice, caravanserai 235
rikhw: rikhawāt al-tikak with loose trouser waists 111
riyāsh home comforts 64
rubʿ measurement of weight 41
rubbāḥ ape 243
rubbān captain 243
rūhīniyā finest Indian steel 59
ruqaʿ roka tree 89
rūsī type of cloth 161
rustāq district 42
ruṭab fresh, ripe dates 36, 105
rutbah garrison 185

ṣabā v float along 106
sabara v measure in spans 162
sabirah/ṣabir aloes 107
ṣabiyyah: ṣabāyā jawbone/pupil (of eye) 244
ṣadaf shell
safaqa v block off 212
safarjal quince 196
saffārah trader 160
safiy(y)ah/safīh species of fish 244
sāḥah courtyard 242
saḥaqa v grind 55
sāʾibah mother of *baḥīrah 220*
sākhil: sukhkhal type of date 288
salam acacia 166
sallaba v II plunder 245
salwā quail 244
samak: al-samak al-ʿarabī mullet 243
ṣamqah: ṣimāq milk 173
ṣanbūq small in-shore boat 143 n. 10, 278 n. 7
sandarūs species of tree 108
sandās rubbish dump 133
sāqah retinue 228
sarḥ/ṣarḥ eel wood 46
sariyyah military force 200
ṣarraʿa v II cast down 211
saʿtar thyme 270
ṣawāfī confiscated palms 106
sawāsī: sawāsī al-kattān al-kibār large Sousse linen 158
sawsan lily 52
sayfī type of dirham 114

sayyaba v II leave to pasture at will 220
sayyaḥa v II: *sayyaḥa qiṭaʿ qiṭaʿ* tear limb from limb 216
shaddah: shaddatan shaddatan piece by piece 155
shaḥm suet 40
shaʿīrah barley corn/measurement of weight 287
shakk doubt/penetration 285
shammāmah small melon 86
shaqaḥ (for *tashqīḥ*) reddening (of dates) 105
shaʿrah pubic hair 152
sharyān/shiryān species of tree 219
shawānī galleys 156
shawḥaṭ species of tree 202
shaydhar striped plaid 115
shīḥ white wormwood 113
shīraj sesame oil 40
shuqduf litter 204
sidr nabk tree 68
sikand chameleon 237
silq beet 59
ṣināʿah boatyard 138
sīsbān sesban 90
siyāsah Sousse cloth 233
subāʿī/subāʿiyyah loincloth 115, 158
ṣufr brass 265
sukurrujah/sukurrajah bowl 240
summān quail 244
sunnah: sunan religious observance 29, 62
ṣūrī picture seller/maker 152
surrah navel/centre 29

tabaddada spill over 222
ṭabbaqa v II be opposite 235
ṭaḥan: ṭaḥawāt plain 90
takḥīmu repressing 151 n. 12
ṭalʿ spadix 105, 286
ṭāla v: *ṭālat yadu-h* feel strong 230
talḥ acacia 113 n. 10
tall: ʿalā tall al-salāmah in a safe place 284
talqīḥ see *laqaḥ*
tanḍūb species of plant 150
ṭāq bale 41
taqallaba v V come up against 205
ṭaraf bag 233
ṭaraḥa v *ʿalā* impose a price on 163
ṭarfāʾ tamarisk 91
ṭarḥ marriage money 35
tarib species of plant? 149
tasabbaba v V achieve 125
tashqīḥ see *shaqaḥ*
taslīm handing over ceremony 240
tawaʿʿada v V go/do something once a week 202
ṭaysūj/ṭassūj measurement of weight 287
tawzīr: tawāzīr beam 280
thaqifa v come across 48
thaqīl: al-thiqāl heavy leathers 42 n. 10
thaqqafa v II give discipline, tend 48
tharada v crumble for *tharīd* 228
tharīd name of a dish 186, 228
ṭiḥṭāḥ: ṭiḥṭāḥ raḥrāḥ scattered far and wide and ample (rain) 203
tikkah: tikak see *rikhw*
tīn figs 196
ṭurṭur hoopoe bird/bonnet 252
tūt mulberry 50

ʿufw see *ʿafw*
ʿumariyyah see *dhirāʿ*
umm: umm ḥubayn chameleon 237
ʿunnah see *ʿinnah*
ʿuqbūl/ʿuqbūlah: ʿaqābil/ʿaqābīl last trace 184
ʿuqdah 1 land abounding in herbage 96
ʿuqdah/ʿaqdah 2 silk cloth 157
uqḥuwān camomile 53
ūqiyyah measurement of weight 40
ʿurr mountain/bedrock 129
ʿury without a saddle 252
ʿushar French cotton 150, 210
ushnān saltwort 159
utrunjah/utrunj citron 168
uyyal see *iyyal*

waʿd week 161
waʿd: awʿād tariff 161
waḍaḥ visible reef 120
waḥsh ugly/disfigured 241
wakālah agency tax 160
warqāʾ dove 74

wars Flemingia 194
wāsiʿ/wasīʿ non-virgin 285
waṭāʾ something to make softer 51
wuzz geese 84

yasamīn/yāsimīn jasmine 52
yasʿūb leader/queen bee 43
yūsufī type of dirham 75

zabadī/zubdī measure of weight 114
zabūr/zibr Psalms 241
zaʿfarān saffron 157
ẓahr spine (of land) 84
zāmilah: zawāmil camel 212 n. 3
zaradiyyah chain-mail 215
ẓarf clay vessel 212
zayt: zayt al-ḥārr flax oil 159
zubbah beard 83
zubdah best 96
zubrah piece of iron 241
zulāl sweet, cool water 291
zunjufr/zinjafr cinnabar 265

BIBLIOGRAPHY

al-ʿAbdalī, Aḥmad Faḍl b. ʿAlī Muḥsin, *Hadiyyat al-zaman fī akhbār mulūk Laḥj wa-ʿAdan*, Cairo, AH 1351.

Abū Nuwās, al-Ḥasan b. Hāniʾ al-Ḥakamī, *Der Dīwān des Abū Nuwās*, ed. Ewald Wagner, Wiesbaden and Stuttgart, Bibliotheca Islamica 20, 4 vols, 1958–82.

——, *Dīwān Abī Nuwās*, ed. ʿUmar Fārūq al-Ṭabbāʿ, Beirut, 1998.

Abun-Nasr, Jamil, *A History of the Maghrib*, Cambridge, 1975.

Agius, Dionisius, *Arabic Literary Works as a Source of Documentation for Technical Terms of Medieval Culture*, Berlin, 1984.

——, 'Classifying Vessel-Types in Ibn Baṭṭūṭa's *Riḥla*' in David Parkin and Ruth Barnes, eds, *Ships and the Development of Maritime Technology in the Indian Ocean*, London, 2002, pp. 174–209.

——, *In the Wake of the Dhow. The Arabian Gulf and Oman*, Reading, 2002.

——, Medieval Qalhat: 'Travellers, Dhows and Stone Anchors in South-East Oman' in Himanshu Prabha Ray, ed., *Archaeology of Seafaring. The Indian Ocean in the Ancient Period*, Delhi, 1999, pp. 173–221.

Ahmad, S. Maqbul, *India and the Neighbouring Territories in the* Kitāb Nuzhat al-mushtāq fikhtirāq al-āfāq *of al-Sharīf al-Idrīsī*, Leiden, 1960.

al-Akwaʿ, Ismāʿīl b. ʿAlī, *al-Amthāl-Yamāniyyah*, 2 vols, Ṣanʿāʾ, 1984.

——, *al-Buldān al-Yamāniyyah ʿinda Yāqūt al-Ḥamawī*, Kuwait, 1985.

——, *al-Madāris al-Islāmiyyah fī al-Yaman*, Ṣanʿāʾ, 1980.

al-ʿAlawī, Ṣāliḥ b. Ḥāmid, *Tārīkh Ḥaḍramawt*, 2 vols, Jeddah, 1968.

ʿAlī b. Muḥammad, al-ʿAbbāsī al-ʿAlawī, *Sīrat al-Hādī ilā al-Ḥaqq Yaḥyā b. al-Ḥusayn*, ed. Suhayl Zakkār, Damascus, 1972.

Allouche, Adel, *Mamluk Economics – a Study and Translation of al-Maqrīzī's* Ighāthah, Salt Lake City, 1994.

Ambraseys, N. N., Melville, C. P. and Adams, R. D., *The Seismicity of Egypt, Arabia and the Red Sea – a Historical Review*, Cambridge, 1994.

Amīn, Muḥammad Muḥammad and Ibrāhīm, Laylā ʿAlī, *al-Muṣṭalaḥāt al-miʿmāriyyah fī al-wathāʾiq al-Mamlūkiyyah*, Cairo, 1990.

al-Amri, Hussein Abdullah, 'A Document Concerning the Sale of Ghayl al-Barmakī and al-Ghayl al-Aswad by al-Mahdī ʿAbbās, Imam of the Yemen' in R. L. Bidwell and G. R. Smith, eds, *Arabian and Islamic Studies – Articles Presented to R. B. Serjeant on the Occasion of his Retirement from the Sir Thomas Adams's Chair of Arabic at the University of Cambridge*, London and New York, 1983, pp. 29–38.

al-ʿAqīlī, Muḥammad Aḥmad, *al-Muʿjam al-jughrāfī li-l-Bilād al-ʿArabiyyah al-Suʿūdiyyah: Muqtaʿat Jāzān*, Cairo, 1979.

Arberry, A. J., 'A Baghdad Cookery Book', *Islamic Culture*, 13, 1939, pp. 21–47, 189–214.

van Arendonk, C., *Les Débuts de l'imāmat zaidite*, Leiden, 1960.

al-Aṣmaʿi, ʿAbd al-Malik b. Qurayb, *Kitāb al-Nabāt*, ed. ʿAbdallāh Yūsuf al-Ghunaym, Cairo, 1972.

al-Balādī, ʿĀtiq b. Ghayth, *Muʿjam maʿālim al-Ḥijāz*, 10 vols, Mecca, 1978–84.

Balog, Paul, 'Dirhems ayoubites inédits du Yémen', *Bulletin de l'Institut d'Egypte*, 36, 1953–4, pp. 347–55.

Bartold, W., *Turkestan down to the Mongol Invasion*, 4th edn, London, E. J. W. Gibb Memorial Trust, 1977.
al-Bayḍāwī, ʿAbdallāh b. ʿUmar, *Anwār al-tanzīl wa-asrār al-taʾwīl*, ed. H. O. Fleischer, Leipzig, 1846–78.
Beckingham, C. F., 'Arabic Texts and the Hakluyt Society', *Address to the Annual Meeting of the Hakluyt Society, 1979*, London, 1979, pp. 1–13.
Beeston, A. F. L., 'The Chain of al-Mandab' in *On Both Sides of al-Mandab – Ethiopian, South-Arabic and Islamic Studies Presented to Oscar Löfgren on his Ninetieth Birthday 13 May 1988 by Colleagues and Friends*, Istanbul, Swedish Research Institute Transactions, 2, 1989, pp. 1–7.
——, 'Two Biʾr Ḥimā Inscriptions Re-examined', *Bulletin of the School of Oriental and African Studies*, 48/1, 1985, pp. 42–52.
Beeston, A. F. L., Ghul, M. A., Müller, W. W. and Ryckmans, J., *Sabaic Dictionary/Dictionnaire sabéen*, Louvain-la-Neuve and Beirut, 1982.
Ben Shemesh, A., *Taxation in Islam – Abū Yūsuf's* Kitāb al-Kharāj, Leiden and London, 1969.
Bidwell, Robin, and Smith, G. Rex, eds, *Arabian and Islamic Studies and Articles Presented to R.B. Serjeant on the Occasion of his Retirement from the Sir Thomas Adams's Chair of Arabic at the University of Cambridge*, London and New York, 1983.
Bikhazi, Ramzi J., 'Coins of al-Yaman 132–569 A.H.', *al-Abḥāth*, 23, 1970, pp. 3–127.
Bindagji, Hussein Hamza, *Atlas of Saudi Arabia*, Oxford, 1980.
al-Bīrūnī, Muḥammad b. Aḥmad, *The Book of Instruction in the Elements of the Art of Astrology (Kitāb al-Tafhīm li-awāʾil ṣināʿat al-tanjīm)*, trans. R. Ramsey Wright, London, 1934.
——, *Chronologie Orientalischer Völker von AlBeruni (Kitāb al-Āthār al-bāqiyah ʿan al-qurūn al-khāliyah)*, ed. C. Eduard Sachau, Leipzig, 1923.
Blau, Joshua, *The Emergence and Linguistic Background of Judaeo-Arabic*, Oxford, 1965.
——, 'The State of Research in the Field of the Linguistic Study of Middle Arabic', *Arabica*, 28, 1981, pp. 187–203.
de Blois, François, *Persian Literature, a Bio-bibliographical Survey*, V, *Poetry of the pre-Mongol Period*, London, 1997.
Bombay, Government of, *An Account of the Arab Tribes in the Vicinity of Aden*, Bombay, 1909.
Bosworth, Clifford Edmund, *The Mediaeval Islamic Underworld. The Banū Sāsān in Arabic Society and Literature*, 2 vols, Leiden, 1976.
——, The *New Islamic Dynasties – a Chronological and Genealogical Manual*, Edinburgh, 1996.
——, 'The Quf or Kūfichīs in Early Islamic History', *Iran*, 14, 1976, pp. 9–17.
Botta, P. E., 'Extraits de la relation d'une excursion au Mont Sabir etc.', *Bulletin de la Société de Géographie*, 12, 1839, pp. 369–81.
Botting, Douglas, *Island of Dragon Blood*, London, 1958.
Brockelmann, C, *Geschichte der Arabischen Literatur*, 2 vols, 3 supplements, Leiden, 1937–49.
Brockett, A. A., *The Spoken Arabic of Khābūra on the Bāṭina of Oman*, Manchester, 1985.
Brouwer, C. G., *al-Mukhā: Profile of a Yemeni Seaport as Sketched by Servants of the Dutch East India Company (VOC) 1614–1640*, Amsterdam, 1997.
Brown, Francis, Driver, S. R. and Briggs, Charles A., *A Hebrew and English Lexicon of the Old Testament*, Oxford, 1962.
Browne, Edward G., *A Literary History of Persia*, 4 vols, Cambridge, 1928.
Burton, Capt. Sir Richard F., *Personal Narrative of a Pilgrimage to al Madinah and Meccah*, ed. Lady Burton, 2 vols, London, 1913.
Busse, H., trans., *History of Persia under Qājār Rule*, New York, 1972.
Cahen, C. and Serjeant, R. B., 'Fiscal Survey of the Medieval Yemen: Notes Preparatory to a Critical Edition of the *Mulaḫḫaṣ al-fiṭan* of al-Ḥasan b. ʿAlī al-Šarīf al-Ḥusaynī', *Arabica*, 4, 1957, pp. 22–33.
The Cambridge History of Arabic Literature: ʿAbbasid Belles-Lettres, ed. Julia Ashtiany et al., Cambridge, 1990.

The Cambridge History of Arabic Literature: Arabic Literature to the End of the Umayyad Period, ed. A. F. L. Beeston et al., Cambridge, 1983.
The Cambridge History of Arabic Literature: Religion, Learning and Science in the ʿAbbasid Period, ed. M. J. L. Young et al., Cambridge, 1990.
Cambridge History of Iran, III, ed. Ehsan Yarshater, Cambridge, 1983.
Cambridge History of Islam, IA and B, ed. P. M. Holt, Ann K. S. Lambton and Bernard Lewis, Cambridge, 1970.
Carter, M. G., 'Arabic Grammar' in M. J. L. Young et al., eds, *Cambridge History of Arabic Literature: Religion, Learning and Science in the ʿAbbasid Period*, Cambridge, 1990, pp. 118–39.
——, 'Arabic Lexicography', ibid., pp. 106–18.
Caskel, Werner, *Ǧamharat an-nasab: Das Genealogische Werk des Hišām ibn Muḥammad al-Kalbī*, Band I, Einleitung von Werner Caskel, Tafeln von Gert Strenziok, Band II Erläuterungen zu den Tafeln von Werner Caskel, Register begonnen von Gert Stenziok, Leiden, 1966.
Chelhoud, J., 'Introduction à l'histoire sociale et urbaine de Zabīd', *Arabica*, 25, 1978, pp. 48–88.
CHIr, see *Cambridge History of Iran*.
CHIs, see *Cambridge History of Islam*.
Costa, Paolo M., *Historic Mosques and Shrines of Oman*, Oxford, 2001.
——, 'The Mosque of al-Janad' in Robin Bidwell and G. Rex Smith, eds, *Arabian and Islamic Studies and Articles Presented to R. B. Serjeant on the Occasion of his Retirement from the Sir Thomas Adams's Chair of Arabic at the University of Cambridge*, London and New York, 1983, pp. 43–68.
——, 'The Study of the City of Ẓafār (al-Balīd)', *Journal of Oman Studies*, 5, 1979, pp. 111–50.
D *see* Dozy.
Daftary, Farhad, 'Ḥasan-i Ṣabbāḥ and the Origins of the Nizārī Ismaʿili Movement' in Farhad Daftary, ed., *Mediaeval Ismaʿili History and Thought*, Cambridge, 1996, pp. 181–205.
——, *Mediaeval Ismaʿili History and Thought*, Cambridge, 1996.
Dallimore, W. and Jackson, A.B., *A Handbook of Coniferae and Ginkgoaceae*, revised by S. G. Harrison, 4th edn, London, 1966.
Darley-Doran, Robert E., 'Examples of Islamic Coinage from Yemen' in Werner Daum, ed., *Yemen, 3000 Years of Art and Civilisation in Arabia Felix*, Innsbruck and Frankfurt/Main, 1987, pp. 182–204.
De Gaury, Gerald, 'Note on Masira Island', *The Geographical Journal*, 123/4, 1957, pp. 499–502.
——, *Rulers of Mecca*, London etc., 1951.
De Goeje, M. J., 'Communication sur le livre d'Ibn al-Modjâwir', *Actes du Onzième Congrès International des Orientalistes, Paris, 1897*, Paris, 1899, pp. 23–33.
Derenbourg, H., *Les Manuscrits arabes dans la collection Schefer de la Bibliothèque Nationale*, Paris, 1901.
——, *Ousama ibn Mounḳidh*, Paris, 1886.
DeShazo, A. S. and Bates, Michael L., 'The Umayyad Governors of al-ʿIrāq and the Changing Annulet Pattern on their Dirhams', *Numismatic Chronicle*, 7th ser., 14, 1974, pp. 107–15.
Dey, Nundo Lal, *Geographical Dictionary of Ancient and Mediaeval India*, 3rd edn, Delhi, 1971.
al-Dhahabī, Muḥammad b. Aḥmad, *al-Mushtabih fī al-rijāl asmāʾi-him wa-ansābi-him*, ed. ʿAlī Muḥammad al-Bajawī, Cairo, 1962.
al-Dihās, Fawwāz ʿAlī, 'Edition of al-Fākihī's *Akhbār Makkah*', PhD thesis, University of Exeter, 1983.
al-Dimyāṭī, Maḥmūd Muṣṭafā, *Muʿjam asmāʾ al-nabātāt al-wāridah fī* Tāj al-ʿarūs *li-l-Zabīdī*, Cairo, 1965.
al-Dīnawarī, Abū Ḥanīfah, *The Book of Plants of Abū Ḥanīfa ad-Dīnawarī*, ed. Bernhard Lewin, Uppsala and Wiesbaden, 1953.
Doe, Brian, *Socotra – Island of Tranquility*, London, 1992.

Donaldson, W. J., 'The Pre-Metric Weights and Measures of Oman in the 1970s', *New Arabian Studies*, 1, 1993, pp. 83–107.
Donzel, Emeri Johannes van, *A Yemenite Embassy to Ethiopia 1647–1649*, Stuttgart, 1986.
al-Doy, Ali, 'Bahrain According to Arab Geographers and Historians from the Ninth Century AD to Ibn Battuta' in Shaikh Abdullah bin Khalid al-Khalifa and Michael Rice, eds, *Bahrain through the Ages – the History*, London and New York, 1993, pp. 158–67.
Dozy, R., *Dictionnaire détaillé des noms de vêtements chez les Arabes*, Amsterdam, 1845.
——, *Supplément aux dictionnaires arabes*, 2 vols, Paris, 3rd edn, 1967.
Dunn, Ross E., *The Adventures of Ibn Battuta – a Muslim Traveler of the 14th Century*, Berkeley and Los Angeles, 1986.
EI, see *Encyclopaedia of Islam*, 2nd edn.
EIran, see *Encyclopaedia Iranica*.
EJ, see *Encyclopaedia Judaica*.
Encyclopaedia Iranica, New York, 1985–.
Encyclopaedia of Islam, 2nd edn, Leiden, 1960–2003.
Encyclopaedia Judaica, Jerusalem, 1971–2.
Fakhry, Ahmed, *An Archaeological Journey to Yemen (March–May, 1947)*, 3 parts (Part II by G. Ryckmans), Cairo, 1951–2.
Faris, Nabih Amin, see al-Hamdānī, *Iklīl*, VIII.
Farsi, Zaki M. A., *National Guide and Atlas of the Kingdom of Saudi Arabia*, Jeddah, 1989.
Ferrand, G., 'L'Elément persan dans les textes nautiques arabes des XVe et XVIe siècles', *Journal asiatique*, 204, 1924, pp. 193–257.
al-Fīrūzābādī, Majd al-Dīn Muḥammad b. Yaʿqūb, *al-Qāmūs al-muḥīṭ*, 4 vols, Cairo, 1952.
Forand, P. '*ʿUshr* and *maks*', *Arabica*, 13, 1966, pp. 137–41.
Forbes, Henry O., *The Natural History of Sokotra and Abd-el-Kuri*, Liverpool, 1903.
Freeman-Grenville, G. S. P., *The Muslim and Christian Calendars*, London, New York and Toronto, 1963.
Garcin, Jean-Claude, *Un centre musulman de la Haute-Egypte médiéval: Qūṣ*, Cairo, 1976.
Garrett, John, *A Classical Dictionary of India*, Delhi, 1871.
Gavin, P. J., *Aden under British Rule, 1839–1967*, London, 1975.
Geddes, C. L., 'The Apostasy of ʿAlī b. al-Faḍl', in Robin Bidwell and G. Rex Smith, eds, *Arabian and Islamic Studies Articles Presented to R. B. Serjeant on the Occasion of his Retirement from the Sir Thomas Adams's Chair of Arabic at the University of Cambridge*, London and New York, 1983, pp. 80–86.
Ghaznawī, Ḥasan, *Dīwān*, Tehran, 1951.
Gibb, Sir Hamilton, *The Life of Saladin*, Oxford, 1973.
Gibbon, Edward, *The History of the Decline and Fall of the Roman Empire*, VI, *Mohammed and the Rise of the Arabs*, ed. with an introduction by Felipe Fernández-Armesto, London, 1988.
The Glorious Koran, a Bi-lingual Edition with English Translation, Introduction and Notes, by Marmaduke Pickthall, London, 1976.
Goitein, S. D., 'New Light on the Beginnings of the Kārim Merchants', *Journal of the Economic and Social History of the Orient*, 1, 1957, pp. 175–84.
——, *A Mediterranean Society. The Jewish Communities of the Arab World as Portrayed in the Documents of the Cairo Geniza, I, Economic Foundations*, Berkeley, Los Angeles and London, 1967.
——, *Travels in Yemen – an Account of Joseph Halévy's Journey to Najran in the Year 1870 Written in Sanʿani Arabic by his Guide Hayyim Habshush*, Jerusalem, 1941.
Golius, Jacobus, *Lexicon Arabico-Latinum*, Leiden, 1653.
Golvin, Lucien, and Fromont, Christine, *Thula, architecture et urbanisme d'une cité de haute montagne en République arabe du Yémen*, Paris, 1984.
Groom, Nigel, *Frankincense and Myrrh: a Study of the Arabian Incense Trade*, London and New York, 1981.

Grosset-Grange, Henri, *Glossaire nautique arabe ancien et moderne de l'Océan indien*, Texte établi par Alain Rouaud, Paris, Mémoires de la Section d'Histoire des Sciences et des Techniques 5, 1993.
Guest, R., 'Ẓufâr in the Middle Ages', *Islamic Culture*, 9, 1935, pp. 402–10.
Guidi, I, see al-Iṣfahānī, *Kitāb al-Aghānī*.
Guillaume, A., *The Life of Muhammad: a Translation of Isḥāq's* Sīrat Rasūl Allāh, Lahore etc., 1967.
Habshush, Hayyim, *Travels in Yemen – an Account of Joseph Halévy's Journey to Najran in the Year 1870*, ed. S. D. Goitein, Jerusalem, 1941.
al-Ḥaḍramī, ʿAbd al-Raḥmān b. ʿAbdallāh, *Jāmiʿat al-Ashāʿir Zabīd*, Ṣanʿāʾ, 1973.
al-Ḥajarī, Muḥammad b. Aḥmad, *Majmūʿ buldān al-Yaman wa-qabāʾili-hā*, ed. Ismāʿīl b. ʿAlī al-Akwaʿ, 4 vols, [Ṣanʿāʾ], 1984.
al-Ḥakīm, Abū al-Ḥasan ʿAlī b. Yūsuf, *al-Dawḥah al-mushtabikah fī ḍawābiṭ dār al-sikkah. Regimen de la Casa de la Moneda*, ed. Ḥussain Monés, Madrid, 1960.
al-Hamdānī, al-Ḥasan b. Aḥmad, *al-Iklīl*, I, ed. Muḥammad b. ʿAlī al-Akwaʿ al-Ḥiwālī, Cairo, 1963.
——, VIII, *The Antiquities of South Arabia, Being a Translation from the Arabic with Linguistic, Geographic, and Historic Notes of the Eight Book of al-Hamdānī's* al-Iklīl, trans. Nabih Amin Faris, Princeton, 1938.
——, *al-Iklīl*, X, ed. Muḥibb al-Dīn al-Khaṭīb, Cairo, AH 1368 [1948–9].
——, *Kitāb Ṣifat Jazīrat al-ʿArab, al-Hamdânî's Geographie der Arabischen Halbinsel*, ed. David Heinrich Müller, Leiden, 1968.
——, *K. Ṣifat Jazīrat al-ʿArab*, ed. Muḥammad b. ʿAlī, al-Akwaʿ, Ṣanʿāʾ, 1983.
——, *Südarabisches Muštabih Verzeichnis Homonymer und Homographer Eigennamen*, ed. Oscar Löfgren, Uppsala etc., Bibliotheca Ekmaniana 57, 1953.
al-Hamdānī, Ḥusayn b. Fayḍ Allāh, *al-Ṣulayḥiyyūn wa-al-ḥarakah al-Fāṭimiyyah fī al-Yaman*, Cairo, 1955.
al-Hamadhānī, Aḥmad b. Ibrāhīm Ibn al-Faqīh, *Kitāb al-Buldān*, ed. M. J. De Goeje, Leiden, Bibliotheca Geographorum Arabicorum 5, 1885.
al-Ḥarbī, Abū Isḥāq, *Kitāb al-Manāsik wa-amākin ṭuruq al-ḥajj wa-maʿālim al-Jazīrah*, ed. Ḥamad al-Jāsir, Riyadh, 1969.
Harris, Walter B., *A Journey through the Yemen and Some General Remarks upon That Country*, London, 1893.
Ḥasan, Yūsuf Faḍl, *The Arabs and the Sudan*, Edinburgh, 1967.
al-Ḥasan, Aḥmad Yūsuf, *Ṣināʿat al-fūlādh al-Dimashqī fī al-tārīkh al-ʿArabī*, n.p., 1972.
Healey, John F., *The Nabataean Tomb Inscriptions of Madaʾin Salih*, Oxford, Journal of Semitic Studies Supplement 1, 1993.
Healey, J. F. and Porter, V., eds, *Studies on Arabia in Honour of Professor G. Rex Smith*, Oxford, Journal of Semitic Studies Supplement 14, 2002.
Hepper, F. Nigel and Friis, I., *The Plants of Pehr Forsskål's 'Flora Aegyptiaco-Arabica' Collected on the Royal Danish Expedition to Egypt and the Yemen 1761–63*, Kew, 1994.
Hinz, Walther, *Islamische Masse und Gewichte*, Leiden and Cologne, 1970.
Hitti, Philip K., *Memoirs of an Arab-Syrian Gentleman or an Arab Knight in the Crusades: Memoirs of Usmah ibn Munqidh*, New York, 1929.
——, *Usāmah's Memoirs entitled* 'Kitāb al-Iʿtibār *by Usāmah ibn Munqidh*, Princeton, 1930.
Holt, P. M., *The Age of the Crusades: The Near East from the Eleventh Century to 1517*, London and New York, 1986.
Hopkins, J. F. P., 'Geographical and Navigational Literature' in M. J. L. Young et al., eds, *Cambridge History of Arabic Literature: Religion, Learning and Science in the ʿAbbasid Period*, Cambridge, 1990, pp. 301–27.
Hopkins, Simon, *Studies in the Grammar of Early Arabic*, Oxford, 1982.
Hunter, Captain F. M., *An Account of the British Settlement of Aden in Arabia*, 2nd impress., London, 1968.

Ibn ʿAbd Rabbi-h, Aḥmad b. Muḥammad al-Andalusī, *Kitāb al-ʿIqd al-farīd*, ed. Aḥmad Amīn et al., 6 vols, Cairo, 1948–9.
Ibn al-ʿAydarūs, *al-Nūr al-sāfir*, Baghdad, 1934.
Ibn Baṭṭūṭah, Muḥammad b. ʿAbdallāh, *The Travels of Ibn Baṭṭūṭa A.D. 1325–1354. Translated with Revisions and Notes from the Arabic Text Edited by C. Defrémery and B. R. Sanguinetti*, 5 vols, I–III ed. by H. A. R. Gibb, IV ed. by C. F. Beckingham, V (index by A. D. H. Bivar), London, Hakluyt Society, 2nd ser. 190, 1958–2000.
Ibn al-Daybaʿ, ʿAbd al-Raḥmān b. ʿAlī, *Kitāb Qurrat al-ʿuyūn bi-akbār al-Yaman al-maymūn*, ed. Muḥammad b. ʿAlī al-Akwaʿ, 2 vols, Cairo, 1977.
Ibn Fahd, ʿIzz al-Dīn ʿAbd al-ʿAzīz b. ʿUmar, *Ghāyat al-marām bi-akbār salṭanat al-Balad al-Ḥarām*, ed. Fahīm Muḥammad Shaltūt, 3 vols, Mecca, 1986–9.
Ibn Faraj, ʿAbd al-Qādir b. Aḥmad, *Kitāb al-Silāḥ wa-al-ʿuddah fī tārīkh bandar Juddah*, *Bride of the Red Sea, a 10th/16th Century Account of Jeddah*, Arabic text edited, translated and annotated by G. Rex Smith and Aḥmad ʿUmar al-Zaylaʿī, Durham, 1984.
Ibn Ḥātim, Muḥammad, al-Yāmī al-Hamdānī, *Kitāb al-Simṭ al-ghālī al-thaman fī akhbār al-mulūk min al-Ghuzz bi-al-Yaman*, ed. Rex Smith, London, 1974, volume I of G. R. Smith, *The Ayyūbids and Early Rasūlids in the Yemen*.
Ibn Ḥawqal, Abū al-Qāsim, *Ṣūrat al-arḍ*, ed. M. J. de Goeje, Leiden, Bibliotheca Geographorum Arabicorum 2, 1873.
Ibn Ḥazm, ʿAlī b. Aḥmad al-Andalusī, *Jamharat ansāb al-ʿArab*, ed. ʿAbd al-Salām Muḥammad Hārūn, Cairo, 1962.
Ibn Hishām, ʿAbd al-Malik, *al-Sīrah al-nabawiyyah*, ed. Muṣṭafā al-Saqqā et al., 2 vols, Cairo, 1955.
Ibn al-Ḥusayn, Yaḥyā, *Ghāyat al-amānī fī akhbār al-quṭr al-Yamānī*, ed. Saʿīd ʿAbd al-Fattāḥ ʿĀshūr, 2 vols, Cairo, 1968.
Ibn al-ʿImād, ʿAbd al-Ḥayy b. Aḥmad, *Shadharāt al-dhahab fī akhbār man dhahab*, Cairo, V, Cairo, 1351 H.
Ibn Jubayr, Muḥammad b. Aḥmad, *The Travels of Ibn Jubayr/Rilat Ibn Jubayr*, ed. William Wright, 2nd edn, revised by M. J. De Geoje, Leiden and London, E. J. W Gibb Memorial Series 5, 1907.
Ibn al-Kalbī, Hishām b. Muḥammad, *Kitāb al-Aṣnām*, ed. Aḥmad Zakī Bāshā, Cairo, 1924.
Ibn Khaldūn, ʿAbd al-Raḥmān, *The Muqaddimah*, trans. by Franz Rosenthal, 3 vols, New York, 1958.
Ibn Khurdādhbeh, Abū al-Qāsim ʿUbayd Allāh b. ʿAbdallāh, *Kitāb al-Masālik wa-al-mamālik*, ed. M. J. de Geoje, Leiden, Bibliotheca Geographorum Arabicorum 6, 1889.
Ibn Manẓūr, Jamāl al-Dīn Muḥammad b. Mukarram, *Lisān al-ʿArab*, 15 vols, Beirut, 1955–6.
Ibn Mammātī, Asʿad, *Kitāb Qawānīn al-dawāwīn*, ed. ʿAzīz Ṣuryāl ʿAṭiyyah, Cairo, 1943.
Ibn al-Mujāwir, *Ibn al-Muǧāwir, Descriptio Arabiae Meridionalis ..., Ṣifat bilād al-Yaman wa-Makkah wa-baʿḍ al-Ḥijāz al-musammā Taʾrīkh al-Mustabṣir*, ed. Oscar Löfgren, 2 vols (with continuous pagination), Leiden, 1951–4.
——, *Ṣifat bilād al-Yaman wa-Makkah wa-baʿḍ al-Ḥijāz al-musammā Tārīkh al-Mustabṣir li-Ibn al-Mujāwir*, ed. Mamdūḥ Ḥasan Muḥammad, Cairo, 1996.
——, *Tārīkh al-Mustabṣir*, MS Aya Sofya Istanbul Nr 3080, now preserved in the Süleymaniye Kütüphanesi.
——, *Tārīkh al-Mustabṣir*, MS University Library Leiden Or. 5572 (Ar. 2450).
Ibn Rasūl, ʿUmar b. Yūsuf, *Ṭurfat al-aṣḥāb fī maʿrifat al-ansāb*, ed. K. W. Zetterstéen, Damascus, 1949.
Ibn Rustah, Aḥmad b. ʿUmar, *Kitāb al-Aʿlāq al-nafīsah*, ed. M. J. De Goeje, Leiden, Biblioteca Geographorum Arabicorum 7, 1892.
Ibn Samurah, ʿUmar b. ʿAlī al-Jaʿdī, *Ṭabaqāt fuqahāʾ al-Yaman*, ed. Fuʾād Sayyid, Cairo, 1957.
Ibn Taghrī Birdī, Yūsuf, *al-Nujūm al-zāhirah fī mulūk Miṣr wa-al-Qāhirah*, VIII, Cairo, 1939.

al-Idrīsī, Abū ʿAbdallāh Muḥammd b. Muḥammad, *Opus Geographicum* (text of *Kitāb Nuzhat al-mushtāq fī ikhtirāq al-āfāq*), ed. E. Cerulli, F. Gabrieli et al., 2 vols, Naples and Rome, 1970.

Imruʾ al-Qays, *Dīwān*, ed. Yāsīn al-Ayyūbī, Beirut, Damascus and Amman, 1998.

Ingrams, Harold, *Arabia and the Isles*, London, 1966.

Iraq and the Persian Gulf, London, Naval Intelligence Division Geographical Handbook Series, 1944.

al-Iryānī, Muṭahhar ʿAlī, *al-Muʿjam al-Yaman fī al-lughah wa-al-turāth*, Damascus, 1996.

al-Iṣfahānī, Abū Faraj, *Kitāb al-Aghānī*, 20 vols, Būlāq, 1285 [1868] with I. Guidi, *Tables alphabétiques du* Kitāb al-Aghānī, Leiden, 1900.

al-Iṣfahānī al-Ḥasan b. ʿAbdallāh, *Bilād al-ʿArab*, ed. Ḥamad al-Jāsir and Ṣāliḥ al-ʿAlī, Riyadh, 1968.

al-Iṣṭakhrī, Ibrāhīm b. Muḥammad, *al-Masālik wa-al-mamālik*, ed. Muḥammad Jābir ʿAbd al-ʿĀl al-Ḥīnī, Cairo, 1961.

al-Jāḥiẓ, ʿAmr b. Baḥr, *Kitāb al-Bukhalāʾ*, ed. Ṭāhā al-Ḥājirī, Cairo, 1958.

Jawad, M., 'Petites découvertes dans les manuscrits arabes de la Bibliothèque Nationale de Paris', *Revue des études islamiques*, cahiers 2–3, 1938, pp. 285–7.

Johnstone, T. M., *Jibbāli Lexicon*, Oxford, 1981.

——, *Mehri Lexicon and English-Mehri Word-List, with Index of the English Definitions in the* Jibbāli Lexicon *compiled by G. Rex Smith*, London, 1987.

Kaḥḥālah, ʿUmar Riḍā, *Muʿjam qabāʾil al-ʿArab al-qadīmah wa-al-ḥadīthah*, 5 vols, Beirut, 1982.

Kahl, Oliver, *Sābūr ibn Sahl, the Small Dispensatory*, Leiden and Boston, 2003.

Kammerer, A., *Le Routier de Dom Joam de Castro – l'exploration de la Mer Rouge par les Portugais en 1541*, Paris, 1936.

Kay, Henry Cassels, *Yaman, its Early Mediaeval History*, London, 1892.

Kazimirski, A. de Biberstein, *Dictionnaire arabe–français*, 2 vols, Paris, 1860.

al-Khalifa, A. M., 'Fishing in Bahrain: Some Techniques and Technical Terms' in Robin Bidwell and G. Rex Smith, eds, *Arabian and Islamic Studies – Articles Presented to R. B. Serjeant on the Occasion of his Retirement from the Sir Thomas Adams's Chair of Arabic at the University of Cambridge*, London and New York, 1983, pp. 229–34.

al-Khazrajī, ʿAlī b. al-Ḥasan, *The Pearl-strings; a History of the Resūliyy Dynasty of Yemen (al-ʿUqūd al-luʾluʾiyyah fī tārīkh al-dawlah al-Rasūliyyah)*, translated and annotated by J. W. Redhouse (I, II, III), edited by Muḥammad ʿAsal (IV, V), 5 vols, Leiden and London, E. J. W. Gibb Memorial Series 3, 1906–18.

Khoury, Raif Georges, *Chrestomathie de papyrologie arabe. Documents relatifs à la vie privée, sociale et administrative dans les premiers siècles islamiques*, préparée par Adolf Grohmann, retravaillée et élargie par Raif Georges Khoury, Leiden, New York etc., 1993.

Kindermann, Hans, *'Schiff' im Arabischen*, Zwickau i. Sa., 1934.

al-Kindī, Sālim b. Muḥammad, *Tārīkh Ḥaḍramawt al-musammā bi-al-ʿUddah al-mufīdah al-jāmiʿah al-tawārīkh qadīmah wa-ḥadīthah*, ed. ʿAbdallāh Muḥammad al-Ḥabshī, 2 vols, Ṣanʿāʾ, 1991.

Lajnat al-Jughrāfiyyah al-ʿAdaniyyah (Aden Geographical Board), *Jughrāfiyyat ʿAdan wa-Bilād al-ʿArab*, Cairo, 1932.

Landberg, Le Comte de, *Critica Arabica II: H. Derenbourg, Ousama ibn Mounqidh*, Leiden, 1888.

——, *Etudes sur les dialectes de l'Arabie méridionale*, 3 vols, Leiden, 1901–13.

——, *Glossaire daṯînois*, 3 vols, Leiden, 1920–42.

Lane, Edward William, *An Arabic–English Lexicon*, 8 parts, London and Edinburgh, 1863–93.

Lane-Poole, Stanley, *The Mohammadan Dynasties*, Westminster, 1894.

Lankester Harding, G., *Archaeology in the Aden Protectorates*, London, 1964.

Lassner, Jacob, *The Shaping of ʿAbbāsid Rule*, Princeton, 1980.

Lemmens, R. H. M. J. and Wulijarni-Soetjipto, N., eds, *Plant Resources of South-East Asia No. 3. Dye and Tannin-producing Plants*, Wageningen, 1991.

Le Strange, G., *The Lands of the Eastern Caliphate*, London, 1966.

——, *Palestine under the Moslems*, London, 1890.

Lewcock, Ronald and Smith, G. Rex, 'Two Early Mosques in the Yemen: a Preliminary Report', *Art and Architectural Research Papers*, 4, 1973, pp. 117–30.

Liddell, Henry George and Scott, Robert, *A Greek-English Lexicon*, New York, 1879.

Löfgren, Oscar, *Arabische Texte zur Kenntnis der Stadt Aden im Mittelalter*, 2 vols, Uppsala etc., 1936–50.

Løkkegaard, Frede, *Islamic Taxation in the Classic Period*, Copenhagen, 1950.

Lorimer, J. G., *Gazetteer of the Persian Gulf, 'Oman, and Central Arabia*, I/3, Historical, Tables and Maps (Map of the Persian Gulf etc., compiled by F. F. Hunter in consultation with J. G. Lorimer and M. O. Tandy); IIA/B, Geographical and Statistical, Calcutta, 1908.

Lowick, Nicholas, *Coinage and History of the Islamic World*, Aldershot, 1990.

——, 'Coins of the Najāḥids of Yemen: A Preliminary Investigation', *Actes du 8ème Congrès international de numismatique (New York–Washington, septembre 1973)*, Paris, 1976. Art. II of Lowick, *Coinage*.

——, 'The Mint of Ṣan'ā'', in R. B. Serjeant and Ronald Lewcock, eds, *Ṣan'ā', an Arabian Islamic City*, London, 1983, pp. 303–10. Art. I of Lowick, *Coinage*.

——, 'The Religious, the Royal and the Popular in the Figural Coinage of the Jazra' in Julian Raby, ed., *The Art of Syria and the Jazīra, 1100–1250*, Oxford, 1985, pp. 159–74.

——, 'Some Unpublished Dinars of the Ṣulayḥids and Zuray'ids', *Numismatic Chronicle*, 7th ser., 4, 1964, pp. 261–70.

Lyons, Malcolm Cameron and Jackson, D. E. P., *Saladin – the Politics of the Holy War*, Cambridge, 1982.

al-Mad'aj, 'Abd al-Muḥsin Mad'aj M., *The Yemen in Early Islam 9–233/630–847 – a Political History*, London, Centre for Middle Eastern and Islamic Studies, University of Durham, 1988.

al-Maqḥafī, Ibrāhīm Aḥmad, *Mu'jam al-buldān wa-al-qabā'il al-Yamaniyyah*, Ṣan'ā', 1988.

al-Mas'ūdī, 'Alī b. Ḥusayn, *Kitāb Murūj al-dhahab wa-ma'ādin al-jawhar*, ed. Barbier de Meynard and Pavet de Courteille, 7 vols, Beirut, 1966–74.

Matsumoto, Hiroshi, 'The Traditional and Modern Regional Divisions and the Tribes in North Yemen', unpublished PhD thesis, University of Manchester, 1994.

Mermier, Franck, 'Les Fondations mythiques de Sanaa et d'Aden' in *Yémen, passé et présent de l'unité, Revue du Monde Musulman et de la Méditerranée*, 67, 1994, pp. 131–41.

Miles, George C., 'The Ayyūbid Dynasty of the Yaman and their Coinage', *Numismatic Chronicle*, 5th ser., 19, 1939, pp. 62–97.

Miller, Anthony G. and Morris, Miranda, *Plants of Dhofar the Southern Region of Oman: Traditional, Economic and Medicinal Uses*, Oman, 1988.

Miquel, Andre, *La Géographie humaine du monde musulman jusqu'au milieu du 11e siècle*, Paris, 1967.

Morony, Michael G., *Iraq after the Muslim Conquest*, Princeton, 1984.

Morrison, George, *Vis and Ramin. Translated from the Persian of Fakhr al-Dīn Gurgānī*, New York and London, 1972.

Mortel, Richard T., 'Zaydī Shi'ism and the Ḥasanid Sharifs of Mecca', *International Journal of Middle Eastern Studies*, 19, 1987, pp. 455–72.

——, 'Weights and Measures in Mecca during the Late Ayyūbid and Mamlūk Periods', *Arabian Studies*, Cambridge, 1990, pp. 177–87.

al-Mubarrad, Muḥammad b. Yazīd, *al-Kāmil fī al-lughah*, ed. Muḥammad Abū al-Faḍl Ibrāhīm and al-Sayyid Shaḥātah, 4 vols, Cairo, n.d.

al-Muqaddasī, Muḥammad b. Aḥmad, *Aḥsan al-taqālīm fī ma'rifat al-aqālīm*, *Descriptio Imperii Moslemici*, ed. M. J. de Geoje, 2nd edn, Leiden, Bibliotheca Geographorum Arabicorum 3, 1906.

al-Nakhīlī, Darwīsh, *al-Sufun al-Islāmiyyah 'alā ḥurūf al-mu'jam*, Alexandria, 1973.

Nashwān b. Saʿīd al-Ḥimyarī, *Shams al-ʿulūm wa-dawāʾ kalām al-ʿArab min al-kulūm*, ed. Ḥusayn b. ʿAbdallāh al-ʿAmrī, Muṭahhar b. ʿAlī al-Iryānī and Yūsuf Muḥammad ʿAbdallāh, 12 vols, Beirut and Damascus, 1999.
Nicholson, Reynold A., *A Literary History of the Arabs*, Cambridge, 1956.
——, *Translations of Eastern Poetry and Prose*, Cambridge, 1922.
Niebuhr, Carsten, *Description de l'Arabie faite sur des observations propres et des avis recueillis dans les lieux mêmes*, Amsterdam and Utrecht, 1774.
Noeldeke, Th., *Delectus Veterum Carminum Arabicorum*, Wiesbaden, 1961.
——, 'H. Derenbourg: Ousāma ibn Mounqidh', *Wiener Zeitschrift zur Kunde des Morgenlandes*, 1, 1887, pp. 237–45.
Norris, H. T., 'Fables and Legends' in Julia Ashtiany et al., eds, *The Cambridge History of Arabic Literature: Arabic Literature to the End of the Umayyad Period*, Cambridge, 1983, pp. 136–46.
Norris, H. T. and Penhey, F. W., *An Archaeological and Historical Survey of the Aden Tanks*, Aden and London, 1955.
al-Nuʿmān b. Muḥammad, al-Qāḍī, *Risālat Iftitāḥ al-daʿwah*, ed. Wadād al-Qāḍī, Beirut, 1970.
Nūr al-maʿārif fī nuzum wa-qawānīn wa-aʿrāf al-Yaman fī ʿahd al-muzaffarī al-wārif, ed. Muḥammad ʿAbd al-Raḥīm Jāzim, 2 vols, *Sanʿāʾ*, 2003–5.
Ockley, Simon, *The History of the Saracens; Comprising the Lives of Mohammed and his Successors*, 4th edn, London, 1847.
Oxford Dictionary of the Christian Church, ed. F. L. Cross, London, 1957.
Payne Smith, R., *A Compendious Syriac Dictionary*, Oxford, 1903.
Pellat, Charles, *Le Livre des avares de Ǧāḥiẓ*, Paris, 1951.
Penrice, John, *A Dictionary and Glossary of the Kor-ân*, London, 1873.
Piamenta, Moshe, *Dictionary of Post-Classical Yemeni Arabic*, 2 vols, Leiden, New York etc., 1990–1.
al-Qināʿī, Najāḥ, ʿAbd al-Qādir al-Jāsim and al-Khuṣūṣī, Badr al-Dīn ʿAbbās, *Tārīkh ṣināʿat al-sufun fī al-Kuwayt wa-anshiṭatu-hā al-mukhtalifah*, Kuwait, 1982.
al-Rashid, Saad A., *Darb Zubaydah – the Pilgrim Road from Kufa to Mecca*, Riyadh, 1980.
——, *al-Rabadhah – a Portrait of Early Islamic Civilisation in Saudi Arabia*, Riyadh, [1986].
al-Rawas, ʿIsam ʿAli Ahmed, 'Early Islamic Oman (ca. 1–280/622–893) – a Political History', PhD thesis, University of Durham, 1990.
——, *Oman in Early Islamic History*, Reading, 2000.
al-Rāzī, Aḥmad b. ʿAbdallāh, *Tārīkh madīnat Ṣanʿāʾ*, ed. Ḥusayn b. ʿAbdallāh al-ʿAmrī, Ṣanʿāʾ, 1981.
Red Sea and Gulf of Aden Pilot, London, Hydrographic Department, Admiralty, 10th edn, 1955.
Rodwell, J. M. trans., *The Koran*, London and New York, 1971.
Rosenthal, Frantz, *A History of Muslim Historiography*, Leiden, 1968.
Rossi, Ettore, *L'arabo parlato a Ṣanʿāʾ*, Rome, 1939.
Runciman, Steven, *A History of the Crusades*, 3 vols, Harmondsworth, 1951–4.
Rypka, Jan, *History of Iranian Literature*, Dordrecht, 1968.
Sadek, Noha, 'Ẓabīd: the Round City of Yemen' in J. F. Healey and V. Porter, eds, *Studies on Arabia in Honour of Professor G. Rex Smith*, Oxford, Journal of Semitic Studies Supplement 14, 2002, pp. 215–27.
al-Saʿīdān, Ḥamad Muḥammad, *al-Mawsūʿah al-Kuwaytiyyah al-mukhtaṣarah*, Kuwait, 1981–.
Sale, George, *The Koran*, London, n.d.
SEI, see *Shorter Encyclopaedia of Islam*.
Schen, I., 'Usāma Ibn Munqidh's Memoirs: Some Further Light on Muslim Middle Arabic', *Journal of Semitic Studies*, 17/2, 18/1, 1972–73, pp. 218–36, pp. 64–97.
Schönig, Hanne, 'Traditional Cosmetics of Women in Yemen. The Black Dye *ḫiḍāb*: Traditional and Modern Ways of Fabrication', *Proceedings of the Seminar for Arabian Studies*, 26, 1996, pp. 135–44.

Schuman, Lein Oebele, *Political History of the Yemen at the Beginning of the 16th Century – Abū Makhrama's Account of the Years 906–927 H. (1500–1521 A.D.) with Annotations*, Groningen, 1960.

Serjeant, R.B., *Abū 'Uthmān ibn Bar al-Jāhiẓ, the Book of Misers*, Reading, 1997.

——, 'The Coastal Population of Socotra' in Brian Doe, *Socotra – Island of Tranquillity*, London, 1992, pp. 133–81. Art. XVII of Serjeant, *Society*.

——, 'The Cultivation of Cereals in Mediaeval Yemen', *Arabian Studies*, 1, 1974, pp. 25–74. Art. VII of Serjeant, *Farmers*.

——, 'The Customary Law of South-west Arabia and Bedouin Justice in Jordan', *Recueils de la Société Jean Bodin pour l'histoire comparative des institutions LII: la coutume/custom, troisième partie*, Brussels, 1992, pp. 269–80. Art. V in Serjeant, *Society*.

——, *Customary and Sharī'ah Law in Arabian Society*, Aldershot, 1991.

——, *Farmers and Fishermen in Arabia*, ed. G. Rex Smith, Aldershot, 1995.

——, 'Forms of Plea: a Šāfi'ī Manual from al-Šiḥr', *Rivista degli studi orientali*, 30, 1955, pp. 1–15. Art. XI in Serjeant, *Customary and Sharī'ah Law*.

——, 'A Fortified Tower-house in Wādī Jirdān (Wāḥidī Sultanate) – I and II', *Bulletin of the School of Oriental and African Studies*, 38, 1975, pp. 1–23, 276–95. Art. XV in Serjeant, *Society*.

——, 'The Ḥaḍramī Network' in Denys Lombard and Jean Aubin, eds, *Marchands et hommes d'affaires asiatiques dans l'Océan Indien et la Mer de Chine, 13e-20e siècles*, Paris, 1988. Art. II in Serjeant, *Society*.

——, 'The Interplay between Tribal Affinities and Religious (Zaydī) Authority in the Yemen, *al-Abhath*, 30, 1982, pp. 11–50. Art. III in Serjeant, *Customary and Sharī'ah Law*.

——, *Islamic Textiles*, Beirut, 1972.

——, 'Maritime Customary Law off the Arabian Coasts' in M. Mollat, ed., *Société et compagnies de commerce en Orient et dans l'Océan Indien. Actes du VIIIième Colloque International Maritime (Beyrouth, 5–10 septembre 1966)*, Paris, 1970. Art. XV in Serjeant, *Customary and Sharī'ah Law*.

——, '*Miḥrāb*', *Bulletin of the School of Oriental and African Studies*, 22. 1959, pp. 439–53. Art. IV in Serjeant, *Arabian History*.

——, 'The Ports of Aden and Shihr (Mediaeval Period)', *Les Grandes Escales I. Receuils de la Société Jean Bodin*, 32 (10e Colloque d'histoire maritime), Brussels, 1974, pp. 207–24. Art. XII in Serjeant, *Studies*.

——, *The Portuguese off the South Arabian Coast*, Oxford, 1963.

——, with Arthur Lane, 'Pottery and Glass Fragments from the Aden Littoral with Historical Notes', *Journal of the Royal Asiatic Society*, 1948, pp. 108–33. Art. XI in Serjeant, *Studies*.

——, 'Saint Sergius', *Bulletin of the School of Oriental and African Studies*, 22, 1959, pp. 574–5. Art. II in Serjeant, *Studies*.

——, *Society and Trade in South Arabia*, ed. G. Rex Smith, Aldershot, 1996.

——, *Studies in Arabian History and Civilisation*, London, 1981.

——, 'Sunnah, Qur'āh, 'Urf' in Christopher Toll and Jakob Skovgaard-Petersen, eds, Munksgaard, 1995, pp. 33–48. Art. VII in Serjeant, *Society*.

——, 'Tihāmah Notes' in Alan Jones, ed., *Arabicus Felix: Luminosus Britannicus – Essays in Honour of A. F. L. Beeston on his Eightieth Birthday*, Reading, Oxford Oriental Institute Monographs, 1991, pp. 45–60. Art. XVI in Serjeant, *Society*.

——, 'The White Dune at Abyan: an Ancient Place of Pilgrimage in Southern Arabia', *Journal of Semitic Studies*, 16, 1971, pp. 74–83. Art. X in Serjeant, *Customary and Sharī'ah Law*.

——, 'Yāfi', Zaydīs, Āl Bū Bakr b. Sālim and Others: Tribes and Sayyids', in *On Both Sides of al-Mandab – Ethiopian, South-Arabic and Islamic Studies presented to Oscar Löfgren on his Ninetieth Birthday 13 May 1988 by Colleagues and Friends*, Swedish Research Institute in Istanbul, Transactions, Vol. 2, 1989, pp. 83–105. Art. VI in Serjeant, *Customary and Sharī'ah Law*.

——, 'The Yemeni Coast in 1005/1597: an Anonymous Note on the Flyleaf of Ibn al-Mujāwir's *Tārīkh al-Mustabṣir*', *Arabian Studies*, 7, 1985, pp. 187–91. Art. III in Serjeant, *Society*.

——, 'Yemeni Merchants and Trade in Yemen, 13th–16th Centuries', in Denys Lombard and Jean Aubin, eds, *Marchands et hommes d'affaires asiatiques dans l'Océan Indien et la Mer de Chine, 13e–20e siècles*, Paris, 1988, pp. 61–82. Art. I in Serjeant, *Society*.
——, 'A Zaidī Manual of Ḥisbah of the 3rd Century (H)', *Rivista degli studi orientali*, 28, 1957, pp. 1–34. Art. VII in Serjeant, *Studies*.
——, 'Zinā, Some Forms of Marriage and Allied Topics in Western Arabia', in Andre Gingrich, Sylvia Haas, Gabriele Paleczek and Thomas Fillitz, eds, *Studies in Oriental Culture and History. Festschrift for Walter Dostal*, Frankfurt am Main, 1993, pp. 145–59. Art. XII in Serjeant, *Society*.
Serjeant, R. B. and Lewcock, Ronald, eds, *Ṣanʿāʾ, an Arabian Islamic City*, London, 1983.
Serjeant, R. B., Costa, Paolo and Lewcock, Ronald, 'The *Ghayls* of Ṣanʿāʾ', in R. B. Serjeant, and Ronald Lewcock, eds, *Ṣanʿāʾ, an Arabian Islamic City*, London, 1983, pp. 19–32.
Shaban, M.A., *Islamic History – a New Interpretation, 1, AD 600–750 (AH 132)*, Cambridge, 1971.
——, *Islamic History – a New Interpretation, 2, A.D. 750–1055 (A.H. 132–448)*, Cambridge, 1976.
al-Shāfiʿī, Muḥammad b. Idrīs, *Dīwān al-Imām al-Shāfiʿī*, ed. Naʿīm Zarzūr, Beirut, 1986.
Shahîd, Irfan, *The Martyrs of Najrân – New Documents*, Brussels, 1971.
al-Sharjī, Aḥmad b. Aḥmad, *Ṭabaqāt al-khawāṣṣ ahl-al-ṣidq wa-al-ikhlāṣ*, Ṣanʿāʾ, 1986.
al-Shāṭirī, Muḥammad b. Aḥmad, *Adwār al-tārīkh al-Ḥaḍramī*, 2 vols, Jeddah, 1983.
Shorter Encyclopaedia of Islam, Leiden and London, 1961. [*SEI*]
al-Sijistānī, Abū Ḥātim Sahl b. Muḥammad, *Kitāb al-Nakhl*, ed. Ibrāhīm al-Sāmmarāʾi, Beirut, 1985.
de Slane, MacGluckin, *Le Diwan d'Amro'lkaïs*, Paris, 1837.
Smith, Clive, 'Kawkabān: Some of its History', *Arabian Studies*, 6, 1982, pp. 35–50.
——, *Lightning over Yemen – a History of the Ottoman Campaign (1569–71) being a Translation from the Arabic of Part III of* al-Barq al-Yamānī fī al-Fatḥ al-ʿUthmānī *by Quṭb al-Dīn al-Nahrawālī al-Makkī as published by Ḥamad al-Jāsir (Riyadh 1967)*, London and New York, 2002.
Smith, G. R., *The Ayyūbids and Early Rasūlids in the Yemen (567–694/1173–1295)*, 2 vols, London, E. J. W. Gibb Memorial Trust 26/1–2, 1974–78. (See also Ibn Ḥātim above.)
——, 'The Ayyubids and Rasulids – the Transfer of Power in 7th/13th Century Yemen' article XII in Smith, *Studies*, a revised and corrected version of that in *Islamic Culture*, 43, pp. 175–88. Art. XII in Smith, *Studies*.
——, 'Ibn al-Mujāwir on Dhofar and Socotra', *Proceedings of the Seminar for Arabian Studies*, 15, 1985, pp. 79–92. Art. III in Smith, *Studies*.
Smith, G. Rex, 'The Early and Medieval History of Ṣanʿāʾ, ca. 622–953/1515', in R. B. Serjeant and Ronald Lewcock, eds, *Ṣanʿāʾ, an Arabian Islamic City*, London, 1983, pp. 49–68.
——, 'Have You Anything to Declare? Maritime Trade and Commerce in Ayyubid Aden – Practices and Taxes', *Proceedings of the Seminar for Arabian Studies*, 25, pp. 127–40. Art. X in Smith, *Studies*.
——, 'Ibn al-Mujāwir's 7th/13th Century Arabia – the Wondrous and the Humorous', in A. K. Irvine, R. B. Serjeant and G. Rex Smith, eds, *A Miscellany of Middle Eastern Articles: in Memoriam Thomas Muir Johnstone 1924–83*, Harlow, 1988, pp. 111–24. Art. IV in Smith, *Studies*.
——, 'Ibn al-Mujāwir's 7th-13th Century Guide to Arabia: the Eastern Connection', *Occasional Papers of the School of Abbasid Studies, University of St Andrews*, 3, 1990, pp. 71–88. Art. V in Smith, *Studies*.
——, 'The Kuria Muria Islands 1959–60. A Footnote of British Colonial History' in Ian Richard Netton, ed., *Studies in Honour of Clifford Edmund Bosworth, I, Hunter of the East: Arabic and Semitic Studies*, Leiden, Boston and Cologne, 2000, pp. 280–97.
——, 'The Language of Ibn al-Mujāwir's 7th/13th Century Guide to Arabia, *Tārīkh al-Mustabṣir*, in J. R. Smart, ed., *Tradition and Modernity in Arabic Language and Literature*, Richmond, 1996, pp. 327–51. Art. VII in Smith, *Studies*.

——, 'Magic, Jinn and the Supernatural in Medieval Yemen: Examples from Ibn al-Mujāwir's 7th/13th Century Guide', *Quaderni di studi arabi*, 13, pp. 7–18. Art. VIII in Smith, *Studies*.

——, 'Masqaṭ in the Arab Lexicographers and Geographers', *Journal of Oman Studies*, 6, 1983, 145–8. Art. XVIII in Smith, *Studies*.

——, *A Medieval Administrative and Fiscal Treatise from the Yemen: the Rasulid* Mulakhkhaṣ al-fiṭan *by al-Ḥasan b. al-Ḥusaynī*, Journal of Semitic Studies Supplement 20, Oxford, 2006.

——, 'More on the Port Practices and Taxes of Medieval Aden', *New Arabian Studies*, 3, 1996, pp. 208–18. Art. XI in Smith, *Studies*.

——, 'The Political History of the Islamic Yemen down to the First Turkish Invasion (1–945/622–1538)', in Werner Daum, ed., *Yemen: 3000 Years of Art and Civilisation in Arabia Felix*, Innsbruck and Frankfurt-am-Main, 1988, pp. 129–39. Art. I in Smith, *Studies*.

——, 'The Rasulids in Dhofar in the VIIth–VIIIth/XIII–XIVth Centuries – Part I, the Historical Background', *Journal of the Royal Asiatic Society*, pt 1, 1988, pp. 26–32. Art. XIII in Smith, *Studies*.

——, 'Robert Bertram Serjeant 1915–1993', *Proceedings of the British Academy*, 87, *1994 Lectures and Memoirs*, London, 1994. Art. XX in Smith, *Studies*.

——, 'Some Anthropological Passages from Ibn al-Mujāwir's Guide to Arabia and Their Proposed Interpretations', in A. Gingrich, S. Haas, G. Paleczek and T. Fillitz, eds, *Studies in Oriental Culture and History: Festschrift for Walter Dostal*, Frankfurt-am-Main, 1993, pp. 160–71. Art. VI in Smith, *Studies*.

——, *Studies in the Medieval History of the Yemen and South Arabia*, Aldershot, 1997.

——, review of Varisco, *Agriculture*, *Journal of the Royal Asiatic Society*, 1995, pp. 11–13.

——, 'Three Tales from Arabia – Story-telling in Ibn al-Mujāwir's 7th/13th Century Guide', *New Arabian Studies*, 6, 200, pp. 124–32.

——, 'The Yemenite Settlement of Tha'bāt: Historical, Numismatic and Epigraphic Notes', *Arabian Studies*, 1, 1974, pp. 119–34. Art. XIV in Smith, *Studies*.

——, *The Yemens*, Oxford, Santa Barbara, CA, and Denver, CO, World Bibliographical Series 50, 1984.

Snouck Hurgronje, C., *Mekka*, 2 vols, The Hague, 1888 .

Sobhy Bey, Georgy, *Common Words in the Spoken Arabic of Egypt of Greek or Coptic Origin*, Cairo, 1950.

Sourdel, D., 'The 'Abbāsid Caliphate', in P. M. Holt, Ann K. S. Lambton and Bernard Lewis, eds, *The Cambridge History of Islam*, IA, Cambridge, 1970, pp. 104–41.

Sprenger, A., *Post- und Reiserouten des Orients*, Leipzig, Abhandlungen der *Deutschen Morgenländischen Gesellschaft*, III Band, No. 3, 1864.

Stern, S.M., 'Rāmisht of Sīrāf, a Merchant Millionaire of the Twelfth Century', *Journal of the Royal Asiatic Society*, 1967, pp. 10–14.

Stone, Francine Lida, 'Tihāmah Gazetteer. The Southern Red Sea Coast of Arabia to 923/1517', unpublished PhD thesis, University of Manchester, 1999.

——, ed., *Studies on the Tihāmah*, Harlow, 1985.

al-Sulamī, 'Arrām b. al-Aṣbagh, *Kitāb Asmā' jibāl Tihāmah wa-sukkāni-hā wa-mā fī-hā min al-qurā wa-mā yanbutu 'alay-hā min al-ashjār wa-mā fī-hā min al-mā'*, ed. 'Abd al-Salām Muḥammad Hārūn, Cairo, 1373 H.

al-Ṭabarī, Muḥammad b. Jarīr, *The History of al-Ṭabarī, I, General Introduction and from the Creation to the Flood*, translated and annotated by Franz Rosenthal, Albany, NY, 1989.

——, *The History of al-Ṭabarī, III, The Children of Israel*, translated and annotated by William M. Brinner, Albany, NY, 1991.

——, *The History of al-Ṭabarī, IV, The Ancient Kingdoms*, translated and annotated by Moshe Perlmann, Albany, NY, 1987.

——, *The History of al-Ṭabarī, V, The Sasānids, the Byzantines, the Lakhmids, and Yemen*, translated and annotated by C. E. Bosworth, Albany, NY, 1999.

——, *The History of al-Ṭabarī, VI, Muḥammad at Mecca*, translated and annotated by W. Montgomery Watt and M. V. McDonald, Albany, NY, 1988.

——, *The History of al-Ṭabarī, VII, The Foundation of the Community*, translated by M. V. McDonald, annotated by W. Montgomery Watt, Albany, NY, 1987.

——, *The History of al-Ṭabarī, VIII, The Victory of Islam*, translated and annotated by Michael Fishbein, Albany, NY, 1997.

——, *The History of al-Ṭabarī, XII, The Battle of al-Qādisiyyah and the Conquest of Syria and Palestine*, translated and annotated by Yohanan Friedmann, Albany, NY, 1992.

——, *The History of al-Ṭabarī, XIV, The Conquest of Iran*, translated and annotated by G. Rex Smith, Albany, NY, 1994.

——, *The History of al-Ṭabarī, XXVII, The 'Abbāsid Revolution*, translated and annoted by John Alden Williams, Albany, NY, 1985.

——, *The History of al-Ṭabarī, XXXII, The Reunification of the 'Abbāsid Caliphate*, translated and annotated by C.E. Bosworth, Albany, NY, 1987.

——, *Tārīkh al-Rusul wa-al-mulūk*, ed. Muḥammad Abū al-Faḍl Ibrāhīm, 10 vols, Cairo, 1969.

el Tayib, Abdullah, 'Abū Firās al-Ḥamdānī', in Julia Ashtiany et al., eds, *Cambridge History of Arabic Literature 'Abbasid Belles-Lettres*, Cambridge, 1990, pp. 315–24.

Thackston, W. M. Jr, *The Tales of the Prophets of al-Kisa'i*, Boston, 1978.

al-Thenayian, Mohammed A. Rashed, *An Archaeological Study of the Yemeni Highland Pilgrim Route between Ṣan'ā' and Mecca*, Riyadh, 1999.

——, 'Rilat al-Sulṭān al-Malik al-Mujāhid al-Rasūlī min Ta'izz ilā Makkah al-Mukarramah', *al-Dārah*, 25/1, 1999, pp. 117–80.

Tibbetts, G. R., *Arab Navigation in the Indian Ocean before the Coming of the Portuguese*, London, Oriental Translation Fund, New Series, Vol. XLII, 1971.

al-Tibrīzī, Abū Zakariyyā Yaḥyā, *Kitāb Sharḥ al-qaṣā'id al-'ashr*, ed. Charles James Lyall, Calcutta, 1894.

Tritton, A. S., *The Rise of the Imams of Sanaa*, London and New York, 1925.

'Umārah b. 'Alī, Najm al-Dīn al-Yamanī, *Tārīkh al-Yaman*, see Kay.

——, *Tārīkh al-Yaman al-musammā al-Mufīd fī akhbār Ṣan'ā' wa-Zabīd wa-shu'arā'i-hā wa-mulūki-hā wa-a'yāni-hā wa-udabā'i-hā*, ed. Muḥammad b. 'Alī al-Akwa' al-Ḥiwālī, Ṣan'ā', 1985.

Varisco, Daniel Martin, 'Agriculture in Rasulid Zabīd' in J. F. Healey and V. Porter, eds, *Studies on Arabia in Honour of Professor G. Rex Smith*, Oxford, Journal of Semitic Studies Supplement 14, pp. 323–53.

——, *Medieval Agriculture and Islamic Science – the Almanac of a Yemeni Sultan*, Seattle and London, 1994.

——, 'The Production of Sorghum (*Dhurah*) in Highland Yemen', *Arabian Studies*, 7, 1985, pp. 53–89.

——, 'A Royal Crop Register from Rasulid Yemen', *Journal of the Economic and Social History of the Orient*, 34, 1991, pp. 150–54.

Vire, François, *Le Traité de l'art de volerie (Kitāb al-Bayzara)*, Leiden, 1967.

Voorhoeve, P., *Handlist of Arabic Manuscripts*, Leiden, 1957.

Wahb b. Munabbih, *Kitāb al-Tījān fī mulūk Ḥimyar*, Ṣan'ā', 1347 H.

Walker, John, *A Catalogue of the Arab-Sassanian Coins*, London, 1967.

al-Wāqidī, Muḥammad b. 'Umar, *Kitāb al-Maghāzī*, ed. Marsden Jones, 3 vols, Oxford, 1966.

Weapons of the Islamic World – Swords and Armour, Riyadh, 1991.

al-Wāsi'ī, 'Abd al-Wāsi' b. Yaḥyā, *Tārīkh al-Yaman*, Cairo, 1346 H.

al-Waysī, Ḥusayn b. 'Alī, *al-Yaman al-kubrā*, Cairo, 1962.

Wehr, Hans, *A Dictionary of Modern Written Arabic*, ed. J. Milton Cowan, 3rd print., Wiesbaden and London, 1971.

Werdecker, Josef, 'Contribution to the Geography and Cartography of North-West Yemen (Based on the Results of the Exploration by Eduard Glaser, Undertaken in the Years 1882–1884)', *Bulletin de la Société Royale de Géographie d'Egypte*, 20, 1939, pp. 1–160.
Western Arabia and the Red Sea, London, Naval Intelligence Division Geographical Handbook Series, 1946.
Whitehouse, David, 'Excavations at Sīrāf; First Interim Report', *Iran*, 6, 1968, pp. 1–3.
Wilkinson, John C., *The Imamate Tradition of Oman*, Cambridge, 1987.
——, *Water and Tribal Settlement in South-East Arabia. A Study of the* Aflāj *of Oman*, Oxford, 1977.
Wilson, Robert T. O., *Gazetteer of Historical North-West Yemen in the Islamic Period to 1650*, Hildesheim, Zürich and New York, 1989.
al-Wohaibi, *The Northern Hijaz in the Writings of the Arab Geographers*, Beirut, 1973.
Wood, J. R. I., *A Handbook of the Yemen Flora*, London, 1997.
Wright, W., *A Grammar of the Arabic Language*, 3rd edn revised by W. Robertson Smith and M. J. de Goeje, 2 vols, Cambridge, 1955.
al-Wuṣābī, ʿAbd al-Raḥmān b. Muḥammad, *Tārīkh Wuṣāb al-musammā al-Iʿtibār fī al-tawārīkh wa-al-āthār*, ed. ʿAbdallāh Muḥammad al-Ḥabshī, Ṣanʿāʾ, 1979.
Wüstenfeld, Ferdinand, *Die Chroniken der Stadt Mekka*, 4 vols, Leipzig, 1858–61.
Yajima, Hikoichi (ed.), *A Chronicle of the Rasulid Dynasty of Yemen*, Tokyo, 1974.
Yāqūt b. ʿAbdallāh al-Ḥamawī, *Muʿjam al-buldān*, 5 vols, Beirut, 1979.
al-Zabīdī, Muḥammad Murtaḍā al-Ḥusaynī, *Tāj al-ʿarūs min jawāhir al-qāmūs*, ed. ʿAbd al-Sattār Aḥmad Farāj et al., Kuwait, 1965– .
al-Zabīdī, al-Murtaḍā, *Tarwīḥ al-qulūb fī dhikr al-mulūk Banī Ayyūb*, ed. Ṣalāḥ al-Dīn al-Munajjid, Damascus, 1971.
al-Zahrānī, ʿAlī b. Ṣāli al-Salūk, *al-Muʿjam al-jughrāfī li-l-Bilād al-ʿArabiyyah al-Suʿūdiyyah – Bilād Ghāmid wa-Zahrān* (II), Riyadh, 1971.
Zakī, ʿAbd al-Raḥmān, *al-Silāḥ fī al-Islām*, *Vocabulary Relating to Arms and Armour in Islam*, Cairo, 1951.
Zettersteén, K. V., *Die Arabischen Handschriften der Universitätsbibliothek zu Uppsala*, Uppsala, 1930.
Ziriklī Khayr al-Dīn, *al-Aʿlām*, 8 vols, Beirut, 1988.
al-Zulfa, Mohammed, 'Village Communities in Bilād Rufaydah: their Political and Economic Organisation', *Arabian Studies*, 6, 1982, pp. 77–96.

MAPS

Arabian Peninsula, 1:3,000,000, John Bartholomew and Son Ltd., Edinburgh, 1983.
Socotra, 1:150,000, War Office and Air Ministry, [London], 1960.
Southern Arabia, part of Aden Protectorate, 1:500,000, made by Hermann von Wissman, Royal Geographical Society, London, 1958.
Yemen Arab Republic, 1:1,000,000, Survey Authority, Ṣanʿāʾ, n.d., and Orell Fussli Graphic Arts Ltd., Zurich, 1986.

INDEX